Protecting Migrant Children

Protecting Migrant Children

In Search of Best Practice

Edited by

Mary Crock

Professor of Public Law, Sydney Law School, The University of Sydney, Australia

Lenni B. Benson

Professor of Law, New York Law School, USA

Edward Elgar
PUBLISHING

Cheltenham, UK • Northampton, MA, USA

Published by
Edward Elgar Publishing Limited
The Lypiatts
15 Lansdown Road
Cheltenham
Glos GL50 2JA
UK

Edward Elgar Publishing, Inc.
William Pratt House
9 Dewey Court
Northampton
Massachusetts 01060
USA

A catalogue record for this book
is available from the British Library

Library of Congress Control Number: 2018944032

This book is available electronically in the **Elgar**online
Law subject collection
DOI 10.4337/9781786430267

Printed on elemental chlorine free (ECF)
recycled paper containing 30% Post-Consumer Waste

ISBN 978 1 78643 025 0 (cased)
ISBN 978 1 78643 026 7 (eBook)

Typeset by Servis Filmsetting Ltd, Stockport, Cheshire
Printed and bound in the USA

Contents

PART V CHILDREN AND IMMIGRATION DETENTION

PART VI CHALLENGES AND SOLUTIONS

About the authors

THE EDITORS

Mary Crock has worked in the area of immigration and refugee law since 1985. She is Professor of Public Law in the University of Sydney's Law School. Co-founder in 1989 of the specialist community legal service now known as Refugee Legal in Melbourne, Victoria, she has been recognized as an Accredited Specialist in Immigration Law since 1994. She has served on a variety of national, state and NGO bodies relating to immigration, refugees, disability and child protection. She has written extensively on issues related to immigration and refugee law, authoring 13 books and over 75 book chapters and refereed articles. Mary has had a research focus on the laws, policies and practices involving migrant children since 2004, working with Jacqueline Bhabha on the three-country 'Seeking Asylum Alone' Project and later on the Australian-based 'Small Mercies, Big Futures' Project. Her most recent book (with L. Smith-Khan, B. Saul and R.C. McCallum) is *The Legal Protection of Refugees with Disabilities: Forgotten and Invisible?* (Edward Elgar Publishing, 2017).

Lenni B. Benson is a Professor of Law at New York Law School. In 2012, she founded the Safe Passage Project, a non-profit organization that has aided over 1,500 unaccompanied youth by recruiting and mentoring *pro bono* counsel. She is a member of several national task forces on the needs of migrant youth, and has been a speaker for the federal government at national trainings. In 2012 she completed, with Russell Wheeler, a study of the immigration courts for the Administrative Conference of the United States. She has won many honors and served in leadership positions related to her work in immigration law. Her book *Immigration and Nationality Law: Problems and Strategies* (with L.A. Curcio, V.M. Jeffers and S.W. Yale-Loehr) was published in 2013 and is updated annually.

CONTRIBUTORS

Edwin Odhiambo Abuya is Associate Professor in Law at the University of Nairobi who lectures in Legal Research and Human Rights. His research focuses on forced migrants, statelessness, persons with disabilities and issues around access to information. His publications include a 2010 report on statelessness for Kenya's National Commission on Human Rights and UNHCR.

Farrin R. Anello is a Senior Staff Attorney at the American Civil Liberties Union of New Jersey, where she conducts litigation and advocacy to advance the rights of immigrants, Muslim Americans, and members of other vulnerable communities. She has taught at various law schools across the United States, and has supervised law students on a wide variety of immigration matters.

Timnah Baker (BA/LLB Monash and LLM Boston) is a researcher at the Peter McMullin Centre on Statelessness, Melbourne Law School and Ph.D candidate Sydney Law School. From 2009–2017 she was based at Harvard University as visiting scholar at the Weatherhead Center for International Affairs and Research Associate for the International Policy and Law Analysis (IMPALA) Project.

Syd Bolton is a children's human rights lawyer (solicitor, non-practising), former legal and policy officer including for Coram Children's Legal Centre; The Children's Legal Centre; Medical Foundation for the Care of Victims of Torture; Islington Law Centre, Wilford Monro Solicitors. He has conducted strategic litigation on children's rights, spoken about and delivered training on the rights of children, in particular, refugee, asylum-seeking and migrant children, both nationally and internationally, and was an adviser to the Children's Commissioner for England. He is co-convenor with Catriona Jarvis of 'The Last Rights Project' which calls for the development of new frameworks to deal with missing and dead refugees and migrants.

Kate Bones is a migration lawyer working at Refugee Legal, a specialist community legal centre in Melbourne, Australia. She has worked previously as research assistant to Professor Mary Crock and Professor Ben Saul at the University of Sydney, and in the Civil Justice Program at Victoria Legal Aid.

Carmelo Danisi is a Research fellow at the University of Sussex, UK, and Adjunct Professor of International Law at the University of Bologna, Forlì campus. He has been Endeavour Research Fellow at the Australian National University, College of Law, and is involved in the ERC SOGICA project. His research interests include human rights, especially with regard to the European system of protection, non-discrimination, migration and refugee law.

Daniel Ghezelbash is a senior lecturer at Macquarie Law School. His research focuses on comparative law with a particular interest in refugee and immigration law. He has a particular interest in the diffusion of restrictive asylum-seeker policies across jurisdictions. He is a practising refugee and immigration lawyer and the founder and director of the Macquarie University Social Justice Clinic.

pamela goldberg is a recognized expert in international refugee, human rights and protection law and policy and has written and spoken widely on these issues. She has been in the forefront of developing law and policy for refugee claims of women and gender-based violence.

Carlos Holguín is General Counsel with the Centre for Human Rights and Constitutional Law Foundation. He has over 30 years of legal experience and has litigated multiple class actions on behalf of immigrants and refugees. He currently serves as lead counsel for over 35 faith-based groups and human rights organizations in a petition to the Inter-American Commission on Human Rights of the Organization of American States challenging a joint program of the United States and Mexico to interdict and summarily deport persons, including thousands of children and families, fleeing rampant violence in Central America's 'Northern Triangle': Honduras, Guatemala and El Salvador.

Catriona Jarvis is a former judge of the United Kingdom Upper Tribunal (Immigration and Asylum Chamber), who retired in 2013 with 21 years' experience as a judge in the fields of immigration, asylum and human rights law. She has extensive experience working internationally on refugee rights, especially in relation to women and children, including publications and training work with the United Nations Refugee Agency (UNHCR), the European Council on Refugees and Exiles (ECRE) and other organizations. She is a Trustee and former Chair of the Board of Prisoners of Conscience Appeal Fund; a Trustee and former Chair of the Inderpal Rahal Memorial Trust; Chair of the Unaccompanied Migrant Children's Court Steering Group and member and former Rapporteur of The International Association of Refugee Law Judges (IARLJ, now IARMJ). She is Co-convenor with Syd Bolton of 'The Last Rights Project' and author of 'In Potters' Fields' which addresses issues around missing and dead refugees and migrants.

Kavita Kapur is an international human rights and immigration lawyer, focusing on asylum and refugee protection and migrants' rights. She has previously been involved with UNHCR operations in the Dominican Republic, Haiti, Malaysia and the United States, and has volunteered in detention centres in Greece. She has been involved in litigation on behalf of migrants' rights, both in the United States and internationally.

Mary Anne Kenny is an Associate Professor at the School of Law at Murdoch University, Perth Western Australia. She teaches and researches in the area of refugee and immigration law. She is an adjunct Associate Professor in the Centre for Human Rights Education at Curtin University. She is a member of the Australian Government's Minister of Immigration Advisory Council on Asylum Seekers and Detention (MCASD).

Joseph Lelliott holds an LLB(Hons)/BA from the University of Queensland. He is a doctoral candidate, undertaking a thesis examining the smuggling of unaccompanied minors. He has served as a consultant to the United Nations Office on Drugs and Crime (UNODC), and is particularly interested in the intersections between migrant smuggling, human trafficking and international human rights law.

Maryanne Loughry is a Sister of Mercy and a psychologist and has worked in refugee work with the Jesuit Refugee Service since 1988. Dr Loughry is a visiting research scholar at the School of Social Work, Boston College, a Research Associate at the Refugee Studies Centre, University of Oxford, and a member of the Australian Government's Minister of Immigration Advisory Council on Asylum Seekers and Detention (MCASD).

Arezo Malakooti is an Australian trained lawyer, independent migration researcher and an adviser to IOM's Global Migration Data Analysis Centre in Berlin. She is an expert on the migratory movements from North Africa to Europe and across the Mediterranean and assists European governments in designing and evaluating migration policies and programs. Between 2011 and 2016 she was the Director of Migration Research at Altai Consulting.

Hannah Martin completed her Bachelor of Arts (Hons) and Bachelor of Laws (Hons) at the University of Sydney in 2012. She has worked as a research assistant to Professor Mary Crock and Emeritus Professor Ron McCallum, AO. She now works as a solicitor, and is an Honorary Research Affiliate at the Sydney Law School.

Isabel Martinez is an Assistant Professor of Sociology at John Jay College of Criminal Justice at City University of New York. Dr Martinez is also the Director of the Unaccompanied Latin American Minor Project that focuses on providing academic, social and legal support to recently arrived immigrant minors. Her book, *Becoming Transnational Youth Workers: Independent Mexican Teenage Migrants and Pathways of Survival and Social Mobility* is forthcoming.

Gerald L. Neuman is the J. Sinclair Armstrong Professor of International, Foreign and Comparative Law at Harvard Law School. From 2011 to

2014, he was a Member of the Human Rights Committee, the monitoring body created by the International Covenant on Civil and Political Rights.

Agnes Olusese is a humanitarian actor working with refugee and other displaced populations in East Africa around issues of protection, child protection, trafficking and rule of law as it affects displaced populations. She has a Master's in Law and Diplomacy from Fletcher, Tufts University, a second Master's from Yale University and Bachelor of Law from University of Nairobi.

Shamm Petros is a former refugee from Eritrea who has designed programs in economic development, education and protection for refugees and displaced populations across the Middle East and East Africa. She is currently a Master's Candidate at the University of Pennsylvania studying Counseling and Mental Health Services.

Geraldine Sadoway is a lawyer and law professor in Canada specializing in refugee law and international human rights. She is co-author of *Canadian Human Rights Law and Commentary* (3rd edn, 2016) and is a Director of the International and Transnational Law Intensive Program at Osgoode Hall Law School.

Andreas Schloenhardt is Professor of Criminal Law at the University of Queensland in Brisbane and Professorial Research Fellow in the Department of Criminal Law and Criminology at the University of Vienna. He serves as a consultant to the United Nations Office on Drugs and Crime (UNODC) and the Council of Europe. Andreas is a Visiting Professor at the University of Zurich and the University of St Gallen.

Savitri Taylor is an Associate Professor in the La Trobe Law School, Melbourne. Her main area of research is international, regional and Australian refugee law and asylum policy. Her current research project, funded by the Australian Research Council, is entitled 'Protecting Non-citizens: An Australian Legal and Political History, 1945–89'.

Claire R. Thomas is an Adjunct Professor at New York Law School where she directs the Asylum Clinic. She is the former director of training at the Safe Passage Project, a non-profit that aids unaccompanied minors. She was recently a Visiting Scholar at the New School's Zolberg Institute on Migration and Mobility. As a practising attorney she has represented many young people and asylum-seekers, including those held in detention.

David B. Thronson is Professor of Law and Associate Dean for Experiential Education at the Michigan State University College of Law.

His research focuses on the intersection of family law and immigration law, with particular emphasis on the impact of immigration law on children.

Gillian Triggs is the former President of the Australian Human Rights Commission. She was Dean of the Faculty of Law and Challis Professor of International Law at the University of Sydney from 2007 to 2012 and Director of the British Institute of International and Comparative Law from 2005 to 2007. She is a former Barrister and a former Governor of the College of Law. Her focus at the Commission was on the implementation in Australian law of the human rights treaties to which Australia is a party. She is the author of many books and papers on international law, including *International Law: Contemporary Principles and Practices* (2nd edn, 2011).

Kasey Tyler uses her qualifications in law and child protection to promote the rights of vulnerable children, both in Australia and internationally. Kasey is a member of three emergency humanitarian rosters and has been a Child Protection Officer for UNICEF Pacific and the United Nations Mission in South Sudan.

Kathryn (Kate) E. van Doore is an international children's rights lawyer and an academic at Griffith Law School, Australia. Kathryn currently researches the intersections of children's rights, human trafficking and modern slavery in international law. She was the recipient of the 2017 Anti-Slavery Freedom Award recognizing her significant contribution to this area.

Shelly Whitman is the Executive Director of the Romeo Dallaire Child Soldiers Initiative located at Dalhousie University, Canada. She is a Professor in International Development and Political Science. Shelly has published on issues related to children and armed conflict. Key appointments have included working on the peace process in the Democratic Republic of the Congo, as a professor at the University of Botswana, and as a consultant to UNICEF, New York.

Phoebe Yule is a graduate from Sydney Law School and former research associate for Professor Mary Crock at the University of Sydney. She works as a solicitor and migration agent in Sydney, delivering legal advice to asylum-seekers as part of a government-funded legal service.

Mimi Zou is the Career Development Fellow in Chinese Commercial Law at the University of Oxford. She has previously taught at Columbia, Chinese University of Hong Kong, Oxford, Utrecht University and

Sydney University. Dr Zou has been a consultant at the International Labour Organization since 2007. She received her law degree from Sydney Law School and her doctorate from Oxford where she was a Commonwealth Scholar.

Foreword: the plight of the migrant child

The situation of children displaced by armed conflict and other disasters is rightly a matter of great concern to the international community. In July 2017, I reported on the situation in Myanmar following a 12-day visit as Special Rapporteur on Human Rights in that country. In the five months following my visit, no less than 604,000 Rohingyas were forced to flee Myanmar into Bangladesh.[1] More than half of these refugees were children who in no time were facing starvation and death from disease and injury in conditions that can only be described as appalling.[2]

As the contributors to this volume attest, the sheer number of children on the move, both alone and with family members, is without precedent. The tragedy unfolding in Bangladesh finds parallels in the outflow of refugees from Syria, Yemen, Iraq and Afghanistan. Children continue to flee violence in unprecedented numbers from Central American states into the United States. The hardships children endure in displacement are all too predictable. Even where they seek safety in wealthy countries, however, escape from misery and even persecution cannot be assured. In even the most developed of the world's countries, migrant and refugee children remain in immigration detention; they are selected arbitrarily for transfer to other countries for 'processing'; they are denied access to basic social supports and to the education that is so critical to their wellbeing and human development.

---

1 My report is available at www.ohchr.org/EN/NewsEvents/Pages/DisplayNews.aspx?NewsID=21900&LangID=E. See Report from International Organization for Migration, Inter Sector Coordination Group, available at https://reliefweb.int/report/bangladesh/iscg-situation-update-rohingya-refugee-crisis-cox-sbazar-24-oct-2017.

2 See M. Berak 'Bangladesh is now home to almost 1 million Rohingya refugees', *Washington Post*, 25 October 2017, available at www.washingtonpost.com/news/worldviews/wp/2017/10/25/bangladesh-is-now-home-to-almost-1-million-rohingya-refugees/?utm_term=.533727373b37; and UNICEF Child Alert, *Outcast and Desperate: Rohingya Children Face a Perilous Future* (October 2017), available at www.unicef.org/publications/files/UNICEF_Rohingya_refugee_children_2017.pdf.

The dire situation facing so many child migrants stands in curious contrast to the steps that have been taken to create legal protections for children under international law – and, in consequence, under many domestic legal systems. Ten years in the making, the 1989 United Nations Convention on the Rights of the Child (CRC) will come of age on 2 September 2018.[3] The CRC is the distillation of many different legal systems and cultural traditions, underpinned by universally agreed, non-negotiable, norms and standards. It is founded on respect for the dignity and worth of each and every individual, regardless of race, colour, gender, language, religion, ability, social or ethnic origin. The CRC is the only human rights instrument with almost universal ratification.[4] All but one country globally (the United States) have committed to promote, protect and uphold the rights of all children. Until 2006, when the Convention on the Rights of Persons with Disabilities (CRPD)[5] was adopted, the CRC was also the only international human rights instrument that provided legal effect to the promotion and protection of the rights of children with disabilities.[6] As Crock and Martin attest in this volume,[7] the CRC and the CRPD share a similar structure and focus in the way that they operate to truly universalize the concept of human rights for children everywhere. The truly global reach of this book, with contributors from every major continent, illustrates well the impact that the UN human rights systems have had on law and increasingly practice relevant to protecting migrant children.

---

3 Convention on the Rights of the Child, opened for signature 20 November 1989, 1577 UNTS 3 (entered into force 2 September 1990) (CRC). The following account of the CRC and the operation of the CRC Committee is drawn in part from Y.H. Lee, 'Creating New Futures for All Children: The Promise of International Human Rights Law' (2013) 20 *Australian Journal of International Law* 3.

4 See the current list of the status of Ratification, Reservations and Declarations, available at United Nations Treaty Collection, http://treaties.un.org/Pages/ViewDetails.aspx?src=TREATY&mtdsg_no=IV-11&chapter=4&lang=en.

5 Convention on the Rights of Persons with Disabilities, opened for signature 30 March 2007, (2008) 2515 UNTS 3 (entered into force 3 May 2008) (CPRD); Optional Protocol to the Convention on the Rights of Persons with Disabilities, opened for signature 30 March 2007, (2007) 46 ILM 443 (entered into force 3 May 2008). The texts of both instruments are available at www.ohchr.org/EN/HRBodies/CRPD/Pages/ConventionRightsPersonsWithDisabilities.aspx.

6 CRC, Arts 2 and 23, address the rights of children with disabilities. Article 2 establishes that disability should not be grounds for discrimination and recognizes disability as a 'human rights' issue. In addition, Art. 23 explicitly addresses children with disabilities.

7 See Mary Crock and Hannah Martin, Chapter 4.

The CRC is underpinned by four general principles: Non-discrimination (Article 2); best interests of the child (Article 3); life, survival and development (Article 6); and respect for the views of the child (Article 12). All rights are indivisible and interdependent, providing for a holistic approach and avoiding hierarchy of rights. The CRC made a very significant departure from most other human rights instruments, declarations and strategies with respect to children. It established the view that children, both girls and boys, from birth to 18 years of age, are not simply the property of their parents, caregivers or the state. They are citizens, rights holders and social agents with the rights to participate and be heard in the shaping of their own development and destiny, according to their age and level of maturity. The Convention recognized that childhood is a transient state and that children are always changing and must be considered according to their 'evolving capacities' (Article 5).

Containing 42 substantive provisions for the guarantee and protection of economic, social, cultural, civil and political rights of children, the CRC has been supplemented by three Optional Protocols. The Optional Protocol on the involvement of children in armed conflict[8] raised the legal age of recruitment of children in armed conflict from 15 years to 18 years. The Optional Protocol on the sale of children, child prostitution and child pornography,[9] added further protection for children. Both Protocols were adopted in 2000 and entered into force in 2002. These two protocols significantly strengthened the rights of children to protection from the worst forms of human rights violations. As Tyler and Whitman show us in this book, they are of particular relevance to refugee children.[10]

The third Optional Protocol is close to my heart. When I was elected as the Chairperson of the CRC Committee in 2007, I made it my mission to complete the journey towards the full realization of children's rights. Working with the NGO Group for the CRC and the EU-GRULAC Group, a discussion of a communications procedure was reopened. The Chairperson of the CRC Committee reports to the Third Committee of the General Assembly each year. I brought this issue to the 63rd General Assembly for rigorous debate. A Human Rights Council Resolution[11]

---

[8] Optional Protocol to the Convention on the Rights of the Child on the Involvement of Children in Armed Conflict, opened for signature 25 May 2000, 2173 UNTS 222. See General Assembly Resolution A/RES/54/263.

[9] Optional Protocol to the Convention on the Rights of the Child on the Sale of Children, Child Prostitution and Child Pornography, opened for signature 25 May 2000, 2171 UNTS 227. See General Assembly Resolution A/RES/54/263.

[10] See Kasey Tyler and Shelly Whitman, Chapter 23.

[11] *Open-ended Working Group on an Optional Protocol to the Convention on the*

was later adopted to establish a working group to explore the possibility of elaborating an optional protocol to the CRC to provide a communications procedure. On 9 June 2011, the Third Optional Protocol to the CRC was accepted by consensus[12] and was adopted at the 66th General Assembly on 2 November 2011.[13] It entered into force on 14 April 2014 and by November 2017 had 51 signatories and 36 parties.[14]

As I wrote in 2013,[15] much was lost during negotiations, but we did achieve an instrument that provides children and/or their representative with the right to seek remedy for violations of their rights. Rights have no meaning if there are no timely and effective remedies available. The third Optional Protocol represented a significant step towards the full realization of children's rights, consistent with Article 12, the right of the child to be heard.

This Protocol was of special significance for the CRC Committee as it empowered the Committee to hear individual complaints in addition to performing the functions of reviewing the policies and practices of states parties to ensure compliance with the Convention's various provisions. Over time, I have watched with interest as the Committee has taken more and more interest in the particular challenges facing migrant children. Initiatives to improve respect for the rights and needs of refugee children include the adoption of a series of General Comments on children on the move, including General Comment No. 6, which is devoted to the particular challenges facing unaccompanied and separated migrant children.[16] The Committee has also conducted days of General Discussion on migrant children.[17]

Rights of the Child to Provide a Communications Procedure, Human Rights Council Res., UN GAOR, 11th Sess., Agenda item 3, UN Doc. A/HRC/11/L.3 (12 June 2009).

[12] Optional Protocol to the Convention on the Rights of the Child, Human Rights Council Res., UN GAOR, 17th Sess., A/HRC//RES/17/18 (17 June 2011).

[13] Optional Protocol to the Convention on the Rights of the Child on a Communications Procedure, GA, UN GAOR, 3rd Comm., 66th Sess., Agenda item 64, UN Doc. A/C.3/66/L.66 (2 November 2011).

[14] See https://treaties.un.org/Pages/ViewDetails.aspx?src=TREATY&mtdsg_no=IV-11-d&chapter=4&lang=en.

[15] See Lee, 'Creating New Futures for All Children', above n. 3.

[16] See CRC, Part II, especially Arts 42, 44 and 45; and UNCRC, *General Comment No. 6: Treatment of Unaccompanied and Separated Children Outside Their Country of Origin*, 39th Sess., UN Doc. CRC/GC/2005/6 (1 September 2005).

[17] The UNCRC devoted its 2012 Day of General Discussion to the rights of all children in the context of international migration. The discussion took place on Friday, 28 September 2012. See www.ohchr.org/EN/HRBodies/CRC/Pages/Discussion2012.aspx for links to the program, Background Paper and Report.

In commending this book to everyone, I would like to thank Lenni Benson, who is the founder and director of the Safe Passage Project, established to assist unaccompanied and separated migrant youth in New York, one of the top four locations for unaccompanied youth. This work is crucial in terms of navigating US migration and asylum laws, for our young people who have had to make a very difficult decision to migrate.

My deepest thanks go to my dear, long-time friend Mary Crock. Her dedication on the topic of migration and refugees is so profound and of great conviction. I will never forget the work she has done as an academic and as a practising lawyer to improve the law and practice for refugee children, including those with disabilities, in Australia and internationally. If there is any question surrounding issues for vulnerable migrants, Mary Crock and her work is where one should always start. Without a doubt, this book will serve as an important source for protecting migrant children.

Yanghee Lee[18]
Seoul, 6 December 2017

[18] UN Special Rapporteur on the situation of human rights in Myanmar, Former Chairperson of UN Committee on the Rights of the Child, Professor, Department of Child Psychology and Education, Sungkyunkwan University, Seoul.

Acknowledgements

The two editors of this book are best described as 'hands-on' academics. We have both maintained our credentials as lawyers after moving into the academy from legal practice. A co-founder (in 1989) of Melbourne's first community legal centre specializing in immigration and refugee law (known now as Refugee Legal), Mary has taken a particular interest in the plight of migrant children over many years. In 2006, Lenni began holding trainings for *pro bono* attorneys at New York Law School to expand the pool of attorneys prepared to represent child migrants. In 2012, as the numbers of unaccompanied minors arriving at the south west border of the United States grew exponentially, she founded the Safe Passage Project, a law school clinic combined with a non-profit representing hundreds of children via direct and mentored *pro bono* services.

This book has involved considerable work and commitment on the part of many people. We are deeply grateful to each of our contributors and for their patience in reviewing and revising their work so as to give a sense of unity and fluency to what would otherwise be a very diverse collection. Research for this book was made possible through the support of private donor, Ms Judy Harris; research funding by New York Law School and private donor, Sheila Wellington; and before that, the Australian Research Council, Linkage Project LP100200596 'Small Mercies, Big Futures: Enhancing Law, Policy and Practice in the Selection, Protection and Settlement of Refugee Children and Youth'. In 2015, many of the authors met at the University of Sydney (supported by Sydney Law School) and later that year New York Law School convened a meeting of many of the US authors. We thank NYLS alumnus Lap J. Wong who donated funds to support the second of these gatherings.

For research assistance, we owe a particular debt of gratitude to Dominic Wilcox-Watson who helped us with research and a very considerable amount of editing. Thanks are due also to: Phoebe Kiat, Hannah Martin, Anna Pejovic and Laura Smith-Khan. We thank and pay special tribute to Jason Pobjoy who read and commented on two chapters and whose recent work on refugee children underpins many more. We acknowledge also the work and support of Jacqueline Bhabha, Judy Cashmore, Michelle Foster, Jane McAdam, Ben Saul, Rebecca Wallace,

Mark Capaldi, John R. Campbell, Jennifer Nagda, Elizabeth Frankel, Ilham Kumar and Elizabeth Kennedy.

We are deeply grateful for the support of our respective faculties, in particular Dean Joellen Riley, Julia Robertson and Kimberley Wetherall at Sydney Law School and Dean Anthony Crowell and William LaPiana at New York Law School. Finally, we both acknowledge the love, wisdom and scholarly support provided by Ron McCallum.

This book was prepared during a time of enormous need and fast paced change. It brings together authors from across the globe to write on various aspects of law, policy and practice relevant to children on the move both generally and in specific regions. Unless otherwise indicated, the material is current to November 2017. The views expressed by each of the individual authors are theirs alone and should not be attributed to other authors or to organizations they may represent.

Mary would like to dedicate this book to Gerard, Daniel, Kate, Virginia, Liang (Pheap), Riz, and Ali; and to all the migrant children they (and others) have brought into her life. Lenni dedicates this book to her family: John, Max, Lily, Bill, Shelly, Timm and Jacque. She also remembers her grandmother Hilda Baer, an unaccompanied minor child smuggled into the United States in 1907 by a desperate family fleeing persecution. Finally, she thanks the remarkable staff and volunteers of the Safe Passage Project who every day defend the rights of migrant children.

Abbreviations

AAT	Administrative Appeals Tribunal (Aus)
AAT MRD	Administrative Appeals Tribunal (Migration and Refugee Division) (Aus)
ACRWC	African Convention on the Rights and Welfare of the Child
ACTIP	ASEAN Convention and Plan of Action Against Trafficking in Persons, Especially in Women and Children
ASEAN	Association of South-East Asian States
ASIO	Australian Security Intelligence Organisation
ATD	alternatives to detention
AU	African Union
BIA	Board of Immigration Appeals (US)
BID	Best Interest Determination
CAAFAG	child associated with armed force or armed group
CAM	Central American Minors Refugee/Parole Program
CARSI	Central American Regional Security Initiative
CAT	Convention Against Torture
CBP	Customs and Border Protection (US)
CBSA	Canadian Border Services Agency
CCI	Charitable Children's Institution (Kenya)
CCP	Chinese Communist Party
CEAS	Common European Asylum System
CFR	Charter of Fundamental Rights of the European Union
CJEU	Court of Justice of the European Union
CoE	Council of Europe
COMAR	Mexican Commission for Assisting Refugees
CRC	Convention on the Rights of the Child
CRC-OPAC	Optional Protocol to the Convention on the Rights of the Child on the Involvement of Children in Armed Conflict
CRC-OPCP	Optional Protocol to the Convention on the Rights of the Child on Communications Procedure
CRC-OPSC	Optional Protocol to the Convention on the Rights of

	the Child on the Sale of Children, Child Prostitution and Child Pornography
CRPD	Convention on the Rights of Persons with Disabilities
CRRF	Comprehensive Refugee Response Framework
CUNY	City University of New York
DACA	Deferred Action for Childhood Arrivals
DCO	District Children's Officer (Kenya)
DFN	designated foreign national
DHHS	Department of Health and Human Services (US)
DHS	Department of Homeland Security (US)
DIBP	Department of Immigration and Border Protection (Aus)
DOS	Department of State (US)
DR	designated representative
DRA	Department of Refugee Affairs (Kenya)
DCR	Democratic Republic of the Congo
DR-CAFTA	Dominican Republic-Central American Free Trade Agreement
ECHR	European Convention on Human Rights
ECOWAS	Economic Community of West African States
ECtHR	European Court of Human Rights
EOIR	Executive Office for Immigration Review (US)
ESC	European Social Charter
EU	European Union
FGM	female genital mutilation
FJDA	Federal Juvenile Delinquency Act (US)
FRONTEX	European Border and Coastguard Agency
GBV	gender-based violence
HEV	Humanitarian Evacuation Program
HPG	Humanitarian Policy Group
HRC	Human Rights Committee (UN)
HRW	Human Rights Watch
IAA	Immigration Assessment Authority (Aus)
IAAAS	Immigration Advice and Application Assistance Scheme (Aus)
IACHR	Inter-American Commission on Human Rights
IACtHR	Inter-American Court of Human Rights
ICCPR	International Covenant on Civil and Political Rights
ICE	Immigration and Customs Enforcement (US)
ICESCR	International Covenant on Economic, Social and Cultural Rights
IDP	internally displaced person

IGC	Intergovernmental Consultations on Migration, Asylum and Refugees
IGOC Act	Immigration (Guardianship of Children) Act (Aus)
IHL	international humanitarian law
IIRIRA	Illegal Immigration Reform and Immigrant Responsibility Act 1996 (US)
ILO	International Labour Organization
IMF	International Monetary Fund
INA	Immigration and Nationality Act (US)
INS	Immigration and Naturalization Service (US)
IOM	International Organisation for Migration
IRB	Immigration and Refugee Board (Canada)
IRIN	Integrated Regional Information Networks (Kenya)
IRO	International Refugee Organisation
IRPA	Immigration and Refugee Protection Act 2002 (Canada)
ISAP	Intensive Supervision Appearance Program
LGBTI	lesbian, gay, bisexual, transgender and intersex
MCFD	Ministry of Children and Family Development (Canada)
MENA	Middle East and North Africa
MNI	minimum necessary income
MOU	Memorandum of Understanding
MRM	Monitoring and Reporting Mechanism
NAFTA	North American Free Trade Agreement
NGO	non-governmental organization
NTCA	Northern Triangle of Central America (El Salvador, Honduras and Guatemala)
OAS	Organization of American States
OCL	Office of the Children's Lawyer (Canada)
OLAP	Office of Legal Access Programs (US EOIR)
ORR	Office of Refugee Resettlement (US)
PACE	Parliamentary Assembly of the Council of Europe
PAIS	Primary Application Information Service (Aus)
PJCHR	Parliamentary Joint Committee on Human Rights (Aus)
POM Act	Migration Amendment (Protection and Other Measures) Act 2015 (Aus)
PRC	People's Republic of China
PSG	particular social group
RRT	Refugee Review Tribunal (Aus)
RSD	Refugee Status Determination

SAR	Syrian Arab Republic
SCWG-CAAC	Security Council Working Group on Children and Armed Conflict
SPLA	Sudan Peoples' Liberation Army
SPLAiO	Sudan Peoples' Liberation Army in Opposition
SRSG-CAAC	Special Representative of the Secretary-General for Children and Armed Conflict
STCA	Safe Third Country Agreement
TCN	third country national
TEU	Treaty on the European Union
TFEU	Treaty on the Functioning of the European Union
TVPRA	Trafficking Victims Protection Reauthorization Act 2008 (US)
UAM	unaccompanied minor
UASC	unaccompanied and separated children
UASC Leave	Unaccompanied Asylum-Seeking Child Leave to Remain (UK)
UDHR	Universal Declaration of Human Rights
UK	United Kingdom
U-LAMP	Unaccompanied Latin American Minor Project
UMA	unauthorized maritime arrival
UN	United Nations
UNCRC	United Nations Committee on the Rights of the Child
UNCRPD	United Nations Committee on the Rights of Persons with Disabilities
UNDESA	United Nations Population Division, Department of Economic and Social Affairs
UNHCR	United Nations High Commissioner for Refugees
UNICEF	United Nations International Children's Emergency Fund
UNODC	United Nations Office on Drugs and Crimes
UNRWA	United Nations Relief and Works Agency for Palestine Refugees in the Near East
US	United States
USC	United States Code
USCIS	United States Citizenship and Immigration Service
VAWA	Violence Against Women Act (US)
WHO	World Health Organization

1. Central issues in the protection of child migrants

Mary Crock and Lenni B. Benson

1. SEEING AND HEARING THE MIGRANT CHILD

In September 2015, images of a three-year-old Syrian child washed ashore on Turkey's Aegean coast dominated media around the world. Aylan Kurdi's tiny, lifeless body was photographed face down on the water's edge; watched by solemn-looking Turkish policemen; lifted and carried gently to dry land. Returning to the village from which the family had fled, the grieving father buried the toddler along with the child's mother and older brother.[1] These children became the faces of the tragedy unfolding in Syria. Their deaths brought home the dangers and human cost of the mass forced migration sweeping across Europe. Yet the tragedies continue. As this book was going to press, thousands of Rohingyan refugees were fleeing religious, ethnic and political violence in Myanmar. Between August and October 2017, the United Nation's International Children's Emergency Fund (UNICEF) estimated that 230,000 Rohingyan children had crossed the border into Bangladesh. Unable to secure work and legal status, many of these children were immediately vulnerable to trafficking and slavery.[2]

We write at a time of relentless change, if not crisis. In the West, long-standing cooperative frameworks of the European Union (EU) are threatened with disintegration after Britain's decision to withdraw from the Union.[3] Minority communities in the United States of America (US)

---

[1] See, e.g., H. Smith, 'Shocking images of drowned Syrian boy show tragic plight of refugees', *The Guardian* (online), 2 September 2015, available at www.theguardian.com/world/2015/sep/02/shocking-image-of-drowned-syrian-boy-shows-tragic-plight-of-refugees.

[2] UNICEF, *Outcast and Desperate: Rohingya Refugee Children Face a Perilous Future* (UNICEF, October 2017) available at www.unicef.org/publications/files/UNICEF_Rohingya_refugee_children_2017.pdf.

[3] See, e.g., the collection of articles published in *The Economist*, available at www.economist.com/Brexit.

have been unsettled by sweeping anti-immigrant Executive Orders and other measures following the election of President Donald Trump.[4] For its part, the EU has put unprecedented pressure on an external state, Turkey, to accept the return of people seeking protection in EU countries. Already playing host to millions of refugees from the Syrian conflict, an attempted coup in that country prompted dangerously repressive measures from President Recep Tayyip Ergodan.[5] The threat of terrorism seemed to spread even as the 'Caliphate' of fundamentalist groups such as the Islamic State (Isis or Daesh) diminished.[6] Candidates with increasingly extreme (often xenophobic) views have been elected or nominated for high office across the world.[7]

In many instances, political movements to the right appear to have roots in public concern about (uncontrolled) migration.[8] The percentage of people on the move around the world may have remained relatively stable (at 3.3 per cent of the world's population).[9] However, numbers

---

[4] For a collection of the Executive Orders restricting the admission of refugees and cancelling some of the special programmes for resettlement of children in the United States see, generally, https://pennstatelaw.psu.edu/immigration-after-election.

[5] See, e.g., E. Cunningham, L. Sly and Z. Karatas, 'Turkey rounds up thousands of suspects in failed coup attempt', *Washington Post*, 16 July 2016, available at www.washingtonpost.com/world/after-bloody-night-turkeys-president-declares-coup-attempt-foiled/2016/07/16/9b84151e-4af7-11e6-8dac-0c6e4accc5b1_story.html.

[6] See, e.g., K. Yourish, D. Watkins, T. Guratikanon and J.C. Lee, 'How many people have been killed in ISIS attacks around the world?', *New York Times*, 16 July 2016, available at www.nytimes.com/interactive/2016/03/25/world/map-isis-attacks-around-the-world.html?_r=0.

[7] Examples in 2016 include: Norbert Hofer won 47.6 per cent of the vote in Austria and narrowly lost the national election after running on a nationalist and anti-immigrant platform. Donald Trump won the US Presidency after promising mass deportations and tough new border controls. Pauline Hanson and three other members of an extreme right wing anti-immigrant party, One Nation, were elected to the Australian Senate. See the collection of articles at www.theguardian.com/world/far-right. See also M. Hirsch, 'Why the New Nationalists are Taking Over', *Politico*, 27 June 2016, available at www.politico.com/magazine/story/2016/06/nationalism-donald-trump-boris-johnson-brexit-foreign-policy-xenophobia-isolationism-213995.

[8] See, e.g., S. Collinson and J. Diamond, 'Trump on immigration: no amnesty, no pivot', CNN, 1 September 2016, available at http://edition.cnn.com/2016/08/31/politics/donald-trump-immigration-speech/ and A. Travis, 'Fear of immigration drove the leave victory – not immigration itself', *The Guardian* (online), 24 June 2016, available at www.theguardian.com/politics/2016/jun/24/voting-details-show-immigration-fears-were-paradoxical-but-decisive.

[9] See UN Department of Economic and Social Affairs (DESA), *International*

migrating to developed countries have risen sharply in recent decades. If forced migration between developing and developed countries has become one of the world's great problems, the movement of children as migrants represents compounding complexity. By the start of 2017 it was estimated that nearly 51 per cent of the world's 65.6 million forcibly displaced people were children and that approximately 22.5 million were in need of humanitarian protection.[10] Using UN data, UNICEF claims that one in 200 children in the world was a child refugee in 2015, representing a doubling of the global population of such children in one decade.[11] In some instances, the rise in the number of children travelling alone has been so extreme that systems are overwhelmed, eroding support for the protection of these most vulnerable of migrants.[12]

After years of uncertainty and mass international movements of children, the United Nations (UN) has begun to address the need for express

---

Migration Report 2015 (September 2016), available at www.un.org/en/development/desa/population/migration/index.shtml.

[10] UNHCR, *Global Trends: Forced Displacement in 2016* (December 2016), available at www.unhcr.org/5943e8a34.pdf. These estimates exceed the mid-year all-time high, see A. Edwards, *Global Forced Migration Hits Record High* (UNHCR, 20 June 2016), available at www.unhcr.org/en-us/news/latest/2016/6/5763b65a4/global-forced-displacement-hits-record-high.html.

[11] See, e.g., UNICEF, *Uprooted: The Growing Crisis for Refugee and Migrant Children* (7 September 2016), available at http://weshare.unicef.org/Package/2AMZIFQP5K8. In 2017, UNICEF and IOM estimated that 100,000 children under the age of 18 had crossed into Europe since 2016 and that over 20 per cent of those who sought asylum were unaccompanied. See UNICEF and IOM, *Harrowing Journeys: Children and Youth on the Move Across the Mediterranean Sea, at Risk of Trafficking and Exploitation* (2017), p. 31, available at www.unicef.org/publications/files/Harrowing_Journeys_Children_and_youth_on_the_move_across_the_Mediterranean.pdf. For a discussion of the statistical data, see Arezo Mallakooti, Chapter 2.

[12] In 2017, the United Kingdom was thought to host as many as 65,000 unaccompanied migrant children whose right to remain would be contested as they reached their 18th birthday (the age of legal majority in that country). See Law Society of Scotland, 'Legal Services Agency Co-Founds Migrant Children Project', *The Journal*, 24 May 2016, available at www.journalonline.co.uk/News/1021800.aspx#.V8oiNJgrKM8. One Interpol report suggests that in 2015–16 one in every nine unaccompanied children was unaccounted for in Europe. See UNICEF Press Release, *Unaccompanied Refugee and Migrant Children in Urgent Need of Protection, Warns UNICEF* (6 May 2016), available at www.unicef.org/media/media_91069.html. With its extensive undocumented population, the United States also plays host to very large numbers of undocumented migrant children. A 2014 survey estimated that there were 1.4 million people under 21 years of age, of an estimated 11 million undocumented migrants. See American Community Survey 2014 data available at http://cmsny.org/cms-research/democratizingdata/.

principles that will guide and govern the treatment of children on the move. In September 2016, on the eve of his departure from US political life, President Barack Obama hosted a leaders' Summit on Refugees, an event that paralleled the High Level Summit organized by the UN General Assembly on the large-scale movement of refugees and migrants.[13] The resulting New York Declaration for Refugees and Migrants, adopted unanimously by UN member states, has been described as 'a milestone for global solidarity with refugees and the global refugee regime'.[14] The Declaration is in three parts, beginning with a section that applies to both migrants and refugees, followed by two parts relating separately to refugees and to migrants. One of the most significant aspects of the instrument is that for the first time UN member states committed to sharing responsibility for refugees. It reads:

> We underline the centrality of international cooperation to the refugee protection regime. We recognize the burdens that large movements of refugees place on national resources, especially in the case of developing countries. To address the needs of refugees and receiving States, we commit to a more equitable sharing of the burden and responsibility for hosting and supporting the world's refugees, while taking account of existing contributions and the differing capacities and resources among States.[15]

The Declaration includes two important appendices: Annex I, the 'Comprehensive Refugee Response Framework', and Annex II, entitled 'Towards a Global Compact for Safe, Orderly and Regular Migration'. These contain the elements of frameworks for a comprehensive 'people centred' response to the challenges of forced and mass migration. They task UNHCR and the International Organisation for Migration (IOM) with initiating the application of the agreed frameworks through the conclusion of two 'Global Compacts'. The objective of the Compacts is to improve international responses to large movements of refugees and migrants, including protracted refugee situations. They are to be included in the Secretary General's 2018 Annual Report to the UN General Assembly.

The period following the New York Declaration saw a flurry of activity as UNHCR and IOM worked together and separately to convene a whole range of meetings – thematic, regional, academic, 'stakeholder',

---

13 See http://refugeesmigrants.un.org/summit.

14 UNHCR, 'Towards a Global Compact on Refugees: A Roadmap', available at www.unhcr.org/58e625aa7.

15 New York Declaration for Refugees and Migrants, 3 October 2016, para. [68], available at www.un.org/en/ga/search/view_doc.asp?symbol=A/RES/71/1.

'stocktaking', all with a focus on a 2018 deadline. For us, these initiatives give reason for at least cautious optimism. In mid-December 2017, President Trump made a show of declaring that the United States would play no part in the Global Compact on migrants.[16] However, no mention was made of the process relating to refugees, which suggests that the United States may continue its involvement in this facet of the Global Compact process. If they are concluded, the two Compacts will be extraordinary achievements. However, even if this is not the case, the very process associated with their negotiation has worked to generate a sense of energy and enthusiasm for cooperation and change. Across Africa and parts of the Americas, a number of countries moved immediately to adopt the Comprehensive Refugee Response Framework (CRRF).[17]

As many have noted, the Global Compacts will be political instruments, rather than documents that directly bind states. In the recent past, the device of a 'Compact' was used to frame a multilateral agreement to compensate states hosting refugees from Syria on the understanding that the host states would impede or discourage onward movements (notably to Europe).[18] The Global Compacts will be less specific in application and proscriptions. Their significance lies in the fact that they build on existing legal frameworks, including the 1951 Refugee Convention and the various UN human rights instruments. For international migrants, the Compact

---

[16] Secretary of State Tillerson claimed that the gesture was necessary to affirm US state sovereignty. He rejected assertions that international cooperation was the best means to address large migration flows, including those of children. See www.state.gov/secretary/remarks/2017/12/276190.htm. See also R. Gladstone, 'US quits Migration Pact, saying it infringes on sovereignty', *New York Times*, 3 December 2017, available at www.nytimes.com/2017/12/03/world/americas/united-nations-migration-pact.html?_r=0.

[17] See, e.g., D. Endres, 'Update on the Practical Roll-out of the CRRF', Address at the Annual NGO Consultations, UNHCR, 14 June 2017, available at www.unhcr.org/en-us/594248734. The CRRF has four key aims: (1) ease pressure on countries that welcome and host refugees; (2) build self-reliance of refugees; (3) expand access to resettlement in third countries/other complementary pathways; (4) foster conditions that enable refugees voluntarily to return to their home countries. By December 2017, there had been agreed adoption of the framework in Djibouti, Ethiopia, Kenya, Uganda, Tanzania, Zambia, and Somalia. Belize, Costa Rica, Guatemala, Honduras, Mexico and Panama were taking similar steps.

[18] See, e.g., Government of Jordan, 'The Jordan Compact: A New Holistic Approach between the Hashemite Kingdom of Jordan and the International Community to Deal with the Syrian Refugee Crisis', *ReliefWeb*, 7 February 2016, available at https://reliefweb.int/report/jordan/jordan-compact-new-holistic-approach-between-hashemite-kingdom-jordan-and; and EU–Lebanon Partnership, *The Compact* (European Commission, August 2017), available at https://ec.europa.eu/neighbourhood-enlargement/sites/near/files/lebanon-compact.pdf.

has the potential to act as a real agent for change, if only because of the paucity of the legal frameworks that exist for the governance of migration outside of the refugee context.[19] For present purposes, it is noteworthy that the undertakings of the states include a statement that they commit to:

> protect the human rights and fundamental freedoms of all refugee and migrant children, regardless of their status, and giving primary consideration at all times to the best interests of the child, and to comply with their obligations under the Convention on the Rights of the Child.[20]

Of course, there are limitations inherent in the Global Compact process. Perhaps most disappointing is the decision to treat separately the issue of refugees and forced migration on the one hand and migration generally on the other. This decision will entrench the tendency to 'silo' law and practice in two areas that in reality are intrinsically linked. The complexity of refugee status determination processes everywhere reflects the fact that most mass migration events tend to involve mixed populations of both migrants and refugees. Moreover, the Compacts also exclude internally displaced persons (IDPs) who can be just as vulnerable (and as numerous) in displacement as refugees and international migrants. The side-events organized by UNICEF and specialist non-governmental organizations (NGOs) around the Global Compacts process underscore the fact that effort and organization continue to be required if the voices of children and of other vulnerable migrants are to be heard. The inclusion of these voices is critical if the Compacts are to achieve their full potential.

On 17 November 2017, two of the UN human rights treaty bodies issued Joint General Comments that address directly the protection needs of child migrants and refugees.[21] The two comments outline key concerns

---

[19] This point is made by T. Gammeltoft Hansen et al., 'The Normative Impact of the Global Compact on Safe, Orderly and Regular Migration' in *What is a Compact? Migrants' Rights and State Responsibilities Regarding the Design of the UN Global Compact for Safe, Orderly and Regular Migration* (Raoul Wallenberg Institute, 11 October 2017), available at https://papers.ssrn.com/sol3/papers.cfm?abstract_id=3051027. See also the other papers from the conference held by the Raoul Wallenberg Institute in October 2017; and E. Ferris, 'Negotiating Two New Global Compacts: Processes, Politics and Problems', Kaldor Centre Conference 2017, available at www.kaldorcentre.unsw.edu.au/kaldor-centre-conference-2017-global-compacts-refugees-and-migration.

[20] General Assembly Resolution 71/1, para. [32].

[21] Joint General Comment No. 3 (2017) of the Committee on the Protection of the Rights of All Migrant Workers and Members of Their Families and No.

and articulate minimum protections essential for the health and safety of these children. At last, the international community seems to be recognizing the wisdom in demanding that member states adapt their procedures and substantive protections to recognize the unique challenges facing young migrants, particularly when travelling alone.

Around the globe children are migrating with and without their families in search of freedom, safety or simply a better life. They travel for education, for work, for pleasure, or for a complex combination of reasons. This book has at its centre the millions of children who are being or who have been displaced across borders by wars and other catastrophes. However, our collective concern is not just with these most vulnerable of children, but also with other young migrants whose experiences and needs are more finely nuanced.

We agree with the criticism advanced by UNICEF that child migrants are presented in the literature too frequently as 'passive, vulnerable and exploited'.[22] At one extreme there are children who are subjected to human trafficking, a modern version of slavery.[23] On the other hand, an increasing number of children travel abroad in situations of relative freedom in search of work or for other, facially benign reasons. As explored in the concluding parts of the book, stories of child migration can also involve threat and danger to receiving countries. Child soldiers are one iteration of children viewed by societies as a menace. Young people fleeing gang violence are perceived as another threat by some receiving communities. The growth of the smuggling industry is fuelled in part by child labour as smugglers leverage the fact that juveniles are less likely to face criminal

---

22 (2017) of the Committee on the Rights of the Child on the General Principles regarding the human rights of children in the context of international migration (Joint General Comment No. 3); and Joint General Comment No. 4 (2017) of the Committee on the Protection of the Rights of All Migrant Workers and Members of Their Families and No. 23 (2017) of the Committee on the Rights of the Child on State obligations regarding the human rights of children in the context of international migration in countries of origin, transit, destination and return (Joint General Comment No. 4). The two General Comments are available at www.ohchr.org/EN/NewsEvents/Pages/DisplayNews.aspx?NewsID=22408&LangID=E.

[22] See Committee on the Rights of the Child, *The Rights of all Children in the Context of International Migration, Background Paper* (August 2012), available at www.ohchr.org/Documents/HRBodies/CRC/Discussions/2012/2012DGDBackgroundPaper.pdf.

[23] The International Labour Organization (ILO) provides estimates of people trafficked or in forced labour. In 2016, the ILO estimates 21 million trafficked people and children (<18) represent 26 per cent (5.5 million). See ILO, *Statistics on Forced Labour, Modern Slavery and Human Trafficking* (2016), available at www.ilo.org/global/topics/forced-labour/policy-areas/statistics/lang--en/index.htm.

prosecution.[24] Not all migrant children are innocent. Not all move without agency and intent.

As Jacqueline Bhabha notes, it was not until the 1990s that either policy-makers or scholars paid much attention at all to the drivers of child migration.[25] Nor was any attempt made to address the obvious and unique vulnerabilities of children travelling and living as migrants in host countries. While children living out of home care have suffered and continue to suffer abuse and deprivation all around the world, the focus of child welfare initiatives until very recently has been on children who are *citizens* of a state. Bhabha points to two factors that have operated as agents of change. The first is the global rise in the number of children on the move as solo migrants, travelling either alone or separated from responsible family members. She argues that the phenomenon has resulted in conflicting responses to children on the move. The vulnerability of unaccompanied or separated child migrants to human rights abuse has elicited sympathetic responses. Yet, real or imagined threats posed by young migrants with lived experience of violence and lawlessness have prompted punitive measures.

The second factor that has led to changes in attitude towards child migrants is legal. As we explore in Part II of this book, recent decades have seen a virtual explosion in international, regional and domestic laws and policies relevant to child migrants. These initiatives are recent but, sadly, have not necessarily ensured either uniformity in state practice nor uniformly sympathetic responses to young people on the move. The least that can be said is that migrant children are now included on the agenda of law-makers around the world.

Global developments in law and policy reflect a growing awareness of diversity in both the reasons children move across borders and the

---

[24] Many nations do not criminally prosecute juveniles engaged in human smuggling. In the United States, the federal statutes require a transfer to the state for juvenile delinquency prosecution unless the state declines to prosecute. 18 USC s. 5032. Federal prosecutions of juveniles using the alien smuggling statute are very rare. In Arizona, juveniles are being prosecuted under a state delinquency statute. See E.S. Eaton and D. Gonzalez, 'Should young teens face trial as adults for aiding Mexican drug cartels?', *Arizona Republic (Phoenix)*, 14 August 2016. Australia similarly does not prosecute young people engaged in smuggling if they are under the age of 18. See E. McKenzie, *Prosecution of Juveniles or People Smuggling Offences*, Practice Group Instruction No. 1, Human Exploitation and Border Protection (CDPP, 30 October 2014), p. 1. For a discussion of the US consideration of children with a criminal history, see also Farrin Anello, Chapter 22.

[25] See J. Bhabha, *Child Migration and Human Rights in a Global Age* (Princeton University Press, 2014).

situations they face. Academics have at last begun the task of analysing and deconstructing this complexity.[26] Our aim is to complement this work, focusing on issues around the protection of migrant children. The range of scholars who have joined us in this venture stand testament to the growing interest within the academy in these issues. While many of the contributors in this book are legal scholars, almost all are actively engaged in direct advocacy or policy development. We are joined also by scholars from non-legal disciplines and by human rights workers. Our joint concern is to create a collection of chapters that will foster greater understanding of how and why children are on the move. Together we explore ways in which laws, policies and practices can or should operate to protect and nurture young migrants. Providing a broad survey of developments throughout the world, the chapters in this collection build a foundation for assessment and improvement in the rather chaotic and haphazard way in which states react to large movements of children.

Today, there are a multitude of legal schemes that intersect and press upon the lives of migrant children. Yet few nations, if any, have fully integrated norms of child welfare law into their migration laws and policies. Too often, immigration enforcement trumps the values and systems designed to promote the welfare of children. The universal notion that children's best interests should predominate is often not acknowledged at all in immigration adjudication.[27] Migration systems need both greater substantive and procedural coherence to protect children on the move, even as they acknowledge the sovereignty and security concerns of host states.

In this introductory chapter we identify themes that will be carried throughout the book. We begin in section 2 with a discussion of the human rights challenges presented by children on the move, posing questions that our contributors will address as they build on the themes we identify. This is followed by an examination of obstacles that have been created to recognizing child migrants as rights bearers. After setting out in section 4 a brief outline of the book's structure, the chapter concludes with some comments on global initiatives that have been made to address the challenges associated with mass migration, on the one hand, and of forced movement of refugees on the other. We will argue that the uncertainty and

---

[26] See, in particular, J. Bhabha, D. Senovilla Hernandez and J. Kanics (eds), *Handbook on Migration and Childhood* (Edward Elgar Publishing, 2018).

[27] See discussion of the best interest standard in the UN Joint Committee Report No. 4, para. [11] (liberty and family life protection), paras. [14]–[15] (protections in proceedings and in tribunal determinations), para. [34] (assessing benefit of reunification with family), and para. [65] (in developing bilateral agreements).

risks facing the world in the new millennium certainly constitute problems – but they also offer opportunities for positive change.

2. MIGRATION AND CHILDHOOD: CHALLENGES AND QUESTIONS

Four foundational principles inform our discussion of how states should respond to children on the move. The first is that childhood is unique in that the status of being a child is transitory and (absent disabilities) the capacities of children evolve as children age. Second, it follows that children require special protection and assistance, most particularly in their younger and adolescent years, if they are to develop and thrive. The third point is that procedural accommodations should be made for children in recognition of the physical and cognitive stages of their development. The fourth and final principle both flows from and unites the three that precede it. It is that the treatment of child migrants matters because it has long-term consequences, both for the children themselves and for their host communities. It is a truth too frequently demonstrated that the abuse of children affects how they develop and grow. Damaged children too frequently become damaged (and even potentially dangerous) adults. Conversely, making adequate provision for the protection of young ones displaced from hearth and home can lead to the enrichment not just of the young people themselves but also of the societies into which they are received. In what follows we will address each of these principles in turn.

2.1 The Unique Status of Childhood: But Who Is a Child?

By definition, the status of child is not static: childhood is a temporary condition that, for most, ceases with the passage of time. In many cultures, the attainment of a certain chronological age is set as the marker for transition into adulthood. Article 1 of the Convention on the Rights of the Child[28] (the most subscribed of all the UN Conventions other than the UN Charter itself) defines children as persons aged less than 18 years. However, this provision acknowledges that state laws may provide for majority to be attained earlier. It recognizes that concepts of childhood vary across cultures and legal regimes. For example, the United States defines majority age as 18 years for many purposes. However, for family

---

[28] Convention on the Rights of the Child, adopted 20 November 1989, 1577 UNTS 3 (entered into force 2 September 1990) (CRC).

reunification in migration law the age of 21 is used, unless the child has married:[29] a valid marriage ends legal childhood regardless of a person's actual chronological age.[30] In some countries, childhood is bounded by physical development such as the attainment of puberty or special rites of passage. Age may not be marked by the celebration of birthdays at all.[31]

In many countries, the determination of age in a child migrant will trigger a suite of procedural and substantive rights. But how accurate are the age determination processes used in migration processes in developed countries playing host to child migrants? In Chapter 17, Kenny and Loughry show that the mechanisms adopted by countries to determine chronological age can be intrusive, intrinsically harmful and not particularly accurate. Receiving nations can adopt sharp line definitions of childhood that do not comport with cultural or developmental reality. So we ask: if the aim of accommodating laws and procedures is to address vulnerability, should physical age alone be determinant of rights in young migrants?[32]

Cross-cultural expectations complicate all migration law but are particularly harmful when assumptions about agency and vulnerability interfere with acknowledging the needs of young people. In some cultures and communities of origin, adolescents may have greater agency and adult responsibilities than is the case in the countries to which the children

---

29 Thronson has highlighted the essential problem that statutory law requires pages to define who is a 'child'. He notes: 'not all children are "children" for immigration purposes. Under immigration law, a child is recognized as a "child" only if she meets the criteria of a "particularly exhaustive" statutory definition'. See David Thronson 'Entering the Mainstream: Making Children Matter in Immigration Law' (2010) 38 *Fordham Urban Law Journal* 393, at 397. The US Immigration and Nationality Act, s. 101(b) (fundamental definition of 'child') contains four different ages that define childhood. Adoptions must occur before 16 in most cases; step-child relationships must form before the age of 18; marriage ends childhood; and all other children are under 21 years of age. The statute devotes over 1,500 words to defining who is a child. Independently, the term 'unaccompanied alien minor' is found in the Trafficking Victims Reauthorization Act 2008, defining an unaccompanied child as under 18 at time of apprehension by the government at the US border. See TVPRA, 6 USC s. 279(g). See www.law.cornell.edu/uscode/text/6/279.

30 This is the case in many countries. In the United States, see, e.g., 8 USC s. 1101(b).

31 See T. Smith and L. Brownlees, *Age Assessment Practices: A Literature Review and Annotated Bibliography*, UNICEF Discussion Paper (2010), available at www.unicef.org/protection/Age_Assessment_Practices_2010.pdf.

32 Similar concerns about age assessments are expressed in the UN Joint Committee General Comment No. 4, above n. 21, paras. [3]–[4].

migrate. Imposing infantilizing restraints upon such youth may be disproportionately restrictive and even counter-productive. For example, both of the editors have encountered 16-year-old migrants, regarded squarely as children in US and Australian cultures respectively, who were already parents to children of their own by the time of their migration.[33]

Closely related to the physical age of a child and the child's cultural expectations of maturity is the fact that a child's mental and emotional capacity may vary over time and with experience. For some, past experiences of trauma or displacement may have impeded their mental and physical development such that chronological age is an inappropriate determinant of capacity. Legal systems need to be flexible and adapt to the reality of the needs of the young person. In all societies children are recognized as having abilities that evolve over time as the child grows and develops. This basic fact holds obvious significance for migrant children. The transient nature of childhood increases the likelihood that young people can experience the force of migration law in different ways, affecting both the substantive and procedural rights of an individual. In some instances, 'aging out' of childhood can be the difference between the right to remain in a host country and becoming susceptible to removal and return to a country of origin.

The administration of migration laws may require bright-line tests in some instances. Problematically, however, rigid rules based on chronological age can create perverse incentives for children to migrate before attaining majority. Such rules can also result in unfair or harsh treatment for children who have just crossed the line into a putative maturity. It will be our argument that a better approach is to adopt a more holistic assessment of need and vulnerability in young migrants that is not based solely on chronological age – even where this can be determined with any certainty. Precedents can be found in practices used to protect people with diminished capacity. We will argue that adjudication models should be built and managed such that the subject of the adjudication, the migrant child, is paramount. Our contributors are not the first to posit that fun-

[33] Further complicating the legal treatment of these young parents is that their children may not qualify for the same benefits or legal treatment they receive if the child is also in need of protection. In the United States, birth in the territory confers citizenship on the child but the parent has no right to immigrate through this child's citizenship until the child is over 21 and only if the parent is not barred by previous law violations or grounds of inadmissibility. For an article discussing birthright citizenship see P. Weil, 'From Conditional to Secured and Sovereign: The New Strategic Link Between the Citizen and the Nation-State in a Globalized World' (2011) 9 *International Journal of Constitutional Law* 615.

damental fairness for children cannot be achieved in systems designed for the adjudication of adult claims for protection.[34] One size does not fit all.

2.2 Migrant Children Need Substantive Protection and Care

A migrant's status as a minor child does not confer any inherent right to enter or remain in a foreign country.[35] It will be our argument, however, that states should respond to the presence of children in migratory flows by moderating the otherwise damaging and punitive effects of domestic immigration laws. In Chapter 4, Crock and Martin argue that international law has now developed to the point where it is possible to assert that states are obliged to extend special protections to children presenting as humanitarian migrants, because of their status as children. Put another way, child migrants are children first and, as such, deserve special treatment, including being afforded the immediate and temporary protection of the state. Any child who articulates relevant fears or who a government is aware is at risk due to war, natural disaster, or great economic and civil instability should be offered some form of stable and temporary protection. While the length and rights that attach to the sojourners' respite may vary, we believe that international law and existing regional and national legal regimes require states to offer children a safe and secure opportunity to seek protection from refoulement or return to danger.

These obligations should mean that states never submit children to interdiction and turn-back operations without first determining that these actions can be done without harming children.[36] The same principles should apply to the transfer of asylum-seeking children to processing facilities in third countries where the security and basic human rights of the children could be at risk.

Part III of the book pursues issues around the substantive protection of migrant children in the domestic laws of countries that play host to these young people. It is here that we see examples of both good and bad practice

---

[34] See, e.g., J. Bhabha and W. Young, 'Not Adults in Miniature: Unaccompanied Child Asylum Seekers and the New US Guidelines' (1999) 11 *International Journal of Refugee Law* 87.

[35] See V. Chétail, 'The Transnational Movement of Persons under General International Law: Mapping the Customary Law Foundations of International Migration Law' in V. Chétail and C. Bauloz (eds), *Research Handbook on International Law and Migration* (Edward Elgar Publishing, 2014), p. 27 ff.

[36] See, e.g., Human Rights Watch, *Closed Doors: Mexico's Failure to Protect Central American Refugee and Migrant Children* (2016), available at www.hrw.org/sites/default/files/report_pdf/mexico0316web_0.pdf.

in the jurisprudence created in the application of the Refugee Convention and of other relevant systems of human rights law. Contributors from Europe, North America and Oceania explore questions such as: How should children's claims for protection under the Refugee Convention be adjudicated and how should domestic legal regimes adapt to the special context of a child making a claim? Do children experience persecution in ways that are unique to childhood? When do children constitute a 'particular social group' for the purposes of invoking international protection from harm?

It is a fundamental tenet of child welfare in most developed countries that the state must provide children with the essentials of life, including adequate housing, food and access to education. While not every nation has the capacity to provide for the needs of all children, too often migrant children are seen and treated as exceptions to the general rule, even where resources are not an issue. Legal systems can ignore the needs of these children, creating impoverishment and neglect – a second class childhood for the foreign born.

It is beyond the scope of this book to discuss issues around the integration of migrant children into receiving nations. However, we will address immediate problems and concerns with the treatment of children apprehended upon arrival or identified in the course of enforcement or deportation operations. Too often governments detain migrant children and justify the detention as a means of protecting the children in question. The use and misuse of incarceration for migrant youth is a matter of global concern that has become the subject of considerable international and domestic jurisprudence and a vast body of literature in the fields of medicine, law and social science. The recent Joint General Comments from the UN Committee on the Rights of the Child (UNCRC) and the Committee on the Rights of Migrant Workers reject the use of detention for children as part of migration control.[37] Research shows that when used, detention disproportionately harms the migrant child's psychosocial development and can leave children with a sense of abandonment and a lasting mistrust of authority. It can also compromise their ability to adequately prepare and present claims for protection.[38]

Because most youth on the move are treated as migrants first rather than as children, legal regimes around the world often lack some of the basic protections found in child welfare systems designed to promote the

---

[37] UN Joint General Comment No. 4, above n. 21, paras. [5]–[10]. Detention should be brief and only as a last resort. *Ibid.*

[38] These issues are discussed in Part V of the book.

'best interests of the child'. In many countries, immigration processes bypass child welfare systems, relying instead on arrangements that either 'warehouse' migrant children or outsource the care and protection to border enforcement agencies. What does respecting the 'best interests of the child' require in these circumstances? Can detention ever be justified or seen as necessary for child migrants?

2.3 Children Require Procedural Assistance

If it is accepted that children have evolving capacities, there should be little contest that children require competent adult assistance if they are to adequately navigate complex legal systems.[39] Again, in most developed nations, if a citizen child is the subject of a legal proceeding, he or she is provided with a skilled guardian and/or legal advocate. Too often, the same rights are not afforded to children in immigration processes. Our own research and experience show that without adequate interim care and skilled advocacy, child migrants are much less able to petition successfully for protection. Children need guidance in telling their stories to tribunals or decision-makers. Preliminary studies in the United States indicate that a child trying to secure protection in the immigration court without counsel is more than 84 per cent likely to fail. Conversely, children assisted by competent legal counsel obtain a form of relief in nearly 78 per cent of cases.[40] These statistics align roughly with the findings of Australian researchers in the *Seeking Asylum Alone* project in 2004–2007.[41]

Almost all of the child migration systems discussed in this book permit a child to have legal assistance but none guarantees universal free representation. While chapters in this text will set out specific reasons why

---

[39] See UN Joint General Comment No. 4, above n. 21, para. [16] expressly stating that children deserve free legal counsel: 'States should ensure standardized policies to guide authorities in offering free, quality legal advice and representation for migrant, asylum-seeking and refugee children, including equal access for unaccompanied and separated children in local authority care and undocumented children'.

[40] Estimates based on published data available for cases begun in fiscal year 2014 and completed as of August 2016, available at http://trac.syr.edu/phptools/immigration/juvenile/. See, e.g., *Representation for Unaccompanied Children in Immigration Court* (TRAC at Syracuse University, 2015), available at http://trac.syr.edu/immigration/reports/371/, which finds a 14-fold increase in positive outcomes for youth who are represented).

[41] See M. Crock, *Seeking Asylum Alone: Unaccompanied and Separated Children and Refugee Protection: A Study of Laws, Policy and Practices in Australia* (Themis Press, 2006), p. 125.

legal counsel is necessary, a persistent obstacle to achieving this goal is the lack of transparency in the warehousing and processing of children's claims. Young migrants who are not mainstreamed into child welfare protection adjudication inevitably suffer. The burden of finding legal assistance often falls upon the child and specialist pro bono organizations.

What does it mean to incorporate the 'best interests of the child' standards into migration policy and processes? What are the costs and benefits of including this standard and what type of adjudication system is needed to fully implement the standard? When may a nation apply rapid adjudication models to children? Do the same standards of interdiction at sea, expulsion and return to countries of origin apply to children as to adult migrants? What are the essential protections that children need in rapid adjudication models? Should there ever be a blanket prohibition on deportation or expulsion of children?

We urge governments to evaluate child migration controls and adjudication against the same standards they would apply to child welfare adjudication regimes for their citizens. While foreign born children might not have the same substantive claims to financial support, there is no real justification for ignoring the lessons of child welfare law and process when designing and implementing child migration controls.

2.4 Why Protection Matters for Child Migrants: The Long-term Consequences of Abuse

Traumatic experiences resulting in cross-border displacement change lives in obvious ways. For children, however, the consequences of harmful early experiences can be truly profound, crippling a child's physical and/or psycho-social development. Migration and border processes are focused typically on national security and control. Insufficient attention is paid to designing systems that address the long-term consequences of the migration experience on children. Even where long-term status is not provided, experience all around the world suggests that asylum-seeking children are likely to spend significant time in the receiving country.[42] Whatever their stage of development, the 'immigration years' are critical to a child's

[42] The length of processing time varies greatly by country and whether complementary protection is available. Further, many states do not actively seek to remove youth until they reach the age of majority so it is likely many young people will spend their childhood in the receiving state. See, e.g., Catriona Jarvis and Syd Bolton in Chapter 12 discussing leave to remain for children under age 18. See Joint General Comment No. 4, above n. 21, para. [59] encouraging equality in access to education for migrant children.

future. A failure to address the specific needs of these children can result in social costs for the receiving society as much as for the children themselves.

Ample evidence exists of the crippling effect on children of prolonged and punitive incarceration.[43] Denial of access to appropriate care can produce education and emotional deficits that endure for the child's entire life. It will be our argument that states ultimately act against their own best interests when they ignore the short-term needs of migrant children, justifying the denial of care and protection because a child may not have a right to long-term resettlement or naturalization.

Of course, evidence also abounds that children can be remarkably resilient. Migrant children who suffer great hardships can grow up to become independent and successful adults who cherish their new home country and take full advantage of resettlement opportunities. This only happens, however, with thought and action on the part of receiving states.[44] Childhood resilience should never be an excuse for affirmative neglect or abuse. Legal systems must have safeguards in place that allow for inspection, reporting, and correction of systems that are harming children. In this collection we address some of the most challenging tasks facing states playing host to children affected by war and conflict. These include the reception and rehabilitation of child soldiers and of children who are players themselves in trafficking and smuggling enterprises. When may a nation-state criminally prosecute a child migrant for violating border entrance laws or regulations? What are the consequences of criminalizing immigration violations for the juvenile? What strategies can be adopted to maximize the chance of rehabilitation of damaged young people while assuring the security of the host or resettlement communities?

---

[43] See, e.g., UNHCR, *Beyond Detention: Progress Report Mid 2016* (UNHCR, August 2016), available at www.unhcr.org/53aa929f6.pdf; see also Australian Human Rights Commission, *A Last Resort? National Inquiry into Children in Immigration Detention* (2004), available at www.humanrights.gov.au/human_rights/children_detention_report/ind ex.html; I. Bronstein and P. Montgomery, 'Psychological Distress in Refugee Children: A Systematic Review' (2011) 14(1) *Clinical Child and Family Psychological Review* 44; M. Dudley, Z. Steel, S. Mares and L. Newman, 'Children and Young People in Immigration Detention' (2012) 25 *Current Opinion in Psychiatry* 285; and A. Lorek et al., 'The Mental and Physical Health Difficulties of Children Held Within a British Immigration Detention Centre: A Pilot Study' (2009) 33 *Child Abuse and Neglect* 573. See also J. Everitt, *The Bitter Shore* (Pan Macmillan, 2008), describing the impact of detention on a young child held in an Australian centre.

[44] For a discussion of the Australian case see M. Crock (ed.), *Creating Futures: Settling Children and Youth from Refugee Backgrounds* (Federation Press, 2015).

3. OBSTACLES TO THE ACKNOWLEDGEMENT OF RIGHTS IN MIGRANT CHILDREN

In spite of the growing interest in the phenomenon and plight of children on the move around the world, migration laws, policies and processes everywhere continue to pose particular problems for young people. In this section we examine some of the obstacles to the recognition of rights in child migrants that will recur as themes throughout the chapters that follow.

Like their adult counterparts, migrant children are being affected by the increasing restrictiveness of immigration regimes all around the world. If international travel has never been easier from a technological perspective, the legal constraints of visa regimes have made true freedom of movement the province of a relative minority of individuals from developed countries and/or from wealthy backgrounds. On the one hand, the administrative requirements attending lawful movement between countries have become increasingly complex. On the other, countries are resorting more frequently to erecting physical barriers in the fight against irregular migration. Such systems operate to both impede and endanger child migrants. Ironically, restrictive policies can create perverse incentives for irregular movement. For example, one could argue that the exponential increase in irregular child migrants from Central and South America to the United States is a product (at least in part) of restrictive policies that prevent parents living in the United States from sponsoring children as regular migrants.[45] Another example is the almost immediate spike in the number of asylum-seeker children travelling to Australia by boat following the

[45] In 2014, UNHCR published a report based on over 400 interviews of migrant children and found that 49 per cent of El Salvadoran children had at least one parent in the United States; 27 per cent of Guatemala children; and 47 per cent of Honduran youth. See UNHCR, *Children on the Run* (2014), available at www.unhcr.org/en-us/children-on-the-run.html. One 2015 study of migrant children entering the United States estimates that children are unlikely to migrate alone unless a parent has migrated before the child. See K.M. Donato and B. Sisk, 'Children's Migration to the United States from Mexico and Central America: Evidence from the Mexican and Latin American Migration Projects' (2015) 3(1) *Journal of Migration and Human Security* 58 (data does not include Honduran children and is based on data prior to 2014 dramatic increase in Central American migration). The US government did create an expanded humanitarian parole programme allowing parents living within the United States to sponsor children for refugee processing in the country of origin. This programme is limited to children of people who are living in the United States with some form of status, which has greatly narrowed the programme. See www.uscis.gov/humanitarian/humanitarian-parole/central-american-minors-cam-refugeeparole-program-

institution of temporary protection visas in the late 1990s that removed family reunification rights.[46]

While respect for human rights and immigration restriction need not be mutually exclusive, the reality is that enforcement measures often lead to a diminished focus on human rights. Children die crossing seas and deserts in attempts to reach safety because regular migration routes are closed to them. Even where they manage to gain admission, migrant children are being detained and denied access to basic entitlements. Subscribing to the dualist approach to international law,[47] Australia is one country in which domestic migration laws that are abusive of human rights prevail even when inconsistent with obligations assumed under international law.[48] The United States similarly has not afforded full constitutional protection to non-citizens, especially to those apprehended upon arrival.[49] United Nations High Commissioner for Refugees (UNHCR) research suggests that these countries are far from unique.[50]

Another, egregious, obstacle to the realization of human rights in migrant children is what we term 'deterrence theory'.[51] The justification given so often for punitive and restrictive immigration control measures

---

information-conditionally-approved-applicants. This programme is discussed in Chapter 24 by pamela goldberg.

[46] See Crock, *Seeking Asylum Alone*, above n. 41, at 38–9.

[47] See G. Triggs, *International Law: Contemporary Principles and Practices* (LexisNexis Butterworths, 2006), pp. 105 para. [3.4], 142–3 para. [3.65].

[48] See, e.g., H. Charlesworth, M. Chiam, D. Hovell and G. Williams (eds), *The Fluid State: International Law and National Legal Systems* (Federation Press, 2005).

[49] See the discussion of the 'plenary power doctrine' in M. Taylor and K. Johnson, 'Vast Hordes . . . Crowding in Upon Us: The Executive Branch's Response to Mass Migration and the Legacy of *Chae Chan Ping*' (2015) 68 *Oklahoma Law Review* 185; and K. Knop, 'Here and There: International Law in Domestic Courts' (2000) 32 *New York University Journal of International Law and Politics* 501.

[50] See UNHCR, *Beyond Detention*, above n. 43.

[51] See M. Crock, 'Of Relative Rights and Putative Children: Re-thinking the Critical Framework for the Protection of Refugee Children and Youth' (2013) 20 *Australian Journal of International Law* 33; and M. Crock and D. Ghezelbash, 'Do Loose Lips Bring Ships? The Role of Policy, Politics and Human Rights in Managing Unauthorised Boat Arrivals' (2010) 19 *Griffith Law Review* 238. See also *RIL-R* v. *Johnson*, 80 F Supp 3d 164 (DDC 20150) (District Court rejects deterrence as legitimate reason to detain mothers and children seeking asylum) and the US government told the Ninth Circuit Court of Appeals it was no longer arguing that detention was necessary for deterrence. See also *Flores* v. *Lynch*, 2016 US App. LEXIS 12439 (9th Cir., July 6, 2016, No. 15-56434). This decision reaffirms the obligation on US authorities to release children as soon as possible, including children apprehended with a parent.

is that they are necessary to deter irregular migration. The theory finds extreme expression in assertions by politicians in Australia that the country's interdiction and offshore processing regime is necessary to save lives at sea.[52] The politicians point to the fact that thousands of people have died trying to reach the country by boat, and that the restrictive policies have been effective in bringing the maritime people smuggling trade in Australia to a virtual halt. The policies have resulted in individuals recognized as Convention refugees spending years in remote, tropical detention centres, surrounded in the case of Papua New Guinea's Manus Island by a hostile local population. The policy has led to refugees dying from disease, suicide (including by self-immolation) and from interpersonal violence. Women and children have been raped and subjected to other gross human rights breaches.[53] The embodied refugee children have been abused in the interests of saving the lives of putative children whose parents would otherwise have sent them on a risky path in search of a better life.[54]

Migrant children also face obstacles that are both legal and attitudinal. In what may be characterized as institutional blindness, children on the move have literally and figuratively slipped under relevant radars. An obvious manifestation of the invisibility of children in migration flows is the dearth of statistical information on how many children are on the move and why they migrate.[55] Where children travel with parents or other responsible adults, young people are rarely seen as having rights independent of the family collective of which they are perceived to be part. The children's rights will be determined often by the rights of adults with whom they are associated by relationship or responsibility. When parents are arrested or excluded as irregular migrants or as security risks, their children will often suffer collateral damage in decisions made about adults' legal standing. Children can benefit from derivative status, for example, when parents or guardians are granted protection in asylum processes. However, a one-in-all-in approach can also disadvantage children if no separate consideration is given to a child's specific protection claims.[56] The global rise in the number of children traveling as solo migrants has increased attention on the fact that children can experience persecution and disadvantage in unique ways. While examples of good practice in the

[52] See M. Gleeson *Offshore: Behind the Wire on Manus and Nauru* (Newsouth Press, 2016), ch. 1.

[53] See *ibid.* and the 'incident reports' published by the *Guardian Australia* newspaper, at www.theguardian.com/news/series/nauru-files.

[54] See Crock, 'Of Relative Rights and Putative Children', above n. 51.

[55] See UNICEF, *Uprooted,* above n. 11.

[56] See further discussion of remedies for children in David Thronson, Chapter 13.

interpretation of international and domestic laws can now be identified, this remains an area where jurisprudence and practical experience are somewhat impoverished.[57]

The rightlessness of children relative to responsible adults can also be manifest in an imbalance between parents and children in family reunification laws and policies. This is an area where the law can tend to commodify children in the sense that migrating parents are seen as having rights to live and travel with their offspring. Conversely, national laws rarely confer equal rights on migrant children to sponsor their parents. Rather, the child's right to family unity is commonly qualified by conditions requiring parents to meet economic or stringent health criteria.[58]

Yet another obstacle to the realization of rights in migrant children has been the failure in international organizations to adopt a human rights focus in cooperative measures relating to migration control and transnational crime. As Ghezelbash documents, there are now a plethora of fora in which states meet to discuss these issues.[59] However, the emphasis in these meetings is most often on measures to control immigration and on the punishment of offenders, rather than on the protection of migrant victims of abuse. In this book, a number of contributors address questions that have arisen in relation to international measures targeting human trafficking and the smuggling of migrants. In spite of the universal acceptance that children are rendered most vulnerable in these situations, here again domestic laws, policies and practices continue to emphasize state sovereignty over child protection.

The final problem we identify and discuss in this book is the pervasive failure in states to adopt a child rights focus in administrative procedures involving child migrants. Ironically, however widespread the failures in process, we will argue that this obstacle may well be the easiest one to remove. It is our hope that this book will increase awareness of the challenges facing both children and governments when young migrants engage with our immigration laws and policies. Through sharing the wisdom and experience of experts and practitioners, it is also our aspiration that the book itself may act as an agent for change within migration bureaucracies around the world.

---

[57] See, e.g., Geraldine Sadoway, Chapter 15, discussing Canada; and Kate Bones and Timnah Baker, Chapter 14, comparing the United States and Australia.

[58] Part III of the book contains chapters exploring the legal rights of children in Canada, Europe and the United Kingdom, the United States, Australia and Mexico.

[59] See Daniel Ghezelbash, Chapter 21.

4. STRUCTURE OF THE BOOK

The central argument we make in this book is that children on the move, and how they are treated, matter. We all have a stake in processes that experience suggests will end with young migrants settling and integrating into the communities of which we are part. If only for this reason, it is in everyone's interest to engage with the challenges posed by children travelling as forced or irregular migrants.

The book begins in Part I with two chapters in which the authors attempt to put numbers and faces on the children on the move around the world and the reasons they are migrating. The task is not an easy one, because statistical data disaggregated by age and gender across countries has never been created or collected in a uniform way. There are some regions of the world (South America and parts of Africa, for example) where information is sparse or non-existent. Malakooti's generalist chapter is paired with a case study by Martinez on Mexican and Central American children.[60] Her chapter explores some of the historical and socio-political motivations of why children leave their homes and seek entry in the United States.

Part II of the book contains a series of chapters that provide the international and regional context for the more detailed consideration of the laws, policies and practices affecting children on the move in different parts of the world. The first block of three chapters in this part addresses aspects of international law. Chapter 4 by Crock and Martin has as its focus the international foundations that protect migrant children, and Chapter 5 by Crock and Yule focuses on the Convention on the Rights of the Child (CRC) and other human rights conventions, as well as children as subjects of international refugee law.[61] In Chapter 6, Schloenhardt and Lelliot examine critical frameworks created to deal with human trafficking and the smuggling of migrants across borders.[62]

The second group of chapters in this Part takes us to the regional frameworks relevant to the protection of migrant children. Danisi reminds us in Chapter 7 that two systems of protection interact in Europe when a migrant child arrives in one of the EU Member States.[63] Both acknowledge the importance of respecting the best interests of the child. First, the European Union has developed a normative framework grounded in the 1951 Refugee Convention and the CRC. This finds expression in the

---

60 See Arezo Malakooti, Chapter 2 and Isabel Martinez, Chapter 3.

61 See Mary Crock and Hannah Martin, Chapter 4 and Mary Crock and Phoebe Yule, Chapter 5.

62 See Andreas Schloenhardt and Joseph Lelliott, Chapter 6.

63 Carmelo Danisi (with Mary Crock), Chapter 7.

fundamental rights (re)affirmed in the Charter of Fundamental Rights of the EU (CFR)[64] and the Treaty on the European Union itself. Second, EU Regulations and Directives in the field of asylum and migration must conform with minimum standards of protection enshrined in the European Convention on Human Rights (ECHR) as interpreted by the European Court of Human Rights (ECtHR). If the European systems and laws are well known, the two chapters that follow provide insights into regional human rights frameworks that have attracted less academic attention. In Chapter 8, human rights workers Petros and Olusese join with Nairobi University's Professor Abuya to set out the elements of the African system, offering a case study of how unaccompanied child migrants are treated in Kenya.[65] Holguin and Kumar explain in Chapter 9 the workings of the Organization of American States (OAS) and special instruments that should protect migrant children.[66] They report on current litigation brought on behalf of Central American women and children challenging detention and expedited deportation procedures as violations of essential human rights guaranteed by the OAS instruments.

Part II.2 complements these framework chapters with two case studies looking at protection issues surrounding children at work. In Chapter 10, Van Doore takes the discussion of initiatives targeting human trafficking into South East Asia.[67] She argues against a simplistic characterization of Asian children at work as victims of trafficking, noting that cultural attitudes and economic necessity create an environment in which children can be expected to join the workforce at a young age. The search for remunerative employment can lead young adults to make reasoned decisions to cross borders. The second chapter in this series concerns young people moving for work within one of the world's most populous nations: China. Zou's more historical piece is included at Chapter 11 because of the scale of child migration within this country and the place China is assuming as a powerhouse economy in the world as it sheds its status as a developing country.[68]

---

[64] Adopted in Strasbourg [2012] OJ C326/391. Article 51 of the CFR states that the Convention is addressed 'to the institutions, bodies, offices and agencies of the Union with due regard for the principle of subsidiarity and to the Member States *only when they are implementing Union law*'. See S Peers et al., *The EU Charter of Fundamental Rights, A Commentary* (Hart Publishing, 2014), p. 661.

[65] See Agnes Olusese, Shamm Petros and Edwin Odhiambo Abuya, Chapter 8.

[66] See Carlos Holguín and Kavita Kapur, Chapter 9.

[67] See Kathryn Van Doore, Chapter 10.

[68] See M Zou, Chapter 11.

Part III of the book gathers experts from several nations to describe and examine the adequacy of domestic law and how nations are implementing legal schemes designed to protect migrant children and child asylum-seekers. In Chapter 12, Jarvis and Bolton begin by examining the UK and EU experience of offering complementary protection to some child migrants while not fully offering refugee protection.[69] This chapter necessarily discusses the intersection of international and domestic laws as they protect children. In contrast, Thronson explains in Chapter 13 the reality faced by migrant children found within the United States or at its borders. There, domestic laws include a complex amalgam of federal and state child welfare measures.[70]

In Chapter 14, Baker and Bones expand our understanding by providing a comparative chapter on asylum law for children in Australian and US law.[71] Their assessment illuminates the critical role of adjudication and charts the development of common law jurisprudence on asylum protections for children. In Chapter 15, Sadoway describes the procedure and substantive law that is used to adjudicate children's asylum claims in Canada. She notes the need to improve the role of guardians and to adjust the adjudication models to the needs of vulnerable children.[72]

In Part IV of the book we study the interaction of migrant children with protection processes. Kenny and Loughry argue in Chapter 16 that techniques that prioritize the identification of physical markers of age often involve harmful and intrusive procedures such as bone scans, yet producing results of doubtful accuracy.[73] Benson and Thomas in Chapter 17 and Taylor in Chapter 18 provide detailed country-specific chapters on the procedural entitlements and treatment of unaccompanied children, including the right to counsel.[74]

Part V of the book contains three quite diverse chapters on children and immigration detention. It begins in Chapter 19 with Neuman's piece on the UN Human Rights Committee's General Comment on detention that he helped to draft when serving as a member of that Committee.[75] This body has oversight of the International Covenant on Civil and Political Rights (ICCPR). In a thought-provoking chapter, Neuman argues that if the best interests of the child are to be respected, detention may sometimes

---

[69] See Catriona Jarvis and Syd Bolton, Chapter 12.

[70] See David Thronson, Chapter 13.

[71] See Kate Bones and Timnah Baker, Chapter 14

[72] See Geraldine Sadoway, Chapter 15.

[73] See Mary Anne Kenny and Maryanne Loughry, Chapter 16.

[74] See Lenni B. Benson and Claire Thomas, Chapter 17 and Savitri Taylor, Chapter 18.

[75] See Gerald Neuman, Chapter 19.

be the best option, for example, for young migrants who would otherwise lack any form of care and protection. In Chapter 20, Triggs provides stark contrast material in her description of the at times gross abuses of children's rights that have occurred in detention centres across Australia, as well as in facilities run and funded by that country in Nauru and Papua New Guinea's Manus Island.[76] Ghezelbash concludes in Chapter 21 by exploring the tendency in states to copy each other's laws and policies – often with disastrous consequences for migrant children.[77] His chapter tracks the apparent transfer or borrowing of immigration detention laws and policies between Australia and the United States.

The book continues in Part VI with three chapters exploring different facets of child migrants and the interface between migration law and criminal law. In Chapter 22, Anello explores how the criminalization of immigration status or prosecution for criminal acts severely reduces or eliminates protections for child refugees and others.[78] There follows a chapter examining the treatment at law and in practice of child soldiers. Writing from practical experience in South Sudan, in Chapter 23, Tyler and Whitman describe the problems inherent in the post-conflict (re-) integration of children who have been forced into war.[79]

The book concludes in Chapter 24 with a contribution by pamela goldberg on UNHCR's search for regional solutions in partnership with the US government to process (at point of origin or transit) the claims of migrant youth in Central America.[80]

*

In 2016, UNICEF articulated six goals and practical suggestions to improve the lives of child migrants and refugees that we think capture well the essence of the contributions made by the authors in this volume.[81] These relate to the protection of children from exploitation and violence; the use of detention; family unity; access to education; the need for action on the underlying causes of large-scale movements; and measures to combat xenophobia, discrimination and marginalization in countries of transit and destination.[82] While our various contributors write as

---

76 See Gillian Triggs, Chapter 20.
77 See Daniel Ghezelbash, Chapter 21.
78 See Farrin Anello, Chapter 22.
79 See Kasey Tyler and Shelly Whitman, Chapter 23.
80 See pamela goldberg, Chapter 24.
81 UNICEF, *Uprooted*, above n. 11.
82 These goals and suggestions find expression in the principles for the

individuals and no claim is made that they adopt the views of any other contributor, there is a unity in the messages conveyed. This is found in the view that children deserve *protection*, but also *respect* insofar as they have both a right to be heard and a right to exercise agency to the extent that their capacities allow. If nations continue to ignore the special vulnerabilities and characteristics of child migrants, they will fail to meet the protection standards demanded by international and domestic law.

No single volume can suffice to capture the complex and rapidly changing legal treatment of child migrants. We trust that this book will help to illuminate some common concerns, failures and shortcomings but that it will also identify examples of best practice as we adapt to the reality of child migration. For us, the evidence and arguments presented by our contributors compel action and reform. We should strive for uniform definitions and measures that enable us to better understand the reality and challenges of child migration. Countries everywhere need to integrate the essentials of child welfare and child protection into border control and immigration controls. Mechanisms for adjudication and assessment of children's claims should be devised and run so as to protect the fundamental rights of children as children – and to do no harm.

As we stand on the brink of achieving a new global consensus on migrants and refugees, it is well to recall that migrant children everywhere are part of our future. Critically, the fulfilment of their potential is in our hands.

---

treatment of migrant children enshrined in the more recent Joint General Comments issued by the Committee on the Rights of the Child and the Migrant Workers Committee. See the two Joint General Comments, above n. 21.

PART I

Displacement stories

2. The where, when and how of children on the move

Arezo Malakooti

1. THE BIG PICTURE

While the scope and characteristics of child migration vary across different regions of the world, the phenomenon of children 'on the move' is a global one. The rate of child migration tends to be increasing everywhere – along with the associated risks for the children displaced from hearth and home. At any given time it is estimated that approximately 3 per cent of the world's population is on the move as migrants. As the global population has increased over time, the proportion that are migrants has increased by a few percentage points year on year. In absolute terms, this means that there have been significant increases in the number of international movements. The growth rate of child migrants has been even higher than the growth rate for migrants in general. Of 244 million international migrants in 2015, 13 per cent were estimated to be children under the age of 18.

War, famine and natural disasters have played a role in increasing the number of people on the move both within and across borders. More children are travelling as refugees than as simply migrants. At 10 per cent, the growth rate for child refugees between 2010 and 2015 was significantly higher than the growth rate for child migrants (2 per cent). Children make up 51 per cent of all refugees under the mandate of the United Nations High Commissioner for Refugees (UNHCR). Most find asylum in their region of origin. However, the paucity of safe and orderly migration routes in many parts of the world has led asylum-seekers to take irregular and dangerous journeys in order to reach a country of safe haven. In such scenarios, children are particularly vulnerable, from not only a physical but also a psychological perspective.

In this chapter, I will provide an overview of the global data on child migration, and explore how and why children travel in the regions covered by the various contributors to this book. At the outset, I acknowledge that data on international migration is not particularly precise or reliable.

Statistics in many regions are scarce or non-existent, so that numbers are generally based on estimates. Specific data on child migration is even more difficult to come by. According to UNHCR, only a few countries supply refugee data disaggregated by age. In 2015, data disaggregated by age was available for 21.2 million people only, which represented 33 per cent of the estimated global number of refugees.[1] In this chapter I draw heavily on the ground-breaking report prepared by the United Nations' Children's Fund (UNICEF) in 2015, *Uprooted: The Growing Crisis for Refugee and Migrant Children*, which represents a laudatory effort to compile all of the data then available on the topic of children on the move around the world.[2]

In this chapter the term migrant is used broadly to refer to all people on the move, unless a distinction is otherwise made. This means that the term includes labour migrants, asylum-seekers, refugees, children in family units, and unaccompanied and separated children.

2. NUMBER OF CHILDREN ON THE MOVE

According to the United Nations Population Division, Department of Economic and Social Affairs (UNDESA), in 2015 there were 244 million international migrants in the world,[3] representing 3.3 per cent of the world's population. While the number of international migrants has been on an upward trend for some time, it has risen sharply in recent decades. International migrant stocks increased from 153 million in 1990 to 160 million in 1995; with 173 million in 2000; 191 million in 2005; 222 million in 2010; reaching 244 million in 2015.[4] Migrants comprised 2.9 per cent of the world's population in 1990, increasing to 3.2 per cent in 2013, and 3.3 per cent of the global population in 2015.[5] This means that the international movements experienced a growth rate of 2 per cent between 2000

---

[1] UNHCR, *Global Trends Report 2015* (UNHCR, 2016), p. 52.

[2] See E. Garin, *Uprooted: The Growing Crisis for Refugee and Migrant Children* (UNICEF, 2016), available at www.unicef.org/emergencies/childrenonthemove/uprooted/.

[3] 'International migrants' refers to people living in a country or region other than where they were born. In cases where information on the country of birth was not available, it refers to people living in a country other than that of their citizenship.

[4] See 'Total International Migrant Stock' dataset, available at www.un.org/en/development/desa/population/migration/data/estimates2/estimates15.shtml.

[5] UNDESA, *Population Facts No. 2013/2* (September 2013), available at https://esa.un.org/unmigration/documents/The_number_of_international_migrants.pdf.

and 2005, accelerating to 3 per cent between 2005 and 2010, with a further 1.9 per cent increase between 2010 and 2015.[6]

In 2015, Europe was the region that hosted the most international migrants in absolute terms (76 million), followed closely by Asia (75 million), Northern America (54 million) and Africa (21 million). There were also 9 million international migrants residing in Latin America and the Caribbean and 8 million in Oceania. Asia experienced the greatest increase in terms of international migrants in the period 2000–2015 (26 million in total or 1.7 million per year).[7] In terms of single countries, the United States of America (US) hosted the highest number of international migrants in 2015 (47 million), followed by Germany and the Russian Federation (12 million each).[8] Australia hosted the ninth largest number of international migrants in 2015, with a total of 7 million.[9]

Of the 244 million international migrants globally in 2015, it is estimated that 31 million were under the age of 18.[10] This means child migrants accounted for 13 per cent of the total number of international migrants in that year. Between 1990 and 2005, the number of international child migrants (under the age of 18) remained fairly stable, ranging between 24 and 25 million. Between 2005 and 2010, the number increased from 25 million to 28 million and between 2010 and 2015 it increased to 31 million.[11] This means that the growth rate for international child migrants was 2 per cent for the period 2010–2015, which is slightly higher than the overall growth rate for all international migrants in the same period (1.9 per cent).

In contrast to the main hosting regions for all international migrants, Asia was the region that hosted the greatest number of international child migrants (12 million or 39 per cent of the total child international migrant population) in 2015. It was followed by Africa (6.5 million or 21 per cent) and then Europe (5.5 million or 18 per cent). In Northern America, 14 per cent of all international migrants were children in 2015, 6 per cent in Latin America and the Caribbean, and 2 per cent in Oceania.[12]

When these figures are compared against the proportion of the total population that is accounted for by children, variations emerge across the regions. For example, in Asia, children account for 56 per cent of the

---

6 UNDESA, *International Migration Report 2015 Highlights* (UNDESA, 2016), p. 5.

7 *Ibid.* 6.

8 *Ibid.* 8.

9 *Ibid.* 7.

10 Garin, *Uprooted*, above n. 2, at 18.

11 *Ibid.*

12 *Ibid.* 24.

total population but child migrants account for 39 per cent of all migrants. Similarly, in Africa, Latin America and the Caribbean, the share of all migrants that is accounted for by children is less than the share of the total population that is accounted for by children. However, in Europe, children account for 6 per cent of the total population while child migrants account for 18 per cent of all migrants and in North America, children account for 4 per cent of the total population but child migrants account for 14 per cent of all migrants.[13]

Analysed by demographics, the available global data on international child migration reveals that boys and girls are migrating in almost equal numbers at both global and regional levels. This is quite different from the data on adult migration, which shows parity at the global level but reveals quite significant differences at the regional level. Boys and girls are also equally represented among refugees; however, the risks faced by the two groups may vary. For example, recruitment by armed forces is a risk more commonly faced by boys, whereas sexual and gender-based violence is a risk faced by girls.[14]

3. PROFILES OF CHILDREN ON THE MOVE

Children on the move are classified in various ways under international and national laws. Regardless of why they move, all children are exposed to risk and vulnerabilities. All require protection. The Convention on the Rights of the Child (CRC) is the main guiding legal instrument in this area.[15] The most widely ratified human rights treaty in history, the CRC outlines a very clear and solid set of protections for children, recognizing the particular vulnerabilities of children on the move. Most importantly, the CRC obliges states to respect and protect the rights of all children within their territories, regardless of a child's background or migration status.[16]

3.1 Child Refugees

UNHCR defines the term 'refugee' to include individuals recognized under the 1951 Convention relating to the Status of Refugees and its 1967

---

13 *Ibid.*

14 *Ibid.* 21.

15 Convention on the Rights of the Child, adopted 20 November 1989, 1577 UNTS 3 (entered into force 2 September 1990) (CRC).

16 See further Mary Crock and Hannah Martin, Chapter 4.

Protocol,[17] the 1969 Organization of African Unity (OAU) Convention Governing the Specific Aspects of Refugee Problems in Africa,[18] those recognized in accordance with the UNHCR Statute,[19] individuals granted complementary forms of protection, and those enjoying temporary protection. The refugee population also includes people in refugee-like situations.[20] According to the Refugee Convention, a refugee is:

> Someone who, owing to a well-founded fear of being persecuted for reasons of race, religion, nationality, membership of a particular social group or political opinion, are outside the country of their nationality and are unable or, owing to such fear, unwilling to avail themselves of the protection of that country; or who, not having a nationality and being outside the country of their former habitual residence as a result of such events, is unable or, owing to such fear, is unwilling to return to it.[21]

Of the 31 million child migrants in 2015, 26 per cent (or 8 million children) were child refugees under UNHCR's mandate. This made nearly one in every 200 children in the world a child refugee.[22] As noted earlier, the share of the total number of child migrants who were refugees increased between 2005 and 2015 from 4 million in 2005 (14 per cent of all child migrants), to 5 million in 2010, to 8 million in 2015 (26 per cent of all child migrants).[23] The growth rate for child refugees between 2010 and 2015 was just under 10 per cent, compared to 2 per cent for child migrants in general.

While child migrants (including refugees) comprised 13 per cent of all international migrants in 2015, child refugees made up 51 per cent of all refugees under UNHCR's mandate in the same year (16.1 million refugees in total). When children account for 31 per cent of the global population, it

---

17 See Convention relating to the Status of Refugees, adopted 28 July 1951, 189 UNTS 137 (entered into force 22 April 1954); and the Protocol relating to the Status of Refugees, adopted 31 January 1967, 606 UNTS 267 (entered into force 4 October 1967) ('Refugee Convention').

18 Convention Governing the Specific Aspects of Refugee Problems in Africa, adopted 10 September 1969, 1001 UNTS 45 (entered into force 20 June 1974).

19 See UN General Assembly, Statute of the Office of the United Nations High Commissioner for Refugees, UN Doc. A/RES/428(V) (14 December 1950).

20 *Global Trends Report 2015*, above n. 1, at 54. People in refugee-like situations include individuals who may be stateless or denied the protection of the government in their countries of citizenship or habitual residence, but who have not been recognized as refugees.

21 See Art. 1A(2) as amended by the 1969 Protocol.

22 Garin, *Uprooted*, above n. 2, at 18.

23 *Ibid.* 19.

is apparent that children are overrepresented in refugee statistics. In terms of absolute numbers, the number of child refugees more than doubled between 2005 and 2015.[24] While the proportion of child refugees was high throughout that entire decade (greater than 40 per cent), the increase since 2011 was steep.[25] This rise coincides with the start of the Syrian crisis.

In fact, half of all child refugees in 2015 came from just two countries: the Syrian Arab Republic and Afghanistan.[26] If Syrian children are excluded from global refugee demographic data, the proportion of the refugee population that is accounted for by children drops to 49 per cent from the total figure of 51 per cent. Thus, the number of Syrian refugee children is slightly higher than the average for all refugee children.[27] However, the increase in refugees in 2015 also reflects new or reignited conflicts in Burundi, Iraq, Libya, Niger and Nigeria, as well as unresolved crises in the Central African Republic, Democratic Republic of the Congo, South Sudan and Yemen.[28]

In terms of the geographic spread of Syrian refugee children, the vast majority are hosted by countries in the Middle East and North Africa (MENA). In Egypt and Iraq, 43 per cent of the Syrian refugee population is accounted for by children (below the age of 18), 51 per cent in Jordan, 55 per cent in Lebanon and 45 per cent in Turkey.[29]

When the proportion of refugees accounted for by children is explored from a regional perspective, the most recent data is from 2014 and based on UNHCR registration data (and inherently limited in coverage). According to UNHCR figures from that year, 58 per cent of all refugees in the Horn and East Africa were children, 55 per cent in Central Africa, 56 per cent in West Africa and 47 per cent in Southern Africa. In the MENA region, 51 per cent of all refugees are children, 35 per cent in Europe and 24 per cent in the Americas. This suggests that children are represented more in refugee statistics in Africa and the Middle East than in industrialized countries (with the United States a possible outlier).[30]

---

[24] *Ibid.*

[25] *Global Trends Report 2015*, above n. 1.

[26] Garin, *Uprooted*, above n. 2, at 6. Note that the flows from Central America were also very high in this period, but the characterization as refugees has not always been consistent.

[27] UNHCR, *Statistics Yearbook 2014* (2015), p. 65.

[28] *Global Trends Report 2015*, above n. 1, at 16.

[29] This data is from the Syria Regional Refugee Reponse: Inter-Agency Information Sharing Portal, available at http://data.unhcr.org/syrianrefugees/regional.php.

[30] It should be noted that UNHCR's data coverage per region varies. In East and Horn of Africa it stood at 97% for 2014, 98% for Central Africa, 88% for West

3.2 Unaccompanied and Separated Children

When an armed conflict or other disasters occur, many children become separated from their parents or other care-givers. Because their status is not always immediately clear, they are referred to as 'separated' or 'unaccompanied children'. *Separated children* are those separated from both parents, or from their previous legal or customary primary care-giver, but not necessarily from other relatives. These may, therefore, include children accompanied by other adult family members. *Unaccompanied children* (also called unaccompanied minors) are children separated from both parents and other relatives and who are not being cared for by a responsible adult.[31] When children leave their homes, they are exposed to many risks, including exploitation, abuse and trafficking. These risks are heightened when they are not accompanied by parents or other responsible adults.

According to UNHCR data, asylum applications made by children considered to be unaccompanied or separated (UASC) also increased between 2010 and 2015, rising from 15,600 in 2010 to 21,300 in 2012 and 34,300 in 2014. Between 2014 and 2015, the numbers increased almost threefold from 34,300 to 98,400.[32] The 2015 figure was the highest number on record since UNHCR started collecting such data in 2006. The proportion of UASC among all asylum applications also increased from 2 per cent in 2013 to nearly 5 per cent in 2015.[33] The statistical jump mirrors the large increase in the number of individuals applying for asylum in the EU in 2015, evidenced also in the nationalities of UASC applying for asylum. Most applications (52 per cent) were made by UASC from Afghanistan, followed by the Syrian Arab Republic (15 per cent), Eritrea (8 per cent), Iraq (6 per cent) and Somalia (4 per cent).[34] Afghans, Syrians and Iraqis were the three top nationalities of arrivals along the Eastern Mediterranean route for 2015 and 2016. Somalis and Eritreans dominated arrivals along the Central Mediterranean route. Moreover, 14 per cent

---

Africa, only 27% for Southern Africa, 19% for Europe and 13% for the Americas. This should be factored in when interpreting the data. Note that forced migration flows from Central America include a great many children. See Carlos Holguin and Kavita Kapur, Chapter 9, for a discussion of the Central American children on the move.

31 *Inter-agency Guiding Principles on Unaccompanied and Separated Children* (Red Cross Central Tracing Agency and Protection Division, 2004), p. 13.

32 Data source: *UNHCR Global Trends Reports, 2010–2015.*

33 *Global Trends Report 2015*, above n. 1, at 3, 44.

34 *Ibid.*

of all arrivals on the Central Mediterranean route in 2016 were UASC, accounting for 88 per cent of all child arrivals.[35]

Sweden and Germany not only registered the most asylum applications from UASC across the European Union but also the highest number of asylum claims from UASC *among all countries reporting* such statistics.[36] In Sweden, 35,800 UASC applied for asylum in 2015 (compared with 98,400 globally), an almost fivefold increase from 2014 and accounting for almost one-fifth of all asylum applications received in Sweden in 2015. Most applications were made by Afghan UASC (23,600), followed by UASC from the Syrian Arab Republic (3,800); Somalia (2,200); Eritrea (1,900); and Iraq (1,100). Germany received 14,400 claims from UASC in 2015, compared to 4,400 in 2014, most lodged by Afghan children (4,700).[37] While the total number of Syrian refugee children globally is greater than other nationalities, Syrian children are more likely to travel in family units than alone.

In the African region, Kenya had 2,300 asylum applications lodged by UASC. Most of these applications were made by children from the Democratic Republic of the Congo and Sudan.[38] While figures are difficult to source, trends show that there is a high and increasing number of vulnerable children moving on their own in the Americas.

3.3 Internally Displaced Children

Children do not always cross international borders to seek safety; they also move to different locations within their own country. Such journeys also present numerous risks and dangers. The challenges that children face when they are forced out of their homes are often the same, regardless of whether they cross a border. Moreover, most refugees who cross international borders attempt an internal migration first and only leave when they cannot find safety within their country.

In 2015, 41 million individuals were recorded as 'internally displaced' by conflict and violence, up from 28 million in 2010. Most internally displaced persons (IDPs) were recorded in Asia (19.2 million individuals or 47 per cent of the total). In the Middle East, the Syrian Arab Republic,

---

[35] This data is from Operational Portal: Refugee Situations, available at http://data.unhcr.org/mediterranean/regional.php.

[36] Not all countries report information on the numbers of UASC seeking asylum, most notably South Africa and the United States. This means that total figures are likely to underrepresent the reality.

[37] *Global Trends Report 2015*, above n. 1, at 44.

[38] *Ibid.*

Iraq and Yemen together accounted for nearly one-third of the world's IDPs; while the African region accounted for 30 per cent (12.4 million people) with the highest numbers coming from Nigeria, Democratic Republic of the Congo, Central African Republic and South Sudan. These four African countries were also among the top 10 countries globally for new, violence-induced internal displacements in 2015.[39]

Of the 41 million conflict-related IDPs in 2015, UNICEF estimates that 17 million were children (41 per cent). Like data on migration in general, data on internal displacement is irregular and rarely disaggregated by age, making it difficult to generate reliable estimates on the number of internally displaced children. The figure of 17 million is based on the assumption that the proportion of children among persons internally displaced by violence is the same as the proportion of children amongst the national population. If children are overrepresented in internal displacement numbers in the same way that they are in refugee numbers, the total would be even higher.[40]

In addition, an estimated 19 million people were displaced by natural disasters such as earthquakes, tsunamis and flooding in 2015. At 60 million, the total figure for IDPs in 2015 was significantly higher than the global total for refugees (16.1 million).[41] While the total number of conflict-related IDPs almost doubled between 2010 and 2015 (from 28 to 41 million), the number of IDPs related to natural disasters remained stable, ranging between 19 and 21 million.[42] The increase in global displacement is thus demonstrably a product of conflict and war.

3.4 Child Victims of Trafficking

Children are often more prone to exploitation and abuse on migratory journeys, particularly when unaccompanied or separated from family. Research also suggests that risks are higher along routes where children move with different smugglers for different legs of the journey and pay step by step. This is because the child often does not have enough money

---

[39] Garin, *Uprooted*, above n. 2, at 7.

[40] *Ibid.* 33.

[41] The global figure of 16.1 million refugees refers to refugees under the mandate of the UNHCR. However, it should be noted that there were an additional 5.2 million Palestinian refugees in 2015 who are registered by the United Nations Relief and Works Agency for Palestine Refugees in the Near East (UNRWA).

[42] Internal Displacement Monitoring Centre, *DMC Global Report on Internal Displacement 2016 Conflict Dataset* (11 May 2016), available at www.internal-displacement.org/globalreport2016.

for the entire journey at the outset and must work along the way to make the money required to continue the journey. This makes children vulnerable to traffickers who promise to deliver them to their destination in return for particular services.

According to the UN Office on Drugs and Crime (UNODC) 2016 *Trafficking in Persons Report*, children were the second most commonly detected victims of trafficking for the period 2012–2014 (after women), representing 25–30 per cent of all victims globally. While this represents a decrease of 5 percentage points from 2011,[43] it is still high.

Detections of child victims of trafficking vary across regions. Between 2012 and 2014, 64 per cent of detected victims in Sub-Saharan Africa were children, a trend consistent since 2003. In Central America and the Caribbean, 62 per cent of detected victims were children. Conversely, adult victims were more common than child victims in the wealthier regions of North America (19 per cent children), the Middle East and North Africa (25 per cent children) and Europe (25 per cent children in Western and Southern Europe and 26 per cent in Central and South-Eastern Europe). As a general rule, countries with younger populations tend to have higher levels of child trafficking.[44]

Between 2012 and 2014, UNODC reports that trafficking appears to have been predominantly for sexual exploitation and for forced labour. Other victims were used as beggars, for forced or sham marriages, for benefit fraud, for the production of pornography or for organ removal.[45]

Conflict can drive trafficking: refugees become particularly vulnerable to traffickers who leverage their desperation to deceive them into exploitation. So, the number of Syrian victims of trafficking has increased sharply since the start of the Syrian conflict. The presence of large numbers of troops in conflict zones also creates demand for labour and sexual services. When coupled with degraded rule of law and weak institutions, this can generate trafficking flows into conflict or post-conflict zones.[46]

Trafficking aside, there are also cases of children engaging in 'survival sex' to finance their journeys. Evidence of this has been found on routes to and within Europe, where children stranded without money reach a point where they feel the only option is to sell their bodies.

---

43 UNODC, *Global Report on Trafficking in Persons 2016* (2016), p. 25.

44 *Ibid.*

45 *Ibid.* 8.

46 *Ibid.* 10.

3.5 Migration and Detention

Across the world, how countries treat migrants entering or remaining without valid permits has become a matter of concern. Migrants can be detained for irregular entry or even for attempting to leave a country without authorization. For example, Egypt has traditionally served as a departure point for irregular journeys to Europe through the Central Mediterranean. In 2013, Egyptian authorities began detaining anyone detected as trying to depart the Egyptian coast using smugglers.

In theory, asylum-seekers should not be detained for irregular entry into a country, as seeking refugee protection is not a crime under international law. When an individual enters a country without the required documents, they should be given the chance to apply for asylum before being determined an irregular migrant. Yet, in many instances asylum-seekers are detained – both in countries which are not party to the Refugee Convention (Libya is an example) and those that are (such as Australia, where all irregular entrants must be detained).[47]

Some countries that detain migrants distinguish between different types of migrants. For example, asylum-seekers and irregular migrants might be detained in separate facilities. Families may be detained together and in separate facilities to individual migrants. Women and vulnerable migrants might have specific detention facilities; and sometimes children are separated from their families and detained in designated childcare centres. Until 2015 (when the policy was abandoned), this was the case in Malta, for example.

In many countries, detected UASC who cannot be matched with parents or legal guardians in the country, are also prevented from continuing their journeys and placed in state care. The state becomes the legal guardian of the child and makes decisions for the child's accommodation and upbringing (as deemed in the child's best interests) until the child becomes of age. This usually means that the child will spend some years in a state institution or in foster care.

Statistics on the number of migrant children (or even migrants in general) who are detained are generally poor. However, it is estimated that over 100 countries detain child migrants, with hundreds of thousands of children in detention for immigration reasons. This includes countries such as Australia, Malaysia, Israel, South Africa, Greece, Mexico and the United States.[48] In the case of Australia, the Department of Immigration

---

[47] See Gerald Neuman, Chapter 19 and Daniel Ghezelbash, Chapter 21.

[48] End Immigration Detention of Children, *The Issue*, http://endchilddetention.org/issue/.

and Border Protection provides statistics on the number of children in immigration detention: as of 31 January 2017, there were less than five children in closed immigration detention facilities in Australia, with 234 living in the community under a 'Residence Determination' status and 3,925 on 'Bridging E' visas (both regimes for conditional and supervised release pending status determination). The average time for those held in closed detention was 493 days, with some held more than 730 days.[49] These figures do not include the 70 children detained in the Regional Processing Centre in Nauru since late 2013.[50]

Another country where the incarceration of migrant children, including refugee children, has been of concern is the United States. The law states that children, if detained, should be placed in shelters appropriate for juveniles. However, shortage of space does not always allow this. Due to recent increases in the arrival of unaccompanied children, the US government expanded its capacity to 10,000 housing spaces for children. However, in fiscal year 2016, the government detained 59,170 children referred by immigration authorities. The majority are released within 34 days to relatives.[51]

4. REGIONAL FOOTPRINTS

Why are children on the move? Some flee their country of origin alone or with their families simply to find safe haven elsewhere. Some are sent by families to make the journey alone, to claim asylum and facilitate a family reunification later on. Some are sent abroad to work and send money back to the family. All seek a better future for themselves in a country that promises better opportunities. Children may set out on a migratory journey with their family but become separated along the way; the clandestine nature of many migratory journeys and the risks that they present can often lead to family members dying or becoming lost.

The decision to migrate is usually motivated by a number of factors combined together: factors that relate to both the conditions at home

---

[49] See Australian Border Force, *Immigration Detention and Community Statistics* (Department of Immigration and Border Protection, 31 January 2017) available at www.border.gov.au/ReportsandPublications/Documents/statistics/immigration-detention-statistics-31-jan-2017.pdf.

[50] Australian Human Rights Commission, *Information about Children in Immigration Detention* (6 January 2016), available at www.humanrights.gov.au/information-about-children-immigration-detention.

[51] See data posted at www.acf.hhs.gov/orr/about/ucs/facts-and-data.

that make life unbearable (push factors), as well as the conditions at destination that hold the potential for a brighter future (pull factors). When children are involved it can cause families to prioritize these factors differently. For example, in the case of Syrian families in the Middle East, secondary movements to Europe were often motivated by the lack of long-term options for their children. That is, an inability to naturalize has much graver consequences for children than parents. Lack of educational opportunities for children, while rarely a primary driver, can also be a factor encouraging onward movement. Decisions to leave are rarely taken lightly.

While the discourse around migration tends to paint a picture of mass movements to the industrialized world, in 2015 the reality was that 53 per cent of refugees and migrants globally moved to new countries within their region of origin. For refugees, this was even more common: 90 per cent of all refugees worldwide found asylum in their region of origin. Only 10 per cent sought protection further afield.[52]

4.1 Africa

Movements within the region

Africa is a region characterized by regional migratory movements. In 2015, 16.2 million African migrants moved to another country in the region.[53] These movements are usually facilitated by free movement protocols, such as those guaranteed by the Economic Community of West African States (ECOWAS).

Africa is also the region of origin for one-third of all refugees under UNHCR's mandate, with 5.4 million refugees coming from African countries; 86 per cent of African refugees (4.6 million in total) find asylum in other African countries.[54] The largest populations are hosted by Ethiopia, Kenya and Uganda. The protracted nature of the crises in sending countries means that some refugee communities have been living in camps for generations. Many African children have lived their entire lives in refugee camps (for example, Eritreans in Sudanese camps, Somalis and South Sudanese in Kenya).

The conflicts responsible for the large number of African refugees also produce a staggering number of IDPs. A total of 12 million people were internally displaced by conflict in Africa in 2015, more than double the

---

52 Garin, *Uprooted*, n. 2 above, at 27.
53 *Ibid.* 53.
54 *Ibid.* 58.

number of refugees and roughly 30 per cent of the global IDP total. In Nigeria, the Democratic Republic of the Congo, Central African Republic and South Sudan, 1.7 million people were newly displaced by conflict and violence in 2015, one-fifth of the global total. An estimated 1.1 million children were displaced in Nigeria.[55]

Movements out of the region

While 16 million African migrants were living in another African country in 2015, a further 16 million Africans emigrated to: Europe (57 per cent); Asia (26 per cent); North America (14 per cent); Latin America and the Caribbean (6 per cent); and Oceania (3 per cent).[56] It should be noted, however, that secondary movements out of the region are usually only made once the migrant does not find what they seek regionally. In practical terms, this means that most Africans who migrate out of the region have been regional migrants at some point.

In terms of African migration to Europe, the most prominent countries of origin amongst boat arrivals through the Mediterranean are from Sub-Saharan Africa. Here, the main movements occur through the Western and Central Mediterranean routes.

The Western Mediterranean route tracks from North Africa to Spain. It encompasses a sea passage from North Africa to the Iberian Peninsula, by way of boat across the Strait of Gibraltar from Tangier (Morocco) to Tarifa (Spain), a land route through the enclaves of Ceuta and Melilla that are surrounded by Morocco, as well as a sea passage to the Canary Islands in Spain. Until 2006, most West African migrants used this route to access Europe: the number of irregular arrivals through the Canary Islands peaked at 30,000 in that year. The Spanish government has since worked with origin countries in a regional response to control borders and stop the boats. In 2012, only 173 migrants arrived through the Canary Islands. By 2016, the total number of arrivals through the Western Mediterranean route, across all of Spain's sea and land borders, had fallen to 8,162 individuals. The main countries of origin were Cote d'Ivoire (21 per cent), Algeria (18 per cent), Guinea Conakry (14 per cent), Gambia (10 per cent), Cameroon (10 per cent) and Morocco (8 per cent). In 2017, the number increased again to 28,349 arrivals across the land and sea arrival points.[57]

The Central Mediterranean route refers to the mixed migratory flow

---

55 *Ibid.*

56 Garin, *Uprooted*, above n. 2, at 53.

57 This data is from Operational Portal: Refugee Situations, available at http://data.unhcr.org/mediterranean/regional.php.

from Northern Africa to Italy and Malta. Libya has traditionally been the major transit and departure point for these boat journeys. Although there have also been variations in the departures from the Egyptian, Tunisian, Algerian and Moroccan coasts over the years, the relative number of boats leaving from Libya has continued to increase. The proportion of boats that arrived in Italy, ex-Libya, increased from 38 per cent in 2012; to 62 per cent in 2013; 84 per cent in 2015; to 93 per cent in 2016.[58] As arrivals through the Western Mediterranean decreased, arrivals through the Central Mediterranean have increased, moving from just over 15,000 arrivals in 2012 to 181,436 arrivals in 2016. In 2016, the main countries of origin for migrants travelling along the Central Mediterranean route were Nigeria (21 per cent), Eritrea (12 per cent), Guinea (7 per cent), Cote d'Ivoire (7 per cent), Gambia (7 per cent), Senegal (6 per cent), Mali (5 per cent), Sudan (5 per cent), Bangladesh (4 per cent) and Somalia (4 per cent).[59]

The evolution of migratory flows through the Western and Central Mediterranean between 2012 and 2016 is mapped on Figure 2.1 Movements along Mediterranean routes, 2012–2016.

Child migration

Africa has one of the lowest rates of child migration: only one in 90 African children live outside their country of birth. However, African children make up a large proportion of all migrants from Africa: nearly one-third are children, more than twice the global average. Burkina Faso, Cameroon and Chad are three of four countries in the world where the immigrant population comprises mostly children.[60] Moreover, nearly 3 million, or 53 per cent, of the refugees originating from Africa are children. The largest number of these child refugees come from Somalia, followed by South Sudan, Sudan, Democratic Republic of the Congo and Central African Republic.[61]

Child migration varies across the region. For example, UASC make up a large share of all Egyptians arriving in Europe through the Central Mediterranean. In 2015, 65 per cent of all Egyptian arrivals in Italy were UASC, up from 49 per cent in 2014.[62] It is thought that Egyptian families

---

[58] Data source: Italian Ministry of the Interior.

[59] *Ibid.*

[60] Garin, *Uprooted*, above n. 2, at 55.

[61] *Ibid.* 56.

[62] International Organization for Migration, *Why Unaccompanied Egyptian Children are Migrating to Europe* (22 April 2016), available at www.iom.int/news/why-unaccompanied-egyptian-children-are-migrating-europe.

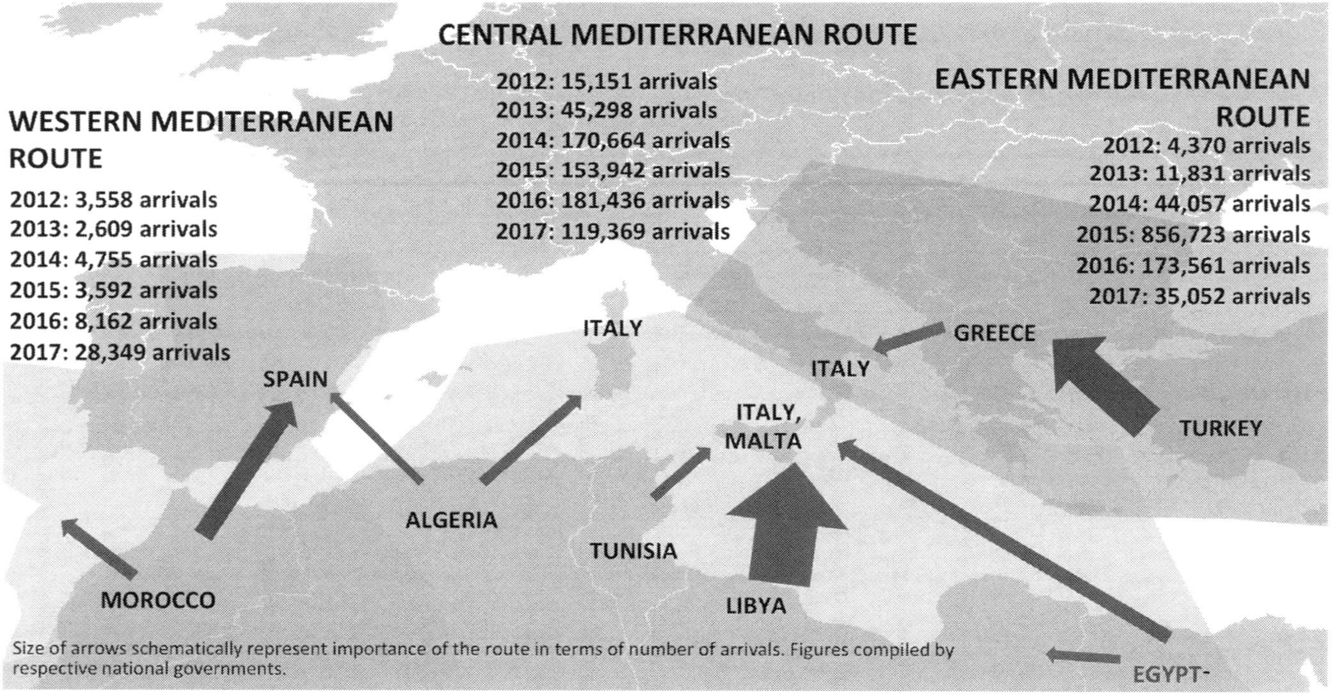

Figure 2.1 Movements along Mediterranean routes, 2012–2016

send their young boys to Europe (Egyptian UASC are generally aged 14–17) because they will not be returned until they are 'of age' (over 18), thereby allowing them to create a foothold for the family in Europe. These boys are expected to find jobs and send money back home.

West African UASC tend to be sent to Libya to find jobs and send money home to families who struggle with poverty. The lack of income-generating opportunities at origin either encourages these children to migrate or leads to family members pushing them out to support the family. The age of these child migrants is decreasing, with UASC as young as 12–14 being sent to Libya for work. Some arrive in Libya and hear about Europe and decide to try their luck or are pushed out of Libya and on to Europe by the high levels of insecurity, which worsened after the 2014 Libyan Political Crisis.[63]

East African UASC tend to be asylum-seekers from countries such as Eritrea and Somalia, following the route from the Horn of Africa to Libya, via Sudan, and on to Europe. They tend to be sent by families in search of a better life, without expectation of remittances. Some leave on their own accord after losing parents in conflict, which has been observed amongst Somali minors.[64]

4.2 Europe

African and European migration dynamics are linked by the three Mediterranean routes: Western, Central and Eastern (see Figure 2.1 Movements along Mediterranean routes, 2012–2016). As noted earlier, the Western and Central Mediterranean routes involve movements from Sub-Saharan Africa to the Sahel, then to North Africa and then on to Europe. The Eastern Mediterranean route generally involves movements from Turkey to Greece, across the Aegean. While the Western and Central Mediterranean routes are followed by African nationals, the Eastern Mediterranean route is more commonly favoured by migrants from Central Asia and the Middle East, and thereby links the Middle East to Europe.

In 2015, movements along the Eastern Mediterranean route reached a record high, with over 850,000 individuals travelling by boat from Turkey to Greece. This was the first time that arrivals along the Eastern Mediterranean route surpassed arrivals along the other two

---

[63] Author's own research in the region between 2012 and 2016.

[64] A Malakooti, *Mixed Migration: Libya at the Crossroads* (UNHCR and Altai Consulting, 2013).

Mediterranean routes (see Figure 2.1 Movements along Mediterranean routes, 2012–2016). In that year, most migrants on this route originated from Syria, followed by Afghanistan and Somalia (all refugee producing countries). There were also increasing numbers of migrants coming from Sub-Saharan Africa along this route, although their numbers remained small. Most moved north, leaving Greece through its border with the former Yugoslav Republic of Macedonia, continuing through the Balkans to enter Germany. According to UNHCR,[65] 35 per cent (or just under 300,000) of the arrivals along the Eastern Mediterranean route in 2015 were children. This represented the highest proportion of children of all three routes. In 2015, an estimated 11 per cent of arrivals through the Central Mediterranean and 9 per cent of arrivals through the Western Mediterranean were children.

What is interesting to note about migration in the European context is that while much of the discourse has focused on irregular migration to Europe through the Mediterranean, the data suggests that this represents a very small proportion of all migration to Europe. In 2016, Figure 2.1 Movements along Mediterranean routes, 2012–2016 records 363,159 irregular migrants entering the EU through the Mediterranean across the Western (8,162), Central (181,436) and Eastern Mediterranean routes (173,561). One year earlier, just over 1 million migrants arrived through the Mediterranean. This exceptional number mainly comprised asylum-seekers from Syria, Afghanistan and Iraq. Even so, this represented less than 3 per cent of the total number of non-European migrants living in Europe and just over 1 per cent of all migrants in Europe in 2015.

Like Africa, Europe is also a region that is characterized by regional migratory movements that are facilitated by free movement protocols, specifically those of the European Union (EU). In 2015, 76.1 million international migrants (31 per cent of the global total of 244 million) lived in Europe. Just over half (39.9 million in total) were Europeans living in different European countries from those of their birth.[66] The other 35.4 million non-European migrants living in Europe came from Asia (20.2 million individuals, being 57 per cent of all non-European migrants) and Africa (9.2 million individuals, being 25 per cent of all non-European migrants).[67]

---

65 UNHCR, *Mediterranean Sea Arrivals, 2015 Data, by Location, Country of Arrival, Demographic and Country of Origin* (22 January 2016), Operational Portal: Refugee Situations, available at https://data2.unhcr.org/en/documents/details/34990.

66 Garin, *Uprooted*, above n. 2, at 90.

67 *Ibid.*

In addition to the 39.9 million European migrants that resided within their region of origin in 2015, 19.7 million Europeans were living in countries outside of their region of origin. The destinations for these European migrants were North America (7.5 million) and Asia (6.9 million), which together host 75 per cent of all European migrants living outside of Europe. An additional 3 million live in Oceania; 1.3 million in Latin America and the Caribbean; and 1 million in Africa.[68]

Child migration

Of the migrants living in Europe in 2015, children made up only 7 per cent (5.4 million), the smallest share of international child migrants in any region in the world. However, child migrants in Europe made up 17 per cent of the global number of child migrants.[69]

More than 300,000 child migrants were detected crossing irregularly into Italy (through the Central Mediterranean) and Greece (through the Eastern Mediterranean) in 2015.[70] There were stark differences between the profiles of children arriving in Italy and Greece. For example, Italy received a larger share of UASC. Of 16,500 entering through the Mediterranean in Italy, over 12,000 (72 per cent) were UASC. In Greece, the figure was around 10 per cent,[71] or approximately 30,000 children. In Greece in 2015, most were from the Syrian Arab Republic, Afghanistan, Pakistan, Iraq and the Islamic Republic of Iran, whereas arrivals in Italy were from Nigeria, Eritrea, Gambia, Côte d'Ivoire and Sudan.[72] In 2016, 100,264 children[73] were detected crossing irregularly into Greece, Italy, Spain and Bulgaria, and UNHCR estimates that 33,424 were UASC.[74] While slightly lower than the 2015 figure, children accounted for a much larger percentage of total arrivals as the overall numbers decreased significantly in 2016. In 2017, 32,963 children arrived in Greece, Italy, Spain and Bulgaria, of whom 19,858 (60 per cent) were UASC. While the number of

---

68 *Ibid.*

69 *Ibid.*

70 UNHCR, *Mediterranean Sea Arrivals, 2015 Data*, above n. 64.

71 The Greek authorities do not make an official distinction between accompanied and unaccompanied children at entry, so no official figure exists. However, UNHCR estimates that at least 10% of the children who arrived in Greece in 2015 were UAMs.

72 IOM Global Migration Data Analysis Centre, Data Briefing Series No. 5 (September 2016), p. 1.

73 Figure quoted in UNHCR, UNICEF and IOM, *Refugee and Migrant Children in Europe: Overview of Trends*, 2017, p. 1.

74 Figure quoted in UNICEF, *Refugee and Migrant Crisis in Europe Humanitarian Situation*, Report No. 20 (UNICEF, 2017), p. 1.

child arrivals decreased by 67 per cent between 2016 and 2017, the proportion of children that were unaccompanied or separated increased from 34 per cent in 2016 to 60 per cent in 2017.[75]

Migration through the Mediterranean is far more dangerous than other routes into the European Union (EU). According to the International Organisation for Migration (IOM)'s Missing Migrants project, there were 3,777 detected deaths in the Mediterranean in 2015.[76] In the first 11 months of 2015, one in every three people who lost their lives in the Eastern Mediterranean was a child.[77] More restrictive migration policies in the EU in 2015–2017, such as the agreement between the EU and Turkey and the actions of governments in the Balkans, are likely to make these journeys even riskier and more clandestine.

With the EU–Turkey Agreement and consequent closure of the Balkans route, migrants have continued to seek other pathways. According to Frontex, by March 2016, most migrants were making their way into the EU from Croatia's border with Serbia. After April in that year, irregular migration through Croatia and Slovenia was stopped and routes were opened first through Hungary (with 100 recorded crossings) and Serbia where 11,000 individuals broke through border fences.[78]

Refugees

In 2015, Europe hosted 1.8 million refugees, 11 per cent of the global total. This compares with the 4.6 million which were hosted by African nations. Roughly half a million came from other European countries, especially Ukraine. It is difficult to determine the total share of the child refugees in Europe, as not all national governments provide data disaggregated by age. However, 30 per cent of all asylum-seekers in Europe were children (389,000), more than twice the number for 2014. Nearly 70 per cent of claims came from children from the Syrian Arab Republic, Afghanistan and Iraq. About 90,000 were UASC.[79]

Since 2015, the lack of legal pathways to asylum in Europe has led to some Syrian and Iraqi families sending their children to Europe alone, using smugglers, to anchor family reunification for the rest of the family. Such strategies expose children to great risks. In most cases, family reun-

---

[75] UNHCR, UNICEF and IOM, above n. 73.

[76] International Organization for Migration, 'Missing Migrants' in *Latest Global Figures: Migrant Fatalities Worldwide* (2017), available at http://missingmigrants.iom.int/latest-global-figures.

[77] Garin, *Uprooted*, above n. 2, at 92.

[78] *FRAN Quarterly: Quarter 2 April–June 2016* (Frontex, 2016), p. 8.

[79] IOM, Data Briefing Series No. 5, above n. 71, at 1.

ion takes many years to effect, such that the remainder of the family often resort to smugglers and irregular migration anyway.

4.3 The Americas

The Americas are also characterized by regional migratory movements. In fact, migration in the Americas is more highly concentrated within the region than in any other part of the world. In 2015, 33.1 million migrants from the Americas moved within the same region and only 7.1 million (18 per cent) migrated out of the region. Most of these intra-regional movements end in North America but there are different characteristics per subregion. That is, the majority of migrants from the Caribbean and Central America head to North America but migrants from South America move in almost equal proportions to North America, within South America, and to Europe. Of the 7.1 million individuals that migrated out of the region, 5.7 million moved to Europe (80 per cent).[80] The United States hosts the largest number of migrants of other countries in the region, in absolute terms, and Canada hosts the largest number of migrants in terms of per capita ratio.

In terms of child migrants, there were 6.3 million residing in the Americas in 2015, which constitutes 21 per cent of the global total. Of the 6.3 million child migrants, the majority were residing in the United States (59 per cent), followed by Mexico (12 per cent) and Canada (10 per cent). Not only does the United States host the largest number of child migrants in the region (3.7 million children) but also the largest number of child migrants of any single country in the world.[81]

In 2015, there were a total of 747,000 refugees residing in the Americas, 453,000 of whom originated from the region (61 per cent). Three-quarters of the refugees from the region came from Colombia and half of all refugees from Colombia were children. Three-quarters of refugees from the region received asylum in Latin America and the Caribbean and 100,000 in Northern America (United States and Canada).

More than 7.3 million people were considered internally displaced by conflict in the Americas in 2015. Just as with the refugees, the majority of IDPs in the region are from Colombia (6.3 million individuals, accounting for 86 per cent of conflict-induced internal displacements in the region),[82] followed by El Salvador (289,000), Guatemala (251,000),

---

80 Garin, *Uprooted*, above n. 2, at 66.

81 *Ibid*. 67.

82 It should be noted that these figures are an estimate of all people that have

Mexico (287,000) and Honduras (174,000).[83] In Colombia, internal conflict between various groups who wish to exert their influence over the country has created five decades of instability and violence.

The violence in El Salvador, Guatemala, Honduras (referred to collectively as the Northern Triangle) and Mexico not only creates internal displacement but also departure, particularly in the case of children. Most of the unaccompanied and separated children apprehended by immigration authorities at the southern border of the United States originate from one of these four countries. In 2016 (fiscal year), a total of 17,512, 18,913 and 10,468 unaccompanied minors (UAMs) were apprehended at the southern borders of the United States from El Salvador, Guatemala and Honduras, respectively. These figures have been generally on the increase since 2009 when the figures were 1,221, 1,115 and 968 for El Salvador, Guatemala and Honduras, respectively. There were also 11,962 Mexican UAMs that were apprehended at this border in 2016; however, the United States repatriates arrivals from Mexico almost immediately, even UAMs.[84] The total number of UAMs apprehended on the southern borders of the United States in 2016 (59,692) made up roughly 15 per cent of all irregular migrants apprehended. In addition to the UAMs, a further 77,674 family units were apprehended (19 per cent of all apprehensions), which includes accompanied children.[85]

Migration from the Northern Triangle to the United States, through Mexico, has a long history and is usually driven by a combination of the following factors: instability created by decades of civil war; resulting economic downturn; social exclusion derived from poverty and/or belonging to a minority group; as well as displacement due to natural disasters. Children, in particular, face high risks of gang-related recruitment, violence and extortion. These factors are exacerbated by impunity for perpetrators of crime/violence and lack of access to justice for victims.

UNHCR has established certain risk profiles for asylum-seekers from the Northern Triangle and advises that all of these profiles may be in need

---

been displaced over the course of more than five decades of conflict in Colombia. As some may be deceased or no longer displaced, the estimate may be overstated.

[83] Many of the UAMs qualifying for refugee protection in the United States are youth fleeing from Central America, meaning that the number of IDPs in the region may be lower than current estimates indicate and may need reviewing. See Kate Bones and Timnah Baker, Chapter 14.

[84] US Customs and Border Protection, *United States Border Patrol Southwest Family Unit Subject and Unaccompanied Alien Children Apprehensions Fiscal Year 2016* (2016).

[85] *Ibid.*

of international protection under the 1951 Refugee Convention. These risk profiles are: persecution by a gang for not having complied with the gang's authority (particularly relevant in the face of increasing amounts of territory coming under the control of gangs); persons working or involved in activities susceptible to extortion; victims and witnesses of crimes committed by gangs or members of the security forces; children and youth from areas where gangs operate; women and girls in areas where gangs operate; and LGBTI people.[86]

There is also an increasing trend of minors from Central America moving to the United States to reunite with family that previously made the journey. In 2013, 22 per cent of Mexican children who crossed into the United States had at least one parent resident in the country, as did 49 per cent from El Salvador and 27 per cent from Honduras.[87]

4.4 Oceania

A total of 1.8 million people from Oceania are living outside the country in which they were born. Of these, 1.1 million remain within the region but in a country other than their birthplace. Of the 800,000 living outside the region, half reside in Europe, around 40 per cent in North America and the rest in Asia. In 2015, 6.9 million migrants moved to Oceania from countries outside of the region – more than nine times the number of migrants who left the region. Europe and Asia each supplied approximately 3 million migrants. The remaining 900,000 came from Africa (approximately 500,000) and the Americas (approximately 400,000).

In 2015, it was estimated that 670,000 child migrants resided in the region, comprising only 8 per cent of all migrants and 2 per cent of all child migrants globally. Even so, child migrants in Oceania represented a high proportion of all children in the region: 6 per cent of all children in the region were migrants. Three-quarters of all child migrants in the region lived in Australia, with an additional 17 per cent in New Zealand.

The two migration dynamics that have received the greatest attention in Oceania are the movement of asylum-seekers by boat to Australia, and climate change induced migration that affects small island nations in the Pacific.

Oceania is the region of origin for less than 1,400 refugees, which is a

---

[86] Lesbian, gay, bisexual, transgender and intersex (LGBTI). Amnesty International, *Home Sweet Home? Honduras, Guatemala and El Salvador's Role in a Deepening Refugee Crisis* (Amnesty International, 2016), p. 5.

[87] Garin, *Uprooted*, above n. 2, at 70.

number much lower than any other region in the world. Moreover, the region hosts approximately 48,000 refugees or people that are living in refugee-like situations, which is less than 1 per cent of the global total. There are an additional 22,000 asylum-seekers awaiting processing; however, even if this 22,000 was added to the total number of refugees in the region, it would still be the lowest number of any region in the world. The main refugee communities in Oceania are from Asia: 9,300 Indonesian refugees lived in Papua New Guinea, and 7,800 Afghan and 5,200 Iranian refugees lived in Australia in 2015.[88]

The movement of asylum-seekers to Australia by boat, and the response of the Australian government, has become the subject of a great deal of controversy since 2013. Since that year, the Australian government has implemented a policy of interception and pushback at sea for migrants travelling irregularly, most of whom are asylum-seekers. The decision has been criticized for the fact that it prevents access to asylum and creates serious risks for those on board. The boats are often in serious disrepair and unfit for the extended journey from Asia to Australia and so pushbacks create tremendous risks for all on board, with children being most at risk, both in terms of physical danger but also psychological trauma.

Under the Regional Resettlement Agreement of the Australian government, when boats are intercepted, the migrants on board are directed to neighbouring countries where they will wait until their applications for asylum are processed. In some cases, they are taken to detention facilities in Papua New Guinea. The detention of these migrants, and the conditions of the centres that they are held in, have been criticized harshly by NGOs, the international community and the United Nations. Particularly in the case of children, reports of maltreatment, poor mental health and self-harm have prompted many to speak out against the detention of children.[89]

In terms of climate-induced migration, most Pacific Island countries and territories experience climatic extremes, such as tropical cyclones, droughts and high wave events. These disasters create a whole host of challenges for these small nations, including rising sea levels and reduced arable land, drinkable water and sustainable fish stock. Moreover, rising sea levels threaten the entire existence of certain islands, which are predicted to be completely underwater within a few decades (for example, Kiribati).

Disasters are often followed by migration as individuals seek greater

---

88 *Ibid.* 104.

89 *Ibid.*

livelihood opportunities elsewhere as a way to address consequent poverty at home. The young and fit are usually able to migrate out while the elderly and children remain at home and rely on remittances that are sent back. Usually, these remittances are not enough to lift the family that remains out of poverty, meaning that it is the children and the elderly that suffer the most. Moreover, even when children themselves are not migrating, they may still experience the risks of migration. For example, when family members migrate abroad for long periods of time, the separation can cause children to experience neglect, psychological trauma and vulnerability to exploitation. In the case of many of the Pacific Islands, the great distances between these islands and other countries means that when parents/other family members migrate for economic reasons, their ability to visit home regularly is limited.[90]

5. CONCLUSION

In conclusion, while the number of migrants (as a proportion of the total population) has been increasing in recent years, the number of international child migrants has been increasing at an even higher rate. Children are particularly overrepresented in refugee statistics (as opposed to migrant statistics) and the growth rate for child refugees has been much higher than the growth rate for child migrants. Contrary to popular opinion, more child migrants and refugees are hosted by countries in Africa and the Middle East than by countries in the industrialized world. In fact, 90 per cent of all refugees worldwide found asylum in their region of origin in 2015.

In terms of recent issues of concern, the lack of legal pathways to asylum in some countries (particularly in Europe) has led to children being sent ahead of the rest of the family in the hope that they will pave the way for a family reunification (particularly in the case of Syrians and Iraqis), thereby leading to increases in asylum applications made by UASC. Increases in conflict globally are also leading to increases in IDPs, a large proportion of whom are children. Cases of child victims of trafficking are also increasing, with children being the second most commonly detected victims of trafficking after women between 2012 and 2014.

---

[90] *Ibid*. 106.

3. Why they leave: Latin American immigrant youths and their quest for survival

Isabel Martinez

1. INTRODUCTION

In 1918, at the age of 16, my grandmother left her home in El Molino, Guanajuato, Mexico and walked over 500 miles to escape the growing violence that was surrounding her home. From 1912 until 1920, revolutionaries battled Federales, and then each other, in a civil war sparked by, among other acts, privatization and foreign economic control, both accelerated under Mexican dictator Porfirio Diaz.[1]

Fleeing the rumors of rape, robbery and kidnapping that surrounded this war, this young girl, who would become affectionately known as Mama Chepa to over 100 US-born children, grandchildren and great-grandchildren, would finally arrive and settle 30 miles north of the Mexico–United States border in south Texas, almost 60 days after she had left her childhood home.[2]

Almost 100 years after my grandmother's arrival, young teenagers are still fleeing economic and physical violence that has been manufactured by neocolonial agreements between United States, Mexican and Central American 'elites'.[3] Similar to the migrations incited by a revolution that was in no small part a response to Mexico's increasing embrace of US investment, subsequent exoduses from Mexico and Central America have been incited by US-backed economic and security policies. In both post-revolution Mexico and in mid to late twentieth century Central America, Mexican and Central American families have been subjected

---

[1] J.M. Hart, *Revolutionary Mexico: The Coming and Process of the Mexican Revolution* (University of California Press, 1987).

[2] F. Salazar, *The Martinez Family* (Unpublished Monograph, 2000).

[3] G.G. Gonzalez, *Guest Workers or Colonized Labor: Mexican Labor Migration to the United States* (Paradigm Publishers, 2005).

to increased, not decreased, poverty, violence and displacement.[4] Due to the United States' accelerated deportation of US-manufactured criminal organizations and agents, current policies, including the Dominican Republic-Central American Free Trade Agreement (DR-CAFTA) and the Central American Regional Security Initiative (CARSI), families are again being forced to seek alternative strategies for economic as well as physical survival.[5]

Unfortunately, discussions of these policies have ignored the youngest victims of this long-standing neocolonial relationship between the United States, Mexico and Central America: independent teenage migrants. Based on years of archival research, primary interviews and observations across myriad sites, including schools, homes and courts in Puebla, Mexico, New York City, and south Texas, this chapter places their migrations into a socio-historical context so that this phenomenon can be better understood as a byproduct of seemingly endless US (and foreign) interventions. Largely subsumed into accounts of adult and family migration, where minors were assumed simply to be 'luggage' or following their parents, the trickles of independent teenage migrants that came before today's waves have mostly gone ignored.[6] Entitled to economic and physical security with and away from their families, these youths have actively responded to the ebb and flow of interventions in their countries by immigrating for nearly a century; today's Mexican and Central American teenage migrants are simply making the old new again.

---

[4] P. Fernandez-Kelley and D. Massey, 'Borders for Whom? The Role of NAFTA in Mexico-US Migration' (2007) 610 *Annals of the American Academy of Political and Social Science* 98; S.B. Coutin, *Exiled Home: Salvadoran Transnational Youth in the Aftermath of Violence* (Duke University Press, 2016).

[5] Approved in 2006, DR-CAFTA is a Free Trade Agreement between the United States and the following Latin American countries: Dominican Republic, El Salvador, Guatemala, Honduras, Nicaragua and Costa Rica. Critics have described it as exacerbating poverty, dislocation and violence among Central America's poorest denizens. An offshoot of the Merida Initiative, CARSI is a collaborative regional program funded by the United States that aims to promote safety and security in Northern Triangle countries by combatting local and transnational criminal organizations.

[6] J. Bhabha, *Child Migration and Human Rights in a Global Age* (Princeton University Press, 2014); M.F. Orellana, B. Thorne, A. Chee and W.S.E. Lam, 'Transnational Childhoods: The Participation of Children in Processes of Family Migration' (2001) 48 *Social Problems* 572.

2. IMPERIALISM AND INDEPENDENT TEENAGE MIGRATION

Across examples of US economic and political domination in Mexico and Central America, displacement is the common denominator. Repeatedly, peaceful and non-peaceful interventions have uprooted poor individuals in Mexico and Central America.[7] For example, just prior to the Mexican Revolution in the 1880s and 1890s, 90 percent of the peasant class had been displaced from their communally held lands due to agreement between Mexican elites and US corporations.[8] Once displaced, these individuals have either been forced to become surplus labor for corporations benefitting from these interventions, been confronted with and resisted violence and/or became internal, and later, external, migrants.[9]

Some Mexican and Central American teenagers have responded to this economic and political violence by emigrating without their parents. Unlike dependent child and adolescent migrants, independent teenage migrants make, to varying degrees, their own choices that include leaving their parents behind in search of economic and/or physical security.[10] These decisions, however, are not abruptly made or without precedents. In fact, rather than enjoying the extended childhoods that are generally espoused by international and national policies, these youths make choices while enduring accelerated childhoods, or shortened periods of emotional and economic dependence on adults.[11] Long prior to emigration, many of the youths have participated in the labor market, left school in their home countries and/or experienced threats to their security. In the case of youths pursuing economic migration, the decision to leave is made after being born into and witnessing the economic effects of remittances. Others leave amidst threats of violence that have infiltrated their communities and even households. Upon reaching certain ages, the youths themselves even become targets of threats. Regardless of the reason, emigration becomes a highly desirable, if not the only, option for their survival and/or social mobility.

---

[7] J. Gonzalez, *Harvest of Empire* (Viking Press, 2000); N. Hamilton and N. Chinchilla, 'Central American Migration: A Framework for Analysis' (1991) 26 *Latin American Research Review* 75.

[8] Gonzalez, *Guest Workers or Colonized Labor*, above n. 3.

[9] *Ibid.*; Hamilton and Chinchilla, 'Central American Migration', above n. 7.

[10] Bhabha, *Child Migration and Human Rights in a Global Age*, above n. 6.

[11] I. Martinez, 'Supporting Two Households: Unaccompanied Mexican Minors and Their Absences from US Schools' (2016) 15 *Journal of Latinos and Education* 229.

Strong notions of family obligation or familism also drive the actions of youths.[12] From early ages, these young teenagers are taught to act in the best interests of the family. This may include alleviating household financial stresses by working. Those leaving in search of physical security may relocate. In many contemporary cases, gangs attempt to recruit children and teenagers and if the youths refuse, they risk endangering their families. Rather than subject them to harm, the youths are forced to leave.

Using these frameworks, the following sections seek to recover previous trickles and waves of independent teenage migration from Mexico and Central America to demonstrate that this is not a new phenomenon. In spite of nearly 100 years of independent teenage migration from Latin America, it has only been recently that minors and their reasons for migration have been considered, with and/or apart from adults.[13] By placing independent teenage migration into a socio-historical context that spans nearly 100 years, it becomes evident that the most recent waves of youth migration from Mexico and Central America are not occurring in isolation, but rather are simply recycled consequences of reoccurring US intervention in the region.

3. MEXICO

3.1 Underage and Independent: Mexico's Youngest Braceros

After the end of the Mexican Revolution, migration flows from Mexico to the United States were described as the result of the 'relentless pressure of United States agricultural, financial and oil corporate interests' on the development of Mexico as a nation-state.[14] Massive repatriations in the 1930s and increasing 'birthrates, life expectancies and literacy levels' due to US backed social programs created two interrelated conditions

---

12 *Ibid.* 229–43; and R.F. Schoeni and K.E. Ross, 'Material Assistance from Families During the Transition to Adulthood' in R.A. Settersten, F.F. Furstenberg and R.G. Rumbaut (eds), *On the Frontier of Adulthood: Theory, Research and Public Policy* (University of Chicago Press, 2005), pp. 396–416; M. Suarez-Orozco and C. Suarez-Orozco, *Transformations: Immigration, Family Life and Achievement Motivation among Latino Adolescents* (Stanford University Press, 1995).

13 Bhabha, *Child Migration and Human Rights in a Global Age*, above n. 6, at 3. Bhabha points to two factors that emerged in the late 1990s to explain this 'new' approach to child immigration, which includes (a) growing numbers of unaccompanied child migrants, and (b) increased attention to non-citizen children in international law.

14 E. Galarza, 'Program for Action, 1949' in E. Galarza, *Man of Fire: Selected Writings* (University of Illinois, 2013), p. 37.

that had been unanticipated. First, there was a strain on the existing agricultural system that had not been sufficiently expanded to feed a growing and aging population. Second, this created an expanding working-age population without a simultaneous expansion of the labor market or wages.[15] In search for a panacea, the temporary worker program, officially known as the Mexican Farm Labor Program, was designed to alleviate un- and underemployment and pressure mounting, especially in Central Mexico.[16] With many of Mexico's poor desperate for employment and 'willing to take arduous jobs at wages scorned by most Americans', the bilateral program provided the safety-valve Mexico needed, as Mexican workers would fill the void left by labor-age men fighting in World War II. Citing the need for higher wages and keenly aware of Mexico's inability to provide them, adult Mexican males began to both enlist in the program but to also emigrate to fill other agricultural jobs without authorization.[17]

Joining these adult males were also young teenage male minors. Seeking an escape from poverty, independent teenage migrants would leave their parents behind and seek work across the United States-Mexico border, both prior to and as Braceros. Ignoring both immigration laws that prohibited unaccompanied minor migration and/or the required minimum age of enlistment set by the Bracero Program, these minors simply blended in with adult Mexican males seeking work in *el norte*.[18] While some young teenage Mexican males immigrated to the United States and returned just in time to enroll into the Bracero program as adults, others would simply lie about their ages and enlist into the Bracero Program as minors. Both groups of youths, however, were leaving for the same reasons: to work so that they could help alleviate their families' poverty and economic precariousness.

One such youth, Alvaro Hernandez, was born in Julimes, Chihuahua, to a *campesino*, or farmer, and a schoolteacher. Although his family moved to the capital of Chihuahua and he was able to attend school until the sixth grade, when he was only 13, Alvaro returned to his hometown to help his father work in the fields. Aware of the financial difficulties

---

[15] D. Cohen, *Braceros: Migrant Citizens and Transnational Subjects in the Postwar United States and Mexico* (University of North Carolina Press, 2011), p. 23; Gonzalez, *Guest Workers or Colonized Labor*, above n. 3; J.J. Dwyer 'The End of US Intervention in Mexico: Franklin Roosevelt and the Expropriation of American-Owned Agricultural Property' (1998) 28 *Presidential Studies Quarterly* 495.

[16] Cohen, *Braceros*, above n. 15.

[17] *Ibid.*; R.L. Mize and A.C.S. Swords, *Consuming Mexican Labor: From the Bracero Program to NAFTA* (University of Toronto Press, 2011).

[18] Immigration Law 1907 (US); Cohen, *Braceros*, above n. 15.

his family endured, after turning 14, Alvaro borrowed 15 pesos and left without telling his parents. He first migrated to Ciudad Juarez, and then, lured by stories of labor opportunities in the United States, crossed over the Chihuahua-Texas border into El Paso, Texas.[19]

Alvaro describes easily procuring work in Texas after crossing into El Paso on a chilly November day with his similarly aged friend, Francisco Uribe. At the immigration booth, an immigration officer pointed him towards a cluster of trucks and let them cross the border. After passing and walking a few blocks, he found the trucks waiting for laborers to pick cotton. He and Francisco Uribe were selected to accompany a man to Mesquite, New Mexico, where he would pick cotton until February of the following year. Returning to Julimes with his pockets full of money, he could not resist returning the next year as a 16-year-old. By 1946, when he was 18, he returned to Chihuahua and sought work as a Bracero. He worked for the next several years for a man named Neil Armstrong; when the astronaut Neil Armstrong walked on the moon, he would wonder whether or not his boss was the astronaut's father.[20]

Other youths lied about their ages to enlist in the Bracero Program. Although there was a minimum age requirement of 18 years, age verification was sometimes lax. Ismael was only 17 when he became a Bracero. Completing only four years of school, Ismael worked from a very young age to help his siblings and his mama 'get ahead'. He described recruiters for the Bracero Program arriving in Aguascalientes and setting up an enlistment center in a downtown hotel. They did not ask for any papers or requirements, he said; the only requirement was knowing how to work in the fields. Having the *voluntad* or the will to work was the only prerequisite.[21]

Seventeen-year-old Duranguense Antonio Garcia prepared to enter the Bracero Program underage. Mindful of the age requirements, he arranged for his Mexican Military ID card to state that he had been born a year earlier. With an altered ID, he enlisted at a contracting center in Durango, Mexico, and was soon on his way to fulfill his first contract in the cotton fields of south Texas. He was unable to stomach American food and within a week of arriving, he fell so ill that he could not work. He eventually returned to Mexico, where after a few months, he enlisted as a Bracero again.[22]

---

19 A. Hernandez, 'Interview by Myrna Parra-Mantilla' (Bracero History Archive, 5 February 2003).

20 *Ibid.*

21 I. Diaz de Leon, 'Interview by Myrna Parra-Mantilla' (Bracero History Archive, 4 February 2003).

22 A. Garcia, 'Interview by Claudia Morales Haro' (Bracero History Archive, 12 March 2003).

These three youths exemplify cases of independent Mexican teenage migrants who were responding to the socio-economic contexts of post-Revolution Mexico. From households with limited economic needs and communities with limited work and wage opportunities, these teenage minors were lured independently and through a bilateral work program to work in the United States. Circumventing lax age requirements to cross the United States-Mexico border and to join the Bracero Program, these teenage minors would join the adult remittance-sending population. By the 1950s, their monies would become 'fundamental for Mexico's economy and the State's modernization projects' as Mexico's third largest source of income.[23] In light of a conglomeration of insufficient and outright damaging social and economic policies from both sides of the United States-Mexico border, these youths, in addition to their adult counterparts, left in order to prop up their country's and their households' economies.

3.2 New Deals, Old Consequences: The Case of NAFTA

Fifty years after the Bracero Program, the United States and Mexico entered into another agreement that compelled the migration of Mexican adults and independent teenage minors to the United States. In 1994, the North American Free Trade Agreement (NAFTA), as well as a bundle of other economic reforms dictated by the World Bank and IMF, became the vehicles through which, according to the chief Mexican negotiators, millions of Mexicans would be lifted out of poverty and the country would achieve 'national prosperity'.[24]

Unfortunately, for many rural Mexican communities, NAFTA was a 'death sentence'.[25] Several of NAFTA's tenets dealt damaging blows to nearly four-fifths of the 2.6 million small farms located in the rural south. This included the deregulation of the agricultural market, the elimination of tariffs, the removal of subsidies, and the favoring of larger rather than smaller farms.[26] Subsistence farmers would be the most harmed as they bore witness to the collapse of their meager income-bearing endeavors, and ultimately their survival.

---

[23] Cohen, *Braceros*, above n. 15, at 24.

[24] P. Fernandez-Kelly and D. Massey, 'Borders for Whom: The Role of NAFTA in Mexico-US Migration' (2007) 610 *Annals of American Academy of Political and Social Science* 104.

[25] Mize and Swords, *Consuming Mexican Labor*, above n. 17, at 195.

[26] M.G. Marroni, *Fronteras Perversa, Familias Fracturadas: Los indocumentados mexicanos y el sueño Americano* (BUAP, 2009).

But how did this occur? As part of NAFTA, Mexico ended an era of trade protectionism and lift tariffs that had previously kept heavily subsidized American fruits, grains and vegetables out of the Mexican market.[27] By removing tariffs and price controls, US goods could now flood the Mexican markets at prices lower than those of Mexican foodstuffs. Compounded by the elimination of pre-NAFTA subsidies, these aforementioned developments left Mexican small farmers unable to set competitive prices.[28] When tariffs that had long protected '*lo Mexicano*' or corn, a national symbol of Mexico and staple of all agrarian households, were completely removed, Mexican corn would see its production fall by two-thirds.[29] Unable to compete with highly subsidized corn from the United States, small farmers whose lifeblood had depended on this crop for generations could not continue this trade or tradition.

To offset the economic devastation inflicted on their families, teenage minors would immigrate to the United States, including 5,000 to the tri-state region of New York, New Jersey and Connecticut.[30] I would notice this phenomenon after riding alongside peach-fuzz faced young Mexican workers late at night on New York City's subways. After conducting a study examining these youths' reasons for remaining out of school, I found that they had immigrated to help their families survive and become socially mobile, an endeavor they felt that they could not achieve if they remained in Mexico.[31]

Hailing mostly from the most adversely affected southern states of Puebla, Oaxaca and Guerrero, youth reported considering or actually immigrating to New York City after being unable to continue their schooling or encountering a scarcity of informal or formal employment and low wages. As members of communities and families with high levels of outmigration, they were surrounded by evidence that immigration is a viable vehicle for their own and their families' economic security. As a result, these youths would begin to imagine their own departures at early ages, oftentimes waiting until they were both old enough and conditions were severe enough that they could not remain in Mexico.

Manuel shared his story about why and how he immigrated at the age of 16. After his father died when he was an infant, his older brothers

---

[27] J.C. McKinley, 'Mexican farmers protest end of Corn Import Tax', *New York Times*, 1 February 2008.

[28] E. Malkin, 'Nafta's promise, unfulfilled', *New York Times*, 23 March 2009.

[29] Marroni, *Fronteras Perversa, Familias Fracturadas*, above n. 26.

[30] R. Fry, personal communication with author, 2012.

[31] I. Martinez, *Making Transnational Adults from Youth: Mexican Immigrant Youth in Pursuit of the Mexican Dream* (Unpublished Dissertation, 2011).

immigrated to New York City. Their remittances would help pay for household expenses and his and his siblings' schooling. One time, he fondly recalled, his mother used the monies to purchase a new, sturdier backpack to hold his notebooks. This was especially significant because Manuel was studious and dreamed of becoming a teacher.

Even with his brothers' remittances, however, Manuel's schooling was always vulnerable to his household's economic precariousness. Supporting the family with her sons' inconsistent remittances and by raising and selling chickens and goats, his mother would sometimes cry alone after worrying about how she would pay for food, his and his siblings' schooling and other necessities. Overhearing her sobbing, Manuel knew that even though he was awarded a partial scholarship to attend high school his continued schooling would only cause more severe financial distress.

By October of his first semester, the financial stresses were too much to bear. Unable to pay the balance on his school account, Manuel considered dropping out. After his brother-in-law shared how much he could earn by working even a limited amount of time in New York City, he decided that he had no other choice but to emigrate. He would free himself of his school debts by dropping out of high school and joining his brothers in New York City. From there, he could send monies home to his mother and siblings.

Samuel immigrated after a long bout of unemployment. He had dropped out of school to work years before, but after his father's death, he began to give his earnings to his mother and his sister so that she could continue her studies. Although he had enjoyed moderate success in the labor market, after his latest temporary job ended and he was unable to find work, he began to seriously consider his friend's invitation to join him and to work in Brooklyn. Desperate, he borrowed money to pay for the trip and left for the Big Apple.

Little attention has been paid to the effects of NAFTA on distinct age populations. By isolating this group of youths we see how, at such young ages, they reacted to their families' economic need and communities' labor challenges. By placing them into a broader socio-historical context, we also see that, like their compatriots before them, these youths were reacting to the effects of agreements with the United States (as well as Canada) which had left their communities and households economically insecure. With little hope of finding economic stability in Mexico, these youths looked and travelled north of the United States-Mexico border to escape debt and to support their households back home.

In more recent years, unaccompanied minors arriving from Mexico have not only encountered a different reception to those mentioned above, but they have also decreased in number. Recent laws have mandated that rather than being apprehended and released, unaccompanied Mexican minors detained by Border Patrol would undergo rigorous screenings to determine whether or not they were victims of trafficking or possessed credible fears of violence or persecution in Mexico.[32] If youths do not meet either criterion, they are 'voluntarily repatriated' to Mexico.[33] Critics, including Appleseed, however, have questioned Border Patrol's ability to effectively interview minors as well as acting in the best interests of these youths and found that the majority of Mexican minors were immediately repatriated.[34] My conversations in spring 2015 with child advocates in south Texas confirmed these fears, as I was told of minors who, in spite of being targeted by gangs, were dropped off in the middle of the night across Veteran's Memorial Bridge in Matamoros, Tamaulipas, by Border Patrol agents.[35]

Additionally, the apprehensions of unaccompanied Mexican minors at the United States-Mexico border has declined every year since 2009. This has mirrored the overall rates of migration from Mexico which have been negative since 2008, with the exception of 2013. Between 2009 and 2016, apprehensions declined by 25 percent, from 16,114 in 2009 to 11,926 in 2016.[36] Like youths before them, these minors include those who are and will be unaccompanied both in travel and destination, as well as those who are arriving to reunify with one or more parents. It is this latter population who are commonly seen as 'Dreamers': undocumented youths who were brought by their parents, have lived and attended school in the United States, and mostly identify as 'American'. Often conflated with Dreamers, of the nearly 6 million undocumented Mexicans in the United States, approximately 548,000 are youths and young adults who possess Deferred Action for Childhood Arrivals (DACA) status. Signed in 2012 by then President Barack H. Obama, DACA provides young undocumented adults who meet criteria that largely reflects those outlined in DREAM Acts with work permits and deportation reprieves.[37]

---

[32] Unaccompanied Alien Children Protection Act 2005; William Wilberforce Trafficking Victims Protection Reauthorization Act 2008 (TVPRA).

[33] L. Zamora, *Unaccompanied Alien Children: A Primer* (Bipartisan Policy Center, 12 July 2014), available at http://bipartisanpolicy.org/blog/unaccompanied-alien-children-primer/.

[34] B. Cavendish and C. Maru, *Children at the Border: The Screening, Protection and Repatriation* (Appleseed, 2011).

[35] Diana Donahue, Attorney, personal communication with author, 2016.

[36] See www.cbp.gov/newsroom/stats/southwest-border-unaccompanied-children/fy-2016.

[37] R. Rosenblum and G.R.S. Ariel, *An Analysis of Unauthorized Immigrants in the United States by Country and Region of Birth* (Migration Policy Institute, August 2015), available at www.migrationpolicy.org/sites/default/files/publications/Unauth-COB-Report-FINALWEB.pdf. 'Dreamer' is a label associated with unauthorized

While the aforementioned cases of independent teenage migration could be considered the effects of 'peaceful' economic conquests, the policies impacting Central America have resulted in much bloodier and physically violent outcomes. The next section turns to this region and the United States' complicity in the conditions driving the arrival of thousands of unaccompanied Central American minors, both at and after the end of the twentieth century.

4. CENTRAL AMERICA

4.1 Uncivil Wars: The Displacement of Central American Teenagers

Deemed attractive due to geopolitical positioning and economic benefits and in the name of anti-communism, Northern Triangle countries such as El Salvador, Guatemala and Honduras have been the focus of persistent US intervention and militarization. Although each country is distinct, the United States adopted similar orientations towards them, acting as an essential neocolonial ally in shaping the region's conflicts.[38] Thirty years after El Salvador's large-scale massacre of approximately 30,000 indigenous peasants and farmers known as *La Matanza*, Central American oligarchs, backed by and reliant upon the US government for economic and military support, again confiscated land from peasants for foreign economic expansion in the early 1960s. In El Salvador alone, the numbers of landless people quadrupled between 1961 and 1975. Between 1978 and 1984, nearly 30 percent of the population were displaced due to related counter-insurgency and repression.[39]

To quell unrest, these land reforms were accompanied by increases in

---

immigrant youths in the United States who would/do qualify for criteria widely included in versions of federal and (in absence of its passage by the US Congress) State Dream Acts and the executive Deferred Action for Childhood Arrivals (DACA). Under federal and state Dream Acts and DACA, Dreamers are youths who are at least age 15 but arrived to the United States prior to age 16; have continuously resided in the United States since 2007; are or have been enrolled in a US school and/or possess a high school diploma/equivalency and/or are in the military or honorably discharged; and have not been convicted of a felony, significant misdemeanor, three or more misdemeanors or otherwise pose a national security or public threat.

[38] A. Lauria-Santiago, 'The Culture and Politics of State Terror and Repression in El Salvador' in C. Menjivar and N. Rodriguez (eds), *When States Kill: Latin America, the US and Technologies of Terror* (University of Texas Press, 2005), p. 89.

[39] Gonzalez, *Harvest of Empire*, above n. 7; Lauria-Santiago, 'The Culture and Politics of State Terror and Repression in El Salvador', above n. 38, at 85–114.

military-led repression that were disguised as necessary to ward off the communism at the United States' 'backdoor'. Peasants who resisted displacement were characterized as communists and guerillas and became the targets of the military. Between the 1960s and the 1990s, Central American military and paramilitary groups controlled the population by becoming death squads: murdering, torturing and disappearing peasants, farmers, dissidents, sympathizers who resisted these reforms.[40] Entire villages were killed or 'disappeared', with survivors fleeing or forced to resettle into military controlled villages, oftentimes so that they could become surplus labor for foreign companies.[41]

The US funded many of these human rights violations. By the 1980s, over US$5 billion was funneled to these governments, including US$3.7 billion to El Salvador, and US$10.3 billion to Guatemala in 1986 alone. By 1985, Honduras was the eighth highest receiving country of US military and economic assistance, with most of the money paying for weapons, training and war assistance.[42]

Central American youths were not spared from these aggressions. In their 1990 study of unaccompanied and undocumented minors from Central America, Rodriguez and Urrutia-Rojas documented nearly identical conditions pushing these youths' migration as those reported by Central American youths today. Subject to dislocation and poverty, targeted for recruitment by both the military and guerillas, and witnesses and victims of violence themselves, many minors fled this region for the United States. By 1990, between 10,000 and 20,000 unaccompanied Central American minors, of whom most were male teenagers, were entering the United States without documents annually.[43]

---

[40] Gonzalez, *Harvest of Empire*, above n. 7; Lauria-Santiago, 'The Culture and Politics of State Terror and Repression in El Salvador', above n. 38, at 85–114; M.G. Torres, 'Bloody Deeds/ Hechos Sangrientes: Reading Guatemala's Record of Political Violence in Cadaver Reports' in C. Menjivar and N. Rodriguez (eds), *When States Kill: Latin America, the US and Technologies of Terror* (University of Texas Press, 2005), pp. 143–69.

[41] D. Paley, *Drug War Capitalism* (AK Press, 2014).

[42] Gonzales, *Harvest of Empire*, above n. 7; Lauria-Santiago, 'The Culture and Politics of State Terror and Repression in El Salvador', above 38, at 85–114; J. Kruckewitt, 'U.S. Militarization of Honduras in the 1980s and the Creation of CIA-backed Death Squads' in C. Menjivar and N. Rodriguez (eds), *When States Kill: Latin America, the US and Technologies of Terror* (University of Texas Press, 2005), pp. 170–97; Paley, *Drug War Capitalism*, above n. 41.

[43] A. Gonzales, *Reform Without Justice: Latino Migrant Politics and the Homeland Security State* (Oxford University Press, 2014); M. Berdal and D.M. Malone, 'Introduction' in M. Berdal and D.M. Malone (eds), *Greed and Grievance: Economic Agendas in Civil Wars* (Lynne Riehnner, 2000), pp. 1–13.

In the case of Rebeca, a 17-year-old female who, in June 1990, left El Salvador for the United States with her younger brother and cousin, the reasons for departure sound eerily similar to accounts disclosed by recent Central American youth arrivals. At age 10, a bomb destroyed her house and killed two of her brothers. At age 13, her school was attacked. By the time she was 15, her family members, including her mother, father, romantic partner and cousins, had been murdered at the hands of Salvadoran military and guerillas. After enduring several more years of intimidation and harassment, she would convince her younger brother, a 14-year-old who was at risk of being forcibly recruited into the army, to leave for the United States.[44]

Although the region's long history of US interventions have been cited to assist in explaining current unaccompanied Central American minor migration, their predecessors often go unmentioned. This is an oversight, as it is critical to examine unaccompanied minor migration from this particular era as a separate phenomenon specific to the period's interests and interventions. Publicly naming Communism as the enemy, US and Central American elites utilized violence to quell uprisings against displacement by US and other corporations. Unbeknownst to unaccompanied minors, and more specifically, independent teenage migrants like Rebeca, youths would flee to the same country liable for much of the violence occurring in their home countries. Twenty years later, history repeats itself with new enemies and old tactics.

4.2 Remilitarizing and Criminalizing the Northern Triangle: Different Enemies, Same Victims

By the end of the civil wars and the 1996 signing of peace accords, an economically and politically fragile region was poised to demilitarize and enter an era of prosperity. By the early twenty-first century, however, new wars would replace the Cold War. Shifts in narco-trafficking (en-route to satisfy US consumption) and post-9/11 security concerns would officially warrant new reasons and means for foreign intervention, but frankly, an appetite for the region's natural resources had not been satiated.[45] Considering not only the remnants from the civil wars, but also new

---

[44] N. Rodriguez and X. Urrutia-Rojas, *Undocumented and Unaccompanied: A Mental Health Study of Unaccompanied Immigrant Children from Central America* (Institute for Higher Education Law and Governance, University of Houston Law Center, 1990).

[45] Gonzales, *Reform Without Justice*, above n. 43; Berdal and Malone, 'Introduction', above n. 43.

US-backed economic, security and immigration policies, the proposed demilitarization of Central America never stood a chance.

After the signing of the peace accords, Hurricane Mitch (1998) impacted the region's fragile coffee, maize and banana plantations and displaced over 2 million Central Americans. This included over 500,000 people in El Salvador and 80,000 in Guatemala.[46] Disaster assistance was tied to neoliberal economic reforms, so loans and debt restructuring laid the groundwork for DR-CAFTA with increased private foreign investment.[47] In spite of significant opposition, by 2006, DR-CAFTA was signed into law.

Ten years later, DR-CAFTA is attributed with worsening environmental as well as economic conditions.[48] Most harmful have been the prioritizing of multinational company rights over those of the regions' citizens and the acceleration of 'mega-projects' focusing on resource extraction. For example, in 2014, over 30 percent of Guatemala and Honduras was authorized for private mining.[49] Attempts to stave off multinational corporations have been met with lawsuits permitted by a clause included in DR-CAFTA, the Investor-State Dispute Settlement Provision. With countries deeming it cheaper to harm their citizens than to pay corporations, these lawsuits are often settled in secret tribunals hosted by the World Bank.[50]

These actions have not occurred without conflict. In order for private corporations to confiscate national lands, thousands of indigenous Central Americans whose families have resided in these lands for generations have been evicted.[51] Corporate elites have hired paramilitary groups to intimidate and remove indigenous peoples from valuable lands and to protect their interests. These clashes between corporate interests and indigenous peoples fighting displacement have largely been ignored or recast as attacks between neutral corporations and criminals or terrorists.[52]

This is not to say that transnational criminal organizations do not imperil the region's security; they are a major threat with some estimates placing over 60 percent of countries' territories under the control of

---

[46] National Climatic Data Center (NCDC), *Mitch: The Deadliest Atlantic Hurricane Since 1780* (2009), available at www.ncdc.noaa.gov/oa/reports/mitch/mitch.html; Paley, *Drug War Capitalism*, above n. 41.

[47] *Ibid.*

[48] M. Perez-Rocha and J. Paley, *What 'Free Trade' Has Done to Central America*, Foreign Policy in Focus (2014), available at http://fpif.org/free-trade-done-central-america/.

[49] Paley, *Drug War Capitalism*, above n. 41.

[50] Perez-Rocha and Paley, *What 'Free Trade' Has Done to Central America*, above n. 48.

[51] *Ibid.*

[52] Paley, *Drug War Capitalism*, above n. 41.

transnational crime organizations.[53] Proliferating in contexts marked by weak institutions, drug-related crime is also tied to several US policies, including anti-narcotic efforts in Mexico and Colombia and immigration policies. In Mexico, strategies to curb trafficking in the last decade have pushed Mexico-based Los Zetas into Central America and forced shifts in the transport of drugs to short-range land, maritime and aerial routes that include stopover points in Central America.[54] In Colombia, more severe deportation policies have provided Los Zetas with armies of transporters and *sicarios,* or enforcers and assassins comprising members of Mara Salvatrucha (MS-13) and 18th Street (M-18) gangs. First under the 1996 Illegal Immigration Reform and Immigrant Responsibility Act and now under the Department of Homeland Security's Operation Community Shield, Central American youths are subject to higher rates of immediate removal due to the broadening of deportable offenses, including minor offenses such as shoplifting or speeding.[55]

Between 2010 and 2012, these changes resulted in the expulsion of over 100,000 offenders, more than had been deported in the previous six years, into insecure areas of El Salvador, Guatemala and Honduras.[56] Policies such as El Salvador's Plan Mano Dura have aggravated the region's problems by criminalizing perceived gang affiliation. As a result, former gang members were placed in jails together where they organized and crystallized their networks.[57]

Meant to curb the violence, the United States-backed security plans such as CARSI aggravated the situation. Beginning as a component of the Merida Initiative in 2008, CARSI was introduced independently in 2011 as an initiative focusing on regional security in Central America.[58] Officially charged with disrupting criminal organizations through law enforcement cooperation, capacity building and prevention programs,

---

53 P.J. Meyer and C.R. Seelke, 'Central America Regional Security Initiative: Background and Policy Issues for Congress' (2011) *Current Politics and Economics of South, Southeastern and Central Asia* 721.

54 *Ibid.*

55 Paley, *Drug War Capitalism*, above n. 41; Meyer and Seelke, 'Central America Regional Security Initiative', above n. 53, at 721–66; Gonzales, *Reform Without Justice*, above n. 43.

56 A. Chardy, 'Deportation of criminals blamed for exodus from Central America', *Miami Herald*, 3 August 2014.

57 Paley, *Drug War Capitalism*, above n. 41; M.H. Johnson, *National Policies and the Rise of Transnational Gangs* (Migration Policy Institute, 2006); Gonzales, *Reform Without Justice*, above n. 43.

58 M. Alexander 'The U.S. Remilitarization of Central America and Mexico', North American Congress on Latin America, 3 July 2014.

CARSI has been criticized for funding and even providing training to law enforcement agencies in spite of their high rates of corruption and blatant human rights violations.[59] Strong evidence exists that suggests that members of communities inhabiting lands desirable for extraction were disappeared, tortured and murdered by CARSI-backed military and paramilitary.[60] By 2015, proposals addressing the root causes of violence would reflect a break from past priorities. Instead of only providing funding to police and military forces, this package, which was triple the previous funding, focused on building up economic development and civil society.[61] By 2016, funding was based on efforts made to thwart migration to the United States.[62]

A discussion of intervention in Central America is incomplete without mention of the 2009 coup in Honduras that further destabilized the region. The removal of President Manuel Zelaya, a democratically elected moderate whose decisions had alarmed Honduran and US elites, was at first seemingly devoid of Washington influence.[63] After his removal and in spite of calls from the Organization of American States and the UN General Assembly to reinstate Zelaya, the US State Department financially supported efforts to hold elections and to rapidly recognize a far-right post-coup government that had 'consistently supported US interests'.[64] Over the past seven years, the subsequent far-right presidential administrations have been characterized by rampant human rights violations and the highest homicide rates in the world.

Because of these regional conflicts, we have seen nearly 150,000 unaccompanied children and teenagers, many of whom are independent teenage migrants, seek refuge in the United States. Harkening back to earlier incidents of independent teenage migration, the underlying reasons for their departures are the same: US-backed policies that displace and threaten Central America's poorest and most vulnerable denizens.

---

59 A. Korthuis, *The Central American Regional Security Initiative in Honduras*, Working Paper prepared for the Woodrow Wilson Center Latin American Program (2014); Paley, *Drug War Capitalism*, above n. 41.

60 Paley, *Drug War Capitalism*, above n. 41.

61 A. Isacson, *What's in a Billion Dollar Aid Request for Central America?* (Washington Office on Latin America, 3 February 2015).

62 *FACT SHEET: The United States and Central America: Honoring Our Commitments* (The White House, 14 January 2016).

63 Paley, *Drug War Capitalism*, above n. 41; M. Weisbrot, 'Hard choices: Hillary Clinton admits role in Honduran coup aftermath', *Al Jazeera America*, 29 September 2014.

64 F. Dana 'Hopeless in Honduras? The Election and the Future of Tegucigalpa', *Foreign Affairs*, 22 November 2013; Weisbrot, 'Hard choices', above n. 63.

This was certainly true for 17-year-old Carlos, a Salvadoran youth who one of my students, Cristina, met while providing legal support through the Unaccompanied Latin American Minor Project (U-LAMP).[65] In his hometown in El Salvador, rising threats of gang violence compelled other youths to depart but he was scared because of the long journey and his parents did not want him to leave. One day, however, as he was riding his bicycle to church through a gang-controlled area, members of the transnational MS-13 or Mara Salvatrucha gang stopped him to ask him for his gang affiliation. After responding that he was not affiliated with any gang, the young adult men insisted that his haircut suggested that he was part of their rival gang, the 18th Street gang. After he continued to deny that membership, they demanded that he join their gang, threatening to kill him if he did not. He was terrified but they let him go.

With his sister and her husband already in the United States, his parents called them frantically to see if they could send money to bring Carlos to New York City. After over a week and feeling safer, Carlos left home to go shopping. Within blocks, a total of 12 gang members surrounded him and again demanded that he join their gang. After showing him their guns, a 9 mm and a 38 mm pistol and then accurately naming him, where he lived, and who he lived with, the members threatened to come after him if he did not agree. After he was released a second time, it would take two days for his siblings to wire funds for him to leave. Afraid to step outside, his family paid a human smuggler extra monies to pick him up from his home.

After being picked up, he took a bus from El Salvador to Guatemala where officers arrested part of the group that he was traveling with, but all of the minors were let go. After finally arriving at the Guatemala-Mexico border, they crossed, but they had to stay in a hotel in Mexico for six nights because the 'coyote' who was hired to accompany them through Mexico was not answering his phone. After finally meeting their coyote, they would travel throughout Mexico for nearly two days by bus. During their journey, Mexican authorities stopped them but their coyotes simply bribed them and they were released. Finally, Carlos and his fellow travelers arrived at the United States-Mexico border near Brownsville, Texas.

---

[65] The Unaccompanied Latin American Minor Project (U-LAMP) is a hybrid research-service project that focuses on providing academic, legal and social support to recently arrived immigrant minors who are in removal proceedings. U-LAMPers are CUNY (City University of New York) students who are immigrants or children of immigrants and bilingual English-Spanish. These students work with attorneys, youths and their families to facilitate their integration into New York City (ulamp.weebly.com). Carlos's story is based on notes and interviews with Cristina (pseudonym), a former U-LAMPer.

Here, he got into an inner tube and attempted to cross the river. After he crossed, the coyote left him and the others. After walking through thick brush and hearing helicopters overhead, they ran into Border Patrol who hauled them to Harlingen, Texas, to be processed. After processing, he was first sent to an Office of Refugee Resettlement contracted detention shelter in Chicago where he received his paperwork, including a Notice to Appear in Court, and then he was reunited with his older sister in New York City. After appearing in New York City's Immigration Court at 26 Federal Plaza, he was screened and then represented by the Safe Passage Project. When asked by Cristina what he feared the most, he answered that he worried that what happened to him would happen to his little brothers: gangs would try to recruit them and, if unsuccessful, kill them.

Unfortunately, Carlos's story is not an unfamiliar one to those representing and/or supporting unaccompanied minors who have arrived from Central America, both during the civil wars in the last half of the twentieth century or more recently. Over and over again, young people share terrifying and horrific experiences that forced them to escape settings that fail to provide them and their families with the economic and physical security that they deserve.

5. CONCLUSION

Over the past 100 years, the inextricable relationships between the United States and its southern neighbors have produced one particular outcome that has gone largely undiscussed: independent teenage migration. Recent arrivals of nearly 150,000 youths at the United States-Mexico border has illuminated this one outcome, but it has been lumped in with unaccompanied minor migration, as well as viewed and discussed as an isolated event occurring during this particular moment of neocolonialism. Rather, this phenomenon has repeated itself for at least a century. Due to the United States' orientation towards Latin America, teenage minors have fled their homes in search of economic and physical security denied to them. While earlier trickles and waves of independent teenage migrants from Latin America may not have been treated as minors in need of safeguarding, under the Convention on the Rights of the Child (1989), countries are compelled to consider them as separate human beings deserving of protection in their own right.[66] Fundamentally, in order to prevent future

[66] See Convention on the Rights of the Child, opened for signature 20 November 1989, 1577 UNTS 3 (entered into force 2 September 1990).

trickles and waves of youth migration, countries and entities must be held accountable for disparate impacts on youths in the future. They must be denied the ability, intended or unintended, to violate young people's rights to economic and physical security.

PART II.1

Protection frameworks: international and regional frameworks

4. First things first: international law and the protection of migrant children

Mary Crock and Hannah Martin

1. INTRODUCTION

The treatment of children under international law has mirrored societal attitudes to childhood across the world and across time. Starting from a low base,[1] trends in child protection over the course of the last century have generally been positive, at least in developed countries. For the subset of children displaced within or across borders as migrants or victims of armed conflict or disaster, however, the gaps and silences in domestic and international law have been stark. The changing nature of warfare in the twentieth century has meant that civilians have increasingly lost their immunity from involvement in armed conflict.[2] Like the very old and persons with disabilities, children have become increasingly vulnerable to conflict-related injury and deprivation.[3] While concern about the effects of conflict and displacement on children is not so new, it is only in very recent years that the law has developed to the point of recognizing children as rights bearers rather than as passive objects of charity or welfare.

In this chapter we discuss the evolution of international law relative to the protection of child migrants. After a brief historical account of the traditional protective frameworks of international humanitarian

---

[1] See G. Van Bueren, *International Documents on Children* (2nd edn, Save the Children, 1998), p. xv; and L. de Mause, *The History of Childhood* (Harper and Row, 1974).

[2] See R.K. Dixit, 'Special Protection of Children During Armed Conflicts Under the Geneva Convention Regime' (2001) *ISIL Yearbook on International Humanitarian and Refugee Law* 1.

[3] In some recent conflicts there have been suggestions that children have been actively targeted for persecution. See Save the Children, *Horrors I will Never Forget* (November 2017), available at www.savethechildren.org/atf/cf/%7B9def2ebe-10ae-432c-9bd0-df91d2eba74a%7D/HORRORS_I_WILL_NEVER_FORGET.PDF.

law (IHL), refugee law and general human rights law, section 3 turns to a closer analysis of the United Nations Convention on the Rights of the Child (CRC).[4] We examine the ways in which this Convention has changed thinking about children on the move. In this context, two core legal precepts are explored. The first is the concept of the 'best interests' of the child.[5] The second is the injunction that affording a child dignity and respect must include allowing children to participate in relevant decision-making processes.[6] While the concept of best interests has a long lineage, we argue that it is the participation provisions that have been truly transformative in the discourse on children's rights. Section 4 follows with a brief case study of the rights of children displaced by armed conflict and/or natural disasters enshrined in the more recent UN Convention on the Rights of Persons with Disabilities.[7] This Convention is modelled in more than one respect on the CRC.[8] The chapter concludes with an acknowledgement of the many ways that states have found to deny children the protective force of international human rights laws.

2. RECOGNIZING MIGRANT CHILDREN AS RIGHTS BEARERS IN INTERNATIONAL LAW

World War I and its aftermath was a catalyst for early international recognition of the effects of conflict and displacement on children. The special vulnerability of children displaced by that conflict and its aftermath pushed Eglantine Jebb and others to found the international relief agency Save the Children. Claiming that 'all wars are waged against children', Jebb was the driving force behind the 1924 Geneva Declaration on the Rights of the Child.[9] Although one of the first to associate children with rights, this aspirational document was very much a product of its time.

---

4 See Convention on the Rights of the Child, opened for signature 20 November 1989, 1577 UNTS 3 (entered into force 2 September 1990) (CRC).

5 CRC, Art. 3.

6 *Ibid.* Art. 12.

7 See Convention on the Rights of Persons with Disabilities, opened for signature 30 March 2007, 2515 UNTS 3 (entered into force 3 May 2008) (CRPD).

8 See, e.g., the parallels between CRC, Art. 3 and CRPD, Art. 7(2); and CRC, Art. 12 and CRPD, Arts 7(3) and 12.

9 See G. Van Bueren, *The International Law on the Rights of the Child* (Kluwer Law International, 1998), p. 8. For Jebb's writings on the subject, see E. Jebb, *International Responsibilities for Child Welfare* (Save the Children International Union, 1927).

Steeped in the language of charity and welfare, the Declaration posited children as subjects of nurturing and assistance, but not as rights bearers.[10]

The plight of unaccompanied and separated children was recognized formally in laws developed around international efforts to protect refugees and humanitarian migrants after World War II. Again, the model was one predicated on welfare rather than rights.

The Constitution of the International Refugee Organisation (IRO), the UN agency created in 1946 to coordinate relief efforts for displaced persons, made express provision for the care of children. Its definition of 'refugee' included a separate category of 'unaccompanied children who are war orphans or whose parents have disappeared, and who are outside their countries of origin'. Other than an upper age limit of 16, no further qualification (such as race or country of origin) applied. The IRO mandate stated that refugee children were entitled to 'all possible priority assistance, including, normally, assistance in repatriation in the case of those whose nationality can be determined'.[11]

The four Geneva Conventions and the two Additional Protocols that dominate the framework of modern IHL also address the protection needs of children.[12] The Fourth Geneva Convention focuses on civilian

---

[10] Adopted 26 September 1924, [1924] LN OJ Spec. Supp. 21, 43. Expressed as coming from 'men and women of all nations', the Declaration stated that all should 'accept it as their duty that, beyond and above all considerations of race, nationality or creed: (1) The child must be given the means requisite for its normal development, both materially and spiritually; (2) The child that is hungry must be fed; the child that is sick must be nursed; the child that is backward must be helped; the delinquent child must be reclaimed; and the orphan and the waif must be sheltered and succored; (3) The child must be the first to receive relief in times of distress; (4) The child must be put in a position to earn a livelihood, and must be protected against every form of exploitation; (5) The child must be brought up in the consciousness that its talents must be devoted to the service of fellow men'. Jebb drafted the initial document which was tabled before the League of Nations in 1922. On Jebb's life, see Clare Mulley, *The Woman Who Saved the Children: A Biography of Eglantine Jebb Founder of Save The Children* (Oneworld Publications, 2009).

[11] See Constitution of the International Refugee Organization, adopted 15 December 1946, 18 UNTS 3 (entered into force 20 August 1948) Annex 1, Part IA, para. [4]. Mention should also be made here of the creation of the United Nations International Children's Emergency Fund (UNICEF) around the same time. That organization was created by Resolution of the UN General Assembly 'for the benefit of children and adolescents of countries which were the victims of aggression' (see General Assembly Resolution A/RES/57(I), 11 December 1946). See further J. Pobjoy, *The Child in International Refugee Law* (Cambridge University Press, 2017), pp. 16–19.

[12] See Geneva Convention for the Amelioration of the Condition of the

populations, which are assumed always to include children. Article 24 is of particular significance to children affected by war as it creates an express obligation to assist children in the migration process, this time marking 15 as the upper age limit. It provides that:

> The Parties to the conflict shall take the necessary measures to ensure that children under fifteen, who are orphaned or are separated from their families as a result of the war, are not left to their own resources, and that their maintenance, the exercise of their religion and their education are facilitated in all circumstances. The Parties to the conflict *shall facilitate the reception of such children in a neutral country* for the duration of the conflict. (emphasis added)

As well as benefitting from the specific protections set out in this instrument, children affected by armed conflict of any description are entitled to 'special protection' under IHL. Children rate special mention in 25 Articles across the Geneva Conventions and Protocols.[13] Examples include Article 77 of Additional Protocol I, which emphasizes respect of the child and protection against any form of indecent assault. Article 4 of Additional Protocol II extends the duties of states to the protection of children at risk through the actions of non-international armed conflicts. It states that 'children shall be provided with the care and aid they require'.[14]

Perhaps the most critical source of rights for migrant children post-dating World War II is the UN Convention relating to the Status of Refugees ('Refugee Convention') and its attendant Protocol.[15] In fact,

---

Wounded and Sick in Armed Forces in the Field, adopted 12 August 1949, 75 UNTS 31 (entered into force 21 October 1950); Geneva Convention for the Amelioration of the Condition of the Wounded, Sick and Shipwrecked Members of the Armed Forces at Sea, adopted 12 August 1949, 75 UNTS 85 (entered into force 21 October 1950); Geneva Convention Relative to the Treatment of Prisoners of War, adopted 12 August 1949, 75 UNTS 135 (entered into force 21 October 1950); Geneva Convention Relative to the Protection of Civilian Persons in Time of War, adopted 12 August 1949, 75 UNTS 287 (entered into force 21 October 1950) ('Fourth Geneva Convention').

[13] See G. Goodwin-Gill, 'Unaccompanied Refugee Minors: The Role and Place of International Law in the Pursuit of Durable Solutions' (1995) 3 *International Journal of Children's Rights* 405, at 413.

[14] For a detailed account of the extent to which IHL mandates the 'special protection' of children during armed conflicts, see Dixit, 'Special Protection of Children During Armed Conflicts', above n. 2.

[15] See Convention relating to the Status of Refugees, adopted 28 July 1951, 189 UNTS 137 (entered into force 22 April 1954); and the Protocol relating to the Status of Refugees, adopted 31 January 1967, 606 UNTS 267 (entered into force 4 October 1967) ('Refugee Convention'). See further the discussion in Mary Crock and Phoebe Yule, Chapter 5.

this Convention is remarkably short on direct references to children, leaving the protection of refugee children a matter of inference.[16] While the Refugee Convention and Protocol do not differentiate between rights provided to children and adults, some rights are of obvious and particular relevance to children, notably the right to public education (Article 22). As we explore further in Chapter 5, the process of 'reading children into' the Refugee Convention definition of refugee has proved problematic for domestic decision-makers.[17] However, in recent years the UN High Commissioner for Refugees (UNHCR) and the General Assembly have shown no reticence in affirming the protection needs of refugee children.[18]

The concept of the 'best interests' of the child was first adopted by the UN General Assembly in 1959 with the proclamation of the Declaration of the Rights of the Child. Again, however, the child remained an object of protection rather than a subject with rights and voice. Principle 2 read:

> The child shall enjoy special protection, and shall be given opportunities and facilities, by law and by other means, to enable him to develop physically, mentally, morally, spiritually and socially in a healthy and normal manner and in conditions of freedom and dignity. In the enactment of laws for this purpose, the best interests of the child shall be the paramount consideration.

The creation of the international Bill of Rights in the 1960s extended the protective mandate of international law for children.[19]

---

[16] The only express references to children are in Art. 4, referring to refugee parents' freedom to religious education of their offspring; and Art. 17(2)(c) which relates to the working rights of refugee parents whose children are nationals of a host country.

[17] See Pobjoy, *The Child in International Refugee Law*, above n. 11, at 32 ff; J. Pobjoy, 'A Child Rights Framework for Assessing the Status of Refugee Children' in S. Juss and C. Harvey (eds), *Contemporary Issues in Refugee Law* (Edward Elgar Publishing, 2013); and M. Crock, 'Re-thinking the Paradigms of Protection: Children as Convention Refugees in Australia' in J. McAdam (ed.), *Forced Migration, Human Rights and Security* (Hart Publishing, 2008), pp. 155, 161 ff.

[18] Note, however, that the first such affirmation was not until 1988, when UNHCR released its Guidelines on Refugee Children. See UNHCR Executive Committee, *UNHCR Policy on Refugee Children*, UN Doc E/SCP/82 (6 August 1993); UNHCR, *Refugee Children: Guidelines on Protection and Care* (UNHCR, 1994); UNHCR, *Guidelines on Policies and Procedures in Dealing with Unaccompanied Children Seeking Asylum* (February 1997); see further J. Pobjoy, 'Article 22' in P. Alston and J. Tobin (eds), *The UN Convention on the Rights of the Child, A Commentary* (Oxford University Press, forthcoming), notes 7 and 8.

[19] This is the phrase used to describe the 1948 Universal Declaration of Human Rights, GA Res. 217A (III), UN GAOR, Third Session, 183rd Plen Mtg, UN Doc. A/810 (10 December 1948); together with the International Covenant

While the recognition of children in these instruments and by their supervisory bodies suggests a growing awareness of children's special status, the sense of children as rights bearers was still lacking. Geraldine Van Bueren argues that real change occurred only in 1979. Proclaimed as the International Year of the Child, it was in this year that serious steps were taken towards conclusion of the CRC.[20] The reasons for the delayed development of a child rights perspective for children were twofold. As Van Bueren and others note,[21] the human rights regime developed in the 1960s and early 1970s was predicated on a paternalistic and welfare approach. This provided little scope for acknowledging and fostering agency and autonomy in children and at its worst tended to commodify children as the possessions of adults.[22] A second problem can be identified in the tendency for relevant areas of law – IHL, refugee law and international human rights law – to be somewhat siloed. Each was regarded as *lex specialis* or a discrete area of international law.[23] This view impeded the growth and development that occurred once the true universality of human rights law was accepted.

As we explore in the balance of this chapter, recent years have seen dra-

---

on Civil and Political Rights, opened for signature 19 December 1966, 999 UNTS 171 (entered into force 23 March 1976) (ICCPR); the two Optional Protocols to this instrument; and the International Covenant on Economic, Social and Cultural Rights, opened for signature 16 December 1966, 993 UNTS 3 (entered into force 3 January 1976) (ICESCR). See generally, S. Joseph, J.A. Schultz and M. Castan, *The International Covenant on Civil and Political Rights: Cases, Materials, and Commentary* (Oxford University Press 2004); and B. Saul, D. Kinley and J. Mowbray, *The International Covenant on Economic, Social and Cultural Rights: Commentary, Cases, and Materials* (Oxford University Press, 2014).

20 See Van Bueren, *International Documents on Children*, above n. 1, at xv. She argues that until 1979 the child's perspective in international law was 'either absent or assumed to be co-terminus with that of adults'.

21 See *ibid.*; J. Bhabha and W. Young, 'Not Adults in Miniature: Unaccompanied Child Asylum Seekers and the New US Guidelines' (1999) 84 *International Journal of Refugee Law* 93; Pobjoy, *The Child in International Refugee Law*, above n. 11, at 5 ff; and Pobjoy, 'A Child Rights Framework for Assessing the Status of Refugee Children', above n. 17.

22 On this point see also M. Crock, 'Of Relative Rights and Putative Children: Re-thinking the Critical Framework for the Protection of Refugee Children and Youth' (2013) 20 *Australian Journal of International Law* 33.

23 On IHL as *lex specialis*, see Legality of the Threat or Use of Nuclear Weapons (Advisory Opinion) ICJ Rep. 225 (8 July 1996), at 240. Compare International Committee of the Red Cross's (ICRC) authoritative statement of customary IHL produced in 2005: J.-M. Henckaerts and L. Doswald-Beck, *Customary International Humanitarian Law*, vol. I, *Rules* (Cambridge University Press, 2005).

matic change in the treatment of children generally, and migrant children in particular, as subjects of international law. In many respects the starting point for the modern regime was the adoption of the CRC which came into force in 1990. The CRC is now the most widely subscribed of all UN treaties apart from the United Nations Charter itself.[24]

The significance of acknowledging the interactive and evolving nature of international law becomes apparent when considering the other instruments emerging as significant elements of a protective regime for migrant children. In addition to the core human rights treaties, these include the Migrant Workers' Convention; the Trafficking and Smuggling Protocols; the Optional Protocols to the CRC itself; and the Convention on the Rights of Persons with Disabilities (CRPD).[25] There are then the various human rights instruments devised as supra-national law in different regions of the world.[26]

The youngest of the core human rights treaties, the CRPD shares a number of similarities with the CRC. Both reflect the modern trend away from seeing any of the protective areas of international law as *lex specialis*. Both give precedence to the best interests of the child, but acknowledge squarely the voice and agency of children. In fact, the CRPD can hold particular significance for migrant children. There can be close connections between disability and refugee status insofar as war and displacement are prime causes of impairment.[27] In the absence of a dedicated chapter

---

[24] See the current list of the Status of Ratification, Reservations and Declarations, available at United Nations Treaty Collection, available at http://treaties.un.org/Pages/ViewDetails.aspx?src=TREATY&mtdsg_no=IV-11&chapter=4&lang=en. The CRC is so widely subscribed that every member state of the United Nations, except the United States, has now ratified it. See E. Bartholet, 'Ratification by the United States of the Convention on the Rights of the Child' (2011) 633(1) *Annals of the American Academy of Political and Social Science* 80.

[25] See Optional Protocol to the Convention on the Rights of the Child on the Sale of Children, Child Prostitution and Child Pornography, opened for signature 25 May 2000, A/RES/54/263 (entered into force on 18 January 2002) (CRC-OPSC); Optional Protocol to the Convention on the Rights of the Child on the Involvement of Children in Armed Conflict, opened for signature 25 May 2000, A/RES/54/263 (entered into force 12 February 2002) (CRC-OPAC); and Human Rights Committee, Optional Convention on the Rights of the Child on Communications Procedure, 17th Sess., UN Doc. A/HRC/RES/17/18 (14 July 2011) (CRC-OPCP).

[26] Many of these are considered in the chapters that follow in this Part of the book.

[27] UN CRC, *General Comment No. 9 (2006): The Rights of Children with Disabilities*, CRC, 43rd Sess., UN Doc. CRC/C/GC/9 (27 February 2007), pp.

on migrant children with disabilities, we will consider the CRPD and its relevance to migrant children in section 4 below.

3. EXPANDING THE PROTECTIVE REACH OF INTERNATIONAL LAW FOR MIGRANT CHILDREN: AN OVERVIEW OF THE CRC

3.1 Giving Content to Rights

The CRC stands as the centrepiece and key unifying element in an integrated legal regime for recognizing the rights of all children that stems from all human rights law, IHL and refugee law. Article 4 obliges states to ensure that the convention's principles and standards are reflected and given full effect in domestic laws and policies. Like many of the other UN human rights Conventions,[28] the CRC establishes an oversight Committee: the UN Committee on the Rights of the Child (UNCRC).[29] This committee operates to review states parties' compliance with the terms of the instrument (on a five-yearly rotation); it issues General Comments on the interpretation and application of the CRC; and it engages in other activities including public days of discussion.[30] This oversight mechanism has been enhanced by a Protocol allowing the UNCRC to hear individual complaints.[31]

Perhaps the most notable aspect of the CRC is that it establishes normative rules that all apply to children, regardless of citizenship or immigration status. Article 2(1) requires states parties to 'respect and ensure the rights set forth in the present Convention to *each child* within their jurisdiction' and prohibits discrimination 'irrespective of the child's or his or her parent's or legal guardian's . . . birth or other status'.[32]

21–2, para. [79]. Note, however, the prevalence of disability within migrant and refugee populations has traditionally been underrecognized and underreported. See L. Smith-Khan, M. Crock, B. Saul and R. McCallum, 'To Promote, Protect and Ensure: Overcoming Obstacles to the Identification of Disability in Displacement' (2014) 27 *Journal of Refugee Studies* 38.

[28] For an overview of the working of these bodies see S. Egan, *The UN Human Rights Treaty System: Law and Procedure* (Bloomsbury, 2011).

[29] CRC, Art. 43.

[30] See generally CRC Part II, especially Arts 42, 44 and 45.

[31] See CRC-OPCP.

[32] Emphasis added. See UNICEF, *Implementation Handbook for the Convention on the Rights of the Child* (3rd edn, United Nations Children's Fund, 2007), p. 23; Office of the High Commissioner for Human Rights (OHCHR),

At one level, the universality of the CRC echoes Article 24 of the International Covenant on Civil and Political Rights (ICCPR). The right to family life enshrined in that provision is not conditional on a child's migration status or citizenship. However, countries have considerable scope in how they interpret and implement this right.[33] The critical difference between the ICCPR and the CRC is that the CRC extends *as a whole* to children within a state's jurisdiction, regardless of their status under domestic migration laws. As Pobjoy documents, the CRC's coverage was a reasoned decision made by the drafters of the Convention. The matter was not without controversy during the drafting of the Convention, expressed particularly by the US representative who urged limitations based on a child's 'lawful status' within a country.[34] The reference to children in the CRC therefore includes children who lack status, undocumented migrants, refugees and asylum-seekers.

Article 22 of the CRC drives home the universal reach of the Convention by stipulating that states parties should afford to children who are 'seeking refugee status or who (are) considered a refugee':

> appropriate protection and humanitarian assistance in the enjoyment of applicable rights set forth in the present Convention *and in other international human rights or humanitarian instruments to which the said States are Parties.* (emphasis added)

This provision is unique amongst the human rights Conventions. It makes direct reference to other instruments in both IHL and human rights Conventions, including the Refugee Convention. It is our view that the

---

Study of the OHCHR on Challenges and Best Practices in the Implementation of the International Framework for the Protection of the Rights of the Child in the Context of Migration, Human Rights Council, 15th Sess., UN Doc. A/HRC/15/29 (5 July 2010), p. 3, para. [3]; and UNCRC, *General Comment No 6: Treatment of Unaccompanied and Separated Children Outside Their Country of Origin*, 39th Sess., UN Doc. CRC/GC/2005/6 (1 September 2005), para. [18] ('GC6').

33 The matters based on which the country must not discriminate in provision of the Art. 24 right include 'race, colour, sex, language, religion, national or social origin, property or birth'. See generally UN Human Rights Committee, *General Comment No. 17: Article 24 (Rights of the Child)*, 35th Sess., UN Doc. HRI/GEN/1/Rev.9 (7 April 1989), para. [3], see also para. [4]: 'The right to special measures of protection belongs to every child because of his status as a minor'.

34 See Pobjoy, 'Article 22', above n. 18. For the contrary view (in favour of universality), see *Note Verbale Dated 5 October 1979 Addressed to the Division of Human Rights by the Permanent Representation of the Polish People's Republic to the United Nations in Geneva,* UN Doc. E/CN.4/1349 (1979).

effect of Article 22 should operate to expand quite radically the protective reach of the Refugee Convention because it requires states to take the same approach to those rights for both children recognized as Convention refugees and for asylum-seeker children.[35]

In his comprehensive analysis of Article 22, Pobjoy suggests that as a bare minimum the provision operates to oblige all states parties to consider whether children meet the Convention definition of refugee – and to offer protection where this is the case. The significance of this is that such an interpretation of the CRC would give the Refugee Convention universal coverage in the case of children, drawing in states not otherwise party to the Refugee Convention.[36] As explored further in this book, the Refugee Convention has at its centre the obligation not to return or *refoule* refugees to a place where they may face persecution on one of the five Convention grounds.[37] However, it also contains a range of rights and obligations that apply over the life-course of a refugee's journey.[38] This Convention provides a hierarchy of rights to persons depending on their status within the host country, according to whether they are a refugee under the Refugee Convention's own definition of that term. Here, we note simply that the CRC operates to require states to consider the unique features and vulnerabilities of children and childhood in determining the application of the definition to both refugees and asylum-seeker children. As an organ of the United Nations, UNHCR is bound by the CRC. Together with UNICEF, this agency has played a critical role in operationalizing the Convention for refugee children through the development of policies, guidelines and protection programmes.[39]

The generic reference to the 'protection of refugees' in Article 22 of the

---

[35] For a comprehensive discussion of Art. 22 and its effects, see Pobjoy, 'Article 22', above n. 18.

[36] Pobjoy, *The Child in International Refugee Law*, above n. 11, ch. 6 and Pobjoy, 'Article 22', above n. 18. In September 2016, there were 145 states parties to the Refugee Convention and 146 states parties to the Protocol, compared with 196 states parties to the CRC.

[37] Refugee Convention, Art. 33: 'No Contracting State shall expel or return ("refouler") a refugee in any manner whatsoever to the frontiers of territories where his life or freedom would be threatened on account of his race, religion, nationality, membership of a particular social group or political opinion.'

[38] See J.C. Hathaway, *The Rights of Refugees under International Law* (Cambridge University Press, 2005).

[39] See P. Alston, 'The Best Interests Principle: Towards a Reconciliation of Culture and Human Rights' in P. Alston (ed.), *The Best Interests of the Child: Reconciling Culture and Human Rights* (UNICEF and Clarendon, 1994). See further Mary Crock and Phoebe Yule, Chapter 5.

CRC also implies inclusion of other protective regimes for refugees, of which there are a number around the world (including some of the regional frameworks discussed elsewhere in this book).[40] Where children do not meet the Convention definition of refugee, we agree with those scholars who suggest that the CRC operates in and of itself as an alternative or complementary regime for the protection of children.[41] This is because the CRC is a capstone Convention for children in that it draws in the protective elements of all of the human rights Conventions. This includes the traditional non-refoulement provisions of not only the Refugee Convention, but also of the Convention Against Torture and the ICCPR.[42]

Specific non-refoulement obligations can be found in Articles 6 and 7 of the CRC and Article 38 of the OPAC. We would go further to argue that if return to their place of origin or transit country is against a child's best interests, then it runs counter to the CRC. This is important because considerations relevant to a child's best interests extend well beyond assessments of whether a child is at risk of torture or physical harm upon return, as we will discuss further.

The CRC is the first of the modern human rights Conventions to make express reference to the protective measures enshrined in IHL. Article 38 requires states parties 'to respect and to ensure respect' for IHL applicable to them in armed conflicts which are relevant to children. States parties must ensure 'protection and care of children who are affected by an armed conflict', and avoid using children as soldiers.[43] The CRC thus gives further force and effect to IHL. It imposes on states parties an obligation not only to ensure protection and care of children during armed conflict, but also to do so in a manner that respects the best interests and views of the child. The embrace of IHL in the CRC, which provides for a monitoring body, also increases scope for enforcement and potential remedy.

---

[40] See Carmelo Danisi (with Mary Crock), Chapter 7; Carlos Holguin and Kavita Kapur, Chapter 9; Kathryn Van Doore, Chapter 10.

[41] See Pobjoy, *The Child in International Refugee Law*, above n. 11, ch. 6; G. Goodwin-Gill, 'The United Nations Convention on the Rights of the Child and Its Application to Child Refugee Status Determination and Asylum Processes: Introduction' (2012) 26(3) *Journal of Immigration Asylum and Nationality Law* 226; and J. McAdam, 'Seeking Asylum under the Convention on the Rights of the Child: A Case for Complementary Protection' (2006) 14 *International Journal of Children's Rights* 251.

[42] Convention Against Torture and Other Cruel, Inhuman or Degrading Treatment or Punishment, opened for signature 10 December 1984, 1465 UNTS 65 (entered into force 26 June 1987), Art. 3; ICCPR, Art. 7.

[43] See also Optional Protocol on the Involvement of Children in Armed Conflict, opened for signature 25 May 2000, GA Res. A/Res/54/263 (12 February 2002).

3.2 Best Interests Principle

As noted earlier, the notion that children deserve special protection is embedded in most of the major frameworks developed to protect human rights through history. The idea that adults who make decisions must do so considering the interests of the child has a similarly long lineage. The concept was central to the Declaration on the Rights of the Child.[44] This made best interests the 'paramount' consideration, however only in relation to 'the enactment of laws' (Principle 2). In the context of education, it was to be 'the guiding principle' (Principle 7). The CRC requires consideration of a child's best interests by a much broader range of administrative decision-makers (including, relevantly, those charged with making decisions in relation to refugee status determination and durable solutions). The 'interests' of children feature also in the Convention on the Elimination of Discrimination Against Women.[45] The obligation to consider the 'best interests of the child' has become a *grundnorm* in international human rights law.

In its General Comment No. 14, the UNCRC explains that the notion of best interests stands at the very heart of the Convention, operating as a right, a principle and a rule of procedure to benefit a child who is fully the subject of rights.[46] Philip Alston and Bridget Gilmour-Walsh make the point that 'there is no article in the convention, and no right recognized therein, with respect to which this principle is not relevant'.[47]

Article 3(1) of the CRC creates a substantive right in that it enjoins states parties to ensure that the best interests of children within its care are considered as a matter of primary concern.[48] The provision contains language of strong legal obligation: it commands that states 'shall' make best interests a primary consideration.[49] In practical terms this should

---

[44] Declaration on the Rights of the Child, GA Res. 1386 (XIV), 14th Sess., UN Doc. A/4354 (20 November 1959), Art. 2.

[45] Convention on the Elimination of All Forms of Discrimination Against Women, opened for signature 1 March 1980, 1249 UNTS 13 (entered into force 3 September 1981) Arts 5(b), 16(1)(d). It has also been adopted by treaty bodies including the Human Rights Committee and UNHCR. See Alston, 'The Best Interests Principle', above n. 39, at 4.

[46] UNCRC, *General Comment No. 14 (2013) on The Right of the Child to Have His or Her Best Interests Taken as a Primary Consideration (Art. 3, para. 1)*, 62nd Sess., UN Doc. CRC/C/GC/14 (29 May 2013), p. 14, para. [21].

[47] P. Alston and B. Gilmour-Walsh, *The Best Interests of the Child: Towards a Synthesis of Children's Rights and Cultural Values* (UNICEF, 1996), p. 1.

[48] UNCRC, *General Comment No. 14*, above n. 46, p. 14, para. [6].

[49] *Ibid.* 10, para. [36].

mean that every child is *entitled* as a matter of first priority to consideration of what is and is not in their best interests. The inquiry should focus on *the child* whose interests are in question. This, in itself, is revolutionary. It frees the law from what Australian judges (in applying the CRC to children with disabilities) have described as 'the degrading doctrines of earlier times which gave priority to parental or, more particularly, paternal rights to which the interests of the child were subordinated'.[50] It identifies the child as a rights bearer with value and interests separate from surrounding adults.

However, the CRC does not confer a right to best interests as an outcome. Article 3(1) enjoins decision-makers and other actors to make the best interests of the child '*a* primary consideration'. Though it exhorts states to give 'high priority' and 'larger weight' to what serves the child best, the UNCRC acknowledges that states are not required to make best interests an overriding or conclusive consideration.[51]

In only two circumstances does the CRC demand that the best interests of a child be the determining factor: adoption (Article 21) and separation of a child from their parents against their will (Article 9). Thus, domestic child welfare laws and policies frequently oblige officials to make the best interests or the welfare of the child *the paramount* consideration in those situations.[52] It follows that the CRC does place an onus on persons minded to act against a child's best interests to justify the action.[53]

But what does the best interests principle means in practice? The first challenge is the indeterminacy of the notion of best interests.[54] Brennan J. of Australia's High Court noted in 1992:

> in the absence of legal rules or a hierarchy of values, the best interests approach depends on the value system of the decision maker. Absent any rule or guideline, that approach simple creates an unexaminable discretion in the repository of power.[55]

However, as the majority stated in the same case, 'It is true that the phrase "best interests of the child" is imprecise, but no more so than the "welfare of the child" and many other concepts with which courts must

---

[50] *Secretary, Department of Health and Community Services* v. *JWB and SWB* (*Marion's* Case) (1992) 175 CLR 218, para. [13].

[51] UNCRC, *General Comment No. 14*, above n. 46, p. 10, para. [39].

[52] S. Parker, 'The Best Interests of the Child: Principles and Problems' (1994) 8 *International Journal of Law and the Family* 26, at 27–8.

[53] Alston, 'The Best Interests Principle', above n. 39, at 4.

[54] Parker, 'The Best Interests of the Child', above n. 52.

[55] *Marion's* Case, above n. 50, para. [14].

grapple'.[56] For us the imprecision or poly-centricity of the phrase is one of its strengths, because it requires decision-makers to grapple with the needs and circumstances of the individual, rights-bearing child before them.[57] In what follows, we will argue that the best interests principle can be both explained and operationalized – as a command that migrant children be afforded full enjoyment of *all* their rights.

The UNCRC notes that there is no hierarchy of rights in the CRC: all rights are deemed to embody the notion of best interests. This is a point made in other General Comments. Relevantly, and most particularly, in General Comment No. 6 relating to unaccompanied and separated asylum-seeker children, the CRC Committee affirmed that all CRC rights, and indeed all human rights, are 'indivisible and interdependent'.[58]

While universality and equality of children's rights may be correct as a matter of law and theory, the rights embodied in the CRC necessarily fall into something of a practical hierarchy. At the apex must be the child's right to life, aligned with other rights that go to the child's ability to subsist. Thereafter, the transient nature of childhood dictates that a child's health and wellbeing must include those elements necessary for growth and development, namely family, health and education. It is at this point that the treaty intersects with the International Covenant on Economic, Social and Cultural Rights (ICESCR), which obliges states parties to progressively realize the full enjoyment of economic, social and cultural rights for every person within a state's jurisdiction.[59] The participation Articles in the two Conventions stand out as the elements that deliver children agency as rights bearers, underscoring the foundational shift from a model of social paternalism to a model of rights.

'Best interests' operates as a unifying concept, transforming these rights into outcomes. The CRC enjoins states parties to ensure that children are safe; achieving material basics; healthy; learning; and participating.[60] The

---

56 *Ibid.* para. [75] (Mason CJ, Dawson, Toohey and Gaudron JJ).

57 The indeterminacy and poly-centricity of the best interests principle may explain why the CRC Committee did not produce a General Comment on Art. 3(1) until 2013, 23 years after the CRC came into force. See UNCRC, *General Comment No. 14*, above n. 46.

58 UNCRC, *General Comment No. 6 (2005) on Treatment of Unaccompanied and Separated Children Outside Their Country of Origin*, CRC, 39th Sess., UN Doc. CRC/GC/2005/6 (1 September 2005), para. [6].

59 See ICESCR, Art. 2 and CESCR, *General Comment 3 on the Scope of States' Obligations*, E/1991/23 (14 December 1991).

60 This list of outcomes derives from The Nest, a plan developed by the Australian Research Alliance for Children and Youth (ARACY), albeit there the reference is to 'loved and safe'. The Nest is an agenda for the improvement of

EU Reception Directive takes a similar approach. In the article dealing with minors, it echoes the CRC in demanding that best interests be a primary consideration, and goes on to say 'Member States shall ensure a standard of living adequate for the minor's physical, mental, spiritual, moral and social development'.[61]

The transformative effect of the CRC is that even if best interests is taken as a relative concept, and even if rights do fall into a hierarchy, the CRC demands that at every stage and in every process, a child's best interests must be considered. Even if there is no way to invoke a legal right under domestic law to any of a child's other entitlements under the CRC, international law operates (in theory at least) to require every decision-maker and authority to think about children and about what is in the children's best interests. It is possible to use the concept of best interests to identify and to promote *outcomes* that ensure a child is safe, healthy and happy. In short, 'best interests' bridges the gap between rights on paper, actions by governments, and protected children in reality.

The absence of a hierarchy of rights in the CRC stands in contrast to the Refugee Convention which does create different tiers of rights. The scope of a refugee's rights (including children) depends on the legal status conferred by a host state. While the basic non-refoulement obligations inhere in all refugees who are present within a state's territory, rights to work, education and other social welfare vary according to the degree of attachment within the state, namely, whether the refugees are lawfully present or lawfully resident within a state. As such, the Refugee Convention gives greater primacy to state sovereignty, and particularly to the power of states to control access to rights within its territory. A state party to the CRC has no such ability to limit access to rights among children in its territory.

The 'best interests' principle offers neither a guarantee of a child's welfare nor a set of universal rules. While courts have struggled with the indeterminacy of the concept, we argue nonetheless that the best interests approach – if done in accordance with the UNCRC's General Comment – *does* offer 'a hierarchy of values' to guide the exercise of a discretionary

---

child wellbeing in Australia. We argue that its five outcomes capture the outcomes sought by the CRC. See further Australian Research Alliance for Children and Youth, 'The Nest: A National Plan for Child and Youth Wellbeing', *The Nest* (2012), available at www.thenestproject.org.au/. See also G. Lansdown, 'Children's Rights' in B. Mayall (ed.), *Children's Childhoods: Observed and Experienced* (Falmer Press, 1994), p. 36.

[61] Directive 2013/33/EU of the European Parliament and of the Council of 26 June 2013 laying down standards for the reception of applicants for international protection (recast) [2013] OJ L96/107.

power. It need not mean a vacuum into which the decision-maker can simply insert his or her own priorities. One example of progress towards an articulated standard is the revised EU Reception Directive.[62] The Directive requires EU Member States to 'seek to ensure full compliance with the principles of the best interests of the child and of family unity', in accordance with the various applicable instruments (including the CRC). The Directive articulates a non-exhaustive list of factors that must be taken into account when assessing the best interests of a child. These include: family reunification possibilities; the minor's wellbeing and social development, taking into particular consideration the minor's background; safety and security considerations, in particular where there is a risk of the minor being a victim of human trafficking; and the views of the minor in accordance with his or her age and maturity.[63]

3.3 Children and the Right to Participate

If the CRC has operated to expand the reach of international human rights law, its greatest impact has been in the ways in which it conceives of children as individual rights bearers. The central message is that personhood or human status is indivisible: all are equally worthy of respect and protection, not merely as the objects of the law, but as active subjects. In this section we examine the 'participation' provisions that underscore the shift from charity and welfare to rights in human rights law.

The CRC broke new ground by acknowledging the fact that childhood and the abilities of children are not monolithic concepts, stressing the need for cognizance of the 'evolving capacities of the child'.[64] The central message is that the Convention operates to acknowledge dignity, worth and rights in *every* child, whatever their attributes or stage of development. Allowing for children's participation is a necessary consequence of recognizing their evolving capacity. Article 12 of the CRC requires states to ensure that the child with the appropriate capacity has the right to express their views and to be heard in any administrative proceeding affecting them, either directly or through a representative or appropriate body.

As others explore in this book, the right to participate has considerable significance for migrant children, particularly those seeking protection as

---

62 *Ibid.* See further Carmelo Danisi (with Mary Crock), Chapter 7.

63 *Ibid.*

64 See CRC, Arts 5 and 14(2). Note that Art. 3(h) of the CRPD echoes this, stating as one of the Principles of the CRPD: 'Respect for the evolving capacities of children with disabilities and respect for the right of children with disabilities to preserve their identities.'

refugees. As a bare minimum, it should operate to require states to consult children and/or consider the claims of children in any process affecting them. Unless children present as unaccompanied or separated minors (and sometimes even then), this often does not occur. In our view, equal attention should be paid to children who present as part of a family group. The provision serves as a reminder that children should not be defined by their relationship to adults. Wherever possible, they should be treated as persons with a right to determine their own destinies.

This is particularly powerful in the case of separated or unaccompanied migrant children, without parents or other family members to speak on their behalf. The CRC enjoins states not to let these children merely drift through administrative processes, but to require and encourage their active participation in those processes. As Lenni Benson and Claire Thomas consider further in Chapter 17, however, this does not mean that children should be left to their own devices. The duty to accept children's participation in administrative processes carries with it a duty to facilitate and enable that participation. This includes, where necessary, allowing a child to have proper representation.

4. PROTECTING THE HUMAN RIGHTS OF MIGRANT CHILDREN WITH DISABILITIES

There are close links between the CRC and the CRPD that create an integrated and mutually reinforcing framework for the protection of children's rights. Interestingly, the CRC was the first of the human rights Conventions to address expressly the rights and protection needs of persons with disabilities. Article 23(1) recognizes that:

> a mentally or physically disabled child should enjoy a full and decent life, in conditions which ensure dignity, promote self-reliance and facilitate the child's active participation in the community.

The UNCRC has acknowledged the significance of the extended protections for disabled children articulated in Article 23 in its early General Comments.[65] In 2007, the Committee adopted a General Comment

---

[65] See, e.g., UNCRC, *General Comment No. 1 (2001): Article 29(1): The Aims of Education*, 26th Sess., UN Doc. CRC/GC/2000/1 (17 April 2001), p. 4, para. [10]; UNCRC, *General Comment No. 4 (2003): Adolescent Health and Development in the Context of the Convention on the Rights of the Child*, 33rd Sess., UN Doc. CRC/GC/2003/4 (1 July 2003); UNCRC, *General Comment No. 7 (2005): Implementing*

dealing specifically with children with disabilities. It recognized that refugee children with disabilities, and especially girls, are vulnerable to multiple forms of discrimination. The Committee strongly endorsed giving these children 'high priority for special assistance, including preventative assistance, access to adequate health and social services, including psycho-social recovery and social reintegration'.[66] However, the UNCRC did not include a discussion of disability issues in the issues paper prepared for its day of general discussion on migrant children. The omission underscores how recent and novel consideration of these issues have been.[67]

While the CRPD does not refer expressly to migrant children, there can be no doubt that this Convention follows the CRC in the universality of its coverage. The fact that the CRPD refers to situations of both armed conflict and other emergencies without distinction based on nationality supports the view that the drafters of the CRPD did not intend the protective function of the Convention to apply to citizens alone.[68]

The CRPD did not set out to create new rights in persons with disabilities, including children. Rather its purpose is to 'promote, protect and ensure the full and equal enjoyment of all human rights and fundamental freedoms by all persons with disabilities, and to promote respect for their inherent dignity'. That this injunction includes children is underscored by paragraph (r) of the Preamble, which makes express reference to the CRC. Article 3 then sets out the eight guiding principles. These require governments and all private and public actors to treat all persons with disabilities with respect because of their inherent dignity, and to ensure that their disabilities do not restrict their full participation in society. Again, the place

---

Rights in Early Childhood, 40th Sess., UN Doc. CRC/C/GC/7/Rev 1 (20 September 2006), p. 17, para. [36(d)].

[66] UNCRC, *General Comment No. 9 (2006): The Rights of Children with Disabilities*, 43rd Sess., UN Doc. CRC/C/GC/9 (27 February 2007), p. 1, para. [1].

[67] See R. McCallum and H. Martin, 'Comment: The CRPD and Children with Disabilities' (2013) 20 *Australian International Law Journal* 17.

[68] For longer discussion of this issue see M. Crock, C. Ernst and R. McCallum, 'Where Disability and Displacement Intersect: Asylum Seekers and Refugees with Disabilities' (2012) 24 *International Journal of Refugee Law* 735, at 739–41. See also UNHCR Executive Committee (ExCom), *Conclusion on Refugees with Disabilities and Other Persons with Disabilities Protected and Assisted by UNHCR*, Conclusion No. 110 (LXI) (12 October 2010), available at www.unhcr.org/4cbeb1a99.html. When the CRPD Committee saw the ExCom Conclusion on Refugees and Disability there was no dissent from members on the universal reach of the CRPD: the Committee expressly congratulated UNHCR on its Conclusion. See CRPD, *Report of the Committee on the Rights of Persons of Disability on its Fourth Session,* 4th Sess., UN Doc. CRPD C/4/3 (4 October 2016), para. [16].

of children with disabilities is acknowledged, using the same language as the CRC in the reference to the 'evolving capacity' of such young ones. Article 7 requires states parties to:

> ensure that children with disabilities have the right to express their views freely on all matters affecting them, their views being given due weight in accordance with their age and maturity, on an equal basis with other children, and to be provided with disability and age-appropriate assistance to realize that right.

Like the CRC, the CRPD enjoins states parties to demonstrate acceptance of Convention obligations through national laws and policies. These should include mechanisms allowing binding, effective and accessible remedies for individuals affected by breaches of the instrument. Article 34 establishes the CRPD Committee to perform the same functions as the UNCRC.[69]

One other shared feature of the CRC and the CRPD is worth highlighting. Unlike the older human rights Conventions,[70] neither contains a derogation clause allowing for suspension of provisions in times of emergency. To the contrary, the CRC aligns itself with IHL, as noted earlier. The CRPD goes further in Article 11 to provide expressly that it shall apply in situations involving both armed conflict and natural disasters. It requires that states parties:

---

[69] See also Optional Protocol to the Convention on the Rights of Persons with Disabilities, opened for signature 30 March 2007, 46 ILM 443 (entered into force 3 May 2008) ('CRPD Optional Protocol'). In cases of egregious breaches, the Committee can recommend 'interim measures' to 'avoid possible irreparable damage' to an alleged victim (Art. 4). It may suggest measures to prevent or stop the violation and repair any damage caused (Art. 5). The Committee may also launch an inquiry into allegations of grave or systematic violations under Art. 6. The Optional Protocol creates a mechanism for hearing complaints from individuals alleging breach of their Convention rights by a state party.

[70] Article 4 of the ICCPR and Art. 15 of the European Convention on Human Rights (ECHR) both allow for the temporary repeal or suspension of human rights guarantees in extreme cases. The preconditions for such action are strict: a situation must constitute 'a threat to the life of the nation' and must be 'officially proclaimed' and notified internationally. Derogation is permitted only 'to the extent strictly required by the exigencies of the situation, provided that such measures are not inconsistent with . . . other obligations under international law; do not involve discrimination (as defined); and do not affect non-derogable rights'. See further M. Crock, 'The Protection of Vulnerable Groups' in S.C. Breau and K.L.H. Samuel (eds), *Edward Elgar Research Handbook, Disasters and International Law* (Edward Elgar Publishing, 2016), p. 393; and W. Kälin, 'The Human Rights Dimension of Natural or Man Made Disasters' (2012) 55 *German Yearbook of International Law* 119, at 131 n. 46.

> take, in accordance with their obligations under international law, including international humanitarian law and international human rights law, all necessary measures to ensure the protection and safety of persons with disabilities in situations of risk, including situations of armed conflict, humanitarian emergencies and the occurrence of natural disasters.

This provision has particular significance insofar as it represents the first occasion in international law where states are enjoined to respect the human rights of persons with disabilities in emergency situations, which often cause or are followed by migrant and refugee flows. As explored elsewhere,[71] the provision marked the beginning of truly revolutionary change in thinking about rights and obligations around the most vulnerable members of the human family.

Just as children have been treated as objects of charity and welfare, so too have persons with disabilities. The revolution wrought by the CRPD is that it does more than merely confirm the rights of persons with disabilities to respect and equal treatment. It acknowledges disability as a social construct, being the inability or failure to make 'reasonable accommodations' of a person's impairment to facilitate their participation in society. Article 1 states that:

> Persons with disabilities include those who have long-term physical, mental, intellectual or sensory impairments, which *in interaction with various barriers* may hinder their full and effective participation in society on an equal basis with others. (emphasis added)

In other words, impairments alone do not create disabilities. Rather, it is the failure in society to accommodate the person's impairment in a way that allows the person to fully participate in that society. This Convention demands that persons with disabilities be afforded respect, dignity and assistance rather than being treated as 'objects of charity, medical treatment and social protection'.[72] Again, the emphasis is on facilitating *full*

---

[71] See Crock, Ernst and McCallum, 'Where Disability and Displacement Intersect', above n. 68; N. Hart, M. Crock, B. Saul and R. McCallum, 'Making Every Life Count: Ensuring Equality for Persons with Disabilities in Emergency Situations' (2014) 40(1) *Monash Law Review* 148; and M. Crock, L. Smith-Khan, R. McCallum and B. Saul *The Legal Protection of Refugees with Disabilities: Forgotten and Invisible?* (Edward Elgar Publishing, 2017).

[72] Statement by Louise Arbour, UN High Commission for Human Rights, on the Ad Hoc Committee's adoption of the International Convention on the Rights of Persons with Disabilities, 5 December 2006, cited in R. Kayess and P. French, 'Out of Darkness into Light? Introducing the Convention on the Rights of Persons with Disabilities' (2008) 8(1) *Human Rights Law Review* 1.

participation in society, which expressly includes political and public life and legal proceedings.[73] These rights are powerful for migrants with disabilities, including children. Already marginalized by society or circumstance in the places from which they have fled, persons with disabilities can find status determination processes and starting life in a strange land especially challenging. The CRC and the CRPD work together such that the migrant children with disabilities deserve respect and accommodation on an equal basis with others.

5. IF THE ARC OF THE MORAL UNIVERSE BENDS TOWARDS JUSTICE, THE JOURNEY IS LONG

The pressure of world events,[74] together with increasing sensitivity to the justice claims of child migrants, have fed interest in laws, policies and practices in this area. Ours has been a necessarily cursory overview of the broad legal frameworks for the protection of migrant children. The chapters that follow will take us to more specialized protection regimes, for child victims of trafficking and child migrant workers, and thence to regional and national frameworks.

For present purposes, it suffices to acknowledge that states everywhere have tended to honour the CRC as much in the breach as in compliance with its precepts. Governments justify repressive measures despite obvious dissonances with the rights of migrant children. They employ interpretative tricks to assert (superficial) compliance with international law or assert that deterrent measures are necessary to save children who would otherwise engage in harmful behaviours.[75] Egregious examples are

---

[73] CRPD, Arts 1, 13(1), 29, 30. On the Convention generally, see M. Schulze, *Understanding the UN Convention on the Rights of Persons with Disabilities: A Handbook on the Human Rights of Persons with Disabilities* (Handicap International, 2010); R.C. McCallum and H. Martin, 'The CRPD and Children with Disabilities' (2013) 20 *Australian International LJ* 17; Kayess and French, 'Out of Darkness into Light?', above n. 72; and AS. Kanter, 'The Promise and Challenge of the United Nations Convention on the Rights of Persons with Disabilities' (2007) 34(2) *Syracuse Journal of International Law and Commerce* 287.

[74] The title of this section references an oft-cited statement by Martin Luther King, quoting in turn Theodore Parker, American Transcendentalist and reforming minister of the Unitarian church who fought hard for the abolition of slavery in America. See H.S. Commager (ed.), *Theodore Parker: An Anthology* (1960).

[75] See, e.g., arguments that irregular migrant children have no right to family reunion in a host state because the host state played no role in separating the children from their families in the first place. See *Explanatory Statement to Migration*

found in claims by Australian politicians that the mandatory detention of undocumented refugee children and/or their deflection to regional processing centres are necessary to prevent deaths at sea. As Crock explains:

> The idea is that policies must be set so as to deter adults from placing refugee children and youth in situations of peril by sending them alone in search of asylum. So it is that the protection of the *putative* child is invoked in defence of policies that are acutely harmful to embodied children.[76]

In February 2018, a class action suit was filed against a new US policy to separate parents and children arriving at US borders and seeking asylum.[77] The suit alleges that the separation directly frustrates the ability of the children to seek asylum and violates the due process rights of both the parent and the child. The *New York Times* reports that more than 700 children have been separated from parents at the US border.[78] These separations are a change in US policy.[79]

Migrant children continue to suffer in holding camps, in detention centres, in the streets of nations where disadvantage and danger are the constant companions of the young and the vulnerable. For many, the rights enshrined under international law have all the substance of a mirage. The challenge for all of us – practitioners, advocates and academics – is to identify and reaffirm the protective function of the laws that ultimately shape the arc of our moral universe.

Amendment Regulation 2012 (No. 5), Select Legislative Instrument 2012 No. 230 (Cth) (Austl.).

[76] See Crock, 'Of Relative Rights and Putative Children', above n. 22, at 35.

[77] *Ms. L and Ms. C. v. US Immigration and Customs Enforcement*, Case No. 18-cv-00428-DMS-MDD filed in the US Dist. Ct. S.D. Ca. Mar. 9, 2018. Litigation materials available at: https://www.aclu.org/cases/ms-l-v-ice.

[78] C. Dickerson, 'Hundreds of Children Have Been Taken From Parents at US Border', *New York Times*, 20 April 2018.

[79] See Benson and Thomas Ch. 17.

5. Children and the Convention Relating to the Status of Refugees

Mary Crock and Phoebe Yule

1. IMPORTANCE OF REFUGEE STATUS

Although children constitute over half of the world's refugees and are widely recognized as having both special vulnerabilities and rights,[1] the Convention Relating to the Status of Refugees and its attendant Protocol[2] are remarkably short on references to children and childhood.[3] Its mandate is age-neutral, applying to all individuals irrespective of age and containing no explicit provision for refugee children. As noted in the previous chapter, however, the Convention has been treated in recent years as a 'framework' document that can be read to evolve over time. The UN High Commissioner for Refugees (UNHCR) and the United Nations General Assembly have encouraged and supported a child-focused approach to refugee law, affirming the protection needs

---

[1] According to UNHCR data, in 2015 children below the age of 18 years constituted 51% of the world's refugee population, and 98,400 asylum applications were lodged by unaccompanied minors. This was the highest number on record since UNHCR started collecting such data in 2006: UNHCR, *Global Trends: Forced Displacement in 2015* (2016), p. 3.

[2] Convention Relating to the Status of Refugees, adopted 28 July 1951, 189 UNTS 137 (entered into force 22 April 1954) and the attendant Protocol Relating to the Status of Refugees, adopted 31 January 1967, 606 UNTS 267 (entered into force 4 October 1967). Hereafter referred to collectively as the 'Refugee Convention'. Note that the Protocol removed the geographical and temporal limitations of the Convention which was confined in 1951 to fugitives from the conflict in Europe during and after World War II.

[3] The only references to children in the Refugee Convention itself relate to refugee parents' freedom regarding the religious education of their children (Art. 4), and the effect on an adult refugee's right to employment of having one or more children possessing the nationality of the country of residence (Art. 17(2)(c)). See J. Pobjoy, *The Child in International Refugee Law* (Cambridge University Press, 2017), p. 32.

of refugee children on a great many occasions.[4] For example, guidelines issued by the UNHCR in 2009 make the following statement about asylum claims made by children:

> As noted by the UN Committee on the Rights of the Child, the refugee definition 'must be interpreted in an age and gender-sensitive manner, taking into account the particular motives for, and forms and manifestations of, persecution experienced by children'.[5]

The UNHCR Guidelines affirm the responsibility of states to take special measures to protect refugee children and stress the importance of reading the various human rights instruments as an integrated and mutual supportive framework for protecting children's rights: 'age is relevant to the entire refugee definition'.[6]

We will not revisit here the terms of the Convention on the Rights of the Child (CRC),[7] other than to stress again the central importance of Article 22 of that Convention. We agree with those who argue that this provision operates as an express link between the CRC and the Refugee Convention. Article 22's effect is twofold. First, it serves to underscore that all children affected by human conflict have an inherent right to

---

[4] Note, however, that the first such affirmation was not until 1988, when UNHCR released its Guidelines on Refugee Children. See UNHCR Executive Committee, *UNHCR Policy on Refugee Children*, UN Doc. E/SCP/82 (6 August 1993); UNHCR, *Refugee Children: Guidelines on Protection and Care* (UNHCR, 1994); UNHCR, *Guidelines on Policies and Procedures in Dealing with Unaccompanied Children Seeking Asylum* (1997). See further Pobjoy, *The Child in International Refugee Law*, above n. 3; and J. Pobjoy, 'Article 22' in P. Alston and J. Tobin (eds), T*he UN Convention on the Rights of the Child, A Commentary* (Oxford University Press, forthcoming), ch. 22, notes 7 and 8.

[5] See UNHCR, *Guidelines on International Protection: Child Asylum Claims under Articles 1(A)2 and 1(F) of the 1951 Convention and/or 1967 Protocol relating to the Status of Refugees,* 22 December 2009, UN Doc. HCR/GIP/09/08, p. 3 ('UNHCR Guidelines on Child Asylum Claims'). Reference is to Committee on the Rights of the Child, *General Comment No. 6: Treatment of Unaccompanied and Separated Children Outside Their Country of Origin*, UN Doc. CRC/GC/2005/6 (3 June 2005), para. [74].

[6] *Ibid.* 4. For a deeper analysis, see J. Bhabha and M. Crock, 'Children and Refugee Status: Who Gains Protection as a Refugee' in *Seeking Asylum Alone: A Comparative Study – Unaccompanied and Separated Children and Refugee Protection in Australia, the UK and the US* (2007), ch. 7. See also M. Evenhuis, 'Child-Proofing Asylum: Separated Children and Refugee Decision Making in Australia' (2013) 25 *International Journal of Refugee Law* 535.

[7] Convention on the Rights of the Child, adopted 20 November 1989, 1577 UNTS 3 (entered into force 2 September 1990) (CRC).

protection, embracing both refugees and those 'seeking refugee status'.[8] Second, it works to draw in the CRC as an aid in interpreting the Refugee Convention.

The focus of this chapter is on the second of these matters. We examine in detail the Convention definition of refugee and how this can be interpreted to accommodate the needs and lived experiences of children. We will argue that the Convention is the most appropriate protective scheme for children who cross borders to escape the most commons threats and harms experienced by children. This could include trafficking for sexual exploitation, bonded labour or other forms of contemporary slavery; harmful traditional cultural practices; or persecution arising out of membership of marginalized and disenfranchised groups, such as street children, orphans, the disabled, victims of domestic abuse. All of these types of persecution are capable of falling within the province of refugee law.

This is not to say that all the harms facing children who cross borders can be addressed through the refugee system. However, our central argument in this chapter is that the Refugee Convention can and should be read in a manner that considers the experiences and particular vulnerabilities of children. We begin in section 2 with a (necessarily brief) examination of the Convention definition of the term 'refugee', exploring how the various elements can and should be read to accommodate the protection needs of children. Section 3 looks at the Convention's exclusionary provisions and how these can affect children who have been embroiled in violence and conflict. We conclude with some reflections on the substantive rights that should flow in acknowledging the application of the Refugee Convention to children on the move as forced migrants.

2. REFUGEE CONVENTION DEFINITION OF REFUGEE

Article 1A(2) of the Refugee Convention, as amended by the Refugee Protocol, defines a refugee as a person who:

> owing to a well-founded fear of being persecuted for reasons of race, religion, nationality, membership of a particular social group or political opinion, is outside the country of his nationality and is unable or, owing to such fear, is unwilling to avail himself of the protection of that country.[9]

---

[8] See Mary Crock and Hannah Martin, Chapter 4. For a comprehensive overview of Art. 22, see Pobjoy, 'Article 22', above n. 4.

[9] Refugee Convention, Art. 1A(2).

Children are no different from adults insofar as they must meet each element of this definition in order to be considered a Convention refugee. Yet, each aspect of the definition presents its own issues for child applicants.[10] An applicant must establish that he or she 'fears' being persecuted, involving both a subjectively held fear, and that the fear is objectively 'well-founded'.[11] Children may express their fears differently to adults,[12] or may not be able to articulate a subjective fear.[13] Their experience of 'persecution' can be different. In this section, we examine in turn the meaning of the phrases or terms: 'well-founded fear'; 'persecution'; 'for reasons of' (sometimes referred to as the 'nexus' requirement); and the five Convention grounds. The section concludes with a short reflection on the significance of geography and the child refugee's position relative to their country of origin.

2.1 Well-founded Fear

The first marker of a Convention refugee is his or her inability or unwillingness to return home due to a 'well-founded fear' of being persecuted. It is generally accepted that this phrase requires an applicant to demonstrate both subjective fear and an objective risk of prospective harm. UNHCR has stated:

> To the element of fear – a state of mind and a subjective condition – is added the qualification 'well-founded'. This implies that it is not only the frame of mind of the person concerned that determines his refugee status, but that this frame of mind must be supported by an objective situation. The term 'well-founded fear' therefore contains a subjective and objective element.[14]

---

[10] For a comprehensive analysis, see Bhabha and Crock, 'Children and Refugee Status', above n. 6, ch. 7. See also M. Evenhuis, 'Child-Proofing Asylum: Separated Children and Refugee Decision Making in Australia' (2013) 25 *International Journal of Refugee Law* 535.

[11] UNHCR, *Handbook on Procedures and Criteria for Determining Refugee Status under the 1951 Convention and the 1967 Protocol Relating to the Status of Refugees*, UN Doc. HCR/IP/4/Eng/REV.3 (2011), paras [37]–[38] ('UNHCR Handbook').

[12] UNHCR, *Guidelines on Policies and Procedures in Dealing with Unaccompanied Children Seeking Asylum* (1997), para. [8.6].

[13] M. Crock, *Seeking Asylum Alone: A Study of Australian Law, Policy and Practice Regarding Unaccompanied and Separated Children* (2006), p. 170.

[14] UNHCR Handbook, above n. 11, para. [38], quoted in J.C. Hathaway and M. Foster, *The Law of Refugee Status* (2nd edn, Cambridge University Press, 2014), p. 91.

This two-part approach to 'well-founded fear' has been adopted by most leading courts of the common law world.[15] Although one of the least contentious elements for adults seeking protection as refugees, the fear requirement can be inherently problematic for children, for two reasons. First, depending on their age and cognitive maturity, children may be unable to conceive of or articulate a future apprehension of harm.[16] The second problem is related to the first: the procedures used to elicit information from adult claimants may simply not work for children.[17] Absent special accommodations, a child may have difficulty articulating fear for reasons that include trauma, parental instructions, lack of education, fear of state authorities, or reliance on ready-made testimony fed to them by smugglers. Children may be too young or immature to evaluate the sort of information that will be important to making a protection claim. They may be unable to connect their trepidation to a relevant risk. This is particularly so when the decision to flee is made by parents, guardians or other adults conscious of a threat to the minor, rather than by the child him- or herself.[18]

The consequence of insisting that a child prove subjective fear is that the child's claim may be rejected even though he or she is actually at risk of harm as a matter of objective evidence. In order to avoid this situation and to deal with the practical challenges of implementing the bipartite standard, decision-makers have devised a number of strategies to circumvent the purported requirement of subjective fear.[19] One has been to dispense with the inquiry into subjective fear altogether when a child is unable to

---

[15] The highest courts in Canada, Australia, the United States, the United Kingdom and Ireland have all adopted this understanding of the phrase. New Zealand is the only notable exception.

[16] UNHCR Handbook, above n. 11, paras [213]–[215]; UNHCR, *Guidelines on International Protection No. 8: Child Asylum Claims under Article 1A(2) and 1F of the 1951 Convention and/or 1967 Protocol Relating to the Status of Refugees*, UN Doc. HCR/GIP/09/08 (2009), para. [72] ('2009 Guidelines'); J. Bhabha and M. Crock, *Seeking Asylum Alone: A Comparative Study* (Themis Press, 2007), para. [157].

[17] For a full discussion of these issues, see Part IV of this book.

[18] In the *Seeking Asylum Alone* project researchers across the three countries' studies found that children most often had little agency in either decisions to leave home countries or decisions to choose particular states as destinations. See Bhabha and Crock, *Seeking Asylum Alone*, above n. 16, at 44–5; and Pobjoy, *The Child in International Refugee Law*, above n. 3, at 84ff.

[19] See J.C. Hathaway and W.S. Hicks, 'Is there a Subjective Element in the Refugee Convention's Requirement of "Well-Founded Fear"?' (2004) 26 *Michigan Journal of International Law* 505; Hathaway and Foster, *The Law of Refugee Status*, above n, 14, para. [92].

express their fear or connect it to a relevant risk. Others strategies are for decision-makers to impute fear from the parent to the child or to simply give greater regard to objective factors when dealing with children.[20]

Each of these strategies is important in rectifying the discriminatory impact this requirement can have on children applying for refugee status. However, it is our view that they also go to demonstrating the futility and undesirability of insisting on the subjective fear criterion for all.[21] In this context, we note the consensus that has developed around the interpretation of the objective element of the phrase 'well-founded fear'. Some early country jurisprudence adopted approaches akin to those used in civil or even criminal litigation, reading the phrase 'real chance' to require refugee claimants to demonstrate likely future harm on something akin to a balance of probabilities.[22] Accepted wisdom in more recent times has been that refugees do not bear a conventional onus of proof at all. Rather, the question for decision-makers is whether, in all of the known circumstances, there is a 'real chance' that claimants could face persecution if returned to the country from which they have fled.[23] This more nuanced approach should work in favour of children and young adults seeking recognition as Convention refugees. We acknowledge, however, the challenges children often face in having their claims taken seriously, with credibility often raised as an issue in denying protection. As Crock wrote:

> What is needed is a re-orientation in approach to the situation of children within the asylum regime, acknowledging harms when they threaten children and hearing the voices of children when they speak. This needs to occur both at the level of decision-making and advocating the claims of children seeking asylum – most particularly children seeking asylum alone.[24]

---

[20] UNHCR, 2009 Guidelines, above n. 16, para. [11]; Hathaway and Foster, *The Law of Refugee Status*, above n. 14, para. [103].

[21] That the bipartite approach to the definition of 'well-founded fear' is neither desirable as a matter of principle nor defensible as a matter of international law is examined in depth in Hathaway and Hicks, 'Is there a Subjective Element', above n. 19. Hathaway and Foster also support the proposition: *The Law of Refugee Status*, above n. 14, para. [92], as does Pobjoy, see *The Child in International Refugee Law*, above n. 3, at p. 84.

[22] See, e.g., *R* v. *Home Department State Secretary, ex parte Sivakumaran* [1988] AC 958, 992–4, 996–7 and 1000.

[23] See, e.g., *Chan Yee Kin* v. *Minister for Immigration* (1989) 169 CLR 376.

[24] M. Crock, 'Children as Convention Refugees' in J. McAdam (ed.), *Forced Migration, Human Rights and Security* (Bloomsbury, 2007), pp. 155, 180.

2.2 Persecution from the Perspective of the Child

A child will only be a refugee if he or she is threatened by a harm that constitutes a risk of 'being persecuted'. The term 'persecuted' is accepted widely as requiring evidence of a 'sustained or systemic violation of basic human rights demonstrative of a failure of state protection'.[25] In other words, persecution for the purposes of the Refugee Convention has two elements: human rights abuse plus failure of state protection.

The Convention itself offers no definition of the word 'persecution', a fact that can work in favour of children as an implicit acknowledgement of the plasticity of the term.[26] In fact, for a child to be recognized as a Convention refugee it is crucial to consider how 'persecution' can differ for children as opposed to adults. The CRC is vital in this regard because it recognizes that children have a distinct set of human rights. In enumerating such rights, the Convention identifies forms of harm that satisfy the persecutory threshold in claims involving children.[27] As the Federal Court of Canada has stated:

> If the CRC recognizes that children have human rights and that 'persecution' amounts to the denial of basic human rights, then if a child's rights under the CRC are violated in a sustained or systemic manner demonstrative of a failure of state protection, that child may qualify for refugee status.[28]

The rights enumerated and protected by the CRC acknowledge the reality that children's development needs and heightened sensitivities mean that they may experience harm differently from adults. For example, risk of denial of an opportunity to obtain an education is particularly compelling in the case of children since the right to education is integral to a child's evolving capacities, dignity and full development of human personality.[29]

---

[25] This phrase was first set out in J.C. Hathaway, *The Law of Refugee Status* (Butterworths, 1991), p. 101, and has been extensively adopted in the modern jurisprudence. For an overview of this jurisprudence see Hathaway and Foster, *The Law of Refugee Status*, above n. 14, paras [185], [196]–[197].

[26] See M. Crock, 'Re-thinking the Paradigms of Protection: Children as Convention Refugees in Australia' in J. McAdam (ed.), *Moving On: Forced Migration and Human Rights* (Hart Publishing, 2008), pp. 155–80.

[27] Pobjoy, 'Article 22', above n. 4.

[28] *Kim* v. *Canada (Minister of Citizenship and Immigration)* [2011] FCR 448, para. [51].

[29] UN Committee on the Rights of the Child (UNCRC), *General Comment No. 1: The Aims of Education*, UN Doc. CRC/GC/2001/1 (17 April 2001). This is reflected in Art. 28 of the CRC which stipulates a child's right to education.

Similarly, recruitment and engagement of children in armed conflict more readily amounts to persecution than an adult claiming subjection to military service as persecution due to the particular vulnerability of children as recognized in international human rights law.[30] There are also harms that are specific to children. Examples include child marriages and the sale or trafficking of children.[31] The CRC (including the CRC Protocols) provide a principled and widely accepted means for adapting the persecutory threshold for cases involving children.[32]

Both UNHCR and the UN Committee on the Rights of the Child (UNCRC) have issued guidance encouraging 'persecution' as used in the Refugee Convention to be read in conjunction with the CRC and other international human rights instruments. The UNHCR stated in its 2009 Guidelines:

> A contemporary and child-sensitive understanding of persecution encompasses many types of human rights violations, including violations of child-specific rights. In determining the persecutory character of an act inflicted against a child, it is essential to analyse the standards of the CRC and other relevant international human rights instruments applicable to children.[33]

The second key element of 'being persecuted' is failure of state protection. Refugee law is not designed simply to enable persons to escape the risk of serious harm. Rather, its purpose is 'to serve as a back-up to the protection one expects from the state of which an individual is a national'.[34] Refugee law is thus 'substitute protection' in the sense that it is a response to disenfranchisement from the usual benefits of nationality.[35]

---

[30] UNCRC, *General Comment No 6: Treatment of Unaccompanied and Separated Children Outside their Country of Origin*, UN Doc. CRC/GC/2005/6 (3 June 2005), p. [59]. This is reflected in Art. 38 of the CRC which requires states to take all feasible measures to ensure that children under 15 years do not participate in hostilities. Also see Mary Crock and Hannah Martin, Chapter 4, for a discussion of how the four Geneva Conventions and the two Additional Protocols address the special protection needs of children in this context.

[31] See, e.g., Optional Protocol to the Convention on the Rights of the Child on the Sale of Children, Child Prostitution and Child Pornography, opened for signature 25 May 2000, A/RES/54/263 (entered into force 18 January 2002) (CRC –OPSC).

[32] Pobjoy, *The Child in International Refugee Law*, above n. 3, at pp. 101–30.

[33] UNHCR, 2009 Guidelines, above n. 16, para. [13]. See also UNCRC, *General Comment No. 6*, above n. 30, para. [74].

[34] *Ward* v. *Canada (Attorney General)* [1993] 2 SCR 689, 709 (Can. SC, 30 June 1993).

[35] Hathaway and Foster, *The Law of Refugee Status*, above n. 14, para. [292].

Pobjoy notes that there are three pertinent issues in this regard for claims involving children.[36] First, there can be a failure of state protection even where the risk emanates from a private actor, so long as there is evidence that the state is unwilling or unable to respond to the risk. This is particularly important in claims involving children where persecution is frequently at the hands of non-state actors such as local criminal gangs, insurgency groups or family members. A child at risk of domestic violence may therefore satisfy the refugee definition if the country of origin has failed to satisfy its protective obligations required under Article 19 of the CRC. Second, it will rarely be appropriate for a decision-maker to draw an inference about the availability of state protection from the fact that a child has not previously sought protection from state authorities.[37] Status as a minor must be taken into account in assessing the reasonableness of an applicant's willingness to seek protection. Hence, in the Canadian case of *Bueckert*, the Court said of a three-year-old child: '[It] is not immediately apparent how anyone that age could ever personally test the adequacy of state protection.'[38] Finally, in assessing whether a child has an internal protection alternative in their country of origin, a decision-maker must have regard to the applicant's age and whether relocation would be in the best interests of the child.[39]

2.3 Nexus Requirement

Proving persecution is not sufficient in itself to ground an asylum claim. A person's well-founded fear of being persecuted must be 'for reasons of' an enumerated ground: race, religion, nationality, political opinion or membership of a particular social group.[40] Refugee law thus requires that there be a nexus or causal link between the risk of being persecuted and a Convention ground (these grounds will be examined in the following section). Two initial points can be made here. First, it is generally not necessary for an applicant to identify correctly the ground upon which their fear of persecution is based.[41] However, there must be a demonstrable

---

36 Pobjoy, 'Article 22', above n. 4, at 16; and Pobjoy, *The Child in International Refugee Law*, above n. 3 at pp. 116–56.

37 See also Hathaway and Foster, *The Law of Refugee Status*, above n. 14, para. [329]; UNHCR, 2009 Guidelines, above n. 16, para. [39].

38 *Bueckert* v. *Canada (MCI)* 2011 FC 1042, para. [18]. See also *Zhu* v. *Canada (Minister of Citizenship and Immigration)* 2001 FCT 884, para. [28], approved in *Lorne* v. *Canada (MCI)* 2006 FC 384, para. [18].

39 UNHCR, 2009 Guidelines, above n. 16, paras [53]–[57].

40 Refugee Convention, above n. 1, Art. 1(A)(2).

41 *Ward* v. *Canada*, above n. 34, para. [745]; *Suvorova* v. *Canada (Minister of*

link between feared persecution and a Convention ground, even if not referenced by the applicant.[42] Second, the applicant need not possess the relevant Convention-related characteristic. It is sufficient that a potential persecutor attributes or has attributed the ground to the applicant.[43] This is significant for children because they may attract persecution because of characteristics of their parents or relatives. For example, children born to political dissidents or adherents to a particular religion may be assumed themselves to be dissidents or adherents to a persecuted faith.

While these core principles are widely accepted, controversy persists over whether the Convention ground must be linked to the intention of the persecutor or to the state withholding protection. We support Hathaway and Foster's proposition that while evidence of intention to harm or withhold protection is relevant and sufficient to satisfy the nexus clause, it is not a necessary condition for establishing that the risk of being persecuted is linked to a Convention ground. Rather, the nexus requirement is met where the reason for the applicant's exposure to their well-founded fear of being persecuted is linked in fact to a Convention ground.[44] We hold this view because a focus on persecutorial intention places an unfair burden on applicants to adduce evidence of and explain the motives of past and future persecutors. It can also divert attention from the wider societal context of discrimination and oppression that often explains why an applicant is at risk. For children, it can be surpassingly difficult to engage with these issues, underscoring the importance of taking an objective and flexible approach.

With regard to the strength of the nexus required, the Convention ground need not be the sole motive for the persecution.[45] For example,

---

Citizenship and Immigration) [2009] FCJ 443; UNHCR Handbook, above n. 11, para. [67].

[42] UNHCR Handbook, above n. 11, para. [67].

[43] *Ward* v. *Canada,* above n. 34, para. [120]; *RT (Zimbabwe) v Secretary of State for the Home Department* [2012] 3 WLR 345, para. [363]; *Singh v. Gonzalez* (2005) 406 F.3d 191 (USCA, 3d Cir., May 5, 2005), para. [196]; UNHCR Handbook, above n. 11, para. [80]; UNHCR, *Guidelines on International Protection No. 7: The Application of Article 1A(2) of the 1951 Convention and/or 1967 Protocol relating to the Status of Refugees to Victims of Trafficking and Persons at Risk of Being Trafficked,* UN Doc. HCR/GIP/06/07 (7 April 2006), para. [29].

[44] Hathaway and Foster, *The Law of Refugee Status*, above n. 14, paras [367]–[368].

[45] *R (Sivakumar)* v. *Secretary of State for the Home Department* [2003] 1 WLR 840, paras [853]–[854]; *Applicant in V488 of 2000* v. *Minister for Immigration and Multicultural Affairs* [2001] FCA 1815, para. [36]; UNHCR, 2009 Guidelines, above n. 16, para. [20]; UNHCR, *Guidelines on International Protection No.7*, above n. 43, para. [29].

in a trafficking context, the overriding economic incentive involved need not exclude the possibility of Convention-related grounds influencing the targeting and selection of trafficking victims.[46] The majority of judicial preference and international guidance has adopted a 'one factor' test such that the Convention ground need only be a contributing factor to the risk of being persecuted.[47]

2.4 Five Convention Grounds and Children's Claims

The Refugee Convention requires an applicant to demonstrate fear of persecution for reasons of one of the five reasons or grounds: race, religion, nationality, membership of a 'particular social group' or political opinion. Although independent, all concern fundamental socio-political disenfranchisement defined by reference to core norms of non-discrimination law.[48] Each may apply in claims concerning children, although two are worthy of special attention: membership of a particular social group and political opinion.

The grounds of race and nationality have raised few issues because these grounds are based generally on features such as physical appearance that are readily apparent. 'Race' is interpreted broadly to include not only membership in a particular racial category, but also groups such as Europe's Roma people or the Hazara in Afghanistan who are defined by physical, linguistic or cultural features.[49] 'Nationality' has been interpreted in the same way to encompass stateless persons (such as Palestinians),[50] as well as persons whose citizenship is defined or perceived in terms of allegiance to a predecessor state. An example is ethnic Russians born in Estonia after Estonian independence.[51] Like an adult, a child may face persecution because of their race or nationality. This may occur when a child faces legal disqualification or exclusion amounting to persecution for being born stateless, or discrimination due to their ethnicity. In this context it is worth noting that children can face discrimination

---

46 *Ibid.* para. [31].

47 For a brief overview of the authorities see Hathaway and Foster, *The Law of Refugee Status*, above n. 14, para. [389].

48 G.S. Goodwin-Gill and J. McAdam, *The Refugee in International Law* (3rd edn, 2007), paras [100]–[102]; Hathaway, *The Law of Refugee Status*, above n. 25, paras [135]–[141].

49 *Horvath* v. *Secretary of State for the Home Department* [1999] Imm. AR 121, paras [131], [137]–[138]; *Calado* v. *Minister for Immigration and Multicultural Affairs* (1997) 81 FCR 59, para. [445].

50 For example, *Refugee Appeal No. 73861* (NZ RSAA, 2005), para. [118].

51 *Stserba* (USCA, 6th Cir., 2011), para. [975].

by virtue of being born abroad to persons whose home country does not recognize children born to its nationals either abroad or out of wedlock.[52] Unfortunately, it is rare for such children to be recognized as refugees, even if no state is prepared to admit them. In these cases, denial of access to a nationality also operates as a denial of refugee protection.[53]

In accordance with international human rights law, 'religion' in the Refugee Convention is interpreted to include theistic, non-theistic and atheistic beliefs, as well as the right not to profess any religion or belief.[54] A child may therefore be at risk of persecution not only because of what they believe, but also because of what they do not believe. A child need not show that they are an active practitioner; it is enough that they are perceived to belong to a particular sect or religion.

With regard to 'political opinion', decision-makers often assume falsely that children are apolitical; that they are incapable of holding political opinions or engaging in political activity.[55] Many counter-examples demonstrate that this is a radical misconception, particularly in highly polarized and politicized societies. Examples include the engagement of Palestinian children in the first and second Intifadas; and the role of Soweto school children in political opposition to the Apartheid regime in South Africa. That children can indeed be politically active and aware is recognized in Articles 12 and 15 of the CRC which imply that children have a right to express political opinion and engage in political activity. It has also been acknowledged in the UNHCR's 2009 Guidelines, which emphasize that 'children can be politically active and hold particular political opinions independently of adults . . . for which they may fear being persecuted'.[56]

A second flawed assumption that impacts on children's claims for asylum on the ground of political opinion is that persecutors would

---

52 Bhabha and Crock, 'Children and Refugee Status', above n. 6, para. [164].

53 In Australia this led to the incarceration for three years of a child born in immigration detention to a Malaysian mother detained as an unlawful non-citizen. See *Singh* v. *Commonwealth* (2004) 222 CLR 322; and M. Foster, 'Membership in the Australian Community: *Singh v The Commonwealth* and its Consequences for Australian Citizenship Law' (2006) 34 *Federal Law Review* 161; and Bhabha and Crock, 'Children and Refugee Status', above n. 6, para. [164].

54 UNHCR, *Guidelines on International Protection No. 6: Religion-based Refugee Claims under Article 1A(2) of the 1951 Convention and/or the 1967 Protocol Relating to the Status of Refugees*, UN Doc. HCR/GIP/04/06, para. [10]; International Covenant on Civil and Political Rights, adopted 19 December 1966, 999 UNTS 171 (entered into force 23 March 1976) Art. 18(1) (ICCPR).

55 Bhabha and Crock, 'Children and Refugee Status', above n. 6, para. [164]; Pobjoy, *The Child in International Refugee Law*, above n. 3, at pp. 166 ff.

56 UNHCR, 2009 Guidelines, above n. 16, para. [45].

not take a child's view seriously because they are too insignificant or ignorant.[57] This is again acknowledged by the UNHCR as it notes in its Guidelines that 'dismissing a child's claim based on the assumption that perpetrators would not take a child's views seriously or consider them a real threat could be erroneous'.[58]

Membership of a 'particular social group' is the most nebulous and contentious of the Convention grounds,[59] yet has been critical to giving children voice in seeking to establish refugee status.[60] We concur with the proposition put forward by Hathaway and Foster, justified by reference to the context, object and purpose of the Refugee Convention: that is, that a 'particular social group' exists where members of a group share an innate characteristic or common background that cannot be changed; or share a characteristic or belief that is so fundamental to identity or conscience that a person should not be forced to renounce it.[61] Size of the group is irrelevant; it may be a very small group (such as family) or a very large group (such as women).[62] Voluntary association or cohesion amongst group members is not a requirement.[63]

In relation to children, decision-makers have appropriately recognized particular social groups defined in whole or in part by reference to a child's age. For example, decision-makers have found that groups such as 'children',[64] 'minors'[65] and 'young people'[66] can constitute particular social groups. In other cases, it is the intersection of other factors with

---

57 Bhabha and Crock, 'Children and Refugee Status', above n. 6, para. [164].

58 UNHCR, 2009 Guidelines, above n. 16, para. [11].

59 For an overview of this engagement and controversy, see Hathaway and Foster, *The Law of Refugee Status*, above n. 14, paras [426]–[432].

60 UNHCR, 2009 Guidelines, above n. 9, paras [48]–[52]; Hathaway and Foster, *The Law of Refugee Status*, above n. 14, para. [451].

61 *Ibid.* para. [432]. This definition originated in the decision of *Acosta* (USBIA, 1985), para. [233] and now also represents the position in Canada and New Zealand.

62 *Applicant A* v. *Minister for Immigration and Ethnic Affairs* (1997) 190 CLR 225, para. [241]; UNHCR, *Guidelines on International Protection No. 2: 'Membership of a Particular Social Group' Within the Context of Article 1A(2) of the 1951 Convention and/or its 1967 Protocol Relating to the Status of Refugees*, UN Doc. HCR/GIP/02/02 (7 May 2002) paras [18]–[19].

63 *Ibid.* para. [15].

64 *Xiao* v. *Canada (Minister of Citizenship and Immigration)* [2001] FCT 195, para. [14].

65 *Canada (Minister for Immigration and Citizenship)* v. *Li* (2001) 203 FTR 154, para. [11].

66 The High Court in *Applicant S* v. *Minister for Immigration and Multicultural Affairs* (2004) 217 CLR 387 recognized as a group 'young able-bodied men', para. [16].

a child's age that has exposed them to a risk of being persecuted. Hence 'orphaned children',[67] 'impoverished children',[68] 'girls'[69] and '*hēiháizi*' (children ineligible for registration in China due to violation of the one-child policy)[70] have been recognized as social groups. Recognition of age as an immutable or innate characteristic has thus been a significant development for the independent refugee claims of children.

Further to earlier discussions on the interaction between the Refugee Convention, CRC and the Convention on the Rights of Persons with Disabilities (CRPD),[71] children with disabilities provide an interesting case study. While not heavily litigated, existing case law (reinforced by the CRPD) confirms that a group defined by reference to disability is within the ambit of social group.[72] Decision-makers have accepted that a social group may be constituted by a range of disabilities and illness, including autism,[73] visual impairment,[74] congenital deafness[75] and mental illness.[76] In the assessment of such claims it has been recognized that '[w]hile not all disabilities are "innate" or "inherent" . . . they are usually, unfortunately, "immutable"'.[77] In 2005, a US Appeal Court found that disabled children and parents who provide care for them constituted members of a particular social group such that a family, taken as a whole, had suffered persecu-

---

67 *Re WBT, V98-00787* [1999] CRDD 199 (Can. IRB, 4 June 1999); UNHCR, 2009 Guidelines, above n. 16, para. [50].

68 *JDJ (Re), No. A95-00633b* [1998] CRDD 12; UNHCR, 2009 Guidelines, above n. 16, para. [50].

69 UNHCR, 2009 Guidelines, above n. 16, para. [50].

70 *Chen* (USCA, 7th Cir., 2010), paras [333]–[334]; UNHCR, 2009 Guidelines, above n. 16, para. [50].

71 Adopted 13 December 2006, 2515 UNTS 3 (entered into force 3 May 2008) (CRPD). See also Mary Crock and Hannah Martin, Chapter 4.

72 M. Crock, C. Ernst and R. McCallum, 'Where Disability and Displacement Intersect: Asylum Seekers and Refugees with Disabilities' (2012) 24(4) *International Journal of Refugee Law* 735; M. Foster, *The 'Ground with the Least Clarity': A Comparative Study of Jurisprudential Developments Relating to Membership of a Particular Social Group*, UNHCR Legal and Protection Policy Research Series, PPLA/2012/02 (2012).

73 M. Foster, *International Refugee Law and Socio-Economic Rights: Refuge from Deprivation* (Cambridge University Press, 2007), pp. 322–3.

74 *Re BOG, VAO-03441* [2001] CRDD 121 (Can. IRB, 16 July 2001), cited in Foster, *The 'Ground with the Least Clarity'*, above n. 72, para. [319].

75 *Re H (GY), T94-05654 and T94-05655* [1995] CRDD 70 (Can. IRB, 1 February 1995), para. [4], cited in Foster, *The 'Ground with the Least Clarity'*, above n. 72, para. [319].

76 *Kholyavskiy* (USCA, 7th Cir., 2008).

77 *Tchoukhrova* v. *Gonzales* (2005) 404 F.3d 1181 (USCA, 9th Cir., April 21, 2005), para. [1189].

tion. The court held that the disabled child's asylum claim provided the basis for a derivative claim by his parents, reversing the usual situation where adult claims are the basis for protection of dependent children.[78] This is significant for it demonstrates how recognition of this social group enabled decision-makers to depart from the traditional adult-centred approach to refugee protection. Matters concerning the definition of Convention refugee are considered at greater length by other contributors writing in Part III of this book.

3. EXCLUSION CLAUSES

Space constraints do not permit anything like a comprehensive discussion of the protective reach for children of the Refugee Convention. However, we include in this section a brief discussion of the Convention's 'exclusion clauses'.

Article 1F of the Refugee Convention provides that persons seeking to evade legitimate prosecution or punishment for serious domestic crimes, those who have committed serious international crimes, and anyone who is guilty of actions contrary to the principles and purpose of the United Nations must be denied refugee status.[79] These clauses apply in principle to children and could have significant ramifications for asylum claims made by child soldiers, whose actions may amount to war crimes or crimes against humanity. However, UNHCR has noted that 'as with any exception to human rights guarantees, the exclusion clauses must always be interpreted restrictively and should be used with great caution'.[80] In particular, the exclusion clauses should only apply where a child has reached the age of criminal responsibility.[81] For children over the minimum age or where no such limit exists:

> [t]he maturity of the particular child should still be evaluated to determine whether he or she has the mental capacity to [be] held responsible for the crime in question. The younger the child, the greater the presumption that such mental capacity did not exist at the relevant time.[82]

---

78 *Ibid.*

79 Refugee Convention, Art. 1(F)(a), (b) and (c).

80 UNHCR, *Background Note on the Application of the Exclusion Clauses: Article 1F of the 1951 Convention Relating to the Status of Refugees* (2003), para. [4].

81 Convention on the Rights of the Child, Art. 40, requires states to set a minimum age of criminal responsibility, although there is no universal minimum age.

82 UNHCR, *Background Note on the Application of the Exclusion Clauses*, above n. 80, para. [91].

4. TOWARDS A CHILD-CENTRED INTERPRETATION OF THE REFUGEE CONVENTION

If there are countries willing to offer protection to migrant children simply because they are minor children, the question arises as to the worth of fighting to have such children recognized as Convention refugees. Our view is that the grant of asylum under the Refugee Convention constitutes the most protective and comprehensive state response for someone fleeing persecution. This instrument offers long-term security, access to state benefits and (potentially) family reunion rights that continue beyond the temporal limitations of childhood.[83] It is the most widely accepted international legal framework for the protection of persons displaced by fears of persecution. It articulates the obligations of states to respond to the tragedies and adversities that cause people to flee across borders.

The sheer number of children on the move around the world in search of protection is forcing states to consider more closely the relevance of the Refugee Convention to this most vulnerable of groups. In this chapter we have considered the application of the Convention definition of refugee to children in need of protection. Others will consider some of the substantive protections that this Convention affords to children recognized as refugees. These include the critical right not to be returned to a place where the child might suffer persecution on one of the five Convention grounds,[84] as well as the right not to be detained.[85]

While the jurisprudence on children as Convention refugees is growing, it is fair to say that this remains an underdeveloped area of both international and domestic law and policy. While some states make concessions in the procedures adopted to determine refugee status, there remain many instances where children struggle to be heard in administrative processes. Without assistance, formal status determination proceedings can present insurmountable barriers for young asylum-seekers. As the contributors to

---

[83] Alternative (childhood-specific) protection options generally lack one of the following important attributes: immediate access to permanent legal residency (and eventually citizenship); entitlement to family reunion; and access to welfare and education benefits on an equal footing with children who are citizens. For example, unaccompanied children are often granted protection during minority; however long-term legal residency which guarantees a safe and secure future is more elusive: Bhabha and Crock, 'Children and Refugee Status', above n. 6, at 175–82.

[84] Refugee Convention, Art. 33. See further the chapters in Part III of the book.

[85] See the chapters in Part V of the book.

this book document, there is a pervasive need for states to adopt processes that acknowledge the need of asylum-seeking children for the personal protections of a guardian and the legal protections of an appropriate advisor and advocate *ad litem*.

Of equal importance is the need to increase knowledge and understanding of the conditions within countries that explain why children are on the move in such large numbers. Recognizing children as Convention refugees depends not only on the correct interpretation of the law, but also on knowledge of the country conditions that force children to move in the first place. If the best interests of children are acknowledged as a 'primary' consideration, the protection of migrant children must involve multiple strategies: addressing root causes of displacement, inclusive processing and reception, through to finding durable solutions for children at risk. It is to these many and diverse matters that we will turn in the chapters that follow.

6. Migrant children and the United Nations Protocols against smuggling of migrants and trafficking in persons

Andreas Schloenhardt and Joseph Lelliott

1. INTRODUCTION

Irregular migration of children is a worldwide phenomenon that has grown considerably in recent years. Many children are smuggled to destinations where they hope to find safety and prosperity. Others find themselves in situations of trafficking where they face exploitation and abuse. Regrettably, irregular migration of children, including the causes, conditions and the true scale of the phenomenon, remains poorly understood and researched. This is despite evidence that both trafficking and smuggling of children are increasing. Global asylum applications by children reached new heights in 2014, and children account for a growing proportion of smuggled migrants globally.[1] Trafficking in children has similarly increased in recent years: about one in three trafficking victims worldwide is a child.[2]

Irregular migrant children are particularly vulnerable to exploitation and abuse. Current policies, laws and regulations addressing smuggling and trafficking, however, mostly serve to prevent and suppress irregular migration, and do not adequately protect the rights of children. In international law, the United Nations (UN) Protocol against the Smuggling of Migrants by Land, Sea and Air[3] and the Protocol to Prevent, Suppress

---

1 See UNHCR, *Global Trends: Forced Displacement in 2014* (UNHCR, 2015); UNODC, *Smuggling of Migrants: A Global Review and Annotated Bibliography of Recent Publications* (United Nations, 2011), p. 2.

2 UNODC, *Global Report on Trafficking in Persons 2014* (UNODC, 2015), p. 11.

3 Opened for signature 15 December 2000, 2241 UNTS 507 (entered into force 28 January 2004).

and Punish Trafficking in Persons, especially Women and Children,[4] do little to protect children who are caught up in irregular migration.

The purpose of this chapter is to provide some insight into the smuggling and trafficking of children, examine the application of the Smuggling of Migrants and Trafficking in Persons Protocols to this phenomenon, and explore avenues on how to better protect migrant children in international law.

2. CONDITIONS AND RISKS

Growing migration pressures led by war, persecution and poverty, combined with a lack of legal avenues for migration and asylum, have caused a considerable increase in irregular migration worldwide. To cross international borders, especially those that are marked by fences, walls and tight immigration restrictions, many migrants have come to rely on smugglers who offer to transport and guide them to their destinations. This often involves hazardous smuggling methods, and many smugglers exploit the desperation of their clientele. Trafficking in persons and smuggling of migrants exist along a continuum and in many cases migrant journeys that start as free and voluntary decisions to move abroad end in situations involving coercion, abuse and exploitation. Over the past decade, thousands of people have suffocated in containers, perished in deserts or drowned at sea. Other migrants are thrown into huge debt and are often left with little choice but to comply with the demands of their smugglers and traffickers. For many migrants, however, the illegal services offered by their smugglers represent the only way to escape persecution, violence or discrimination. For others, migrant smuggling and trafficking in persons are seen as the only or most immediate avenues to escape poverty and unemployment, and to better their lives and those of their families.

2.1 Smuggling of Children

The many challenges, obstacles and dangers associated with migrant smuggling are of particular concern if children are involved. The vulnerabilities, helplessness and young age of many children make them dependent on the smugglers or the adults they are travelling with. Children, especially if they are young, often cannot anticipate particular threats, do

---

4 Opened for signature 12 December 2000, 2237 UNTS 319 (entered into force 25 December 2003).

not know how to avoid certain dangers, and generally lack the experience, knowledge and skills to master the challenges associated with irregular migration or react to changing conditions and circumstances.

The methods used by smugglers are frequently dangerous, and in many cases threaten the lives of smuggled migrants. Smuggling by sea is particularly dangerous, and children are especially at risk as they embark on dangerous journeys in overcrowded and unseaworthy boats. Smuggling vessels are often undersupplied with water, food and life jackets, use rudimentary navigational equipment, and are equipped with unreliable engines. These circumstances increase the risks of sickness and malnutrition during smuggling journeys, as well as the dangers of sinking and getting lost in open waters. Smuggling by land also presents significant dangers. Children travelling in trucks may hide in closed compartments, which can result in death if there is inadequate ventilation, or if they are left inside for too long. They may also be threatened by adult co-travellers fighting for room. Some smuggling ventures place children on top of trains or between wheel axles, exposing them to risks of death or serious injury if they fall off. Moreover, many smuggled children are forced to undertake long treks through harsh terrain or swim across rivers. Smuggling by air is by comparison less risky, though migrants may be placed in danger if they travel as stowaways on planes or try to hide in the undercarriage of aeroplanes.

In some cases, smuggled children may become involved in assisting the smuggling process. This may be voluntary, but in many instances migrants are forced into such situations. For example, migrants may be required to sell smuggling services to other potential migrants. In other instances, unaccompanied children may be used as guides for border crossings, or as crew members on smuggling vessels.

2.2 Exploitation and Trafficking

The vulnerability of children places them at the mercy of their smugglers and creates additional risks of abuse and exploitation. This is particularly the case if children are smuggled unaccompanied, without a parent or legal guardian, and if they have to fight for themselves, even if they are smuggled in larger groups of migrants. The UN Rapporteur for Human Rights has noted that 'children who are unaccompanied or separated from their parents are particularly vulnerable to human rights violations and abuses at all stages of the migration process'.[5] They may be extorted for

---

[5] UN Human Rights Council, *Promotion and Protection of all Human Rights, Civil, Political, Economuc, Social and Cultural Rights, including the Right to*

smuggling fees, forced to work to pay off debts in transit countries, and may be sexually and physically harassed.

Young unaccompanied girls are particularly vulnerable to sexual exploitation, which may include providing sexual favours to migrant smugglers in exchange for protection or for assistance in crossing borders. They may also be placed in situations of sexual servitude, used for child pornography, or raped by smugglers or other persons they encounter during the smuggling process. Although sex trafficking is particularly common, children may be forced to work in various sectors such as agriculture, mining, manufacturing, or by begging.[6] Children may be put into situations of forced labour while in transit or in destination countries. This is particularly evident in cases where migrants are placed into debt-bondage in order to pay smuggling-related debts. In such cases they may spend months or years working in exploitative conditions in transit and destination countries. If they are apprehended, children are often placed in immigration detention, sometimes in centres with poor hygienic conditions, little food and medical care, and that are ill-suited for the mental and physical health of children.

3. SMUGGLING OF MIGRANTS; TRAFFICKING IN PERSONS

3.1 Smuggling of Migrants

Supplementing the Convention Against Transnational Organized Crime,[7] the Smuggling of Migrants Protocol is the principal international instrument that defines and criminalizes the smuggling of migrants, fosters international cooperation, and protects the rights of smuggled migrants. Article 3(a) of the Protocol defines the term 'smuggling of migrants':

> [to] mean the procurement, in order to obtain, directly or indirectly, a financial or other material benefit, of the illegal entry of a person into a state party of which the person is not a national or a permanent resident.

Development; Report of the Special Rapporteur on the Human Rights of Migrants Jorge Bustamente, UN Doc. A/HRC/11/7 (14 May 2009), para. [23].

[6] ILO, UNICEF and UNGIFT, *Training Manual to Fight Trafficking in Children for Labour, Sexual and Other Forms of Exploitation: Understanding Child Trafficking* (ILO, 2009), pp. 28–9.

[7] Opened for signature 15 December 2000, 2225 UNTS 209 (entered into force 29 September 2003).

The term 'illegal entry' used in the definition of smuggling of migrants is defined in Article 3(b) to mean 'crossing borders without complying with the necessary requirements for legal entry into the receiving State'. It is further required that the object of migrant smuggling, i.e. the smuggled migrant, is 'a person [who] is not a national or a permanent resident [of the country entered]'.

The 'financial or other material benefit' serves as the purpose element in the definition of smuggling of migrants. The Interpretative Notes emphasize that:

> the reference to 'a financial or other material benefit' as an element of the definition in subparagraph (a) was included in order to emphasise that the intention was to include the activities of organised criminal groups acting for profit, but to exclude the activities of those who provided support to migrants for humanitarian reasons or on the basis of close family ties. It was not the intention of the Protocol to criminalise the activities of family members or support groups such as religious or non-governmental organisations.[8]

The inclusion of the 'financial or other material benefit' in the definition of smuggling of migrants thus articulates clear boundaries about the types of migrant smuggling that are viewed as criminal, and those that are not, and makes it abundantly clear to states parties what type of circumstances would, and should, fall outside the criminalization requirements. The term 'benefit':

> should be understood broadly to include, for example, crimes in which the predominant motivation may be sexual gratification, such as the receipt or trade of materials by members of child pornography rings, the trading of children by members of paedophile rings, or cost-sharing among ring members.[9]

3.2 Trafficking in Persons

The Trafficking in Persons Protocol sets out a uniform approach to trafficking in persons to be taken by all states parties, and to facilitate

---

[8] UN Ad Hoc Committee on the Elaboration of a Convention Against Transnational Organized Crime, *Report of the Ad Hoc Committee on the Elaboration of a Convention Against Transnational Organized Crime on the Work of its First to Eleventh Sessions: Addendum: Interpretative Notes for the Official Record (Travaux Préparatoires) of the Negotiations of the United Nations Convention Against Transnational Organized Crime and the Protocols Thereto*, UN Doc. A/55/383/Add.1 (3 November 2000), p. 16, para. [88], p. 17, para. [89] ('*Interpretative Notes*').

[9] *Ibid.* 2, para. [3].

international cooperation among them. Article 3(a) of the Protocol defines 'trafficking in persons' as:

> the recruitment, transportation, transfer, harboring or receipt of persons, by means of the threat or use of force or other forms of coercion, of abduction, of fraud, of deception, of the abuse of power or of a position of vulnerability or of the giving or receiving of payments or benefits to achieve the consent of a person having control over another person, for the purpose of exploitation. Exploitation shall include, at a minimum, the exploitation of the prostitution of others or other forms of sexual exploitation, forced labor or services, slavery or practices similar to slavery, servitude or the removal of organs.

This definition combines elements relating to the acts involved in each stage of the trafficking process, the means used by the traffickers against victims, and the purpose of trafficking in persons. In instances that involve the trafficking of children, Article 3(c) states that 'the recruitment, transportation, transfer, harbouring or receipt of a child is trafficking, even if one of the means above is not used'.

3.3 Distinctions and Overlap

Although the two Protocols provide universally accepted definitions of smuggling of migrants and trafficking in persons, confusion and overlap between the phenomena and other forms of irregular migration persist. The distinction between smuggling and trafficking of children can be particularly difficult to draw, and situations of smuggling often morph into trafficking.

The offences of smuggling of migrants and trafficking in persons serve different objectives, which have major implications for the way in which smuggled migrants and victims of trafficking are protected. The offence of trafficking in persons seeks to protect the rights, integrity and freedoms of trafficked persons, while punishing people who traffic others for exploitative purposes. Because the definition of trafficking does not involve an element of transnationality, the offence does not purport to protect national interests such as border control and national security. The offence of smuggling of migrants, on the other hand, serves to protect national sovereignty, borders and immigration systems. The protection of smuggled migrants and their rights and liberties are not primary objectives of the Smuggling of Migrants Protocol, and accordingly the protection provisions are only rudimentarily developed.

The two offences can also be differentiated by their purpose elements that reflect the intention of the perpetrator. The primary purpose of trafficking in persons is exploitation. The purpose of migrant smugglers is to obtain a 'financial or other material benefit', and they typically have 'no intention to exploit the smuggled migrant after having enabled him or her to irregularly enter or stay in a country'.[10]

For the smuggling of migrants there must be 'illegal entry of a person into a state party of which the person is not a national or a permanent resident'.[11] Alternatively, migrant smuggling may arise by enabling a person to remain illegally in a country that he or she has entered (legally or illegally). There is thus both a cross-border element as well as a requirement of illegal entry or illegal stay. Trafficking in persons, in contrast, may involve illegal or legal entry into a country and does not require the crossing of a border. There is no requirement that trafficking in persons occurs transnationally; it can also occur completely within one country.

A further difference between smuggling and trafficking is the issue of consent, which is considered to be irrelevant by the Trafficking in Persons Protocol.[12] Although the Smuggling of Migrants Protocol does not address the issue, in practice smuggling of migrants involves an agreement whereby a person may pay or give some other benefit to a smuggler in order to facilitate that person's irregular migration. Smuggled migrants may retract their initial consent during a smuggling venture but be forced to continue on the journey.[13] The issue of consent is less relevant for smuggling and trafficking of children, who are generally regarded to lack the capacity to consent. Neither offence includes consent, or the lack thereof, as an element.

3.4 Criminalization versus Protection

The Smuggling of Migrants Protocol and the Trafficking in Persons Protocol are supplements to the Convention Against Transnational Organized Crime, and as such primarily serve to address the criminal justice aspects of the two phenomena. The original drafts of the Protocols contain few provisions to protect the rights of smuggled migrants and victims of trafficking, prioritizing prevention and criminalization over the

---

[10] UNODC, *A Short Introduction to Smuggling of Migrants* (UNODC, 2010), p. 10.

[11] Smuggling of Migrants Protocol, Art. 3(a).

[12] Trafficking in Persons Protocol, Art. 3(b); see also UNODC, *A Short Introduction to Smuggling of Migrants*, above n. 10, at 10.

[13] UNODC, *Legislative Guides for the Implementation of the United Nations Convention Against Transnatipnal Organized Crime and the Protocols Thereto* (United Nations, 2004), pp. 340–1('*Legislative Guides*'); UNODC, *A Short Introduction to Smuggling of Migrants*, above n. 10, at 10.

protection of smuggled migrants and victims of trafficking in persons. It was only following interventions by an Inter-Agency Group comprising several international organizations led by the UN High Commissioner for Human Rights that provisions recognizing the vulnerability and human rights of migrants were inserted into the Protocols.

Smuggling of Migrants Protocol

To preserve the rights of smuggled migrants, the initial idea was to include a savings clause referring to international human rights law treaties and, in particular, the Convention and Protocol Relating to the Status of Refugees.[14] A note by the Office of United Nations High Commissioner for Human Rights (OHCHR), UNICEF (the UN Children's Emergency Fund), and the International Organisation for Migration (IOM) called for the specific consideration of smuggled migrants who are women and children, as well as recognition of the right of return with respect to the principle of non-refoulement to ensure migrants who are covered by protection obligations under international refugee law are afforded protection by the relevant state.[15] In particular, the note argued that the 'Protocol should include an explicit acknowledgement of the fact that children have special rights under international law', and that their best interests should be 'paramount'.[16] In response, the Ad Hoc Committee drafted a provision incorporating protection and assistance measures for smuggled migrants, which became Article 16 of the Smuggling of Migrants Protocol. The protection of the rights of smuggled migrants was subsequently also included as an express purpose of the Protocol in Article 2.[17]

---

[14] Convention Relating to the Status of Refugees, opened for signature 28 July 1951, 189 UNTS 150 (entered into force 22 April 1954); Protocol Relating to the Status of Refugees, opened for signature 31 January 1967, 606 UNTS 267 (entered into force 4 October 1967) ('Refugee Convention').

[15] UN General Assembly, Ad Hoc Committee on the Elaboration of a Convention against Transnational Organized Crime, *Note by the Office of the United Nations High Commissioner for Human Rights, the United Nations Children's Fund and the International Organisation for Migration on the Draft Protocols Concerning Migrant Smuggling and Trafficking in Persons*, 8th Sess., UN Doc. A/AC.254/27 (8 February 2000); see also UN General Assembly, Ad Hoc Committee on the Elaboration of a Convention Against Transnational Organized Crime, *Informal Note by the United Nations High Commissioner for Human Rights*, 4th Sess., UN Doc. A/AC.254/16 (1 June 1999).

[16] UN Ad Hoc Committee on the Elaboration of a Convention Against Transnational Organized Crime, *Note by the Office of the United Nations High Commissioner for Human Rights, the United Nations Children's Fund and the International Organisation for Migration*, above n. 15, at 6.

[17] T. Obokata, 'The Legal Framework on Immigration Control at Sea' in

Despite these inclusions, the Smuggling of Migrants Protocol takes a 'vague, discretionary' approach to the goal of protecting smuggled migrants, as opposed to its primary goal of criminalizing migrant smuggling.[18] Unlike trafficked persons, smuggled migrants are withheld 'victim' status and, as a result, do not enjoy the 'special protections afforded to victims of crime and human rights violations under international law'.[19] In addition, apart from a token acknowledgement in Article 16(4), the special needs and vulnerabilities of smuggled children are not addressed by the Protocol.

Trafficking in Persons Protocol

Although early drafts of the Trafficking in Persons Protocol acknowledge the rights of victims of trafficking, these lack specific mandatory provisions to protect victims and assist them when they exit the trafficking situation. The Protocol, too, has been criticized for placing too much emphasis on the criminal justice aspects of trafficking and paying too little attention to the rights and needs of victims, many of whom are women and children. The submission by the Inter-Agency Group during the negotiations of the Trafficking in Persons Protocol called for an explicit acknowledgement that children have special rights under international law, and for a greater focus on the special needs of child victims of trafficking, including rights to physical and psychological recovery, social integration, and the provision of non-discretionary assistance and protection.[20] The drafters of the Protocol responded with the inclusion of Article 3(c), which modifies and reduces the standard definition of trafficking for cases involving children.

Article 3(c) has been both criticized for falling far short of the standard expected by UN agencies, and praised as a major step forward in addressing child trafficking. Commentators like Lisa Kurbiel have noted approvingly that the removal of the 'means' requirement takes into account the special vulnerability of children, especially in situations where they are obeying

---

B. Ryan and V. Mitsilegas (eds), *Extraterritorial Immigration Control: Legal Challenges* (Martinus Nijhoff, 2010), pp. 151, 164. See also UNODC, *Travaux Préparatoires of the Negotiations of the United Nations Convention Against Transnational Organized Crime and the Protocols Thereto* (United Nations, 2006), p. 461.

[18] A. Schloenhardt and K.L. Stacey, 'Assistance and Protection of Smuggled Migrants: International Law and Australian Practice' (2013) 35 *Sydney Law Review* 53, at 64.

[19] A.T. Gallagher and F. David, *The International Law of Migrant Smuggling* (Cambridge University Press, 2014), p. 556.

[20] A.T. Gallagher, 'Human Rights and the New UN Protocols on Trafficking and Migrant Smuggling' (2001) 23 *Human Rights Quarterly* 975, at 989.

orders from parents or other authoritative figures in their communities.[21] This approach is based on the accepted assumption that children do not sufficiently understand their likely fate in order to give informed consent. Nonetheless, others have noted that a plan to increase the scope of the offence was rejected. Some authors have criticized the limited scope of the definition of exploitation and called for an expansion to cover all forms of child labour.[22] A stand-alone instrument to specifically address child trafficking has also been suggested,[23] but has not materialized.

4. PROTECTION OF CHILDREN UNDER THE SMUGGLING OF MIGRANTS PROTOCOL

The statement of purpose in Article 2 of the Smuggling of Migrants Protocol provides for the protection of the rights of smuggled migrants, in addition to the purposes of preventing and combatting smuggling and promoting international cooperation.[24] Despite this explicit reference to protection, the Protocol does not grant smuggled migrants any rights additional to those under other international instruments.

4.1 Assistance to Smuggled Migrants

Article 16 of the Smuggling of Migrants Protocol contains several provisions relating to assistance measures. These 'provisions are intended to set an appropriate standard of conduct for officials who deal with smuggled migrants and illegal residents and to deter conduct on the part of offenders that involves danger or degradation to the migrants'.[25]

Article 16(2) requires states parties to protect smuggled migrants from physical violence, but contains no specific guidelines about the way in which such protection may be provided. For example, there is no explicit

---

[21] L. Kurbiel, 'Implementing the UN Trafficking Protocol to Protect Children' (2004) 24 *Children's Legal Rights Journal* 73, at 75.

[22] A.T. Gallagher, 'Human Rights and the New UN Protocols on Trafficking and Migrant Smuggling' (2001) 23 *Human Rights Quarterly* 975, at 989.

[23] N. Ollus, *The United Nations Protocol to Prevent, Suppress and Punish Trafficking in Persons, Especially Women and Children*, UNAFEI Resource Material Series No. 62 (2004), pp. 16, 23.

[24] See also Smuggling of Migrants Protocol, Art. 4 'Scope of Application': 'This Protocol shall apply . . . to the protection of the rights of persons who have been the object of such offences.'

[25] *Legislative Guides*, above n. 13, at 364.

requirement that the host country provide safe accommodation or other types of physical protection.

Article 16(3) calls on states parties to 'afford appropriate assistance to migrants whose lives or safety are endangered by reason of being [smuggled migrants]'. The *Legislative Guide for the Implementation of the United Nations Convention Against Transnational Organised Crime and the Protocols Thereto* states that Article 16(3) imposes a new obligation on states to provide 'basic assistance', though explicitly precludes the existence of a corresponding right.[26] The Model Law Against the Smuggling of Migrants suggests a number of measures, including provision of urgent medical care, access to food and shelter, and protection of physical security, may stem from the Article 16(3) obligation.[27]

Article 16(4) includes the only reference to children in the Smuggling of Migrants Protocol. It does not include any reference to the rights or best interests of the child but does mandate that states parties take into account the special needs of children. There is no further explanation of what these 'special needs' are or how they are to be accounted for. The United Nations Office on Drugs and Crime (UNODC)'s *Basic Training Manual on Investigating and Prosecuting the Smuggling of Migrants* provides some limited guidance, recommending that, at a minimum, children should be removed, immediately, from the source of any danger; not be allowed further contact with any suspects; be seen by a medical professional (for health issues but also for possible evidential issues); be provided with additional clothing or nappy changes (if required); fed, given refreshments and if old enough, given at least a pencil and paper to provide them with something to do; and be dealt with thereafter by trained officers.[28]

4.2 Protection of the Rights of Smuggled Migrants

Article 16(1) of the Smuggling of Migrants Protocol preserves the rights of smuggled migrants under international law, requiring that each state party:

> take, consistent with its obligations under international law, all appropriate measures, including legislation if necessary, to preserve and protect the rights

---

[26] *Ibid.* 365, para. [71].

[27] UNODC, *Model Law Against the Smuggling of Migrants* (United Nations, 2010), p. 69.

[28] UNODC, *Basic Training Manual on Investigating and Prosecuting the Smuggling of Migrants: Module 9: Human Rights* (United Nations, 2010), p. 8.

> of persons who have been the object of conduct set forth in article 6 of this Protocol as accorded under applicable international law, in particular the right to life and the right not to be subjected to torture or other cruel, inhuman or degrading treatment or punishment.

While this paragraph refers to specific rights such as life and protection from torture, cruel, inhuman or degrading treatment or punishment, Article 16(1) is generally seen as emphasizing the protection of all fundamental human rights and freedoms as accorded in relevant international treaties, especially the International Covenant on Civil and Political Rights (ICCPR)[29] and the International Covenant on Economic, Social and Cultural Rights (ICESCR).[30] Article 16(1) does not create any new obligations for states parties.[31]

Article 16(5) implies an obligation on states parties to facilitate communication between smuggled migrants and their relevant consular missions, especially in situations in which the receiving country detains smuggled migrants because of their illegal entry, or to facilitate their removal.[32] Reflecting provisions under the Vienna Convention on Consular Relations,[33] this encompasses assistance measures, such as informing migrants of their right to contact their relevant consulate, notification of a migrant's request to do so, and facilitation of this communication, in person or otherwise.[34]

5. PROTECTION OF CHILDREN AND THE TRAFFICKING IN PERSONS PROTOCOL

Article 2 of the Trafficking in Persons Protocol cites victim protection as one of the Protocol's core purposes. While children benefit from all the protection provisions in the Protocol, there is recognition that child victims of trafficking suffer heightened levels of harm and are thus deserving

---

29 Opened for signature 16 December 1966, 999 UNTS 171 (entered into force 23 March 1976) art 6(1); see also Art. 12(1).

30 Opened for signature 16 December 1966, 993 UNTS 3 (entered into force 3 January 1976); cf. *Interpretative Notes*, n. 8 above, para. [108].

31 *Interpretative Notes,* n. 8 above, para. [109]; *Legislative Guides*, above n. 13, at 365.

32 Smuggling of Migrants Protocol, Art. 16(5).

33 Opened for signature 24 April 1963, 596 UNTS 261 (entered into force 19 March 1967), Art. 36.

34 UNODC, *Model Law Against the Smuggling of Migrants*, above n. 27, at 73.

of greater protection, taking into account their special rights and needs.[35] Although there are no specific provisions addressing child victims in the Protocol, the relevant provisions should be construed in a child-sensitive manner, cognisant of their vulnerabilities and lack of agency.

5.1 Accommodation and Material Assistance

Article 6(3) of the Trafficking in Persons Protocol asks states parties:

> to consider implementing measures to provide for the physical, psychological, and social recovery of victims of trafficking, including, in appropriate cases, in cooperation with NGOs and other relevant agencies and members of civil society.

Article 6(5) reiterates the points raised in paragraph (3) by calling on states parties to endeavour to provide for the physical safety of victims of trafficking.[36] These requirements only apply to victims who are in the territory of the respective country, i.e. the receiving state, until the victim has returned to his or her country of origin (and/or to the country of origin thereafter).[37] Specific assistance measures should include:

(a) appropriate housing;
(b) counselling and information, in particular as regards to their legal rights, in a language that the victim can understand;
(c) medical, psychological and material assistance; and
(d) employment, educational and training opportunities.[38]

In applying these provisions, states parties should take into account the special needs of children.[39] The Legislative Guide encourages the appointment of a guardian for child victims until a durable solution for protection has been implemented.[40] Persons responsible for the care of children

---

[35] UN Trafficking Principles and Guidelines, Principle 9, Guideline 47; see, e.g., Convention on the Rights of the Child, opened for signature 20 November 1989, 1577 UNTS 3 (entered into force 2 September 1990), Art. 20(1) ('CRC'); see also A.T. Gallagher, *The International Law of Human Trafficking* (Cambridge University Press, 2010), pp. 323–4.

[36] See also Convention Against Transnational Organised Crime, Art. 25(1).

[37] *Travaux Préparatoires*, n. 17 above, para. [71].

[38] Trafficking in Persons Protocol, Art. 6(3).

[39] *Ibid.* Art. 6(4).

[40] *Legislative Guides*, above n. 13, at 289–90; D. McClean, *Transnational Organized Crime: A Commentary on the UN Convention and its Protocols* (Oxford University Press, 2007), p. 340.

should be specially trained, and accommodation for children should take account of their age and special needs.[41]

The supplementary material to the Protocol also recommends that where the 'age of a victim is uncertain, and there are reasons to believe the victim is a child', the victim should be treated as a child until their age is verified.[42] It is also suggested that victims of trafficking, children or not, are referred to assistance agencies at the earliest possible time,[43] and that assistance is provided regardless of the willingness of the victim to participate in the investigation or prosecution of his or her alleged trafficker.[44]

5.2 Legal Assistance and Access to Courts; Protection of Victim-Witnesses

In order to encourage and facilitate participation in legal proceedings, Article 6(1) of the Trafficking in Persons Protocol obliges states parties to protect the privacy and identity of victims, inter alia, by making legal proceedings relating to such trafficking (especially against the traffickers) confidential. Where threats against victims and witnesses are particularly imminent, it may also be necessary to take measures to relocate the victim or witness and take additional steps to limit the disclosure of personal information.[45] The acceptability and use of these measures will vary between jurisdictions and some measures may not be permissible in all legal systems.

If child victims of trafficking are involved in legal proceedings of any kind, including proceedings that may be directed against their traffickers, it is important that they have access to legal assistance in order to understand relevant proceedings, participate in them effectively, and to facilitate the expression of their views and concerns.[46] Accordingly, the Trafficking in Persons Protocol requires states parties to provide victims of trafficking with information on relevant court and administrative proceedings and with counselling and information, in particular about their legal rights, in a language they can understand.[47] While the Protocol itself is silent on the

---

41 *Legislative Guides*, above n. 13, at 290.

42 *Ibid.* 289; UNODC and UNGIFT, *Model Law Against Trafficking in Persons*, above n. 27, at 47–8.

43 *Ibid.* 56.

44 *Ibid.* 57.

45 *Ibid.* 62–3, 64–6; *Legislative Guides*, above n. 13, at 283.

46 Trafficking in Persons Protocol, Art. 6(2); see also Convention Against Transnational Organised Crime, Art. 25(3).

47 UNODC, *Toolkit to Combat Trafficking in Persons* (2nd edn, United Nations, 2008), p. 430.

specific issue of involvement of child victims in criminal proceedings, the Legislative Guide notes that legal safeguards and protection measures for child witnesses must be 'strongly emphasised' and steps should be taken to ensure their safety.[48]

5.3 Victim Compensation

Article 6(6) of the Trafficking in Persons Protocol obliges states parties to ensure that their domestic legal systems contain measures that offer victims of trafficking the possibility of obtaining compensation for damage suffered.[49] The Protocol also requires states to provide trafficked persons with 'information on relevant court and administrative proceedings'. This provision may be interpreted to include information and assistance with respect to obtaining compensation through criminal or civil proceedings. The Protocol does not specify the source from which victims may obtain compensation. It has been noted that one possible source could be the traffickers themselves, either as a result of compensation orders made in criminal proceedings, or some national compensation scheme funded from the public revenue.[50] To that end, the Model Law Against Trafficking in Persons also recommends the establishment of a fund to which victims can apply for compensation for the damages suffered by them.[51]

5.4 Immigration Status of Victims of Trafficking in Persons

Article 7(1) of the Trafficking in Persons Protocol encourages states parties to consider adopting legislative or other appropriate measures that permit foreign trafficked persons to remain in the territory of the host country, temporarily or permanently, in appropriate cases. In implementing such measures, Article 7(2) calls on states parties to give appropriate consideration to humanitarian and compassionate factors. It is understood that 'humanitarian factors' refer to rights that are established in international human rights instruments, such as the ICCPR, the Refugee Convention, and the Convention on the Rights of the Child (CRC). 'Compassionate factors' is meant to refer to personal circumstances such

---

48 *Legislative Guides*, above n. 13, at 290.

49 See also Convention Against Transnational Organised Crime, Art. 25(2).

50 UNODC, *Toolkit to Combat Trafficking in Persons*, above n. 47, at 436–7; McClean, *Transnational Organized Crime*, above n. 40, at 341.

51 UNODC and UNGIFT, *Model Law Against Trafficking in Persons*, above n. 27, at 69, 70.

as family situation, age, gender, de facto relationships, and other factors that should be considered on an individual and case-by-case basis.[52]

5.5 Return and Repatriation

Article 8 creates several obligations for countries seeking to repatriate victims of trafficking in persons to their home country.[53] Article 8(2) requires that the state party returning the victim must have due regard for the safety of the victim and for the status of any legal proceedings relating to the trafficking. This provision relates to the timing of any return of the victim, recognizing that decisions to return victims of trafficking in persons require consideration of the two factors.

The safety of the victim must be paramount in the decision to repatriate. Accordingly, 'it may well be best for the return of the victim to his or her home state to be delayed in order to allow at least some aspects of [the physical, psychological, and social] recovery process to have been completed'.[54] Victims of trafficking in persons may be needed in criminal proceedings in the receiving state before they are returned to their home country. Preferably, child victims should not be repatriated unless doing so is in their best interests and, prior to their return, a suitable relative or guardian has agreed and is able to take responsibility and offer care and protection for the child.[55] All necessary steps should also be taken to carry out family reunification, where in the best interests of the child.[56] In cases where return is carried out, the Protocol obliges states parties to cooperate in the course of the return procedure.[57]

Article 8(2) further mandates that the repatriation of victims 'shall preferably be voluntary'. While the Protocol does not prohibit compulsory repatriation against the known wishes of the victim, it calls on states parties not to use force in order to compel victims to return to their home country.

---

[52] UN General Assembly, Ad Hoc Committee on the Elaboration of a Convention Against Transnational Organised Crime, *Revised Draft Protocol to Prevent, Suppress and Punish Trafficking in Persons, Especially Women and Children*, UN Doc. A/AC.254/4/Add.3/Rev.6 (4 April 2000), para. [55].

[53] See further A. Schloenhardt and M. Loong, 'Return and Reintegration of Human Trafficking Victims from Australia' (2011) 23 *International Journal of Refugee Law* 143, at 149–59.

[54] McClean, *Transnational Organized Crime*, above n. 40, at 347.

[55] *Legislative Guides*, above n. 13, at 290.

[56] *Ibid.* 290; see also CRC, Art. 10(1).

[57] Trafficking in Persons Protocol, Art. 8(3) and (4); *Legislative Guides*, above n. 13, at 290–91.

6. OTHER INTERNATIONAL HUMAN RIGHTS AND REFUGEE LAW INSTRUMENTS

Article 19(1) of the Smuggling of Migrants Protocol and Article 14(1) of the Trafficking in Persons Protocol preserve the rights of smuggled and trafficked migrants established under international refugee and human rights law. The wording of each Article is identical, stating that:

> [n]othing in this Protocol shall affect the other rights, obligations and responsibilities of States and individuals under international law, including international humanitarian law and international human rights law and, in particular, where applicable, the 1951 Convention and the 1967 Protocol Relating to the Status of Refugees and the principle of non-refoulement as contained therein.

These savings clauses do not create new obligations for states parties or new rights for smuggled or trafficked migrants, but rather seek to uphold those already recognized by international law.[58] It is there that important protection provisions relevant to smuggled and trafficked children can be found.

6.1 International Refugee Law

Articles 19(1) and 14(1) draw particular attention to the specific obligations stemming from the Refugee Convention and Protocol. The key aspect of the protection granted under the Refugee Convention is that a refugee must neither be expelled nor returned (refouled) to 'the frontiers of territories where his [or her] life or freedom would be threatened'.[59] A country is in breach of this non-refoulement obligation if its authorities fail to properly identify and protect persons who are entitled to the benefits of refugee status.[60]

The Refugee Convention does not contain special provisions or references to refugee children. Nevertheless, UNHCR and the United Nations Committee on the Rights of the Child recommend that definitions of 'persecution' and 'well-founded fear' should be interpreted in a child sensitive manner.[61] In particular, children should be afforded a

---

[58] *Legislative Guides*, above n. 13, at 255–6, 364–5.

[59] Refugee Convention, Art. 33.

[60] See further UNODC, *Basic Training Manual on Investigating and Prosecuting the Smuggling of Migrants*, above n. 28, at 6.

[61] See UNHCR, *Guidelines on International Protection: Child Asylum Claims under Articles 1(A)2 and 1(F) of the 1951 Convention and/or 1967 Protocol relating to the Status of Refugees*, UN Doc. HCR/GIP/09/08 (22 December 2009), para. [13];

greater benefit of the doubt as to whether they have a well-founded fear, and special attention should be given to 'child-specific forms and manifestations of persecution'.[62] Procedural aspects of refugee proceedings should also take into account the needs and vulnerabilities of children.[63]

6.2 Rights of the Child

Despite drawing specific attention to the principle of non-refoulement under the Refugee Convention, the savings clauses in the two Protocols have a wide ambit. They ensure the unimpeded operation of international law generally, including the rights, obligations and responsibilities provided for in international instruments. Given the limited protection measures in the Convention and Protocols, the savings clauses are integral to safeguarding the rights of smuggled and trafficked children. Children gain the benefit of the rights provided for in numerous instruments, including the ICCPR and, in particular, the CRC.

Article 3 of the CRC is a fundamental part of the legal framework protecting smuggled and trafficked children. It mandates that in all actions concerning children the best interests of the child must be a primary consideration. The principle is cited numerously in supplementary materials to the Protocols.[64] Importantly, non-rights-based considerations, including those relating to migration control, should not displace the best interests of a child.[65]

The CRC grants children a number of rights, including rights to healthcare and education.[66] Articles 32 and 34, respectively, oblige states parties to protect children from economic and sexual exploitation, while Article 37(b) mandates that states parties only place children in detention as a last resort, and only for the shortest appropriate period of time.[67] Pertinently, deterrence of migrant smuggling is not a legitimate purpose

---

see also United Nations Committee on the Rights of the Child, *General Comment No. 6 (2005): Treatment of Unaccompanied and Separated Children Outside their Country of Origin*, 39th Sess., UN Doc. CRC/GC/2005/6 (1 September 2005), p. 21.

62 *Ibid.* 21.

63 See UNHCR, *Guidelines on International Protection*, n. 61 above, para. [1].

64 See, e.g., *Legislative Guides*, above n. 13, at 289–90; UNODC, *Model Law Against Smuggling of Migrants*, above n. 27, at 70.

65 United Nations Committee on the Rights of the Child, *General Comment No. 6 (2005)*, above n. 61, para. [85]; see also UNHCR, *UNHCR Guidelines on Determining the Best Interests of the Child* (UNHCR, 2008), p. 76.

66 CRC, Arts 24, 28.

67 See also ICCPR, Art. 9(1).

for the detention of children.[68] The CRC also includes an implicit non-refoulement obligation in Article 37, where there is a risk children would be 'subjected to torture or to cruel, inhuman or degrading treatment or punishment'.[69] Importantly, all the rights in the CRC must be applied without discrimination, including discrimination based on a child's migration status.[70]

7. CONSEQUENCES AND CONCLUSIONS

On the surface, it appears that the Smuggling of Migrants Protocol and, in particular, the Trafficking in Persons Protocol provide an extensive web of protection mechanisms that build on and, in some cases, expand protections provided to smuggled and trafficked children under other international human rights treaties. A closer look, however, reveals that the Protocols do little more than restate the status quo. The protection of the rights of smuggled migrants and victims of trafficking, including children, is little more than an afterthought of international law and a matter that is frequently overlooked in national laws and by national agencies.

Whilst the Smuggling of Migrants Protocol suggests that states parties 'shall take' appropriate steps to provide basic assistance and protect the fundamental human rights of smuggled migrants, relevant provisions in the Protocol are not mandatory. It is left to states' discretion to provide assistance and protection as they consider appropriate.[71] This rather vague, discretionary approach to assistance and protection of smuggled migrants is reflective of the Protocol's criminal justice focus.[72] The Protocol primarily serves a criminal justice purpose through criminalizing the smuggling of migrants and establishing a system to

---

68 See, e.g., UNHCR, *Detention Guidelines: Guidelines on the Applicable Criteria and Standards relating to the Detention of Asylum-Seekers and Alternatives to Detention* (UNHCR, 2012), p. 7.

69 See also ICCPR, Arts 6 and 7. It has also been argued that Art. 3 of the CRC contains an implicit non-refoulement obligation. See, e.g., J. McAdam, *Complementary Protection in International Refugee Law* (Oxford University Press, 2006); J. Pobjoy, 'The Best Interests of the Child Principle as an Independent Source of International Protection' (2015) 64(2) *International and Comparative Law Quarterly* 327.

70 CRC, Art. 2(1).

71 Smuggling of Migrants Protocol, Art. 16(3).

72 S. Pickering, 'Transnational Crime and Refugee Protection' (2007) 34(2) *Social Justice* 47, at 52.

facilitate the prosecution of perpetrators. The Protocol does not view smuggled migrants as victims of this crime and deliberately avoids using such terminology.[73] As a result, measures relating to the protection and assistance of smuggled migrants are only marginally developed. The special causes, conditions and circumstances of smuggling of migrant children, many of them unaccompanied, are not recognized in the Protocol and children are not given any special protection. Tom Obokata further remarks that the Protocol fails to recognize the human rights aspects of migrant smuggling, and that it shows little regard for 'political, social and economic solutions' to the problem.[74] The protection mechanisms for victims of trafficking in persons, including children, in the Trafficking in Persons Protocol are more elaborate and far-reaching, but the actual treatment, accommodation and detention of trafficked children in many countries casts doubt over the practical implementation of these mechanisms.

An analysis of the two Protocols shows that in international law smuggling and trafficking of migrant children is seen primarily as a criminal justice problem. Most domestic responses to these phenomena also show that states are generally more concerned about stopping and deterring irregular migration than protecting the rights of children who may have endured considerable suffering, trauma and exploitation. By failing to recognize them as victims of their smugglers, smuggled migrants are commoditized as objects of this offence, a point that is also reflected in the language of Article 5 of the Smuggling of Migrants Protocol.[75] To this end, migrant smuggling is conceptualized in the same way as offences such as drug trafficking and arms smuggling, which involve the illicit transfer of contraband across international borders, without adequately recognizing the vulnerability and frequent exploitation of smuggled migrants.[76] While many official sources acknowledge that the division between smuggling and trafficking is often unclear and shifting,[77] the Smuggling

---

[73] *Travaux Préparatoires*, n. 17 above, p. 461; cf. Obokata, 'The Legal Framework on Immigration Control at Sea', n. 17 above, at 151, 164.

[74] T. Obokata, 'Smuggling of Human Beings from a Human Rights Perspective: Obligations of Non-State and State Actors under International Human Rights Law' (2005) 17(2) *International Journal of Refugee Law* 394, at 414–15.

[75] Smuggling of Migrants Protocol, Art. 5 states: 'Migrants shall not become liable to criminal prosecution under this Protocol for the fact of having been the *object* of conduct set forth in Article 6 of this Protocol' (emphasis added).

[76] Pickering, 'Transnational Crime and Refugee Protection', above n. 74, at 48.

[77] See, e.g., UNODC, *A Short Introduction to Smuggling of Migrants*, above n. 10, at 6; F. David, *Human Smuggling and Trafficking: An Overview of the Response at a Federal Level* (Australian Institute of Criminology, 2000), pp. 9–10.

of Migrants Protocol deliberately omits the extensive protection and assistance provisions included in the Trafficking in Persons Protocol.

Despite the clear prioritization of the criminalization of smuggling of migrants and trafficking in persons, there is a growing body of literature that attempts to construct and assess the two Protocols against a human rights framework, often drawing on the international protection principles for asylum-seekers and refugees to highlight the Protocols' inadequacies insofar as the assistance and protection of smuggled and trafficked migrants are concerned.[78] In reality, there is often little difference between the experiences of smuggled migrants and victims of trafficking in persons. This justifies calls to equate the protection of smuggled migrants accordingly, by offering smuggled migrants assistance with 'return and reintegration and medical, psychological, counselling and legal support'.[79]

There has been, and continues to be, little support by the international community for a stronger human rights focus in official responses to migrant smuggling. Some authors also argue that more extensive, mandatory protection and assistance measures in the Smuggling of Migrants Protocol would deter countries from signing and ratifying this instrument.[80] The lack of support for a 'comprehensive international human rights treaty in the field of migration'[81] is similarly evidenced by the International Convention on the Protection of the Rights of All Migrant Workers and Members of their Families.[82] This treaty was first opened for signature on 18 December 1990, but it took over 12 years to find the

[78] See, e.g., A.T. Gallagher, 'Human Rights and the New UN Protocols on Trafficking and Migrant Smuggling: A Preliminary Analysis' (2001) 23 *Human Rights Quarterly* 975; C. Brolan, 'An Analysis of the Human Smuggling Trade and Protocol Against the Smuggling of Migrants by Land, Sea and Air (2000) from a Refugee Protection Perspective' (2003) 14(4) *International Journal of Refugee Law* 561; E. Feller, 'Asylum, Migration and Refugee Protection: Realities, Myths and the Promise of Things to Come' (2006) 18(3–4) *International Journal of Refugee Law* 509; Pickering, 'Transnational Crime and Refugee Protection', above n. 74, at 47; Obokata, 'Smuggling of Human Beings from a Human Rights Perspective', n. 74 above, at 394; Obokata, 'The Legal Framework on Immigration Control at Sea', n. 17 above, at 151.

[79] S. Haque, 'Ambiguities and Confusions in the Migration-Trafficking Nexus: A Development Challenge' in K. Beeks and D. Amir (eds), *Trafficking and the Global Sex Industry* (Lexington Books, 2006), pp. 3, 10.

[80] Gallagher, 'Human Rights and Human Trafficking: Quagmire or Firm Ground?', n. 78 above, at 793.

[81] A. Pécoud, 'The UN Convention on Migrant Workers' Rights and International Migration Management' (2009) 23(3) *Global Society* 333.

[82] Opened for signature 18 December 1990, UNTS 2220 (entered into force 1 July 2003).

necessary 20 signatories for this Convention to enter into force on 1 July 2003.[83] Even today, over 27 years since its creation, the Convention lacks ratification by a number of major receiving nations.

The dramatic pictures of smuggled migrants drowning at sea, of bodies of dead children washing up at the shore, and of many children undertaking long and arduous journeys to reach countries in which they seek protection, safety, or simply a better life show the hardship and dangers smuggled and trafficked children frequently have to endure. With thousands of migrants, many of them children, dying on their quest to find a safer life and better existence abroad, and many other children suffering sexual or labour exploitation at the hands of smugglers and traffickers, there is an urgent need to develop better and more comprehensive international frameworks to protect the rights of migrant children.

---

[83] United Nations Treaty Collections, *Status of Treaties: International Convention on the Protection of the Rights of All Migrant Workers and Members of their Families* (30 August 2011), available at http://treaties.un.org/pages/Treaties.aspx?id=4&subid=A&lang=en.

7. Immigration control and the best interests of the child in Europe

Carmelo Danisi (with Mary Crock)*

1. ONE REGION, TWO SYSTEMS OF HUMAN RIGHTS PROTECTION

Issues around migration control featured strongly in the domestic and regional politics within the European Union (EU) in 2016. The United Kingdom's decision to withdraw from the EU is a stark example of the prevailing mood in the region. In the attempt to answer criticisms, the EU itself opted for controversial solutions.[1] These contrast sharply with the 'constitutional' principles of the EU legal order, including rights and freedoms as protected by the European Convention on Human Rights.[2]

The number of children on the move in the EU region is without historical precedent. In theory, these children should enjoy protections as rich as anywhere in the world. European laws promote the realization of children's best interests as a guiding principle, drawing on the full catalogue of rights enshrined in the UN Convention on the Rights of the Child (CRC).[3] In reality, European practices have often been based on minimum standards of protection with a focus on specific (often procedural) rights.

Europe as a region is unusual if not unique in the legal structures developed to influence the way countries behave. Europe was the crucible of two World Wars, but also the birthplace of the Convention relating to the Status of Refugees[4] and of the Universal Declaration of Human Rights

---

* This chapter was written substantially by Carmelo Danisi. Mary Crock assisted with English expression and editing for meaning.

[1] See, e.g., European Council Press Release, *EU-Turkey Statement*, 144/16 (18 March 2016) discussed further below.

[2] European Convention for the Protection of Human Rights and Fundamental Freedoms, opened for signature 4 November 1950, ETS No. 5 (entered into force 3 September 1953).

[3] Convention on the Rights of the Child, adopted 20 November 1989, 1577 UNTS 3 (entered into force 2 September 1990) (CRC).

[4] Convention relating to the Status of Refugees, adopted 28 July 1951, 189

upon which the modern human rights regime is constructed.[5] Countries within Europe have become party to various international human rights Conventions. However, they have also created regional governance structures which include courts and common policy Directives in matters relevant to protecting human rights. These give substance to international instruments that have remained rather aspirational in countries and regions with no enforcement mechanisms.

This chapter examines the two systems operating in Europe to protect human rights: the Council of Europe and the EU. Considering the limited academic consideration of the issues, I will explore how notions of the best interests of the child have been embedded in the Council of Europe and EU's frameworks, using the Refugee Convention and the CRC as a base. I draw on rulings by the two European judicial bodies: the European Court of Human Rights (ECtHR) and the Court of Justice of the EU (CJEU). However imperfect the system, the variety of measures adopted at national and supranational levels show that European legal frameworks do provide something of a life-belt for migrant children, including those moving between EU countries. Section 2 begins with an overview of the protective structures established by the Council of Europe and the EU. Sections 3 and 4 explore in greater detail how the two systems have and have not protected migrant children. The chapter concludes with discussion of issues affecting the operation of Europe's two-part human rights regime.

2. THE COUNCIL OF EUROPE AND THE EU: TWO COMPLEMENTARY SYSTEMS

When a migrant child arrives in Europe, two systems of protection (based on the principle of 'subsidiarity') come into play within different regional institutions. I will examine in turn the operation of the Council of Europe and relevant structures within the European Union.

2.1 Council of Europe

The Council of Europe (CoE) was founded in 1949 to promote the rule of law and respect for human rights. With 47 members, the Council

---

UNTS 137 (entered into force 22 April 1954) and the attendant Protocol relating to the Status of Refugees, adopted 31 January 1967, 606 UNTS 267 (entered into force 4 October 1967) (the 'Refugee Convention').

[5] Universal Declaration of Human Rights, GA Res. 217A (III), UN GAOR, 3rd Sess., 183rd Plen Mtg, UN Doc. A/810 (10 December 1948).

has greater state coverage than the EU but less real power.[6] Its signal achievements were the conclusion of the European Convention on Human Rights (ECHR) and the establishment of the ECtHR which operates as an enforcement mechanism.[7] The ECtHR plays a key role in interpreting the ECHR, a 'living instrument'[8] that can be adapted to meet the human rights challenges attending recent mass migration flows from Africa and Asia. The Council's member states have all ratified the ECHR. Access to the ECtHR extends to 'any person, non-governmental organisation or group of individuals' claiming to be victim of a violation of the Convention's rights.[9] Only violations attributable to states parties may be referred to the court.[10] The ECtHR cannot examine acts or omissions of supranational European entities giving rise to an alleged breach of the ECHR unless these entities are parties to the Convention. This includes the EU itself, which in 2016 was still negotiating access to the ECHR.[11]

The ECHR is complemented by Additional Protocols safeguarding 'second generation rights' which have the same application *ratione personae* as the ECHR.

The Council of Europe also promoted the conclusion of a European Social Charter (ESC), which established the ESC Committee to adjudicate violations of protected rights.[12] Article 17 of this Charter creates a specific right in children and young persons to 'social, legal and economic

---

[6] The Council includes every state situated in the European geographical continent, except Belarus and the Vatican City State. Comparators are the Organisation for American States (OAS) in the Americas and the African Union (AU) in Africa.

[7] European Convention for the Protection of Human Rights and Fundamental Freedoms.

[8] Among others, *V* v. *United Kingdom*, ECtHR App. No. 24888/94 (16 December 1999).

[9] See Art. 34. An inter-state mechanism is also in place (Art. 33) but is rarely used.

[10] In terms of actions, omissions or combinations of both: see *Draft Articles on Responsibility of States for Internationally Wrongful Acts*, UN GA Res. A/56/10, in (2001) 11(2) *Yearbook of the International Law Commission*. The evolution of the concept of jurisdiction (Art. 1 ECHR) has been fundamental to protecting migrants arriving by sea: *Hirsi Jamaa and others* v. *Italy*, ECtHR App. No. 27765/09 (23 February 2012), paras [70]–[82].

[11] Until the EU accedes to the ECHR, the principles guiding the relationship between the EU's own actions and the ECHR are summarized in *Bosphorus* v. *Ireland*, ECtHR App. No. 45036/98 (30 June 2005), paras [155]–[156].

[12] European Social Charter (revised), opened for signature 3 May 1996, ETS No. 163 (entered into force 1 July 1999). The Charter had been ratified by 34 CoE member states in March 2017 (ESC).

protection'. The ESC Committee has affirmed that Article 17 binds states parties to ensure 'the full development of children's personality' through the adoption of 'appropriate' measures. It also protects children 'not lawfully present' on the territory of states parties. The Committee has stated:[13]

> The Charter treats children as individual rights' holders since human dignity inherent in each child fully entitles her/him to all fundamental rights granted to adults. [The] specific situation of children, which combines vulnerability, limited autonomy and potential adulthood, requires States to grant them specific rights, such as those enshrined [in the ESC].

The right to life and rights crucial for human dignity, such as the right to housing, may find protection in the ESC in addition to the ECHR framework.[14]

The Council of Europe has no express authority to regulate matters relating to immigration and refugees. Through its Committee of Ministers and the Parliamentary Assembly, it may only adopt non-binding recommendations for improving, at national level, respect and protection of human rights while controlling migration flows. Having said this, the Parliamentary Assembly of the CoE has taken a keen interest in the plight of unaccompanied children in Europe, elaborating standards to protect such children's rights in the context of migration.[15] It has made recommendations on matters ranging from the living conditions of diverse groups of migrant children;[16] access to guardians and legal assistance in administrative proceedings;[17] the arrival, stay and return of unaccompanied children;[18]

---

[13] *Defence for Children International (DCI)* v. *The Netherlands*, European Committee of Social Rights, Complaint No. 47/2008 (20 October 2009), para. [25]. See also paras [29], [64].

[14] To appreciate the value of this decision, note that, according to Art. 1 of the ESC's Appendix, 'the persons covered by articles 1 to 17 and 20 to 31 include foreigners only in so far as they are nationals of other Parties lawfully resident or working regularly within the territory of the Party concerned'.

[15] For instance, Parliamentary Assembly of the Council of Europe (PACE), *The Alternatives to the Immigration Detention of Children*, Recommendation 2056 (3 October 2014); PACE, *Undocumented Migrant Children in an Irregular Situation*, Recommendation 1985 (7 October 2011); Committee of Ministers, *Council of Europe Strategy for the Rights of the Child* (3 March 2016), especially points 22 and 32. These attempts were all aimed at applying the best interests principle.

[16] See PACE, *Situation of Young Migrants in Europe*, Recommendation 1596 (31 January 2003).

[17] See PACE, *Protection and Assistance for Separated Children Seeking Asylum*, Recommendation 1703 (18 April 2005)

[18] See PACE, *Unaccompanied Children in Europe: Issues of Arrival, Stay*

and the treatment of children transitioning to adulthood.[19] As explored further, litigant migrants have enjoyed some success by invoking the ECHR, arguing that regressive policies and actions breach various human rights.

2.2 European Union

The European Union is an atypical, supranational organization created after World War II with a precise aim.[20] This was to enhance economic cooperation between European countries through the development of a common market. In recent years the project has evolved into a greater (political) union, expanding geographically and in terms of the matters regulated, including migration and human rights protection.[21]

In the 1970s it became clear that implementation of EU law could compromise respect for human rights at national levels. The CJEU stepped in to ensure that EU action was in accordance with human rights standards. This court recognized the ECHR rights as general principles of EU law – parameters of legitimacy for all EU actions. The EU has had its own binding human rights instruments since 2009. Adopted first as a non-binding declaration in 2001, with the entry into force of the Lisbon Treaty, the Charter of Fundamental Rights of the European Union (CFR)[22] was regarded as part of the EU's constitutional documents. While it does not extend the powers of the Union or establish any new power, every piece of EU legislation must align with this Charter. It binds both EU institutions and Member States when they are implementing EU law.

The Charter embraces the human rights regime established by the Council of Europe, yet in some respects introduces a more modern and progressive framework for its rights regime. When they correspond,

---

and Return, Recommendation 1969 (15 April 2011) and PACE, *Unaccompanied Children in Europe: Issues of Arrival, Stay and Return*, Recommendation 1810 (15 April 2011).

[19] See also PACE, *Report on Migrant Children: What Rights at 18?*, Doc. 12678 (30 June 2011). For a discussion of these reports and recommendations, see C. Pelaia, 'The Council of Europe and Unaccompanied Minors' in R. Rosskopf (ed.), *Unaccompanied Minors in International, European and National Law* (BWV, 2016), p. 39.

[20] Among others, see P. Craig and G. de Búrca, *European Union Law: Text, Cases, and Materials* (Oxford University Press, 2015).

[21] Consolidated Version of the Treaty on the European Union and the Treaty on the Functioning of the European Union [2012] OJ C326/01. The Lisbon Treaty provided for the most recent reform of EU founding Treaties.

[22] Proclaimed 7 December 2000, [2000] OJ C326/02 (entered into force 1 December 2009), Art. 51.

Charter rights must be given the same meaning and scope as rights enshrined in the ECHR.[23] Considering post-ECHR changes in European society and scientific/technological developments, the Charter gives expression to a wider catalogue of human rights and freedoms grouped under six key concepts. These are: Dignity, Freedoms, Equality, Solidarity, Citizenship and Justice. It is worth noting that the CFR has introduced at regional level the rights of the child *as autonomous rights* filling an apparent gap in the ECHR system of protection. The decision to introduce Article 24 (on the rights of children) under the 'Equality' Chapter of the Charter has highlighted the 'equal worth' of children as independent human rights bearers. Having the protection of dignity as its cornerstone (Article 1), the Charter requires that children's rights and their best interests must be interpreted, applied and realized as underlying values in all contexts, including migration. The Charter has also expanded the ECHR's reach to include a 'right to asylum' with no limitations of any kind, such as age. The Charter's explanatory document suggests Article 18 reflects EU commitment to respect the Refugee Convention and must be read in light of EU competences in this field.[24] Hence, it should be read as a 'procedural' right that grants to 'anyone' the access to a 'fair' asylum procedure. In contrast, the ECHR contains no explicit provisions related to asylum, and certainly not a right to asylum per se.[25] Within the ECHR system, protection has been granted through more general provisions, e.g. the right to life, the prohibition of torture and cruel and degrading treatment, the prohibition of refoulement and the right to an effective remedy. The consequences for migrant child are explored below.

EU competences in the field of migration and asylum are governed by the founding Treaties – the Treaty on the European Union (TEU) and the Treaty on the Functioning of the European Union (TFEU). Both entered into force in 2009 and empower the EU to legislate with respect to specific aspects of immigration.[26] Among the EU's most important initiatives are laws and policies governing the movement of 'third country nationals' (TCNs) in the context of migration and asylum. Two separate frameworks with internal *and* external dimensions were created in line with the European Commission's 'Global Approach to Migration and Mobility'. These include

---

23 *Ibid.* Art. 52.

24 *Explanations relating to the Charter of Fundamental Rights* [2007] OJ C303/02.

25 Among others, *VM and others* v. *Belgium*, ECtHR App. No. 60125/11 (July 2015), para. [130].

26 See Treaty on the Functioning of the European Union, Art. 78 ff.

different regulatory instruments. Unlike national law and policies, they only cover matters where EU action will deliver better results (at Union level).

This complex system reflects a long process that has allowed the EU to broaden its competences, changing deeply the cooperation of European states in these fields. Its origin can be traced to the Schengen Agreement, concluded in 1985 between central European states (Germany, France, Belgium, the Netherlands and Luxembourg) which created an area for the free movement of people. Controls over people moving across common borders were gradually eliminated. Then, rules for the control over people entering in this area were defined through a common visa policy and the systematic exchange of data. As other European states joined the Schengen area, this intergovernmental cooperation was eventually incorporated into the EU legal framework by the Treaty of Amsterdam, amending the EU's founding Treaties in 1997. Since the entry into force of the Amsterdam Treaty, the original Schengen Agreement has been revised and new common rules have been made to achieve the same original aims. Interestingly, not all EU Member States decided to participate in the Schengen arrangements within this new framework. For example, the United Kingdom cooperates only to a certain extent. In contrast, other European states that are not members of the EU have joined the Schengen area (i.e. Iceland, Norway, Liechtenstein and Switzerland).

In line with the Schengen system, the new TFEU aims to create in the Union an 'area of freedom, security and justice' which, while safeguarding freedom of movement for EU citizens, 'should be fair towards TCNs'. Although the meaning of 'fair' is disputable, it seems to indicate that *at least* this area should guarantee that TCNs' human rights will be protected, including in the context of external border control. The TFEU empowers the Council and the European Parliament to discuss and jointly adopt proposals for Directives or Regulations elaborated by the European Commission. This process has produced two complementary 'policies': a general common immigration policy and a more specific common asylum policy.

The common regulatory instruments are mostly known as Directives. First are those defining conditions for the legal entry and stay of TCNs within the EU. The greatest protections are given to highly qualified TCNs. Relevant Directives also provide baseline rules for the integration or treatment of TCNs residing legally in Member States.[27] Second, special

[27] See Council Directive 2009/50/EC of 25 May 2009 on the conditions of entry and residence of third-country nationals for the purposes of highly qualified employment [2009] OJ L155/17; Council Directive 2011/98/EU of 13 December 2011 on a single application procedure for a single permit for third-country nationals to reside and work in the territory of a Member State and on a common

attention is given to measures to combat illegal immigration. The Return Directive outlines safeguards and procedures that Member States must respect when returning TCNs who are not entitled to stay in the EU, for example because their visa has expired.[28] Readmission agreements have been concluded to fast-track the repatriation of irregular migrants from certain countries. Through this policy, the EU is increasingly committed to the fight against human trafficking. While this may include broader transnational cooperation with non-EU countries and other international organizations, a specific Directive provides an internal framework for dealing with victims of trafficking, including women and children.[29] Relying on vulnerability as a rationale for intervention, the Directive includes several safeguards to ensure children's physical and psycho-social recovery.

Despite its name, the EU's Common European Asylum System (CEAS) is far from a comprehensive framework. Grounded in the 1951 Refugee Convention, the CEAS aims to achieve common treatment of asylum-seekers within EU Member States.[30] After its recast, this System consists mainly of the following EU secondary legislation: the Dublin Regulation,[31] the Reception Directive,[32] the Procedures Directive[33] and the Qualification

---

set of rights for third-country workers legally residing in a Member State [2011] OJ L343/1; and Council Directive 2003/109/EC of 25 November 2003 concerning the status of third-country nationals who are long-term residents [2004] OJ L16/44 (modified to apply also to refugees).

28 Council Directive 2008/115/EC of 16 December 2008 on common standards and procedures in member states for returning illegally staying third-country nationals [2008] OJ L348/98 ('Return Directive').

29 Directive 2011/36/EU of the European Parliament and of the Council of 5 April 2011 on preventing and combating trafficking in human beings and protecting its victims, and replacing Council Framework Decision 2002/629/JHA [2011] OJ L101/1.

30 See C. Costello, *The Human Rights of Migrants and Refugees in European Law* (OUP, 2016) and on children, C. Smyth, *European Asylum Law and the Rights of the Child* (Routledge, 2014).

31 Regulation (EU) 604/2013 of the European Parliament and of the Council of 26 June 2013 establishing the criteria and mechanisms for determining the Member State responsible for examining an application for international protection lodged in one of the Member States by a third-country national or a stateless person [2013] OJ L180/31, arts 2(j), 4, 6, 8. Together with the EURODAC Regulation, this is the only CEAS Act adopted through a Regulation. Directly applicable within EU Member States, this legislative tool promotes greater uniformity in the EU compared with Directives.

32 Directive 2013/33/EU of the European Parliament and of the Council of 26 June 2013 laying down standards for the reception of applicants for international protection [2013] OJ L180/96 ('Reception Directive').

33 Directive 2013/32/EU of the European Parliament and of the Council of

Directive.[34] The Dublin Regulation has evolved from the 1990 Dublin Convention, the first international instrument concluded to regulate the responsibility of EU states to evaluate asylum requests. Included in the EU legal framework after the EU was given power in this field, this Regulation prevents asylum-seekers from forum shopping between EU states. It sets out criteria that identify relationships between the asylum-seeker and the European state which will be responsible for examining a protection request. All applicants are fingerprinted upon arrival in one of the 'Dublin Regulation' states. No exceptions are made for children.[35] The three Directives contain rules for the treatment of asylum-seekers and status determination processes. After arrival, the Reception Directive sets out minimum standards for the reception of asylum-seekers. These refer mostly to basic needs such as housing and healthcare with specific attention paid to detention. As for status determination, the CEAS includes minimum procedural rules for evaluating each request for international protection. In theory, TCNs have rights to a fair asylum decision, including at the borders, within a reasonable period (six months). Finally, the Qualification Directive aims to guide national authorities in the application of the Refugee Convention, establishing who is a refugee and the rights associated to this status. Rights include a renewable three-year residence permit; access to education and training, social assistance and healthcare under the same conditions as the state's nationals; and access to integration programmes. The Qualification Directive introduces an additional form of international protection. When an applicant cannot qualify as refugee but, nonetheless, has a reasonable fear of serious abuses

---

26 June 2013 on common procedures for granting and withdrawing international protection [2013] OJ L180/60 ('Procedures Directive').

[34] Directive 2011/95/EU of the European Parliament and of the Council of 13 December 2011 on standards for the qualification of third-country nationals or stateless persons as beneficiaries of international protection, for a uniform status for refugees or for persons eligible for subsidiary protection, and for the content of the protection granted [2011] OJ L337/9 ('Qualification Directive').

[35] See Regulation (EU) 603/2013 of the European Parliament and of the Council of 26 June 2013 on the establishment of EURODAC for the comparison of fingerprints for the effective application of Regulation (EU) 604/2013 establishing the criteria and mechanisms for determining the Member State responsible for examining an application for international protection. This also amended Regulation (EU) 1077/2011, establishing a European Agency for the operational management of large-scale IT systems in the area of freedom, security and justice. See [2013] OJ L180/1 ('EURODAC Regulation'). All EU Member States, including the United Kingdom, are bound by the Dublin Regulation together with Iceland, Norway, Switzerland and Liechtenstein.

in the country of origin, he/she may be granted subsidiary protection with the recognition of a (limited) number of rights.

All legislative acts can be examined by the CJEU, which oversees compliance with the EU founding Treaties. Most importantly, the preliminary ruling procedure enables national courts to question the CJEU on the interpretation or validity of EU secondary law when they have specific concerns about potential human rights violations resulting from the national implementation of EU law.[36] This mechanism guarantees uniform application of EU law in all Member States. The CJEU can indicate what interpretative solutions are most consistent with the EU legal order and its fundamental rights standards. As explored below, this role has proved critical in realizing the best interests of the child in migration and asylum contexts.

Through this comprehensive framework, the EU is progressively implementing its motto 'An open and secure Europe serving and protecting citizens'.[37] 'Open' should be read as absence of internal controls, with advantages for those already residing lawfully in EU territory. 'Secure' implies strong external border controls with adverse consequences for all outsiders, especially those who cannot articulate a need for international protection at EU borders. In this respect, there has been a gradual change from local interventions to a more comprehensive migration strategy. The EU's role in this field has grown, as the 2015 European Commission Communication 'A European Agenda on Migration' demonstrates.[38] This policy document identifies four pillars for the adoption of new measures. These are aimed first at reducing incentives for irregular migration through cooperation with immigrants' countries of origin and the fight against smugglers and traffickers. The second pillar relates to border management. In the Commission's plan, the EU seems to move from emergency interventions, often connected with mass immigration flows in the Mediterranean, to more stable operations to be used inter alia for saving lives. A direct consequence is the reinforcement of the European Border and Coast Guard Agency, FRONTEX. This operates through operations to return irregular immigrants and the coordination of EU and non-EU states' activities in sea, land and air surveillance to control irregular

---

[36] See Treaty on the Functioning of the European Union, Art. 267.

[37] The Stockholm Programme: An Open and Secure Europe Serving and Protecting Citizens [2010] OJ C115/1.

[38] European Commission, *Communication from the Commission: The European Agenda on Migration*, COM(2015)240 final (13 May 2015); European Commission, *Communication from the Commission: A New Partnership Framework with Third Countries*, COM(2016)385 final (7 July 2016).

migration flows.[39] The third pillar is focused on a stronger common asylum policy, through reform of existing rules and the establishment of Reception and Identification Centers. The 'Hotspot system' is designed to assist frontline Member States, such as Greece and Italy, to quickly identify, register and fingerprint incoming migrants. The general intention is to speed the process of identification. In practical terms, this means that the EU will support states in two ways. First, to detect irregular migrants and return them, with the involvement of FRONTEX; and second to channel those in need of international protection to status determination processes, with the help of the European Asylum Support Office. The fourth pillar is aimed at establishing new policies on legal migration. Here, focus is placed on attracting skilled workers to Europe, and assuring social cohesion and integration. It is no coincidence that the only references to children in this agenda are to children in need of international protection and, more generally, those involved in the asylum policy. As explored in section 4, the migrant child's interests are mostly defined by the CEAS.

3. ECHR AND THE MIGRANT CHILD

Although the CoE and the EU fulfil different roles within Europe, they are based on the same values: the rule of law; the promotion of peace; and respect and protection of human rights. For migrant children, the two European systems are guided by similar, sometimes complementary, considerations. In this and the following section I examine how this complex framework works to realize the best interests of the child. It is worth stressing that all EU Member States have ratified the ECHR. Therefore, within their jurisdictions, both EU law (including the Charter) and the ECHR apply and must be respected. Those European countries that are not part of the EU are bound only by the ECHR. This will be the case for the United Kingdom as soon as the process of withdrawing from the EU Treaties is completed.

The absence of provisions protecting children's rights did not stop the ECtHR from acknowledging developments within the universal human rights system. As all CoE's member states have ratified the CRC, the ECtHR concluded that the obligations imposed by the ECHR must be interpreted in light of the CRC.[40] Hence, in every case involving a child,

---

[39] On human rights implications, see PACE, *Frontex: Human Rights Responsibilities*, Resolution 1932 (2013).

[40] See Vienna Convention on the Law of Treaties, opened for signature 23 May 1969, 1155 UNTS 331 (entered into force 27 January 1980), Art. 31.3(c).

the Court has stressed that the best interests of the child should be a primary consideration as well as the CRC's underlying values.[41] The ECtHR has acknowledged that the concept of best interests does not have a unique or static meaning. In *Jeunesse* v. *The Netherlands*, it affirmed: '[w]hilst alone [best interests] cannot be decisive, such interests certainly must be afforded significant weight'.[42]

Considering the subsidiary nature of the ECHR system, the Court's role is focused on determining whether national authorities have given 'appropriate' weight to the best interests of the child. What is 'appropriate' will turn on the circumstances of each case. In asylum and migration cases, the ECtHR has stated generally that 'children have specific needs that are related in particular to their age and lack of independence, but also to their asylum-seeker status'.[43] In accordance with the CRC, states parties are thus called to ensure that a child seeking asylum enjoys protection and humanitarian assistance, irrespective of the fact that he/she is alone, separated from or accompanied by any family members. As I explore in the following sections, the Court has developed principles to guide a best interests' assessment in migratory contexts.

3.1 Prohibition of Torture and the Right to Non-Refoulement

As noted, the ECHR comes into play most frequently through Article 3 which protects in absolute terms the migrant child against torture and/or cruel and degrading treatment, and the risk of refoulement.[44] This provision has always been given a 'dynamic' interpretation. To fall within Article 3, treatment must attain a minimum level of severity. However, the assessment of this minimum has always been deemed relative. Not only are the duration and physical or mental effects of harmful actions considered, but also the age, sex and state of health of the alleged victim. When child asylum-seekers are involved, the Court has stressed their vulnerability due to the 'particularly underprivileged' situation they face.[45]

---

[41] Among others, *Neulinger and Shuruk* v. *Switzerland*, ECtHR (GC) App. No. 41615/07 (6 July 2010), para. [135].

[42] *Jeunesse* v. *The Netherlands*, ECtHR (GC) App. No. 12738/10 (3 October 2014), para. [118].

[43] *Mubilanzila Mayeka and Kaniki Mitunga* v. *Belgium*, ECtHR App. No. 13178/03 (12 October 2006), para. [55]; *Popov* v. *France*, ECtHR App. Nos 39472/07, 39474/07 (19 January 2012), para. [91].

[44] Among others, D. Harris et al., *Law of the European Convention on Human Rights* (OUP, 2014), ch. 6.

[45] The concept of vulnerability has been recently developed by the ECtHR to address minorities' rights in light of a more robust idea of equality: see

All these considerations have led to the conclusion, in the *Tarakhel* decision that, for the purpose of Article 3 of the ECHR, when a migrant child is under the control of a state party, his/her vulnerability is 'the decisive factor which takes precedence over considerations relating to the status of illegal immigrant'.[46] The implication for CoE member states in relation to the 'appropriate' weight to be given to the interests of the involved child is immediate. When balanced with other rights and interests, for example, the right to control borders, children's special needs should prevail in principle. When a child is involved, a lower level of severity is required to identify a treatment as falling within the scope of Article 3 of the ECHR.

The *Tarakhel* decision demonstrates how these general 'guidelines' operate. This case concerned the implementation of the Dublin Regulation. It is unusual for a EU Member State to be found in breach of the non-refoulement principle in sending an asylum-seeker to another European state. It has happened only in very exceptional circumstances.[47] However, when children are involved, the consideration of their best interests leads the 'exceptional' to be applied as the 'ordinary' rule. So, when Switzerland wanted to move six Afghan children, with their parents, to Italy as the European state responsible for examining their asylum request, the ECtHR found the transfer decision unlawful because 'appropriate' weight had not been given to the children's best interests. The Swiss authorities had relied on a 'general presumption' that Italy would have protected the Afghan children but no evidence was provided of specific guarantees in case the children were returned to Italy.

Article 3 of the ECHR read with the CRC requires that relocation of children be based on specific analysis of the conditions of transfer, reception and asylum procedures in the receiving country. Transfer will only be lawful if the conditions in the country of destination are adapted to children seeking asylum having regard to the children's age, levels of stress and anxiety and the need to keep their family together. Best interests' assessments must include specific and consistent assurances which national authorities should request and receive.[48]

L. Peroni and A. Timmer, 'Vulnerable Groups: The Promise of an Emerging Concept in European Human Rights Convention Law' (2013) 11(4) *International Constitutional Law Journal* 1056.

[46] *Tarakhel* v. *Switzerland*, ECtHR (GC) App. No. 29217/12 (4 November 2014), para. [99].

[47] *MSS* v. *Belgium and Greece*, ECtHR (GC) App. No. 30696/09 (21 January 2011).

[48] In all subsequent cases related to transferrals of asylum-seekers to Italy, the ECtHR found differently because no children were involved: see *AS* v.

3.2 Right to Personal Security and Liberty

The second provision of significance to migrant children is Article 5 of the ECHR which prohibits arbitrary interference with children's right to liberty. The Convention does allow states parties to detain irregular migrants for the purpose of their expulsion (see Article 5(1)(f)). However, this does not mean that states parties are free to detain migrants. *Khlaifia and others* v. *Italy* reaffirmed that any deprivation of liberty of migrants must be 'in accordance with a procedure prescribed by law' and deportation or extradition proceedings must be in progress.[49] If such proceedings are not prosecuted with due diligence, or if less severe measures are available and are found sufficient to protect public interest, detention will cease to be permissible under the ECHR.

For migrant children, the ECtHR has adopted a more restrictive interpretation of Article 5(1)(f). Having regard to the best interests principle, it has ruled that the 'automatic' application of a national law allowing deprivation of liberty of migrant children cannot comply with Articles 3 and 37 of the CRC. A few examples serve to illustrate this point.

In *Rahimi* v. *Greece*, an unaccompanied boy child from Afghanistan alleged that he was unlawfully detained by Greece. The Greek authorities argued that the boy's rights were respected because he was being held in anticipation of expulsion from the country. The ECtHR accepted that Article 5(1)(f) applied to children in principle. However, it found that when a child is involved, national authorities must demonstrate that alternative measures to detention are not available and that the expulsion cannot be achieved without detention. For the ECtHR, this 'extraordinarily hard test' is necessary to ensure that children's best interests prevail over the circumstance that they are irregularly present in the state's territory.[50]

Although this interpretation of the ECHR does not place an absolute ban on the detention of migrant children, two points should be made. First, this unusual test is applied for both unaccompanied children and those who arrive in Europe with a family member. In *Popov* v. *France*, the detention prior to expulsion of two children along with their parents was deemed not to be a measure of last resort, resulting in a breach of

---

Switzerland, ECtHR App. No. 39350/13 (30 June 2015); *AME* v. *The Netherlands*, ECtHR App. No. 51428/10 (13 January 2015).

49 *Khlaifia and others* v. *Italy*, ECtHR App. No. 16483/12 (1 September 2015), paras [60]–[65].

50 *Rahimi* v. *Greece*, ECtHR App. No. 8687/08 (5 July 2011), para. [108]; *Neulinger and Shuruk* v. *Switzerland*, above n. 41, para. [135].

the ECHR.[51] Second, the ECtHR also operates to protect the migrant child against arbitrary detention through the prohibition of torture. In *Kanagaratnam and others* v. *Belgium*, the consequences of detention on children's personal development was held to raise issues under Article 3 of the ECHR.[52] Hence, in a number of subsequent cases brought against France, the ECtHR found three factors critical to determining whether the detention of children amounts to torture or inhuman or degrading treatment contrary to Article 3 of the ECHR. These are: the age of the child; the duration of the detention; and the conditions in the holding centre. In all cases, the Court found that, despite the short duration of the detention (from four days to three weeks) and the presence of their parents, all involved children suffering anxiety and distress due to the cumulative effects of deprivation of liberty, the presence of security forces, participation in their parent's interviews and noise and disruption from the airport close to the centre.[53] This interpretation is particularly welcomed because, unlike Article 5, Article 3 does not provide for any limitations.

3.3 Additional Guarantees: Right to an Effective Remedy and Interim Measures

Two other aspects of the ECHR warrant mention in the context of migrant children. Article 13 of the ECHR provides for a right to an 'effective' remedy, while Article 39 of the internal Rules of the ECtHR allows for the institution of 'interim measures'.[54] Both have immediate relevance for migrant children because of the Court's affirmation that special considerations apply for such children.

In *Rahimi*, the ECtHR examined the remedies available to children during their stay in Greece. It ruled that the nominal provision of information (in the form of a leaflet) and assistance to unaccompanied minors was in breach of Article 13 of the ECHR.[55] Although Greece faced a crisis,

---

51 *Popov* v. *France*, above n. 43, para. [119].

52 *Kanagaratnam and others* v. *Belgium*, ECtHR App. No. 15297/09 (13 December 2011), para. [68].

53 See *AB and others* v. *France*, ECtHR App. No. 11593/12 (12 July 2016); *RK and others* v. *France,* ECtHR App. No. 68264/14 (12 July 2016); *RM and others* v. *France,* ECtHR App. No. 33201/11 (12 July 2016); and *RC and VC v. France*, ECtHR App. No. 76491/14 (12 July 2016).

54 See Court Registry, European Court of Human Rights, Rules of Court (14 November 2016), available at www.echr.coe.int/Documents/Rules_Court_ENG.pdf.

55 *Rahimi* v. *Greece*, above n. 50, paras [120]–[121].

the ECtHR found that when formal guarantees are granted but cannot be effectively enjoyed by migrant children, the ECHR is breached.

The same reasoning may be applied to migrant children attempting to reach Italy through Greece by hiding themselves in commercial boats.[56] Once discovered by Italian border authorities, these children are usually returned quickly to Greece without considering their personal situation. In *Sharifi* v. *Italy and Greece*, the ECtHR affirmed in clear terms that in such situations it is irrelevant whether migrants disembark.[57] When children are placed under the control of the destination country, Article 13 applies. By denying the children access to the asylum procedure or to any other judicial authority, Italian authorities improperly prevent the children from accessing procedural guarantees, especially the *suspension* of their removal orders in light of their vulnerable situation. In fact, when there are reasonable grounds for believing that children would be exposed through their expulsion to torture or inhuman and degrading treatment, Article 13 requires suspension of the removal process.[58]

Children's protection is finally reinforced by Article 39 of the Rules of the Court which allows the ECtHR to make interim orders to protect the interests of applicants, especially when they belong to a vulnerable group. Article 39 is a procedural tool allowing the recognition of a potential specific danger. It would be interesting to see whether the ECtHR might order provisional measures to prevent the transfer of children from an EU country to Turkey in the context of the 2016 EU-Turkey Agreement.[59] This agreement will be explored in the following part.

4. EUROPEAN UNION AND THE MIGRANT CHILD

The post-Lisbon version of the founding Treaties confirms that the EU is fully responsible for protecting migrant children. Article 3 of the TEU refers explicitly to 'the protection of the rights of the child' as one of the EU founding values and primary aims. As the Charter applies to migration and asylum policies, its child-specific provision should guide any related

---

[56] See Human Rights Watch, *Turned Away: Summary Returns of Unaccompanied Migrant Children and Adult Asylum Seekers from Italy to Greece* (2013).

[57] *Sharifi* v. *Italy and Greece*, ECtHR App. No. 16643/09 (21 October 2014).

[58] *De Souza Ribeiro* v. *France*, ECtHR App. No. 22689/07 (13 December 2012), in relation also to the right to respect for private and family life.

[59] See *Mohammadi* v. *Austria*, ECtHR App. No. 71932/12 (3 July 2014), para. [60]; *LM and others* v. *Russia*, ECtHR App. Nos 081/14, 40088/14, 40127/14 (15 October 2015).

action. Reflecting this primary law framework, children are identified as a vulnerable group with special needs.

Although expressed in very general terms, this approach is confirmed in the 2015 'European Agenda on Migration' calling for a more comprehensive (*qua* less sectorial) EU intervention in this area. However, neither this Agenda nor other policy documents call for the integration of child-related provisions in a comprehensive legislative framework to enhance their protection, and their clarity, above current minimum standards.[60]

At EU level, each common policy may nonetheless contain different levels of protection for migrant children. When we move from the general obligation to consider the best interests of the child to the elaboration of concrete solutions in migration control, results may differ. Interestingly, the latest legislative measures in this field are far more sensitive to migrant children's needs. It is the external action that seems more problematic, as the following sections explore.

4.1 Best Interests of the Child as a Substantive Right: Migration and Asylum Policies

Analysed as a comprehensive legislative framework, the EU's common migration and asylum policies show an ambivalent attitude. On the one hand, they characterize the child as vulnerable, setting safeguards for addressing special needs.[61] On the other, they seem to prioritize the child's migration status, with derogations to basic standards permitted and little consideration given to the specific situation of the child. This leads to children being treated as adults in miniature. Interestingly, the factor that seems to dictate which of these two opposing approaches is used will often be determined by the existence of a manifest situation of danger or uncertainty. For unaccompanied minors, their status as children will usually prevail. The same is true for child victims of trafficking or children who request international protection. In all other situations, the general requirement of considering the best interests of the child applies. Most legislation in the comprehensive migration and asylum package use this principle as guide in accordance with the CRC. This means that, when the implementation of EU rules at national level is deemed to have disregarded a child's best interests, it may be challenged before national courts

---

60 See European Commission, *Communication from the Commission to the European Parliament and the Council: The Protection of Children in Migration*, 12 April 2017, COM (2017), 211 final.

61 See, for example, Qualification Directive, Art. 20.

and, indirectly, before the CJEU. In other words, what is included as a guiding principle is to be viewed as a substantive right which the migrant child may enjoy directly.

With the exception of Directives aimed at attracting highly skilled workers, EU migration has a strong control agenda. Attention is paid to the migrant children especially where it is thought that this group may follow illegal channels to reach European shores. That is why the minimum common rules for returning irregular migrants, the Return Directive, sets special standards for vulnerable groups including all children, not only unaccompanied minors.[62] However, these more favourable measures do not extend to an absolute suspension on returning children or to a similar prohibition of detention pending removal. Provided that the principle of non-refoulement is respected, Member States can return an unaccompanied minor to 'a member of his or her family, a nominated guardian or adequate reception facilities in the State of return' (Article 10). No reference is made to the general conditions of the country of return or whether these are suitable for the child's development. Although restricted, detention is allowed for children illegally staying in the EU with the sole proviso that healthcare, education and recreational activities should be provided (Article 17).

A more CRC-based approach is apparent in the Anti-Trafficking Directive. In setting procedural standards to protect and assist the child victim of trafficking, this Directive calls for the elaboration of 'durable solutions'. Significantly, individual assessments must be carried out to determine which solution, including return, resettlement or integration in the Member States' society, would be in the child's best interests (Article 16).

Considering FRONTEX's practical role in returning TCNs, combatting trafficking[63] and, more generally, in external border controls, its legal basis is worthy of comment. Following the standards elaborated by the ECtHR in *Hirsi Jamaa and others* v. *Italy*,[64] it became clear for Member States that, during interception operations, collective expulsion or ill-treatment was unlawful. Individuals intercepted at sea have the right to an effective remedy and the possibility of claiming asylum and to be disembarked at

---

[62] Above n. 28.

[63] See European Border and Coast Guard Agency, FRONTEX Archive of Operations, *Archive of Operations: Joint Operation VEGA Children* (5 October 2015), aimed at 'Combating child trafficking and detection of children at risk on the move at air borders'.

[64] *Hirsi Jamaa and others* v. *Italy* above n. 10, *re* Art. 4 of Protocol 4 on collective expulsions.

a safe harbour. These human rights commitments were made clear in the reform of the Agency in 2016.[65] The 2016 Regulation is less ambivalent, ensuring that interception activities must be compliant with the CRC, as well as with the CFR. This general commitment is translated into practical duties that include: ensuring staff training in child-related issues; involving experts in the field when children are returned; addressing the special needs of children (whether accompanied or not); and laying down procedures for all borders operations intended to guarantee children's rights. Reforms in 2016 mirrored the EU strategy on migration that includes a strong engagement of the Agency in designated 'hotspots'. Considering that the EU has not yet regulated hotspots through separate legislation,[66] the new FRONTEX obligations enhance children's protection in the field.

As for asylum policy, the recast of the CEAS also provided for a stronger human rights framework with special attention to children's rights. It is no coincidence that this result was achieved through the integration of the standards progressively elaborated by the ECtHR and the CJEU.

First, the CEAS clarifies the meaning of the best interests of the child principle. The Procedures Directive states that, in assessing these interests, national authorities should consider the 'minor's well-being and social development, including his or her background'.[67] Although different interpretations are possible, the express reference to the CRC seems to require Member States to consider the rights protected by the UN Convention for identifying which solution best suits the child's development.

Second, with all child asylum-seekers treated as a vulnerable group, a number of procedural and substantial 'accommodations' were introduced. For instance, EU asylum law ensures protection of the migrant child through: the appointment of a representative with appropriate expertise; priority processing of children's claims; the prohibition of expedited hearings at the border or in transit zones, unless specific conditions are satisfied; and child-friendly interviews. Where doubts arise about the age of a child, she or he must be informed and must consent to medical examinations or other inquiries. Although there are no instructions on what method is more appropriate to protect the child, EU asylum law prevents states from using the refusal to undergo medical examination to

---

[65] Regulation (EU) of the European Parliament and of the Council of 14 September 2016 on the European Border and Coastguard [2016] OJ L251/1.

[66] D. Neville, S.S. Sy and A. Rigone, *On the Frontline: The Hotspot Approach to Managing Migration* (EU, 2016).

[67] Procedures Directive, Preamble 33. See also the Qualification Directive, Preamble 18.

deny international protection. Significantly, in line with the CRC, states must also offer appropriate assistance and care during the process. In status determinations, EU law complements Article 1(A) of the Refugee Convention, embracing contemporary understandings of children's rights violations as relevant for protection purposes. Child-specific forms of persecution, such as female genital mutilation, are therefore recognized as the basis of claims by reason of 'membership of a particular social group'.[68]

Notwithstanding this attempt to protect the child, EU minimum standards can fall short. For example, despite the consensus that the best interests of the child principle requires states to avoid detention of migrant children,[69] EU asylum law allows asylum-seeking children to be detained in exceptional circumstances. Unaccompanied minors must never be detained in prison. Yet EU law affirms that 'minors shall be detained only as a measure of last resort and after it having been established that other less coercive alternative measures cannot be applied effectively' (Article 11 of the Reception Directive). In monitoring the implementation of the Reception Directive, the European Commission acknowledged that detention of children is not such an extraordinary measure in some Member States. The Commission's attempts to introduce an absolute prohibition on detaining children were challenged successfully during the CEAS' recast process.[70]

In sum, while EU asylum policy was conceived as providing minimum common standards of protection, its value cannot be underestimated when children are involved. Not all Member States are able to grant the same level of protection, especially for reception conditions. The Refugee Convention is not sufficient considering that it does not contain any provisions on children's protection. Forced to implement the CEAS at national level, Member States are called to give expression to children's best interests. This effort is not only facilitated through *a priori* procedural and substantive standards in the EU 'Geneva-plus scheme'. National

---

68 Qualification Directive, Preamble 28 and Art. 9(2)f.

69 See, e.g., UNHCR, *Guidelines on Determining the Best Interests of the Child* (UNHCR, May 2008); *Rights and Guarantees of Children in the Context of Migration and/or in Need of International Protection* (Advisory Opinion) (Inter-American Court of Human Rights, Advisory Opinion OC-21/14, 19 August 2014).

70 See European Commission, *Proposal for a Directive of the European Parliament and of the Council Laying Down Minimum Standards for the Reception of Asylum Seekers*, COM(2008) 815 final.

authorities may also be supported by the CJEU to give the best interests of the child concrete meaning.

4.2 Best Interests of the Child as an Interpretative Tool: CJEU's Role

The CJEU is not a human rights court and is not 'directly' available to individuals (unlike the ECtHR). However, it has fulfilled a similar role to the ECtHR in practice since the 1970s. After the Lisbon reform, the CJEU acquired full jurisdiction in migration and asylum matters. The Court has worked to ensure that the wide range of exceptions and derogations open to Member States are implemented in accordance with the EU's human rights catalogue.

The CJEU plays a dual role in ensuring realization of the best interests of the child. While the EU has its own Charter of Fundamental Rights, the CJEU must apply the minimum standards of protection set by the ECtHR. The rights and the freedoms protected by the ECHR are considered general principles of EU law. Therefore, in migration and asylum matters, the CJEU indirectly monitors the compliance of the CEAS with the ECHR. This creates a 'common' minimum ground of protection between the two European systems.

At the same time, the CJEU can set higher levels of protection for children by interpreting EU law in line with the CRC. As mentioned, through its preliminary ruling procedure, when a national judge has specific concerns about the violation of children's rights in the implementation of EU law, the CJEU may indicate how legislation is to be interpreted so as to comply with the best interests of the child principle.

A good example is found in the *Queen* case.[71] There, the CJEU found that the Dublin Regulation did not give due consideration to the child's best interests. In its original iteration, the Dublin Regulation provided that, if no family member could be identified in the EU, the asylum request of an unaccompanied minor should be determined in the European state where they first articulated a desire to seek refugee protection. This enabled national authorities to transfer a child from one country to another if he/she was found outside the responsible state. The CJEU ruled that the Dublin Regulation was inconsistent with Article 24 of the CFR. The Court found that the child's best interests will only be respected if an unaccompanied child can have an asylum application determined promptly. Hence, in its view, it is irrelevant where an unaccompanied child lodges an asylum application. The

---

[71] C-648/11 *MB and others* (CJEU, 6 June 2013).

important rule is that such children should be protected against the suffering that could flow from drawn out procedures for determining which state is responsible for determining their asylum claim.[72]

The same principle was also used by the CJEU as an interpretative tool in relation to asylum-seekers' material conditions of reception. The Reception Directive obliges Member States to ensure an 'adequate standard of living' for all applicants. However, no definition of 'adequacy' is provided other than the need to grant subsistence and protecting physical and mental health of the people of concern. As a result, EU Member States provide very different standards of living for migrants, including children. According to the CJEU's ruling in *Saciri*,[73] 'adequacy of living' must be understood as 'dignified living'. The rule permits no derogation, even where national reception networks are stretched to breaking point. In line with the CRC Committee's comments,[74] best interest determinations require Member States to determine appropriate material conditions by considering the individual needs of migrant children. National authorities are thus required to consider the children's needs in terms of well-being and social development, safety and security and taking into account the views of the children.

In sum, adopting an approach that echoes the CRC, the CJEU has combined considerations based on vulnerability with the concepts of dignity and wellbeing. There is no reason to believe that this cannot apply to all aspects of the CEAS in case of referral for preliminary ruling by national judicial authorities when children are involved. A different approach may be taken with regard to the external dimension of EU migration policy. From a best interests of the child perspective, attempts to externalize migration control may indeed require a preliminary analysis of compliance with EU primary law, including with the CFR.

---

72 After this ruling, proposals were drafted to amend the Dublin Regulation but they have not been adopted yet. See the new set of reforms elaborated in 2016 by the Commission, below.

73 C-79/13 *Saciri* (CJEU, 27 February 2014). In a situation involving a TCN who was not an asylum-seeker but was staying illegally in an EU Member State, the CJEU reached a similar interpretation applying Directive 2008/115/EC: see C-562/13 *Abdida* (CJEU, 18 December 2014).

74 See UN Committee on the Rights of the Child, *General Comment No. 14 (2013) on the Right of the Child to Have His or Her Best Interests Taken as a Primary Consideration*, UN Doc. CRC/C/GC/14 (29 May 2013), para. [6(c)].

4.3 Best Interests of the Child as a Legitimacy Tool: EU External Action

Difficulties around the implementation of EU migration and asylum laws drew the European Commission in 2016 to propose new common rules, beyond the minimum standards discussed earlier. These include a more effective mechanism for sharing responsibility among EU Member States.[75] Interestingly, as far as migrant children are concerned, the Commission's attempts are aimed at protecting children of all ages, whether accompanied or not. The rules include a general right to apply for international protection (until now, a discretion left to states despite Article 18 of the CFR) as well as a right to a personal interview. Put another way, this shows that the lack of uniformity in the management of migration in Europe, coupled with unclear rules, has been preventing migrant children from enjoying the minimum standards of protection supposedly in place.

These developments have been accompanied by EU attempts to establish safe legal channels for people in need of international protection through the support of third countries. In the aftermath of massive migration flows, the 2016 EU-Turkey 'Statement' provides a good example of the 'new' strategy underpinning the EU Agenda on Migration. This agreement provides for the return to Turkey of migrants in Greece who are not applying for asylum or whose applications are determined to be either unfounded or inadmissible. A number of concerns have been raised from a human rights perspective.[76]

Although the text states that human rights obligations must be observed,

---

[75] See European Commission, *Proposal for a Regulation of the European Parliament and of the Council Establishing a Common Procedure for International Protection in the Union*, COM(2016)467 final, Arts 21–2; European Commission, *Proposal for a Regulation of the European Parliament and of the Council on Standards for the Qualification of Third-Country Nationals or Stateless Persons as Beneficiaries of International Protection, for a Uniform Status for Refugees or for Persons Eligible for Subsidiary Protection and for the Content of the Protection Granted,* COM(2016)466 final; European Commission, *Proposal for a Directive of the European Parliament and of the Council Laying Down Standards for the Reception of Applicants for International Protection (Recast)*, COM(2016)465 final, recital 32. The European Commission has turned to 'Regulations', which are directly applicable in Member States, with the only exception being for the Reception Standards Directive. See V. Chétail, P. De Bruycker and F. Maiani (eds), *Reforming the Common European Asylum System: The New European Refugee Law* (Martinus Nijhoff, 2016).

[76] See CoE Committee on Migration, *Refugees and Displaced Persons' Report*, Doc. 14028 (18 April 2016); European Commission, *Second Report on the Progress Made in the Implementation of the EU-Turkey Statement*, COM(2016)349, pp. 4–5, 8.

no effective guarantees are made that transfers from Greece to Turkey will be based on individual evaluations. Further, from a practical point of view, the commitment to observe minimum standards of protection enshrined in the CEAS Directives does not provide a sound basis for human rights protection for the reasons already analysed. There is no certainty that the same international obligations and EU rules will apply to those migrants, including children, intercepted before reaching EU shores. As the main executor of the agreement, Turkey is bound by the ECHR. As a consequence, it must respect at least the minimum standards of protection enshrined in the ECtHR's case law, including when people are intercepted at sea.[77] At the same time, everyone (children included) who is subject to Turkey's jurisdiction may refer an alleged violation of ECHR rights to the Court which, in turn, may apply interim measures. In contrast, because the EU has not yet accessed the ECHR, the same opportunities are not available to those migrants who are solely under EU control (unless EU Member States can be considered internationally responsible for their actions).

From a 'legislative' point of view, this was the first time in a migration-related act involving EU states that the usual approach on children was not followed. The Agreement is a very short statement that, aside from the general reference to human rights, is silent on the treatment of vulnerable groups. Children, with or without families, attract no measures for special protection (or exemptions) against removal. While both Greece and Turkey face serious problems in managing huge migration flows, controversially the EU supposes Turkey to be a 'safe country' opening to an easier return of people reaching the EU from that country (Article 38 of the Procedures Directive).[78] In this context it is worth noting that the ECtHR has ruled repeatedly that ratification of human rights treaties is not *per se* a sufficient guarantee that 'the country of destination will respect human rights, especially the non-refoulement principle'.[79] Finally, the Agreement does not include a 'saving clause' to suspend its execution in case of serious human rights abuses.

In sum, the EU-Turkey Statement has a legitimacy problem because it is

---

[77] *Hirsi Jamaa and others* v. *Italy*, above n. 10.

[78] See Amnesty International, *No Safe Refuge: Asylum-Seekers and Refugees Denied Effective Protection in Turkey* (2016); J. Hathaway, 'Taking Refugee Rights Seriously', *Verfassungsblog* (12 March 2016), available at http://verfassungsblog.de/taking-refugee-rights-seriously-a-reply-to-professor-hailbronner/.

[79] For a recent example of potential violation of non-refoulement following a forced return to Turkey from Greece, see *BAC* v. *Greece*, ECtHR App. No. 11981/15 (13 October 2016).

poorly aligned with the EU legal order's fundamental principles, including human rights. Having regard to Article 24 of the Charter, the agreement may hamper best interests-based evaluations both from an individual and a collective perspective. It undermines the practical right of a child to receive a thorough examination of his/her case, in accordance inter alia with Article 18 of the CFR. The Statement also disregards children's best interests as a group since no special measures relating to their wellbeing and social development are included. Surprisingly, in an action challenging the EU-Turkey Statement's compliance with EU primary law, the CJEU ruled that the Agreement is not an EU act. Nonetheless, it may be affirmed that, since it seems to bind the EU, all EU-related implementing measures should respect the legal framework protecting, among others, migrant children.[80] The real danger is now in the replication of similar initiatives with other countries. For example, following the UK referendum, the United Kingdom will wish to negotiate agreements in this field with the EU. The matter is of particular concern given the United Kingdom's specific position in the EU's area of freedom, security and justice that has led to a lower degree of integration in asylum and migration than in any other field of EU law.[81]

5. CONCLUSION: THE TYRANNY OF MINIMUM STANDARDS AND LOW EXPECTATIONS

For children affected by immigration control measures, Europe's two systems have worked increasingly to fill the gaps left in the 1951 Geneva Convention relating to the Status of Refugees. For the EU, the best interests principle has evolved as part of a normative process, driven especially by the adoption of the Charter of Fundamental Rights. With regard to the ECHR, the ECtHR has worked consciously to interpret the Convention in accordance with more specialized universal human rights treaties. Both systems have considered the CRC and the CRC Committee as guidance for every context involving children, including for asylum and migration.

---

[80] C. Danisi, 'Taking the Union Out of the EU: The EU-Turkey Statement on the Syrian Refugee Crisis as an Agreement Between States under International Law', *EJIL Talk* (20 April 2017), available at www.ejiltalk.org/taking-the-union-out-of-eu-the-eu-turkey-statement-on-the-syrian-refugee-crisis-as-an-agreement-between-states-under-international-law/.

[81] Note that, thanks to an opting-out clause granted by the EU founding Treaties, the United Kingdom decided to be bound only by the first phase of the CEAS legislation and to opt out of its recast (with the exception of the Dublin Regulation). See Protocols 21 and 22 to the Treaties.

While CoE and EU standards are said to establish 'minimum' guarantees, even this core protection is sometimes disregarded by European states. More generally, as De Schutter notes, a peculiar trend seems to be developing. Provided they comply with the minimum standards, European states are convincing themselves that they act in conformity with human rights law. No attention is given to affording higher levels of protection,[82] with very few exceptions.[83] This may prove a great obstacle for attempts to elaborate common European solutions that truly consider the best interests of migrant children.

It is true that the EU bears almost all responsibility for setting higher standards in comparison with the CoE and the ECtHR in its different roles. In some situations, the EU legislator itself is unable to give the 'appropriate' weight to children's rights in the elaboration of internal and external strategies. The need to protect national and/or European boundaries continues to dominate the policy discourse.

However, when the EU legislator evades its human rights obligations or EU Member States implement EU law incorrectly, the CJEU still holds the power to restore the primacy of the Charter and uphold the general principles of the EU legal order. In turn, the ECtHR can work as a 'last resort protection mechanism' for migrant children who are subject to a CoE member state's jurisdiction. When the United Kingdom withdraws from the EU, in the absence of specific agreements with the EU on common rules for managing migration flows, the ECtHR will be the only body supervising the United Kingdom's compliance with human rights standards as it is for all non-EU members of the Council of Europe. In the grey areas (such as where international responsibility for human rights protection lies with the EU), EU accession to the ECHR will empower children who have a valid claim against the EU to refer their case to the ECtHR.

While controversies persist, the CoE and the EU do provide a common protective foundation for migrant children that tries to be aligned with the CRC. These guarantees carry potential for more sophisticated best interests-friendly solutions to prevail over raw economic or financial considerations. Acknowledging the vulnerability of migrant children as

---

[82] O. De Schutter, *The Implementation of the EU Charter of Fundamental Rights Through the Open Method of Coordination*, Jean Monnet Working Papers 7(4) (2004), pp. 21–2.

[83] Italy has tried to set a new model for Europe with the adoption of a comprehensive text defining protection standards for unaccompanied minors. See Disposizioni in materia di misure di protezione dei minori stranieri non accompagnati, Law no. 47, 7 April 2017.

a group with special needs, they stress the importance of integrating the best interests principle at legislative and administrative levels to pursue the 'social development' of children whatever their immigration status. It is here that the rights of the child are embraced as a comprehensive and indivisible catalogue. The challenges ahead in this area of the world may be huge. However, if taken as a whole, the European protection system seems to be based increasingly on the right rationale. It acknowledges the 'migrant' child less as an alien and more as a child.

8. Under siege: alternative care for urban unaccompanied and separated refugee children in Kenya

Agnes Olusese, Shamm Petros and Edwin Odhiambo Abuya

1. INTRODUCTION: KENYA REFUGEE POLICY AND ENVIRONMENT

Kenya is home to 585,646 registered refugees and asylum-seekers, of whom 63,940 (11 percent) reside within the capital, Nairobi. Experts estimate that thousands more remain unregistered and out of reach of service providers.[1] The urban refugee population in Kenya continues to grow despite the unfavorable legal and policy environment.[2] The refugees in Kenya are from over 21 countries of origin including Somalia (69 percent), South Sudan (17 percent), Democratic Republic of the Congo (DRC) (5 percent), Ethiopia (5 percent) and Burundi (1 percent).[3] Only about 10 percent of Kenya's refugee population resides in Nairobi, while the rest have settled between camps in Kakuma, Dadaab and Alinjugur.[4] According to UNHCR's people of concern status update in 2016, more than half (328,923 or 56 percent) of the registered refugees in Kenya were children (that is, persons under 18 years)[5] of whom 7 percent are recorded as unaccompanied and separated children (UASC). Amongst the asylum-seekers, a total of 7,776 children, of whom 34 percent are girls, were recorded as unaccompanied or separated.

---

1 UNHCR, *Refugees and Asylum Seekers in Kenya* (February 2016).

2 Norwegian Refugee Council/Internal Displacement Monitoring Centre (NRC/IDMC), *A Review of the Normative Framework in Kenya Relating to the Protection of IDPs: In the Context of the Kampala Convention and Other Supranational Frameworks* (August 2015).

3 UNHCR, *Refugees and Asylum Seekers in Kenya by Country of Origin* (February 2016).

4 UNHCR, *Kenya: Factsheet* (16 April 2016).

5 Children Act 2001 (Kenya), s. 2.

Kenya is also known as a source, transit and destination country for men, women and children trafficked for the purposes of forced labor and sexual exploitation.[6] UASC are trafficked within the country for domestic servitude, forced labor and for commercial sexual exploitation.[7] While the Counter-Trafficking in Persons Act 2010 (Kenya) is geared towards curbing these crimes, it is seldom applied because of the high threshold of evidence required to obtain a conviction. Reliable statistics on the actual number of victims of trafficking are hard to come by because of the clandestine and criminal nature of the industry. However in 2014, 658 child trafficking victims were identified. Of these only 65 cases were prosecuted.[8] The International Organisation of Migration (IOM) estimates that at least 50 girls aged between 10 and 15 are sold every week as sex workers in Nairobi and Mombasa.[9] Girls mainly from Somalia are trafficked from North Eastern Kenya to Nairobi or Mombasa for prostitution and forced labor. Kenya's extremely porous borders combined with high demand for cheap labor and sexual trafficking markets in Kenya and beyond mean it is possible for thousands of other UASC to enter and remain within Kenya, unregistered and unprotected. With the backdrop of an Encampment Policy and the recent disbandment of Kenya's Department of Refugee Affairs, many urban UASC are fearful of the registration process or accessing services.

In response to security threats, notably the Westgate attacks in September 2013, the government of Kenya reinforced the Encampment Policy.[10] Among other things, it abolished the legal status of urban refugees in Nairobi.[11] The policy originates from long-standing, legitimate security fears of the conflict in Somalia and its history of deadly terrorist acts. The Kenyan government's attitude towards the Somali refugee community, in particular, has been dominated by a national security agenda, rather than humanitarian efforts. The effect of Kenya's hostility and policy actions towards Somali refugees has affected all refugees within the

---

[6] US Department of State, *2015 Trafficking in Persons Report: Kenya* (27 July 2015).

[7] *Ibid.*

[8] 'Kenya lands on US human trafficking list', *Daily Nation* (Kenya), 28 September 2015.

[9] UK Home Office, *Country of Origin Information Report: Kenya* (22 May 2013).

[10] UNHCR, *Submission by the United Nations High Commissioner for Refugees for the Office of the High Commissioner for Human Rights' Compilation Report, Universal Periodic Review: Kenya* (January 2014).

[11] *Ibid.*

country's borders.[12] The Kenyan Interior Ministry considers the presence of unregistered urban refugees to be a high threat to national safety.[13] This policy has forced refugees to retreat further into the margins of society to avoid harassment and violence by both Kenyans and law enforcement personnel. The Encampment Policy predisposed refugees to more insecurity and invisibility from service providers, such as NGOs, faith-based organizations and community-based organizations offering protections and livelihood services. For UASC within Nairobi, this meant accessing support was even more difficult.[14]

To further exacerbate the difficulties faced by refugees, on 6 May 2016, Kenya's Ministry of Interior announced the disbandment of the Department of Refugee Affairs (DRA). Kenya planned to subsequently close the Dadaab refugee camp, the largest refugee camp in Africa, by November 2016 and repatriate about 350,000 Somali refugees.[15] This did not occur. An action by the Kenya National Commission on Human Rights and Legal Advice Centre to challenge the legality of the directive to shut the camp succeeded in the Kenyan High Court.[16]

Since the disbandment of the DRA, the United Nations High Commission for Refugees (UNHCR)'s capacity to administer Movement Passes and Mandates has been affected. Without official recognition from UNHCR or DRA, it is difficult to access the protection, education and health services that asylum-seekers and refugees are entitled to. The absence of the DRA and lack of capacity to fill in the gap from UNHCR has hindered the ability for urban refugees, especially UASC, to access the services they need to sustain a safe lifestyle.

The lack of viable, sustainable employment and youth focused programming in livelihood and secondary education, has left many UASC susceptible to the use of survival sex work and negative coping strategies.[17] This issue is compounded by the inability to identify foster families

---

[12] Human Rights Watch, *'Welcome to Kenya', Police Abuse of Somali Refugees* (17 June 2010).

[13] Human Rights Watch, *'You are All Terrorists': Kenyan Police Abuse of Refugees in Nairobi* (29 May 2013).

[14] UNHCR, *Building on the Foundation: Formative Evaluation of the Refugee Status Determination (RSD) Transition Process in Kenya* (April 2015).

[15] UNHCR Press Release, *UNHCR Appeals to Kenya Over Decision to End Refugee Hosting* (9 May 2016).

[16] See *Kenya National Commission on Human Rights and another* v. *Attorney General and others* (2016), Constitution Petition No. 227 of 2016 (9 February 2017), per Mativo, J.

[17] UNHCR, *Living on the Edge: A Livelihood Status Report on Urban Refugees Living in Nairobi, Kenya* (7 November 2012).

and secure well-structured and monitored alternative care for UASC in Nairobi.[18] After registration with UNHCR, UASC are referred to implementing partners who then conduct assessments and a Best Interest Determination (BID) session to establish the applicable intervention. The UASC is sometimes referred to as a safe shelter awaiting placement in a family. However, there are very limited options for family placement for these minors for a number of reasons. Most of the UASC are placed with refugee families who already have their own challenges and are often unable and unwilling to take additional commitments. Some families accept these children but only because they are gaining financial assistance from UNHCR and implementing partners. If the assistance is withdrawn the refugee child is abandoned at UNHCR and partners' premises, exploited or evicted. Unfortunately, the informal system of alternative care used by UNHCR and partners is not captured in the legal framework for alternative care, consequently leaving refugee children vulnerable to abuse, exploitation and violence.

In this chapter, we argue that the informal system of alternative care adopted in the urban areas has a number of shortcomings which leave the UASC vulnerable to violence, abuse and exploitation. These shortcomings are: the lack of a proper grounding in the child protection framework; the absence of reporting mechanisms; and a failure in law enforcement. The chapter concludes with a number of recommendations for the different actors. It argues that in order to enhance the protection of UASC in urban areas, UNHCR, the government and implementing partners need to coordinate activities and adhere to the guidelines set up for alternative care. Furthermore, this chapter advocates for the introduction of mandatory reporting of abuse cases irrespective of the severity of the abuse claimed, so as to ensure there is some follow-up action upon reporting.

2. METHODOLOGY

This chapter adopted a case study design[19] due to the narrow focus of the topic: effectiveness of alternative care arrangements for unaccompanied urban refugee children in Nairobi. The focus was on the Kenyan

---

[18] UNHCR, *Newcomers to Nairobi: The Protection Concerns and Survival Strategies of Asylum Seekers in Kenya's Capital City* (July 2013).

[19] For further discussion of this data collection mode, see P. Verschuren, 'Case Study as a Research Strategy: Some Ambiguities and Opportunities' (2003) 6(2) *International Journal of Social Research* 121; B. Flybvjerg, 'Five Misunderstandings About Case-Study Research' (2006) 12(2) *Qualitative Inquiry* 219.

government, UNHCR and implementing partners engaged in child protection services for refugee children, past and present, within Nairobi. Data is principally qualitative and collected through desk review of existing literature. There is a significant lack of data and literature on the topic, which further deteriorates the mechanism for securing safe alternative care for urban refugee children. The authors also conducted key informant interviews with staff from the aforementioned agencies. The objective of each informant interview was to analyse the alternative care arrangements that exist for urban refugee children in Nairobi and to highlight gaps present in the protection of this demographic.

3. LEGAL FRAMEWORK ON CHILD PROTECTION IN KENYA

An efficient and effective legal and policy framework plays an important role in strengthening of child protection mechanisms and systems. It is a legal and policy framework that should set the standard for practice in protection of children, specifically in implementation of alternative care arrangements.[20] The analysis will consider both the national and international legal frameworks and the ways they have been implemented in Kenya and its impact on child protection. The all-important question that an analysis of the legal and policy framework should seek to answer is whether the laws and standards that exist afford unaccompanied and separated refugee children sufficient protection from abuse, exploitation and violence.

3.1 National Legal Framework

The Constitution of Kenya is acclaimed as being among the most progressive Constitutions in the region and the world in terms of its inclusion of social, economic and cultural rights.[21] Article 53 of the Constitution delineates the rights of the child, including the right to healthcare, education, shelter and nutrition. In addition to these basic rights of the child, the Constitution indicates that every child in Kenya has a right to parental care and protection. The Constitution further provides that children should not be detained except as a measure of last resort. If a child is to be

---

[20] UN Committee on the Rights of the Child, *Consideration of Reports Submitted by State Parties under Article 44 of the Convention*, 44th Sess., UN Doc. CRC/C/KEN/3-5 (1 April 2015), pp. 9–10.

[21] See, e.g., UNDP, *Four Years On: Assessing the Gains Made in the Kenya Constitution* (2014).

detained, it should be for the shortest time possible and in a place separate from adults.

The Children Act 2001 was enacted to provide for parental responsibility, fostering, guardianship, maintenance, care and protection of children and the administration of relevant institutions charged with this mandate. The Children Act provides in section 4(2) that the best interests of the child shall be of paramount importance in all actions concerning a child. In section 6, the Act instructs that every child is entitled to protection and parental care. In recognition of these provisions, legislators have also set up mechanisms by which children in need of parental care and protection can be assisted and by which other individuals can acquire parental responsibility. The law does not usually support the separation of children from their parents unless as a last option.[22] However, during conflict, natural disasters and instances of abuse and violence children usually are separated from their parents/caregivers. The Children Act 2001 as it currently exists explicitly recognizes alternative care options as guardianship, fostering, adoption or placement in institutions.

Legally the arrangements through which individuals can obtain orders to provide parental care and protection are guardianship, fostering or adoption.[23] The law is very specific on the set of circumstances in which one acquires parental responsibility over a child. The applicant must be the biological parent of the child or a relative in cases where both parents are deceased.[24]

Guardianship refers to a scenario where a person is appointed by deed by the parent of the child, a will or court order to assume parental responsibility over a child.[25] In this instance, at least one child of the parent must be dead and responsibility could be over the child and his/her estate.[26] Where a guardian fails to fulfill their obligations, the law prescribes a penalty of up to one year's imprisonment.[27] Fostering or foster care refers to a situation where a child who has been committed by a court order to a rehabilitation school or a charitable children's institution (CCI) is placed with a foster parent. A foster parent is defined as an individual, other than a child's parent, relative or guardian, willing to be responsible for the care and maintenance of a

22 Children Act 2001 (Kenya), s. 6(2).
23 *Ibid.*
24 *Ibid.* s. 24.
25 *Ibid.* ss. 2, 102.
26 *Ibid.* s. 102.
27 *Ibid.* s. 111.

child.[28] The Children Act recognizes parallel mechanisms of obtaining parental responsibility, apart from being the biological parent or one married to a biological parent. These others (as mentioned above) are guardianship,[29] fostering[30] and adoption.[31] Once an individual is on a specific track of parental responsibility (for example, appointment as a guardian) they cannot also be considered as a foster parent or adoptive parent. The status of being a guardian will have to cease for the individual to acquire the other status. Adoptive parent is more final, unlike guardianship and fostering which can be terminated by court orders.

However, there is a serious gap in the Children Act: the statute does not recognize any informal alternative care arrangements. Thus, it does not provide measures to safeguard children under these sorts of arrangements. In many cases children who are orphaned are usually taken in by relatives who assume parental responsibility over the child, but such arrangements are not acknowledged by law.[32] Recognizing this gap, the government in October 2014 released *Guidelines for the Alternative Family Care of Children in Kenya*. These regulations provide the principles to consider in adopting alternative care arrangements. They also discuss different forms of alternative care that could be utilized in the country.

3.2 International Legal Framework

Kenya ratified the United Nations Convention on the Right of the Child (CRC)[33] in 1990 and acceded to the African Charter on the Welfare and Rights of the Child (ACRWC)[34] in 2000. Under Article 2(5) and (6) of the Constitution of Kenya, international (and regional) treaties to which Kenya is a party have the same force of law as national laws. Within Kenya, the CRC and Children's Act are implemented with the same level of authority and regard.

Article 20 of the CRC requires states to take steps to provide care and protection to children temporarily or permanently deprived of the family

---

[28] *Ibid.* s. 2. See also UNDP, *Four Years On*, above n. 21.

[29] Children Act 2001 (Kenya), Part III.

[30] *Ibid.* Part XI.

[31] *Ibid.* Part XII.

[32] H.K. Akibaya, 'Towards Functional Alternative Care for Children in Kenya', *Nairobi Law Monthly*, 1 April 2016, available at www.pressreader.com/kenya/nairobi-law-monthly/20160401/281831462899399.

[33] Opened for signature 20 November 1989, 1577 UNTS 3 (entered into force 2 September 1990) (CRC).

[34] Adopted by the Assembly of Heads of State and Government of the OAU, 26th Sess., Addis Ababa, Ethiopia (July 1990).

environment. Internationally, family-style arrangements are recognized as the best set-up to raise a child. Article 20 goes further to necessitate that states consider alternative care arrangements as per their national laws and customs. The CRC recognizes the following forms of alternative care arrangements: guardianship, fostering, adoption, *kafalah* and, where suitable, placement in institutions.[35] *Kafalah* is an alternative care system under the Islamic faith where vulnerable children without parental care and protection can be taken in by relatives or a member of the community for upbringing.[36] This individual assumes parental responsibility and is obliged to provide for the rights of the child and their basic needs while maintaining the child's heritage.

Article 25 of the ACRWC has provisions similar to that of Article 20 of the CRC. It requires states parties to ensure alternative care arrangements exist for children deprived of the family environment. The treaty further acknowledges that such children are in need of special protection and assistance. Consequently, it goes ahead to list some of the alternative care arrangements as fostering or placement in institutions among other youth.[37] This indicates that the ACWRC is cognizant of the fact that other arrangements exist and it has left this open to the member states to actualize.

Other instruments that are useful in the child protection system are the 1951 UN Refugee Convention, which requires that unaccompanied minors should be accorded alternative care such as guardianship or adoption where possible.[38] The CRC is explicit in its declaration that refugee children should be accorded the same treatment as national children.[39] There is also the *United Nations Guidelines on Alternative Care* of 2010 ('UN Guidelines'), which recognize other forms of alternative care not considered by previous legal instruments, especially informal arrangements such as kinship, customary forms of alternative care, and supervised independent group living, among others.[40] Although these guidelines are not necessarily binding on the Kenyan government, they were formulated to inform policy and practice in the area of alternative care. They also offer important guidelines for treatment of UASC. The Kenyan government

35 CRC, Art. 20.

36 Government of Kenya, *Guidelines for the Alternative Family Care of Children in Kenya* (2014), p. 49 ('Guidelines').

37 See ACWRC, Art. 25.

38 Convention relating to the Status of Refugees, adopted 28 July 1951, 189 UNTS 137 (entered into force 22 April 1954) ('Refugee Convention'), Part B.

39 CRC, Art. 20.

40 A/RES/64/142 (24 February 2010).

through the conception of the *Guidelines on Alternative Care* in Kenya of October 2014[41] is working to ensure observance of the principles set in the *UN Guidelines on Alternative Care.*

4. UNACCOMPANIED AND SEPARATED REFUGEE CHILDREN

Kenya receives a significant number of unaccompanied and separated children, especially from Somalia, South Sudan and the Democratic Republic of the Congo, among other states. More than half of the refugees in Kenya are children (328,923 or 56 percent) of whom 7 percent are recorded as unaccompanied or separated.[42] Conflict, persecution and oppression as exacerbated by drought or climatic factors tend to pose new protection risks for children.[43] Moreover, existing risks are aggregated by the weak, informal child protection systems that leave children who are separated from their families extremely vulnerable. These vulnerabilities are augmented when the child seeks asylum, as their level of protection will be dependent on the child protection system and mechanism that exist in the country of asylum. An effective system needs to be sensitive to the needs of refugee children who have gone through trauma and are now seeking refuge in foreign land.[44] As Matthew Hodes writes, a 'multi-agency collaboration is required' to ameliorate the difficulties UASC have undergone.[45]

The Refugees Act 2006 requires that the Commissioner of Refugee Affairs ensures that all unaccompanied children are accorded the same protection as children temporarily or permanently deprived of parental care and protection.[46] A similar obligation is imposed by the ACRWC.[47]

---

41 UNICEF, *Guidelines for the Alternative Care of Children in Kenya* (Government of Kenya and UNICEF, October 2014).

42 UNHCR, *Population Statistics: Persons of Concern* (2016), available at http://popstats.unhcr.org/en/persons_of_concern.

43 Integrated Regional Information Networks (IRIN), *Go South Young Man: Migration in the Developing World* (23 April 2016).

44 For further discussion of intervention mechanisms, see C. Montgomery, C. Rosseau and M. Shermarke, 'Alone in a Strange Land: Unaccompanied Minors and Issues of Protection' (2001) 1 *Canadian Ethnic Studies* 102, at 107–12; R. Kohil and R. Mather, 'Promoting Psychosocial Well-being in Unaccompanied Asylum Seeking Young People in the United Kingdom' (2003) 8 *Child and Family Social Work* 2001.

45 M. Hodes, 'Psychologically Distressed Refugee Children in the United Kingdom' (2000) 5 *Child Psychology and Psychiatry Review* 57, at 65.

46 Refugees Act 2006 (Kenya), s. 23(4).

47 ACRWC, Art. 20.

The National Council of Children Services is charged with enhancing the best interests of displaced or unaccompanied children in refugee camps.[48] There is a presumption here that all unaccompanied refugee children reside in a camp, which is not a reflection of the reality, as there are a large number of unaccompanied children residing in urban areas who are unregistered.[49]

In determining placement in alternative care, consideration goes to the child's cultural, religious, linguistic, social and ethnic background.[50] In refugee camps, unaccompanied children are quickly identified, registered and matched with families based on the above criteria. However, this situation is much more difficult in the urban setting where unaccompanied children can reside for years without detection, identification or registration with the proper authorities. The Refugees Act 2006 places the onus of care and protection of refugee children on the Commissioner of Refugee Affairs.[51] However, the Children Act requires the Director of Children Services and the National Council of Children's Services to oversee protection of all children in Kenya, including refugee children.[52] These pieces of legislation require these two government actors to work very closely to ensure the protection and care of refugee children in the country. According to the *UN Guidelines on Alternative Care*, no unaccompanied child should be without the support of and protection of a legal guardian or other recognized adult or competent public body at any time.[53] The Kenyan guidelines of 2014 require that all 'alternative care providers should be registered, licensed, authorized and monitored by the Government of Kenya'[54] and every child in alternative care should be afforded all basic rights as stipulated in the Constitution of Kenya and the Children Act 2001. These provisions must be observed if UASC are to be protected.

Specific to refugee children, the UNHCR has provided the UNHCR Framework for Child Protection which provides a mechanism to assist governments fill in gaps in the care and protection of children during emergencies not anticipated by the government. The Kenyan government does not have a national refugee policy or measures that are specific

---

48 Children Act 2001 (Kenya), s. 32.

49 UNHCR, *Navigating Nairobi: A Review of the Implementation of UNHCR's Urban Refugee Policy in Kenya's Capital City* (January 2011).

50 See generally Sch. 4 to the Children Act 2001. See also ACRWC, Art. 25(3).

51 Refugees Act 2006 (Kenya), s. 23(4).

52 Children Act 2001 (Kenya), s. 32.

53 Guidelines, above n. 36, at 23.

54 *Ibid*. 20.

to the identification, care and protection of refugee children. This role has been filled by UNHCR and partners concerned with refugee child protection. The partners in collaboration with UNHCR and sometimes an officer from the Department of Children's Services conduct Best Interest Determinations (BIDs) for refugee children and determine what interventions should be provided to the refugee child. The BIDs are conducted in accordance with the *UNHCR BID Guidelines* and the *Field Handbook for the Implementation of BID Guidelines*[55] set by UNHCR, which include conditions to consider prior to placement in alternative care arrangements. The intent is that these processes will complement national child protection systems.

According to the *UNHCR BID Guidelines*, alternative care arrangement considerations should be informed by the BID conducted for the specific child, national laws and policies, as well as the child's cultural, religious, linguistic, ethnic background and nationality.[56] In most instances, refugees are placed within families of other refugees. Refugee children are rarely placed with a Kenyan family unless it is through self-selection and the arrangement has been thoroughly scrutinized. Usually these alternative care arrangements are informal as they do not involve the Director of Children Services or the courts, and are unofficial arrangements between the organization placing the child and the refugee family taking them in. There are several challenges that arise in these conditions, due to the lack of supervision and monitoring of the care arrangements. The government charges the Director of Children's Services with the responsibility of monitoring these homes at least every month for the first three months and afterwards once a quarter.[57] For the system to work, the placing organizations must feed information back to government. Data on the number of UASC placed in each home, as well as the profile of the receiving family, must be supplied to government. Otherwise there will be a gap in information, which can work against a child. As of now, the government cannot by itself provide up-to-date data on how many unaccompanied refugee children reside in the urban areas and who their care-givers are. This is in direct contradiction to what is recommended by the guidelines instituted by the Kenyan government in 2014. It is also against the Children Act, the CRC and the ACRWC, all of which call on government to ensure that children in their jurisdiction are protected at all times.

---

55 UNHCR, *Field Handbook for the Implementation of UNHCR BID Guidelines* (November 2011).

56 *Ibid.*

57 Guidelines, above n. 36, at 20.

5. CURRENT PRACTICES IN ALTERNATIVE CARE ARRANGEMENTS OF UASC

Adopting a chronicle framework, this section will examine the alternative care mechanisms utilized by UASC upon initial arrival to Nairobi, registration as a refugee, and once in the care of an implementing partner, if and when that does occur. At each stage, this section will discuss the current practices of implementing partners, government agencies and UASC. Information for this section was acquired through a number of key informant interviews with acting personnel of each aforementioned agency. There is a deficit in data and literature about UASC in urban areas, especially in regard to their protection needs. This section will shed light on the realities of Nairobi for UASC in need of safe, reliable shelter.

5.1 Initial Care Arrangements

Although most refugees in Kenya reside within camp settings, there are over 60,000 registered refugees in Nairobi. Within their first few weeks in Nairobi, UASC move between several homes, often making arrangements to live with strangers they interact with on the streets or people of their own ethnic group.[58] UASC are likely to move around frequently between informal hosts, which complicates efforts by cooperative partners or government agencies to monitor their whereabouts or protection status. The initial care arrangements are quite crucial. As with any individual in a foreign land, how one is received and treated in the first few weeks determines to a large extent their perceptions about the host state. Considering the trauma and violence most UASC have experienced in their home or transit states,[59] it is important for the initial arrangements to take cognizance of these. Hence, the environment UASC find themselves in initially must be one that goes towards ameliorating the pain and suffering undergone. Failure to deal with these issues can have serious consequences on the life of UASC.[60]

Unfortunately, the conditions of the shelters available to UASC are

---

[58] UNHCR, *Newcomers to Nairobi*, above n. 18.

[59] See also S. Schmeidl, 'Exploring the Causes of Forced Migration: A Pooled Time-Series Analysis, 1972–1990' (1997) 78 *Social Science Quarterly* 284; S. Thomas, B. Nafees and D. Bhugra, 'I was Running Away from Death: The Pre-Flight Experiences of Unaccompanied Asylum Seeking Children in the UK' (2004) 30 *Child: Care, Health and Development* 113.

[60] See CRC, Art. 6 and Children Act 2001 (Kenya), s. 4, requiring the government to ensure the survival and development of any child.

typically unsafe, and often require for both unaccompanied and unconnected adults and children to work in exchange for housing.[61] Contrary to restrictions on child labor,[62] female minors are often taken in as domestic workers. While they tend not to be paid, they are given food and shelter during this vulnerable period.[63] One Somali female new arrival described how she entered into such an arrangement, in a study conducted by Refuge Point and UNHCR, *Newcomers to Nairobi* in 2013. She was dropped in Eastleigh, an area of Nairobi heavily occupied by Somalis and Ethiopians, where she met a Somali woman selling tea on the street, who agreed to take her in and provide her one meal a day in return for cleaning her house. For UASC not able to arrange a similar living condition or meet the high cost of living in Nairobi, they find themselves at the mercy of strangers. For new UASC entering Nairobi, there is a higher rate of survival among those that can identify members of their own ethnic community upon arrival.[64] Somalis represent a large portion of the refugee community in Kenya, nearly 77 percent in 2015,[65] and subsequently maintain a strong level of support for newcomers. Many Somali refugees, both women and children, are taken in as domestic workers and provided small amounts of food and temporary shelter. While Somali new arrivals can usually rely on the support of their communities, refugees from minority groups or of mixed ethnicity (e.g. Ethiopian-Eritrean or Tutsi-Hutu)[66] can be isolated. The high cost of living in Nairobi usually means hosts can't afford to take care of UASC for long periods of time, resulting in frequent evictions. Consequently, this exposes this vulnerable population to further risks.

UASC moving between temporary, unverified hosts face a high risk of sexual exploitation.[67] Gender-based violence (GBV) is one of the most reported protection issues.[68] Across Nairobi, slum residents are vulnerable to high levels of criminal violence, including sexual violence, exploitation and domestic abuse. Health and social workers report sexual violence, including rape, sexual abuse and prostitution, is prevalent in the slums

---

61 Amnesty International, *Kenya: From Life Without Peace to Peace Without Life: The Treatment of Somali Refugees and Asylum-seekers in Kenya* (8 December 2010), p. 13.

62 See Children Act 2001 (Kenya), s. 10, and ACRWC, Art. 19.

63 Human Rights Watch, *'Welcome to Kenya'*, above n. 12.

64 UNHCR, *Newcomers to Nairobi*, above n. 18.

65 UNHCR, *Population Statistics*, above n. 42.

66 S. Elhawary and S. Pantuliano, *Hidden and Exposed Urban Refugees in Nairobi, Kenya* (Humanitarian Policy Group, 2010).

67 UNHCR, *Newcomers to Nairobi*, above n. 18.

68 Global Protection Cluster (GPC), *Handbook for Coordinating Gender-based Violence Interventions in Humanitarian Settings* (July 2010).

and informal settlements where UASC reside.[69] In its study on Kenya, Amnesty International found that 'women and girls live under constant threat of violence in their everyday lives – at home, at work and on the street', with an acute risk of rape in home settings that is perpetrated by parents, relatives and/or neighbors.[70] While females underreport the incidences of sexual assault, qualitative data suggest that the actual figures are very high.[71] Female new arrivals are especially vulnerable if they arrive without any prior contacts in Nairobi. Often they resort to living with strange men or persons to avoid sleeping on the street. After their initial period in Nairobi, UASC continue to depend on strangers for their well-being. This is particularly true of UASC who have not identified service or care providers. UNCHR's *Newcomers to Nairobi* reports:

> female new arrivals were often dependent for their survival upon the goodwill of strangers, who could offer them accommodation or employment but later demand sexual favors in return. They could be kept within a confined environment, and be unable to seek help. One young Somali woman experienced such a situation – she was kept in captivity by her host, forcibly raped, and had five children before she was discovered during a home visit by a community worker.[72]

Unfortunately this is true of many UASC who have not accessed formal or informal foster care.

A Human Rights Watch report titled *Protection Problems for Refugees* in Nairobi shared the story of Pauline F, a 16-year-old Rwandan refugee whose mother was killed and whose father was abducted. As an orphan Pauline had to care for her five-year-old sister, in Nairobi's unsafe living conditions:

> I slept outside at the UNHCR compound for one night, then a good Samaritan kept me for one week in her house. Then, she told me I had to look for a place to stay. I found a small shelter, where we pay Ksh. 500 per month [US$6], but I cannot pay this yet . . . The main thing I am worried about is not those thieves, but the men who live around me, they keep on coming back to me, because anyone can break into our little house and they come and beat on the door and tell me to let them in. They come at night like that – I am very scared. I am afraid of that day and night.[73]

---

69 Elhawary and Pantuliano, *Hidden and Exposed Urban Refugees in Nairobi*, above n. 66.

70 Amnesty International, *Risking Rape to Reach a Toilet: Women's Experiences in the Slums of Nairobi, Kenya* (2010).

71 UNHCR, *Newcomers to Nairobi*, above n. 18.

72 *Ibid.*

73 Human Rights Watch, *Interview with Refugee* (Nairobi, 3 April 2002).

Future research should focus on young boys. Data capturing experiences of male UASC is still scarce, yet they too are vulnerable to sexual violence.

5.2 Identifying UASC by the Authorities

Before they can receive the entitlements due to them, UASC must first be correctly identified and registered. Once UASC have been documented, s/he can be referred to relevant agencies for registration. Recognizing UASC is also key as it enables us to know their number in places where they find themselves.

These data are of immense use to the protection regime. Among other reasons, they assist service providers when it comes to planning programs (short- and long-term) for and offering services to UASC.[74] They are also key in fund-raising, as well as mapping out the extent of the problem. Considering the value of this stage of the process, identification should be done immediately. But in an urban setting this is often problematic. In a large city like Nairobi, identifying the vulnerable UASC can be daunting and costly. Unless refugee children are aware of the process and implementing partners have mechanisms to identify them, it may be quite hard to locate them.[75] Interviews with staff engaged in assisting with child protection cases for UASC revealed that usually refugee children were identified by community leaders, NGO interpreters or neighbors who had spotted them in their community. Once an implementing partner was aware, a brief bio-data assessment was conducted by a case-worker, the child was referred to the DRA and this information was sent to UNHCR for initiation of the Refugee Status Determination (RSD) process.

Prior to Kenya's disbandment of the DRA, it was responsible for the registration of all refugees. In the absence of the DRA, UNHCR has taken on the responsibility of registering unaccompanied minors (UAMs) and separated children as vulnerable protection cases. Separated children cases without a heightened protection threat must wait until a more permanent solution is determined with regard to the role of the government in registering refugees. During this time, the implementing partners also initiate family tracing, which is organized by the Kenya Red Cross. Once family tracing has been initiated and UNHCR is aware of the presence of the refugee child, the search for alternative care arrangements begins.

While a refugee child is under self-made arrangements, fieldwork

---

74 See also UN Guidelines, paras 145 and 147, making a similar argument.

75 See ACRWC, Art. 15(2), requiring government to promote dissemination of information.

established that most crimes committed against them are not investigated. This is inconsistent with the law.[76] An interview with an official of a prominent CCI, Heshima Kenya, revealed that in cases where UASC report sexual abuse or domestic crimes in self-made arrangements, prior to registration, those crimes are not investigated and in some cases not even reported since no one was tracking this host family in the first place. The priority, given the capacity of the agency, is to rescue the child first and then find a safe care arrangement. For reports of sexual abuse to be investigated, the refugee child must receive a medical report from a government hospital or some specific numbered hospitals or Kenya Red Cross and file a report with the police.[77] The historically tense relationship between Kenyan police and refugees deters reporting.[78] Furthermore, many agencies don't have the capacity to retroactively penalize care-givers who have committed crimes. Kenya's child protection services are organized by counties and districts within the country. District Children's Officers (DCOs), at each district level, are the actors tasked with responding to children who face trouble/conviction with law or have protection issues.[79] Given the lack of capacity and funding for DCOs, they are rarely involved with refugee cases. Although not grounded legally, cases with refugee children are outsourced to implementing partners.

5.3 Accessing Services for UASC

Access to services, including food, security, shelter and accommodation,[80] from government and non-state agencies is of upmost importance to the life and livelihood of USAC. Absent these services, life will be very challenging for this already vulnerable population. Historically, urban refugees are a blind-spot in international policies, primarily UNHCR's policies, which often assume refugees are either in camps or an urban environment of a

---

[76] ACRWC, Art. 16 and CRC, Art. 19, respectively, require relevant government agencies to investigate comprehensively any claim of child maltreatment.

[77] See National Police Service Act 2011 (Kenya), Part VII.

[78] Integrated Regional Information Networks (IRIN), *Kenya: Urban Refugees Need Legal Clarity, Says Report* (25 March 2010). This situation is not unique to Kenya. See, e.g., E. Abuya and D. Nyaoro, 'Between a Rock and a Hard Place: Victims of Persecution and Armed Conflict in South Africa' (2009) 32(1) *Hastings International and Comparative Law Review* 1.

[79] UNHCR, *Options Paper 1: Options for Governments on Care Arrangements and Alternatives to Detention for Children and Families* (2015).

[80] See Children Act 2001 (Kenya), s. 4 (underlining every child's inherent right of life). See also Refugees Act 2006 (Kenya), s. 16 (entitling refugees to rights contained in domestic and international laws).

developed country governed by able systems. It was not until 2011 that the UNHCR published a revised Urban Refugee Policy after the first one failed miserably. The management of urban refugees is a new concept and a challenge for many actors. For example, the *UNHCR Guidelines on the Protection of Refugee Women* make detailed recommendations for alleviating infringements on the protection of women and children in the refugee camp setting, but not in cities. There is a need for similar guidelines to stipulate the status and demands of refugees in urban centers within transition countries. Moreover, the *UNHCR Guidelines on the Protection and Care of Refugee Children* does not claim any agency-wide accountability in serving refugee children in urban environments of transition countries. While the *UNHCR Guidelines on Policies and Procedures in Dealing with Unaccompanied Children Seeking Asylum* do acknowledge the needs of UASC, they are mostly aimed at governments in the developed countries where UASC could be resettled. Most alarming is the Guidelines' ignorance of the challenges of identifying large numbers of UASC in urban areas, which is a particularly handicapping challenge implementing partners meet in protecting UASC in Nairobi.[81] The minute space urban refugees occupy in international policies of UNHCR, paired with Kenya's discriminatory urban refugee policy, creates a vulnerable environment for urban refugees, which is visible in their everyday realities. Perhaps the most jarring ramification of this policy environment lies in an urban refugee's inability to access proper services in a timely manner. Without proper acknowledgement of the problems faced by urban refugees, UNHCR subsequently fails to assume appropriate responsibility for protecting this population.

UASC newcomers to Nairobi find services from UNHCR insubstantial, given their particular heightened need.[82] UASC's ability to locate and access services is dependent on several factors, especially their ability to identify and integrate into a community upon arrival. Quite often, UASC are unaware of the existence of service providers unless informed by others, contrary to the legal obligation to provide adequate information to UASC.[83] The most financially consuming aspect of accessing services is acquiring refugee status and legal documentation. Identification allows UASC to stabilize their life and ward off arbitrary harassment from law enforcement and civilians.[84] With the recent disbandment of the DRA, it is likely this process will be further delayed. UNHCR offers limited

[81] UNHCR, *Evaluation of the Implementation of UNHCR's Policy on Refugees in Urban Areas* (December 2001), p. 1.

[82] UNHCR, *Newcomers to Nairobi*, above n. 18.

[83] See, e.g., ACRWC, Arts 14–15, 23.

[84] E. Campbell, 'Urban Refugees in Nairobi: Problems of Protection,

services to assist refugees with basic needs, but UASC cases are given a priority. Apart from UNHCR and NGOs, faith-based organizations do provide support for UASC but only when they are made aware of a case. Furthermore, support from faith-based organizations is contingent on funding sources, which doesn't allow for reliable and long-term assistance for vulnerable individuals. The vast majority of humanitarian agencies interviewed for a study conducted by the Humanitarian Policy Group (HPG) stated their inability to properly meet the protection and assistance needs of urban refugees and citied overstretched capacity, limited resources and funding for urban programs, in comparison to funding provided for refugee camps in Kenya.[85] With Kenya's recent Encampment Policy deterring urban settlements, refugees in Nairobi find that there is limited protection and assistance available compared to assistance provided to refugees in a formal camp setting.[86]

5.4 Access to Care Arrangements for UASC

If and when UASC can identify a service provider, the process to equip them with basic needs and care arrangements begins. These service providers play a crucial role in the protection regime. In the first place, they handle the day-to-day needs of UASC. Considering their status, one would additionally expect them to intervene when there is a problem between UASC and any third party, such as law enforcement officials. Knowing these duty bearers is also important when it comes to dealing with complaints lodged by or against UASC. In view of their central role, service providers must be on top of their game at all times.[87] However, fieldwork found several problems with the services offered. The quality and efficiency of these services are erratic, iniquitous and in need of a reassessment. In January 2016, the Kenyan government declared that the formulation of a progressive legal and policy framework, to ensure displaced children receive proper care, was a key concern.[88] Article 22

Mechanisms of Survival, and Possibilities for Integration' (2006) 19(3) *Journal of Refugee Studies* 396.

[85] S. Pavanello, S. Elhawary and S. Pantuliano, *Hidden and Exposed Urban Refugees in Nairobi, Kenya* (Overseas Development Institute, 2010).

[86] Human Rights Watch, *Hidden in Plain View: Refugees Living Without Protection in Nairobi and Kampala* (21 November 2002).

[87] See Children Act, Part II and ACRWC, Part I, respectively, outlining safeguards due to children in Kenya.

[88] Akibaya, 'Towards Functional Alternative Care for Children in Kenya', above n. 32.

of the CRC stipulates that states must ensure that all refugee children are provided with appropriate protection and humanitarian assistance, including family tracing and reunification. In cases where reunification is not viable, the refugee child should be provided with the same alternative care protection provided for other children of that state.

Legally in Kenya, the recognized options are guardianship, fostering and adoption.[89] Adoption as a practice is not considered an option for UASC in Kenya. As for guardianship and fostering, it has been noted that many families willing to assist refugee children are wary of legal processes or only do so to obtain financial assistance from agencies. Many refugees would not want to have legally binding documentation because they believe the process of acquiring such documentation to be long and burdensome. In most cases, UASC are placed with other refugee families and they are sometimes afraid that an additional member can affect their resettlement process and some are willing to consider the child if it means options of resettlement then become open to them. For UAMs in Nairobi, CCIs, group homes and informal hosts are the most viable options. But if these options are not monitored closely, especially in the case of informal hosts, it is likely that reports of abuse or exploitation by care-givers will persist.

5.5 Identifying Care-givers

According to the Kenyan government's *Guidelines on Alternative Care*, DCOs should be involved in the selection and verification of host care-givers.[90] Despite this requirement, the position on the ground is quite different. Fieldwork established that DCOs are absent from this stage. When UASC are identified and the registration process is initiated, case-workers or appointed personnel from an agency look at the specific cultural, ethnic, religious and national background of the child to determine a proper home setting.[91] Cultural background often helps direct the search in foster care arrangements.[92] When a mutual language, religion or cultural background exists, forging care arrangements becomes easier.[93] In the search for a care-giver, agencies do not utilize an official reference

---

89 See Children Act 2001 (Kenya), Parts XI and XII.

90 *Guidelines on Alternative Care*, p. 62.

91 For an interesting discussion of these factors, see D. Steinbock, 'Unaccompanied Refugee Children in Host Country Foster Families' (1996) 18 *International Journal of Refugee Law* 6, at 28–31.

92 Guidelines, above n. 36.

93 See also L. Chile, 'The Imported Underclass: Poverty and Social Exclusion

list of candidates, but care-givers are informally nominated by respected community leaders. Community leaders are often pastors, nuns, school teachers and other persons with status in a neighborhood. However, recognition from a community leader doesn't always mean the person is willing and able to take in a refugee child at the moment. In some instances, the person needs to be convinced that there is need for them to become an informal foster parent. Refugees fear that becoming a formal foster parent will delay their resettlement process, draw heightened attention to their whereabouts, or restrict their access to services available to vulnerable populations. Unfortunately, as discussed with regard to the legal and policy framework above, these kinds of arrangements are not recognized legally and it is only recently that the government has provided guidelines to consider other alternative care arrangements not in statute.[94]

When identifying care-givers of UASC, the two pressing requirements are willingness and reputation of previous assistance. This is not to imply that those without any previous record are not considered, if they were enthusiastic to help. Support given to care-givers depends on the financial status of each household, which is assessed in the earlier stages. Quite often the care-giver is provided a small stipend, a mattress and a food basket to help meet the needs of UASC. This financial support is only available in the short term, and care-givers often abandon the refugee child they are responsible for when the support terminates. Over time, care-givers who have exploited or provided poor foster care are eventually removed from the list of service providers. They are also removed if they continuously volunteer to host refugee children and then abandon them after financial support is terminated. These culprits are known as child collectors. Other offenders are care-givers who host unofficial CCIs in their private home, without proper legal registration. These care-givers are usually refugees who once owned or managed the equivalent of a CCI in their country of origin.

During the key informant interviews, one informant stated that when a potential care-giver is identified, no legally binding agreement is made between the care-giver, refugee child and implementing partner. In some cases, implementing partners use a simplified version of the Foster Care Agreement,[95] which requires the care-giver to provide essential care, such as feeding the refugee child two meals a day. Under the terms of these

---

of Black African Refugees in Aotearoa New Zealand' (2002) 43 *Asia Pacific Viewpoint* 355 (advocating for the 'community development approach').

[94] Akibaya, 'Towards Functional Alternative Care for Children in Kenya', above n. 32.

[95] These draw on Children Act 2001, s. 26.

agreements care-givers undertake to ensure that the refugee child attends school and that they (care-givers) will meet other basic needs. Fieldwork established that DCOs have abdicated their duties as far as these agreements are concerned. While they are expected to administer these accords (between an agency and foster parent), they are hardly ever present. In the rare situations that they are available and a refugee child is placed with a care-giver, a volunteer or incentive staff is usually tasked with monitoring the conditions of the arrangement.[96] This step, which draws on section 32 of the Children Act 2001, is a positive one in the sense that it checks the conditions under which USAC are kept. If there is any problem, one would expect it to be dealt with immediately it is identified. For the measure to deliver, the visits have to be regular and interactive. The objective of these is to ensure that 'violations can be reported, prosecuted, and remedied without delay'.[97] Hence, routine or one-off visits will not work. Therein lies the problem. We found that the monitoring in Nairobi was sporadic in nature. It was also difficult to manage, considering the wide reach of Nairobi's urban borders. Considering this state of affairs, it is reasonable to assume that a number of UASC suffered at the hands of their care-givers.

5.6 Alternatives to Individual Care-givers

Refugee children not in self-identified care arrangements or urgently in need of a home are initially placed in CCIs, while the acting agency searches for other more suitable alternative care arrangements. If family-style arrangements cannot be confirmed, CCIs become the next available option. When CCIs are utilized, DCOs are often involved because government regulations require that these CCIs have documentation from the DCO authorizing placement of refugee children in the CCI. Implementing partners must request placement forms from DCOs to lawfully place refugee children in CCIs. Placing children in CCI is a challenge, since accommodations can only be confirmed for a one- to two-week span. Heshima Kenya is one of the only CCIs in Nairobi that offer longer (three to nine months) accommodation for vulnerable protection cases. Where refugee children demonstrate psycho-social vulnerability, severe protection needs and symptoms of trauma, group homes or CCI are considered for care.

---

[96] This is pursuant to Children Act 2001, s. 32. See also rule 13 of Sch. 4 to this Act.

[97] M. Kures, 'The Effect of Armed Conflict on Children: The Plight of Unaccompanied Refugee Minors' (2001) 25 *Suffolk Transnational Law Review* 141, at 157.

5.7 Reporting and Accountability Procedures

Legally, states are required to take measures that will facilitate reporting to authorities' instances of child abuse and neglect.[98] These systems should be easily accessible to children and their care providers, if they are to be effective. In Kenya, reporting procedures have been built into the protection framework. These are vital in any protection regime. Primarily, they check any allegation by UASC of ill-treatment by the care-giver. In other words, they promote accountability as care-givers are aware that they are under scrutiny. These procedures also ensure that children taken on by a home conduct themselves well.[99] Geraldine Sadoway argues that in addition to 'checks and balances' ensuring these arrangements are 'satisfactory', they also 'provide appropriate support to the de facto guardian'.[100] If there are claims of severe abuse on UASC, particularly sexual abuse, a child is rescued from the home immediately and transferred somewhere else. The DCOs are involved in all rescue missions. Afterwards, if the acting agency has the capacity to do so, they investigate to verify claims, but this is atypical. Claims regarding domestic labor take longer to verify and settle. If the employee of the acting agency believes mitigation is possible, that method is used to manage conflict between a care-giver and the refugee child. In cases where relatives are hosting separated children, mitigation has a higher success rate. In juxtaposition, care-givers of UAMs are not very responsive to mitigation methods, since there are not family ties to the refugee child.

Verbal and emotional abuses are the most reported claims amongst UASC living with care-givers. Care-givers who display symptoms of trauma, anger or depression are offered counselling sessions by service providers, as a way towards ameliorating these difficulties. The depth and frequency of counseling services depends on the acting agency's ability to identify the need and fund the service. In cases where refugee children report sexual abuse, UNHCR is made aware of this during regularly administered BID panels in which several implementing partners attend. Issues regarding care arrangements that are brought to the BID panel typically concern custody issues, fraudulent cases, and cases in which the refugee child has been served before.

Although the standard practice is to report incidences of abuse,

---

98 See ACRWC, Art. 16(2) and CRC, Art. 19(2), respectively.

99 For duties and responsibilities of a child see Children Act 2001 (Kenya), s. 21.

100 G. Sadoway, 'Canada's Treatment of Separated Refugee Children' (2001) 3 *European Journal of Migration and the Law* 347, at 366.

exploitation or violence to the police and the DCO or a Volunteer Children's Office, this is usually not the position on the ground. A key informant from UNHCR stated that UNHCR and implementing partners work closely with DCOs when serving refugee children. However, an interview with an official of Heshima Kenya revealed that DCOs are only involved when a refugee child needs to be rescued, placed in a CCI, or when claims of abuse have been lodged and need to be investigated. The interview with UNHCR staff identified that the low capacity and funding provided to DCOs limit their involvement when serving refugee children. This is less than ideal considering DCOs have a legal obligation to protect children.[101] Issues surrounding the lack of funding can not be used as an excuse. Put simply, DCOs must perform their work at all times.

Owing to the fear of authorities, refugees are usually afraid of approaching police officers or stations on their own.[102] This trepidation is heightened for refugees residing in urban areas who live in the perpetual fear that the authorities could easily force their relocation to the refugee camps. It is therefore only a small percentage of refugees who do report crimes committed against them. Usually they report to an assisting agency and it is the agency which makes the decision whether to approach the police or not. For cases involving sexual abuse, medical verification is required, which in itself can be a traumatizing experience that further deters reporting.

Employees of agencies usually determine whether to report any complaint to the police. Some of the factors they consider include: the severity of the violence or abuse; whether the claim is verifiable; the difficulty in tracking down a suspected perpetrator; the resources that may be required to intervene; and the time that will be utilized in this matter vis-à-vis other competing demands. In the face of these challenges, most incidents unfortunately go unreported either because it seems like it will be a lost cause or the focus is more on removing the child from the abusive situation. After a child is removed, further action is rarely taken. However, if the Director of Children's Services were tracking these unaccompanied or separated refugee children and monitoring their situation, perhaps this department of government could be pressured to take action. Failing this, we have many instances of individuals who abuse children and are able to get away with it. Since most care-givers who host UASC are refugees themselves, they are likely to be in the process of resettlement to a third country.

---

[101] See also Children Act, s. 68, Sch. VIII, requiring regular inspection of facilities by an Inspection Committee appointed by the Minister. CRC, Art.3(3) places a similar obligation.

[102] Amnesty International, *Kenya: From Life Without Peace to Peace Without Life*, above n. 61.

Currently, UNHCR and implementing partners are not able to provide data on how a refugee's RSD case is affected if they are found guilty of abusing or neglecting a refugee child they are caring for. That said, one would expect the exclusion clause of the Refugees Act 2006 to kick in when such claims are proven.[103]

That offenders must be held accountable cannot be overemphasized. The Children Act 2001 lays down penalties for anyone who is found guilty of infringing on the rights of a child.[104] Indeed, the Director of Children's Service, which has the mandate of safeguarding the 'welfare of children' in Kenya,[105] must take an active role in the protection of UASC. As demonstrated above, the lack of monitoring and reporting framework allows for exploitation of this vulnerable population. Since very few cases of abuse against UASC are even reported, it is extremely difficult to find statistics of individuals prosecuted for abusing children. The Director of Children's Services would be the expected office to have this information. But due to its limited involvement in matters affecting urban refugee children, the Department cannot provide any data on this issue. This by itself has serious consequences for the protection regime.

In cases not considered severe by agencies, these individuals are excluded by the specific agency. While this may be seen as a positive step, for this initiative to deliver, the information gathered must be shared with other partners in the system. A central database, with profiles of all care-givers, would go a long way towards deterring future abuse. Additional requirements, such as the production by a care-giver of a clearance certificate from the Law Enforcement Agencies, should also be built into the screening process. Absent these, there is a high risk of individuals excluded by one agency approaching successfully another agency. Involvement of the office of the Director of Children's Services and the imposition of a requirement for mandatory reporting would lead to these individuals being red flagged and avoided if it is determined that legal action cannot be sustained against them.

---

[103] Refugees Act 2006, s. 4 disqualifies from refugee protection any person who 'has committed a serious non-political crime inside Kenya after the person's arrival and admission into Kenya as a refugee'.

[104] See Children Act 2001 (Kenya), s. 20 (the penalty for those who are found guilty is up to one year's imprisonment or a fine of KShs 50,000, or both).

[105] Children Act 2001 (Kenya), s. 38(1).

6. CONCLUSION

A child protection system comprises a number of elements. These include child protection coordination mechanisms, data management, legal and policy frameworks, monitoring, referral mechanisms, advocacy and inter-agency response mechanisms. For there to be a change in ways that child protection is undertaken, all the actors need to ensure the components mentioned above are active and efficient. These safeguards could contribute to the protection of this vulnerable group.

For UASC and refugees in general, the social and political tension of Nairobi is not conducive to a safe protection environment. Police harassment and abuse of refugees have historically shaped the relationships between legal authorities and refugees in Nairobi.[106] Communities known for hosting refugees are targets of raids, financial exploitations and harassments from police. This reality discourages formal reporting of abuse or crimes committed against refugees or UASC.

Courts can play a key role in the protection regime. As mentioned earlier, the High Court of Kenya in February 2017 handed down a decision stopping the government from closing Dadaab refugee camp. While it is said that the government will appeal this decision to the Court of Appeal, the jurisprudence that Judge Mativo propounded will contribute a great deal to our understanding of the protection of refugees in general and UASC in particular. But for court cases to deliver, lawyers must craft their pleadings in a manner that makes a judge appreciate the infractions that have been committed and reliefs being sought. In-depth research on international and domestic laws is essential towards this end. Partnerships, too, with local and international academics and other interested players, are critical.[107] Legal interventions that are poorly packaged can lead to the setting of dangerous precedents. Eventually, these could harm those whom the interventions were designed to protect.

In order to enhance the protection environment and formalize the alternative care system undertaken in protection of refugee children, it is crucial to ensure that these arrangements are licensed, authorized and regularly monitored to reduce incidences of abuse and exploitation by care-givers. Different actors should increase their efforts and work closely together so as to promote a strong and cohesive child protection system

---

[106] IRIN, *Kenya: Urban Refugees Need Legal Clarity, Says Report*, above n. 78.

[107] ACRWC, Art. 23(2), also underlines the need for such alliances. Several authors have also made this point. See, e.g., A. Christie, 'Responses of the Social Work Profession to the Unaccompanied Children Seeking Asylum in the Republic of Ireland' (2002) 5 *European Journal of Social Work* 187, at 197.

for UASC in Nairobi and other urban areas. If the recommendations flagged in this chapter are ignored by the Director of Children's Services and other duty bearers, there is a risk that the protection due to UASC will fall way below the legal standards.

9. Defending migrant children and youth in the inter-American system

Carlos Holguín and Kavita Kapur

1. INTRODUCTION

The Center for Human Rights and Constitutional Law has advocated for immigrant and refugee youth since 1985. In 1997, the Center concluded a nationwide settlement that continues to regulate the treatment and conditions juveniles experience during immigration-related detention in the United States (US).[1]

With the 'surge' of Central American families and children arriving at the US southern border in the summer of 2014, the settlement buttressed a broader campaign to end the US policy of detaining Central American families indefinitely in order to deter other youth and families fleeing violence in El Salvador, Honduras and Guatemala (known collectively as the Northern Triangle of Central America (NTCA)) from seeking refuge in the United States.

In addition to pursuing its family detention policy, however, the United States also enlisted the governments of Mexico and the NTCA countries to stop Central Americans from journeying to the United States.[2] This strategy of 'border externalization'– in effect, refugee interdictions – elevated what might have remained a matter of domestic law and policy to one of international dimensions.

US-sponsored interdiction of Central American migrants afflicts adults as well as juveniles. But the engine of the current NTCA diaspora – endemic criminal gang-violence – disproportionately targets the young, as the following anecdote demonstrates:

> In February 2015 my brother[s], 16 and 23 years old, my niece, 13 years old and I, 17 years old, decided to leave [El Salvador] . . . My parents were in agreement

---

1 *Flores* v. *Sessions*, No. CV45-4544-DMG (CD Cal., 1997).

2 See C. Ribando Seelke, *Mexico's Recent Immigration Enforcement Efforts* (Congressional Research Service, 2016).

> that we should leave because of the danger in El Salvador. We left because the gang wanted to force my niece, who lived with us, to sell drugs for them. The gang members use young people because they think the police will not check them as much as older people. Many gangsters lived in the United States, where they learned the tactics of delinquency, and after being deported they practice those tactics in El Salvador. The gangsters threatened my niece, that if she refused to sell drugs they would kill her and all of the family, including me. Inasmuch as my niece refused to become a drug dealer, we made the decision to leave El Salvador.[3]

According to the United Nations High Commissioner for Refugees (UNHCR), children and youth in the NTCA live under the 'rampant threat of . . . inter-gang conflict and . . . the control gangs exercise in different neighborhoods, such as determining who may enter and exit these neighborhoods', as well as with the 'potentially life-threatening dangers of being misidentified as a member of one gang while in rival territory of another gang'.[4] The UN body notes that gangs systematically beat, rob and threaten youth, who struggle to 'avoid gang recruitment, harassment by gangs while commuting to school, and the extortion exacted by gangs on children and their families'. As a result, the UNHCR concludes, some 58 per cent of children of the NTCA diaspora are prima facie eligible for international protection.[5]

The combination of border externalization – a strategy effectively beyond remediation by domestic US courts[6] – and unbridled violence disproportionately affecting the young in the NTCA lends new importance to the inter-American system for protecting the human rights of migrant children and youth. Although the reports and conclusions of international tribunals have only the power of moral persuasion, it is arguable that the inter-American system is the last, best tool to draw attention to the plight of interdicted refugee youth through juridical process.

---

[3] Declaration of Margarita del Carmen Barrios, interviewed January, 2016, in the *Adolescentes en El Camino* migrant shelter, Oaxaca, Mexico, on file with the Inter-American Commission of Human Rights; see also Inter-American Commission on Human Rights (IACHR), *Situation of Human Rights in Honduras*, OEA/Ser.L/V/II (2015), p. 11 (Honduras's homicide rate 'remains one of the highest in the region and the world, and it particularly affects youth').

[4] UNHCR, *Children on the Run: Unaccompanied Children Leaving Central America and Mexico and the Need for International Protection* (2014), p. 26.

[5] *Ibid.* 6.

[6] In *Sale* v. *Haitian Centers Council, Inc.*, 509 US 155, 159 (1993), the Supreme Court held that the principle of non-refoulement posited by Art. 33 of the Convention relating to the Status of Refugees, adopted 28 July 1951, 189 UNTS 137 (entered into force 22 April 1954) at least as incorporated into US law, does not protect persons outside US territory.

In this chapter, we summarize the inter-American treaties and conventions we think speak most forcefully to governments that would deny Central American children and youth the right to refuge or other international protection. We then discuss the jurisdiction and procedures of the institutions charged with promoting adherence to the inter-American human rights framework. Finally, we describe recent examples of advocacy within the inter-American system we hope will illustrate the potential and limitations of this system as a tool to advocate for *adolescentes en el camino* (migrant adolescents).

2. INTER-AMERICAN HUMAN RIGHTS SYSTEM, TREATIES AND CONVENTIONS

The inter-American human rights system is established and governed by the Charter, treaties and conventions of the Organization of American States (OAS). Signed in Bogotá, Colombia, in 1948 and entered into force in 1951,[7] the Charter establishes the OAS and defines its structure and 'legal architecture'.[8] The Charter provides for an inter-American system for the protection of human rights:

> There shall be in Inter-American Commission on Human Rights whose principal function shall be to promote the observance and protection of human rights and to serve as a consultative organ of the Organization in these matters.[9]

The Charter itself provides few details regarding regional human rights supervision, instead stipulating that '[a]n inter-American convention on human rights shall determine the structure, competence, and procedure of this Commission, as well as those of other organs responsible for these matters'.[10] The member states of the OAS agreed unanimously to these provisions, and they are thus binding throughout the hemisphere.

Concurrently with founding the OAS, the member states adopted the American Declaration of the Rights and Duties of Man ('American Declaration').[11] Eighteen years later, in 1969, a majority of the OAS's

---

[7] Charter of the Organization of American States, opened for signature 30 April 1948, 119 UNTS 3 (entered into force 13 December 1951).

[8] D. Rodríguez-Pinzón, 'Precautionary Measures of the Inter-American Commission on Human Rights: Legal Status and Importance' (2013) 20(2) *Human Rights Brief* 13.

[9] Charter of the OAS, Art. 106.

[10] *Ibid.*

[11] (1948) OAS Res XXX, OAS Off. Rec. OEA/Ser.L/V/I 4 Rev.

member states signed (and 25 later ratified) the American Convention on Human Rights ('American Convention'), which reinforces and elaborates upon the American Declaration.[12]

In sum, all OAS member states are bound by the American Declaration by virtue of their OAS membership and ratification of the OAS Charter. Member states that have ratified the American Convention are bound by it as well. The American Declaration and American Convention are the chief statements of the substantive law of human rights in the Americas.

2.1 American Declaration of the Rights and Duties of Man

The American Declaration remains the cornerstone of the inter-American system for the protection of human rights. Adopted following the Ninth International Conference of American States in 1948, '[t]he [Inter-American] Commission [on Human Rights] and the Inter-American Court have both held that the Declaration, although not initially adopted as a legally binding treaty, is now a source of legal obligation for OAS Member States'.[13]

The American Declaration contains 28 articles positing basic human rights which all OAS member states are pledged to respect.[14] The enumerated rights encompass both civil and political rights, as well as key economic, social and cultural rights.

The Declaration begins with the fundamental rights of every human being: the 'right to life, liberty and security of his person',[15] and to equality before the law 'without distinction as to race, sex, language, creed or any other factor'.[16] The Declaration then proceeds to protect specific

---

[12] Opened for signature 22 November 1969, 1144 UNTS 123 (entered into force 18 July 1978).

[13] Rodríguez-Pinzón, 'Precautionary Measures of the Inter-American Commission on Human Rights', above n. 8, at 13 (citing *Roach and Pinkerton* v. *United States* (1987) Inter-Am. Comm'n HR Report No. 147, OEA/Ser.L/V/II.71 Doc. 9 Rev. 1, paras [46]–[49]; *Interpretation of the American Declaration of the Rights and Duties of Man within the Framework of Article 64 of the American Convention on Human Rights (Advisory Opinion)* (1989) Inter-Am Ct HR (Ser. A) No. 10, paras [35]–[45].

[14] American Declaration, above n. 11.

[15] *Ibid.* Art. 1.

[16] *Ibid.* Art. 2. Other basic rights, including those to freedom of religion, freedom of expression and to private and family life are codified in Arts 3, 4, 5 and 6. Articles 8, 9 and 10 guarantee the right to establish a residence and to move freely within the territory, together with preserving the inviolability of the home and of correspondence.

rights: to health, education, culture, work with fair remuneration, leisure time, social security, and property,[17] as well as civil and political rights, including the right to due process of law and freedom from arbitrary arrest.[18]

Most germane to present purposes, the American Declaration contains two provisions that combine to protect children fleeing violence in their countries of origin: Articles 7 and 27. Article 7 declares that 'all children have the right to special protection, care and aid'.[19] Meanwhile Article 27 guarantees all persons the right 'to seek and receive asylum in foreign territory, in accordance with the laws of each country and with their international agreements'.[20]

The Inter-American Commission on Human Rights (IACHR) holds that these rights should be construed in conformity with evolving international law respecting children: that is, they 'should be considered in the context of the broader international and Inter-American human rights systems *to include the incorporation of the principle of the best interests of the child*' (emphasis added).[21]

2.2 American Convention on Human Rights

Twenty-five of the OAS's 35 member states have ratified the American Convention, including Mexico.[22] Notably, the United States has signed, but not ratified, the American Convention.[23]

The American Convention elaborates upon the American Declaration with respect to the general obligations of states and inter-American protections for civil, political, economic, social and cultural rights.[24] Most importantly, it guarantees the right of every person 'to leave any country freely, including his own', as well as 'to seek and be granted asylum in

17 *Ibid.* Arts 10–16, 23.

18 *Ibid.* Arts 17–22, 24–6.

19 *Ibid.* Art. 7.

20 *Ibid.* Art. 27.

21 Inter-American Commission on Human Rights, *Refugees and Migrants in the United States: Families and Unaccompanied Children* (July 2015), p. 46.

22 *Signatories and Ratifications: American Convention on Human Rights*, available at www.oas.org/dil/treaties_B-32_American_Convention_on_Human_Rights_sign.htm.

23 *Ibid.* For a detailed analysis of the United States' position vis-à-vis the American Convention, see J. Diab, 'United States Ratification of the American Convention on Human Rights' (1992) 2(2) *Duke Journal of Comparative and International Law* 323.

24 American Convention, Ch. I-III.

a foreign territory',[25] and prohibits the collective expulsion of aliens.[26] Elaborating on the right to humane treatment, the American Convention also protects the right of every individual 'to have his physical, mental and moral integrity respected'.[27]

3. INTER-AMERICAN INSTITUTIONS

In addition to providing one of the most comprehensive statements of human rights in the world, the American Convention also defines the present-day structure, jurisdiction and rules of procedure of IACHR and its sister entity, the Inter-American Court of Human Rights (IACtHR). Together, these institutions are charged with promoting member states' compliance with the substantive human rights set out in the American Declaration and the American Convention:

> The Inter-American System is composed of two entities: a Commission and a Court. Both bodies can decide individual complaints concerning alleged human rights violations and may issue emergency protective measures when an individual or the subject of a complaint is in immediate risk of irreparable harm. The Commission also engages in a range of human rights monitoring and promotion activities, while the Court may issue advisory opinions on issues pertaining to the interpretation of the Inter-American instruments at the request of an OAS organ or Member State.[28]

3.1 Inter-American Commission on Human Rights

The IACHR was created by the OAS in 1959 and has its headquarters in Washington, DC. It is composed of seven independent members who are charged with the mission to 'promote and protect human rights in the American hemisphere'.[29] The Commission carries out this mission through a variety of mechanisms: adjudication of individual petitions, thematic hearings, and both thematic and country-specific reporting.[30]

---

[25] *Ibid.* Art. 22(2), (7).

[26] *Ibid.* Art. 22(9).

[27] *Ibid.* Art. 5.

[28] International Justice Resource Center, *Inter-American Human Rights System*, available at www.ijrcenter.org/regional/inter-american-system/.

[29] Organization of American States, Inter-American Commission on Human Rights, *What is the IACHR?* (2011), available at www.oas.org/en/iachr/mandate/what.asp.

[30] Organization of American States, Inter-American Commission on Human

The Commission includes separate Special Rapporteurs on the Rights of the Child and on the Rights of Migrants.

The procedures for presenting individual petitions to the Commission are set out in Articles 23 *et seq.* of the Rules of Procedure of the Inter-American Commission on Human Rights.[31] Examples of the IACHR petitioning process brought for the benefit of migrant children are described below.

The Office of the Rapporteur on the Rights of the Child is tasked with promoting respect for the human rights of children and adolescents in the Americas.[32] The Special Rapporteur has called attention to the plight of Central American children and families detained in the United States.[33]

The present mandate of the Rapporteur on the Rights of Migrants is to advocate for 'the rights of migrants and their families, asylum seekers, refugees, stateless persons, victims of human trafficking, internally displaced persons and other vulnerable groups of people in the context of human mobility'.[34] Among the more salient reports in which this Rapporteurship has figured is *Human Rights of Migrants and Other Persons in the Context of Human Mobility in Mexico*,[35] which paints a disturbing picture of the crime, violence, impunity and corruption Central American migrants experience in Mexico.

3.2 Inter-American Court

Only member states or the IACHR itself may initiate actions before the Inter-American Court, and then only if the member state being sued has accepted the contentious jurisdiction of the IACtHR. Among the 20

Rights, *About the IACHR: Composition*, available at www.oas.org/en/iachr/mandate/composition.asp#tab3.

31 Organization of American States, Inter-American Commission on Human Rights, *Rules of Procedure* (2011), available at www.oas.org/en/iachr/mandate/Basics/rulesiachr.asp ('Rules of Procedure').

32 OAS Rapporteurship on the Rights of the Child, Inter-American Commission on Human Rights, *Rights of the Child*, available at www.oas.org/en/iachr/children/.

33 See the Commission's report, *Human Rights Situation of Refugee and Migrant Families and Unaccompanied Children in the United States of America*, OAS/Ser.L/V/II 155, Doc. 16 (24 July 2015), available at www.oas.org/en/iachr/reports/pdfs/Refugees-Migrants-US.pdf.

34 Organization of American States, Inter-American Commission on Human Rights, *Rapporteurship on the Rights of Migrants*, available at www.oas.org/en/iachr/migrants/default.asp.

35 OEA/Ser.L/V/II, Doc. 48/13 (30 December 2013), available at www.oas.org/en/iachr/migrants/docs/pdf/Report-Migrants-Mexico-2013.pdf.

OAS member states accepting the Court's contentious jurisdiction are El Salvador, Guatemala, Honduras and Mexico, but not the United States.[36]

However, if a non-state petitioner prevails before the IACHR against a member state subject to the Court's contentious jurisdiction, he or she may ask the Commission to submit the matter to the Court.[37] Similarly, if the Commission determines that a member state has failed to comply with its recommendations, it may submit the matter to the IACtHR for binding adjudication provided the state is subject to the Court's contentious jurisdiction.[38]

4. APPLICATION

4.1 Precautionary Measures: Matter of EGS and AESG

Securing final disposition of a petition to the IACHR takes time – often a lot of time.[39] Where irreparable injury will occur before the Commission may be expected to decide a case, a petitioner may request that the Commission issue 'precautionary measures'. These are interim measures requesting states to take or refrain from action pending disposition of the underlying petition.[40] Such precautionary measures may be conceived as an inter-American analogue to a domestic court's issuing a preliminary injunction.

The Commission's rules provide that such requests may be granted in 'serious and urgent' situations which irreparable violations of human rights appear imminent.[41] The requirements for receiving precautionary measures are three-fold: seriousness, urgency and irreparable harm.

---

[36] Organization of American States, Secretariat for Legal Affairs, *American Convention on Human Rights: Signatories and Ratifications* (2014), available at www.oas.org/dil/treaties_B-32_American_Convention_on_Human_Rights_sign.htm.

[37] Rules of Procedure, art. 44(3).

[38] *Ibid.* art. 45.

[39] Among other reasons for delay, the Commission's funding, or lack thereof, sometimes delays the adjudication of petitions. In May 2016, for example, the Commission announced that for want of adequate funding it would lay off 40 per cent of its staff, suspend visits, and cancel its 159th and 160th regular sessions. Although the financial crisis has eased somewhat, the Commission remains hobbled. News and developments regarding the Commission's financial crisis are available at www.oas.org/en/iachr/media_center/crisis-iachr.asp.

[40] Rules of Procedure, art. 25.

[41] *Ibid.* art. 25(2).

The IACHR's Resolution 30/2016 in *Matter of EGS and AESG* illustrates the potential of precautionary measures in protecting migrant children.[42] On 28 March 2016, lawyers for two Salvadoran citizens, a mother and her 12-year-old daughter, requested the Commission issue precautionary measures recommending against their clients' being repatriated from the United States pursuant to an order of expedited removal, a truncated deportation procedure applied to certain non-citizens apprehended shortly after entry.[43]

The petitioners alleged that repatriating the mother and daughter without affording them a meaningful opportunity to be heard would violate the American Declaration's rights to life and personal security (Article 1), protection and care of children (Article 7), a fair trial (Article 18), to petition (Article 24), to protection from arbitrary arrest (Article 25), to due process of law (Article 26), and to seek asylum (Article 27). The repatriation of the family was scheduled to take place within a few days.[44]

On 11 May 2016, the IACHR granted precautionary measures, finding that the information submitted suggests a prima facie case of 'seriousness and urgency, since [the beneficiaries'] lives would be at risk if they were deported'. The Commission requested the United States refrain from deporting the family so it could reach a judgment on whether the expedited removal proceeding comported with international law.[45] The Commission found the need for precautionary measures serious because of the risks to the beneficiaries' lives were they returned to El Salvador.[46] The Commission was moved by the 'context of violence' that the beneficiaries had experienced in El Salvador, including having been gang-raped twice and threatened with further gang rape.[47]

The Commission ruled that the beneficiaries had likely been denied an 'adequate and effective' asylum adjudication, which, considered in light of the grave risks to their lives, warranted precautionary measures. The Commission found that 'the execution of the deportation order will eventually prevent the Inter-American Commission from properly assessing the merits of the petition'. Further, it found a likelihood of irreparable

---

[42] *Matter of EGS and AESG regarding the United States of America (Precautionary Measure No. 297-16)* (Inter-American Commission on Human Rights, Resolution 30/2016, 11 May 2016).

[43] See 8 USC 1235.3.

[44] *Matter of EGS and AESG*, above n. 42.

[45] *Ibid.*

[46] *Ibid.*

[47] *Ibid.*

harm because 'the possible effect on the right to life and physical integrity represents the highest irreparable situation'.[48]

A member state's complying with the Commission's precautionary measures is, of course, another matter. In *Garza* v. *United States*, for example, the Commission granted precautionary measures to a prisoner sentenced to death and requested the state

> preserve the life and physical integrity of Mr Garza until the IACHR would decide on the individual petition, in order for the processing of his case before the Inter-American System not to be rendered moot.[49]

About one month later, Mr Garza was executed regardless.[50] Lifting the precautionary measures as moot, the Commission wrote:

> this disregard by a member State of the Organization of American States of a request to preserve the life of a person sentenced to death, while the petition he has filed is examined, contravenes the State's international obligations. Noncompliance with this precautionary measure is detrimental to the effectiveness of the Commission's procedures, depriving sentenced persons of their right of petition in the inter-American system of human rights and affects his right to life in a serious and irreparable manner.[51]

Despite such instances of flagrant disregard for international law, precautionary measures remain an important, if limited, tool in advocating for migrant children, if only to draw attention to injustice that might otherwise go unnoticed.[52]

4.2 Petitions and Thematics: *Adolscentes en El Camino* v. *United States and Mexico*

On 14 April 2016, over 35 faith-based groups and human rights organizations filed a petition with the IACHR denouncing the joint campaign

---

48 *Ibid.*

49 Resolution to Lift Precautionary Measures 10/2014 (Precautionary Measure No. 255-13) (Inter-American Commission on Human Rights, 5 May 2014), para. [2].

50 *Ibid.* para. [10].

51 *Ibid.* para. [11].

52 The Commission's action in *Matter of EGS and AESG*, for example, garnered at least some media coverage. See, e.g., R. Feltz, 'Human rights body makes rare bid to halt Salvadorian woman's deportation', *The Guardian* (online), 12 May 2016, available at www.theguardian.com/world/2016/may/12/deportation-inter-american-human-rights-commission-salvadorian-woman.

of the United States and Mexico – dubbed the *Plan Frontera Sur* – to interdict and summarily deport Central Americans, including thousands of children and families to conditions of rampant violence in NTCA. The petition, *Adolescentes en el Camino, et al. (United States and Mexico)*, Case P-652-16,[53] marshals extensive evidence that the two governments are deporting tens of thousands of men, women and children to jurisdictions in which they run a clear risk of persecution and death, in violation of the long-standing international prohibition against refoulement of refugees. Petitioners ask the Commission to rule, inter alia, that interdicted refugees are entitled to a full and fair process by which their eligibility for international protection in Mexico may be determined. The petition also contends that the two governments unlawfully detain Central America asylum-seekers *en masse* and subject them to conditions of hyper-violence and impunity in Mexico in an unconscionable and illegal effort to deter them from seeking international protection.

Advocates are using the petition to advocate for greater responsibility in US policy in the region. They argue that US support for the *Plan Frontera Sur* should end until and unless the Inter-American Commission certifies that Mexico is in substantial compliance with its obligations to confer refuge or other international protection on deserving Central Americans fleeing the Northern Triangle. Advocates hope that the Commission's adjudicatory process will function as a more credible alternative to State Department certification of compliance with human rights accords.

4.3 Reports: Human Rights Situation of Refugee and Migrant Families and Unaccompanied Children in the United States

The Commission's reports provide yet another important form of human rights protection. Pursuant to Article 60 of its Rules, the Commission may report on the status of human rights in a particular state. Such reports can be highly persuasive in advocating before the Commission, the Court or other regional and international entities on behalf of individual migrant children.

In July 2015, the Commission published a report on human rights of families and unaccompanied children detained in the United States. The report focused

> on the lack of adequate screening and identification of persons arriving to the US who may have international protection needs, the arbitrary and automatic regime of immigration detention being applied to families and children,

---

[53] The petition and related materials are available at www.centerforhumanrights.org/Border_Externalization.html.

> and serious deficiencies in terms of due process guarantees in immigration proceedings.[54]

The report does not expressly conclude that the United States has violated particular articles, but rather recalls and explains the scope of the obligations that the state has acquired by virtue of its acceptance of the OAS Charter and the American Declaration, while also expressing concern and making concrete recommendations for improvement.

Such reports, of course, have only the power to persuade. They lend credibility to the claims of advocates and provide a vehicle to communicate in terms of human rights a general assessment of human rights violations affecting specific groups. The observations and recommendations contained in these reports are important tools for advocacy, not only within the inter-American system but also directly with state actors.

---

[54] IACHR, *Refugees and Migrants in the United States*, above n. 21, at 15.

PART II.2

Protection frameworks: case studies

10. Child migration and trafficking in South-East Asia

Kathryn E. van Doore

The juxtaposition of domestic and regional responses to child trafficking and migration is clearly delineated in the context of South-East Asia due to the proximity of countries and relative ease of access across the region. This ease of access has led to well-established migration flows, or routes, leaving the region split between source countries and destination countries. It is well documented that migration occurs intra-regionally from less developed countries to more developed countries, and that a substantial number of children are making this move.[1] Based on this, this chapter examines how the best interests principle embodied in the Convention on the Rights of the Child intersects with the issue of child migration and trafficking in the Association of South East Asian Nations (ASEAN) region.

Through this contrasting examination in domestic and regional contexts, the chapter draws a conclusion regarding how the law may navigate the best interests of the child paradigm in relation to child migration and trafficking in South-East Asia.

1. WHY ARE CHILDREN ON THE MOVE IN SOUTH-EAST ASIA?

South-East Asia incorporates the nations of Brunei Darussalam, Cambodia, Indonesia, Lao PDR, Malaysia, Myanmar, Philippines, Singapore, Thailand and Viet Nam. Collectively, the nations joined together in 1967 as ASEAN to promote regional peace and stability, and to encourage collaboration and development between the countries. The

---

[1] J. Joudo-Larsen, J. Lindley and J. Putt, 'Trafficking in Persons Monitoring Report July 2007–December 2008' (2009) 6 *Australian Institute of Criminology Monitoring Reports* 14.

region has long been regarded as a 'hot-spot' for trafficking due to its 'socio-economic and developmental disparities, historical intraregional migration patterns and existence of few legal migration alternatives'.[2] The migratory flow of children tends to be from less developed countries to more developed countries in the region.[3]

Children are on the move in, through and out of South-East Asia for independent voluntary migration, or due to forced migration or trafficking. Independent child migration is on the increase in South-East Asia and is occurring both within borders and transnationally,[4] for specific purposes (for example, labour or marriage) or for the general promise of better economic prospects.[5] Research has also shown that children are moving from East Asia to South-East Asia to acquire cheaper education.[6]

Forced child migration is occurring within and to South-East Asia as children flee war, persecution and armed conflicts. In the context of South-East Asia, government development projects resulting in a loss of livelihood, poverty or a deprivation of citizenship, such as the case of the Rohingya in Myanmar and the Hill Tribe people in northern Thailand, can also force people to migrate.[7] Research has shown that many of these forced migrants have not been recognized as refugees and have instead registered as migrant workers.[8] This means that children are not afforded the protection of refugee status and are often forced into various forms of exploitation, blurring the boundaries between forced and voluntary migration and trafficking. Thus, there is a strong link between irregular migration and human trafficking.

Within the region, Joudo-Larsen notes that children are trafficked from Cambodia to Thailand for begging; from Viet Nam and Myanmar to Cambodia and Thailand for sexual exploitation; and from Laos to Thailand for domestic or factory work. Girls travel from Viet Nam and

---

[2] UNICEF, *Reversing the Trend: Child Trafficking in East and South East Asia* (2009), p. 29.

[3] *Ibid.*

[4] H. Beazley, 'Multiple Identities, Multiple Realities: Children who Migrate Independently for Work in Southeast Asia' (2015) 13(3) *Children's Geographies* 296.

[5] J. Joudo-Larsen, 'The Trafficking of Children in the Asia-Pacific' (2011) 415 *Trends and Issues in Crime and Criminal Justice* 2.

[6] K.C. Ho and O. Yoshida, *Advancing the Regional Commons in the New East Asia* (Routledge, 2016), p. 54.

[7] S. Petcharamesree, 'ASEAN and Its Approach to Forced Migration Issues' (2016) 20(2) *International Journal of Human Rights* 173, at 176.

[8] *Ibid.*

Myanmar to China for forced marriage; and boys from Myanmar to Thailand to work in the fishing industry.[9] Children are also trafficked internally within countries throughout the region, for example, girls from rural areas in Cambodia to urban centres for sexual exploitation.[10] The trafficking and migration flows follow the same pattern, as children often do not fall victim to trafficking until they arrive at their destination and are exploited.[11] In some instances, what may begin as voluntary migration may end as trafficking if the destination involves exploitation.[12] Conversely, what may begin as forced migration may transform once a child reaches their destination and does not claim refugee status. In this way, it might be said that the form of migration is as tenuous as the moment of its definition.

Children frequently move to take advantage of labour opportunities. 'Child labour' is usually defined as work that deprives children of their childhood, their potential and their dignity, and that is harmful to physical and mental development.[13] Across South-East Asia, child labour is commonly tolerated and the International Labour Organization (ILO) estimates that there are almost 78 million children working in the Asia Pacific, accounting for 9.3 per cent of the child population.[14] This represents the largest number of children working in any region globally. Beazley notes that the child migration flow in the South-East Asia region is particularly labour-driven, including 'rural to urban migration to work in factories or informal sectors, migration to the streets, migration to work on fishing platforms, migration as child domestic servants and migration into the commercial sex industry'.[15] This is of little surprise as labour migration is generally the dominant form of transnational migration in the region.[16] In South-East Asia, children work in the agricultural, fishing and seafood industries, and as forced and bonded labourers in textiles

---

9 Joudo-Larsen, 'The Trafficking of Children in the Asia-Pacific', above n. 5, at 3.

10 *Ibid.*

11 UNICEF, *Reversing the Trend*, above n. 2, at 63.

12 Y. Rafferty, 'Child Trafficking and Commercial Sexual Exploitation: A Review of Promising Prevention Policies and Programs' (2013) 83(4) *American Journal of Orthopsychiatry* 559, at 560.

13 ASEAN Services Employees Trade Unions Council, *Labour Laws and Practices in ASEAN* (2013), vol. II, p. 111.

14 International Labour Organization, 'Marking Progress Against Child Labour', *Global Estimates and Trends 2000–2012* (2013), p. 17.

15 Beazley, *Multiple Identities, Multiple Realities*, above n. 4, at 296–7.

16 G. Hugo, 'International Labour Migration and Migration Policies in Southeast Asia' (2012) 40(4) *Asian Journal of Social Science* 392.

and manufacturing.[17] They are also often employed as domestic workers, which is considered 'safe and non-stigmatizing'.[18]

The demand for domestic workers has increased due to rapid urbanization and the rise of the middle class in urban areas.[19] This work is often not considered 'labour' and research has previously shown that both employers and members of the general public in countries such as Cambodia[20] and Indonesia[21] do not regard the employment of children as domestic workers as hazardous or exploitative.[22] However, children who are recruited as domestic workers either within a country, or cross-border, often find themselves in very abusive and exploitative domestic situations, or even commercial sexual exploitation.[23]

Children in South-East Asia live with a unique set of pressures which make them vulnerable in the migration process. Of major concern is the prevalence of lack of birth registration resulting in children having limited access to healthcare, education, travel, employment or political representation, and being largely excluded from obtaining both government benefits and protections.[24] This means that children are often on the move without official documentation. Other factors that lead to vulnerability and susceptibility to exploitation in migration include lack of education within a family, birth order, the influence of social networks, and expectations regarding a child's education.[25] Children in South-East Asia also often have a responsibility to generate income for their families which may lead them to seek labour opportunities within and across borders.[26]

---

17 US Department of Labour Bureau of International Labour Affairs, *2014 Findings on the Worst Forms of Child Labor* (Bureau of International Labour Affairs, 2015), p. xxviii.

18 A. Matsuno and J. Blagbrough, *Child Domestic Labour in South East and East Asia: Emerging Good Practices to Combat It* (ILO, 2006), p. 2.

19 *Ibid.* xii.

20 Cambodian Ministry of Planning, *Survey Report: Child Domestic Worker Survey* (National Institute of Statistics, 2004), p. 8.

21 J. Blagbrough, *Child Domestic Work in Indonesia: A Preliminary Situation Analysis* (Anti-Slavery International, 1995), p. 20.

22 Matsuno and Blagbrough, *Child Domestic Labour in South East and East Asia*, above n. 18, at 2.

23 *Ibid.* xii.

24 Joudo-Larsen, 'The Trafficking of Children in the Asia-Pacific', above n. 5, at 2.

25 A. Blackburn, R. Taylor and J.E. Davis, 'Understanding the Complexities of Human Trafficking and Child Sexual Exploitation: The Case of Southeast Asia' (2010) 20(1–2) *Women and Criminal Justice* 105, at 107.

26 E. Goździak, 'On Challenges, Dilemmas, and Opportunities in Studying Trafficked Children' (2008) 81(4) *Anthropological Quarterly* 903, at 919.

Economic issues, including indebtedness, are often a driver for parents choosing to send their children away to work, but it is also the rationale for many children choosing to migrate independently within the region.[27] The promise of better economic opportunities often encourages children to migrate from countries such as Indonesia or Cambodia. Both have low rates of development and are source countries for trafficking. Voluntary migration occurs to countries like Thailand, which is at an intermediate level of development and has a moderate rate of growth.[28] Higher wages in better-developed countries that are easily accessible make migration an attractive option. The prospect of remittances being sent back by the child further enhances the migratory decision.[29] Children are often recruited into these positions by relatives or introduced to work by an acquaintance.

The problem is that child traffickers use the same methods across the region. Children are 'deceived by an acquaintance or relative, taken by use of force, abduction or kidnapping or taken with the consent of parents of guardians, which has been secured through a payment or benefit to the adult'.[30] The purpose of this trafficking is overwhelmingly exploitative labour, however also includes trafficking for sexual exploitation, illegal adoption and begging.[31]

The complexity of the irregular and mixed migration flows within the region makes it difficult to formulate effective legislative responses at domestic and regional levels to ensure that children are protected.

2. LEGAL FRAMEWORKS FOR CHILD MIGRATION AND TRAFFICKING IN SOUTH-EAST ASIA

Turning to examine the legal frameworks relevant to child migration and trafficking in South-East Asia, the initial focus is on the ASEAN Convention Against Trafficking in Persons, Especially Women and Children (ACTIP). I then examine individual responses to child trafficking of Singapore, Cambodia and Thailand, as the first three signatories to ACTIP.

---

27 Blackburn, Taylor and Davis, 'Understanding the Complexities of Human Trafficking and Child Sexual Exploitation', above n. 25, at 108.

28 UNICEF, *Reversing the Trend*, above n. 2, at 32.

29 Goździak, 'On Challenges, Dilemmas, and Opportunities in Studying Trafficked Children', above n. 26, at 919.

30 UNICEF, *Reversing the Trend*, above n. 2, at 28.

31 *Ibid.* 32.

2.1 ASEAN's Response

South-East Asia has long struggled with the issue of human trafficking and migration. Although reliable data is scarce, it is estimated that around one-third of the global trafficking in women and children occurs within or from South-East Asia.[32] Despite a regional mandate, ASEAN countries have long valued sovereignty and national autonomy over cross-border cooperation and external intervention. In turn, this has had significant impact on individual nations' and the region's ability to respond to transnational trafficking. Despite this, ASEAN has attempted to legally respond to the issue through counter-human trafficking strategies in a variety of ways.

In 2004, the heads of ASEAN declared that they would make concerted efforts to address the regional issue of human trafficking through a declaration to reaffirm the Protocol to Prevent, Suppress and Punish Trafficking in Persons, Especially Women and Children 2000 ('UN Trafficking Protocol'). The declaration outlined commitments to share information, to improve the protection of identity documents, to criminalize actions by perpetrators, and to protect victims.[33] However, these commitments only required states parties to take action 'to the extent permitted by their respective domestic laws'. Due to the limited implementation they were largely ineffective.[34]

In recognition that the trafficking of children was most serious in the Greater Mekong Sub-region, the governments of Lao People's Democratic Republic (PDR), Myanmar, Thailand, Viet Nam and China signed the first Regional Memorandum of Understanding (MoU) on Cooperation against Trafficking in Persons in the Greater Mekong Sub-region in 2004. This MoU addressed prevention, repatriation, reintegration, child sensitive investigation techniques, and the extradition and prosecution of traffickers and solicitors of trafficked children.[35] Since then, the counter-trafficking mechanisms have included structural responses such as the

---

[32] 'Key Regional Facts on Child Protection', paper presented at Seventh East Asia and Pacific Ministerial Consultation on Children, 23–25 March 2005, cited in UNICEF, *A Region Where Every Child Counts: Child Protection* (UNICEF EAPRO, 2005), p. 1.

[33] Joudo-Larsen, Lindley and Putt, 'Trafficking in Persons Monitoring Report July 2007–December 2008', above n. 1, at 14.

[34] Petcharamesree, 'ASEAN and Its Approach to Forced Migration Issues', above n. 7, at 182.

[35] UNICEF, *ASEAN Situation Review of Children: A Report by UNICEF to the Association of Southeast Asian Nations* (2007), p. 24.

Roadmap for an ASEAN Community, agreements listing trafficking as a transnational crime, and the designation of two human rights bodies to the issue.[36] However, these measures have also largely been considered ineffective due to failures in implementation and cooperation.[37]

One of the issues with addressing human trafficking in the ASEAN region has been the traditional separation of labour migration and human trafficking at law, when in reality they are closely intertwined. Of most promise in this respect was the establishment of the three-pillar community that aimed to promote and protect people's rights, including protection from human trafficking by 2015. However, the completely separate treatment of protection from human trafficking and labour migration meant that the opportunity was missed.[38] In 2016, this issue was partially solved when children in South-East Asia became specifically protected by the ASEAN Regional Plan of Action on Elimination of Violence Against Children which recognizes child migrants and child labourers separately. The Regional Plan advocates for a child rights-based approach with respect to policies of member states, and requires them to safeguard a child's best interests in accordance with the provisions in the Convention of the Rights of the Child. However, with the focus on child migrants and labourers, the impact on child trafficking victims has been negligible.

The most promising protection introduced against child trafficking in the region is the recently introduced ASEAN Convention and Plan of Action Against Trafficking in Persons, Especially in Women and Children (ACTIP). The ACTIP was introduced on 15 November 2015 and requires six signatories to come into force. It represents a united effort by ASEAN to face the increasing issue of human trafficking and to enable the region as a whole to implement a series of measures designed to be far more powerful than the 2004 Declaration. In contrast to the 2004 Declaration, which was non-binding and unenforceable, the ACTIP is legally binding. It aims to provide ASEAN members with the ability to facilitate cross-border cooperation on anti-trafficking, to strengthen the rule of law and border control, and to place a greater emphasis on prosecution.

The ACTIP was slow to gain momentum and only came into force in early 2017 with six signatory states: Cambodia, Singapore, Thailand, Viet Nam, Myanmar and the Phillipines. Since then, Lao PDR and Malaysia have also ratified it. Indonesia has also indicated that it will ratify,

---

36 N. Kranrattanasuit, *ASEAN and Human Trafficking: Case Studies of Cambodia, Thailand and Vietnam* (Brill Nijhoff, 2014), p. 52.

37 *Ibid.*

38 *Ibid.*

however has not yet done so. Given that Singapore only ratified the UN Trafficking Protocol in November 2015, its early signatory status to the ACTIP appeared to signal a promising turning point in the seriousness with which combatting trafficking is regarded in the region. Indeed, the introduction of ACTIP signalled that there was strong political will for the region to work together on the issue of trafficking. However, even with this promising beginning, ACTIP has since faltered. The hesitancy to ratify appears to lie in the extensive legal obligations that states will be required to assume.

While the hope is that ACTIP will successfully enable states across the region to cooperate on transnational trafficking, the issue of internal domestic trafficking still remains for each state to address independently. To this end, I turn to examining three of the ASEAN states that are representative of the region: Cambodia, which experiences a high level of domestic trafficking; Singapore, which is typically a transit or destination state for transnational trafficking; and Thailand, which experiences both internal trafficking and is both a source and destination state for child trafficking within the region. I examine how each of these states has responded domestically to child trafficking and how the regional operation of ACTIP may assist their efforts.

2.2 Cambodia

Cambodia has long struggled with internal domestic trafficking and trafficking within the Greater Mekong Sub-region. In 1996, Cambodia adopted the Law on Suppression of the Kidnapping, Trafficking and Exploitation of Human Beings, and in doing so was one of the first countries in the region to adopt anti-trafficking legislation. However, while the law prohibited the kidnapping of persons for trafficking, sale or prostitution, it failed to define what was meant by 'trafficking'. This caused immense issues with implementation and prosecution under the law.[39]

Despite their early adoption of anti-trafficking measures, Cambodia remains at Tier 2 on the US State Department's *Trafficking in Persons Report*.[40] This means that they are assessed by the US State Department as

---

[39] International Organization for Migration, *ASEAN and Trafficking in Persons: Using Data as a Tool to Combat Trafficking in Persons* (2007), p. 32.

[40] The annual *Trafficking in Persons Report* is considered a comprehensive resource of anti-human trafficking efforts internationally and the de facto treaty monitoring body of the International Trafficking Protocol. Countries are assessed against the requirements of the Trafficking Victims Protection Act 2000 (US).

a country whose government does not fully meet anti-trafficking minimum standards, but are making significant efforts to meet those standards. The 2016 Report particularly notes that children from impoverished families are often forced into labour such as domestic servitude or street vending in Thailand and Viet Nam, often with complicit approval from their parents.[41] Cambodia has made significant inroads into the prevention of children being trafficked to work in commercial sex establishments, with children making up 2.2 per cent of the total population working in this industry in 2016, a significant improvement from 8.2 per cent in 2013.[42]

Another major issue for Cambodia has been the prevalence of children being trafficked into residential care centres, or orphanages.[43] In 2016, there were 11,788 children residing in these facilities.[44] It was estimated that 80 per cent of them had family that they could be residing with if the family was supported.[45] Despite the number of true orphans decreasing, the number of residential care facilities doubled in the five years before 2016. This reflects an increase in foreign-run orphanages and the growing popularity of orphanage volunteering in the country.[46] These factors have led to an increase of children being removed from their families under fraudulent conditions. They are effectively trafficked into orphanages for the purpose of profit garnered from international volunteers and donors.[47] Further, there is a technicality present in the domestic legislation that results in parents being able to sell their child to a trafficker for the purpose of inter-country adoption without it being legally regarded as trafficking.[48]

While Cambodia has not enjoyed particular success in implementing domestic legislation against child trafficking, as an early signatory to ACTIP, it has recognized the potential of the first regionally binding

---

Countries that are the most compliant are listed as Tier 1, with the least compliant listed as Tier 3.

41 US State Department, *Trafficking in Persons Report 2016* (2016), p. 119.

42 *Ibid.*

43 K.E. van Doore, 'Paper Orphans: Exploring Child Trafficking for the Purpose of Orphanages' (2016) 24(2) *International Journal of Children's Rights* 378, at 403.

44 Ministry of Social Affairs, Veterans and Youth Rehabilitation, *Preliminary Data Compilation and Findings: Mapping of Residential Care Institutions* (2016), p. 7.

45 UNICEF, *With the Best Intentions: A Study of Attitudes Towards Residential Care in Cambodia* (2011), p. 12.

46 *Ibid.*

47 Van Doore, 'Paper Orphans', above n. 43, at 403; also see T. Winkler and L. Delacey, *How (Not) to Start an Orphanage . . . by a Woman Who Did* (Allen & Unwin, 2016).

48 Kranrattanasuit, *ASEAN and Human Trafficking*, above n. 36, at 114.

instrument addressing trafficking in ASEAN. For Cambodia, it is hoped that this regional solution will add strength to the previously poor outcomes for victims of trafficking.

2.3 Singapore

Singapore has taken a firm stance on trafficking both domestically and regionally with the establishment of the Inter-Agency Taskforce on Trafficking in Persons and the adoption of a National Plan of Action 2012–2015. The Inter-Agency Taskforce is a representative body of cross-governmental ministries and agencies, including the Singapore Police Force, established in 2010 to combat human trafficking in Singapore. It has worked strategically through establishing legal frameworks at all levels under the '4P' framework of Prevention, Prosecution, Protection and Partnership. This culminated in the introduction of the Prevention of Human Trafficking Act in March 2015 at the domestic level; acceding to the UN Trafficking Protocol in September 2015 at the international level; and the ratification of the ACTIP in January 2016 at the regional level.

Singapore is regarded widely as an economic powerhouse within the ASEAN region and is largely a destination country for labour trafficking and migration due to its strategic location.[49] Recruitment agencies are known to travel to villages to seek women and children to work in Singapore as domestic help. Where a worker is found to be under-age, legal documents are created to falsify a child's real age and thus facilitate labour trafficking. The US State Department's *Trafficking in Persons Report 2016* also noted that child sex trafficking of both foreign and Singaporean children is an issue for Singapore.[50] In this respect, girls were ostensibly covered under Article 141 of the Women's Charter which prohibits their movement for trafficking. However, the Charter failed to define the meaning of 'trafficking' and boys were not included at all.[51]

This has been corrected with the introduction of the Prevention of Human Trafficking Act 2015 which is gender neutral. However, despite investigating over 50 cases of sex trafficking since the introduction of the Act, Singapore has been successful in securing only one prosecution in relation to child sex trafficking.[52] Children are also afforded special

---

49 N. Piper, 'A Problem by a Different Name? A Review of Research on Trafficking on South East Asia and Oceania' (2005) 43(1–2) *International Migration* 203, at 204.

50 US State Department, *Trafficking in Persons Report 2016*, above n. 41, at 334.

51 *Ibid.*

52 *Ibid.*

protection under the Prevention of Human Trafficking Act 2015. Under this Act, a first-time offender convicted of child trafficking attracts an aggravated sentence, including the potential of up to 10 years' imprisonment, a maximum fine of SGD$100,000, and up to six strokes of the cane. Repeat offenders have harsher penalties, with the potential of 15 years' imprisonment, a fine of up to SGD$150,000 and a mandatory nine strokes of the cane. Child victims must be given shelter as well as access to translation, legal assistance and counselling.[53]

For Singapore, the ACTIP plays a critical role in the government's anti-trafficking mission. Whilst the Prevention of Human Trafficking Act 2015 is transnational in operation, the ACTIP will provide the legally binding mandate necessary for other countries in the region to cooperate with Singapore's efforts towards enforcement.

2.4 Thailand

Thailand is recognized as both a source and destination country for significant levels of child migration and trafficking.[54] In 2016, the US State Department found that children from 'Thailand, Burma, Laos, and Cambodia are victims of sex trafficking in brothels, massage parlours, bars, karaoke lounges, hotel rooms, and private residences' within Thailand and that children were often being recruited using social media.[55] Thailand has the highest number of refugees and asylum-seekers in the ASEAN region, however very few are recognized as such and afforded protection.[56]

Child trafficking in Thailand has come under heavy scrutiny due to slow implementation and weak enforcement of its domestic laws, namely the Prevention and Suppression of Human Trafficking Act (BE 2551) 2008. Many factors were to blame for this, including a low-skilled and lowly remunerated police force that struggled with corruption, subsequently weakening the enforcement system.[57] There is also a concentration on prosecuting the victims of child trafficking under solicitation and begging laws, rather than a focus on securing prosecutions of traffickers, brothel and factory owners.

Although the Thai government is a signatory to the Convention

---

53 *Ibid.*

54 R.M. Pink, 'Child Trafficking in Thailand: Prevention and Prosecution Challenges' (2013) 40(4) *Asian Affairs: An American Review* 163.

55 US State Department, *Trafficking in Persons Report 2016*, above n. 41, at 364.

56 Petcharamesree, 'ASEAN and Its Approach to Forced Migration Issues', above n. 7, at 176.

57 Pink, 'Child Trafficking in Thailand', above n. 54, at 168.

on the Rights of the Child, they have not instituted any effective enforcement regime that will begin to ameliorate the child trafficking situation.[58] As a result, Thailand was ranked at the lowest Tier 3 in the US State Department's *Trafficking in Persons Report* in 2014 and 2015. However, the ratification of the UN Trafficking Protocol in 2013 and the introduction of the Anti-Human Trafficking Amendment No. 2 in 2015 saw the promise of stronger penalties for trafficking, enhanced protection for victims and a reduction in the threat of whistle blowers being intimidated.[59] In a promising move, Thailand was also one of the few early signatories to the ACTIP, lodging their ratification approximately seven months after its introduction. For child trafficking victims in Thailand, ACTIP will reinforce the national legislative amendments and provide further regional support to Thailand's national efforts.

3. STRIKING A BALANCE: BEST INTERESTS OF THE CHILD

Thus far, I have examined the reasons that children are on the move through South-East Asia and the legal frameworks that seek to protect them at domestic and regional levels. I now turn to explore how child migration can become child trafficking at law and the ramifications for children of this characterization. Regardless of whether force, threats or coercion are involved, moving or receiving child labour migrants for the purpose of exploitation is trafficking.[60] Huijsmans notes that most child labour migrants will experience some degree of exploitation and that this has the effect of systemically conflating child labour migration with child trafficking.[61] O'Connell identifies that most of the research focuses on the vulnerabilities that make children susceptible to trafficking, however these factors are identical to the drivers for child migration. This crystallizes the issues when attempting to differentiate between child migrants for labour and trafficked children.[62]

---

58 *Ibid.* 168.

59 US State Department, *Trafficking in Persons Report 2016*, above n. 41, at 376.

60 Joudo-Larsen, 'The Trafficking of Children in the Asia-Pacific', above n. 5, at 3.

61 R. Huijsmans and S. Baker, 'Child Trafficking: "Worst Form" of Child Labour, or Worst Approach to Young Migrants? Trafficked Children or Young Migrants?' (2012) 43(4) *Development and Change* 919, at 923.

62 J. O'Connell Davidson and C. Farrow, *Child Migration and the Construction of Vulnerability* (Save the Children, 2007), p. 35.

The economic disparities that drive irregular migration between ASEAN countries are also drivers of trafficking. Although irregular, the majority of this migration by children begins as voluntary. However, when exploitation occurs, the legal characterization shifts from irregular child migration to child trafficking.[63] The differentiation becomes difficult when considering the 'extremely blurred line between disadvantaged children's labour migration as a strategy for improving difficult life conditions, and "child trafficking"'.[64] The conflation of child labour migration and child trafficking results in criminal justice responses within the region, and anti-trafficking measures that limit migration between countries, which in turn heighten children's vulnerability to exploitation.[65]

The ACTIP facilitates this conflation through rendering 'children's consent to any form of facilitated migration leading to exploitation irrelevant in qualifying as a case of human trafficking'.[66] However, whether children possess sufficient agency to consent to voluntary migration for labour is a question that finds contradictory answers. At law, the assumption is that children do not possess agency and are thus vulnerable to exploitation.[67] The balance between the measure of a child's agency to engage in voluntary migration and the potential of such a decision to result in human trafficking and child exploitation is difficult to conceptualize in a legal framework. For this reason, we turn to the best interests of the child found in the Convention on the Rights of the Child in order to establish how best to approach the protection of the migrant and trafficked child.

3.1 Best Interests of the Migrant or Trafficked Child in South-East Asia?

Unlike most other international agreements, all ASEAN members are signatories to the Convention on the Rights of the Child (CRC).[68] Article 3 of the CRC outlines that:

---

63 Joudo-Larsen, 'The Trafficking of Children in the Asia-Pacific', above n. 5, at 3.

64 O'Connell Davidson and Farrow, *Child Migration and the Construction of Vulnerability*, above n. 62, at 10.

65 *Ibid.* 10.

66 Huijsmans and Baker, 'Child Trafficking', above n. 61, at 923.

67 A. Gallagher, *The International Law of Human Trafficking* (Cambridge University Press, 2010), p. 323.

68 ASEAN Services Employees Trade Unions Council, *Labour Laws and Practices in ASEAN*, above n. 13, at 115.

> In all actions concerning children, whether undertaken by public or private social welfare institutions, courts of law, administrative authorities or legislative bodies, the best interests of the child shall be a primary consideration.[69]

This is reflected in Guideline 8 of the *UN Trafficking Principles and Guidelines*, which states that:

> the best interests of the child must be a primary consideration in all actions concerning trafficking children whether undertaken by public or private welfare institutions, courts of law, administrative authorities or legislative bodies.[70]

As previously stated, the migratory flows throughout South-East Asia suggest that many children undertake the migration process to access better opportunities than they can in their home countries. However, incorporation of the best interests of the child is hardly evident in the anti-trafficking policies that actively discourage child migration for labour. This often results in a policing of the migrant child rather than protection. A balance must be struck between determining when a child has migrated to access these opportunities versus those that end up in exploitative situations. In both situations, children must be protected and their best interests upheld.

Where children migrate for labour, research suggests that a shift from imposing limitations through immigration policies and the resulting policing responses towards a 'more evidence-driven, rights-based approach' to all labour migration would create a model of governance in South-East Asia.[71] In this vein, O'Connell argues for policy frameworks that recognize that migration is 'not inherently bad for children' and have a clear focus 'on the role of government preventing, allowing or creating migratory conditions under which children are vulnerable to abuse or exploitation, while at the same time fully acknowledging children's capacity (including disadvantaged children's) for migratory agency'.[72]

It may be that South-East Asia through ASEAN is in a unique position

---

[69] Convention on the Rights of the Child, adopted 20 November 1989, 1577 UNTS 3 (entered into force 2 September 1990) (CRC).

[70] United Nations High Commissioner for Human Rights, *Recommended Principles and Guidelines on Human Rights and Human Trafficking*, E/2002/68/Add.1 (2002), pp. 348–9.

[71] G. Hugo, 'International Labour Migration and Migration Policies in Southeast Asia' (2012) 40(4) *Asian Journal of Social Science* 392.

[72] O'Connell Davidson and Farrow, *Child Migration and the Construction of Vulnerability*, above n. 62, at 56.

to enable policies with this focus. ASEAN has already established the Children's Forum to:

> serve as the regional voice for children in ASEAN and a channel where children can express their views on urgent regional issues and how these can be resolved by governments with children and young people's participation.[73]

This initiative exemplifies a willingness to engage with, and recognize, children's agency on policy issues, however whether that engagement extends to firm legislative outcomes is yet to be seen.

Of course, this discussion of agency does not translate to protection of the trafficked child, whose agency has been removed. Achieving a child rights-based approach protecting the agency of child migrants while at the same time offering protection to the trafficked child from exploitation is a very difficult task indeed. In this respect, child migration exists on a spectrum, with a child capable of exerting agency and voluntarily migrating at one end, and a child whose rights and agency has been exploited and is trafficked at the other end. At any point in time, a child who believes they are migrating independently may slip into the legal category of trafficked when they find themselves engaged in exploitative labour or sexual exploitation at their destination.

With this in mind, a framework for creating policies with a child rights-based approach should:

- defend the rights of all children throughout the migratory process, whether they are exploited or at risk of exploitation, and despite how, and by whom, the migration was organized;
- promote rights protection through the CRC in both origin and destination countries, especially in relation to the rights that children are attempting to access in making the migratory decision;
- build capacity and expertise in advocating and enshrining children's rights in the migration policy-making processes at regional and national levels.[74]

Building upon the impetus of ACTIP, an ASEAN regional agreement on child migration encapsulating a child rights-based approach would be consistent with the evidence base which calls for a recognition of children's

[73] ASEAN Services Employees Trade Unions Council, *Labour Laws and Practices in ASEAN*, above n. 13, at 114.

[74] O'Connell Davidson and Farrow, *Child Migration and the Construction of Vulnerability*, above n. 62, at 56.

voices and opinions in child migration matters. The incorporation of the best interests of the child principle into a legally binding regional agreement on child migration would be consistent with ASEAN's renewed focus on regional cooperation in relation to trafficking. It would further embed the rights of the child into the forefront of the region's legal framework and serve as a protection mechanism for the ever-expanding number of children engaging in the migration process, whether forcibly or voluntarily.

4. CONCLUSION

In conclusion, child migration and trafficking in South-East Asia poses a series of complex policy issues for ASEAN and the countries in the region. The increasing movement of children through the region, particularly to access perceived better opportunities or to escape atrocities in their home countries, shows no sign of subsiding. The region therefore needs to meet the challenge of responding in a way that places the best interests of the child at the forefront.

While the region has attempted to deal with the issue of trafficking many times in the last decade, the most promising tool introduced in this fight is ACTIP. However, until it is formally enacted through the ratification of at least six member nations, countries in the region are left to their domestic legislation. Cambodia, Singapore and Thailand are countries with differing legislative approaches to the complex issue of child trafficking, both domestically and intra-regionally. Of key importance for all three countries is that ACTIP is enacted to provide further support to the domestic efforts that are increasingly being undertaken.

This chapter has argued that South-East Asia is in a unique position to adopt a child rights-based approach to child trafficking and migration policy regionally with the best interests of the child as the paramount consideration. As all member states of ASEAN are signatories to the CRC, as opposed to other international and regional Conventions, the best interests of the child paradigm should already be at the forefront of domestic policy and legislation. As there are many areas of policy and law where child rights have not been placed as the primary consideration, South-East Asia has the potential to lead the way in embracing a child rights-based approach with respect to child migration and trafficking throughout the region.

11. Regulating child labour in China: a historical perspective of internal child migration

Mimi Zou

1. INTRODUCTION

Thirty years ago, China introduced laws that created a nine-year compulsory education system and a ban on the employment of children of 16 years or younger.[1] Some have argued that child labour has since become negligible in China,[2] existing only in 'pockets' but 'not pervasive' compared to many other developing countries.[3] The International Labour Organization (ILO) has in fact referred to China as an example to illustrate how a country can deploy mass education policies and poverty eradication measures to tackle child labour. It noted:

> In the past 25 years, China has taken more people out of poverty and enrolled more children in school than any other country. There is thus strong circumstantial evidence that this has also had a dramatic impact on child labour in China.[4]

On the other hand, some have pointed to cases involving the exploitation of children workers in diverse sectors and have argued that such practices are more widespread than reported.[5] The problem certainly attracted

---

[1] Compulsory Education Law 1986 (People's Republic of China) Sixth National People's Congress, Fourth Session, 12 April 1986, and amended at the Tenth National People's Congress, 22nd Session, 29 June 2006.

[2] H. He, 'Child Labour and Academic Achievement: Evidence from Gansu Province in China' (2016) 38 *China Economic Review* 130.

[3] A. Chan, *The Exploitation of Labour in a Global Economy* (Armonk, 2001), p. 225.

[4] International Labour Organization, *Global Report on Child Labour, The End of Child labour: Within Reach* (ILO, 2006), p. 11.

[5] P. Lund-Thomsen et al., 'Labour in Global Value Chains: Work Conditions in Football Manufacturing in China, India and Pakistan' (2012) 23(6) *Development*

international media coverage and the attention of top Chinese leaders in 2007–2008 when it was discovered that hundreds of people, including many children, were abducted and forced to work in slave-like conditions in illegal brick kilns in Shaanxi and Henan provinces. The scandal led to a nationwide government crackdown on slavery, human trafficking and child labour.[6] Similar concerns have emerged over the abuse of vocational 'work and study' student internship schemes by Foxconn and other suppliers to multinational brands such as Apple, HP and Dell. Such practices surged in 2012–2013 during a period of acute labour shortages in the manufacturing hub of the Pearl River Delta.[7]

The issues of child labour and internal migration are closely related. In 2016, the reported death of a 15-year-old boy in a rented room next to the undergarment factory that he was working in Foshan city of Guangdong (one of the most prosperous provinces and the largest economic hub of China) prompted the local government to instigate another crackdown on child labour. While the cause of the boy's death remains unknown, his mother (also employed in the same factory) believed that he 'may have died from overwork'.[8] It was reported that both the mother and the boy were rural migrants from a much poorer province (Hunan) and had moved to Foshan to earn some money for supporting family members back home. An investigation by the local government led to a fine of RMB10,000 (around US$1,400) on the company, which was publicly perceived to be a 'light' penalty.[9]

The actual extent of the phenomenon is difficult to ascertain due to the lack of official reporting on cases, data and statistics. As Lieten and Hindman put it, much of the available information has emerged from

---

and Change 1211; China Labour Watch, *Supplier Factory of Samsung, Lenovo Violates Rights of Children and Students* (28 August 2014), available at www.chinalaborwatch.org/newscast/348; K. Lepillez, 'The Dark Side of Labor in China', *University of Denver Research Digest*, available at www.du.edu/korbel/hrhw/researchdigest/slavery/china.pdf.

[6] BBC, 'Chinese police find child slaves', BBC Online, 30 April 2008, available at http://news.bbc.co.uk/2/hi/asia-pacific/7374864.stm.

[7] M. Selden, J. Chan and P. Ngai, 'Interns or Workers? China's Student Labor Regime' (2015) 13(56) *Asia-Pacific Journal* 1.

[8] M. Lau, 'Death of boy, 15, prompts crackdown on child labour in southern Chinese province', *South China Morning Post* (Hong Kong), 9 May 2016, available at www.scmp.com/news/china/society/article/1942616/death-boy-15-prompts-crackdown-child-labour-southern-chinese.

[9] China Labour Watch, *Sudden Death of a 14 Year Old Child Worker from a Factory in Foshan* (27 April 2016), available at www.chinalaborwatch.org/newscast/597.

'anecdotal evidence, news reports, and inference, making inquiry more speculative than scholars would prefer'.[10] This challenge can be gleaned from the Shaanxi brick kiln scandal, where the Chinese media reported thousands of rural children being kidnapped into forced labour. A subsequent police crackdown indicated that the number of rescued child workers was somewhere in the range of 51–109.[11] Shaanxi government officials claimed the figure to be 12, which it later changed to six after conducting its own investigation.[12]

It would seem that, at least on paper, China has developed a relatively comprehensive legal framework in recent decades that is aimed at eliminating and preventing child labour. The most commonly cited problem is the weak monitoring and enforcement of the relevant laws in practice, which is 'then exploited by domestic and foreign businesses'.[13] Demand for low-cost labour and the emergence of labour shortages in a number of coastal regions may have created incentives for some employers to turn to using child labour as a cheaper and more malleable workforce.[14]

This chapter situates China's contemporary child labour regulation and issues concerning internal child migration in the historical context of childhood and the evolution of legal norms that have restricted the use of child labour. There has been little published research (in the English language) that offers historical accounts of child labour issues in China. A few notable exceptions include: a book chapter that provides a historical overview of child labour practices in China;[15] a chapter on child labour reform in a doctoral thesis on pre-school education in China from 1903 to 1953;[16] a book chapter that outlines the changing social views and customs relating to child labour in China;[17] and a book chapter that critiques

---

[10] G.K. Lieten and H.D. Hindman, 'Child Labor in China: An Overview' in H.D. Hindman (ed.), *The World of Child Labour: An Historical and Regional Survey* (M.E. Sharpe Inc., 2009).

[11] China Labour Bulletin, *Small Hands: A Survey Report on Child Labour in China* (September 2007), p. 3, available at www.clb.org.hk/sites/default/files/archive/en/share/File/general/Child_labour_report_1.pdf.

[12] *Ibid.*

[13] U. Liukkunen, 'ILO and Child Labour Regulation in China: Prospects and Complexities' in U. Liukkunen and Y. Chen (eds), *Fundamental Labour Rights in China: Legal Implementation and Cultural Logic* (Springer, 2016), pp. 139, 141, 148–9.

[14] China Labour Bulletin, *Small Hands*, above n. 11, at 4.

[15] J. Howard, 'History of Child Labor in China' in G.K. Lieten and E.N. Meerkerk (eds), *Child Labour's Global Past* (Peter Lang Publishers, 2011), p. 501.

[16] M. Tillman, *Precocious Politics: Preschsool Education and Child Protection in China* (Doctoral Thesis University of California Berkeley, 2013).

[17] S. Lu et al., 'China' in C.L. Schmitz, E.K.J. Traver and D. Larson (eds), *Child Labor: A Global View* (Greenwood Press, 2004).

the historical prevalence of Western ideals underpinning discussions of children's issues in China.[18] This chapter contributes a unique socio-legal and historical perspective to this under-examined area of scholarship.

In the following analysis, I first lay out the key aspects of China's current laws and policies concerning child labour, including the implementation of international child labour standards that it has ratified. Second, I examine how child labour regulation evolved from the Qing dynasty onwards to the founding of the People's Republic of China. In concluding the chapter, I highlight a key contemporary challenge in China's attempts to tackle this issue: the social dislocation arising from mass rural-to-urban migration that has rendered rural migrant children at greater risk of child labour. Millions of rural migrant children coming to the cities with their parents are commonly deprived of access to education, healthcare and social welfare in urban China. Meanwhile, the 60 million children who are 'left behind' in rural hometowns experience a range of physical and psychological problems arising from long-term separation from their parents.

2. CONTEMPORARY REGULATORY FRAMEWORK IN CHINA

China ratified the United Nations' Convention on the Rights of the Child (CRC) in 1992. The CRC, which took effect on 7 September 1990, is the first specific international instrument that covers a full range of human rights that children everywhere in the world should enjoy. The CRC contains the right of children to protection from economic exploitation (Article 32) and the right to education (Article 28). In considering the most recent (2013) report submitted by China on its implementation of the CRC, the Committee on the Rights of the Child noted that:

> China had undertaken to prohibit economic exploitation of child labour; however the Committee was concerned at the absence of disaggregated data with regard to child labour in the country. There was a mismatch between the minimum age of employment and the obligatory school age.[19]

---

[18] A. West, 'Childhood and Children's Rights in China' in B. Franklin (ed.), *The New Handbook of Children's Rights: Comparative Policy and Practice* (Routledge, 2002).

[19] Office of the High Commissioner on Human Rights, *Committee on the Rights of the Child Examines Reports of China of the Convention and on Children in Armed Conflict* (27 September 2013), available at www.ohchr.org/EN/NewsEvents/Pages/DisplayNews.aspx?NewsID=13795&LangID=E#sthash.LNk1LEfF.dpuf.

The two main international instruments on child labour are the ILO's Minimum Age Convention 1973 (No. 138),[20] which China ratified on 28 April 1999, and the Worst Forms of Child Labour Convention 1999 (No. 182),[21] which China ratified on 8 August 2002. These two Conventions on child labour are considered as 'core' Conventions concerning the effective abolition of child labour under the ILO's Declaration on Fundamental Rights and Principles at Work (1998). Regardless of whether or not they have ratified the Conventions, all ILO member states by virtue of their membership in the Organization have an obligation to respect, to promote and to realize the fundamental rights and principles.

ILO Convention No. 138 requires countries to set a minimum age for working children in national laws and regulations. This minimum age cannot be lower than the age for the completion of compulsory schooling, which should be no lower than 15 years (or 14 years for developing countries). The Convention allows for light work to be undertaken by children between the ages of 13 and 15. The minimum age for hazard work must be no lower than 18 years. The competent national authority may exclude certain types of work from the material scope of the Convention after consultation with employers' and workers' organizations.

ILO Convention No. 182 requires countries to adopt 'immediate and effective measures to secure the prohibition and elimination of the worst forms of child labour, as a matter of urgency'. The worst forms of child labour are defined as: all forms of slavery or practices similar to slavery (including the sale and trafficking of children, debt bondage and serfdom and forced or compulsory labour); the use, procuring or offering of a child for prostitution, production of pornography or pornographic performances; the use, procuring or offering of a child for illicit activities; and work which, by its nature or the circumstances in which it is carried out, is likely to harm the health, safety or morals of children ('hazardous work').[22] The Convention allows national governments to define 'hazardous work' after consultation with employers' and workers' organizations and taking into account relevant international standards.

In light of its obligations under these Conventions, China has developed and refined its framework of national laws and regulations aimed at eliminating and preventing child labour. In 1991, the first version of the Law

---

20 ILO, Minimum Age Convention, opened for signature 26 June 1973, C138 (entered into force 19 June 1976).

21 ILO, Worst Forms of Child Labour Convention, opened for signature 17 June 1999, C182 (entered into force 19 November 2000).

22 Law on Protection of Minors 1991 (People's Republic of China) Seventh National People's Congress, 21st Session, 4 September 1991 (repealed).

on the Protection of Minors was promulgated by the National People's Congress, the highest legislative body in China. In 2006, a new version of this law replaced the 1991 legislation.[23] The Law on the Protection of Minors stipulates that children under the age of 16 shall not be employed, except where prescribed by the state.[24] For children between 16 and 18 years old, employers must:

> observe State regulations regarding the types of jobs, working hours, intensity of labour and protective measures. Employers may not assign these children any over-strenuous jobs, jobs exposed to toxic or hazardous substances, or other jobs that imperil their physical or mental health, or any dangerous operations.[25]

Employers who violate these provisions will be subject to fines and revocation of business licence if the circumstances are serious.[26]

Furthermore, the Labor Law of 1994 has a general prohibition on the employment of children under the age of 16.[27] Nevertheless it allows for 'arts, sports and special-skills units that plan to recruit minors under the age of 16' to seek approval according to relevant state regulations, but must guarantee the right of the employed minor to receive compulsory education.[28] The protections under the 1994 Labour Law and the 2008 Labour Contract Law extend only to those in a formal employment relationship with an 'employing unit'. Private individuals and households fall outside this definition, which excludes labour law's coverage to over 20 million domestic workers in China, many of whom are young female rural migrant workers.[29] At the time of writing, China has yet to ratify the ILO's Domestic Workers Convention.

As the highest administrative organ in China, the State Council issued the Provisions on the Prohibition of Using Child Labour 2002 ('the Provisions')[30] to supplement the Law on the Protection of Minors and

---

23 Law on Protection of Minors 2006 (People's Republic of China) Tenth National People's Congress, 25th Session, 29 December 2006.

24 *Ibid.* art. 38.

25 *Ibid.*

26 *Ibid.* art. 68.

27 Labour Law 1994 (People's Republic of China) Eighth National People's Congress, Eighth Session, 5 July 1994, art. 15.

28 *Ibid.*

29 ILO, *Situational Analysis of Domestic Work in China* (1 September 2009), available at www.ilo.org/asia/whatwedo/publications/WCMS_114261/lang--en/index.htm.

30 Provisions on the Prohibition of Using Child Labour (People's Republic of China) State Council, adopted 1 October 2002, effective 1 December 2002.

the Labour Law. The Provisions apply to children working for private and public entities. The recruitment of children by employment agencies is further prohibited.[31] Importantly, employers are required to inspect the worker's identity documents and keep a record of employment registration files.[32] The employer's failure to keep such records or the forgery of identity documents can attract a fine of 10,000 yuan.[33]

Under the Provisions, local labour bureaus at or above the county level are given inspection and supervision responsibilities.[34] The Provisions impose a duty on parents or guardians of minors under the age of 16 to 'protect their physical and mental wellbeing, ensure their right to receive compulsory education, and not allow them to be illegally employed'. It also provides that parents or guardians of children under the age of 16 who allow them to be illegally employed 'shall be reprimanded and educated by local authorities'.[35]

The employer is given a set timeframe by labour bureaus to repatriate children to their place of origin and put them in the care of parents or guardians.[36] A variety of penalties can be imposed on the employer, including: fines of 5,000 yuan per child for each month that they are employed;[37] revocation of business licence;[38] and criminal liability in cases of child abduction, forced labour, dangerous or hazardous work, use of children under 14 years old, and severe injury, disability or death of the child.[39] The Regulations on Labour Protection in Workplaces with Toxic Materials further impose fines of 50,000 to 300,000 yuan for the use of child labour in such workplaces.[40] The employer must bear the medical and living expenses for a child worker requiring medical treatment. In the case of a work-related disability or death, the employer must pay compensation (calculated based on work injury insurance regulations) to the direct family and relatives of the child.[41]

The Provisions also impose direct administrative sanctions (including

---

31 *Ibid.* art. 7.
32 *Ibid.* art. 4.
33 *Ibid.* art. 8.
34 *Ibid.* art. 5.
35 *Ibid.* art. 3.
36 *Ibid.* art. 6.
37 *Ibid.*
38 *Ibid.*
39 *Ibid.* art. 11.
40 Regulations on Labour Protection in Working Places with Toxic Materials (People's Republic of China) State Council, adopted 30 April 2002, effective 2 May 2002, arts 7 and 63.
41 Provisions on the Prohibition of Using Child Labour, art. 10.

demotion or dismissal) on government officials, such as labour inspectors who find the use of child labour but 'do not stop, correct or deal with such instances'; police who violate regulations governing the issue of identity documents or record false dates of birth; officials from industrial and commercial departments who knowingly issue a business licence to an applicant under the age of 16. In some cases, criminal liability can be incurred by acts involving abuse of authority and neglect of duty.[42]

A problematic area of regulation concerns Article 13 of the Provisions, which stipulate:

> minors under the age of 16 involved in educational and experimental labour as well as labour for the purpose of imparting occupational skills which is organised by schools, other educational establishments and occupational training institutes in accordance with relevant regulations set out by the State and which does not endanger their personal safety or physical and mental well-being are not considered to constitute child labour.

However, there has been growing controversy over the abuse of 'work and study' and 'student apprenticeship' programmes that involve students working in poor working conditions and excessive working hours. Reports have suggested that children in some programmes are forced to work to pay for school fees.[43] For rural migrant children, the problem of school fees has been particularly acute.

A number of local law-makers have additionally introduced local-level regulations, frequently in response to potential or actual scandals and exposés. For example, Fujian Province's Regulations on the Ban on the Use of Underage Labourers was introduced in 2003 after local authorities had found 250 children working in the province in the preceding three years. Many of these children were working in the more prosperous coastal regions of Fujian, which tended to have large numbers of small privately owned enterprises.[44] In these types of enterprises, labour laws regulating working hours, working conditions and occupational safety and health are often ignored. In another key hub of China's economic activity, Zhejiang Province introduced a similar regulation in 2008 when

---

42 *Ibid.* art. 12.

43 Selden, Chan and Ngai, 'Interns or Workers?', above n. 9; China Labour Bulletin, *The Mass Production of Labour: The Exploitation of Students in China's Vocational School System* (12 January 2012), available at www.clb.org.hk/sites/default/files/archive/en/share/File/general/vocational_school_system.pdf.

44 China Labour Bulletin, *Child Labour in China: Causes and Solutions* (25 November 2003), available at www.clb.org.hk/en/content/child-labour-china-causes-and-solutions.

a national crackdown on forced labour and child labour was taking place following the brick kiln scandals.[45]

A suite of related laws, policies and programmes have been introduced with a goal of preventing and eliminating child labour, notably the Compulsory Education Law that requires at least nine years of school enrolment for all children. There are also corresponding policy measures to enforce the law and prevent school drop-outs, as reflected in the National Mid- and Long-Term Reform on Education and Development Programme (2010–2020) which includes specific compulsory education targets and measures to raise the quality of education at all levels.

The ILO has emphasized the linkage between efforts to eliminate child labour with other fundamental rights at work, which include the eradication of forced labour, non-discrimination, and the right of workers and employers to form and organize representative associations of their own choosing and to bargain collectively.[46] Notably, there is a close connection between forced labour, child labour and human trafficking, as reflected in the definition of the worst forms of child labour under ILO Convention No. 182.[47] The Law on the Protection of Minors prohibits the 'abducting of, trafficking in, kidnapping or maltreating of minors'.[48] Policy measures against child trafficking can be further found in the National Plan of Action against Human Trafficking (2013–2020) issued by the State Council. In December 2013, China also abolished the controversial 're-education through labour' system which had subjected persons under the age of 18 to hard labour.[49]

The current legal framework forbidding child labour in China appears comprehensive, although significant obstacles remain in its implementation and enforcement. A proper assessment of these contemporary measures requires a broader understanding of the legal culture dealing with the phenomenon of child labour in China, including historical and cultural experiences and attitudes towards child labour and the role of legal institutions and rules.

---

45 Provincial Implementing Measures on Provisions on the Prohibition of Using Child Labour 2008 (People's Government of Zhejiang Province) adopted 30 June 2008, effective 1 August 2008.

46 ILO, Declaration on Fundamental Rights and Principles at Work, adopted 18 June 1998.

47 Liukkunen, 'ILO and Child Labour Regulation in China', above n. 13, at 149.

48 Law on the Protection of Minors, art. 41.

49 ILO, *Observation: Worst Forms of Child Labour Convention 1999 (No. 182) – China*, adopted 2014, published 104th ILC Session (2015).

3. A HISTORICAL PERSPECTIVE OF CHILD LABOUR REGULATION

3.1 Prior to the Twentieth Century

Discussion of child labour and its regulation in imperial China has largely been overlooked in the scholarship. Children in pre-industrial societies generally had an important role in agriculture and household economic activities. Some insights into the life of a child labourer in pre-industrial China can be gleaned from a well-known Chinese novel written in 1750 that detailed the story of Wang Mian, a 10-year-old boy who lived in fourteenth century China.[50] Wang was from an impoverished family and his father had passed away when he was only seven years old. A sympathetic neighbour employed Wang as a cattle boy so he could earn a living to support his family. Wang worked 12 hours a day from 6 am to 6 pm and was paid 2 copper coins per day. His 'employer' also provided him with breakfast and lunch, and sometimes 'discretionary bonuses' of pickled fish and cured meat. Wang was told that he had to be diligent and not shy away from hard work.

While child labour practices did not pose much moral concern in fourteenth-century Chinese society, it emerged as a social issue from the late nineteenth century onwards. Historical materials refer to cases of gin houses in Ningbo that employed eight-year-old children to operate machinery in 1888 and a weaving factory in Wuchang that employed children as the majority of its workforce in 1893.[51] Child labourers were commonly found in the labour force in Shanghai and other treaty ports that had been leased out to foreign powers in the late nineteenth century to early twentieth century.[52] Working conditions for many child labourers at the time could be described as abominable, as they worked in dangerous and dirty environments that exposed them to anaemia, hypoplasia, and other occupational health risks. Some children were killed in industrial accidents, such as being crushed to death by machines and drowning in pits. Some were beaten up and even tortured if they made a mistake in their work.[53]

---

50 J. Wu, *The Scholars* (People's Literature Publishing House, 1956), pp. 1–2.

51 Y. Sun (ed.), *Data of Chinese Modern Industrial History, Series 1, 1840–1895* (China Science Publishing and Media Ltd, 1957), p. 1232.

52 Lieten and Hindman, 'Child Labor in China', above n. 10, at 861.

53 M. Yin, 'Child Labor Protection in the Labor Legislations at the End of the Qing Dynasty and the Beginning of the Republic of China' (2005) 4 *Journal of Shandong Normal University* (Social Science Edition) 122.

Scholars have attributed the situation of child labour in late imperial China to the rise of modern factories, which shared some parallel experiences with the early days of industrialization in England.[54] During this period, there was an absence of legislation or policy for the protection of child labourers. Nevertheless, there were a handful of businesses that had their own internal rules or 'codes of conduct' which regulated the use of child labour. For instance, Kaiping Colliery had its own '33 Regulations' in 1878, of which Article 28 stipulated that 'any children under the age of 13, regardless of gender, were not allowed to be recruited; children between 13 and 18 years old may be recruited but they shall be subject to separate administration'. Furthermore, Article 6 of the company's '15 Principles' specified that: 'a child working in the colliery shall be guided by an adult and the adult shall accompany the child in leaving the colliery when the work has been completed'.[55]

3.2 Republican China (1912–1949)

The downfall of the Qing Dynasty marked the end of imperial rule as China entered the Republican era. Despite the political volatility that underpinned the beginning of the Republic of China, there was an emerging legal system that incorporated elements of child labour protection. During the 1920s, there was a convergence of attention on child labour issues in political, religious, non-governmental and industry circles globally. International organizations such as the ILO exerted pressure on the Chinese government to abolish child labour. The abolition of child labour was formally written into the laws of the Peking (Beiyang) government, which incorporated much of the ILO's recommendations.[56]

The Ministry of Agriculture and Commerce's Provisional Industrial Regulations 1923 prohibited the employment of boys and girls under the ages of 10 and 12, respectively. It also created a special category of 'youth workers' to describe a male worker below the age of 17 and a female worker under the age of 18. The Regulations stipulated various conditions for the employment of youth workers, such as the requirement that they could only be employed for easy and convenient jobs. Youth workers must not be ordered to work for more than 8 hours a day (excluding rest time) or during the night between 8 pm and 4 am, and must be provided at least

54 Lieten and Hindman, 'Child Labor in China', above n. 10, at 861.

55 Yin, 'Child Labor Protection in the Labor Legislations at the End of the Qing Dynasty', above n. 53, at 125.

56 Tillman, *Precocious Politics*, above n. 16, at 102.

three days of holiday per month.[57] Despite these safeguards on paper, the effectiveness of these regulations suffered from a lack of enforcement mechanisms.

Growing child labour activism among different political, religious and social groups and movements emerged in Shanghai at the time. The Shanghai Municipal Government established the Child Labour Commission in 1923, as Tillman argues, 'not necessarily because of a commitment to abolish child labour, but primarily because of a desire to survey factory conditions'.[58] The Child Labour Commission undertook an extensive inquiry and produced a report on the 'Shanghai Child Labour Problem', but failed in its objective to introduce a specific Child Labour Bylaw in 1925.

Based on the labour statistics of the Shanghai Social Census Bureau in 1928, the average proportion of child labour across different industries was over 10 per cent.[59] At a national level, based on the statistics of the Ministry of Industry and Commerce in 1930, there were 55,605 child labourers (around 4.6 per cent) out of 1,204,317 workers in 29 cities of Zhejiang, Anhui, Jiangxi, Hubei, Shandong, Guangdong, Guangxi and Fujian provinces.[60]

During the Nanjing decade (1928–1937), the Nationalist government sought to modernize the legal system and promote various social reforms, including women's rights and labour standards. The revised Industrial Law 1932 provided greater protection for child labourers by deeming all children between 14 and 16 years old as juvenile labourers who could only be employed in easy and convenient jobs.[61] Furthermore, certain categories of work were prohibited, which included: the handling of explosive or toxic materials; work in a dusty or toxic environment; the operation of machinery, high-voltage conductors and boilers; and any jobs that violated the morals or safety of the child. Moreover, the law capped the daily working time of juvenile labourers at 8 hours and prohibited work by youth workers between the hours of 7.30 pm and 6 am.[62]

Despite the existence of legal protections on paper, there were wide-

---

57 D. He, *The Chinese Labor Problem* (Commercial Press, 1936), p. 37.

58 Tillman, *Precocious Politics*, above n. 16, at 113.

59 B. Xing et al. (eds), *The Second Labour Yearbook: Series I* (Beiping Dabei Press, 1932), pp. 17–18; Y. Ding and J. Lue, 'On Child Labour in Shanghai 1920s–1930s' (2008) 2 *Journal of Shanghai University* (Social Sciences Edition) 92.

60 Y. Lu and C. Liu, 'The Phenomenon of Child Labour in Early Republican Era' (2003) 6 *Labour Protection* 54.

61 *Ibid.*

62 *Ibid.*

spread violations by enterprises. Many child labourers continued to work in hazardous environments that harmed their health and safety.[63] Any regulatory developments to combat child labour were halted during the political turmoil that marked the period of 1936 to 1949, which included the second Sino-Japanese war and the civil war between Chiang Kai-Shek's Nationalist government and the Communist Red Army forces led by Mao Zedong.

3.3 People's Republic of China (1949–)

The Chinese Communist Party (CCP) came into power in 1949, with the founding of the People's Republic of China (PRC) under Mao's leadership. The CCP had approached the issue of child labour in the 1920s by focusing on raising the class-consciousness of youth workers.[64] In the first National Labour Conference in May 1922, the CCP considered a policy motion that children under the age of 18 should work less than 8 hours a day and children under the age of 12 should not take up any kind of job.[65] The Communists had criticized much of the work of the Child Labour Commission earlier on. Yet, the CCP government during the 1950s would draw heavily from the Commission's report and general policies.[66]

In the early years of the PRC, the CCP government attempted to increase the number of primary schools, especially in rural China. Under the centrally planned economy, the state provided the so-called 'iron rice bowl' of guaranteed lifetime employment and cradle-to-grave welfare for urban residents who were employed in a 'danwei' work unit.[67] The state's social welfare provision further included housing, health and the provision of education for urban workers' children. However, during the 1960s and 1970s, political chaos, including the Cultural Revolution, destroyed much of the legal system and disrupted Chinese society in an unprecedented manner. Schools and universities throughout the country were closed. Millions of high school students from urban areas were 'sent

---

[63] Ding and Lue, 'On Child Labour in Shanghai 1920s–1930s', above n. 59, at 93.

[64] Tillman, *Precocious Politics*, above n. 16, p. 124.

[65] Y. Lu, 'Earlier Understandings and Propositions on the Issue of Child Labour by the Communist Party of China' (2004) 3 *Journal of Shandong Teachers' University* (Social Science Edition) 141.

[66] Tillman, *Precocious Politics*, above n. 16, at 128.

[67] M. Zou, 'The Evolution of Collective Labour Law with "Chinese Characteristics": Crossing the River by Feeling the Stones?' in R. Blanpain, U. Liukkunen and Y. Chen (eds), *China and ILO Fundamental Principles and Rights at Work* (Kluwer International, 2012), pp. 55–72.

down' to work in the rural countryside for the purpose of 'learning from the peasantry'. Any progress in regulatory efforts to combat child labour by the CCP was halted.

After Deng Xiao Ping's opening-up policy in the late 1970s, the introduction of the Compulsory Education Law in 1986 as part of concerted policy efforts to lift national education levels was a major step towards the goal of eliminating child labour. The One-Child Policy that started from the 1980s also provided a 'countervailing demographic force that kept growth-induced child labour at lower levels than they might have been', as parents were more inclined to devote greater resources to the child's education.[68]

While the early 1990s witnessed the introduction of the Law on the Protection of Minors, China was also experiencing an accelerated transition towards a socialist market economy. A key aspect of this transition was a labour-intensive, export-oriented growth strategy that relied on a large pool of low-cost rural migrant labour. Over the next two decades, dramatic transformations in the labour market saw the breaking of the 'iron rice bowl'. Growing inequalities in income and wealth, inadequacy of social security (especially in rural areas), and limited access to education for migrant children have posed challenges for the quest to eliminate child labour in China. The concluding part of this chapter focuses on the vulnerability of rural migrant children and the need for systematic institutional reform to address the persistent urban and rural divide in China.

4. CHALLENGES FACING RURAL MIGRANT CHILDREN

A global index on child labour developed by Maplecroft in 2014 classified China as a country posing 'extreme risk'. The index evaluates the rate and severity of reported incidents of child labour, the performance of governments in preventing child labour and in ensuring that perpetrators are held accountable. Child labour risks in China largely stem from the 'poor enforcement of child labour laws, exacerbated by significant internal migration population'.[69]

Tang, Zhao and Zhao recently published a statistical study of child

---

[68] Lieten and Hindman, 'Child Labor in China', above n. 10, at 862.

[69] Maplecroft, *Child Labour Index 2014* (15 October 2013), available at https://maplecroft.com/portfolio/new-analysis/2013/10/15/child-labour-risks-increase-china-and-russia-most-progress-shown-south-america-maplecroft-index/.

labour in China, based on data from the government-funded China Family Panel Study in 2010.[70] Their report found that in 2010, around 7.74 per cent of children aged between 10 and 15 years were engaged in some form of work. Importantly, the findings from the study point to the greater likelihood of children living in rural areas and poorer western and central regions being in work, as well as a negative correlation between the incidence of child labour and household assets per capita and household involvement in non-agricultural activities.

The urban and rural divide is a key factor behind the continued occurrence of child labour practices in contemporary China. The country's unprecedented economic growth and industrialization in recent decades has seen the largest rural-to-urban migration of people for work. A salient regulatory feature of this phenomenon has been the *hukou* or household registration system that has placed strict controls on the migration process for over 240 million rural migrant workers. Without a local urban *hukou*, rural migrant workers and their families are usually not entitled to reside permanently in receiving cities or access a full range of social welfare benefits such as pensions, housing and healthcare on an equal basis as urban *hukou* holders.

Rural migrant workers must either leave their children behind in the countryside or bring their children with them to the cities. The number of children accompanying migrant workers has been increasing in recent years, with more rural migrant children likely to be brought up in urban areas.[71] Since the *hukou* is inherited from one's parents, children of rural migrant workers often miss out on decent education opportunities in the cities. This is because many local governments require those without a local urban *hukou* to pay extra levies and/or to provide extensive paperwork such as residential and employment documents in order for their children to attend local state-run schools.

Many rural migrant children find themselves in poorly regulated and low-quality private schools. Despite the nine-year compulsory education system and the central government's attempts to improve access of rural migrant children to urban education, studies have highlighted that many rural migrant children in Chinese cities cannot afford to attend school and are often compelled to work to pay school fees.[72] Furthermore, migrant children tend to have a high school drop-out rate as well as low attendance

---

70 C. Tang, *Child Labor in China*, IZA Discussion Papers 9976 (2016).

71 China Labour Bulletin, *The Children of Migrant Workers in China* (5 August 2009), available at www.clb.org.hk/en/content/children-migrant-workers-china-3.

72 X. Chunli 'Migrant Children and the Right to Compulsory Education in China' (2006) 7(2) *Asia-Pacific Journal on Human Rights and the Law* 29.

and graduation rates.[73] A government survey of migrant children in nine cities showed that only 40 per cent of migrant children aged between 16 and 17 years were in school.[74] Regulations that require migrant children to take university entrance exams in their permanent place of residence (based on their *hukou*) present a further barrier for these children to continue their schooling at the higher levels.[75]

A lack of decent educational opportunities for rural migrant children can undermine the realization of other laws and policies aimed at eliminating child labour in China. While the overhaul of the *hukou* system is not likely to occur any time soon, there have been gradual institutional reforms to address some of the problems that migrant workers face, including education opportunities for their children in the cities. A more recent development has been the State Council's Provisional Rules for Residency 2016, which requires local governments to create a streamlined process for eligible migrants to apply and register for a residential permit from the local public security bureaus. The residential permit holder would have access to key social services in the urban locality, not least public schooling for their children. However, the strict eligibility criteria may substantially limit the scope of applicants due to the requirement of a 'legitimate and stable job, legitimate and stable residence, and consecutive study at local schools'.[76]

5. CONCLUSION

A historical analysis of child labour laws and regulations in China, situated in their social, cultural and economic contexts, provides us with a better understanding of how the contemporary regulatory framework on child labour came into being and the challenges in its implementation. While there may be fewer children like Wang Mian in twenty-first-century China due to changing social norms and legislative reforms, it

---

73 N. Wu et al., 'A Survey on the Education of the Children of Migrant Workers' (2004) *Research and Policy* 5; X. Shen and G. Zhou, *A Study on the Fairness of Education for Migrant Children* (Masses Publishing, 2006), p. 67.

74 China Youth Research Centre, *China's Children and Juveniles Statistical Handbook* (Science Press, 2008), p. 229.

75 China Labour Bulletin, *The Children of Migrant Workers in China*, above n. 71.

76 State Council of the PRC, *China to Implement Provisional Regulation on Residential Permit* (12 December 2015), available at http://english.gov.cn/policies/latest_releases/2015/12/12/content_281475252676348.htm.

is poor families and rural migrant children who are most vulnerable to the problems of child labour. Their vulnerability is shaped, in part, by institutional discrimination entrenched in the *hukou* system. To date there have been few studies investigating China's child labour practices and the operation of relevant laws 'on the ground', especially from a historical and socio-legal perspective. It is hoped that this chapter has put forward some meaningful insights for future research on migrant children at work in China and globally.

PART III

Protecting child migrants: domestic laws

12. Protecting migrant children in the United Kingdom

Catriona Jarvis and Syd Bolton

1. INTRODUCTION

As a former seat of Empire, the United Kingdom (UK) has long been both a source country and reception state for migrant children. While the days have passed that saw thousands of disadvantaged children shipped to the 'new world' countries of Australia, Canada and South Africa,[1] children continue to make up a sizeable proportion of those who seek to enter the United Kingdom each year. Children arrive alone, with family or other carers, in search of refugee status or other forms of international protection, from places of conflict and persecution and from countries with historical and modern-day trading and socio-economic relationships with the United Kingdom. As the dangerous and often deadly Mediterranean refugee and migration crossings to Europe from Africa and the Middle East show little sign of stopping, the drastic nature of European Union refugee policies,[2] and the forcible closure of the informal 'Jungle' camp in Calais, France, have resulted in thousands of children left unaccompanied, uncared for, unprotected and at serious risk of all forms of harm, including trafficking and sexual abuse.[3]

The number of children seeking asylum alone in the United Kingdom or seeking to be reunited with family members has risen steadily in recent

---

[1] See M. Humphreys, *Empty Cradles* (Doubleday, 1994); K. Bagnell, *The Little Immigrants: The Orphans Who Came to Canada* (Dundurn Group, 2001); and M. Crock, *Seeking Asylum Alone – Australia: A Study of Australian Law, Policy and Practice Regarding Unaccompanied and Separated Children* (Themis Press, 2006), ch. 2.

[2] See, e.g., *Report to the Greek Government on the Visits to Greece Carried Out by the European Committee for the Prevention of Torture and Inhuman or Degrading Treatment or Punishment*, CPT/Inf (2017), p. 25.

[3] See T. John, 'Everything to know about the Calais "Jungle" Closure', *Time*, 24 October 2016, available at http://time.com/4542243/calais-jungle-closure-migrants/.

years, climbing back towards the levels of a decade ago, approaching 4,000 per annum in 2015–16. This represents around 10 per cent of the overall asylum claims annually but decreased after 2016,[4] as tougher border security measures were implemented and legislative provisions to relocate unaccompanied asylum-seeking children[5] living in European neighbour states were curtailed.[6] The hardening European regional approach to asylum and migration, the UK government's self-stated 'hostile environment' policies, and the outcome of the referendum on the UK withdrawal from the European Union (so-called 'Brexit'), have all contrived to make children's access to justice to ensure their rights as children, and as refugees and migrants, more challenging than ever.

The United Kingdom has generally been at the forefront in developing normative frameworks of humanitarian and human rights standards since the Breton Woods agreement and the post-World War II establishment of the international institutions and Conventions that have for the most part successfully guided the development of global human rights standards. These include the United Nations itself and the international legal frameworks we now take for granted, such as the overarching 1948 Universal Declaration on Human Rights (UDHR); the 1951 Refugee Convention and its 1967 Protocol (the 'Refugee Convention'); the 1966 Covenant on Civil and Political Rights (ICCPR); and the 1989 Convention on the Rights of the Child (CRC). There are, of course, many more human rights treaties and monitoring bodies, for example, the Office of the UN High Commissioner for Refugees (UNHCR) and the UN Committee on the Rights of the Child (UNCRC), which the United Kingdom can rightly say it has played a significant role in bringing into being. The development of a global jurisprudence in children's rights law has evolved in no small measure from the courts of the United Kingdom and Commonwealth, particularly in relation to refugee and migrant children's rights.[7]

---

[4] UK Home Office, *National Statistics: Asylum* (23 February 2017), available at www.gov.uk/government/publications/immigration-statistics-october-to-december-2016/asylum.

[5] Immigration Act 2016 (UK), s. 67 ('Dubs Amendment') requires the UK Home Secretary to 'make arrangements . . . as soon as possible . . . to relocate unaccompanied refugee children from other European countries to the UK'.

[6] As of July 2017, the UK government had admitted only 200 children in 2016 and none at all in 2017 under the statutory scheme; see A. Travis, 'UK has not taken any child refugees under Dubs Scheme this year', *The Guardian*, 20 July 2017, available at www.theguardian.com/uk-news/2017/jul/19/uk-not-taken-any-child-refugees-dubs-scheme-this-year.

[7] See, e.g., in Australia: *Minister for Immigration and Ethnic Affairs* v. *Teoh* (1995) 183 CLR 273; in Canada: *Baker* v. *Canada* (1999) 2 SCR 817; and in the

It is well-documented history that the United Kingdom received many thousands of children under the volunteer-led 'Kinder Transport' emergency evacuation of child refugees from the brutality of a Europe under Nazi occupation. It is less known that the United Kingdom legislated for the care and protection of these children through the Guardianship (Refugee Children) Act 1944,[8] which was only repealed in the 1950s, as one of many temporary wartime provisions. That legislation acknowledged the special vulnerability of refugee children without their parents but despite the progress made for children's rights since then, it has never been replicated for asylum-seeking children on a statutory footing. This is despite successful pilot schemes and reports identifying the need for and value of guardianship to achieve effective refugee child protection.[9]

Until the 1970s little legislation or case law, let alone an administrative and legal system of refugee protection and immigration, existed. Instead, this was left largely to the discretionary and prerogative powers of the Secretary of State for the Home Department (the Home Secretary). The Immigration Act 1971 was the first major codification of immigration laws in the United Kingdom (still extant and heavily amended). This paved the way over the next four decades for the frequent use of new legislation and comprehensive rules as a means of controlling immigration and asylum, including a specialist tribunal for immigration and asylum appeals and, consequentially, a growing body of asylum case law. There was no right to a substantive asylum appeal until the passing of the Asylum and Immigration Appeal Act 1993. In October 2000, a Labour government brought the Human Rights Act 1998 into force. This made the rights and obligations set out in the 1950 European Convention on Human Rights (ECHR) directly justiciable in domestic law without a claimant having to resort to the European Court of Human Rights in Strasbourg for a remedy. The results helped to shape our understanding of international protection and children's rights, with the UK senior courts increasingly willing to use international jurisprudence and expert guidance to inform its own reasoning on such cases.[10]

United Kingdom: *ZH (Tanzania)* v. *Secretary of State for the Home Department* [2011] UKSC 04.

[8] See National Archives, 'Guardianship, Kindertransport', available at www.nationalarchives.gov.uk/education/resources/kindertransport/guardianship/).

[9] See, e.g., H. Crawley and R.K.S. Kohli, *'She Endures With Me': An Evaluation of the Scottish Guardianship Service Pilot* (Swansea University/University of Bedfordshire, 2013), available at www.scottishrefugeecouncil.org.uk/assets/6798/Final_Report_2108.pdf.

[10] See, e.g., *ID and others* v. *Home Office* [2005] EWCA Civ 38 (migrant child

The subsequent signing of the Treaty of Lisbon in 2007[11] and its incorporated Charter of Fundamental Rights (CFR), together with the United Kingdom's participation as a member state in most aspects of the European Union's Common Asylum Framework,[12] have also served to develop a more consistent Europe-wide set of standards and jurisprudence. Case law on migrant children's rights under the common asylum framework remains in its infancy but is beginning to reflect the principles of the CFR,[13] notably Article 24,[14] which imports from the CRC principles of best interests, the right to be heard and family unity. In a 2013 Court of Justice of the European Union (CJEU) judgment concerning the United Kingdom and a child asylum case about the 'Dublin Regulation' on ascertaining which Member State of the EU should be responsible for considering a child's asylum claim, the Court held that:

> the effect of Article 24(2) of the Charter . . . is that the child's best interests must also be a primary consideration in all decisions adopted by the Member States . . . interpreted as designating as responsible the Member State in which the minor is present after having lodged an application there . . . In the interest of unaccompanied minors, it is important . . . not to prolong unnecessarily the procedure for determining the Member State responsible, and to ensure that unaccompanied minors have prompt access to the procedures for determining refugee status.[15]

The case is most significant in recognizing the primacy of the best interests of the child in asylum laws, recognizing children's rights under the CFR

---

detention); and *AA (Afghanistan v. Secretary of State for the Home Department* [2007] EWCA Civ12 (asylum-seeking child, discretionary leave, procedural error).

[11] See Treaty of Lisbon Amending the Treaty on the European Union and the Treaty Establishing the European Community, opened for signature 13 December 2007, [2007] OJ C306/01 (entered into force 1 December 2009) ('Lisbon Treaty').

[12] See *ibid.* (though with opt-outs on many aspects).

[13] Charter of Fundamental Rights of the European Union [2000] OJ C326/391 (entered into force 1 December 2009) (CFEU).

[14] Article 24 CFEU reads: '1. Children shall have the right to such protection and care as is necessary for their well-being. They may express their views freely. Such views shall be taken into consideration on matters which concern them in accordance with their age and maturity. 2. In all actions relating to children, whether taken by public authorities or private institutions, the child's best interests must be a primary consideration . . . Every child shall have the right to maintain on a regular basis a personal relationship and direct contact with both his or her parents, unless that is contrary to his or her interests.'

[15] See C-648/11 *MA, BT, DA* v. *Secretary of State for the Home Department* ECLI:EU:C:2013:367, paras [59]–[61], available at www.refworld.org/cases,ECJ, 51b0785e4.html.

as direct domestic obligations, and the need for procedural fairness for children.

Successive UK governments have overseen complex and often bureaucratically inadequate management of asylum and immigration systems. The excessive use of rules and legislation to introduce knee-jerk and patch-up solutions to politically charged issues have led to a labyrinthine and arguably dysfunctional system which only accredited and experienced lawyers can navigate.[16] At the same time, more people – children and young adults amongst them – have been deprived of a lawyer and forced to deal with their own cases in person at times of most vulnerability. Legal aid cuts in particular have undermined migrant children's ability to challenge decisions affecting their lives. Critics have been outspoken in their concerns at such measures.[17]

2. LEGAL AND POLICY FRAMEWORKS

As already mentioned, the CFR of the European Union includes core human rights standards and elements of the CRC, all of which are incorporated directly into EU Member State obligations under the Lisbon Treaty and serve as an interpretive aid for domestic compliance with EU laws. The Court of Justice of the European Union (CJEU) acts as the overseeing court, rather than an appellate court, giving judgments on the interpretation of duties under the Union's Treaties and Directives. It is for states and their courts to initiate referrals to the CJEU and not a means of further appeal by individuals. The European Court of Human Rights (ECtHR) by contrast, is not a creature of the EU, but of the Council of Europe which has a wider range of states members than the EU. This includes the United Kingdom. The ECtHR is more like a supra-national court of final appeal, available to individuals, provided that they have (reasonably) exhausted all domestic remedies and the allegation is against a state (including a state agent) for violation of an ECHR right.[18] This court has played a major role in informing member states' jurisprudence on human rights since its inception, including key cases on refugee and

---

[16] Examples include the criminal deportation of families with children, instructions to judges on how to assess the credibility of appellants, removal of appeal rights, and cuts to legal aid and welfare support.

[17] See, e.g., Law Society, *Submission to the Universal Periodic Review – United Kingdom 2017* (September 2016), para. 14 ff, available at https://uprdoc.ohchr.org/uprweb/downloadfile.aspx?filename=3803&file=EnglishTranslation.

[18] See further Carmelo Danisi, Chapter 7.

child rights, across all member states, which have helped to develop a European normative framework.[19] The court also includes a procedure for emergency injunctive relief to prevent an immediate egregious violation of a human right, usually restricted to Article 3 ECHR breaches. The court has been reluctant to grant such stays, usually against deportation, but it remains a last line of protection in extreme cases.

Whilst Brexit may yet see a departure by the United Kingdom from the jurisdiction of the CJEU (this is far from clear as matters stand), it will not trigger departure from the ECHR or ECtHR, though political machinations are never far away on that issue, with strong advocates for a British Bill of Rights to replace both it and the Human Rights Act 1998.

The United Kingdom has incorporated the terms of the Refugee Convention into its domestic immigration rules and has for the most part opted in to the European Union's Directives and Regulations under what is generally referred to as the Common European Asylum System (returns, reception conditions, qualification and subsidiary protection, relocation and transfer of claims) (CEAS). Other Directives embedding human rights and child welfare standards in UK law, for example, the Anti-Trafficking Directive,[20] and the Brussels II Regulation,[21] also assist to bring about uniformity, cooperation and minimum standards across the EU as a whole.

The United Kingdom is a party to the 1989 CRC having been a major advocate and participant in its drafting. It has also adopted two of its three Optional Protocols (on the sale of children and on children and armed conflict). The new Optional Protocol No. 3 provides a direct complaints mechanism for and on behalf of an individual child, but the United Kingdom has not ratified this as at the date of writing and is not expected to do so in the near future.[22] The United Kingdom ratified the

---

[19] For example, identifying violations of children's rights in cases of detention, deportation and separation from parents: *Rahimi* v. *Greece,* ECtHR App. No. 8687/08 (5 July 2011); *Mubilanzila Mayeka and Kaniki Mitunga* v. *Belgium* ECtHR App. No. 13178/03 (12 October 2006).

[20] Directive 2011/36/EU of the European Parliament and of the Council of 5 April 2011 on preventing and combating trafficking in human beings and protecting its victims, and replacing Council Framework Decision 2002/629/JHA [2011] OJ L101/1–11.

[21] Council Regulation 2201/2003 of 27 November 2003 concerning jurisdiction and the recognition and enforcement of judgments in matrimonial matters and the matters of parental responsibility [2003] OJ L338/1.

[22] See Office of the High Commissioner on Human Rights, Committee on the Rights of the Child, *Ratification of the Convention on the Rights of the Child* (2017), available at http://tbinternet.ohchr.org/_layouts/TreatyBodyExternal/Treaty.aspx?Treaty=CRC&Lang=en.

CRC in 1991 but entered a reservation dis-applying the Convention rights in relation to children subject to immigration control. This was for many a controversial and distorting reservation, unlawful according to some legal experts,[23] as it offended against core principles of international treaty law,[24] and gave a green light to discriminate against non-British children, including to detain them alongside adults. Concerted lobbying from the children's rights NGO sector, parliamentarians and legal experts led to its withdrawal in January 2009.

This led directly to a number of new statutory safeguarding provisions and procedures being brought into effect by the UK government to bring migrant children's rights in line with those of British citizen children. This included an express duty under section 55 of the Borders, Citizenship and Immigration Act 2009 upon the Secretary of State 'to ensure that immigration, asylum, nationality and customs functions are discharged having regard to the need to safeguard and promote the welfare of children in the UK'.

That provision corresponds to established welfare and safeguarding duties for all children within the UK care system under the Children Act 1989 (and subsequent Acts). In principle at least, all children in the United Kingdom are now owed the same duties of care irrespective of status. The reality in practice remains different, as unaccompanied asylum-seeking children are often accommodated and their care funded under separate provisions to settled children. Despite the ending of the reservation and the general framework for the welfare and protection of children, the CRC remains a non-incorporated treaty in UK domestic law, save for limited elements by virtue of the EU CFR. Article 24 transposes a hybrid 'child's best interests and right to be heard' provision based on the CRC into EU law. It is not therefore directly justiciable by children claiming a breach of its provisions but can only be used as an interpretive aid in establishing another violation. Examples include a breach of human rights under Article 8 ECHR; an unlawful act based on a failure to apply a domestic law correctly; or an unlawful policy or practice that is non-compliant with a CRC duty.

The primary importance of the best interests of the child has been the subject of a series of UK Supreme Court cases in relation to both settled and migrant children,[25] in the context of immigration control, extradition

---

[23] N. Blake and S. Drew, *In the Matter of the United Kingdom Reservation to the UN Convention on the Rights of the Child* (Opinion, 30 November 2001).

[24] See Vienna Convention on the Law of Treaties, opened for signature 23 May 1969, 1155 UNTS 331 (entered into force 27 January 1980). Article 26 enshrines the good faith principle of *pacta sunt servanda.*

[25] Article 3(1) CRC reads: 'In all actions concerning children, whether

and family disputes.[26] All of these cases identify and elaborate upon the standards required and the weight to be given to children's interests to ensure that UK law *and* process accords with a child rights-based approach, including systems of immigration control, asylum determination and other cross-border issues affecting children. It is also clear from this growing body of cases that the weight to be given to the public interest in implementing government policies must acknowledge that protecting children's interests is an essential part of the equation and cannot be set aside, otherwise not only individual cases will be found against the state, but whole systems may be adjudged unlawful.

The UK courts have started to consider the implications and scope of Article 12 of the CRC (the child's right to participation and to be heard in decisions affecting them) and the extent to which procedural adjustments must be made to ensure these rights are effective, especially for vulnerable asylum-seeking children. Such requirements have been minimal in their implementation despite judicial guidance and practice directions.[27]

3. PROTECTION IN PRACTICE

On paper at least, the UK initial asylum and immigration decision-making system is one that now firmly acknowledges the protection needs of children, focusing attention on their status as children first, rather than as refugees or migrants first. Statute law explicitly establishes provisions on safeguarding asylum-seeking children and their care within the mainstream children's social work system whilst at the same time leaving the international protection and immigration decision-making within the Home Office and the Tribunals' jurisdiction (First-tier Tribunal and Upper Tribunal, Asylum and Immigration Chamber). This leads to a bifurcated system of welfare and immigration status considerations rather than a holistic child-centred approach.

---

undertaken by public or private social welfare institutions, courts of law, administrative authorities or legislative bodies, the best interests of the child shall be a primary consideration.'

[26] *ZH (Tanzania)* v. *Secretary of State for the Home Department* [2011] UKSC 04; *HH* v. *Deputy Prosecutor, Italian Republic* [2012] UKSC 25; *In the Matter of B (A Child)* [2016] UKSC 4; and *MM (Lebanon) and others* v. *Secretary of State for the Home Department* [2017] UKSC 10.

[27] For a comprehensive judgment on the procedural accommodations required to meet child participation standards in asylum appeals, see *AM (Afghanistan)* v. *Secretary of State for the Home Department* [2017] EWCA 1123.

The 2017 operational guidance issued to Home Office decision-makers is clear in the child rights approach needed when making decisions on refugee status and other forms of protective and subsidiary status (often referred to as 'leave') and indeed imports best practice standards from international bodies like UNHCR and the UNCRC.[28] However, an Independent Chief Inspector of Borders and Immigration, established in 2009 to monitor and evaluate Home Office duties including compliance with child safeguarding standards, has often been critical of the Home Office in the discharge of its duties. In 2016, it criticized the Home Office's handling of children's asylum and further leave to remain applications.[29] UNHCR's UK Offices have been involved over several years in evaluating the performance of the Home Office asylum officers, and provided assistance in helping improve standards under its Quality Initiative programme. Its reports, whilst constructive, have also been critical of the quality of decision-making and the approach to consideration of children's and family claims, identifying many concerns about the approach to children's evidence, the refugee definition and credibility issues.[30]

Government statistics show that although there has been a steady improvement in the proportion of positive refugee status determinations in children's asylum applications, the number of children recognized as refugees by virtue of a 1951 Refugee Convention need for protection is very small when compared to the number of claimants annually and the majority are not granted refugee status.[31] Instead, what was for a long time known as Discretionary or Exceptional Leave, in 2013 changed to 'Unaccompanied Asylum-Seeking Child Leave' ('UASC Leave').[32] This is granted to the majority of child applicants for asylum, aged less than 17 years and 6 months, where the child's refugee and subsidiary protection claims (under the CEAS) are refused, but where it is not possible to

---

[28] See UK Home Office, *Children's Asylum Claims* (version 2.0, 9 October 2017) available at www.gov.uk/government/uploads/system/uploads/attachment_data/file/537010/Processing-children_s-asylum-claims-v1.pdf.

[29] See Independent Chief Inspector of Borders and Immigration, *Report on Asylum Casework* (February 2016), available at www.gov.uk/government/publications/inspection-report-on-asylum-casework-february-2016.

[30] See UNHCR, *What We Do: Quality Initiative and Integration*, available at www.unhcr.org/en-us/quality-initiative-and-integration.html.

[31] The 2017 statistical overview and tables are available at www.gov.uk/government/publications/immigration-statistics-october-to-december-2016/asylum#unaccompanied-asylum-seeking-children.

[32] UASC Leave Policy, implementation details are available at www.gov.uk/government/uploads/system/uploads/attachment_data/file/537010/Processing-children_s-asylum-claims-v1.pdf.

return the child to their country of origin because of inadequate reception conditions.[33]

An increasing number of older children (aged 17 and over) are refused asylum or subsidiary protection and given no form of leave. They remain without status of any kind pending removal, on the basis that they will soon reach the age of majority and will no longer need protection as children. It is assumed that they will leave the United Kingdom after turning 18. Children whose claims are not considered until after they have reached 18 are also more likely to be rejected.[34] Those granted leave until 17 years and 6 months are expected to apply for further leave to remain before their initial leave as a child expires. If this is refused, they can appeal to the First-tier Tribunal (Immigration and Asylum Chamber).

As adults by that stage, they are not then afforded any special measures in either procedure or evidential standards, which they otherwise ought to benefit from as a child appellant.[35] Some may regard the approach taken by the UK authorities as cynical and designed to expedite the removal of children as soon after reaching adulthood as possible rather than considering the merits of the individual protection claims on the accepted evidential standards for a child's claims. This attritional approach is wholly inappropriate and many former child asylum claimants will continue to remain at risk of persecution into their adulthood for Refugee Convention reasons. Despite the clear operational instructions, unaccompanied and separated children are still not in the main recognized as at risk of any form of persecution, for example, by way of a particular social group, as children. Rather, they are dealt with mostly by examining the suitability of care arrangements if returned.

The phenomenon of 'age disputes' is becoming more prevalent across Europe and beyond.[36] It is arguable that the United Kingdom's asylum process overly focuses its attention on the age of the asylum-seeking child, as a means of exclusion from child-specific procedures and protections.

---

33 Home Office, *Immigration Rules* (29 February 2016), para. 352ZC-F, available at www.gov.uk/guidance/immigration-rules/immigration-rules-part-11-asylum.

34 Refugee Council, *Children in the Asylum System* (August 2017), available at www.refugeecouncil.org.uk/assets/0004/1347/Children_in_the_Asylum_System_Aug_2017.pdf.

35 See, e.g., *Joint Presidential Guidance Note No. 2 of 2010: Child, Vulnerable Adult and Sensitive Appellant Guidance* (2010).

36 See, e.g., Asylum Information Database, *Detriment of the Doubt: Age-Assessment of Unaccompanied Asylum Seeking Children*, AIDA Legal Briefing No. 5 (December 2015), available at www.asylumlawdatabase.eu/sites/www.asylumlawdatabase.eu/files/aldfiles/AIDA%20Brief%205_AgeAssessment.pdf.

Statistics reveal a high proportion of asylum-seeking children are forced into age dispute procedures, both by the local authority child welfare agencies as well as the Home Office.[37] Age is a 'gateway' issue in determining eligibility for child welfare support as well as child-specific asylum procedures and has become a critical hurdle for children to surmount to enjoy these protections. The UK courts have produced copious case law on age dispute practices by both local authorities and the Home Office since the Supreme Court ruled on the legality of such practices in 2009,[38] which have frequently been found flawed and unlawful. Reports, including by the Children's Commissioner for England,[39] have concluded that the 'science' of age assessment is inadequate, with a wide margin of error. Issues of credibility, consistency, appearance and demeanour are all used against a child to find they are older than claimed. The use of particular techniques, especially the use of x-rays, have been found to be unethical, inaccurate and unlawful. The Upper Tribunal (Immigration and Asylum Chamber) has been given specific jurisdiction to adjudicate on age disputes as a delegated High Court judicial review function. Cases are complex, time-consuming and costly, yet are rarely able to reach satisfactory let alone accurate conclusions. They often lead to children being treated as older than claimed and excluded from welfare as well as from refugee protection.

In 2011, following the Supreme Court's judgment in *ZH (Tanzania)* v. *Secretary of State for the Home Department*,[40] an expert roundtable was convened in the United Kingdom by the Refugee Children's Rights Project to consider whether a wholly new approach and system was necessary. This included an address by Professor Guy Goodwin Gill who has long advocated not only a new system but a new form of protective status derived from the child's rights as a child, primarily under the CRC rather than solely via the Refugee Convention.[41] Other significant

---

[37] Around 25% of the annual child asylum claimants are age disputed and many are not counted in those figures at all based on Home Office counting policies. See Refugee Council, *Quarterly Asylum Statistics* (August 2017), p. 6, available at www.refugeecouncil.org.uk/assets/0004/1243/Asylum_Statistics_Aug_2017.pdf.

[38] In particular, the Supreme Court judgment in *A* v. *Croydon* [2009] UKSC 8.

[39] See L. Brownlees and Z. Yazdani, *The Fact of Age: Review of Case Law and Local Authority Practice Since the Supreme Court Judgment in R(A) v Croydon LBC [2009]* (Children's Commissioner, July 2012), available at www.childrens-commissioner.gov.uk/wp-content/uploads/2017/07/Fact-of-Age.pdf.

[40] [2011] UKSC 4.

[41] For a summary of that exercise, see S. Bolton, 'Promoting the Best Interests of the Child in UK Asylum Law and Procedure' (2012) 26(3) *Journal of Immigration Asylum and Nationality Law* 226.

academic thinkers, such as Professor Jane McAdam,[42] have led the way in demonstrating how both refugee and EU subsidiary protection laws must be interpreted in light of the CRC. Most recently, a study by Jason Pobjoy articulated a comprehensive approach to child refugee protection based on the principles of the CRC.[43]

Legal aid and access to the courts have been significantly eroded by successive UK governments.[44] The UK judiciary has been unusually outspoken, not least the Supreme Court's President in his address to the Australian Bar Association.[45] Recent judgments have rejected a proposed residence test for eligibility to legal aid as unlawful.[46] The Children's Society Report of August 2017, *Cut Off from Justice,* highlights the very negative impact that legal aid cuts have had on the interests of migrant children. The author concluded that this may:

> actively undermine Article 12 [CRC] and the ways in which children can effectively participate in the immigration process, and ultimately, may work against children's right to life, survival and development that is established in Article 6.[47]

Restrictions on the scope of legal aid, excluding legal aid altogether in most immigration cases, is particularly problematic for children. Only asylum and human rights-based applications and appeals work are now eligible for legal aid funding. Non-asylum work, that is, immigration applications, which includes discretionary leave to remain applications, student applications, family entry visas and much more, are outside the scope of legal aid. Similarly, rights of appeal against decisions to refuse entry visas, appeals against deportation in criminal cases, have either been removed or are now only exercisable once the appellant is outside the United Kingdom. This often has the consequence of separating children from a deported parent

---

42 J. McAdam, *Complementary Protection in International Refugee Law* (Oxford University Press, 2007), ch. 5.

43 J. Pobjoy, *The Child in International Refugee Law* (Cambridge University Press, 2017).

44 See O. Bowcott, 'Legal Aid cuts creating two-tier justice system, says Amnesty', *The Guardian* (online), 11 October 2016, available at www.theguardian.com/law/2016/oct/11/legal-aid-cuts-two-tier-system-amnesty-international-law-justice.

45 President of the Supreme Court, Lord Neuberger, 'Access to Justice', speech delivered at the Australian Bar Association Biennial Conference, July 2017, available at www.supremecourt.uk/docs/speech-170703.pdf.

46 *R (Public Law Project)* v. *Lord Chancellor* [2016] UKSC 39.

47 See H. Connolly, R. Crellin and R. Parhar, *Cut Off From Justice: The Impact of Excluding Separated and Migrant Children from Legal Aid* (Children's Society, August 2017), p. 61, para. 3.

for an indefinite period pending appeal, if the parent is even able to pursue such an appeal given the lack of legal aid. The Bach Commission Report of September 2017 which examined the right to justice has called for all cases concerning children to be brought back into the scope of legal aid.[48]

Financial support thresholds set by the Home Office which families must meet in order to show they can support dependants without recourse to public funds are for many families impossibly high and prevent family reunification. The Supreme Court has upheld the lawfulness of the principle of such a policy, whilst finding it had been applied overly restrictively and unlawfully (as we discuss below). Another significant barrier to accessing justice has been the high rise in application and appeal lodgment fees. These must be paid before any engagement with immigration and nationality law rights is possible. This range of financial barriers has been harmful to the interests of children at many levels. They can mean the inability to find or afford a lawyer to pursue any application; attending court as a litigant in person instead of with a representative; the separation of children from a deported parent; or the inability, on account of cost, to apply for citizenship status. All these policy measures prejudice children's rights as a recent report from the Coram Children's Legal Centre has highlighted[49] and head in the opposite direction to the 'progressive implementation' obligations of the CRC.[50]

4. NOTABLE CASE LAW DEVELOPMENTS

The Supreme Court's landmark judgment in *ZH (Tanzania)*,[51] underlining the primacy of best interests in immigration cases involving children, has been mentioned above. This case remains the essential benchmark and has been instrumental in requiring the Home Office and the lower courts to engage with the rights of the child in a way that prior to 2010 was almost totally absent from judicial reasoning. In December 2015, in a bold judgment by the President of the Upper Tribunal (sitting to hear a

---

48 See *The Right to Justice, Final Report of the Bach Commission* (Fabian Policy Report, September 2017), available at www.fabians.org.uk/wp-content/uploads/2017/09/Bach-Commission_Right-to-Justice-Report-WEB.pdf.

49 http://www.childrenslegalcentre.com/wp-content/uploads/2017/06/Thisismyhome_FullReport.pdf.

50 UN Committee on the Rights of the Child, *General Comment No. 5 on General Measures of Implementation of the CRC*, UN Doc. CRC/GC/2003/5 (27 November 2003).

51 [2011] UKSC 4.

judicial review),[52] the court ordered the UK Home Secretary to allow the immediate entry of a number of children who had been left destitute and at risk in the informal settlement known as the 'Jungle' in Calais, France. These unaccompanied children all had family members in the United Kingdom. They were entitled to apply to be relocated to the United Kingdom to have their asylum claims considered and decided there under the so-called Dublin III Regulation,[53] one of the EU CEAS provisions, to which the UK is a party. The Court found that the procedure between the UK and French authorities to manage such requests was so inadequate that it was contrary to the Article 8 ECHR rights of the children. The applicants had been required to wait in substandard living conditions for many months whilst the process was conducted. The Court ruled that as soon as the children had lodged their initial asylum and transfer request with the French authorities, their passage to the United Kingdom should have been expedited as an emergency measure.[54]

The Court of Appeal subsequently overturned that judgment.[55] Allowing the government's appeal, it restricted the legal basis on which further cases could be brought. However, all the children in the initial case were allowed to enter and remain in the United Kingdom pending consideration of their asylum claims. The case nevertheless remains of significance in establishing that procedural barriers and administrative failures cannot simply be used as an obstacle where to do so would materially extinguish a child's rights to family unity.

In *AM (Afghanistan)* v. *Secretary of State for the Home Department*,[56] the Court of Appeal addressed in detail the procedural approach that should be taken by the Tribunals in children's appeals under existing

---

52 *R (ZAT and others)* v. *Secretary of State for the Home Department* [2016] UKUT 00061 (IAC).

53 Regulation (EU) 604/2013 of the European Parliament and of the Council of 26 June 2013 establishing the criteria and mechanisms for determining the Member State responsible for examining an application for international protection lodged in one of the Member States by a third-country national or a stateless person [2013] OJ L180/31, art. 8.

54 In fact, at the time of the Tribunal hearing the children had made no applications to the French authorities. The application to the UK court contended that they did not need to do so for the court to have jurisdiction. The court accepted jurisdiction and found in favour of the children but ordered their entry to the United Kingdom only on condition that they immediately file an application with the French authorities in accordance with the Dublin Regulation procedures.

55 *Secretary of State for the Home Department* v. *ZAT and others (UNHCR Intervening)* [2016] EWCA Civ 810.

56 *AM (Afghanistan)* [2017] EWCA Civ 1123.

Tribunal powers and child-specific Practice Directions.[57] The lead judgment was given by the Senior President of Tribunals, Lord Justice Ryder, sitting as part of the Court of Appeal bench. Significantly, he is a former Family Division judge and also 'Judge in Charge of Modernisation of Family Justice'. The appellant in question was an Afghan child who had been refused recognition as a refugee but had been granted discretionary leave to remain until the age of 17 years 6 months in accordance with the Home Office's then policy for processing child asylum claims. He was 15 at the time of the first decision. The judgment identified multiple failures to establish child-appropriate procedures and evidential standards. The Court held that:

> the [Upper Tribunal] judge took no sufficient steps to ensure that the appellant had obtained effective access to justice and in particular that his voice could be heard in proceedings that concerned him. Procedurally, the proceedings were neither fair nor just. That was a material error of law. The appellant was a vulnerable party with needs that were not addressed.[58]

Critics of the present Tribunal system will no doubt remain to be persuaded that the findings in this judgment alone can meet the needs of migrant children within both the asylum and welfare systems. The Tribunal's remit does not include consideration of the duties of local authorities to the child whilst in their care in the United Kingdom. In 2013, the UK Parliamentary Joint Committee on Human Rights report on the situation of asylum-seeking children included recommendations to pilot a new court for unaccompanied children which might test this approach. The recommendation was not accepted by government.[59]

In other significant developments, the Supreme Court held in the case of *SS (Congo)* v. *Entry Clearance Officer (Nairobi)* that the Minimum Income Rules setting out the financial threshold to be met before dependent relatives could join their families in the United Kingdom were lawful in principle.[60] However, the Court ruled that in that case the officer

---

[57] Tribunals Judiciary, *Practice Direction: Child, Vulnerable Adult and Sensitive Witnesses*, available at www.judiciary.gov.uk/wp-content/uploads/JCO/Documents/Practice+Directions/first-tier-tribunal-practice-direction-child-vulnerable-witnesses.pdf.

[58] *Ibid.* para. 16.

[59] Parliamentary Joint Committee on Human Rights, *Human Rights of Unaccompanied Migrant Children and Young People in the UK*, HL Paper 9/HC 196 (2013), recommendation 22, available at https://publications.parliament.uk/pa/jt201314/jtselect/jtrights/9/9.pdf.

[60] [2017] UKSC 10.

had failed to take proper account of the statutory duty to safeguard and promote the welfare and best interests of children under section 55 of the Borders Citizenship and Immigration Act 2009. The judgment required government to amend the Immigration Rules and instructions to allow consideration of alternative sources of funding when evaluating a claim under Article 8 ECHR (the right to respect for private and family life).

The 2017 term also saw the Supreme Court deliver judgment in the cases of *Byndloss* v. *Secretary of State for the Home Department*[61] and *UNISON* v. *Lord Chancellor*.[62] Neither of these judgments deals expressly with the rights of children but both have significant implications in the context of asylum-seeking and migrant children and their families. The *Byndloss* case concerned the deportation of a father who was a foreign national convicted of serious offences. The relevant appeal provisions permitted only an out of country appeal against deportation, after the fact. The father's deportation affected his children who were separated from him without any consideration of their family relationship and their best interests. The court received lengthy submissions on the child rights aspect of the case. Whilst not addressing the interests and participation rights of the children per se, the Court quashed the Home Secretary's decision to certify the case for an out of country appeal only. The Court found that the decision obstructed the appellant's ability to effectively present his appeal and the Tribunal's assessment, including the quality of his relationships, in particular with his children, partner and other family members.

The *UNISON* case was a challenge to the imposition of a high application fee on would-be litigants before the Employment Tribunal. The Supreme Court held that the Fees Order was unlawful because the high fees effectively prevented access to justice contrary to UK common law and EU law. It found that fees must be affordable not in a theoretical sense, but in the real sense that they can reasonably be afforded. Where households on low to middle incomes can only afford fees by foregoing an acceptable standard of living, the fees cannot be regarded as affordable. Even where fees are affordable, they prevent access to justice where they render it futile or irrational to bring a claim.

These two judgments both have a bearing on the interests of migrant children, by extension, as the Supreme Court's rationale in both cases was based on the evidenced reality of the appellant's lack of access to justice, not their theoretical access. The fees levied in immigration and citizenship applications, including for children, are unaffordable for many applicants

[61] *R (Byndloss)* v. *Secretary of State for the Home Department* [2017] UKSC 42.

[62] *R (UNISON)* v. *Lord Chancellor* [2017] UKSC 51.

and undoubtedly lead to the denial to children of the ability to secure their status in the United Kingdom.

Despite advances in children's rights, the Court of Appeal case of *GD (Ghana)* v. *Secretary of State for the Home Department*[63] highlights the tension that remains between the exercise of executive powers on immigration control and child welfare duties. Conflict of interests (between public and child) still arise frequently. The Court of Appeal considered the effect, within immigration and asylum proceedings, of a residence order made in the Family Division of the High Court, in respect of children whose Ghanaian mother was to be deported from the United Kingdom following a criminal conviction. The Court held:

> The Secretary of State, if she wishes to remove or deport a child or the child's parent, does *not* have to apply for the discharge or variation of any order of the Family Court or Family Division which provides for the child or parent to remain here.[64]

The Court did include a caveat from an earlier judgment, however (referring to an earlier Secretary of State):

> Clearly, any order made or views expressed by the [Family] Court would be a matter to be taken into account by the Secretary of State in the exercise of his powers. If he simply paid no attention to such an order, he would run the risk of his decision being reviewed on the ground that he had failed to take all relevant matters into consideration.[65]

5. LIFE AFTER BREXIT?

In June 2016, a referendum in the United Kingdom on the question whether the United Kingdom should remain a member of the European Union returned a narrow result in favour of leaving the EU. Since that date the United Kingdom has commenced procedures to formally cease membership. In accordance with the Treaty of Lisbon, the separation is scheduled to take place in March 2019, two years after the commencement of cessation procedures. Brexit (the neologism for that process) is, however, both legally and politically extremely complex. It is subject to a lengthy negotiation and renegotiation of relationships, at a state to state

---

63 [2017] EWCA Civ 1126, 25.
64 *Ibid.* para. [51].
65 *Ibid.* para. [50].

and supra-state levels. It requires the unpicking and rebuilding of many legal frameworks, not least the United Kingdom's asylum, immigration and residence controls. Issues of jurisdiction and jurisprudence stand to be re-determined, where at present the CJEU sits as an interpretive and definitive court for the understanding of EU Regulations and Directives as applied in Member States' domestic jurisdictions. Withdrawal will impact freedom of movement and residence rights of all nationals of the (presently) 28 Member States and their families to a greater or lesser degree, including rights of settlement, depending upon the outcome of negotiations. Brexit will affect countless children and their families now and in the future, who would hitherto have enjoyed all the freedoms and legal guarantees that accompanied EU membership.

Brexit may also lead to the United Kingdom no longer participating in cross-border jurisdiction agreements in family proceedings. It may mean withdrawal from the CEAS (including for family reunification and unaccompanied child transfers), anti-trafficking cooperation measures and common definitions and standards on refugee status determination and reception conditions.[66] The CFR of the EU will no longer apply, including the provisions explicitly guaranteeing children's rights.

As things stand, the rights of EU citizens in the United Kingdom and those of UK citizens in the EU are far from settled. Matters of children's rights of residency and nationality, as migrant children, are placed in an even greater state of uncertainty, possibly for many years if transitional arrangements are agreed. Difficulties may arise with inter-country adoption procedures and private family law cases where disputes occur over the country of residence of a child. Children who are settled in the United Kingdom may lose rights of travel and free movement. They may be unable to rely on rights based in EU law which they previously enjoyed. They may be subject to new immigration visa requirements. Asylum-seeking children will no longer have a right to seek transfer between the United Kingdom/EU to join family members under EU regulations nor to exercise free movement once settled. Cooperation provisions on child abduction, anti-slavery and anti-trafficking are at risk and will need to be renegotiated.

As interpretive case law, the jurisprudence of the CJEU prior to Brexit will still be taken into account by domestic courts but thereafter is likely

---

[66] See M. Papadouli, 'Brexit: What's in Pandora's Box for Asylum Seekers and Victims of Human Trafficking?' (Aire Centre, 30 July 2017), available at www.airecentre.org/news.php/282/brexitbrexitbrexitbrexit-whats-in-pandoras-box-for-asylum-seekers-and-victims-of-human-trafficking.

to diverge. However, the ECtHR will still have jurisdiction. The United Kingdom is not resiling from the ECHR nor from other international treaties which will remain effective in the United Kingdom as means of protection for children. These include the Refugee Convention, the CRC, the Convention Against Torture and the ICCPR, though their provisions are not directly justiciable unless incorporated into UK law. A transitional period may delay the final settlement of these changes. The task of repealing and redrafting legislation and statutory instruments to extricate parts that are based in or consequential on EU law is vastly complicated and will take many years.

The European Union (Withdrawal) Act 2018 was given Royal Assent on June 26, 2018 and alongside other related Bills still proceeding through Parliament will import all existing EU law into UK domestic law on the date of actual departure from the EU.[67] If passed as tabled or presently amended, this would import all existing EU law into UK domestic law on the date of actual departure from the EU. It would also give sweeping prerogative powers to the executive to repeal, amend and pass new laws over time, to remove and replace all EU laws and regulations from UK laws and jurisdictions without needing the further consent of Parliament. To that extent migrant children's rights during and after the process of exiting the EU are increasingly uncertain and in potential jeopardy.

6. CONCLUSION

The last decade in UK law and practice has undoubtedly seen significant progress in the recognition of the rights of asylum-seeking and migrant children at all levels: legislative, jurisprudential, policy and practice. The withdrawal of the United Kingdom's reservation against the CRC meant that the discrimination against migrant children was no longer institutionalized. The move finally set the United Kingdom on a journey towards the realization of equality for all children in the United Kingdom as a matter of principle, irrespective of migration status. However, the journey is a very slow and faltering one in the real world for migrant children. The often-conflicting interests of strong immigration controls and 'hostile environment' policies remain ingrained within our political, legal and welfare systems. Changing those practices, particularly in government departments and lower courts, away from a paternalistic, sceptical and even prejudiced perspective, towards a children's rights-based approach

67 http://www.legislation.gov.uk/ukpga/2018/16/contents/enacted/data.htm.

that is substantial not cosmetic, is a continuing challenge. With the complications of Brexit set to continue for many years, political upheaval and economic uncertainty will also play a role in the extent to which priority is given to modernizing and making effective the administrative and legal mechanisms needed to ensure that asylum-seeking and migrant children enjoy the protections and prospects that our international human rights framework and domestic laws accord them. On paper, the direction of travel is positive, with meaningful progress in establishing the primary importance of best interests of the child and increasingly, the voice of the child, nearer to the heart of decision-making. The Supreme Court has shown that it is prepared to lead the way on this and on access to justice. At the same time, hardening attitudes to immigration and border controls, not just in the United Kingdom but globally, have legitimized practices that are inimical to those rights. These include age-testing, immigration detention, splitting deported families, removal of young adults to countries in conflict, cuts to welfare, legal aid budgets and the courts, high application fees and financial thresholds. All vitiate the progress made.

Whilst it is most welcome that the courts have been willing to clarify, define and enforce the rights of some of the most vulnerable children in society, at the same time, deference is still unduly shown to the imperatives of border control by government departments and agencies with responsibility for ensuring that migrant children's best interests are met.[68] The next decade will require a concerted effort from all those who work to promote and protect the rights of asylum-seeking and migrant children to prevent further erosions – let alone make more progress.

[68] https://assets.publishing.service.gov.uk/government/uploads/system/uploads/attachment_data/file/695310/An_inspection_of_the_best_interests_of_unaccompanied_asylum_seeking_children_March_2018.pdf.

13. The legal treatment of immigrant children in the United States

David B. Thronson

1. INTRODUCTION

We pass along many old and used things to children – clothes, cribs, toys and books. These 'hand me downs' can be an efficient use of resources and a great gift to the recipient. Yet hand-me-downs all share the characteristic that they were originally created or acquired with someone else in mind. They may be worn out, patched or even frayed by the use that others have made of them. Despite the best of intentions, it is not unusual for hand-me-downs to be misshapen and ill-fitting. Children wearing hand-me-down clothes may be better off than they would be without them, but perhaps they find themselves floundering in outfits that are too large or squeezing into items that are too small. And for children who need protection, ill-fitting, old clothes may be simply inadequate.

By and large, US immigration law provides children with hand-me-downs, leaving them to stretch or squeeze their need for protection into laws and procedures that were developed for adults and with adult perspectives in mind. US immigration law's substantive criteria for immigration relief, procedural frameworks and protections, expectations for evidence and proof, allocations of burdens and roles, and more, have all been crafted to address the needs and experiences of adults. Children, in this system, are afterthoughts. Even in the few instances where US immigration law has turned its focus directly to children, it has failed to shed antiquated and limited notions of children as dependents. As such, existing adult-oriented frameworks provide an inadequate set of responses to shifting patterns of child migration. And those patterns are shifting.

After a lull in the preceding year,[1] 59,757 unaccompanied children and

[1] Interdiction by Mexico and rapid deportations from that country impacted the reduced numbers of children. See Isabel Martinez, Chapter 3. See also J.M.

77,857 family units including children were apprehended by the US border patrol in fiscal year 2016.[2] These numbers were similar to those from October 2013 through March 2014, when there were 19,830 apprehensions of children with families and 28,579 apprehensions of unaccompanied children.[3] Overwhelmingly, this increase in migration is made up of children from El Salvador, Guatemala and Honduras, while the number of migrant children from Mexico is still significant but decreasing.[4] The large number of child migrants creates a challenge for existing US immigration laws and systems which are simply not designed for the arrival of unaccompanied children and multigenerational families without lawful immigration status.

US immigration law has adapted over time to address other perceived inadequacies or problems in the way in which the law aligned with societal needs or intersected with tumultuous world events. For example, in keeping with its geopolitical positions, the United States has enacted special provisions that create an easy path to permanent residence for Cubans who arrive in the United States.[5] After seeing judges reject asylum for those facing consequences of China's one-child policy, Congress amended US asylum law to specify that such claims warranted relief as persecution

---

Krogstad, *US Border Apprehensions of Families and Unaccompanied Children Jump Dramatically* (Pew Hispanic Center, 2016), available at www.pewresearch.org/fact-tank/2016/05/04/u-s-border-apprehensions-of-families-and-unaccompanied-children-jump-dramatically/.

[2] Department of Homeland Security (DHS), *DHS Releases End of Year Fiscal Year 2016 Statistics* (30 December 2016), available at www.dhs.gov/news/2016/12/30/dhs-releases-end-year-fiscal-year-2016-statistics.

[3] *Ibid.*

[4] Krogstad, *US Border Apprehensions of Families and Unaccompanied Children Jump Dramatically*, above n. 1. See also D. Restrepo and A. Garcia, *The Surge of Unaccompanied Children from Central America: Root Causes and Policy Solutions* (Centre for American Progress, 24 July 2014), available at www.americanprogress.org/issues/immigration/report/2014/07/24/94396/the-surge-of-unaccompaniedchildren-from-central-america-root-causes-and-policy-solutions/. Despite the predominance of Central American migrants, arrivals at the US border increasingly include migrants from more distant locations. See A. Zavis and B. Bennett, 'A changing border: barricades won't solve tough new challenges at the Southwest frontier', *Los Angeles Times*, 31 December 2016, available at www.latimes.com/world/la-fg-immigration-trek-america-solutions-20161231-story.html.

[5] See Cuban Adjustment Act 1966 (US) Pub. L No 89–732, 80 Stat. 1161. Shifting US positions raise the possibility that US immigration law will adjust accordingly. See N. Miroff, 'Fear of immigration policy change triggers new wave of Cuban migrants', *Washington Post*, 27 January 2015, available at www.washingtonpost.com/world/the_americas/fears-of-immigration-policy-change-triggers-new-wave-of-cuban-migrants/2015/01/27/.

on account of political opinion.[6] US immigration statutes have even adapted to provide special considerations to overcome perceived barriers to the admission of very specific categories of people, such as fashion models.[7] While our laws have adjusted for these and other concerns, whether real or imagined, substantive reforms to tailor US immigration law to the experiences and realities of the thousands of migrant children arriving in the United States are conspicuously absent.[8] Unfortunately, this lack of action to address the real situations and experiences of children is consistent with the general disregard for children throughout US immigration law.

2. IMMIGRATION RELIEF OPTIONS FOR CHILDREN IN US IMMIGRATION LAW

US immigration law largely conceives of children not as persons but as dependents and derivatives, and relegates the bulk of its provisions specifically related to children to the law's family-sponsored immigration framework. As such, substantive immigration law that sets forth avenues to obtain lawful status or avoid deportation generally does not provide special provisions for children because of their status as children, but rather subsumes children into provisions designed around adults and adult interests.

2.1 Children in Families, Children as Dependents

Before examining the treatment of unaccompanied children in US immigration law, it is necessary to quickly consider the place of children in families in the broader immigration law frameworks. Family-sponsored immigration comprises the bulk of lawful immigration to the United

---

[6] See Immigration and Nationality Act (US) s. 101(a)(42) (augmenting the general statutory definition of 'refugee' which is derived from the 1951 Convention Relating to the Status of Refugees).

[7] See generally, K. Johnson, 'Importing the Flawless Girl' (2012) 12 *Nevada Law Journal* 831.

[8] Lest it be thought that the lack of responsiveness to children is due to the larger scale and sheer numbers of child migrant arrivals, it is worth noting that with little fanfare or concern '[d]uring the first 10 months of fiscal year 2016, 46,635 Cubans have entered the US via ports of entry – already surpassing full fiscal year 2015's total of 43,159, according to US Customs and Border Protection data obtained through a public records request'. Krogstad, *US Border Apprehensions of Families and Unaccompanied Children Jump Dramatically*, above n. 1.

States, followed by employment-based immigration, including families of employees. Notions of family and family relationship are central to these frameworks, yet these narrowly limit the role of children. Family provisions of US immigration law view children entirely as passive dependents, and the failure here to recognize children as independent persons permeates US immigration law and colors all aspects of its application.[9]

For example, under the immigration law's family-sponsored immigration provisions, legal permanent residents and US citizens may petition for immigrant visas for specified relatives.[10] Petitions by parents for children are favored while petitions by children for parents are prohibited. The ability of a parent to generate immigration status for a child in the absence of the ability of children to do so for their parents reveals a pervasive asymmetry in immigration law. Adults granted asylum or refugee status may generate derivative status for their spouses and children while child asylees and refugees cannot do the same for their parents.[11] When a child obtains legal immigration status through a family petition from one parent or a stepparent, she cannot include the other parent as a derivative.[12]

Immigration law's principal frameworks for family-sponsored and employment-based derivative immigration subordinate children's status to that of their parents. Parents who successfully navigate the immigration system may choose to extend that benefit to their children. But children who obtain lawful immigration status are not able to reciprocate and provide family-based immigration benefits to a parent.[13] This asymmetry is not a reflection of the relationship involved – in all of these instances the same family relationship may allow an extension of immigration status if the legal status holder is the parent, not the child.[14] Moreover,

---

[9] See D.B. Thronson, 'Kids Will be Kids? Reconsidering Conceptions of Children's Rights Underlying Immigration Law' (2002) 63 *Ohio St Louis Journal* 979, at 1014.

[10] See Immigration and Nationality Act, ss. 201(b)(2), 203(a).

[11] See *ibid.* ss. 207(c)(2), 208(b)(2).

[12] *Ibid.* s. 203(d).

[13] 'To the extent that the framework for family-sponsored and derivative immigration tends to achieve family integrity, it does so by ceding control over a child's status to parents and by denying opportunities for children to achieve legal status as children without their parents.' D.B. Thronson, 'Choiceless Choices: Deportation and the Parent-Child Relationship' (2006) 6 *Nevada Law Journal* 1165, at 1182.

[14] See J. Bhabha, 'The "Mere Fortuity" of Birth? Are Children Citizens?' (2004) 15(2) *Differences: A Journal of Feminist Cultural Studies* 91, at 95. Children

once children become adults and are no longer considered children under US immigration law, those who are US citizens may then sponsor their parents.[15]

In US immigration law, therefore, families centered on parents with lawful immigration status are recognized and valued. The law places value on parents' interests in family integrity and provides parents with the possibility to extend lawful status to their children. When only a child in a family has lawful immigration status, the child's concerns for family integrity find no foothold in immigration law. Children are not individuals with rights and agency, but only dependents. As such, US immigration law subordinates children's rights to parents' rights. And by focusing on the adults in children's lives rather than children themselves, US immigration law fails to recognize children as individuals and provides no benefits to children because of their characteristics as children. This has negative impact for those children lacking parents with ability and inclination to successfully navigate the immigration system. Moreover, the pervasive influence of the limiting conception of children as dependent impedes children who migrate on their own.

The major frameworks of US immigration law were established at a time when independent flows of migrant children were unthinkable.[16] With children now migrating alone in substantial numbers, often sent ahead as potential lead immigrants for family or singled out to be saved by families with limited resources, provisions developed for an entirely adult-centric view of families fails to provide solutions for children.

---

also face barriers in other major immigration law programs not directly related to family. Children generally cannot apply under the diversity visa lottery because applicants must be high school graduates or have equivalent education or work experience. See Immigration and Nationality Act, s. 203(c)(2). While children are not directly prohibited from applying for employment-based immigrant visas, it is highly unlikely that they would have the requisite education or job experience to qualify. See Immigration and Nationality Act, s. 203(b).

[15] Immigration and Nationality Act, s. 201(b)(2)(A) (requiring that petitioners for parents 'shall be at least 21 years of age').

[16] 'The principle of family reunification espoused in our contemporary immigration system can be traced to the Emergency Quota Act of 1921, later expanded by the McCarran-Walter Act of 1952 and the Hart-Celler Act of 1965.' A.O. Maddali, 'Left Behind: The Dying Principle of Family Reunification Under Immigration Law' (2016) 50 *University of Michigan Journal of Law Reform* 107, at 129.

2.2 Special Immigrant Juvenile Status: The Exception that Proves the Rule

There is one provision of immigration law that creates a path to lawful permanent immigration status that is unique to children. This, ironically, is perhaps the best example of how US immigration law fails to recognize children as persons and attempts to fit them into adult-centered immigration frameworks that are nonresponsive to their unique situations and experiences. This form of relief, special immigrant juvenile status, doubles down on the conception of children as passive dependents. It requires a determination of a child's best interests but then permits deportation even in instances where it is contrary to such interests, and limits the number of beneficiaries of relief. This is because the statute was arbitrarily situated among the employment-based visa provisions making it subject to numerical limitations perhaps applicable to employment but certainly not to humanitarian relief for children.

The special immigrant juvenile statute was enacted in 1990 to open a path for abandoned undocumented youth to become lawful permanent residents.[17] The children that Congress had in mind at the time were principally children without lawful immigration status who had been removed from their homes in the United States by child protection workers and subsequently were placed in domestic foster care systems. These children routinely faced the problem of living in government care, only to be forced from foster care without lawful immigration status upon reaching the age of majority.

The scheme that was created to address this scenario utilizes a hybrid system of state and federal decision-making, incorporating state court child welfare expertise into federal adjudication of immigration matters. State 'juvenile courts,' defined as 'court[s] located in the United States having jurisdiction under State law to make judicial determinations about the custody and care of juveniles',[18] are asked to make three factual determinations:

(1) The child has been 'declared dependent on a juvenile court' or the child has been 'legally committed to or placed under the custody

---

[17] *Leslie H* v. *Superior Court*, 224 Cal. App. 4th 340, 344 (Cal. Ct Appeals 4th Dist., 2012).

[18] See 8 CFR, s. 204.11(a). 'The reliance upon state juvenile courts anticipated in the SIJ statutory scheme signals Congress' recognition that the states retain primary responsibility and administrative competency to protect child welfare.' G. Zhong and T. Chen, 'Elian or Alien? The Contradictions of Protecting Undocumented Children Under the Special Immigrant Juvenile Statute' (2000) 27 *Hastings Constitutional Law Quarterly* 597, at 609.

of, an agency or department of a State, or an individual or entity appointed by a State or juvenile court located in the United States'.

(2) The child's 'reunification with [one] or both of the [child's] parents is not viable due to abuse, neglect, abandonment, or a similar basis found under State law'.

(3) It 'would not be in the [child's] best interest to be returned to the [child's] or parent's previous country of nationality or last habitual residence'.[19]

With these findings, a child can petition US Citizenship and Immigration Services for recognition as a special immigrant juvenile. Upon approval as a special immigrant juvenile, a child can apply to become a lawful permanent resident.

This provision is the only place in US immigration law where the best interests of a child are statutorily relevant to the grant of a substantive immigration benefit. Assigning the role of determining the child's best interests to the state courts is a natural outgrowth of the presumption that the beneficiaries of this relief would be children already involved with domestic state courts that were tasked with determining their care and custody. These child welfare system roots, with child welfare's characteristic focus on the best interests of the child, are evident in the design and provenance of the statute. While the special state court findings that immigration law demands do encompass the best interests of the child, the provision also meshes with the parent-centric framework of immigration law in some unfortunate ways to undermine the import of the child's best interests.

Even when it is judicially determined that returning a child to his or her country of origin is not in the child's best interests, the child may be deported because reunification with parents is possible or because the requisite dependency on the juvenile court is not established. The special immigrant juvenile law's key requirements regarding dependency and parental reunification direct the focus away from the child as an individual and towards a view of the child as a dependent. Relief turns on whether the child is dependent on the parent or on the state, not on the experiences and needs of the child.

If family-sponsored immigration only aids children as dependents on their parents, special immigrant juvenile status only reaches children named dependent on the court or dependent on a guardian or other adult. This relief thus is patterned precisely on family-sponsored immigration,

---

19 Immigration and Nationality Act, s. 101(a)(27)(J).

down to the prohibition of parents obtaining any immigration benefit from the special immigrant juvenile child.[20] So even when a provision is tailored for children, it is forced into a framework that was established with adults and adult interests in mind. A child welfare agency may benefit from various potential outcomes, either by not having to deal with the consequences that attach to a child without lawful immigration status if the child obtains status, or seeing a child deported. Children may lose in this game, but the adult system never does.

By imposing the requirements regarding dependency and parental reunification, it is evident that a child's best interests are not an overriding, or even primary, consideration. If it is determined both that it is in the child's best interests to remain in the United States and that parental reunification is viable, the child will be denied immigration relief. In this scheme, the best interests of the child are set aside for the possibility of placing the child with parents. Because the child is not a generator of immigration rights and status for the parents, it is not possible to vindicate the child's claims to both immigration relief and an intact family. In other instances, when all the requirements for special immigrant juvenile status have been met and a petition approved, deportation efforts against the child will continue due to a ground of inadmissibility that might attach to the child.[21] In these cases, the United States still deports children, consciously taking action that a court has adjudicated to not be in the child's best interest.

Despite its more limited roots in domestic child welfare realms, special immigrant juvenile status has emerged as a common and successful form of relief from deportation sought by unaccompanied minors arriving in the United States. Generally, children who have been apprehended by the border patrol are placed in removal proceedings, then transferred to the custody of the Office of Refugee Resettlement (ORR). In most instances, ORR then releases children to a parent or other sponsor, or places children in federally funded long-term foster care. Some form of state juvenile court adjudication, such as ratifying the placement in long-term foster care or establishing a guardianship, is then necessary to provide an avenue for the state juvenile court to make the requisite finding.

In fiscal year 2016, US Citizenship and Immigration Services received 19,475 petitions for special immigrant juvenile status, approved 15,101,

---

[20] So central is this prohibition that it appears in the Immigration and Nationality Act twice. See Immigration and Nationality Act, ss. 101(a)(27)(J) and 245(h).

[21] See discussion at 3.4 below.

and finished the period with 8,533 petitions pending.[22] This compares with only 1,646 petitions received in fiscal year 2010.[23] If there is any doubt that the drafters of the special immigrant juvenile statute did not craft a freestanding new approach built around the needs of children, it is the puzzling placement of the provision in the portion of the Immigration and Nationality Act governing employment-based immigration. Because of this placement, the number of children who can be provided lawful permanent residence as special immigrant juveniles is subject to an annual cap.[24] This limitation is entirely unfitting for a humanitarian form of relief.

Special immigrant juvenile status was conceived not to respond to flows of unaccompanied children but rather in response to a different set of circumstances with an eye to the interests of child welfare agencies and an adherence to the adult-centric structures of immigration law. That this status benefits many children in the present flows of unaccompanied minors is true, but it also leaves out many youth in need of humanitarian relief whose situations simply cannot be molded to fit the exacting requirements of special immigrant juvenile status. This relief was not tailored to the flow of unaccompanied minors, and its roots in the child welfare system limit its ultimate usefulness for many child migrants.

3. HUMANITARIAN AND DISCRETIONARY RELIEF

3.1 Protection from Persecution and Torture

Children, like adults, can independently seek humanitarian forms of relief, such as asylum, withholding of removal, and protection from removal under the Convention Against Torture.[25] Problematically, the 'normative

---

[22] US Citizenship and Immigration Services, *Number of I-360 Petitions for Special Immigrant with a Classification of Special Immigrant Juvenile (SIJ) by Fiscal Year and Case Status 2010–2016* (2016).

[23] *Ibid.*

[24] See Immigration and Nationality Act, s. 202. Presently, the caps mean that children from the countries of highest child migration, including El Salvador, Honduras, Guatemala and Mexico, face backlogs of nearly two years. See US Department of State, *Visa Bulletin for January 2017* (2017), available at https://travel.state.gov/content/visas/en/law-and-policy/bulletin/2017/visa-bulletin-for-january-2017.html.

[25] See *Gonzalez* v. *Reno*, 212 F.3d 1338, 1347 n. 8 (11th Cir. 2000). See also J. Bhabha and W.A. Young, 'Through a Child's Eyes: Protecting the Most

and legal substantive framework for unaccompanied children in removal proceedings is based upon an adult framework and does not incorporate a child-oriented framework'.[26] As discussed more fully in Chapter 5, the substantive criteria for children seeking asylum is identical to that applied to adults. Merely being a child does not shift the stringent substantive criteria or lessen the burden of proof.

The William Wilberforce Trafficking Victims Protection Reauthorization Act 2008 (US) amended the procedure for processing asylum applications of unaccompanied children so that an asylum officer from the United States Citizenship and Immigration Service (USCIS) has 'initial jurisdiction' over any asylum application filed by an unaccompanied child, including applications filed by children in removal proceedings.[27] In other words, the law provides that an unaccompanied child in immigration proceedings should have his or her asylum application adjudicated in the first instance by a USCIS asylum officer; if the asylum officer does not grant the child's application, the child may renew it before the Immigration Judge.

In light of their more limited life experiences, the most common claims for child asylum-seekers are those that involve persecution on account of 'membership in a particular social group', and courts have struggled to apply this rubric to the situations presented in child asylum cases.[28] Asylum applicants, regardless of age, bear heavy evidentiary burdens, and the Board of Immigration Appeals has articulated an expectation of corroborating evidence for alleged facts pertaining to the specifics of an applicant's claim.[29]

On one front there has been limited success in forcing adjudicators to acknowledge distinctions between children and adults. In evaluating persecution, the harm that a child suffers must be evaluated differently

---

Vulnerable Asylum Seekers' (1998) 75(21) *Interpreter Releases* 757, at 758. ('Children are, of course, technically eligible for the same protection under international refugee law as adults.')

[26] M.A. Somers et al., 'Constructions of Childhood and Unaccompanied Children in the Immigration System of the United States' (2010) 14 *UC Davis Journal of Juvenile Law and Policy* 311, at 372.

[27] PL 110-457.

[28] See, e.g., *Matter of MEVG*, 26 Immigration and Nationality Decisions 227 (BIA 2014) (discussing, for a third time on a second remand from the US Court of Appeals for the Third Circuit, the evolution of the analysis of particular social groups in a case where applicants claimed persecution as Honduran youths who resisted gang recruitment).

[29] See *Matter of Mogharrabi*, 19 Immigration and Nationality Decisions 439 (BIA 1987); see also Immigration and Nationality Act, s. 208(b)(1)(B)(ii).

to that experienced by an adult. Under guidelines developed by the Immigration and Naturalization Service, 'the harm a child fears or has suffered . . . may be relatively less than that of an adult and still qualify as persecution'.[30] Age thus is a factor in determining whether harm constitutes persecution.[31]

Children in the company of parents have additional concerns to ensure that their independent claims are not lost or subsumed by claims of adults. Children 'within a family may have an independent claim to refugee status and, as with all family dependents, it is important that the asylum process can properly identify, assess and document those claims ensuring that the appropriate rights and status derive from that'.[32] Finally, in keeping with US immigration law's general limitation on parents deriving status from children, asylum-seeking children cannot extend derivative refugee status to parents while they are a child or even later when they become adults.[33]

3.2 Victims of Abuse, Trafficking and Other Crimes

The Violence Against Women Act (VAWA), introduced into US immigration law in 1994, provides battered immigrants abused by their US citizen or lawful permanent resident spouses, parents or children the opportunity to 'self-petition' or independently seek legal immigration status in the United States based on qualifying relationships without having to rely on abusers to file petitions on their behalf.[34] This allows abused children to circumvent the abusers' control of the family immigration process, but is limited in its application to child migrants because it requires that the abuser have lawful immigration status and that the abuse take place in the United States. As such, VAWA is largely a procedural adjustment to the family-sponsored immigration structure discussed above.

Modeled in many ways on VAWA, but expanding its reach, are the T and U visas. The T visa is available to a 'victim of a severe form of

---

[30] US Department of Justice, Immigration and Naturalization Service, Office of International Affairs, *Guidelines for Children's Asylum Claims*, File 120/11.26 (1 December 1998).

[31] *Mejilla-Romero* v. *Holder*, 614 F.3d 572 (1st Cir. 2010) (finding error in failure to follow the Guidelines in consideration of a child's claims).

[32] United Nations High Commissioner for Refugees (UNHCR), *Untold Stories . . . Families in the Asylum Process* (2013), available at www.refworld.org/cgi-bin/texis/vtx/rwmain?page=search&docid=51c027b84&skip=0&query=%22harm%20to%20family%20members%22&coi=GBR.

[33] See generally L.A. Nessel, 'Forced to Choose: Torture, Family Reunification and United States Immigration Policy' (2005) 78 *Temple Law Review* 897.

[34] See Immigration and Nationality Act, s. 204(a)(1)(A)(iv).

trafficking in persons' who, among other qualifications, has 'complied with any reasonable request for assistance' from law enforcement.[35] U visas are for persons who have 'suffered substantial physical or mental abuse as a result of having been a victim of [specified] criminal activity' and who, among other qualifications, are certified by law enforcement as having been or are likely to be helpful in investigating or prosecuting the crime.[36] Technically these are non-immigrant visas, but both T and U visas provide for the possibility of adjustment of status to lawful permanent residence after three years if other requirements are met.[37]

Uniquely in US immigration law, T and U visas provide a means through which immigration status which originates with a child can flow from a child to a parent and even to siblings. When a child granted a T visa or a U visa is under age 21, that visa status also becomes available to the person's 'spouse, children, unmarried siblings under 18 years of age on the date on which such alien applied for status under such clause, and parents'.[38] This means that when a child qualifies for a T or U visa, the child's nuclear family members also may qualify, including the child's parents. This extension of relief to parents based on the child's status is unique in US immigration law, in contrast to the lack of provision for parents when children are granted other forms of relief on their own behalf such as child refugees, asylum-seekers or special immigrant juveniles. The extension of relief not only to the child but often to the entire family increases the likelihood that eligible children will seek and obtain legal immigration status. Without the ability to extend status to parents, unauthorized parents might be wary of an immigration process that could assist one child individually but potentially expose others in the family to risk. Parents, under these provisions, are able to assist their child with the immigration process without fear, and perhaps with the incentive of regularizing their own status. And with legal immigration status the parents are better able to integrate economically and socially for the benefit and support of the child and the family as a whole.

3.3 Deferred Action for Childhood Arrivals

In 2012, the Department of Homeland Security (DHS) announced its Deferred Action for Childhood Arrivals (DACA) initiative under which

---

35 *Ibid.* s. 101(a)(15)(T).
36 *Ibid.* s. 101(a)(15)(T). The crime must have occurred in the United States.
37 *Ibid.* s. 245(l), (m).
38 *Ibid.* s. 101(a)(15)(T)(ii)(I).

certain noncitizens who had arrived in the United States as children could seek deferred action.[39] If successful, this means that the government will defer any action to proceed with their removal. By the terms of the memo, a DACA requestor must show that they arrived in the United States before age 16; continuously resided in the United States since 15 June 2007, i.e. for the five-year period leading up to the date of the memo; was then enrolled in school, had graduated from high school or obtained a GED, or had been honorably discharged from military service; had not committed any of certain crimes and posed no threat to national security or public safety; was at least 15 years of age at the time of applying; and was not above the age of 30.[40] Approval is discretionary even if these criteria are met.[41] Importantly, those approved are provided with temporary employment authorization in addition to deferred removal.[42] Through fiscal year 2016, US Citizenship and Immigration Services had received 910,752 applications and approved 752,154.[43]

This program, together with proposed expansions,[44] has been the focus of litigation and intense political debate.[45] Detractors allege that DACA and its proposed expansions represent executive power grabs and demonstrate a lack of respect for the rule of law, while supporters have rebutted such

---

39 Janet Napolitano, Secretary of Homeland Security, *Memorandum Exercising Prosecutorial Discretion with Respect to Individuals Who Came to the United States as Children* (15 June 2012), available at www.dhs.gov/xlibrary/assets/s1-exercising-prosecutorial-discretion-individuals-who-came-to-us-as-children.pdf [https://perma.cc/H3BQ-MCET.

40 *Ibid.*

41 *Ibid.*

42 *Ibid.*

43 US Citizenship and Immigration Services, *Number of I-821D, Consideration of Deferred Action for Childhood Arrival by Fiscal Year, Quarter, Intake, Biometrics and Case Status, 2012–2016* (30 September 2016).

44 Jeh Charles Johnson, Secretary of Homeland Security, *Memorandum Exercising Prosecutorial Discretion with Respect to Individuals Who Came to the United States as Children and with Respect to Certain Individuals Who Are the Parents of US Citizens or Permanent Residents* (20 November 2014), available at www.dhs.gov/sites/default/files/publications/14_1120_memo_deferred_action.pdf; see also Karl R. Thompson, Principal Deputy Assistant Attorney General, Office of Legal Counsel, US Department of Justice, *Memorandum to the President, The Department of Homeland Security's Authority to Prioritize Removal of Certain Aliens Unlawfully Present in the United States and to Defer Removal of Others* (19 November 2014), available at www.justice.gov/sites/default/files/olc/opinions/attachments/2014/11/20/2014-11-19-auth-prioritize-removal.pdf [https://perma.cc/CL2A-K7HK].

45 *Texas* v. *United States*, 809 F.3d 134 (5th Cir. 2015), aff'd by equally divided Supreme Court, No. 15-674, 579 US (23 June 2016).

allegations through analysis of the strong legal authority and historical precedent for the use of prosecutorial discretion and deferred action.[46] Regardless of the legal analysis, DACA was always an exercise of executive discretion and on 5 September 2017 the new administration announced that it would phase out DACA's protections over a period of approximately two years.[47]

DACA has proven important for hundreds of thousands of people who arrived at a young age. Yet even if a version of DACA's protections is incorporated into another administrative or legislative vehicle, it is hardly a forward-looking reform centered on the rights and perspectives of children. Given its backward-looking criteria and eligibility cutoff date, the program provides no benefit to children who arrived after 2007. In fact, the need for and existence of a program such as DACA highlights the inability of child migrants to obtain relief under extant US immigration law, which DACA in no way changes.

Moreover, DACA does not serve children per se, but rather childhood arrivals, many of whom are now adults. DACA gives a tenuous and temporary relief from deportation not just to children and not because children as children deserve relief. In announcing the framework for individuals eligible for prosecutorial discretion under DACA, Secretary Napolitano noted:

> Our Nation's immigration laws . . . are [not] designed to remove productive young people to countries where they may not have lived or even speak the language. Indeed, many of these young people have already contributed to our country in significant ways.[48]

The narrative, like the relief, is not tailored around children and their needs but rather on young adults and their contributions.

3.4 Barriers to Relief

Just as substantive eligibility criteria for immigration relief apply to children as they do adults, grounds of inadmissibility that can bar relief

---

[46] See A. Kalhan, 'Deferred Action, Supervised Enforcement Discretion, and the Rule of Law Basis for Executive Action on Immigration' (2015) 63 *UCLA Law Review Discourse* 58, at 62–3. See also D.B. Thronson, 'Closing the Gap: DACA, DAPA and US Compliance with International Human Rights Law' (2016) 48 *Case Western Reserve Journal of International Law* 127.

[47] E.C. Duke, Department of Homeland Security, *Memorandum on Rescission of Deferred Action for Childhood Arrivals* (5 September 2017), available at www.dhs.gov/news/2017/09/05/memorandum-rescission-daca.

[48] *Ibid.*

also fail to distinguish between children and adults.[49] Penalties and barriers on persons who enter the United States without inspection and fail to maintain lawful status apply to children as well as adults.[50] This is true regardless of whether the child exercised independent judgment in deciding to enter the United States or the child was brought to the country as a baby. For example, infants who were carried into the United States without inspection are foreclosed from an important immigration law procedure known as adjustment of status.[51] This means that even later in life as adults they will be barred from pursuing regularization of immigration status based on eligibility via marriage or employment. Children thus are held accountable not for choices made on their own but rather are burdened with the consequences of decisions made by adults in their lives.[52] Rather than treatment that acknowledges them as children, immigration law punishes them as adults.

4. CONCLUSION

By failing to develop and tailor immigration law to address the unique experiences of children, especially unaccompanied migrant children, US immigration law leaves children to navigate substantive and procedural hurdles established with adults in mind. Existing adult-oriented frameworks are not responsive to current patterns of child migration and lack adequate protections for children.

---

[49] See, e.g., Immigration and Nationality Act, s. 212(a)(6)(A) (establishing inadmissibility for all persons present without permission or parole regardless of age); *ibid.* s. 212(a)(7)(A) (establishing documents-related inadmissibility grounds regardless of age).

[50] See *ibid.* s. 245(a) (limiting adjustment of status to persons 'inspected and admitted or paroled into the United States'); *ibid.* s. 245(c)(7) (barring adjustment of status of persons 'not in a lawful immigration status').

[51] See *ibid.* s. 245(c)(7).

[52] J. Bhabha, '"Not a Sack of Potatoes": Moving and Removing Children Across Borders' (2006) 15 *Boston University Public Interest Law Journal* 197, at 198–9.

14. Children and refugee law in Australia and the United States

Timnah Baker and Kate Bones

1. CHILDREN AND COMPARATIVE REFUGEE LAW

International and domestic jurisprudence and guidance on the definition of refugee has largely developed around the adult applicant.[1] Decision-makers and courts have often struggled to engage with the different experiences and vulnerabilities of children seeking asylum. Writing in 1999, Jacqueline Bhabha and Wendy Young observed a historical shortcoming in asylum law 'which has failed to acknowledge the unique needs of children seeking refuge from human rights violations, and has required that they meet the same . . . legal rules as have been applied to adult asylum seekers'.[2] In that article, Bhabha and Young commend the United States (US) for implementing the Guidelines for Children's Asylum Claims,[3] which outline a child-sensitive approach to the substantive issues involved in the assessment of children's claims of persecution. The authors urge other countries to follow suit. Almost two decades later, Australia has only limited guidance on the adjudication of child asylum claims. The law has failed adequately to address key issues in the application of the refugee definition to children, most notably the role that an applicant's personal vulnerabilities play in the assessment of whether the person has suffered 'serious harm' amounting to persecution. In the same period, however, US asylum jurisprudence

---

[1] UNHCR, *Guidelines on International Protection: Child Asylum Claims under Articles 1(A)2 and 1(F) of the 1951 Convention and/or 1967 Protocol relating to the Status of Refugees* (22 December 2009), p. 3 ('*UNHCR Guidelines on Child Asylum Claims*').

[2] J. Bhabha and W. Young, 'Not Adults in Miniature: Unaccompanied Child Asylum Seekers and the New US Guidelines' (1999) 11 *International Journal of Refugee Law* 84, at 85.

[3] US Department of Justice, Immigration and Naturalization Service, *Guidelines for Children's Asylum Claims* (10 December 1998) ('*US Guidelines for Children's Asylum Claims*').

has become stuck (or unstuck) around its treatment of 'membership of a particular social group' and the now attendant elements of particularity and visibility/social distinction. The restrictive and conceptually problematic developments in the jurisprudence on this aspect of the refugee definition pose a barrier to protection for many child applicants.

At a normative level, the fact that the strengths as well as some of the most glaring shortcomings of the two asylum regimes have developed along different fault-lines brings into sharp focus the possibilities of cross-jurisdictional exchange,[4] whereby each domestic asylum regime stands to gain important insights about its own system by attending to the technologies of others. Comparative law may afford a measure of distance to (re)examine the state of a system's own jurisprudence.[5] This is all the more pertinent in the field of refugee law, involving as it does a common international status derived from the Convention Relating to the Status of Refugees ('Refugee Convention').[6] Hathaway has remarked that '[s]enior appellate courts now routinely engage in an ongoing and quite extraordinary transnational judicial conversation about the scope of the refugee definition and have increasingly committed themselves to find common grounds'.[7] As a snapshot of the dynamic patterns of cross-jurisdictional exchange, however, the intersection between Australia and the United States around the interpretation of the term 'particular social group' sounds a note of caution. Transnational and cross-jurisdictional 'conversations' in this area have at times produced troubling distortions at the domestic and international levels, weakening rather than strengthening protections for children and other vulnerable groups.

This chapter will examine the application of the refugee definition to children in the law of Australia and the United States, providing

---

4 See, e.g., M. Tushnet, 'The Possibilities of Comparative Constitutional Law' (1999) 108(6) *Yale Law Journal* 1225, at 1310; V.C. Jackson, 'Methodological Challenges in Comparative Constitutional Law' (2010) 28 *Pennsylvania State International Law Review* 319, at 326; M. Tushnet, 'Some Reflections on Method in Comparative Constitutional Law' in S. Choudhry (ed.), *The Migration of Constitutional Ideas* (Cambridge University Press, 2011), p. 81.

5 See G. Frankenberg, 'Critical Comparisons: Re-thinking Comparative Law' (1985) 26 *Harvard International Law Journal* 411, at 456; F.I. Michelman, 'Reflection' (2004) 82 *Texas Law Review* 1737. But see also *ibid.*

6 Convention relating to the Status of Refugees, opened for signature 28 July 1951, 189 UNTS 150 (entered into force 22 April 1954), as modified by the Protocol relating to the Status of Refugees, opened for signature 31 January 1967, 606 UNTS 267 (entered into force 4 October 1967) ('Refugee Convention').

7 J. Hathaway, *The Rights of Refugees under International Law* (Cambridge University Press, 2005), p. 2.

comparative case studies on two aspects of the definition that present particular issues, and potential promise, in the jurisdictions. We begin with a brief overview of the incorporation of the international definition of 'refugee' into Australian and US domestic law. Section 3 provides the first case study on the issue of the level of harm required to amount to persecution. We suggest that looking to the US approach to the relevance of a child's vulnerability may assist Australia to overcome its stagnancy on this important question. Section 4 then considers as the second case study the jurisprudence on defining a 'particular social group' and its impact on protection of children. The chapter concludes by drawing on the two case studies to highlight the possibilities of transnational and cross-jurisdictional dialogue in the field of refugee law. We stress also the need for such dialogue to be careful and principled, in order to ensure the law develops to better engage with the particular circumstances and protection needs of children.

2. REFUGEE DEFINITION IN AUSTRALIAN AND US LAW

The definition of 'refugee' established by the Refugee Convention is set out in Chapter 5, with discussion of the challenges that each element of the definition presents for children. Both Australia and the United States have codified the definition in domestic law, in the process creating some divergence in the definition's terms. In Australia, the refugee definition in Australian law is now codified in the Migration Act 1958 (Cth) (Austl).[8] The legislative definition was inserted in December 2014, removing the prior reference to Australia's protection obligations under the Refugee Convention which operated to incorporate the international definition as interpreted by Australian courts.[9] The intention of the amendments was to 'instead create . . . a new, independent and self-contained

[8] Migration Act 1958 (Cth) (Austl), ss. 5H–5L. The definition was introduced by the Migration and Maritime Powers Legislation Amendment (Resolving the Asylum Legacy Caseload) Act 2014 (Cth) (Austl), passed on 5 December 2014 ('Legacy Caseload Act'). The amended definition applies to applications made on or after 16 December 2014; the preceding definition continues to apply to applications made previously which remain undetermined: Table items 14 and 22 of Sch. 2 and item 28 of Sch. 5; Migration and Maritime Powers Legislation Amendment (Resolving the Asylum Legacy Caseload) Commencement Proclamation (16 April 2015) (FRLI F2015L00543).

[9] Migration Act, s. 36(2)(a) (pre-December 2014). Certain aspects of the definition had been gradually added to the Migration Act: see prior ss. 91R–91U

statutory framework which articulates Australia's interpretation of its protection obligations under the Refugee Convention'.[10] The Minister for Immigration and Border Protection explained that this would ensure Australian law would not be 'subject to the interpretations of foreign courts or judicial bodies which seek to expand the scope of the Refugees Convention well beyond what was ever intended by this country or this parliament'.[11] The codification of the refugee definition is thus intended to restrict the ability of the courts to look to international jurisprudence and developments in other jurisdictions. While the courts are still charged with interpreting the definition as it now stands in the statute, it adds a 'filter' separating Australian domestic law from international law.[12]

The legislative definition largely mirrors the jurisprudence developed on the definition of refugee; but in some instances significantly departs from the existing case law (and international law).[13] Relevantly for the discussion that follows, the term 'well-founded fear of persecution' is defined in section 5J of the Migration Act. It provides that persecution 'must involve serious harm to the person' and 'must involve systematic and discriminatory conduct'.[14] A non-exhaustive list of instances of 'serious harm' is then provided, including a threat to the person's life or liberty; significant physical harassment or ill-treatment; and significant economic hardship or denial of basic services where that 'threatens the person's capacity to subsist'.[15]

(inserted by the Migration Legislation Amendment Act (No. 6) 2001 (Cth) (Austl)).

[10] Explanatory Memorandum, *Migration and Maritime Powers Legislation Amendment (Resolving the Asylum Legacy Caseload) Act 2014 (Cth)*, p. 10.

[11] Hansard, House of Representatives (25 September 2014) 7.

[12] See D.J. Cantor and B. Burson, 'Introduction: Interpreting the Refugee Definition in Light of Human Rights Standards' in D.J. Cantor and B. Burson (eds), *Human Rights and the Refugee Definition* (Brill, 2016), pp. 19–20.

[13] Notably, the definition contained in the Migration Act now requires that 'the real chance of persecution extends to all areas of the receiving country': s. 5J(1)(c). This is a significant change from the internal relocation principle under the Refugee Convention, which considers whether it is reasonable to require a person to relocate to an area within the country to avoid persecution: *SZATV* v. *Minister for Immigration and Citizenship (MIAC)* (2007) 233 CLR 18. This has the potential to be significantly prejudicial to applicants, including children, in circumstances where the persecution may not extend to all areas of the country but nonetheless the child may not be able to reasonably relocate, due to factors such as their young age, dependency and lack of familial or social links: see, e.g., *RRT Case No. 1214218* [2013] RRTA 92 (22 January 2013), paras [141]–[149].

[14] Migration Act, s. 5J(4).

[15] *Ibid.* s. 5J(5). For analysis of this legislative definition in international

The United States codified the Refugee Convention via the Refugee Act of 1980.[16] Its express purpose was to align US asylum law with the nation's international refugee treaty obligations; as Joan Fitzpatrick observed, 'the legislative history of the Refugee Act is replete with general expressions of intent to bring US law into conformity with international norms'.[17] The House Judiciary Committee explained that the amendments were necessary to ensure that 'US statutory law clearly reflects our legal obligations under international agreements'.[18] Aside from the United States' expansion of the definition to include 'past persecution' as a separate and independent ground, the language of Article 1(A)(2) of the Refugee Convention and 8 USC s. 1101(a)(42)(A) of the Refugee Act is almost identical. The Refugee Act has been incorporated into the Immigration and Nationality Act (INA), the relevant section of which reads as follows:

> Any person who is outside any country of such person's nationality, or in the case of a person having no nationality, is outside any country in which such person last habitually resided, and who is unable or unwilling to avail himself or herself of the protection of that country because of persecution or a well-founded fear of persecution on account of race, religion, nationality, membership in a particular social group, or political opinion.[19]

The Supreme Court has confirmed the derivative relationship between US international obligations and the domestic Refugee Act on a number of occasions.[20] In the landmark case of *INS* v. *Cardoza-Fonseca*, the Court affirmed that it is 'clear from the legislative history of the new definition

---

context, see H. Storey, 'What Constitutes Persecution: Towards a Working Definition' (2014) 26 *International Journal of Refugee Law* 272.

[16] Congress passed the Refugee Act of 1980, Pub. L No. 96-212, 94 Stat. 102 (codified as amended in scattered sections of 8 USC). Note that the United States is not a party to the Refugee Convention but has ratified the Protocol.

[17] J. Fitzpatrick, 'The International Dimension of US Refugee Law' (1997) 15 *Berkeley Journal of International Law* 1, at 6. See also C. Blum, 'A Question of Values: Continuing Divergences Between U.S. and International Refugee Norms' (1997) 15 *Berkeley Journal International Law* 38; S. Busby, 'The Politics of Protection: Limits and Possibilities in the Implementation of International Refugee Norms in the United States' (1997) 15 *Berkeley Journal International Law* 27; J. Hathaway and A. Cusick, 'Refugee Rights are Not Negotiable' (2000) 14 *Georgetown Immigration Law Journal* 481, at 540.

[18] HR Rep. No. 96-608, 18 (1979).

[19] Section101(42)A; 8 USC s. 1101(42)(A) (2013).

[20] B. Farbenblum, 'Executive Deference in US Refugee Law' (2011) 60 *Duke Law Journal* 1059, at 1062.

of "refugee", and indeed the entire 1980 Act . . . that one of Congress' primary purposes was to bring US refugee law into conformance with the [Protocol]'.[21] In that case, the Supreme Court remarked in a footnote that while the *UNHCR Handbook on Procedures and Criteria for Determining Refugee Status* does not have 'the force of law', it nonetheless provides 'significant guidance' in light of the congressional intent to bring US law in line with the Protocol.[22] A decade later in *INS* v. *Juan Anibal Aguirre-Aguirre*, the Supreme Court diluted its commitment to UNHCR recommendations. Ruling that the Ninth Circuit erred in holding that the Board of Immigration Appeals (BIA) was required to refer to the Handbook in reaching its decision, the Court held that the 'UN handbook may be a useful interpretive aid, but it is not binding on the Attorney General, the BIA, or United States Courts'.[23]

The Refugee Act does not offer further definition of the component terms, leaving it to the BIA and federal courts to interpret their meaning.[24] This allows opportunity for the courts to look at times outside of the US system when interpreting the refugee definition.

3. LEVEL OF HARM

3.1 Vulnerability and 'Serious Harm' in Australian Law

The term 'persecution' is perhaps the component of the refugee definition that carries the strongest (mis)understandings and assumptions that reflect an adult-centric approach to refugee status. The UN Committee on the Rights of the Child has called for an interpretation that 'tak[es] into account the particular motives for, and forms and manifestations of,

---

21 480 US 421, 436 (1987). The 1980 Refugee Act also amended the INA to reflect the non-refoulement obligation under Art. 33 of the Refugee Convention. It became mandatory for the Attorney General to withhold deportation of a person who would otherwise be sent to a country in which her life or freedom would be threatened on account of a Convention ground (see 8 USC s. 1231(b)(3)).

22 *INS* v. *Cardoza-Fonseca*, 480 US 421, 439 (1987). See generally K. Musalo, J. Moore and R.A. Boswell, *Refugee Law and Policy: A Comparative and International Approach* (4th edn, Carolina Academic Press, 2011).

23 *INS* v. *Juan Anibal Aguirre-Aguire*, 526 US 415 (1999). For further discussion see M.G. Heyman, 'Immigration Law and the Supreme Court: The Flagging Spirit of the Law' (2002) 23 *Immigration and Nationality Law Journal* 303, at 338.

24 8 USC s. 1252 (providing the federal Courts of Appeals with jurisdiction to review decisions by the BIA); 8 CFR s. 1003.1 (establishing the BIA's authority). See S. Rempell, 'Defining Persecution' (2013) *Utah Law Review* 283, at 344.

persecution experienced by children'.[25] Bhabha and Crock identify three categories of situations that may constitute persecution in the case of a child.[26] First, children may face persecution that is the same as that experienced by adults. Second, there are forms of persecution that are specific to children, such as underage recruitment, child trafficking, child labour, female genital mutilation, or domestic violence against children.[27] Third, harm which may not amount to persecution in the case of an adult may arise to the level of persecution in the case of a child. The UNHCR Guidelines acknowledge this principle, explaining that:

> [i]mmaturity, vulnerability, undeveloped coping mechanisms and dependency as well as the differing stages of development and hindered capacities may be directly related to how a child experiences or fears harm.[28]

It is this final category that has the potential to be most contentious in the interpretation of the term 'persecution'.

In the Australian context, guidance and jurisprudence on the application of the refugee definition in children's cases remains limited. Crock noted in the 2006 study *Seeking Asylum Alone* that 'jurisprudence on children and refugee status of any kind is recent and poorly developed'.[29] Ten years on, this remains the case. In particular, there is as yet no case law at an appellate level accepting that a child's vulnerabilities are relevant to the analysis of whether treatment amounts to 'serious harm' required to meet the definition of persecution in Australian law.

The limited development of case law may be attributable to a culture in practice of not raising claims for children who are in family groups.[30] The problem is reflected in decisions of the Federal Court of Australia where it has been argued that the decision-maker failed properly to

---

25 UN Committee on the Rights of the Child, *General Comment No. 6: Treatment of Unaccompanied and Separated Children Outside their Country of Origin*, UN Doc. CRC/GC/2005/6 (1 September 2005), paras [74]–[75].

26 J. Bhabha and M. Crock, *Seeking Asylum Alone: A Comparative Study – Unaccompanied and Separated Children and Refugee Protection in Australia, the UK and the US* (Themis Press, 2007), p. 158.

27 See *UNHCR Guidelines on Child Asylum Claims*, above n. 1, paras [18]–[36].

28 *Ibid.* para. [15]; see also Bhabha and Young, above n. 2, 'Not Adults in Miniature', at 103–5.

29 M. Crock, *Seeking Asylum Alone: A Study of Australian Law, Policy and Practice Regarding Unaccompanied and Separated Children* (Themis Press, 2006), p. 169.

30 *Ibid.* 177. Noting this tendency internationally, see J. McAdam, 'Seeking Asylum under the Convention on the Rights of the Child: A Case for Complementary Protection' (2006) 14 *International Journal of Children's Rights* 251, at 259.

address children's claims, but the Court held that the fears were not sufficiently articulated to be a 'claim' that had to be addressed.[31] Even where independent protection claims are raised for children who are in a family group, they are as a matter of practice unlikely to be considered if a parent is found to be owed protection. This is because the remaining family members are entitled to a protection visa on the basis of forming part of the same family unit,[32] rendering consideration of the other protection claims unnecessary. Such an approach is contrary to the UNHCR Guidelines, which state that '[i]n situations where both the parent(s) and the child have their own claims to refugee status, it is preferable that each claim be assessed separately', thereby increasing the visibility of child applicants.[33]

The tendency to overlook accompanied children is reflected in the policy guidelines used by decision-makers in the Department of Immigration and Border Protection (DIBP), the *Procedures Advice Manual* (*PAM*).[34] For example, the *PAM Refugee Law Guidelines* refers to the need to consider an applicant's personal circumstances in the assessment of persecution, such as 'the particular vulnerabilities of women at risk and unaccompanied minors',[35] but does not address the vulnerability of children more broadly or provide substantive guidance on the assessment of claims brought by children.

At the merits review stage, there is some acknowledgement of age and vulnerability in the Administrative Appeal Tribunal (AAT) *Guide to Refugee Law*.[36] The *Guide to Refugee Law* states:

> There is authority for the proposition that when assessing whether discrimination faced by an applicant amounts to 'serious harm', all the relevant circumstances must be taken into account, including personal circumstances such as the applicant's age and frailty.[37]

---

31 See *WZARN* v. *Minister for Immigration and Border Protection (MIBP)* (2013) 139 ALD 556 (claims based on religion for Iranian children were not sufficiently articulated); *SZOYH* v. *Minister for Immigration and Citizenship (MIAC) and another* (2012) 128 ALD 554 (possible psychological harm to child by seeing parents detained was not raised before the Tribunal).

32 Migration Act, s. 36(2)(b).

33 *UNHCR Guidelines on Child Asylum Claims*, above n. 1, para. [9].

34 See further Savitri Taylor, Chapter 18.

35 PAM3, *Refugee Law Guidelines*, para. [11.4].

36 See Administrative Appeals Tribunal (AAT), *Guide to Refugee Law* (April 2017), available at www.aat.gov.au/migration-and-refugee-division/mrd-resources/guide-to-refugee-law.

37 *Ibid.* ch. 4, p. 10, citing *SZBQJ* v. *Minister for Immigration and Multicultural*

It is difficult to assess the extent to which this guidance is reflected in practice due to the limited number of AAT decisions that are published. However, there are some published decisions demonstrating an approach that appreciates the vulnerability of the child applicant, for example, in the case of young Hazara applicants who have been considered to be more vulnerable to threats due to 'inexperience and unworldliness' and at risk of suffering psychological harm.[38]

This question of the role that vulnerability plays in the assessment of whether certain harm reaches the level of persecution – which Crock and Berg propose could be termed an 'eggshell skull rule for refugees'[39] – has until recently only received limited consideration in case law. Some of the available authority has tended against an approach that would allow for the consideration of the effect of harm on a child. In *Prahastano* v. *Minister for Immigration and Ethnic Affairs*, the Federal Court stated that:

> [I]f the conduct complained of is not, without reference to its impact upon the applicant for refugee status, persecution, it will not become so if it produces in that person fear . . . fear on the part of a claimant does not turn non-persecution into persecution.[40]

This statement was then taken further by the Federal Magistrates Court (as the Federal Circuit Court was previously known) in holding that the test for persecution is an objective one, and if treatment was 'not sufficiently serious to constitute persecution that finding cannot be changed because of the more serious effects that it had on the applicant than it might have had on another person'.[41]

The cases where the circumstances of children have perhaps been best considered have concerned children born in contravention of China's One Child Policy.[42] In the case of *Chen Shi Hai*, the Tribunal had determined

and Indigenous Affairs (MIMIA) [2005] FCA 143 (Tamberlin J, 28 February 2005) and *SZBBP* v. *MIMIA* [2005] FMCA 5 (Driver FM, 18 January 2005).

38 *RRT Case No. 1211431* [2012] RRTA 975 (19 October 2012) (referring to the *UNHCR Guidelines on Child Asylum Claims*); see also *RRT Case No. 1214085* [2012] RRTA 1045 (7 November 2012); *RRT Case No. 1304507* [2013] RRTA 342 (9 May 2013).

39 M. Crock and L. Berg, *Immigration, Refugees and Forced Migration: Law, Policy and Practice in Australia* (Federation Press, 2011), p. 383.

40 *Prahastono* v. *Minister for Immigration and Ethnic Affairs (MIEA)* (1997) 50 ALD 345, at 347.

41 *SZALZ* v. *Minister for Immigration* [2004] FMCA 275 (18 May 2004), para. [8].

42 See, e.g., *Chen Shi Hai* v. *MIMIA* (2000) 201 CLR 293; *VTAO and others* v. *Minister for Immigration and Multicultural Affairs (MIMA)* (2004) 81 ALD 332.

that the applicant would be 'denied access to food, education and to health care beyond a very basic level [and would] probably face social discrimination and some prejudice and ostracism'.[43] There was no issue raised with the Tribunal's finding that such treatment was of a level amounting to persecution. Interestingly, the UNHCR Guidelines cite this case as supporting the proposition that treatment which may not constitute persecution for an adult may do so in the case of a child.[44] The cited passage is from the judgment of Kirby J:

> what may possibly be viewed as acceptable enforcement of laws and programmes of general application in the case of the parents may nonetheless be persecution in the case of the child.[45]

However, in context, this observation in fact addresses a more limited point about the impact of laws of general application. His Honour is reasoning that while adults may be able to alter their behavior to comply with the law, a child born in contravention of the policy could not.[46] Nonetheless, the recognition that children born in contravention of the One Child Policy may be refugees is a positive aspect of Australian law, appreciating the particular circumstances of those children and considering the way that discriminatory treatment may amount to persecution in view of its effect on the child concerned. There is a proper appreciation that the assessment of whether discrimination is of a sufficient level to constitute persecution is fact specific, and must focus on the effect the treatment would have on the individual claimant.[47]

Despite the limited development of other case law considering vulnerability and harm to children, a recent decision of the High Court presents a significant opportunity to move forward. The case of *MIBP* v. *WZAPN and another*[48] addressed the meaning of 'serious harm' as contained in the

---

[43] *Chen Shi Hai*, above n. 42, para. [6].

[44] *UNHCR Guidelines on Child Asylum Claims*, above n. 1, para. [10], citing *Chen Shi Hai*, above n. 42, para. [79] (Kirby J).

[45] *Ibid.*

[46] *Chen Shi Hai*, above n. 42, para. [79] (Kirby J).

[47] *SZBQJ* v. *MIMIA* [2005] FCA 143 (28 February 2005), para. [21]: 'It is obvious that the impact and circumstances surrounding the application of a national policy may impact differently on different persons so that in one instance the impact may constitute persecution but in other cases the impact may not be so substantial as to amount to Convention persecution.'

[48] *MIBP* v. *WZAPN and another*; *MIBP* v. *WZARV and another* (2015) 146 ALD 480.

Migration Act (then section 91R).[49] The question was whether any period of temporary detention, irrespective of the duration, conditions or effect on the person, is a 'threat to liberty' constituting serious harm. This issue had been the subject of divergent approaches in the Federal Court.[50] In a unanimous decision, the High Court rejected the contention that any deprivation of liberty would amount to serious harm.[51] Rather, the assessment requires a 'qualitative judgement' evaluating 'the nature and gravity of the loss of liberty', considering its circumstances and consequences.[52] The Court held that:

> It is persecution, involving serious harm inflicted by the violation of fundamental rights and freedoms, from which the convention and s. 91R of the Act are concerned to provide asylum. *Both the convention and s. 91R of the Act embody an approach which is concerned with the effects of actions upon persons in terms of harm to them.* That approach is not engaged automatically upon the demonstration of any breach, or apprehended breach, of human rights in their country of nationality or former habitual residence.[53] (Emphasis added)

In reaching this conclusion, the Court cited Hathaway and Foster's view that it is relevant to consider the circumstances and consequences of the violation of a human rights norm; and that:

> courts relying on human rights norms to identify serious harm for refugee law purposes have appropriately insisted, for example, that personal attributes such as 'age and frailty' may have an impact on the seriousness of harm.[54]

While the Court's adoption of this interpretation led to a conclusion adverse to the applicants in that case, the decision has the potential to be highly significant for its clear authority that the question of whether treatment amounts to 'serious harm' requires an evaluation of the effects of actions on the individual concerned. It has had some impact in decisions of the AAT in relation to applicants who are vulnerable due to their

---

49 The definition is now in s. 5J(4), (5) of the Migration Act in identical terms, set out in section 2 above.

50 See *WZAPN* v. *MIBP* [2014] FCA 947 (North J); *SZTEQ* v. *MIBP* [2015] FCAFC 39 (Robertson, Mortimer and Griffiths JJ).

51 *WZAPN*, above n. 48, paras [45], [71] (French CJ, Kiefel, Bell and Keane JJ), para. [99] (Gageler J).

52 *Ibid.* para. [45].

53 *Ibid.* para. [71].

54 *Ibid.* para. [66]; quoting J Hathaway and M Foster, *The Law of Refugee Status* (2nd edn, Cambridge University Press, 2014), p. 198.

mental health. In an unreported decision where the authority of *WZAPN* was argued, the AAT accepted that lesser forms of harm could amount to persecution due to an applicant's vulnerability.[55] The applicant in that case was a Tamil man from Sri Lanka, who was suffering from post-traumatic stress disorder and severe depression. The AAT considered that the monitoring and harassment he would face, which would not usually reach the level of 'serious harm', nonetheless amounted to serious harm in his circumstances due to his vulnerability and the effect it would have on his mental health. The decision is indicative of the present opportunity for the development of a greater appreciation of the role of vulnerability in children's claims. In this setting, looking to the treatment of the issue in US jurisprudence provides a view of the possibilities for where the law could develop, moving beyond its present inertia.

3.2 US Law and Level of Harm

As discussed above, children applying for asylum in the United States are subject to the same legal standard as adults.[56] While there is no settled nor fixed definition of persecution, the term is generally understood to mean 'the infliction of suffering or harm . . . in a way regarded as offensive'.[57] In order to establish persecution an applicant must demonstrate that the harm to which he or she was or fears being subjected 'crosses over the severity threshold' such that it 'ceases to be seen as mere harassment or discriminatory conduct'.[58] The *Guidelines for Children's Asylum Claims*, introduced by the US Department of Homeland Security (formerly Immigration and Naturalization Services) in 1988, make clear that '[r]egardless of how sympathetic the child's claim may be, he or she cannot be granted asylum if this standard is not met'.[59] Importantly, the

---

[55] *AAT Case No. 1315451* (2015) (unreported, used with permission).

[56] *US Guidelines for Children's Asylum Claims*, above n. 1, at 17–19; see also *Cruz-Diaz* v. *US INS*, 86 F.3d 330, 331 (4th Cir. 1996) (per curiam) ('In the absence of statutory intent to apply a different standard for a juvenile, and in light of the reasonable interpretation by the INS that the standard as stated takes into consideration the petitioner's age, we are not at liberty to substitute a different interpretation.').

[57] *Desir* v. *Ilchert*, 840 F.2d 723,727 (10th Cir. 1988) (quoting *Kovac* v. *INS*, 407 F.2d 102, 107 (9th Cir. 1969)). Cited in J. Everett, 'The Battle Continues: Fighting for a More Child-Sensitive Approach to Asylum for Child Soldiers' (2009) 21 *Florida Journal International Law* 285, at 356.

[58] S. Rempell, 'Defining Persecution' (2013) 1 *Utah Law Review* 283, at 312.

[59] *US Guidelines for Children's Asylum Claims*, above n. 3, at 19. The INS Guidelines draw from the 1997 UNHCR Guidelines as well as the 1996 Canadian

Guidelines go on to state that '[t] he harm a child fears or has suffered . . . may be relatively less than that of an adult and still qualify as persecution'.[60] This qualification has been applied in a number of Circuit court decisions, producing results and statements that stand as a stark contrast to the Australian system. In *Liu* v. *Ashcroft*, for example, the Seventh Circuit claimed that:

> [a]ge can be a critical factor in the adjudication of asylum claims and may bear heavily on the question of whether an applicant was persecuted or whether she holds a well-founded fear of future persecution.[61]

The Ninth Circuit has similarly held that the degree of harm suffered by a child 'may be relatively less than that of an adult and still qualify as persecution'.[62]

The relatively child-sensitive approach to the question of whether the harm suffered by a child crosses the persecution threshold has to some measure been shaped by the US doctrine of past persecution. The 1980 Refugee Act broadened the Convention refugee definition to include past persecution as an independent (albeit qualified) ground for refugee status.[63] Although applicants must ultimately demonstrate a well-founded fear of persecution, harm suffered by an applicant in the past creates a rebuttable

---

Guidelines. For further discussion, see, e.g., R. Bien, 'Nothing to Declare but Their Childhood: Reforming U.S. Asylum Law to Protect the Rights of Children' (2004) 12 *Journal of Law and Policy* 797, at 842.

[60] S. Hazeldean, 'Confounding Identities: The Paradox of LGBT Children under Asylum Law' (2011) 45 *UC Davis Law Review* 373, at 444.

[61] 380 F.3d 307, 314 (7th Cir. 2004).

[62] *Mendoza-Pablo* v. *Holder*, 667 F.3d 1308, 1313 (9th Cir. 2012). From the Ninth Circuit see also *Mansour* v. *Ashcroft*, 390 F.3d 667, 681 (9th Cir. 2004) (Pregerson J, concurring in part and dissenting in part): 'I have little doubt that, under the international legal standards discussed above, the international legal community would conclude that the harms inflicted on Petitioners while they were children in Egypt amount to persecution and entitle them to relief from removal. I see no reason why our court should not reach the same conclusion . . . Application of a singular definition of persecution to both adult- and child-based claims fails to address adequately the fact that suffering or harm inflicted on children is far more "offensive" than identical suffering or harm inflicted on adults.' For further discussion and case law, see, e.g., Center for Gender and Refugee Studies, *Children's Asylum Claims: CGRS Practice Advisory 31* (2015); D. Anker, N. Kelly, C. Willshire Carrera and S. Ardalan, *Mejilla-Romero: A New Era for Child Asylum*, Immigration Briefings 12-09 (2012). See also Kids in Need of Defense, *Resources for Children's Asylum Claims* (17 June 2015), available at https://supportkind.org/resources/childrens-asylum-claims/.

[63] 8 CFR s. 208.13 (Code of Federal Regulations).

presumption that the applicant has a well-founded fear that he/she will be subjected to persecution in the future.[64] The presumption places the onus on the government to disprove the well-founded fear of persecution.[65] Although inconsistently applied, the expansion of the refugee definition to include an applicant's experience of past persecution as a separate ground has made possible, or at least inflected, the reasoning of several asylum decisions involving children. In the recent case of *Ordonez-Quino* v. *Holder*, for example, the First Circuit found that where the events that form the basis of a past persecution claim took place when the petitioner was a child, the fact-finder must 'look at the events from [the child's] perspective, [and] measure the degree of [his] injuries by their impact on [a child] of [his] age'.[66] It is worth noting that the first decision to properly (if confusedly) parse out the past persecution ground was a 1989 BIA decision involving a child. The applicant in that case, a Chinese national who from the age of eight suffered severe persecution at the hands of public officials,[67] brought his case solely on the grounds of past persecution. Reasoning that 'past persecution and a well-founded fear of persecution are alternative methods for establishing refugee status', the BIA found that 'once an applicant establishes that he has been persecuted in the past for one of the five reasons listed in the statue, he is eligible for a grant of asylum'.[68]

Past persecution claims are often grounded in emotional or psychological trauma as the main or exclusive component of persecutory harm, and have often arisen in cases where the persecution was directed not at the child him or herself, but at the child's family. In *Kahssai* v. *INS*,[69] the Ninth Circuit noted that:

---

64 'Well-founded fear' applicants are not affirmatively barred from asylum eligibility by any of the factors listed in the governing regulation and are automatically eligible for a positive exercise of discretion. Past persecution applicants enjoy only a presumption of eligibility for a grant of asylum. See S.C. Vance, 'An Enduring Fear: Recent Limitations on the Past Persecution Ground for Asylum' (2002) 91 *Kentucky LJ* 957, at 958. Vance notes that the last two decades have seen 'a progressive narrowing of the eligibility of past persecution refugees for discretionary grants of asylum in the United States': at 963.

65 S. Rempell, 'Asylum Discord: Disparities in Persecution Assessments' (2014) 15 *Nevada Law Journal* 142, at 150.

66 760 F.3d 80 (1st Cir. 2014). See also *Jorge-Tzoc* v. *Gonzales*, 435 F.3d 146, 150 (2d Cir. 2006): '[b]ecause the IJ failed to take into account significant evidence and to address the harms Jorge-Tzoc and his family incurred cumulatively and from the perspective of a small child, vacatur of the determination that Jorge-Tzoc failed to establish past persecution is required'.

67 *In re Chen*, 20 1 & N Dec. 16 (BIA 1989).

68 Ibid .17–18, 20–21.

69 16 F.3d 323, 329 (9th Cir. 1994) (Reinhardt J, concurring).

> [t]he fact that [the applicant] did not suffer physical harm is not determinative of her claim of persecution . . . when a young girl loses her father, mother and brother – sees her family effectively destroyed – she plainly suffers severe emotional and developmental injury.[70]

In a more recent decision the Ninth Circuit affirmed that 'additional evidence is not necessary to establish that an eleven or twelve year old girl would be traumatized when her father is beaten and killed and her mother arrested and raped by the police'.[71] Citing a well-known 1879 Circuit Court decision, the judge observed '[w]hen we take our seats on the bench we are not struck with blindness, and forbidden to know as judges what we see as men [and women]'.[72] Once we consider the human significance of child asylum adjudication, it becomes clear that 'no other conclusion [is] possible'.[73]

Yet despite the relatively broad parameters applied to this component of the refugee definition, the US asylum system often fails properly to protect its most vulnerable applicants, many of whom fall through the gaps of its piecemeal and ultimately adult-centered refugee regime. While the US jurisprudence on this issue may provide other countries with a picture of the opportunities for a more child-sensitive approach, the positive work generated by a narrow accommodation of children's particular vulnerabilities can then be undermined by those elements of the refugee determination that do not fall within the scope of the child-sensitive approach.

4. MEMBERSHIP OF A PARTICULAR SOCIAL GROUP

4.1 Children as a Particular Social Group in Australian Law

The UNHCR has noted that '[c]hildren's claims to refugee status most often have been analysed in the context of the Convention ground of "membership of a particular social group", although any of the Convention grounds may be applicable'.[74] This observation is true of the Australian context, where the most substantial jurisprudence around child refugee claims centres on this ground. Cases concerning children

---

70 *Ibid.*

71 *Rusak* v. *Holder*, 734 F.3d 894, 897 (9th Cir. 2013).

72 *Ibid.*, citing *Ho Ah Kow* v. *Nunan*, 12 F Cas. 252, 255 (CCD Cal. 1879) (No. 6546).

73 *Ibid.*

74 *UNHCR Guidelines on Child Asylum Claims*, above n. 1, para. [48].

have been central to the development of this area of Australian law. The jurisprudence concerning children as a particular social group (PSG) is well developed, and the test can readily encompass many situations of harm faced by children.

The leading case on 'membership of a particular social group' is the 1997 decision of the High Court in *Applicant A* v. *MIEA*.[75] In that case, parents of a child born in contravention of China's One Child Policy were determined not to belong to a PSG. The test for identifying the existence of a PSG established in the case was later summarized as follows:

> First, the group must be identifiable by a characteristic or attribute common to all members of the group. Secondly, the characteristic or attribute common to all members of the group cannot be the shared fear of persecution. Thirdly, the possession of that characteristic or attribute must distinguish the group from society at large.[76]

Three years later in *Chen Shi Hai*,[77] the High Court accepted that children born in contravention of the One Child Policy could constitute a PSG. The High Court distinguished between the circumstances of parents contravening the policy, and children born in contravention of it; as 'the group constituted by children born in those circumstances is defined other than by reference to the discriminatory treatment or persecution that they fear'.[78] It is worth noting that there was a child in similar circumstances present when the High Court decided *Applicant A*, with the parents' claims being ultimately unsuccessful; this forms a telling illustration of the failure to recognize children as potential asylum claimants.

Following the decision in *Applicant A*, a line of authority developed in the Federal Court that interpreted the test established by the High Court, in particular the judgment of McHugh J, as including a requirement that 'there must be recognition within the society that the collection of individuals is a group that is set apart from the rest of the community'.[79] In a subsequent case concerning an unaccompanied Afghan minor, the Full Federal Court upheld the conclusion of the RRT that 'young males without a protector' was not 'perceived as a distinct group within Afghan society', denying the applicant protection on this basis.[80] Soon after, the

---

75 (1997) 190 CLR 225.

76 *Applicant S* v. *MIMIA* (2004) 206 ALR 242, para. [36].

77 *Chen Shi Hai*, above n. 42.

78 *Ibid.* para. [22].

79 *MIMA* v. *Zamora* (1998) 51 ALR 1, at 6–7.

80 *MIMIA* v. *VFAY, Minister for MIMIA* v. *SHBB* [2003] FCAFC 191 (22 August 2003), overturning the decision of the Federal Magistrates Court in *SHBB*

issue of whether a PSG must be perceived or recognized within the society as a distinct group was considered by the High Court in *Applicant S* v. *Minister for Immigration and Multicultural Affairs*.[81] The High Court held that there was no such requirement established by its decision in *Applicant A*.[82] The existence of a PSG is to be ascertained objectively, or from a third party perspective, rather than subjectively or from within the society in question.[83]

This approach can make a significant difference to protection outcomes for children. A society may deny the existence of social groups whose shared attributes offend against majority cultural or religious norms, or children in certain circumstances may be invisible within their society; yet that group may nonetheless be identifiable from an outside perspective.[84]

The scope the Australian test has to encompass a range of claims made by children is evident in decisions of the Tribunal, where applicants have been successful on the basis of membership of PSGs, including 'impoverished children in Vietnam',[85] or 'street children or homeless youths in Tanzania'.[86] The Tribunal has accepted that 'girl children'[87] or 'young children'[88] could constitute PSGs. It should be noted, however, that while such broad groups may be recognized, the requirement that the persecution be 'for reasons of' membership of that group still operates to constrain protection.[89] The Tribunal may accept the existence of the

---

v. *MIMIA* (2003) 175 FLR 304. See also the finding concerning the contemporaneous applicant VFAY, where the Full Federal Court found there was no error in the RRT's finding that any harm the applicant would face as an unaccompanied Hazara minor in Afghanistan was 'because of his youth and inexperience and so limited capacity to manage in a difficult environment and the generalised insecurity and hardship' and not because of his membership of a particular social group: paras [29], [57]–[62].

81 (2004) 206 ALR 242.

82 *Applicant S*, above n. 76, para. [50] (Gleeson CJ, Gummow and Kirby JJ).

83 *Ibid.* paras [34]–[35] (Gleeson CJ, Gummow and Kirby JJ).

84 *Ibid.* para. [34]; see Crock, *Seeking Asylum Alone*, above n. 29, at 181.

85 *RRT Case No. 1106185* [2011] RRTA 844 (6 October 2011).

86 *RRT Case No. V96/04555* [1996] RRTA 2087 (12 July 1996).

87 *RRT Case No. 0806954* [2009] RRTA 264 (4 March 2009) (South Africa); *RRT Case No. 1103242* [2011] RRTA 517 (28 June 2011) (Papua New Guinea).

88 *RRT Case No. 0803919* [2008] RRTA 333 (2 September 2008) (Sierra Leone).

89 See B. Casper et al., 'Matter of MEVG and the BIA's Confounding Standard for "Membership in a Particular Social Group"' (2014) 14(6) *Immigration Briefing* 15, discussing the Seventh Circuit Court's view of the limiting function of the nexus requirement.

posited PSG, yet proceed to find that there is not clear evidence that the group is singled out for persecution.[90]

With the codification of the refugee definition in the Migration Act in December 2014, the definition of PSG underwent a significant (albeit relatively little discussed) change. The amendments that were initially introduced proposed to add a further requirement to the existing test, requiring that the characteristic shared by the group either be 'an innate or immutable characteristic' or 'so fundamental to a member's identity or conscience, the member should not be forced to renounce it'.[91] The reason given for the proposed amendment was that the 'broad interpretation' taken by the High Court had 'led to long lists of increasingly elaborate potential particular social groups being drawn', making the test complex and difficult for decision-makers to apply, and that it was 'broader than that being applied in other jurisdictions (e.g. Canada, the United States of America, New Zealand and the European Union)'.[92] The Explanatory Memorandum stated that the legislative definition 'is based on the approach taken in these other jurisdictions'.[93] In fact, by incorporating both the existing requirements of Australian law (sometimes termed a 'social perception' approach) *and* the 'protected characteristics' approach, the proposed test became potentially more onerous than that test as it exists in the other jurisdictions referred to.[94]

This proposed section was subsequently amended in the Senate, with the Explanatory Memorandum to the amendments stating with little explanation that '[t]he Government now intends to modify its approach and specify that the standard for "membership of a particular social group" only requires the satisfaction of either the "protected characteristics" approach or the "social perception" approach'.[95] The test as now contained in section 5L of the Migration Act provides:

---

[90] See *RRT Case No. 0803919* [2008] RRTA 333 (2 September 2008), para. [75]; *RRT Case No. 0806954* [2009] RRTA 264 (4 March 2009), para. [90]; *RRT Case No. 1103242* [2011] RRTA 517 (28 June 2011), para. [74].

[91] See Legacy Caseload Act, Sch. 5, Part 2, s. 5L.

[92] Explanatory Memorandum, *Migration and Maritime Powers Legislation Amendment (Resolving the Asylum Legacy Caseload) Act 2014 (Cth)*, p. 11.

[93] *Ibid.*

[94] See UNHCR, *Guidelines on International Protection: "Membership of a Particular Social Group" Within the Context of Article 1A(2) of the 1951 Convention and/or its 1967 Protocol relating to the Status of Refugees* (7 May 2002) ('*UNHCR Guidelines on Membership of a Particular Social Group*'); J.C. Hathaway and M. Foster, 'Membership of a Particular Social Group' (2003) 15 *International Journal of Refugee Law* 477.

[95] Explanatory Statement to Amendment GH118, *Migration and Maritime*

> For the purposes of the application of this Act and the regulations to a particular person, the person is to be treated as a member of a particular social group (other than the person's family) if:
>
> (a) a characteristic is shared by each member of the group; and
> (b) the person shares, or is perceived as sharing, the characteristic; and
> (c) *any of the following apply*:
>   (i) the characteristic is an innate or immutable characteristic;
>   (ii) the characteristic is so fundamental to a member's identity or conscience, the member should not be forced to renounce it;
>   (iii) the characteristic distinguishes the group from society; and
> (d) the characteristic is not a fear of persecution. (emphasis added)

The result is thus that the legislation has further broadened the test for PSG in Australian law, despite the initial intention being to address what was considered by the government to be an overly broad test developed by the High Court. It is interesting to note that while other aspects of the 2014 amendments evidenced an intention to remove the influence or detach Australia from developments in other jurisdictions, in this area the government attempted to draw on foreign jurisprudence to justify the introduction of a more restrictive approach. Similar tendencies are arguably at play in the developments in US jurisprudence in the same area, with the courts and BIA drawing on foreign jurisprudence and international law, restricting the scope of protection afforded by the PSG ground.

4.2 Particular Social Group in US Law

Over the past decade, US jurisprudence around PSG has become a muddled and muddied domain. From 1985–2006, the standard for PSG was based on the BIA's decision in *Matter of Acosta*, which required that group members share a common immutable or fundamental characteristic.[96] In *Acosta*, the Board looked to the other protected grounds, and, applying the interpretive canon of *ejusdem generis*, determined that a particular social group must be based on a characteristic that group members

---

Powers Legislation Amendment (Resolving the Asylum Legacy Caseload) Bill 2014 (Cth), p. 8.

[96] *Matter of Acosta*, 19 I & N Dec. 211, 232 (BIA 1985) (holding that the criteria for membership in a PSG was defined by an 'immutable, unchangeable characteristic or past or present voluntary association entered into for reasons protected by basic human rights principles that are considered fundamental to human dignity').

cannot change or should not be required to change. As well as forming the cornerstone of PSG in US asylum jurisprudence, *Matter of Acosta* exerted gravitational force in other jurisdictions.[97] Importantly, the definition of PSG in the UNHCR Guidelines merges *Acosta*'s immutable characteristic definition with the 'social perception' approach put forth in Australia's High Court decision of *Applicant A*,[98] presenting the two approaches as alternative grounds for establishing PSG.[99]

In 2006, the BIA began to move away from the *Acosta* framework. Purporting to follow the recently issued UNHCR Guidelines, which according to the BIA, 'combine elements of the *Acosta* immutable . . . approach, as well as the Second Circuit's "social perception" approach',[100] the BIA in *Matter of CA* held that '[t]he social visibility of the members of a claimed social group is an important consideration in identifying the existence of a "particular social group"'. The BIA in that decision also referred to 'particularity' as a 'requirement'.[101] In 2003, the Sixth Circuit followed *Matter of CA*, again citing the UNHCR Guidelines, and

---

97 See, e.g., F.E. Marouf, 'The Emerging Importance of Social Visibility in Defining a Particular Social Group and Its Potential Impact on Asylum Claims Related to Sexual Orientation and Gender' (2008) 27 *Yale Law and Policy Rewiew* 47, at 48.

98 K. Kersh, 'An Insurmountable Obstacle: Denying Deference to the BIA's Social Visibility Requirement' (2013) 19 *Michigan Journal of Race and Law* 153.

99 *UNHCR Guidelines on Membership of a Particular Social Group*, above n. 94, at 2–3. The UNHCR Guidelines defined PSG as 'a group of persons who share a common characteristic other than their risk of being persecuted, or who are perceived as a group by society. The characteristic will often be one which is innate, unchangeable, or which is otherwise fundamental to identity, conscience or the exercise of one's human rights': para. [11]. Marouf observes that the Guidelines 'instruct . . . States Parties to the 1951 Refugee Convention . . . to determine first if there is a protected characteristic and, only if no such characteristic exists, to determine whether the group is recognized by society': F.E. Marouf, 'The Emerging Importance of Social Visibility in Defining a Particular Social Group and Its Potential Impact on Asylum Claims Related to Sexual Orientation and Gender' (2008) 27 *Yale Law and Policy Review* 47, at 49.

100 23 I&N Dec. 951 (BIA 2006). Citing *Gomez* v. *INS*, 947 F.2d 660, 664 (explaining that '[l]ike the traits which distinguish the other four enumerated categories – race, religion, nationality and political opinion – the attributes of a particular social group must be recognizable and discrete'). For a discussion on the misapplication of *Gomez* and the key differences between that decision and the BIA's 'social visibility' standard, see Marouf, 'The Emerging Importance of Social Visibility in Defining a Particular Social Group', above n. 99, at 66–70. See also N.R. Bednar and M. Penland, 'Asylum's Interpretative Impasse: Interpreting Persecution and Particular Social Group Using International Human Rights Law' (2017) 26 *Minnesota Journal of International Law* 145, at 188.

101 *Matter of CA*, 23 I&N Dec. 951 (BIA 2006), para. [957].

referencing in a footnote the Australian decisions of *Applicant A* v. *MIEA* and *MIMA* v. *Applicant Z*.[102]

By 2008, the additional 'considerations' hardened into requirements for the purposes of establishing PSG.[103] In *Matter of SEG* and *Matter of EAG*,[104] the Board stated that 'membership in a purported social group requires that the group have particular and well-defined boundaries, and that it possess a recognized level of social visibility', noting that the two concepts 'give greater specificity to the definition of a social group' as it was defined in *Acosta*.[105] Both cases involved Central American youth who were recruited by gangs and refused to join. As well as leaving unclear the parameters of 'particularity',[106] the decisions created confusion over whether social visibility was to be construed literally or figuratively.[107] The twin decisions generated a split in the Circuit Courts. The Supreme Court has held that Circuit Courts should grant deference to administrative BIA rulings[108] unless such rulings are impermissible interpretations of the statute and thus should not be accorded *Chevron* deference.[109] While a

---

102 *Castellano-Chacon* v. *INS*, 341 F.3d 533, 547–8, n 8 (6th Cir. 2003).

103 See also *In re AME and JGU*, 24 I & N Dec. 69, 74–5 (BIA 2007) (discussing the 'requisite social visibility') affd sub nom. *Ucelo-Gomez* v. *Mukasey*, 509 F.3d 70 (2d Cir. 2007).

104 *Matter of EAG*, 24 I &N Dec. 591, 594 (BIA 2008) (finding that the proposed group of 'persons resistant to gang membership' lack social visibility within Honduran society thus preventing members of society from recognizing these individuals as members of a particular group); *Matter of SEG*, 24 I&N Dec. 579, 590 (BIA 2008) (finding that 'Salvadoran youth who refused recruitment into the MS-13 criminal gang or their family members' do not constitute a particular social group, based in part because a social group 'requires that the group have particular and well-defined boundaries, and that it possess a recognized level of social visibility').

105 *Gatimi* v. *Holder*, 578 F.3d 61, 615 (7th Cir. 2009). See also *Benitez Ramos* v. *Holder*, 589 F.3d 426 (7th Cir. 2009).

106 UNHCR, *In the Matter of MEVG*, Amicus Curiae Brief (10 August 2012), pp. 20–21, available at www.refworld.org/docid/503653562.html.

107 A. Huebner and L. Koop, 'New BIA Decisions Undermine U.S. Obligations to Protect Asylum Seekers', *National Immigrant Justice Centre* (18 February 2014), available at www.immigrantjustice.org/litigation/blog/new-bia-decisions-undermine-us-obligations-protect-asylum-seekers.

108 *Aguirre-Aguirre*, 526 US, above n. 23, at 424–5; see also *Chevron, USA, Inc.* v. *Natural Resources Defense Council, Inc.*, 467 US 837, 842–3 (1984).

109 According to the standard articulated by the Supreme Court in *Chevron* (*ibid.*), federal courts must give deference to agency interpretations. While the *Chevron* case concerned regulations, later cases expanded this deference to BIA administrative rulings. In *Chevron*, the Supreme Court set forth a two-step analysis to determine whether a court reviewing an agency's interpretation of a statute should be granted deference. A court must first determine whether the statutory

majority of the Circuit Courts adhered to the BIA's new standards,[110] the Seventh and Third Circuits refused to grant deference to the BIA rulings, rejecting the requirements as unreasonable interpretations of the statute and inconsistent with prior BIA decisions.[111] The Ninth Circuit also called the validity of the requirements into question, but did not directly reject them.[112] In the first Court of Appeals decision to reject and refuse to award *Chevron* deference to the BIA's social visibility requirement, Judge Posner bitingly questioned the logic of social visibility:

> If you are a member of a group that has been targeted for assassination or torture or some other mode of persecution, you will take pains to avoid being socially visible; and to the extent that the members of the target group are successful in remaining invisible, they will not be 'seen' by other people in the society 'as a segment of the population'.[113]

---

language is clear. In quite a few immigration cases, the Supreme Court has found the statutory intent present in the language and refused to defer to agency interpretation. Such was the case in *Cardoza-Fonseca* decided a few weeks after *Chevron: INS* v. *Cardoza-Fonseca*, 480 US 421 (1986). Where the court finds that the statutory language does not cover the issue, the court will proceed to the second step of the *Chevron* analysis and must defer to any 'permissible construction' of the statute made by the agency charged with interpreting a particular statute. Determining what validly qualifies as a PSG falls under the second step of the *Chevron* analysis. When a Circuit Court reviews a BIA decision, it must always grant *Chevron* deference to the administration's interpretation of the statute unless the BIA's interpretation is unreasonable, i.e. arbitrary, capricious, or clearly contrary to law. See, e.g., K. Kersh, 'An Insurmountable Obstacle: Denying Deference to the BIA's Social Visibility Requirement' (2013) 19 *Michigan Journal of International Law* 153, at 176; K. Bresnahan, 'The Board of Immigration Appeals' New Social Visibility Test for Determining Membership of a Particular Social Group in Asylum Claims and its Legal Policy Implications' (2011) 29 *Berkeley Journal of International Law* 649; K. Ludlum, 'Defining Membership in a Particular Social Group: The Search for a Uniform Approach to Adjudicating Asylum Applications in the United States' (2015) 77 *University of Pittsburg Law Review* 115, at 136.

110 See, e.g., *Rojas-Prez* v. *Holder*, 699 F.3d 74, 77 (1st Cir. 2012); *Fuentes-Hernandez* v. *Holder*, 411 F App'x 438, 438–9 (2d Cir. 2011); *Lizama* v. *Holder*, 629 F.3d 440, 446 (4th Cir. 2011); *Bonilla-Morales* v. *Holder*, 607 F.3d 1132, 1137 (6th Cir. 2010); *Gaitan* v. *Holder*, 671 F.3d 678, 681 (8th Cir. 2012); *Rivera-Barrientos* v. *Holder*, 666 F.3d 641, 648–54 (10th Cir. 2012); *Castillo-Arias* v. *US Attorney General*, 446 F.3d 1190, 1197 (11th Cir. 2006).

111 See *Gatimi* v. *Holder*, 578 F.3d 611, 615 (7th Cir. 2009); *Valdiviezo-Galdamez* v. *Attorneyy General*, 663 F.3d 582, 608 (3d Cir. 2011). The Ninth Circuit called the validity of the requirements into question, but did not unequivocally reject them (*Henriquez-Rivas* v. *Holder*, 707 F.3d 1081 (9th Cir. 2013) (en banc)).

112 *Henriquez-Rivas* v. *Holder*, 707 F.3d 1081 (9th Cir. 2013) (en banc).

113 *Gatimi* v. *Holder*, 578 F.3d 611, 615–16 (7th Cir. 2009).

The Circuit Court critiques of the BIA social visibility and particularity requirements went some way toward bringing US asylum jurisprudence back to the *Acosta* framework and in line with international refugee law. In 2014, however, the BIA issued two companion rulings, *Matter of MEVG* and *Matter of WGR*,[114] in which the Board purported to 'clarify' the PSG standard.[115] Renaming the requirement 'social distinction', the Board explained that social visibility does not require ocular visibility, but instead refers to whether a group is recognized in society as a distinct entity. Aside from reiterating the bounded nature of 'particularity' ('it must not be amorphous, overbroad, diffuse, or subjective'),[116] the Board did not provide any new interpretation of the problematic 'particularity' requirement.

Following the companion decisions, an applicant for asylum or withholding of removal seeking relief based on membership of a PSG must establish that the group is composed of members who share a common immutable characteristic (the *Acosta* standard) *and* that the group is 'defined with particularity' and socially distinct 'as is determined by the perception of the society in question'.[117] The decisions have been criticized widely by the immigration legal community for compounding the confusion generated by *SEG* and *EAG* and increasing the evidentiary burden.[118] As one scholar put it:

> Rather than clarifying the particular social group standard, the BIA's decision in *MEVG* creates a game of semantics that requires an applicant to navigate the fine line between social distinction and particularity . . . To avoid denial of her application due to a lack of either particularity or social distinction, the applicant must define her particular social group with calculated wording.[119]

Ultimately, the 2014 BIA decisions have undone several years of positive Circuit Court development on the murky interpretation of PSG.

---

[114] *Matter of MEVG*, 26 I&N Dec. 227 (BIA 2014) (involving a Honduran youth who was recruited by gang members. The gang members beat him, kidnaped and assaulted him and his family and threatened to kill him if he did not join the gang). *In re WGR*, 26 I&N Dec. 208 (the respondent in *Matter of WGR* was shot in the leg by members of the Mara 18 in El Salvador when he decided to leave the gang).

[115] *Matter of MEVG*, 26 I&N Dec. 227, 288 (BIA 2014).

[116] *Ibid.*

[117] *Ibid.*

[118] See, e.g., Casper et al., 'Matter of MEVG and the BIA's Confounding Standard', above n. 89, at 16–18.

[119] N.R. Bednar, 'Social Group Semantics: The Evidentiary Requirements of Particularity and Social Distinction in Pro Se Asylum Adjudications' (2015–2016) 100 *Minnesota Law Review* 355, at 404.

It was not until the domestic violence case of *Matter of ARCG* that the BIA finally found a proposed group to be recognized as a PSG under the new standard.[120] In the precedential decision, the BIA applied the reformulated analysis as articulated first in 2006 and then in *SEG* and *EAG* to recognize as a PSG 'married women in Guatemala who are unable to leave their relationship'.[121] Although limited for its perpetuation of the 'social distinction' standard, *ARCG* may have a positive spillover effect on children's domestic violence-based asylum claims.[122] Not unlike the Australian decision of *MIBP* v. *WZAPN and another*, *ARCG* holds the potential to improve protection outcomes not only for children but for other categories of vulnerable people seeking asylum. Nonetheless, the confused and convoluted state of this aspect of US law stands likely to present a continuing barrier to children seeking asylum in reliance on the important ground of PSG.

5. CONCLUSION

Asylum jurisprudence in both Australia and the United States is yet comprehensively to address the protection needs of child asylum-seekers, with the shortcomings and relative strengths of each system evolving along different lines. Placing the models side by side and tracing the flow of ideas between the two is suggestive of both the possibilities and the limitations of comparative dialogue in refugee law. The importation into other

---

[120] 26 I&N Dec. 388 (BIA 2014).

[121] *Ibid.* In March of 2018, Attorney General Jeff Sessions certified a BIA case concerning domestic violence to himself for review and requested briefing on the issue of whether any person could establish persecution based on 'private' crime. See Matter of –A-B, 27 I&N Dec. 227 (A.G. certification Mar. 7, 2018). Many are concerned that the Attorney General will vacate the cases that have allowed children as victims of domestic and gang violence to secure refugee protection. See J. Fonda and K. Musalo, 'Her Husband Beat Her and Raped Her. Jeff Sessions Might Deport Her', *New York Times*, 17 May 2018, available at https://www.nytimes.com/2018/05/17/opinion/jeff-sessions-asylum-domestic-violence.html.

[122] See, e.g., S.M. Winfield, '*In re ARCG:* A Game-Changer for Children Seeking Asylum on the Basis of Intrafamilial Violence' (2016) 67 *Hastings LJ* 1153, at 1170 (arguing that 'adjudicators can and should extend In re ARCG's particular social group rationale to children's intrafamilial violence-based asylum claims'). For (attempted) extension of *ARCG* to a child's interfamilial violence-based claim, see Kids in Need of Defense, *Brief of Kids in Need of Defense as Amicus Curiae in Support of the Respondent, In the Matter of ZT* (February 2015), available at https://supportkind.org/wp-content/uploads/2015/04/KIND_Amicus_Brief_Feb_2015-1.pdf.

countries, including now Australia, of the *Acosta* immutable characteristic framework is illustrative of the processes of norm convergence and the impact of cross-jurisdictional dialogue within refugee law.[123] A similar kind of engagement on the question of 'harm' could perhaps help Australia to move beyond its current limitedness. At the same time, however, the introduction of the 'social perception' requirement and its percolation through the UNHCR Guidelines and the US asylum regime cautions us to the potential for transnational dialogue to slip into a distorting game of broken telephone. This is especially true in relation to children, where the Refugee Convention definition does not clearly address the particular circumstances of these applicants, making the interpretation of its terms in jurisprudence critical to whether child applicants fall within or outside the scope of refugee protection. A principled approach is needed to keep in check the international legal community's interpretation of the Convention definition to ensure that states parties to the Convention do not misapply or misconstrue foreign and transnational sources, nor 'cherry-pick' for the most restrictive constructions and policies. Such dialogue can continue the development of domestic jurisprudence towards a consistent interpretation of the Convention definition,[124] and one that better engages with the particular circumstances and vulnerabilities of children and ensures they are visible in the protection system.

---

[123] See, e.g., F.E. Marouf, 'The Role of Foreign Authorities in US Asylum Adjudication' (2013) 45 *NYU Journal of International Law and Policy* 391, at 450–51; Bednar and Penland, 'Asylum's Interpretative Impasse', above n. 100, at 153.

[124] J.C. Hathaway and A.K. Cusick, 'Refugee Rights are Not Negotiable' (2000) 14 *Georgetown Immigration Law Journal* 481, at 540.

15. Protection measures for unaccompanied child migrants in Canada

Geraldine Sadoway

> Canada has no national policy to take care of separated refugee children . . . Separated refugee children seem to fall into the gap between federal responsibility for immigration and provincial responsibility for youth protection.[1]
>
> The Committee [CRC] urges the State party to bring its immigration and asylum laws into full conformity with the Convention and other relevant international standards and reiterates its previous recommendations (CTC/C/15/Add.215, para. 47, 2003).[2]

There are many examples of children and youth who travel alone or with friends, separated from parents or legal guardians, to reach a safe place such as Canada in order to escape danger in their home country.[3] According to recent estimates, as many as 3,000 unaccompanied children arrive in Canada seeking refugee status every year.[4] Sometimes the children are orphans, or have become separated from their parents due to war or civil unrest. Sometimes the parents (or one of the parents) are the source of danger to the child. Some young people have fled their homes due to abuse by a parent or relative and they cannot obtain effective protection from the

[1] Canadian Council for Refugees, *Canada's Treatment of Non-Citizen Children* (January 2012), available at http://ccrweb.ca/files/noncitizenchildrenback grounderen.pdf.

[2] UN Committee on the Rights of the Child (UNCRC), *Concluding Observations: Canada*, 61st Sess., UN Doc. CRC/C/CAN/CO/3-4 (5 October 2012), para. [74].

[3] M.A. Ali, S. Taraban and J.K. Gill, *Unaccompanied/Separated Children Seeking Refugee Status in Ontario: A Review of Documented Policies and Practices* (CERIS, 2003).

[4] D. Hayes, 'Program helps "unaccompanied minors" navigate Canada's refugee process', *Toronto Star*, 17 August 2013, available at www.thestar.com/news/insight/2013/08/17/program_helps_unaccompanied_minors_navigate_canadas_refugee_process.html. See also S. Elgersma, *Unaccompanied and Separated Minors as Refugee Claimants*, Parliamentary Research Brief (2007), available at www.lop.parl.gc.ca/content/lop/researchpublications/prb0715-e.pdf.

authorities in their own country. Children may be victims of illegal trafficking groups or may be targeted for kidnapping in order to extort money from parents or relatives who have travelled abroad to seek employment. Sometimes very young children are sent out of the home country by their parents with friends or relatives or with paid agents, in order to save the life of the child due to serious dangers facing the entire family in the home country, or in the country of first asylum.[5] Although there is no single explanation for the fact that children are crossing international borders on their own, it is very clear that such children constitute an extremely vulnerable group of migrants that require special measures of protection.[6]

1. DESIGNATED REPRESENTATIVES FOR ASYLUM-SEEKING CHILDREN: A COMPARISON BY PROVINCE

Each of the 10 provinces and three territories of Canada has its own system for caring for children who are in that province without their parents. As a result there is *inconsistency* in ensuring immediate care, protection and legal representation for this vulnerable population.

Canada's national immigration law provides for the right to counsel for all persons subject to proceedings before the Immigration and Refugee Board and for the appointment of a designated representative to assist any person under the age of 18, or any person unable to appreciate the nature of the proceedings.[7] The Immigration and Refugee Board (IRB) is responsible for appointing the designated representative (DR) and for

---

[5] For example, the author represented a two-year-old Somali child, born in a refugee camp in Kenya, whose parents had sent her with a woman travelling to the United States, to be taken to the Canadian border and delivered to an older half-sister. The parents sent the child to be cared for by her older half-sibling because she was underweight and in danger of dying in the harsh conditions of the refugee camp. In another case, the author represented a nine-year-old Iranian boy whose parents had sent him with family friends to Canada due to fear of forcible conscription by the Iranian military during the Iran-Iraq war. During that war, conscripted child soldiers as young as nine years old were being used in advance of the regular soldiers to cross minefields. See further UNICEF, 'Children as Soldiers' in *The State of the World's Children 1996: Children in War* (UNICEF, 1997), available at www.unicef.org/sowc96/2csoldrs.htm.

[6] J. Bhabha, *Child Migration and Human Rights in a Global Age* (Princeton University Press, 2014). See particularly, ch. 6, 'David and Goliath: Children's Unequal Battle for Refugee Protection', *ibid.* 203–37.

[7] Immigration and Refugee Protection Act, SC 2001, c. 27, s. 167(2).

paying an honorarium to a DR who is not a friend or relative of the child.[8] The role of the DR is to ensure that the child has appropriate legal representation and that the child understands the process they are involved in. The DR may also help to gather evidence needed for the refugee hearing and may testify on behalf of the child at the hearing. However, there is inconsistency regarding the selection of DRs for separated refugee children in different parts of Canada and in the availability of free legal representation for refugees. For example, in the province of Quebec, a social service organization funded by the provincial Ministry of Health and Social Services provides trained social workers to act as the DR for unaccompanied refugee children. Legal aid for refugee representation in Quebec is minimal, so the role of the DR in retaining counsel to represent the child in their refugee proceeding is very important.

By contrast, in the province of Ontario, the Immigration and Refugee Board has an agreement with a private law firm and Pro Bono Law Ontario to provide lawyers who will act as designated representatives for minors making refugee claims, in the absence of parents or an appropriate guardian in the community. The IRB might also appoint a DR for a child who is accompanied by one of their parents. For example, if the child comes to Canada with one parent and there is concern that the child has been taken to Canada without the permission of the other parent, the IRB might decide that the parent in Canada has a conflict of interest and that it is necessary to appoint a separate DR for the child to ensure that the child's best interests are protected. The provincial Office of the Children's Lawyer (OCL) will sometimes get involved as designated representative for a refugee child in a situation of potential child protection proceedings. If an application under the Hague Convention on Child Abduction is filed by the other parent, the OCL will appoint counsel to represent the child.

In all provinces, however, the DR is only responsible for helping with the hearing process. Provincial child welfare authorities and non-government charitable organizations are called upon to ensure the protection and care for the refugee child or youth. In the province of Ontario, if a child or youth between the age of 16 and 18 arrives unaccompanied by parents or guardians, the Canadian Border Services Agency (CBSA) usually contacts the Canadian Red Cross First Contact program.[9] Through this program the young person is referred to refugee shelters and other

---

[8] See IRB Guidelines, available at www.irb-cisr.gc.ca/Eng/BoaCom/references/LegJur/Pages/GuideIdSi07.aspx.

[9] Canadian Red Cross, *First Contact*, available at www.redcross.ca/what-we-do/migrant-and-refugee-services/first-contact/.

non-governmental services for refugees. Children under 16 arriving in Ontario are referred directly to the Children's Aid Society of Ontario and might then be placed in foster care or referred to a non-government refugee shelter.[10] Unaccompanied minors have access to free legal aid services for representation at their refugee hearing. Lawyers in the Refugee Law Office and the various community legal clinics in Ontario handle these cases and there are about 350 qualified private bar lawyers who will accept legal aid certificates to represent refugees.

In British Columbia (BC), children under the age of 19 arriving in the province may be permitted by border authorities to join relatives or friends in the province. If they do not have such contacts, they are referred to the BC Ministry of Children and Family Development (MCFD). The social workers from MCFD may have little idea of how to process cases involving unaccompanied minors, and it may take weeks or months for a decision to be made about taking the minor into care. Changes were made to the refugee determination process in 2012 which dramatically shortened the timelines for filing documents and hearing the claim. In some cases the hearing is already well under way by the time MCFD makes a decision to take the child into care. If a child is taken into care, a social worker is supposed to contact the Ministry of the Attorney General who then retains counsel to represent the minor in care. Children who are in care have greater access to psychological counselling and other social services and disbursements that might affect the refugee claim. Children who are not in care contact the BC Legal Services Society (LSS) and are usually able to obtain a certificate for representation by a lawyer on the legal aid panel.[11]

The UN Committee on the Rights of the Child has repeatedly made recommendations to Canada to make sure that children arriving alone are provided with guardianship and social services in every part of Canada and that they are not subjected to immigration detention.[12] The International Bureau for Children's Rights has developed a detailed Best Practice Statement: Separated Children in Canada.[13] However, to date the

---

[10] In 2017 the Ontario provincial government passed legislation increasing the age of protection from 16 to 18 years for youth in Ontario. In June 2018, the Ontario Association of Children's Aid Societies launched a new program, the *Child Welfare Immigration Centre of Excellence*, which is intended to respond to the protection and care needs of all unaccompanied minors seeking refugee status in Ontario.

[11] Information provided by Rochelle Appleby of the BC Legal Services Society. See www.lss.bc.ca/about/contactUs.php.

[12] See UNCRC, *Concluding Observations: Canada*, above n. 2, paras [73]–[74].

[13] International Bureau for Children's Rights, *Best Practice Statement: Separated Children in Canada* (2003).

Canadian government has failed to develop a national policy to ensure consistent protection and care for unaccompanied non-citizen children in Canada and, as a result, there is inconsistent reception for child migrants in different parts of the country.

2. SAFE THIRD COUNTRY AGREEMENT: EXCEPTION FOR UNACCOMPANIED MINORS

In December 2002, the United States signed the Safe Third Country Agreement (STCA) with Canada following the 9/11 terrorist attacks against the World Trade Centre and the Pentagon.[14] The STCA came into effect in December 2004 and, under this Agreement, the United States was designated as a safe third country pursuant to section 101(1)(e) of the Immigration and Refugee Protection Act. According to this agreement, refugees who enter Canada at a regular port of entry *by land* from the United States are ineligible to claim refugee status in Canada. Similarly, refugees who arrive in Canada and then attempt to enter the United States are ineligible to claim refugee protection in the United States. In fact, Canada had been seeking such an agreement with the United States for many years in order to cut off the flow of refugees into Canada via the United States across the so-called 'world's longest undefended border'. Following the 9/11 attacks, the STCA was seen as a new security measure for the United States and Canada took advantage of this situation to push for the Agreement.[15]

---

[14] Agreement for Co-operation in the Examination of Refugee Status Claims from Nationals of Third Countries, Canada-United States (signed and entered into force 29 December 2004). Immigration and Refugee Protection Act, s. 101(1)(e) provides that a person is not eligible to make a refugee claim in Canada if that person 'came directly or indirectly to Canada from a country designated by the regulations, other than a country of their nationality or their former habitual residence'. Immigration and Refugee Protection Regulations, reg. 159.3 designates the United States as a country 'that complies with article 33 of the Refugee Convention and Article 3 of the Convention Against Torture, and is a designated country for the purpose of the application of 101(1)(e) of the Act'. However, under paragraph 159.4 of the Regulations, the designation of the United States under s. 101(1)(e) of the Act does not apply to a person who seeks to enter Canada at a location that is not a port of entry, or at a port of entry that is a harbour port or a ferry landing, or a port of entry that is an airport. Regulation 159.5 provides additional exceptions for claimants who have relatives in Canada.

[15] For an excellent analysis of STCA, see L. Sarbit, 'The Reality Beneath the Rhetoric: Probing the Discourses Surrounding the Safe Third Country Agreement' (2003) 18 *Journal of Law and Social Policy* 138.

The land border is Canada's front door. During the 1970s and 1980s, refugees fleeing civil wars and repressive dictatorships in Central and South America and who were not welcome in the United States began making their way to Canada where their refugee claims had a stronger likelihood of success. A twentieth-century 'underground railroad' developed, with advocates in the United States sheltering and advising these refugees about how to reach Canada and how to contact supportive agencies in Canada.[16] Supporters in the United States would often fill out the forms that the refugees needed for Canadian border authorities when they crossed into Canada.[17] Refugees arriving from the United States at the various land border ports of entry did not need to have legal immigration papers or visas, and they did not have to pay smugglers to assist them in reaching a safe haven in Canada: they just had to walk or drive across the bridge and present themselves to Canadian immigration authorities. Canadian lawyers and legal workers or refugee advocates would often arrange to meet the refugees at the border crossing, including arranging for their initial eligibility interview at the border, and connecting them with settlement services in the destination communities.

The STCA put a stop to this civilized, legal entry of refugees from the United States to Canada by land, closing the front door of Canada to refugees, and stimulating illegal smuggling and trafficking enterprises. In the first year after the STCA was signed, the number of new refugee claimants in Canada went down overall by about 35 per cent from 29,680 new claimants in 2004 to 19,562 new claimants in 2005. In fact, the decline of claimants at the land border was more than 51 per cent.[18] Thus, the Safe Third Country Agreement was a major building block of 'Fortress Canada'.

There are specific provisions in the STCA permitting exceptions. In recognition of the fact that refugees might reasonably prefer to claim refugee status in a country where they already have extended family

---

[16] The Underground Railroad was a network of anti-slavery activists and abolitionists in the United States and British North America who assisted black slaves fleeing the US southern states to the US northern states or to Canada in the nineteenth century.

[17] Vive la Casa Refugee Shelter in Buffalo, New York opened its doors in 1984 and has continued to assist refugees seeking to enter Canada. See Associated Press, 'Sale will secure future for shelter for asylum-seekers', *Daily Mail (UK)*, 2 March 2015, available at www.dailymail.co.uk/wires/ap/article-2974608/Sale-secure-future-shelter-asylum-seekers.html.

[18] Canadian Council for Refugees, *Closing the Front Door on Refugees, Report on the First Year of the Safe Third Country Agreement* (December 2005), available at http://ccrweb.ca/sites/ccrweb.ca/files/static-files/closingdoordec05.pdf.

members, refugees coming into Canada via the United States at a land border are eligible to make a refugee claim in Canada, even though they have not sought refugee status in the United States, if they have family members in Canada.[19] They must prove the family relationship, on the balance of probabilities, to the Canadian border authorities and it is best that a member of the refugee's extended family in Canada is present at the border when this interview takes place.

There is another important exception to the STCA for unaccompanied minors who have no parent or legal guardian in either the United States or Canada.[20] This exception was intended to ensure access to the refugee determination process for this vulnerable population travelling on their own but may have the unintended consequence of encouraging parents to send a child on their own or with an agent or smuggler through the United States, rather than seeking refuge in Canada together as a family. If the child does not have reliable contacts in Canada who will assist at the border, it may be difficult for the child to establish to the satisfaction of Canadian border authorities that the child is under 18 years of age, or that the child has no parent or legal guardian either in the United States or in Canada. The child may end up in detention or in the care of child welfare authorities in the province where the child arrives. As noted above, the process for appointing a designated representative for the child varies from one province to another. Furthermore, although generally speaking, most child refugees entering Canada will have access to free legal representation, this also varies from province to province.

3. DETENTION OF REFUGEE CHILDREN

In early January 2016, while Canadians were basking in the warmth of global approval of the newly elected Liberal government's generous response to the crisis of Syrian refugees arriving in Europe,[21] an unaccompanied Syrian teenager arrived at Fort Erie on the Canadian border seek-

---

[19] According to Art. 1 of the STCA: '"Family Member" means the spouse, sons, daughters, parents, legal guardians, siblings, grandparents, grandchildren, aunts, uncles, nieces, and nephews.'

[20] STCA, Art. 1(f): '"Unaccompanied Minor" means an unmarried refugee status claimant who has not yet reached his or her eighteenth birthday and does not have a parent or legal guardian in either Canada or the United States.'

[21] Z. Lum, 'John McCallum says Syrian refugees "super happy" to be in Canada', *Huffington Post (Canada)*, 27 January 2016, available at www.huffingtonpost.ca/2016/01/27/mccallum-syrian-refugees-super-happy_n_9092494.html.

ing refuge. He soon found himself shipped to an immigration detention centre in Toronto where he was held in isolation for three weeks facing deportation to Syria. In February, the case made headlines when lawyers with the Refugee Law Office learned about the detention and acted quickly to prevent this boy's deportation, filing a humanitarian application.[22] Canada's new Minister of Immigration, Refugees and Citizenship, John McCallum, responded quickly, granting a Minister's Permit to the boy so that he could be admitted to Canada as a permanent resident.

There is no question that detention, even in a family detention facility,[23] is harmful to children. In a recent Canadian study[24] of the effect of immigration detention on children, the researchers, who are paediatricians and child psychiatrists, found that:

> immigration detention is acutely stressful and potentially traumatic experience for children. Children reacted with extreme distress, fear and deterioration of functioning . . . Although not directly threatening to children's physical integrity, the detention environment evoked feelings of helplessness and fear. The pervasive under-stimulation and the constant surveillance of the children and of their mothers transformed daily life into an experience of deprivation and powerlessness.

On the issue of imprisonment of children, the Convention on the Rights of the Child (CRC) provides at Article 37:

> State Parties shall ensure that . . . (b) No child shall be deprived of his or her liberty unlawfully or arbitrarily. The arrest, detention or imprisonment of a child shall be in conformity with the law and shall be used only as a measure of last resort and for the shortest appropriate period of time.[25]

---

[22] M. Broshnahan, 'Syrian boy seeking refugee status ordered deported to the United States', *CBC News*, 16 February 2016, available at www.cbc.ca/news/canada/toronto/syrian-teen-detained-toronto-1.3449595; C. Cheung and S. Muscati, 'An inexcusable travesty: Canada sent a Syrian minor to solitary confinement', *The Globe and Mail (Canada)*, 17 February 2016, available at www.theglobeandmail.com/opinion/an-inexcusable-travesty-canada-sent-a-syrian-minor-to-solitary-confinement/article28781118/.

[23] W.S. Hylton, 'The shame of America's family detention camps', *New York Times Magazine*, 4 February 2015, available at www.nytimes.com/2015/02/08/magazine/the-shame-of-americas-family-detention-camps.html?_r=0.

[24] R. Kronick, C. Rousseau and J. Cleveland, 'Asylum Seeking Children's Experiences of Detention in Canada: A Qualitative Study' (2015) 85(3) *American Journal of Orthopsychiatry* 287.

[25] Convention on the Rights of the Child, opened for signature 20 November 1989, 1577 UNTS 3 (entered into force 2 September 1990), Art. 37.

Canadian law appears, at first glance, to recognize this principle. Section 60 of the Immigration and Refugee Protection Act provides as follows:

> For the purposes of this Division, it is affirmed as a principle that a minor child shall be detained only as a measure of last resort, taking into account the other applicable grounds and criteria including the best interests of the child.[26]

Nonetheless new legislation was introduced in 2012.[27] This allows for the mandatory detention for a period of six months without review for refugee claimants aged 16 and over if they are designated by the Minister as foreign nationals who are irregular arrivals (DFNs).[28] This was introduced in order to deter irregular arrivals of refugees in Canada such as the boat arrivals of Tamil refugees off the coast of British Columbia in 2009 and 2010. This legislation may lead to an increase in the numbers of detained migrant children in Canada although to date there have been very few determinations of irregular arrivals.

A more serious problem involving the immigration detention of children, including babies, is the detention of children euphemistically referred to as 'guests' of the detention facility in order to remain with a migrant parent who is detained. The most egregious case of such guest detention involved a Canadian child who was born to his Cameroonian mother while she was in detention. This child remained living with his mother in detention for more than two years until he finally left Canada with his mother when she agreed to be removed to another country (since Cameroon would not provide her with travel documents). (This child's first baby words were 'radio check' – the words he heard on the loud speaker in the detention centre every six hours when the guards changed shifts.[29]) As a result of this case, and other examples of indefinite immigration detention, lawyers have successfully argued that immigration detainees should have access to *habeas corpus* procedures in the regular courts.[30]

---

[26] Immigration and Refugee Protection Act, SC 2001, c. 27, s. 60 (IRPA).

[27] See D. Quan, 'Five years after the MV Sun Sea's arrival, Tory crackdown on irregular arrivals draws praise, scorn', *National Post* (Canada), 6 August 2015, available at http://news.nationalpost.com/news/canada/five-years-after-the-mv-sun-sea-tory-crackdown-on-on-irregular-arrivals-still-going-strong.

[28] IRPA, ss. 20.1, 57.1.

[29] R. Browne, 'What are Babies Doing Behind Bars in Canada?', *McLean's Magazine (Canada)*, 18 June 2015, available at www.macleans.ca/news/canada/what-are-babies-doing-behind-bars-in-canada/.

[30] N. Etienne, 'Habeas Corpus Allowed for Immigration Detainees', *Law Times (Canada)*, 2 November 2015, available at www.lawtimesnews.com/201511025030/headline-news/habeas-corpus-allowed-for-immigration-detainees.

Children, such as the Syrian boy who arrived at Fort Erie in January 2016 seeking refuge in Canada,[31] are victims of the deterrence, interdiction and security measures that have been systematically implemented to prevent refugees coming to Canada on their own. The failure of Federal and Provincial government authorities to develop a consistent policy across Canada to respond to the particular needs of unaccompanied refugee children is clearly demonstrated by this case. Although the case turned out well for this particular individual, it is unknown how many other unaccompanied teens have attempted to enter Canada and have been detained and deported to the United States with no one in Canada realizing that this has happened. The United States-Canada border is not a safe place for children to negotiate on their own.

4. GRANTING REFUGEE PROTECTION TO UNACCOMPANIED MINORS

Canada's Immigration and Refugee Board published guidelines for Board members dealing with the asylum claims of children in 1996. Although submissions had been made to the Board on substantive legal issues of asylum claims by children,[32] the IRB restricted these guidelines for child refugees to procedural and evidentiary matters.[33] However, the IRB guidelines refer specifically to provisions in the Convention on the Rights of the Child and to the guidelines for child refugees published by the UNHCR[34] which include guidance on substantive law issues for the determination of refugee claims by children. In 2009, the UNHCR published very comprehensive guidelines dealing with refugee children and these guidelines are now being referenced by counsel in Canada in cases involving child refugees.[35]

Over the past two decades significant jurisprudence has developed in

---

[31] Broshnahan, 'Syrian boy seeking refugee status ordered deported to the United States', above n. 22.

[32] G. Sadoway, 'Refugee Children before the Immigration and Refugee Board' (1997) 35 *Immigration Law Reporter* 106.

[33] Immigration and Refugee Board of Canada, *Chairperson Guideline 3: Child Refugee Claimants: Procedural and Evidentiary Issues* (1996), available at www.irb-cisr.gc.ca/Eng/BoaCom/references/pol/GuiDir/Pages/GuideDir03.aspx.

[34] UNHCR, *Guidelines on Policies and Procedures in Dealing with Unaccompanied Children Seeking Asylum* (UNHCR, 1997), available at www.unhcr.org/3d4f91cf4.html.

[35] UNHCR, *Guidelines on Child Asylum Claims* (UNHCR, 2009), available at www.unhcr.org/50ae46309.

Canada concerning refugee claims by children, including cases involving the determination of claims of children who are accompanied by their parents. The Federal Court has ruled that the Board must specifically address whether the children are refugees in their own right and threats to the children may affect whether an entire family will be granted refugee status.[36] The IRB guidelines on Child Refugee Claimants are particularly important in dealing with credibility issues that may arise during a child's claim and the Board's decision has been found unreasonable when it fails to take the Guidelines into account in accessing credibility.[37]

Persecution specific to children has also been recognized in the Canadian jurisprudence. In the case of *Cheung* v. *Canada,* the Federal Court of Appeal found that the treatment of a second child, born contrary to the One Child Policy in China, would be persecutory as the child would be a 'black market' person denied the ordinary rights of Chinese children.[38] In *Li* v. *Canada*, the Federal Court found that poor Chinese children who had been trafficked by their parents and were in danger of being trafficked again if returned to China, could be accepted as refugees.[39] In general, the Refugee Board and the Federal Court have accepted the particular vulnerability of child asylum-seekers and found that they come within the Refugee Convention definition.[40]

5. DENIAL OF FAMILY REUNIFICATION FOR CHILD REFUGEES: 'INVOLUNTARY CRUELTY'

> Refugees more than anyone else are people in need of roots. Roots are more than genealogical lineages . . . they are the constituents of a person's family . . .

---

[36] For example, in considering whether an internal flight alternative (IFA) in Colombo was available to a Sri Lankan Tamil family, the Federal Court overturned the Board's decision for failing to consider whether the children would face persecution in Colombo. See a more detailed analysis of the developing jurisprudence in G. Sadoway, 'Canada's Treatment of Separated Refugee Children' (2001) 3 *European Journal of Migration and Law* 372. Some of the cases referred to are: *Nadesalingam and others* v. *Canada* [1994] FCJ 2051; *Frigole* v. *Canada* [1995] 60 ACWS (3d) 596; *Iruthayathas* v. *Canada* [1994] FCJ 1202; *Chehar* v. *Canada* [1997] FCJ 1698; *Gengeswaran* v. *Canada* [1999] FCJ 768; *Sahota* v. *Canada* [1994] FCJ 869.

[37] See *Kankienza* v. *Canada* [2015] FC 478, paras [20]–[22].

[38] *Cheung* v. *Canada* [1993] 2 FC 314 (CA).

[39] *Li* v. *Canada* [2000] FCJ 2037.

[40] See *Re JDJ* [1998] CRDD 12; *Re MZJ* [1999] CRDD 118; *Re RRF* [1999] CRDD 220; *Re B (PV)* [1994] CRDD 12; *Malchikov* v. *Canada* [1996] FCJ 83; *Diaz* v. *Canada* [2011] FC 705.

> It is important that we recognize the genuine refugee and accord such a person the status vouchsafed under the Convention and our law. But to do only this, or to do this and be dilatory about family reunification, is to do either only half the job, or to mix involuntary cruelty with voluntary kindness. (Rabbi W. Gunther Plaut, 1985)[41]

The principle of family unity for refugees was set out in the Final Act of the 1951 UN Refugee Convention:

> Considering that the unity of the family, the natural fundamental group of society, is an essential right of the refugee, and that such unity is constantly threatened . . . [the Committee] recommends to Governments to take the necessary measures for the protection of the refugee's family, especially with a view to:
> (1) Ensuring that the unity of the refugee's family is maintained.[42]

Although the principle of family unity was not incorporated into the refugee definition, according to paragraph 183 of the UN *Handbook on Procedures and Criteria for Determining Refugee Status,* this principle 'is . . . observed by the majority of states, whether or not parties to the 1951 Convention or the 1976 Protocol'.[43]

In 1985, the Supreme Court of Canada ruled in *Singh* v. *Canada (Minister of Employment and Immigration)*[44] that persons seeking refugee protection in Canada had a right to have their status as refugees determined in accordance with the principles of fundamental justice, which included the opportunity to have an oral hearing before the decision-maker. Following this landmark case for refugee rights in Canada, a new refugee determination system was established, based on many of the recommendations contained in the report by Rabbi Gunther Plaut for the Minister of Employment and Immigration, Flora MacDonald. One of the recommendations was to permit family reunification for accepted refugees, and to ensure that it occurred as quickly as possible.

---

41 W.G. Plaut, *Refugee Determination in Canada: A Report to the Honourable Flora MacDonald, Minister of Employment and Immigration* (1985), pp. 151–6.

42 UN Conference of Plenipotentiaries on the Status of Refugees and Stateless Persons, *Final Act of the United Nations Conference of Plenipotentiaries on the Status of Refugees and Stateless Persons*, UN Doc. A/CONF.2/108/Rev. (25 July 1951).

43 UNHCR, *Handbook and Guidelines on Procedures and Criteria for Determining Refugee Status under the 1951 Convention and the 1967 Protocol Relating to the Status of Refugees*, UN Doc. HCR/1P/4/ENG/REV.3 (December 2011), para. [183].

44 *Singh* v. *Canada (Minister of Employment and Immigration)* [1985] 1 SCR 177.

If it is generally understood that refugees need to be reunited with their close family members as quickly as possible, it would seem logical that refugees who are themselves children would need to be reunited with their families on an even more urgent basis. As children they are more vulnerable and dependent upon the care of their family members, particularly their parents. The only situation in which child refugees might not need to be reunited with their parents would be in a situation in which the parents were a source of danger to the child, either through abandonment and neglect or abuse, and the child has actually fled to escape the situation of abandonment or abuse.

The Convention on the Rights of the Child speaks specifically to the rights of a child who is a refugee in Article 22:

> 1. States Parties shall take appropriate measures to ensure that a child who is seeking refugee status or who is considered a refugee in accordance with applicable international or domestic law and procedures shall, whether unaccompanied or accompanied by his or her parents or by any other person, receive appropriate protection and humanitarian assistance in the enjoyment of applicable rights set forth in the present Convention and in other international human rights or humanitarian instruments to which the said States are Parties.
> 2. For this purpose, States Parties shall provide, as they consider appropriate, co-operation in any efforts by the United Nations and other competent intergovernmental organizations or non-governmental organizations co-operating with the United Nations to protect and assist such a child and to trace the parents or other members of the family of any refugee child in order to obtain information necessary for reunification with his or her family. In cases where no parents or other members of the family can be found, the child shall be accorded the same protection as any other child permanently or temporarily deprived of his or her family environment for any reason, as set forth in the present Convention.[45]

Following the Plaut Report, along with the new refugee determination procedure that included an oral hearing, provision was made for reunification of accepted refugees with their dependent family members pursuant to section 46.06 of the Immigration Act, RSC 1985.[46] The Immigration and Refugee Protection Act 2002 (IRPA) included as one of its objectives with regard to refugees, a specific objective for reunification of refugee families. In addition to the general objective of immigration law 'to see

[45] Convention on the Rights of the Child, Art. 22.

[46] Immigration Act, RSC 1985, c. I-2, s. 46.04; 46.04(1): 'Any person who is determined by the Refugee Division to be a Convention refugee may, within the prescribed period, apply to an immigration officer for landing of that person and any dependant of that person.'

that families are reunited in Canada', the IRPA provides in section 3(2) dealing with refugees the following objective:

> (f) to support the self-sufficiency and the social and economic well-being of refugees by facilitating reunification with their family members in Canada;

Furthermore, section 3(3)(f) states:

> (3) This Act is to be construed and applied in a manner that . . . (f) complies with international human rights instruments to which Canada is signatory.

The IRPA provides for protected persons to apply for permanent residence in Canada, and to include their family members in that application, whether their family members are in Canada or abroad. This is accomplished through section 176 of the Regulations:

> (1) An applicant [who is a protected person] may include in their application to remain in Canada as a permanent resident any of their family members.

Section 176(2) provides a further 'one year window' to include a family member after the refugee has been granted permanent residence:

> (2) A family member who is included in an application to remain in Canada as a permanent resident and who is outside Canada at the time the application is made shall be issued a permanent resident visa if:
> (a) the family member makes an application outside Canada to an officer within one year after the day on which the applicant becomes a permanent resident;

However, the family member is defined very restrictively in section 1(3) of the Regulations:

> (3) For the purposes of the Act, other than section 12 and paragraph 38(2)(d), and for the purposes of these Regulations, other than sections 159.1 and 159.5, 'family member' in respect of a person means:
> (a) the spouse or common-law partner of the person;
> (b) a dependent child of the person or of the person's spouse or common-law partner; and
> (c) a dependent child of a dependent child referred to in paragraph (b).

Most significantly, a family member of a protected person does not include parents or siblings of an unaccompanied minor who is found to be a Convention refugee. So if a child or young person in Canada is granted

Convention refugee status (also referred to as protected person status), they cannot include their parent(s) and siblings in their application to become a permanent resident – and they cannot sponsor their parent until they are 18 years of age and earning the minimum necessary income (MNI).

So, for example, a refugee who enters Canada as an unaccompanied minor, if accepted as a Convention refugee or protected person, would not be able to include his parent in his application to become a permanent resident. However, after turning 18 he would be eligible to sponsor his parents if he was earning enough to meet the MNI for sponsorship. In the case of an 18-year-old refugee, seeking to sponsor one parent, he would need to be earning about CAN$36,637 annually, and to have been earning this amount for the previous two years prior to submitting the sponsorship.[47]

So, in the first place, a refugee who is a child cannot apply to have their parent join them in Canada until the child reaches 18. And even if the child waits until he is no longer a child, he will still not be eligible to sponsor his parents until he is earning enough money to meet the MNI. The only way a child can have their parent or parents come to join them in Canada is through a humanitarian and compassionate application filed by the parent outside of Canada.

Advocates from Parkdale Community Legal Services in Toronto and other legal clinics have attempted to challenge this restrictive definition of 'family member' repeatedly on the basis that it discriminates against refugees who are children contrary to the Canadian Charter of Rights and Freedoms by not allowing them to enjoy family reunification. They have been told by Canada Immigration that this is a deliberate restriction to deter unscrupulous parents sending their children with smugglers to establish a 'beachhead' or an 'anchor' for the family in Canada. On cross-examination, these senior immigration officers have admitted that there is no hard evidence that parents would place their children in danger by sending them to Canada with smugglers in order to anchor the family in

---

[47] See Government of Canada policy on sponsorship of parents and grandparents, available at www.cic.gc.ca/english/information/applications/guides/5772ETOC.asp: 'If you are sponsoring a parent or a grandparent, you must meet the minimum necessary income requirement for each of the three years immediately preceding the date of your application. The minimum necessary income requirement is equal to the Low Income Cut offs (LICOs) plus 30%, taking into account the number of family members for whom you are or will be financially responsible'. According to the Federal Income Table, for one person sponsoring one parent, his MNI for 2016 would be CAN$39,371, for 2015 it would be CAN$38,618 and for 2014 it would be CAN$38,272. So the 18-year-old refugee would have had to be earning over CAN$38,000 per year for two years prior to beginning the sponsorship.

Canada and to gain an immigration advantage.[48] Furthermore, if the purpose of sending a child on their own to a country like Canada was really to enable the family to immigrate to Canada, it would be much easier to do that through the various foreign student programs.

The response of the immigration authorities to the issue of denial of access to family reunification for separated refugee children, even when it would clearly be in their best interests to have their parents and siblings with them in Canada, is that those family members could seek to enter Canada on humanitarian and compassionate grounds, under section 25(1) of the IRPA. However, no policy guidelines have been developed for visa officers at posts abroad to instruct them on using section 25(1) for this purpose. Even when counsel for the child in Canada are actively seeking to have the parent(s) of the refugee child admitted to Canada on humanitarian and compassionate grounds, they are met with delaying tactics that go on for years.

Jason Pobjoy dealt with the issue of child refugees being unable extend their protected status to their parents or to reunify with their family members in the country of refuge, in his analysis of the asymmetry of derivative refugee claims. He concluded that 'there is no principled basis under international law for denying children the agency to extend protection to their parents when the child is a refugee' and 'there is no basis for limiting the application of family unity principles'.[49]

6. HUMANITARIAN PROTECTION OF REFUGEE AND MIGRANT CHILDREN IN CANADA

In addition to protection under the Refugee Convention, Canada's Immigration and Refugee Protection Act provides for expanded protection to persons in danger of torture or whose lives are at risk if returned to their country of origin, when the risk is not related to the grounds set out in the Refugee Convention. Section 97 of the IRPA provides that a person may be granted protected person status in Canada even if they don't qualify as a Convention refugee:

---

48 Transcript of cross-examination of John Butt, Manager of Post Determination Procedures Unit in the Refugees Branch of Citizenship and Immigration Canada, in relation to Federal Court File No. IMM-3530-05, on 18 April 2006, in possession of the author.

49 J.M. Pobjoy *The Child in International Refugee Law* (Cambridge University Press, 2017), pp. 76–8.

97.—(1) A person in need of protection is a person in Canada whose removal to their country or countries of nationality or, if they do not have a country of nationality, their country of former habitual residence, would subject them personally:

(a) to a danger, believed on substantial grounds to exist, of torture within the meaning of Article 1 of the Convention Against Torture; or

(b) to a risk to their life or to a risk of cruel and unusual treatment or punishment if:

   (i) the person is unable or, because of that risk, unwilling to avail themself of the protection of that country,

   (ii) the risk would be faced by the person in every part of that country and is not faced generally by other individuals in or from that country,

   (iii) the risk is not inherent or incidental to lawful sanctions, unless imposed in disregard of accepted international standards, and

   (iv) the risk is not caused by the inability of that country to provide adequate health or medical care.[50]

Section 97 is particularly important for persons seeking protection from criminal organizations such as drug traffickers, or criminal gangs seeking to recruit new gang members or to extort money from non-gang members who are perceived as having funds. This section has thus been used successfully to provide protection for young people who have fled forced recruitment by criminal gangs. While it is necessary to show that the young person would be personally subjected to the feared treatment and is not fleeing from a generalized risk, this is easier to argue than attempting to bring the young person into the Refugee Convention grounds of persecution due to membership in a particular social group.

The section 97 criteria is considered by the Immigration and Refugee Board at the same time that the Board is dealing with section 96 which sets out the criteria for refugee protection under the Convention. Counsel usually argue both sections if there is any doubt as to whether the persecution feared is based on a Convention ground. Even if it is not raised by counsel, the Board must consider section 97 grounds for protected person status.

One further protection for refugee children and youth is available under section 25(1) of the IRPA: the special provisions for an exemption from any requirement of the Act or Regulations if there are humanitarian and compassionate reasons, taking into consideration the best interests of any child affected by the decision. Section 25(1) states as follows:

25.—(1) Subject to subsection (1.2), the Minister must, on request of a foreign national in Canada who applies for permanent resident status and who is

---

50 Immigration and Refugee Protection Act, SC 2001, c. 27, s. 97.

> inadmissible – other than under section 34, 35 or 37 – or who does not meet the requirements of this Act, and may, on request of a foreign national outside Canada – other than a foreign national who is inadmissible under section 34, 35 or 37 – who applies for a permanent resident visa, examine the circumstances concerning the foreign national and may grant the foreign national permanent resident status or an exemption from any applicable criteria or obligations of this Act if the Minister is of the opinion that it is justified by humanitarian and compassionate considerations relating to the foreign national, taking into account the best interests of a child directly affected.[51]

There has been considerable litigation in Canada since the IRPA was proclaimed in 2001 on how the best interests of the child principle should be interpreted in deciding humanitarian applications for permanent residence under section 25(1). Immigration officers and judges of the Federal Court have repeatedly tried to limit the scope of the best interests of the child considerations over the years. However, in December of 2015 the Supreme Court decided the case of *Jeyakannan Kanthasamy* v. *Minister of Citizenship and Immigration*,[52] establishing very clearly how the best interests of the child principle must be applied in humanitarian applications.

Jeyakannan Kanthasamy had arrived in Canada as a 16-year-old unaccompanied youth seeking refugee protection based on fear of persecution as a young Tamil male in Sri Lanka. His refugee claim was refused on grounds that the civil war had ended and that his fear of persecution in Sri Lanka was no longer well-founded. His counsel had then applied for him to be allowed to remain in Canada with his extended relatives on humanitarian and compassionate grounds, arguing that it was in his best interests to remain in Canada because of the trauma he had experienced in Sri Lanka and his on-going need for the emotional supports in place for him in Canada. By the time the matter reached the Supreme Court, he was no longer a child since he had passed his 18th birthday but the Supreme Court found that the decision made on his humanitarian application, submitted when he was still under 18 years of age, was an unreasonable decision since it failed to properly assess his best interests.[53] The Court reiterated and approved some of the positive jurisprudence that had developed in the Federal Court on the application of the best interests of the child principle in humanitarian applications.

---

51 *Ibid.* s 25.

52 *Kanthasamy* v. *Canada (MCI)* [2015] SCC 61.

53 *Ibid.* paras [39], [45]–[47], [57]–[60].

7. CONCLUSION

Canada has made it extremely difficult for any refugees, let alone unaccompanied minors, to reach Canada unless they are able to pay agents or smugglers to assist them to enter with false documents. Children and youth do manage to come to Canada as part of refugee families selected abroad to be resettled in Canada, or sponsored by private sponsorship groups or family members. But very few young people reach Canada on their own. This fact has resulted in a certain complacency at the level of the Federal and Provincial governments, not to take this matter seriously, and not to respond effectively to the recommendations of the Committee on the Rights of the Child or the UNHCR. Hopefully, the case of the young Syrian boy who was almost deported from Canada without a refugee hearing and who was shamefully detained in isolation upon his arrival in Canada in January 2016, requiring Ministerial intervention to prevent his removal, will be a wake-up call for the Canadian government to establish procedures and protocols for responding to the needs of refugee children who come to Canada on their own, so that no refugee child falls through the cracks in the system.

PART IV

Process matters

16. 'These don't look like children to me': age assessment of unaccompanied and separated children

Mary Anne Kenny and Maryanne Loughry

1. INTRODUCTION

In October 2016, the United Kingdom (UK) Home Office allowed the first of some 300 child refugees to enter the UK from the so-called 'Jungle' refugee camp in Calais, France. The Home Office stated they had verified that each individual was aged between 14 and 17 years. News outlets in Britain published pictures of the young people, causing a media backlash over whether they were really children. David Davies, a Conservative Member of Parliament, wrote on Twitter '[t]hese don't look like "children" to me. I hope British hospitality is not being abused'. Calls were made to have the group undergo dental x-rays to assess their age.[1]

This case is illustrative of a culture of scepticism and suspicion surrounding the arrival of young people seeking asylum. Considerations around security or immigration control can often overshadow the young person's best interests. Unaccompanied and separated children (UASC) may be viewed as 'delinquents, as pseudo-children, as more threatening than adults'.[2]

In this chapter we will show that where age is disputed, the task of assessing age is complex. Research has consistently demonstrated there is no medical method to accurately determine chronological age of a young person.[3]

[1] S. Goodman, 'Questions over Age of Refugee Children Show How Ugly Britain has Become', *The Conversation*, 20 October 2016, available at https://theconversation.com/questions-over-age-of-refugee-children-show-how-ugly-britain-has-become-67335.

[2] J. Bhabha, 'Demography and Rights: Women, Children and Access to Asylum' (2004) 16(2) *International Journal of Refugee Law* 227, at 241.

[3] Royal College of Paediatrics and Child Health, *The Health of Refugee*

Young people arriving in countries seeking asylum often do so without any (reliable) documentation showing their age. They may not know their age accurately and their appearance may make it difficult to judge how old they are. Age disputes bring into question a child's identity and character, at a time when they are experiencing numerous factors of vulnerability.[4]

Age assessment processes are linked to the provision of support to UASC. In late 2016, the ninth annual United Nations High Commissioner for Refugees (UNHCR) Dialogue on Protection Challenges was focused on the theme of 'Children on the Move' in recognition of the fact that the number of children forcibly displaced has reached historic levels. In 2015, children constituted more than half of the total refugee population. Some 98,400 asylum claims were lodged by UASC in 2015 alone.[5] Numbers of children on the move will not decrease at any time soon and therefore age assessment processes are of increasing importance.

The chapter begins in section 2 with an overview of the contested space of the meaning of age and its relationship to legal, social and cultural constructions of what it means to be a 'child'. Section 3 outlines the international human rights framework relevant to the determination of age disputes. In section 4 we explore some common methods for resolving age disputes. The chapter concludes in section 5 with recommendations for a different approach which focuses less on age and more on particular vulnerabilities.

In this chapter 'age assessment' refers to the procedures through which various government authorities seek to establish the chronological age of an individual, in this case those that arrive in a country seeking asylum without another adult. The purpose is to determine whether they are a child, or under the age of 18 years of age.

2. IMPORTANCE OF AGE

Chronological age is linked to a child having certain legal protections. The United Nations Convention on the Rights of the Child (CRC) estab-

Children: Guidelines for Paediatricians (1999), available at www.rcpch.ac.uk/system/files/protected/news/refugee_1.pdf.

4 Department of Human Services (Victoria), *Child Development and Trauma Guide* (Government of Victoria, 2007), available at www.dhs.vic.gov.au/__data/assets/pdf_file/0006/586167/child-development-and-trauma-guide-1_intro.pdf.

5 See UNHCR, *Concept Paper: High Commissioner's Dialogue in Protection Challenges* (2016), available at www.unhcr.org/en-us/57b46e514.

lishes a common international definition of a child as a 'person below the age of 18 years'.[6] The CRC creates certain obligations on states in respect of separated refugee children.[7] In the asylum and immigration context, the question of age can be of great legal importance. It can determine how an individual's asylum case is processed, whether they are accommodated or detained with adults and whether they can access certain care and support.

An individual's date of birth in developed countries, such as Europe, the United States and Australia, relies heavily upon accurate legal documentation. Official documentation of a child's age provides an important foundation for safeguarding civil and political rights and economic, social and cultural rights. Its importance is recognized in Article 7 of the CRC which specifies that every child has the right to be registered at birth without any discrimination. Many UASC come from countries where there is low birth registration. UNICEF estimates that globally nearly 230 million children under the age of five have never had their births recorded: 59 per cent of those children are in Asia and another 37 per cent are from Sub-Saharan Africa.[8]

UASC may arrive at the borders of a country with no documentation as to their age or identity or with identity documents that may be considered unreliable or even bogus. Families, peers, traffickers, smugglers and advocates may also play a role in influencing a child's perception as to how they should, or should not, answer questions from authorities about their age. Not often recognized is the fact that in some cases children may falsely declare that they are adults. They may have arrived with a relative or friend they fear they will be separated from if they are considered to be a child, or they may hope to have easier access to work or independent living conditions if they are considered an adult.[9]

While the legal definition of age is clearly linked to being under the

---

[6] Convention on the Rights of the Child, opened for signature 20 November 1989, 1577 UNTS 3 (entered into force 2 September 1990) (CRC), Art. 1.

[7] See CRC, Art. 22 which reads: '1. States Parties shall take appropriate measures to ensure that a child who is seeking refugee status or who is considered a refugee in accordance with applicable international or domestic law and procedures shall, whether unaccompanied or accompanied by his or her parents or by any other person, receive appropriate protection and humanitarian assistance in the enjoyment of applicable rights set forth in the present Convention and in other international human rights or humanitarian instruments to which the said States are Parties'. See Mary Crock and Hannah Martin, Chapter 4.

[8] UNICEF, *Every Child's Birth Right: Inequities and Trends in Birth Registration* (UNICEF, 2013).

[9] Separated Children in Europe Programme, *Position Paper on Age Assessment*

age of 18, research shows that social constructions of 'childhood' and 'adulthood' are not fixed across different societies and cultures and may vary through time.[10] Despite the universal legal definition of a child, no one child has the same trajectory of child development. Each child is shaped by gender, personality, genetics, culture and childhood experiences. For asylum-seeking children, these childhood experiences are dislocating, frequently adverse and often traumatic in nature. Such experiences significantly shape how children present themselves to authorities and more significantly how they recount what has caused them to flee their country. Many children seeking asylum have not had a childhood familiar to decision-makers in countries of reception. Their stories have involved extreme challenges, deception, peer rather than family support and sometimes shame because of what they have had to do to survive.[11]

A review for the World Bank of contemporary understandings of child development and the risk exposure of children in low and middle income countries concluded that there was strong evidence of dynamic relations between risk factors in early childhood and later outcomes across multiple developmental domains. This emphasized the heightened effects on children of shocks to the care environment and the cumulative effect of multiple shocks.[12] Risks to childhood are cumulative and it is important to realize that a series of risks that may appear to be of minor significance can have a major impact on a child when viewed collectively.

Children, while defined by age, are shaped by their experiences. These experiences have a differential impact depending on the age of the child at the time of the experience and the multiplicity of factors concurrently influencing the child's development. Source countries for most asylum-seeking children are low-income countries and while in the past the issues of nutrition, status and culture have been accepted as major influences on the perception of a child's age, a 'life course' perspective of child develop-

---

in the Context of Separated Children in Europe (2012), available at www.refworld.org/docid/4ff535f52.html.

[10] A. James and A. Prout, *Constructing and Reconstructing Childhood: New Directions in the Sociological Study of Childhood* (Routledge, 1990); and D. Cipriani, *Children's Rights and the Minimum Age of Criminal Responsibility: A Global Perspective* (Ashgate Publishing, 2009).

[11] Z. Given-Wilson, J. Herlihy and M. Hodes, 'Telling the Story: A Psychological Review on Assessing Adolescents' Asylum Claims' (2016) 57(4) *Canadian Psychology/Psychologie Canadienne* 265.

[12] J. Boyden, S. Dercon and A. Singh, 'Child Development in a Changing World: Risks and Opportunities' (2015) 30(2) *World Bank Research Observer* 193.

ment indicates that significant other factors also influence how a child develops. These include environmental factors, such as housing, land and education settings, and attachment issues if the child has been separated from care-givers at significant developmental stages. There are critical periods in child development and timely interventions within these periods can stall developmental delays and ensure that so-called 'lost generations' are able to resume appropriate lives.[13]

Researchers also point to the fact that children who are seeking asylum are trapped in competing paradigms of child protection versus that of immigration and border control.[14] It is evident from the example referred to at the beginning of this chapter that concerns have been raised by governments that many of those arriving at borders seeking asylum claiming to be children are, in fact, adults.[15] In the European Union, the Dublin Agreement requires asylum claims be determined in the first safe country a person reaches, but children may be able to have their claims transferred to other European countries if they have family living there.

Age assessment can be deployed as part of a number of policies to deter and control unauthorized arrivals. Age disputes are conceptualized as part of an overall effort to '[c]hallenge older applicants and divert them to the adult asylum process',[16] adults posing as children may be viewed as a 'threat to . . . welfare and society'.[17]

Competing against this paradigm of immigration control is the view that, separated from family and support networks, UASC are seen as 'vulnerable children' and are entitled to various protections, support and rights from the state.[18] Bhabha and Crock note that as a corollary

---

[13] Given-Wilson et al., 'Telling the Story', above n. 11; Department of Human Services (Victoria), *Child Development and Trauma Guide*, above n. 4.

[14] Bhabha, 'Demography and Rights', above n. 2; H. Crawley, 'Asexual, Apolitical Beings: The Interpretation of Children's Identities and Experiences in the UK Asylum System' (2011) 37(8) *Journal of Ethnic and Migration Studies* 1171; C. Giner, 'The Politics of Childhood and Asylum in the UK' (2007) 21(4) *Children and Society* 249.

[15] H. Crawley, *When is a Child Not a Child? Asylum, Age Disputes and the Process of Age Assessment* (Immigration Lawyers Practitioners Association, 2007).

[16] UK Home Office, *Secure Borders, Safe Haven: Integration with Diversity in Modern Britain* (HMSO, 7 February 2002), para. [4.56], available at www.gov.uk/government/publications/secure-borders-safe-haven-integration-with-diversity-in-modern-britain.

[17] Giner, 'The Politics of Childhood and Asylum in the UK', above n. 14.

[18] UNHCR, *Guidelines on International Protection: Child Asylum Claims under Articles 1(A)2 and 1(F) of the 1951 Convention and/or 1967 Protocol relating to the Status of Refugees* (2009); Separated Children in Europe Programme, *Position*

of this approach, children are also seen as lacking in capacity and agency.[19]

3. HUMAN RIGHTS FRAMEWORKS

The key international documents on UASC include the United Nations Convention on the Rights of the Child, the United Nations Committee on the Rights of the Child's *General Comment No. 6 on the Treatment of Unaccompanied and Separated Children Outside their Country of Origin* (2005) and the UNHCR's *Guidelines on Policies and Procedures in Dealing with Unaccompanied Children Seeking Asylum* (1997).[20]

Article 3 of the CRC provides that the best interests of the child shall be a primary consideration. Article 7 of the CRC requires that children have their birth registered in order to protect their best interests. Read together, Articles 3 and 7 suggest that for those without a provable date of birth, there should be a presumption of minority. If there is a chance that the person is a child they should be given the 'benefit of the doubt' until proven otherwise.[21] The benefit of the doubt principle has been stressed by the UN Committee on the Rights of the Child, which stated that where there is no proof of age, a child is 'entitled to a reliable medical and social investigation that may establish his/her age and, in the case of a conflict or inconclusive evidence, the child shall have the right to the benefit of the doubt'.[22] In addressing the situation of UASC, the Committee has stated that age assessment:

> must be conducted in a scientific, safe, child and gender-sensitive fair manner,

---

Paper on Age Assessment in the Context of Separated Children in Europe (2012), available at www.refworld.org/docid/4ff535f52.html.

[19] J. Bhabha and M. Crock, *Seeking Asylum Alone – A Comparative Study: Unaccompanied and Separated Children and Refugee Protection in Australia, the UK and the US* (Themis Press, 2007), p. 240.

[20] CRC, above n. 6; United Nations Committee on the Rights of the Child, *General Comment No. 10: Children's Rights in Juvenile Justice*, UN Doc. CRC/C/GC/10 (25 April 2007); United Nations Committee on the Rights of the Child, *General Comment No. 6 on the Treatment of Unaccompanied and Separated Children Outside Their Country of Origin*, UN Doc. CRC/C/2005/6 (1 September 2005).

[21] V. Feltz, *Age Assessment for Unaccompanied Minors: When European Countries Deny Children their Childhood* (Medecins du monde International Network, 2015), available at https://mdmeuroblog.files.wordpress.com/2014/01/age-determination-def.pdf.

[22] UNCRC, *General Comment No. 10*, above n. 20, para. [39].

> avoiding any risk of violation of the physical integrity of the child; giving due respect to human dignity; and, in the event of remaining uncertainty, should accord the individual the benefit of the doubt so that if there is a possibility that the individual is a child, she or he should be treated as such.[23]

The UNHCR *Guidelines for Unaccompanied Children Seeking Asylum* provides that where an age assessment is necessary, authorities should allow for a:

> margin of appreciation inherent to all age-assessment methods [which] needs to be applied in such a manner that, in case of uncertainty, the individual will be considered a child. As age is not calculated in the same way universally or given the same degree of importance, caution needs to be exercised in making adverse inferences of credibility where cultural or country standards appear to lower or raise a child's age.[24]

Similar provisions are found in European Union law. Article 24(2) of the Charter on the Fundamental Rights of the European Union codifies the best interests principle contained in the CRC. Article 25(5) of the recast Asylum Procedures Directive for the EU provides that where there is a doubt in relation to age, Member States may use medical examinations; if after that testing there remains a doubt as to the child's age, then it should be assumed that the person is a minor.

Commentators have noted that despite this range of human rights protections for refugee and asylum-seeker children, the state's best interests often dominate over the child's best interests.[25] The next part of the chapter will examine the various methods used for managing age disputes and consider whether the benefit of the doubt principle is used in practice.

4. CURRENT METHODS FOR AGE ASSESSMENT

There are several different methods for age assessment used in different countries. What is clear is that no method currently available can tell with certainty the exact age of an individual.[26] This part will briefly discuss each of the main methods used and their limitations.

---

23 UNCRC, *General Comment No. 6*, above n. 20, para. [31].

24 UNHCR, *Guidelines on Policies and Procedures in Dealing with Unaccompanied Children Seeking Asylum* (1997), para. [5.11].

25 A. Engebrigtsen, 'The Child's – or the State's – Best Interests? An Examination of the Ways Immigration Officials Work with Unaccompanied Asylum Seeking Minors in Norway' (2003) 8(3) *Child and Family Social Work* 191.

26 European Asylum Support Office, *Age Assessment Practice in Europe* (2013),

4.1 Medical: Wrists/Carpal, Dental, Physical Developments

Several countries, particularly those in the European Union and the United States, use medical examinations such as dental examinations and x-rays of various bones, most commonly of the hands and wrists. To a lesser degree, collar bone and hip x-rays as well as physical development assessments are also used.[27]

Assessment of maturity based on these medical assessments of bone development and teeth have been critiqued extensively by medical experts as being inaccurate, as they only measure maturity, not chronological age.[28] There are particular difficulties in assessing the age for individuals who are between 15 and 18 years of age, with a margin of error that can be 'up to five years either side'.[29] Complications with these assessments also arise due to wide variations in health, nutrition, stress, education and socialization of children from developing countries.[30]

Questions have also arisen about the ethics of such examinations, given the potentially harmful effects of x-rays and the possible traumatic effects of medical examinations on young people who have experienced persecution in the past.[31]

---

available at www.easo.europa.eu/sites/default/files/public/EASO-Age-assessment-practice-in-Europe1.pdf.

[27] T. Smith and L. Brownlees, *Age Assessment Practices: A Literature Review and Annotated Bibliography* (Nova UNICEF, 2011).

[28] G. Noll, 'Junk Science? Four Arguments Against the Radiological Age Assessment of Unaccompanied Minors Seeking Asylum' (2016) 28(2) *International Journal of Refugee Law* 234.

[29] 'In practice, age determination is extremely difficult to do with certainty, and no single approach to this can be relied on. Moreover, for young people aged 15–18, it is even less possible to be certain about age. There may also be difficulties in determining whether a young person who might be as old as 23 could, in fact, be under the age of 18. Age determination is an inexact science and the margin of error can sometimes be as much as 5 years either side.' Royal College of Paediatrics and Child Health, *The Health of Refugee Children: Guidelines for Paediatricians*, above n. 3, at 13.

[30] H. Abbing and D.C. Roscam, 'Age Determination of Unaccompanied Asylum Seeking Minors in the European Union: A Health Law Perspective' (2011) 18(1) *European Journal of Health Law* 11; International Organisation for Migration (IOM), *Resource Book for Law Enforcement Officers on Good Practices in Combating Child Trafficking* (2006), available at https://publications.iom.int/books/resource-book-law-enforcement-officers-good-practices-combating-child-trafficking.

[31] Abbing and Roscam, 'Age Determination of Unaccompanied Asylum Seeking Minors in the European Union', above n. 30.

4.2 Psycho-social Age Assessment

Psycho-social age assessments are aimed at determining the psycho-social maturity of an individual. Focused age assessment interviews are used in the United Kingdom and in Australia. They involve asking an individual a series of questions about their life experiences (for example, education history, family composition, birth dates of other family members) in order to establish a chronology so as to make an assessment of the likelihood of the individual being either above or below the age of 18 years of age.

There are some challenges to achieving reliable results from such interviews. Professor Ansley-Green, former Children's Commissioner for England, has noted that such interviews can be conducted in an environment which may be 'often intimidating' and may seem adversarial. Trust and attachment issues can be significant barriers when being interviewed by authority figures:

> Analysis of the narrative given by the subject is fundamentally important. To be performed properly, however, this demands time, often involving several separate interviews, and expertise in the interviewers in understanding the lives, education and culture of children in the countries from which they have come.[32]

Young people may also have experienced trauma and/or have significant mental health issues which may in turn reduce their ability to cognitively recall dates and times or generally reduce their capacity to engage in a dialogue around complex issues.[33] Researchers have pointed to the fact that age and childhood are experienced differently in other countries: poverty and malnourishment can cause children to age quickly, they may be given responsibilities at an early age which may make them 'appear' older and more mature.[34]

Research undertaken by Professor Heaven Crawley of case studies of age assessments undertaken by local authorities in the United Kingdom

---

32 A. Aynsley-Green, *The Assessment of Age in Undocumented Migrants, A Report for the Office of the Defensor del Pueblo, Madrid, Spain* (2001), p. 14.

33 I. Bronstein, P. Montgomery and E. Ott, 'Emotional and Behavioural Problems Amongst Afghan Unaccompanied Asylum-Seeking Children: Results from a Large-Scale Cross-Sectional Study' (2013) 22(5) *European Child and Adolescent Psychiatry* 285; K. Dorling, *Happy Birthday? Disputing the Age of Children in the Immigration System* (Coram Children's Legal Centre, 2013); Given-Wilson et al., 'Telling the Story', above n. 11.

34 Boyden et al., 'Child Development in a Changing World', above n. 12; Crawley, *When Is a Child Not a Child?*', above n. 15.

found that the quality and consistency of such assessments varied widely.[35] Included in her recommendations for improvement was that assessments be conducted over a period so that behaviour and relationships can be observed. Age assessment should be holistic and allow for input by a range of people involved in a child's life, including teachers, health professionals, psychologists and youth workers. Greater fairness in the process could be achieved by establishing an independent panel that could review decisions to ensure consistency and credibility.[36]

4.3 Holistic Assessments

The Separated Children in Europe Programme *Statement of Good Practice* recommends that:

> [i]f an age assessment is thought to be necessary, the procedures must be multi-disciplinary and undertaken by independent professionals with appropriate expertise and familiarity with the child's ethnic and cultural background.[37]

A 2010 review of practice in 22 European countries showed a majority of countries used dental and bone age assessments. Only Sweden and, in some cases, the United Kingdom carried out multidisciplinary age assessments.[38] In the United States, the Department of Homeland Security (DHS) and the Department of Health and Human Services (DHHS) have joint procedures and policies for reviewing the age of UASC, which include consideration of medical assessments, interviews from the UASC and a range of other sources, including child welfare records.[39]

Researchers in Adelaide, South Australia, conducted a pilot study to estimate the age of 60 refugee children using holistic age assessment methods which included: oral narrative, anthropometric measures, developmental assessment and pubertal assessment.[40] The pilot study showed

---

[35] *Ibid.*

[36] *Ibid.* 130.

[37] Separated Children in Europe Programme, *Position Paper on Age Assessment*, above n. 9, at 25.

[38] European Migration Network (EMN), *Policies on Reception, Return and Integration: Arrangements for, and Numbers of, Unaccompanied Minors, An EU Comparative Study* (2010), available at www.refworld.org/docid/51b0788e4.html.

[39] Office of Refugee Resettlement, *Children Entering the United States Unaccompanied* (2015), available at www.acf.hhs.gov/orr/resource/children-entering-the-united-states-unaccompanied-section-1.

[40] S.A. Sypek et al., 'A Holistic Approach to Age Estimation in Refugee Children' (2016) 52(6) *Journal of Paediatrics and Child Health* 614.

that these methods achieved comparable accuracy to medically based age assessment methods.

One of the difficulties encountered with 'holistic' assessments is identifying exactly what should be considered and what weight should be accorded to the different forms of evidence.[41] In reviewing practices in the United States, the DHS Office of Inspector General found they 'could not identify a single, authoritative definition of what might constitute a holistic approach to age determination . . . [and] several individuals in the medical community noted that psychological testing of individuals to determine exact age would be difficult'.[42]

5. A CONTINUUM OF VULNERABILITY

As set out above, there is no one clear method for determining the age of a young person. Good practice in several countries employs 'child sensitive' psycho-social interviews to assess a child's age. However, while the interviewers need to be skilled in interviewing children from different cultural backgrounds and sensitive to children's cognitive capacity and tolerance for prolonged questioning, an appreciation of issues of child development, particularly within adverse locations, is imperative.[43]

The Separated Children in Europe Programme's *Statement of Good Practice* stresses that the primary aim of age assessments should be the protection of UASC rather than immigration control.[44] The current focus is on chronological age, which in turn establishes whether a child is in need and requires support. However, need and vulnerability are not always directly related to age:[45]

> Somewhere along the line, sensible and considered analysis of the impact of traumatic experiences on a young person is being lost to a dispassionate focus on defining their chronological age. Even if 18 or 19 on arrival, many of these young people will still have left their countries as children, and undergone lengthy journeys alone as children. This issue also raises the question of how we treat those who are young and vulnerable, regardless of their exact age.[46]

---

41 UNICEF, *Every Child's Birth Right*, above n. 8.

42 Department of Homeland Security, Office of Inspector General, *Age Determination Practices for Unaccompanied Alien Children: Update* (2016), available at http://trac.syr.edu/immigration/library/P5048.pdf.

43 Given-Wilson et al., 'Telling the Story', above n. 11.

44 Separated Children in Europe Programme, *Position Paper on Age Assessment*, above n. 9.

45 Dorling, *Happy Birthday?*, above n. 33.

46 *Ibid*. 41.

The UNHCR *Guidelines on Policies and Procedures for Unaccompanied Children Seeking Asylum* provides that the legal significance of age criteria should be reduced and the guiding principle should be whether an individual demonstrates 'an "immaturity" and vulnerability that may require more sensitive treatment'.[47]

The difficulties faced by UASC who lose a range of rights and protections available to them once they turn 18 years of age has been a matter of ongoing concern.[48] The European Parliament also condemned 'the very precarious circumstances with which these [unaccompanied] minors are suddenly confronted when they reach the age of majority'.[49] Upon reaching that age they may find themselves suddenly losing educational, social and economic rights which they were entitled to as children. This can include loss of accommodation, welfare and social supports. At present, there are no international legal instruments designed to protect them and accompany this transition to adulthood.

The issue of youth 'aging out' and losing entitlements and services is not just particular to UASC. Scholars are now recognizing that young people are taking longer periods of time to enter adulthood. Transitions of leaving home, entering the workforce are taking longer.[50] This prolonged transition has implications not only for families but also for institutions that serve children. Around foster care there has been considerable effort to recognize that when children turn 18 years of age, they are not ready to assume all the responsibilities of adulthood. Significant effort has been put into preparing youth for when they 'age out', i.e. turn 18 and are no longer eligible for services provided to children. There has also been a focus on a step-down approach whereby the transition time for youth out of service provision is longer and flexible in response to the capacity of the youth.[51]

It is against this background that the Council of Europe Parliamentary Assembly recently passed Resolution 1996 'Migrant Children: What Rights at 18?', calling on member states of the Council of Europe to a recognize a transition category for young migrants who are between the ages

---

47 UNHCR, *Guidelines*, above n. 24, para. [5.11].

48 A. Macdonald, 'Protection Responses to Unaccompanied and Separated Refugee Children in Mixed Migration Situations' (2008) 27(4) *Refugee Survey Quarterly* 48.

49 European Parliament, Resolution of 12 September 2013 on the Situation of Unaccompanied Minors in the EU [2016] OJ C93/165.

50 R.A. Settersten, Jr and R. Barbara, 'What's Going on with Young People Today? The Long and Twisting Path to Adulthood' (2010) 20(1) *The Future of Children* 19.

51 US Department of Housing and Urban Development, *Housing for Youth Aging Out of Foster Care: A Review of the Literature and Program Typology* (2012).

of 18 and 25, to help young migrants access healthcare, welfare, education, information and housing assistance.[52]

6. CONCLUSION

Age assessment has become central to both the provision of welfare support and immigration. A range of factors means a purely medical assessment will not provide the certainty around age immigration officials may seek. Holistic assessments that include a psycho-social assessment are preferable; those seeking to interview must have an appropriate understanding of the complex interplay of child development, culture and the impacts of torture and trauma.

The most problematic assessments occur in the age ranges of 15–20 years. Part of the media and political response to the example at the beginning of this chapter drive a narrative that refugee children are not really children and therefore not deserving of help. This carries the incorrect assumption that older young people are not in need of support.[53] In many ways, the search for certainty of age may well be at the expense of the overall psychological wellbeing of a young person. An alternative approach is that the focus be turned back upon their needs.

The consideration given to protracted transition for youth in other sectors in society, and the lessons learnt, now needs to be brought to policy and procedures for addressing the needs of UASC. The recent European Parliament Resolution applying this approach recommends recognizing a transition category for young asylum-seekers and refugees and provides a better way forward. It is consistent with international human rights standards which provide that in assessing age, any conflicts should be resolved by giving the benefit of the doubt to an individual, thus ensuring those who are vulnerable are given the protection they need.

---

[52] Council of Europe, Parliamentary Assembly, 'Migrant Children: What Rights at 18?' (2014) Resolution 1996.

[53] Goodman, 'Questions over Age of Refugee Children Show How Ugly Britain Has Become', above n. 1.

17. Procedure deficits in protection for immigrant children in the United States

Lenni B. Benson and Claire R. Thomas

1. INTRODUCTION: PROCEDURE MATTERS

In theory, United States (US) immigration statutes offer many forms of protection and integration for foreign national youth.[1] In practice, however, the ability of young people to access relevant special visa categories is frustrated by process barriers and the lack of adequate information and skilled counsel.[2]

Under US law, migrant children may seek protection as refugees; they may qualify for permanent residence if they have been abandoned, abused or neglected by a parent; they may be protected if victims of crimes or trafficking. Other contributors have defined and explained the substantive requirements for each form of protection.[3] In this chapter, we explore whether US domestic legal systems protect children's procedural rights. We note at the outset that the US Constitution has been applied

[1] Child migration in the United States has a long history. Early laws excluded only those young people judged inadmissible on grounds of disease, lack of mental capacity or likelihood that they would become dependent on public welfare support. Similar exclusions applied for adult applicants for admission. In 1907, Congress adopted the Immigration Act 1907 to prohibit the admission of any child under 16 traveling without one or both parents. Even then, exceptions were made for some unaccompanied children sent to the US to escape war or persecution. See 38 Statutes-at-Large 898 (20 February 1907), s. 2.

[2] In reality, most unrepresented children are unable to identify any form of relief. Based on regular Freedom of Information Act data, 'TRAC' academics at Syracuse University publish information about the juvenile cases in the Immigration Court. The data shows that between 2005 and the end of 2016, only 4% of unrepresented children could secure any relief in Immigration Court, see http://trac.syr.edu/phptools/immigration/juvenile/.

[3] For a discussion of the options available to children, see David Thronson, Chapter 13; Kate Bones and Timnah Baker, Chapter 14.

consistently to protect both citizen and foreign-born children in regards to fundamental rights such as education, safety and criminal punishment.[4]

Between October 2010 and October 2016, the US government initiated 177,561 removal or deportation cases against children.[5] Of these, 41 percent or 73,013 cases remained pending in mid-2017. This suggests that children are given time and process in removal proceedings. In this chapter we examine some of the reasons why 'due process' does indeed require time, as we explore measures that would greatly reduce the procedural protections that have been available.

The presidential election in 2016 led the Department of Homeland Security (DHS), which controls most aspects of immigration enforcement,[6] to rapidly shift its policies and operations. Many of the children who were able to apply for protection at the US Southern border with Mexico may find that new 'fast track', truncated procedures will literally close the door.[7] Others already present within US territory may find an increased focus on apprehension, detention and removal proceedings. As fear of enforcement grows, many have become concerned about the special vulnerability of children, with news reports of a decrease in school attendance in many immigrant communities.[8]

---

[4] In *Plyler* v. *Doe*, 457 US 202 (1982), the US Supreme Court recognized that all children have a right to free public education regardless of the immigration status of the child. Children are not criminally punished for immigration violations and immigration proceedings are characterized as 'civil enforcement'.

[5] Calculations based on reviewing TRAC data between 2010 and end of 2016, see http://trac.syr.edu/phptools/immigration/juvenile/, calculated on 2 April 2017; 19% of the cases were completed with an *in absentia* removal order because the child failed to appear. In the vast majority of these cases the child had no attorney.

[6] The DHS is a cabinet level agency with many divisions, including Customs and Border Protection (CBP), US Citizenship and Immigration Service (USCIS) and its Asylum Directorate, and the Immigration and Customs Enforcement (ICE). The Immigration Court, the Executive Office for Immigration Review (EOIR), is an administrative component within the Department of Justice.

[7] See Secretary John Kelly, Department of Homeland Security, *Implementing the President's Border Security and Immigration Enforcement Improvements Policies* (Memorandum, 17 February 2017), announcing a change in treatment of children and authorizing the use of expedited removal at the border and within the interior of the US ('Kelly Memo'). In 2017 the United States was already returning Mexican and Canadian children to their respective countries under special treaty agreements. Few are admitted to the US unless the child is able to articulate that he or she is a victim of severe trafficking. See discussion below.

[8] See, e.g., V. Yee, 'Immigrants hide, fearing capture on any corner', *New York Times*, 22 February 2017; M. Anderson, 'How Fear of Deportation Harm Kids' Education', *Atlantic Monthly*, 26 January 2017; National Public Radio,

2. LOCATION DEFINES THE SCOPE OF PROCESS

People seeking admission to the US territory have very few statutory or constitutional rights.[9] Traditionally, people who have entered, with or without authorization, enjoy greater procedural and substantive protections. Until the passage of legislation in 2008, children had no greater statutory protections than any other non-citizen seeking admission to the United States. As is discussed below, if border officials agree that a child merits the designation of unaccompanied child, the procedural protections are dramatically increased.

2.1 At the Border

Since 2008, children have had significant procedural protections under the William Wilberforce Trafficking Victims Protection Reauthorization Act 2008 (TVPRA).[10] This statute exempts unaccompanied children from 'expedited removal' procedures.[11] Unaccompanied children hoping to enter the United States present themselves at the Southern border with Mexico at official ports of entry or are apprehended by Customs and Border Protection (CBP) officials within the US.[12] CBP officials intercept the children once they enter the US territory and take them into custody.[13]

'Attendance drops at Maryland High School as deportation fears rise', 16 January 2017.

[9] Since the end of the twentieth century, US case law has given Congress plenary authority to define the scope of procedural due process for people seeking admission to the United States: *Chae Chan Ping* v. *United States*, 140 US 581 (1889); *United States, ex rel. Knauff* v. *Shaughnessy*, 338 US 537 (1950). Only returning lawful permanent residents have been able to secure a greater measure of procedural protections when returning from a brief sojourn abroad: *Landon* v. *Plascencia*, 459 US 21 (1982).

[10] See PL 110-457 (23 December 2008) (TVPRA). While Congress created some procedural protections in this statute, many of the restraints on prolonged detention of children reflect class action litigation that has endured for over 20 years. See *Flores* v. *Reno* settlement, updated to reflect the current US Attorney General as *Flores* v. *Lynch*, discussed below n. 26.

[11] Compare Australia's expedited processing procedures, as discussed by Savitri Taylor in Chapter 18.

[12] The most common entries occur near Brownsville, Texas where children cross the Rio Grande River between Mexico and the United States.

[13] In 1993, the US Supreme Court ruled that the US Coast Guard, now a division of DHS, may refuse to process the asylum applications for people interdicted at sea. See *Sale* v. *Haitian Centers Council*, 509 US 155 (1993). By 2017, very few children were being found in US or international waters. DHS policy announced in February 2017 may encourage irregular maritime migration as children's claims

As a result, hundreds of thousands of children have been initially detained. The majority have been released to close relatives. As most children are arriving from Central America, the children ultimately face removal proceedings in the States with large populations of Central American migrants. The top six States, representing more than 60 percent of the released children, have consistently included: Texas, California, Florida, New York, Maryland and Virginia.[14]

Congress has limited these TVPRA procedural protections for children from Mexico and Canada: children from these two border nations may be immediately returned,[15] unless they can articulate a clear fear of trafficking or immediate harm.[16] Legislation pending in Congress in May 2017 would amend the TVPRA to require processing children's cases at border facilities.[17]

Children who manage to cross into the United States with family members may receive fewer procedural protections. Technically, all people apprehended near the international land border without genuine/valid documents are potentially subject to 'expedited removal'. The effect of such an order is to authorize the immediate expulsion of the individual and bars entry for a minimum of five years. There is no right to counsel in these proceedings.[18]

DHS did not use the expedited removal procedure on unaccompanied

---

are denied or curtailed at international land borders. DHS officials who encounter children at sea do have the option to bring them to the mainland, placing them into removal proceedings.

[14] For State release statistics see www.acf.hhs.gov/orr/programs/ucs/state-by-state-uc-placed-sponsors. In 2016, these States represented 31,796 children out of a total of 52,147 referred from the border to DHHS care.

[15] Between 2013 and fall 2016, 138,611 Central American youth were apprehended at the US Southern border. See statistics generated by CBP at www.cbp.gov/newsroom/stats/southwest-border-unaccompanied-children/fy-2016. In this same time period, an additional 36,400 Mexican youth were apprehended by US border authorities. Almost all were summarily returned to Mexico. There is no statutory right to counsel during the border inspection. No child advocate organization advises children at the early inspection stages.

[16] See agreements between the US DHS and Mexico. See generally B. Cavendish and M. Cortaza, *Children at the Border* (Appleseed, 2011), available at http://appleseednetwork.org/wp-content/uploads/2012/05/Children-At-The-Border1.pdf.

[17] See, e.g., Protection of Children Act 2017, HR 495.

[18] The case law concerns adults as the DHS did not use expedited removal on unaccompanied children. See generally *Castro* v. *United States Department of Homeland Security*, 835 F.3d 422 (3d Cir. 2016) (finding no *habeas* jurisdiction to raise constitutional claims of adults and children subjected to expedited removal and objecting to lack of counsel), en banc review denied, cert. denied US Sup. Ct (17 April 2017), and *United States* v. *Peralta-Sanchez*, 847 F.3d 1124 (9th Cir.

minor children until early 2017, when then DHS Secretary Kelly changed the policy for some of the apprehended children. Again, the entire deportation decision process is made by DHS officials: children only reach an asylum officer or judge if able to articulate a credible fear of persecution.[19] Secretary Kelly stated that children with a parent residing in the United States would no longer be treated as 'unaccompanied' and deserving of the additional process protections and asserted that 60 percent of the unaccompanied children were released to a parent residing without status in the US. Kelly directed DHS to prosecute if the parent had directly or indirectly facilitated the child's unlawful entry into the US. A likely response to this policy is that future children arriving alone will be reluctant to reveal the location of a parent within the US. Thus, more children may remain in Department of Health and Human Services (DHHS) custody until suitable other adults can be found to serve as host families.[20] In addition, as of 2018, DHS has been separating accompanied children from their parents and detaining each separately, adding even more children to the custody of DHHS.[21]

If the government implements a policy of subjecting children to expedited removal, few children are likely to move beyond the initial border assessment. For the adult population, 44 percent of all forced removals are made using these expedited procedures. In theory, if a child is able to articulate a credible fear of persecution or can demonstrate he or she is a victim of trafficking, the child would be entitled to greater procedural protections and an opportunity for an interview with an asylum officer and potentially review before an immigration judge. However, there is no statutory right to counsel at the border assessment. Without counsel, it is our experience that few children are able to explain the context of their fear of return. If the expedited removal of youth does become the norm, the government of Mexico may face a growing population of displaced and unaccompanied youth.[22]

2017) (rejecting collateral attack on an adult's expedited removal order and finding no right to counsel).

19 Kelly Memo, above n. 7.

20 The *Flores* settlement does require DHHS to consider release to other relatives and to third parties who are willing to undertake the duties of a 'sponsor'. One of the primary duties of the sponsor is to ensure the child appears at his or her removal hearing.

21 See C. Dickerson, 'Hundreds of Immigrant Children Have Been Taken from Parents at U.S. Border', *New York Times*, 20 April 2018. The agency is then classifying the children as 'unaccompanied' and initiating removal proceedings separately from the parents.

22 For a general report on the interdiction of Central American youth in Mexico, see Human Rights Watch, *Report: Closed Doors: Mexico's Failure to Protect*

2.2 Inside the Territory

A child born on US territory usually becomes a citizen at birth.[23] A significant number of people enter and overstay an authorized period of visit; in early 2017, the United States had an estimated 11 million undocumented residents. Many are children who have lived most of their lives within the territory but have no clear path to regularization of status. Unless they can navigate the substantive laws or qualify for special protections, these youth are almost as vulnerable to removal as the adult unauthorized population.

Migrant children inside the United States who can prove 'lawful inspection' and admission may seek to extend or change their temporary status. US statutes usually preclude extensions or adjustment to permanent status if a temporary status has expired or if the terms of the original admission were violated. One of the unique protections for children who enter with inspection is that they formally do not begin to acquire unlawful presence in the US until after they turn 18. While they are not formally in status, they don't begin to face the 10-year bar to regularization of status adults face.[24] In theory, such children could regularize their status without the severe penalties such as a 10-year bar to status that are imposed on adults. Nevertheless, the majority of these children grow up to become adults trapped in the unauthorized population because, for most people, there is no statutory path to regularization of status. For over 10 years, the US Congress has refused to pass legislation that would

---

Central American Refugee and Migrant Children (31 March 2017), available at www.hrw.org/report/2016/03/31/closed-doors/mexicos-failure-protect-central-american-refugee-and-migrant-children. The Mexican government has reported that 38% of the children it apprehends are seeking to travel to the United States to join a parent. See Comisión Nacional de Los Derechos Humanos, México, Situación General, available at www.ohchr.org/Documents/HRBodies/HRCouncil/AdvisoryCom/Migrant/MexicoCNDH.pdf. This is smaller than the 60% reported by DHS Secretary Kelly (above n. 7).

[23] The United States began to codify citizenship at the end of the Civil War. Realizing the need to incorporate former slaves born in US territory, the Congress and the States ratified an amendment to the Constitution to guarantee US citizenship to all born in US territory. Thereafter, further regulations were created to allow children born abroad to at least one citizen parent to also acquire citizenship at birth. See INA, ss. 301(g), 309; 8 USC ss. 1401(g), 1409. People claiming citizenship at the border bear the burden of proof.

[24] INA, s. 212(a)(9)(b); 8 USC s. 1182(a)(9)(b) punishes an illegal entrant or person who overstayed for more than 365 days with a 10-year bar if they depart and seek reentry to the United States. Children do not become subject to this penalty until they turn 18.

give permanent residence to individuals brought to the US as children. By 2017, approximately 650,000 youth had been able to secure a form of stay of removal and temporary work authorization under President Obama's Deferred Action for Childhood Arrivals ('DACA') Program. The Trump Administration terminated the DACA Program in an announcement on 5 September 2017, suggesting that only Congress can protect these children raised within the US. As of May 2018, court orders challenging the termination of DACA are still pending. USCIS is accepting DACA renewals, but no new applications for DACA may be made.[25]

The DHS can arrest, detain and deport any individual who fails to maintain status in the United States or who is apprehended within the interior but cannot establish lawful admission. For many years, children were rarely placed in removal proceedings except as part of a parent's deportation case. Children's remedies or opportunities to remain were almost exclusively derivative of the rights of the parent to remain.[26]

As the DHS began to apprehend more children at the border, the agency policy shifted to also initiate removal proceedings against a greater number of unaccompanied children found within the interior. The DHS had focused previously on children who engaged in acts of juvenile delinquency or who were found within close proximity to the border. It is unclear whether the new administration will broaden interior enforcement beyond these categories of children.

3. DETENTION AND INITIATION OF REMOVAL PROCEEDINGS

After the initial apprehension and processing by DHS, the federal government transfers migrant children from border control authorities to the care and custody of the DHHS.[27] For more than 20 years, the *Flores* class

---

[25] See USCIS website on DACA, at https://www.uscis.gov/humanitarian/deferred-action-childhood-arrivals-response-january-2018-preliminary-injunction.

[26] There is no universal procedural mechanism for providing accompanied children with an independent advocate or 'guardian ad litem' to ensure that the best interests of the child are preserved. If the CBP believes a child is being trafficked, the agency may seek intervention of special protection officers who might seek to separate the parent and child. We found no statistics reporting this intervention. Interviews with DHS personnel suggested this rarely occurs.

[27] See Chapters 18 through 21 for a discussion of the detention of children. For a detailed article discussing the rights of child migrants held in detention and similarly arguing for a right to appointed legal counsel, see E. Frankel, 'Detention and Deportation with Inadequate Due Process: The Devastating Consequences

action litigation limited the government's ability to detain children.[28] The *Flores* decision and resulting settlement requires the federal government to release children held in civil detention as soon as possible, and not solely to the child's natural parent.[29] In 2016, a federal court confirmed that these limits apply to all children, whether apprehended alone or with a parent.[30] Children who have a parent or parents in the United States traditionally have been released quickly from federal detention.[31]

While there is no right to appointed defense counsel, Congress has authorized a 'child advocate' program, which has been primarily reserved for children who remain in detention.[32] The child advocate may be a trained attorney who tries to assist the child by serving as an independent evaluator of the child's best interests. She or he makes recommendations about release from federal custody or assesses whether a child can be safely repatriated to his or her country of origin. The role of the advocate is limited and does not include the direct representation of the child before the court, nor assistance in the preparation of applications for relief from removal. Unfortunately, the assessment of a child's best interests is not

---

of Juvenile Adjudications for Immigrant Youth' (2011) 3(63) *Duke Forum on Law and Social Change*, available at http://scholarship.law.duke.edu/dflsc/vol3/iss1/4. The DHHS reported that the detention program cost over US$948 million in fiscal year 2016, see www.acf.hhs.gov/orr/unaccompanied-children-frequently-asked-questions. The DHS spends over US$2 billion annually on the detention of adult non-citizens.

28 *Flores* Settlement Agreement, available at http://centerforhumanrights.org/PDFs/05-19-16_Flores_Press_Statement.pdf. Some of the agreement's terms have been codified at 8 CFR ss. 236.3, 1236.3. See also *Reno* v. *Flores*, 507 US 292 (1993) (related case discussing due process rights of children).

29 See Cavendish and Cortazar, *Children at the Border*, above n. 16, at 32 for a discussion of related litigation on child detention and conditions.

30 *Flores* v. *Reno*, renamed *Flores* v. *Lynch*, 828 F.3d 898 (9th Cir. 2016) (interpreting the settlement agreement and finding it applies to all minors in DHS custody but does not compel release of parents with children).

31 The federal government has reported that 85% of the children are released within 21 days. For fiscal year 2016, the agency reported an average length of detention of 34 days, see www.acf.hhs.gov/orr/about/ucs/facts-and-data.

32 See discussion of the right to counsel below. Congress authorized a pilot Child Advocates program, administered by the Young Center based at the University of Chicago Law School, see www.theyoungcenter.org. See J. Nagda and M. Woltjen, *Best Interests of the Child Standard: Bringing Common Sense to Immigration Decisions* (First Focus, 2015); and Frankel, 'Detention and Deportation with Inadequate Due Process', above n. 25, at 63. The Young Center provides advocacy services for children in several US regions. Again, these child advocates do not serve as 'attorneys' for the child in immigration proceedings. In many instances, the unaccompanied child lacks any legal counsel.

universally incorporated into the adjudications before either the asylum office or the Immigration Court.

4. PROCESS IN REMOVAL PROCEEDINGS

Children apprehended at the border bear the burden of proving eligibility to enter and to remain within the United States. In contrast, when an individual is apprehended in the interior, the DHS must establish by clear and convincing evidence that the person is an alien and is subject to a statutory ground of removal.[33] At the removal hearing, the immigration judge, a form of administrative hearing officer, may entertain applications for relief from removal.[34] All people in removal proceedings have a right to counsel but 'not at expense to the government'.[35]

If a child is able to articulate a request for protection before the court, the resulting procedure is largely dictated by the type of protection the child is seeking. As of 2016, children had greater process protections than adults in removal, with dockets segregated from adult cases. If a child is seeking asylum, the adjudication is taken out of the adversarial process and the child is given an informal hearing with a trained refugee/asylum officer. The asylum procedures are the most protective of a child's needs but almost all applications are made outside the cauldron of the court itself.[36]

Children may seek protection under the Refugee Convention and several other US statutory protections designed for victims of crime or trafficking. Congress has also authorized a form of protection for children who have been subject to a State court family law determination of abuse, neglect or abandonment. In most instances, the first adjudication of eligibility for these forms of protection are made in fora outside the Immigration Court.

Between 2005 and the end of January 2017, the Immigration Court

---

[33] INA, s. 240, 8 USC s. 1229a.

[34] The Immigration Court is formally called the Executive Office for Immigration Review (EOIR) and is an agency within the US Department of Justice (DOJ). It is not an independent court nor a formal part of the judiciary. See www.usdoj.gov/eoir. Immigration Judges are attorneys appointed by the Attorney General. The prosecuting agency within the EOIR is the Immigration and Customs Enforcement (ICE) division of the DHS.

[35] INA, s. 292, 8 USC s. 1362. The need for and right to counsel is explored below.

[36] The T status, the U status and the Special Immigrant Juvenile status forms of protection each involve different procedures outside the Immigration Court. See discussion below (text at n. 47).

adjudicated over 216,000 juvenile cases.[37] The vast majority involved children apprehended at the US border but released into the interior.[38]

4.1 Unaccompanied Children

DHS places all unaccompanied children in the removal system, regardless of whether the child is detained or released to a sponsoring adult. Fearful that delays in adjudication were encouraging youth to seek to enter the United States, the DHS issued directives in 2014 that listed recent border arrivals, including unaccompanied children, as its top enforcement (prosecutorial) priorities.[39] The Executive Office for Immigration Review (EOIR) also prioritized unaccompanied children's removal cases, scheduling the first hearing within 21 days of the DHS lodging the Notice to Appear (the charging document).

In early 2017, President Trump and DHS Secretary Kelly revoked these priorities memoranda and expanded the agency priorities to all who have engaged in any criminal conduct.[40] The Immigration Court priority docket characterizations were also formally rescinded by the Office of the Chief Immigration Judge on 31 January 2017. Only children remaining in DHHS custody will remain priority cases.[41] These policies are likely to produce slower adjudications for children's claims within the Immigration Court.

For the most part, the Immigration Court serves as an expensive, cumbersome monitor of the case while the child must seek substantive protection in other fora. Some cases go to State family courts and then to the United States Citizenship and Immigration Service (USCIS) benefits section.[42] Others go to the USCIS asylum office for primary jurisdiction. Thus, the

---

37 See Juvenile in Immigration Court data available at www.trac.syr.edu/phptools/immigration/juvenile.

38 In contrast, the government's burden is reduced to submitting proof of proper service of the allegations of alienage and charges of inadmissibility.

39 Secretary J. Johnson, Department of Homeland Security, *Memorandum* (25 November 2014), rescinded by Kelly Memo, above n. 7. For many years, ICE was usually willing to close removal or deportation proceedings and allow the migrant child to live temporarily within the United States through a grant of prosecutorial discretion. February 2017 guidance suggests that future prosecution decisions are to be made on a case by case basis: Kelly Memo, above n. 7. Prosecutorial discretion closing the removal case does not give the child formal status nor any affirmation or authorization to work or travel; the child remains in the 'undocumented' population but without threat of immediate removal.

40 See Kelly Memo, above n. 7.

41 Chief Immigration Judge Mary Beth Keller, *Case Processing Priorities* (31 January 2017, on file with author).

42 See above n. 6.

process a child experiences in the removal hearing is highly dependent on having counsel and the specific form of protection. These varied procedures are outlined in more detail below. Once a form of substantive protection is secured, the child can seek a termination of the removal proceedings.

Phrased differently, almost all children's cases are put into adversarial removal proceedings where a child risks a deportation order, yet the opportunities for protection are largely adjudicated elsewhere. Unfortunately, without competent legal counsel, the EOIR procedure is inadequate to both direct the child toward relief or to help the child obtain even minimal substantive protection. Only 12 percent of children who appear in removal proceedings without counsel are granted relief or any discretionary right to remain. In contrast, 86 percent of children who are represented are usually able to obtain an end of the removal and a form of authorization to remain such as asylum or other relief.[43]

Further, in many cases, no form of relief can be found and the government may agree to an administrative closure, allowing the young person to remain. Again, this is much more likely to happen if the child is represented. Between 2014 and 2017, the official DHS policy was to oppose prosecutorial discretion for recent border crossers, including children, who entered after January 2014.[44] The Immigration Judge cannot force the government to accept administrative closure or termination. In most cases, the parties agree to this conclusion. Between 2005 and January 2017, approximately 30,000 children of over 215,000 cases had received a form of administrative closure or prosecutorial discretion.[45]

Even with the high rate of closure, the official policy between 2014 and 2016 was to *discourage* prosecutorial discretion for newly arriving children. In 2017, the Trump Administration issued a policy memorandum that both appeared to broaden the power of government prosecutors to grant administrative closure, while at the same time instructing DHS to investigate

---

[43] Data is based on analysis of rates of representation and outcomes reported by Immigration Judges to staff at TRAC at the Syracuse University, see http://trac.syr.edu/phptools/immigration/juvenile/. One possible explanation may be that counsel select cases of children who have a potential for relief. Until there is a release of data for the small pilot program attempting to provide nearly universal representation in a handful of immigration courts, it is not possible to determine if the provision of counsel alone is the predominate cause for the difference in outcomes. Moreover, many deportation orders for children are issued after the child fails to attend the administrative hearing, as *in absentia* orders of removal. The *in absentia* rate for completed cases 2010–2016 was 19%. Only 5.8% of those subjected to *in absentia* orders were represented.

[44] Johnson, *Memorandum*, above n. 39.

[45] See TRAC data, above n. 5.

whether unaccompanied children can be repatriated to their country of origin.[46] However, on 17 May 2018 the Attorney General of the US, Jeff Sessions, issued a decision ending the ability of Immigration Judges to grant administrative closures if either party objected.[47] At time of writing it was too early to assess how aggressively the new administration will pursue removal of children at the border. What is clear is that Immigration Judges have fewer tools to temporarily close removal cases, even if the child has an application for relief pending before another agency.

4.2 Accompanied Children or Other Juveniles

A child apprehended with a parent and placed into removal proceedings may sometimes qualify for protection when his or her parents do not. If the government and parents consent, the removal cases may be separated.[48] For example, a child may meet the standards for special immigrant juvenile status, a form of permanent residence and successfully obtain legal status and terminate the proceedings. However, his or her parent would have no parallel defence to removal. For most of the statutory forms of protection, a child cannot sponsor his or her parent directly for derivative protection. In these cases, the parent may try to seek prosecutorial discretion to be allowed to remain in the United States until the child reaches the age of majority. There is no statutory or constitutional right to remain in the US because your child is a citizen or has been granted protective status. Only the special visa categories for victims of crimes or of trafficking expressly allow a parent to receive derivative protection based on a child's application.[49]

5. CHILDREN'S ASYLUM CLAIMS: PROCESS ALONE CANNOT PROTECT A CHILD

5.1 Asylum Office Process

People in removal proceedings are not usually able to process their application before the non-adversarial USCIS Asylum Office. In contrast,

---

46 See Kelly Memo, above n. 7.

47 *Matter of Castro-Tum*, 27 I & N Dec. 271 (17 May 2018).

48 A child who is not designated an 'unaccompanied child' is still entitled to child-appropriate procedures under the Immigration Court procedures. See Court Memorandum, OPPM 07-01, discussed below.

49 See U or T status and regulations found in 8 CFR 214.2.

Congress expressly granted unaccompanied children the right to have an application assessed by the Asylum Office even if the child has been placed into removal proceedings.[50] Non-citizen children appear before an Asylum Officer in two contexts: as accompanied minors who appear as derivatives on their parents' asylum applications[51] or as unaccompanied minors who apply for asylum independently.[52]

Normally, an individual has only one year to seek asylum unless he or she can establish extraordinary circumstances to justify a late filing.[53] Under current interpretation, if a child was classified at apprehension as an unaccompanied child, he or she is expressly exempt from this deadline.[54]

Whether an asylum claim is made by a child or an adult, the applicant must show that:

(1) she meets the statutory definition of a 'refugee', as found in Immigration and Nationality Act (INA), section 101(a)(42)(A);
(2) that she is not subject to any statutory bars from asylum; and
(3) that she merits a grant of asylum in the adjudicator's discretion. A child meeting these three criteria may be granted asylum or refugee status under INA, section 208.

While a child must prove the same elements as an adult to be eligible for asylum, a child's asylum claim often differs from an adult's case. One

---

50 TVPRA, above. The USCIS Asylum Office officially created a policy of primary jurisdiction in 2013. See also USCIS, *Affirmative Asylum Procedures Manual* (USCIS, May 2016), s. III.B, 35, available at www.uscis.gov/humanitarian/refugees-asylum/asylum/affirmative-asylum-process.

51 A child can qualify for derivative asylum benefits if he or she is under 21 and unmarried. If the parent secured asylum inside the United States but the child or spouse were abroad, the parent may sponsor the family members for derivative refugee benefits and bring them to the United States.

52 The Kelly Memo, above n. 7, may change the Asylum Office initial jurisdiction for defensive applications filed in immigration court. It is unclear as of this writing. See also Chief Immigration Judge and Asylum Office, *Memorandum on Jurisdiction* (2 April 2013). May be superseded by Kelly Memo, above n. 7.

53 See INA, s. 208(a)(2)(d); 8 USC s. 1158(a)(2)(d). There are exemptions to this deadline such as when an individual can show he or she was suffering a severe mental or emotional impairment.

54 See INA, s 208(a)(2)(e); 8 USC s .1158(a)(2)(e) exempting 'unaccompanied alien children'. The Kelly Memo, above n. 7, suggests reclassification if a child is ultimately reunited with a parent, which implies that children may find asylum claims time-barred in future if they cannot meet the deadline nor utilize an alternative exception.

example of this difference lies in the experience of persecution. For an adult asylum applicant, persecution often entails the applicant directly experiencing mistreatment. However, for a child, merely witnessing violence could be construed as persecution.[55] Further, as scholars note, 'a migrating child exposed to gross violations of social or economic rights may require protection from the United States in circumstances where an adult who endured the same experience might not, because for the child this may amount to persecution'.[56]

The Asylum Office has extensive guidelines that instruct the adjudicators about child protective interviewing policies such as allowing times for breaks or the ability for the child to bring an adult to the interview in a supportive role.[57] One of the most important protections in the guidelines required headquarters review of all decisions where a child was going to be refused asylum. Due to the sharp increase in the number of claims, the Asylum Office instituted a random selection of cases for review.[58] Shortly after the change the number of refused cases began to grow.[59] The cases refused at this Office are returned or referred to the Immigration Court. In January 2018, the Asylum Office adjusted its workload priorities for scheduling cases. Previously, asylum cases for unaccompanied children were prioritized, but following this change, unaccompanied children no longer have a priority in case scheduling. Instead, the Asylum Office will schedule the most recently filed cases first.[60]

5.2 Referred Back to the Immigration Court

When the Immigration Court receives a referred asylum claim, the judge must apply a *de novo* review of the application. The Immigration Judge will allow supplemental filings and new evidence and testimony may be

---

55 For further discussion about the differences between how a child and an adult view persecution, see J. Bhabha, 'Not a Sack of Potatoes' (2006) 15 *Boston University Public Interest Law Journal* 197, at 210.

56 *Ibid.* 210. For more, see Kate Bones and Timnah Baker, Chapter 14.

57 Guidelines available at www.uscis.gov/sites/default/files/USCIS/Laws%20and%20Regulations/Memoranda/Ancient%20History/ChildrensGuidelines121098.pdf.

58 The change was identified in a FOIA request and reported by a private law firm that represented hundreds of children seeking asylum, see https://amjolaw.com/2016/11/12/throwing-children-asylum-applicants-to-the-wolves/.

59 *Ibid.*, reporting a drop from 60% to 41% in 2015 and 38.2% in 2016.

60 See Affirmative Asylum Interview Scheduling, at https://www.uscis.gov/humanitarian/refugees-asylum/asylum/affirmative-asylum-interview-scheduling.

considered in the administrative merits hearing. These hearings are conducted as adversarial trials and the government is represented by a DHS attorney. The burden is on the child to establish his or her eligibility for protection. While formal rules of evidence are not applied as they would be in State and federal courts, the proceedings are governed by the procedural rules of the Immigration Court and evidence is tested for probative value and authenticity.[61]

The statutes do not provide additional procedural protections for children's asylum hearings. However, the Immigration Court has introduced special procedural guidelines that instruct the judge to be aware of the particular vulnerability of juveniles.[62] The procedures expressly explain that the 'best interests of the child' standard 'does not negate the statute or the regulatory delegation of the Attorney General's authority, and cannot provide a basis for providing relief not sanctioned by law'.[63] These procedures identify several areas where a judge may deviate from usual procedure such as appearing before the child without a judicial robe or allowing time for the interpreter to become familiar with the child. The procedures also suggest that judges should recognize 'for emotional and physical reasons, that children may require more frequent breaks than adults'.[64]

The court procedures also suggest that the Immigration Judge attempt to adapt the questioning and structure of the hearing to avoid making it unduly adversarial. It includes examples that illustrate how a judge and/or the attorneys representing the government or the child should use simple questions, avoid leading questions, and understand that children may have difficulty testifying to difficult situations.[65]

While the child is entitled to request a copy of the asylum adjudicator's notes made during the asylum interview, the child does not receive the full written assessment evaluating the application. The DHS prosecutor does have access to the entire application and may use material in the file as a basis for cross-examination or impeachment in the subsequent merits hearing before the Immigration Judge.

If a child's claim for asylum is granted, the removal proceeding is

---

[61] See generally, INA, s. 240, 8 USC s. 1229a. The regulations governing asylum adjudication provide more guidance, 8 CFR 1208 ff.

[62] EOIR, *Operating Policies and Procedures Memorandum 07-01* (22 May 2007) (OPPM 07-01). This OPPM replaced a similar prior set of guidelines issued in 2004.

[63] *Ibid.* s. III.B, at 4.

[64] *Ibid.* s. V6, at 7.

[65] See especially *ibid.* Appendix A for examples of child appropriate questions.

terminated. One year later, a child may seek a formal adjustment of status to full permanent resident status. With this status, once the young person has resided in the United States for four more years and has turned 18, he or she can seek to naturalize as a US citizen.[66]

If the court does not approve the child's application for protection, the child may appeal the decision to the Board of Immigration Appeals and ultimately to the federal Circuit Court of Appeals.[67] Current statistics do not code cases based on the age of the person in the proceedings and this would be a good area for further study.

5.3 Children's Claims Made with Parents

Both accompanied and unaccompanied non-citizen young people run the risk of being rendered voiceless and invisible in the asylum process. For an accompanied child who appears as a derivative on her parent's asylum application, any independent claim to asylum by the child is 'typically subsumed under that of the parent and is not considered separately'.[68] Neither the Asylum Officer nor the Immigration Judge contemplates the derivative child's own claim independently from that of her parent's claim, even if her claim for asylum is much stronger than that of her parent. Should her parent's asylum application be successful, she will be allowed to remain in the United States. But should her parent's asylum application fail, the child will also be ordered removed from the United States.

---

[66] INA, s. 316; 8 USC s. 1416. Children under 18 may not apply for naturalization.

[67] INA, s. 242; 8 USC s. 1252. BIA appeals must be filed within 30 days of the final removal hearing. With the filing of the appeal, the child is granted a stay of removal. If further judicial review is sought, the child must seek a 'stay' of removal while the federal judicial review is pending.

[68] B.A. Carr, 'Incorporating a "Best Interest of the Child" Approach into Immigration Law and Procedure' (2009) 12 *Yale Human Rights and Development Law Journal* 120, at 130. See also Women's Commission for Refugee Women and Children, *Prison Guard or Parent?: INS Treatment of Unaccompanied Refugee Children* (2002), p. 5, available at www.womenscommission.org/pdf/ins_det.pdf>; see also *Salameda* v. *INS*, 70 F.3d 447, 451 (7th Cir. 1995) ('In order to economize on its limited resources, the INS usually does not bother to institute a formal deportation proceeding against an alien who is likely to depart anyway, such as the minor child of parents who are being deported.').

6. SPECIAL IMMIGRANT JUVENILE STATUS: A REMEDY FRUSTRATED BY PROCESS AND LACK OF ACCESS TO COUNSEL

The United States has traditionally delegated all family law and child custody decisions to State authorities. Accordingly, immigrant children straddle a difficult legal line, trapped in the federal authority to make decisions about their deportation and needing the State's power to make decisions for their care and custody. As is explored in David Thronson's discussion of protections for immigrant youth,[69] the US statutes create a bifurcated process that authorizes a child to secure lawful resident status as a special immigrant juvenile provided a State court with power to make care and custody determinations has made specific required findings. In reality, almost all migrant children will need to have a legal guardian or a clear determination of parental custody for permanency planning and integration purposes. As many of the children are living in households with undocumented parents or with families divided across borders, the State court guardianship or custody proceedings may be essential for that child to efficiently and appropriately access insurance benefits, school registration, and related other protections necessary for their long-term health and stability.

Unlike the immigration proceeding, where the federal government initiated the proceeding and the young person is automatically placed into an administrative court proceeding, the child has no direct way to access the family court in the US State where he or she resides. In most States, an adult or a State or local agency must initiate a proceeding and the child is the 'subject' of the proceeding. For example, a parent might bring an action to gain custody over a child and would name the child's other parent as a respondent.[70]

Children in federal detention have almost no ability to access the family court unless an advocate locates them within the detention center and can find a guardian or parent who is willing to seek a custodial determination. In these cases, the family court can only act if DHS consents to the family court proceeding. The conditions of release instruct the parent or other responsible adult to seek a family court guardianship in the appropriate State court. Sponsors are not instructed how to find assistance nor directed to the process in the family court for formal appointment.[71]

---

[69] See David Thronson, Chapter 13. The statute is INA, s. 101(a)(27)(J); 8 USC s. 1101(a)(27)(J).

[70] Custody determinations do meet the immigration law requirement that the child is 'dependent on the family court'.

[71] State procedures vary widely. In some States there is no 'guardianship'

In a few States, it is possible for the child to self-petition and to initiate a proceeding in the family court that will satisfy the requirements of the special immigrant juvenile status findings specified in the federal immigration law.[72] One example is found in Texas, where children have been able to petition to have a guardian or custodian named and the court appoints family law counsel to assist the child in meeting the requirements of service and the development of the factual record.[73]

While some States appoint counsel for children, that appointment is not made until a petition is pending before the court. The obstacles to filing create a significant process barrier. If a child must seek the family court jurisdiction and he or she has no attorney who can help them navigate the web of laws, procedures and rules, the child is unlikely to successfully complete the family court proceeding. If they cannot navigate the State system, they are vulnerable but they also may have lost the opportunity to secure the special immigrant juvenile status defined in the immigration laws.

In 2016, even success in the family court and a filing of a petition for special immigrant juvenile status did not necessarily end the removal proceedings. Congress has limited this special protective visa to a total of 10,000 immigrants annually and no country may exceed more than 7 percent of that total.[74] Accordingly, due to the high volume of applications, there are now multi-year waits for children from Central America, Mexico or India. DHS rarely agrees to a termination of the proceedings when the young person is waiting in this backlog. While the government

---

process but instead adults must seek custody as a parent or a third party grant of custody. See, e.g., North Carolina statutes that do not use a 'guardianship' concept but define only third party custody, available at www.ncga.state.nc.us/EnactedLegislation/Statutes/HTML/BySection/Chapter_50/GS_50-13.2.html. The lack of clear guidance and direction for the parents and sponsors is a significant gap in helping the children secure permanency and integration. Worse still, in some family courts where natural parents have petitioned for custody and special immigrant juvenile findings, the family court clerk's office rejects the filings of the petitioning parent or guardian on the ground that the child doesn't need an order of custody or guardianship. For a report describing a survey of attorneys and the problems with access, see www.fordham.edu/download/downloads/id/3019/findings_from_a_survey_of_lawyers_representing_immigrant_youth_eligible_for_special_immigrant_juvenile_status_in_nys_family_court.pdf.

72 INA, s. 101(a)(27)(J); 8 USC s. 1101(a)(27)(J).

73 Texas FAM, s. 102.003, 'Standing to File Suit', available at http://codes.findlaw.com/tx/family-code/fam-sect-102-003.html.

74 See INA, s. 203(b)(4); 8 USC s. 1203(b)(4). The waiting periods are published monthly by the US Department of State in its Visa Bulletin, available at https://travel.state.gov/content/visas/en/law-and-policy/bulletin.html.

may not vigorously seek deportation, the proceedings are only temporarily suspended.

7. ACCESS TO LEGAL INFORMATION AND REPRESENTATION

7.1 Know Your Rights and Legal Orientation Programs

The existing regulations and court procedures instruct Immigration Judges to advise every child that he or she has the right to have counsel, but the government will not pay for the representation. The judges provide the youth with a copy of the local list of low cost or free providers.[75]

In the past 10 years, a small office, the Office of Legal Access Programs (OLAP), within the EOIR has tried to improve efficiency and to help to identify victims of trafficking by offering 'legal orientation programs'.[76] This Office has funded nonprofit organizations to enter into juvenile detention facilities and to staff a hotline for children's sponsors upon release. The programs are not funded to provide direct legal representation. In 2014, OLAP established a few representation programs and funded legal assistance for a small number of children.[77]

---

[75] The list of free providers is available on the EOIR website. Many of the listed organizations will not accept cases of people in detention and are oversubscribed so that it is very possible that none of the organizations will accept representation of a child who called. See www.justice.gov/eoir/new-york-city-immigration-court for a list of providers and more information.

[76] US Department of Justice, Executive Office for Immigration Review, *Office of Legal Access Programs* (17 May 2017), available at www.justice.gov/eoir/office-of-legal-access-programs. In the spring of 2018, the Department of Justice announced the suspension of the legal orientation program, and then two weeks later reversed its course and opted to temporarily continue the program. See J. Breisblatt, 'Justice Department Will Not Halt Legal Orientation Program for Detained Immigrants, Reversing Course for Now', *American Immigration Council Immigration Impact,* 25 April 2018.

[77] See, e.g., US Department of Justice, Executive Office for Immigration Review, *Baltimore Representation Initiative for Unaccompanied Children (BRIUC)* (16 November 2016), available at www.justice.gov/eoir/baltimore-representation-initiative-unaccompanied-children-briuc. Another novel program was the 2015 creation of the Justice AmeriCorps. The government appropriated approximately US$1 million annually to provide seed grants to qualified hosting nonprofit organizations who hired 'fellows' to represent unaccompanied children younger than age 16. The goal of these pilot projects was to measure the ability of the programs to increase efficiency in the courts and to study the impact of representation for a particularly vulnerable population. The Trump Administration has proposed defunding all AmeriCorps

7.2 Right to Counsel

While children in State court juvenile proceedings are entitled to the appointment of free legal representation, to date, no court has ordered that a child is entitled to free counsel in removal proceedings.[78] The US constitutional guarantee of 'due process' of law is not, by its language, limited to citizens.[79] In July 2014, a coalition of civil rights and nonprofit organizations filed suit on behalf of a proposed class action of unaccompanied juveniles and asserted that the federal government was denying the children a fair hearing because no free attorney was appointed to represent the children.[80] The legal argument built upon the US constitutional law that provides counsel to indigent defendants in criminal cases and has provided counsel to indigent civil respondents where life or liberty was threatened. As of this writing, the class action litigation is stalled, as an appellate court ruled the issue could only be presented after a child had presented the issue in a removal hearing and preserved the issue in agency appeals and through statutory review, as required in the controlling statutes.[81]

A significant number of children appear in Immigration Court without any counsel. While most Immigration Judges will grant a continuance so that the child can try to find representation, the court is not obligated to grant these continuances.[82] As of January 2017, 42 percent of all pending

---

programs. There are no published reports about the program's overall effectiveness. The Vera Institute is expected to release a report, see www.vera.org/projects/evaluation-of-justice-americorps-legal-services-for-unaccompanied-children-program/learn-more.

[78] *In re Gault*, 387 US 1 (1967) (requiring appointed counsel before the State can restrict a juvenile's liberty).

[79] US Constitution, Amendment V.

[80] *JEFM* v. *Holder*, No. 2:14-cv-01026-TSZ, 2015 WL 9839679 (WD Wash. 13 April 2015). The trial court initially refused to certify the full class but eventually certified a group of children seeking asylum protection. Some of the parties changed and the case was renamed *FLB* v. *Lynch*, 2016 US Dist. LEXIS 82653 (WD Wash. 24 June 2016, No. C14-1026 TSZ).

[81] See *JEFM* v. *Lynch*, 837 F.3d 1026 (9th Cir. 2016). While the court found the children likely did have a constitutional claim, it found that Congress had curtailed direct class action challenges in the statute. See INA, s. 242; 8 USC s. 1252. The parties filed a petition for rehearing in December 2016.

[82] It is important to note that in April 2018, the Department of Justice imposed case completion quotas on Immigration Judges tied to their annual performance reviews. This raises concerns that Immigration Judges potentially will refuse continuances in an effort to push through cases to meet these metrics. See N. Miroff, 'Trump administration, seeking to speed deportations, to impose quotas on immigration judges', *Washington Post*, 2 April 2018.

juvenile cases, over 31,000 children, lack representation.[83] The released data appear to indicate that unrepresented children are able to secure relief only 4 percent of the time.[84] To date no legislative remedy has been able to secure sufficient support for adoption.[85]

7.3 Competence of Counsel

One of the continuing challenges within the US system is that the skills and substantive knowledge required to adequately represent children cut across different specialties. Children in immigration removal proceedings need counsel well versed and familiar with the procedures and substantive protections inherent in that system of law.[86] However, equally important is the need for counsel familiar with the State law governing the protection of children and the rules governing the State's power to make permanency and custody arrangements. At the current time in the United States, many States provide children with free appointed counsel but only in proceedings where the State began a proceeding that might remove the child from the care and custody of his or her natural family. Moreover, many of the experienced family law counsel within these systems have tended to ignore the immigration status of the children in family court proceedings. In a sense, this has been a benevolent ignorance, as citizenship is rarely a determinative factor in custody cases.

---

[83] See TRAC, above n. 5.

[84] See above n. 2.

[85] Vulnerable Immigrant Voice Act, HR 1700, introduced in 2015–2016 Congress, available at www.congress.gov/bill/114th-congress/house-bill/1700. This Bill has not been reintroduced in the 2017 Congressional session.

[86] In 2010, the Supreme Court found that the failure to adequately advise a non-citizen of the direct immigration consequences of a conviction meant that the defense counsel had performed inadequately and that failure could be a basis for vacating the underlying conviction. *Padilla* v. *Kentucky*, 559 US 356 (2010). The opinion points out that the entire criminal justice system, not just defense counsel, has an obligation to make sure that the defendant is adequately informed. Accordingly, many criminal law prosecutors and judges are now building a more detailed factual record to demonstrate that the non-citizen is informed about the immigration consequences before any plea agreement. This concept needs to be extended to family and juvenile courts to ensure adequate protection of migrant children's rights. Ignoring a child's citizenship status could be missing an opportunity to assist the child in securing protective status.

8. CONCLUSION: PROCESS CAN SHAPE OUTCOMES

It is difficult to separate the process protections from the statutory substantive protections for youth. Certainly, US law offers a number of varied protections for youth who entered the United States with or without visa documentation. However robust these protections, the complexity of the procedures, and the multitude of agencies a child must navigate in order to benefit from these protections, can be insurmountable. This suggests that the process alone may be one of the single worst barriers to child protection.[87]

If children inside the United States and those apprehended at the border were given appointed counsel to provide them with both orientation and robust representation, the US would be able to protect and integrate many migrant children. Unfortunately, the US is using a removal hearing process without adequate representation and resources, making the promise of protection illusory.

[87] See generally C. Thomas and L. Benson, 'Caught in the Web: Immigrant Children in Removal Proceedings', paper presented at NYLS Impact Seminar on Access to Justice, July 2016, available at http://digitalcommons.nyls.edu/cgi/viewcontent.cgi?article=1015&context=impact_center.

18. Asylum-seeking children and the Australian protection visa process

Savitri Taylor*

1. INTRODUCTION

The principal domestic mechanism through which Australia gives effect to its protection obligations under the UN Convention relating to the Status of Refugees ('Refugee Convention'),[1] and under other human rights treaties is the protection visa.[2] This chapter describes the procedural treatment of asylum-seeking children in Australia and considers whether it is compliant with Australia's obligations under key provisions of the Convention on the Rights of the Child (CRC).[3] While Evenhuis recently undertook a similar project, his work focused on separated children,[4] and has been overtaken by events in some significant respects.[5] This

* The author would like to thank Kate Bones, Mary Anne Kenny, David Manne and Lucy Morgan for their assistance with this chapter. All views and errors are, of course, those of the author alone. The law stated in this chapter was current as at September 2016.

1 Convention relating to the Status of Refugees, opened for signature 28 July 1951, 189 UNTS 137 (entered into force 22 April 1954) as modified by the Protocol relating to the Status of Refugees, opened for signature 31 January 1967, 606 UNTS 267 (entered into force 4 October 1967) ('Refugee Convention').

2 Migration Act 1958 (Cth) (Austl), ss. 35A and 36.

3 Convention on the Rights of the Child, GA Res. 44/25, UN Doc. A/RES/44/25 (20 November 1989), adopted 20 November 1989, 1577 UNTS 3 (entered into force 2 September 1990) (CRC).

4 The Committee on the Rights of the Child defines a 'separated child' as a person under the age of 18 who is 'separated from both parents, or from their previous legal or customary primary care giver, but not necessarily from other relatives'. See Committee on the Rights of the Child, *General Comment No. 6 on Treatment of Unaccompanied and Separated Children Outside Their Country of Origin*, UN Doc. CRC/GC/2005/6 (1 September 2005), para. [8].

5 M. Evenhuis, 'Child-Proofing Asylum: Separated Children and Refugee Decision Making in Australia' (2013) 25(3) *International Journal of Refugee Law* 535.

chapter adds to the existing literature by examining the treatment of all asylum-seeking children and by focusing on legislative and policy changes in 2014 and 2015 affecting procedural rights at the primary and merits review stage of the protection visa application process.

2. RECEPTION AND DETENTION

The treatment of asylum-seekers in Australia differs according to their date of arrival, their manner of arrival, their immigration status upon entry and subsequently, and the manner in which they come into contact with Australian authorities.

2.1 Authorized Arrivals

An authorized arrival holding a valid substantive visa at the time of making a protection visa application will usually be granted a bridging visa that enables them to live freely in the community until their protection visa application is determined. Authorized arrivals who no longer have a visa that is in force must be detained in the first instance.[6] However, they must be advised of the options available to them, including their ability to apply for a visa within seven working days, if notification of intent to apply is made within two working days.[7] Even after the expiry of this time limit, they continue to be able to apply for a protection visa,[8] and will usually be granted a bridging visa enabling them to live freely in the community pending determination of the protection visa application.

2.2 Unauthorized Arrivals

'Unauthorized arrivals' are non-citizens who enter Australia without a visa or other prior permission. Unauthorized arrivals presenting at airports and seaports must be detained. Although not advised of their rights,[9] they are given brief screening interviews for the purpose of identifying *prima facie* protection claims.[10] Supposedly, case by case

---

6 Migration Act, s. 189.

7 *Ibid.* ss 194 and 195(1).

8 *Ibid.* s. 195(2).

9 *Ibid.* ss. 189 and 193.

10 DIBP, *PAM3 – Refugee and Humanitarian – Protection Visas – All Applications – Common Processing Guidelines*, stack date 10 September 2016, available at https://legend.online.immi.gov.au/Pages/Welcome.aspx.

consideration is given to exempting individuals from the screening process because of vulnerabilities such as disability or age, but neither children nor unaccompanied children are exempt as categories.[11] Those who are subject to the screening process are given an opportunity to seek legal assistance upon request,[12] but not otherwise. No provision is made for independent merits review in the event that an individual is 'screened out'. Where practicable, they are returned to their most recent country of departure. The lack of minimum procedural safeguards gives rise to a high risk of refoulement.[13]

Unauthorized air arrivals who are screened in are usually admitted to the protection visa application process. Unauthorized maritime arrivals (UMAs)[14] with *prima facie* protection claims face another hurdle. An UMA detained in Australia's migration zone 'must, as soon as reasonably practicable' be taken from Australia to a regional processing country.[15] This occurs unless the regional processing countries have advised in writing that they will not accept the UMA or the Minister for Immigration exercises a personal and non-compellable power to exempt the UMA from transfer.[16] The Minister has indicated that UMAs arriving on or after 19 July 2013 will only be considered for exemption in two situations.[17] The

---

11 DIBP, *Answer to Question BE13/0117 Taken on Notice at Budget Estimates Hearing 27–28 May 2013*, available at www.aph.gov.au/~/media/Estimates/Live/legcon_ctte/estimates/bud_1314/diac/BE13-0117.ashx. In fact, unaccompanied children have been subjected to the screening process and at least two have been screened out and repatriated: Australian Human Rights Commission (AHRC), *Asylum Seekers, Refugees and Human Rights: Snapshot Report* (2013), p. 14.

12 Migration Act, s. 256.

13 AHRC, *Asylum Seekers, Refugees and Human Rights*, above n. 11, at 13–14.

14 A person is classified as an UMA if they enter Australia by sea and without a valid visa at an 'excised offshore place' or, if after 1 June 2013, at any other place: Migration Act, s. 5AA(1). A person is also classified as an UMA, if born in Australia's migration zone or in a regional processing country to an UMA parent, unless the person is an Australian citizen at birth through their other parent: *ibid.* s. 5AA(1A) and (1AA).

15 Nauru and Papua New Guinea (PNG) have been designated as regional processing countries for the purposes of the Migration Act. Australia's 'migration zone' is the physical area where the Migration Act operates, as explained further below.

16 Migration Act, ss. 198AD, 198AE and 198AG.

17 On 19 July 2013, the then Prime Ministers of Australia and PNG announced that not only would UMAs arriving after that date be subject to the regional processing arrangements, but, if found to be refugees, they would be resettled in PNG or another country but not Australia: Kevin Rudd and Peter O'Neill, *Transcript of Joint Press Conference* (19 July 2013), available at http://pandora.nla.gov.

first situation is where they have made credible claims that they would face persecution or a real risk of serious human rights violations in the regional processing countries. The second situation is where 'independently of any circumstances pertaining to any individual person', the Department of Immigration and Border Protection (DIBP) considers 'that it will not be reasonably practicable to take certain classes of unauthorised maritime arrivals to any regional processing country in the foreseeable future'.[18] In the case of unaccompanied child UMAs who arrived between 12 August 2012 and 19 July 2013,[19] the Minister will also consider exemption on the basis that the best interests of the child require it, as long as that consideration is not outweighed by other considerations.[20]

Despite these regional processing arrangements, Australia was, at the time of writing, hosting a large cohort of UMAs who had not in fact been removed to a regional processing centre. The so-called 'legacy caseload' of about 30,500 UMAs,[21] included 173 unaccompanied and 4,087 other children.[22] As explored below, the Migration and Maritime Powers Legislation Amendment (Resolving the Asylum Legacy Caseload) Act 2014 (Cth) created a fast track process to deal with the bulk of these cases.[23] The DIBP estimates that it will take until the end of 2018 to work through the caseload.[24]

UMAs who are physically present in Australia have no right at law to apply for any kind of visa. Rather, the Minister for Immigration has a broad discretion to allow UMAs to apply. More precisely, a visa application by an UMA in Australia is invalid unless the Minister for Immigration exercises a personal and non-compellable power to 'lift the

---

au/pan/79983/20130731-0937/www.pm.gov.au/press-office/transcript-joint-press-conference-2.html.

18 DIBP, *PAM3 – Refugee and Humanitarian – Regional Processing – Minister's s198AE Guidelines*, stack date 1 July 2016, paras [21], [23], available at https://legend.online.immi.gov.au/Pages/Welcome.aspx.

19 Regional processing was (re)introduced by the then Labor government on 13 August 2012.

20 DIBP, *Minister's s198AE Guidelines*, above n. 18, para. [22].

21 Senate Legal and Constitutional Legislation Committee (SLCALC), *Official Committee Hansard (Estimates)* (25 May 2015), p. 67.

22 SLCALC, *Official Committee Hansard (Estimates)* (26 May 2015), pp. 28, 36.

23 About 6,000 UMAs in the 'legacy caseload' arrived in Australia prior to 13 August 2012 and were permitted to make protection visa applications by the previous Labor government. This group is not subject to the fast track process but its members have been denied eligibility retrospectively for grant of a permanent (as opposed to a temporary) protection visa.

24 SLCALC, *Official Committee Hansard (Estimates)* (25 May 2015), p. 67.

bar'.[25] In practice, a policy decision has been made to allow applications from UMAs who are subject to the fast track process. While processing occurs generally according to order of arrival, DIBP has indicated those with special vulnerabilities, such as unaccompanied minors[26] and families in immigration detention, will be given priority.[27] UMAs are given 60 days from the lifting of the bar to submit a protection visa application with all supporting documentation.[28]

The circumstances in which unauthorized arrivals are eligible for a bridging visa are highly circumscribed. In most cases, a bridging visa can only be granted through Ministerial intervention.[29] At the same time, however, the legislation specifies that minors are to be detained only as a measure of last resort.[30] Hence, the policy preference is to grant bridging visas in order to keep unaccompanied children or families with children out of detention. Where the grant of a bridging visa is not considered appropriate for whatever reason, the Minister can make a residence determination.[31] A person who is subject to a residence determination must live at a designated address and report regularly to the Immigration Department. Although technically they continue to be in immigration detention, they are free to move about in the community.

3. GUARDIANSHIP OF UNACCOMPANIED MINORS

The Minister for Immigration is the guardian of any non-citizen child who has entered Australia with the intention of becoming a permanent resident, unless that child has entered in the charge of, or will be living

---

25 Migration Act, s. 46A. This version of the statutory bar was first introduced in 2013 though it has been tweaked since. It replaced a version in operation since September 2001 which applied to non-citizens entering Australia without a visa at an 'excised offshore place', namely any of the Australian islands and reefs 'excised' from Australia's 'migration zone' (as defined).

26 For immigration purposes, an unaccompanied minor is a non-citizen under the age of 18 years who is in Australia without a parent or relative aged 21 years or over: DIBP, *Common Processing Guidelines*, above n. 10.

27 SLCALC, *Official Committee Hansard (Estimates)* (25 May 2015), p. 66.

28 MA. Kenny, N. Procter and C. Grech, 'Mental Health and Legal Representation for Asylum Seekers in the "Legacy Caseload"' (2016) 8(2) *Cosmopolitan Civil Societies* 84.

29 Migration Act, s. 195A.

30 *Ibid.* s. 4AAA.

31 *Ibid.* s. 197AB.

in the care of, a relative not less than 21 years old.[32] The Minister's functions and powers as guardian can be and usually are delegated to Commonwealth or state officials whose main role is to ensure that the child's basic needs are met.[33] The delegated guardian can in turn place the minor with a custodian who provides day-to-day care.[34] The Minister's guardianship ends upon the child turning 18 or leaving Australia permanently.[35]

The Minister's obligation as guardian is to act in the best interests of the child.[36] At the same time, however, the Immigration (Guardianship of Children) (IGOC) Act, section 8 expressly provides that nothing in it affects the operation of migration law or the performance or exercise of any function, duty or power under the Migration Act or related legislation. DIBP's *Procedures Advice Manual* acknowledges the potential conflict of interest and instructs delegated guardians to take 'reasonable steps' to resolve any conflict that arises, for example, by providing the minor with access to independent advice and support.[37]

4. PROTECTION VISA APPLICATION PROCESS

4.1 Primary Stage

The Minister is able to deal with visa applications in any order that the Minister thinks fit.[38] Processing priority is given to protection visa applications from people with special vulnerabilities such as unaccompanied minors.[39]

Primary stage decision-making is conducted by DIBP officers acting as delegates of the Minister for Immigration. The relevant DIBP guidelines state that in most cases an interview is the most effective way of proceeding. An interview must be offered where the applicant is a 'fast track applicant' (see below) or where the decision-maker is minded to reject the application

---

32 Immigration (Guardianship of Children) (IGOC) Act 1946 (Cth) (Austl), ss. 4AAA and 6.

33 IGOC Act, s. 5.

34 DIBP, *PAM3 – Migration Regulations – Other – PAM – Guardianship of Minors under the IGOC Act*, stack date 10 September 2016, available at https://legend.online.immi.gov.au/Pages/Welcome.aspx.

35 IGOC Act, s. 6.

36 DIBP, *Guardianship of Minors*, above n. 34.

37 *Ibid.*

38 Migration Act, s. 51.

39 DIBP, *Common Processing Guidelines*, above n. 10.

solely on the basis of credibility.[40] Where more than one person in a family unit has made protection claims, the decision-maker has a discretion to interview the applicants separately or together as they think appropriate having regard to factors such as the nature of claims, gender and age.[41]

Applicants can choose to have a representative and/or support person present at the interview. With limited exceptions, only a registered migration agent can act as representative. One such exception is that a child can be represented by a parent or guardian. Anyone can be a support person, but a support person is not entitled to take an active part in proceedings. With unaccompanied minors, it is DIBP policy to have an independent observer, namely a suitably qualified adult engaged by DIBP, present at any interview with DIBP or other government agency to provide support and to ensure appropriate treatment.[42]

DIBP's *Procedures Advice Manual* contains guidelines on interviewing minors.[43] While the guidelines contemplate a situation in which a minor (whether accompanied or unaccompanied) has submitted a protection visa application in their own right, the procedures they outline are described as 'also useful for children's cases in general'. The guidelines state that children making protection claims in their own right should be interviewed by experienced decision-makers and 'if possible, by decision makers who have knowledge regarding the psychological and emotional development of children'. They also deal with how to conduct a hearing, focusing in particular on child sensitive questioning techniques. Whether these guidelines are complied with in practice is a different matter. The available case law suggests that Australian officials do not always get it right.

Interviewing young children is not easy. Where children are part of a family group, there is a temptation to focus on eliciting information about the child's claims through interviews with other family members. *AZAEF* was a case in which the six-year-old appellant's 19-year-old half-brother had made a Protection Obligation Determination request on both their behalves.[44] On 2 May 2012, an Independent Protection

---

40 *Ibid.*

41 *Ibid.*

42 DIBP, *Operations Manual for Service Providers under the IAAAS Version 7* (7 June 2016), Attachment G.

43 DIBP, *Common Processing Guidelines*, above n. 10.

44 *AZAEF (by her litigation guardian Charman)* v. *Minister for Immigration and Border Protection* [2016] FCAFC 3. The appellant and her half-brother had entered Australia without authorization at an excised offshore place on 10 May 2011. They were therefore subject to the non-statutory Protection Obligations Determination Framework then in place.

Assessor interviewed the appellant and her half-brother in the presence of a migration agent and an independent observer. While the Assessor asked the appellant some questions, the bulk of the interview was with her half-brother. The Assessor rejected some parts of the half-brother's evidence on credibility grounds and found that neither he nor the appellant were owed protection obligations by Australia. The case ended up in the Full Federal Court of Australia. The majority held that the appellant had been denied procedural fairness because the Assessor had not given the appellant, or her migration agent or legal guardian (a delegate of the Minister) on her behalf, notice of, and an opportunity to comment on, the Assessor's disbelief of her half-brother's evidence as it pertained to her own claims for protection. In particular, White J, in the majority, noted that the law had considerable experience of reliable information being elicited from young children in other contexts and did not accept that 'the perfunctory questioning by the IP Assessor at the interview on 2 May 2012 exhausted the information which could be provided by the appellant'.

4.2 Standard Merits Review

Protection visa applicants who are refused at primary stage are able to apply for merits review by the Administrative Appeals Tribunal Migration and Refugee Division (AAT MRD) under Part 7 of the Migration Act. Exceptions apply in several circumstances. Other appeal structures apply for refusals made on the basis of an adverse security assessment by the Australian Security Intelligence Organisation (ASIO);[45] where a claimant is otherwise deemed unworthy of protection under provisions which are similar in content to Refugee Convention, Articles 1F and 33(2);[46] or where the refusal is made on character grounds under Migration Act, section 501.[47] Separate regimes operate also where the refusal falls within the definition of a 'fast track decision' (see below); or where the Minister has issued a conclusive certificate in respect of the refusal.[48] Assuming that a decision is Part 7 reviewable, an application for review must be lodged within seven working days after notification of the primary stage decision, if the applicant is in immigration detention, and within 28 days after notification in any other case.[49] The Tribunal does not have power to

45 Migration Act, s. 36(1B).

46 A decision to refuse a protection visa on the basis of Migration Act, ss. 5H(2), 36(1C) or 36(2C) is reviewable by the AAT's General Division: *ibid.* s. 500.

47 *Ibid.* s. 500.

48 *Ibid.* s. 411.

49 *Ibid.* s. 412(1)(b) and Migration Regulations (Cth), reg. 4.31(1), (2).

consider applications lodged out of time. Working out the exact mechanics of making an application for review and what issues to address in the application are hurdles not easily overcome by asylum-seekers who do not have the assistance of a competent adviser. Overcoming the hurdles could well take longer than the period allowed for lodgment of an application for review, resulting in complete denial of the opportunity for review.

The AAT MRD is able to affirm or vary the primary decision or set it aside and substitute its own decision or remit the matter to DIBP for reconsideration in accordance with its directions or recommendations.[50] When reviewing a decision under Part 7, the AAT MRD is, for the most part, able to exercise all of the powers and discretions of the primary decision-maker.[51] However, with the entry into force of the Migration Amendment (Protection and Other Measures) Act 2015 (Cth) ('POM Act'), where an applicant first raises a claim or presents evidence at review and does not have a 'reasonable explanation' for failing to do so earlier, the AAT MRD is required to draw an adverse inference about the credibility of that claim or evidence.[52] According to the government, section 423A is directed at weeding out non-genuine claimants seeking to prolong their stay in Australia by raising new claims at the review stage after having their original claims rejected at primary stage.[53] However, the Parliamentary Joint Committee on Human Rights (PJCHR) pointed out that circumstances ranging from post-traumatic stress disorder to a lack of understanding of legal criteria might result in genuine applicants failing to raise claims or present evidence as early as section 423A required and took the view that the provision did not adequately safeguard against refoulement.[54]

The AAT MRD is not bound by technical rules of evidence but is required to 'act in a way that is fair and just'.[55] Beyond this, the AAT MRD has guidelines on dealing with vulnerable persons which explicitly recognize children as falling into this category.[56] The guidelines suggest

---

[50] Migration Act, s. 415 and Migration Regulations, reg. 4.33.

[51] Migration Act, s. 415.

[52] Migration Act, s. 423A.

[53] Scott Morrison, Migration Amendment (Protection and Other Measures) Bill 2014 (Second Reading Speech), 25 June 2014.

[54] Parliamentary Joint Committee on Human Rights (PJCHR), *Ninth Report of the 44th Parliament* (15 July 2014), paras [1.196]–[1.199].

[55] Migration Act, ss. 420 and 422B(3).

[56] AAT, *Migration and Refugee Division Guidelines on Vulnerable Persons* (July 2015), paras [7]–[8], available at www.aat.gov.au/AAT/media/AAT/Files/MRD%20documents/Legislation%20Policies%20Guidelines/Guidelines-on-Vulnerable-Persons.pdf.

that it may be appropriate in cases involving vulnerable persons for the tribunal to be constituted by a Member with relevant special knowledge or experience (paragraph 16) and also that Members consider whether 'particular procedural arrangements or additional representation or support are desirable in an individual case' (paragraph 19). The AAT MRD must invite an applicant to appear before it to give evidence and present arguments relating to the issues arising at review, unless it is able to make a decision favourable to the applicant on the papers, or the applicant consents to review on the papers, or the applicant is uncooperative.[57] Where members of the same family have made separate review applications,[58] the AAT MRD will 'where practicable and appropriate' seek to conduct a joint hearing nevertheless, provided it obtains the consent of all applicants.[59] Members are provided with guidance on conducting a hearing involving a minor which is similar to the guidance on interviewing minors provided to DIBP decision-makers.[60]

Any applicant can choose to have a support person and/or representative present at their AAT MRD hearing. As at primary stage, the usual rule is that a representative must be a registered migration agent, but a child can be represented by a parent or guardian. In *WZAOT*,[61] the protection visa applicant was a very young child. It was argued that the Refugee Review Tribunal (RRT), the predecessor to the AAT MRD, fell into jurisdictional error by failing to consider whether the circumstances of the case, including the best interests of the child, required the applicant to be represented by an independent person rather than either her mother or the migration agent appointed by her mother. Barker J held that there was no automatic obligation for the Tribunal to appoint an independent representative. The question was whether it was open to the Tribunal to consider that it could meet its statutory obligations to give the applicant a hearing and to act in a just and fair way by allowing the mother and the migration agent appointed by the

---

57 Migration Act, s. 425.

58 Members of the same family can opt to make separate review applications, if they are presenting separate claims. This option remains open even after an initial choice to make a joint application: AAT, *President's Direction: Conducting Migration and Refugee Reviews* (30 June 2015), para. [4.2], available at www.aat.gov.au/AAT/media/AAT/Files/MRD%20documents/Legislation%20Policies%20Guidelines/Presidents-Direction-Conducting-Migration-and-Refugee-Reviews.pdf.

59 *Ibid.* para. [4].

60 *Ibid.* para. [5.3]; AAT, *Guidelines on Vulnerable Persons*, above n. 56, paras [46]–[48], [66].

61 *WZAOT* v. *Minister for Immigration and Citizenship* [2013] FCA 136.

mother to represent the child. A possible further question was whether the hearing might have ceased to be conducted in a just and fair way because of a conflict of interest with the applicant which emerged in the course of such representation. Barker J agreed with the lower court that the mother was 'uniquely placed' to make submissions on behalf of the child and that there was a 'confluence and not a conflict of interest' between the mother and child. Moreover, according to Barker J, it was clear that the migration agent understood that they were representing the interest of the child alone and did so.

In *MZAHU*,[62] the second appellant, who was born in Australia in November 2009, was included as a family member in a protection visa application made by her mother, the first appellant, in March 2014. The first appellant's protection visa application, and hence the second appellant's also, was refused by DIBP in May 2014. That decision was affirmed by the RRT in June 2014. Upon application for judicial review by the Federal Court, it was argued that the RRT had denied the second appellant procedural fairness by not requiring that she be separately represented. Buchanan J held that *WZAOT* was distinguishable on the basis that it dealt with a protection visa application made on behalf of a child in her own right. He noted that, in any event, the argument based on lack of separate representation had been unsuccessful in that case. Buchanan J likewise rejected the argument based on lack of separate representation in the case before him. He held that there was no conflict of interest between the mother and child, noting that 'the notion that [the mother] should not speak for her child should not be encouraged'.

The problem with taking such a stance is that it is not only in cases of conflict of interest that a child may be better served by separate representation. Bridgette Carr illustrates this point well using the hypothetical example of an asylum-seeking mother and her child where the latter would be at risk of female genital mutilation (FGM) if repatriated.[63] The worst case variant on this scenario, of course, is one in which the mother supports FGM and intends that her child will undergo it. In such a scenario, where the parent and child have conflicting interests, there is no likelihood of the separate claim that the child could make surfacing in the asylum proceedings unless the child is separately represented. The best case vari-

---

[62] *MZAHU* v. *Minister for Immigration and Border Protection* [2016] FCA 537.

[63] B. Carr, 'Incorporating a "Best Interests of the Child" Approach into Immigration Law and Procedure' (2009) 12 *Yale Human Rights and Development Law Journal* 120, at 129–32.

ant of the scenario is where the mother opposes FGM and puts forward a separate claim for her child based on that risk. It may well be the case, however, that the mother, though opposed to FGM, puts forward only her own protection claim because the possibility that her child might have a separate claim does not occur to her.[64] In this scenario, if the mother's claim fails, the child faces refoulement.

4.3 Fast Track Merits Review

As mentioned previously, the AAT MRD cannot review a 'fast track decision'. A 'fast track decision' is a decision to refuse to grant a protection visa to a 'fast track applicant', other than one made relying on Migration Act, section 36(1B) (adverse security assessment by ASIO) or section 501 (the character test), or on Migration Act provisions[65] which are similar in content to Refugee Convention, Articles 1F and 33(2).[66] A 'fast track applicant', as defined in the Migration Act, is a UMA who arrived in Australia between 13 August 2012 and 1 January 2014,[67] who has not been taken to a regional processing country.[68] The definition of 'fast track applicant' has been extended by legislative instrument to include specific groups of UMAs who do not quite fall within the primary definition but are regarded nonetheless as being part of the legacy caseload.[69]

The Immigration Assessment Authority (IAA), which is a separate office within the AAT,[70] is empowered to conduct merits review of a subset of 'fast track decisions' which fall within the definition of 'fast track reviewable decisions'. A fast track reviewable decision is automatically referred to the IAA without need for application.[71] The IAA can either affirm the decision or remit it to DIBP for reconsideration in

---

64 See also L. Ottosson and A. Lundberg, '"People Out of Place"? Advocates' Negotiations on Children's Participation in the Asylum Application Process in Sweden' (2013) 27(2) *International Journal of Law, Policy and the Family* 266.

65 Migration Act, ss. 5H(2) and 36(1C), (2C).

66 *Ibid.* s. 5(1). Some of these decisions are reviewable by the General Division of the AAT under Migration Act, s. 500.

67 This is the cut-off date specified by the Coalition government which took office in September 2013.

68 *Ibid.* s. 5(1)(a), (1AC). Note that exceptions are made for children born during this period to UMAs who arrived earlier. Such children acquire the rights and status of their parents.

69 Instrument IMM 16/008 (F2016L00456); Instrument IMM 16/010 (F2016L0 0377); Instrument IMMI 16/049 (F2016L00679).

70 Migration Act, s. 473JA.

71 *Ibid.* s. 473CA.

accordance with its directions or recommendations.[72] By contrast, a fast track decision which is not a fast track reviewable decision receives no merits review at all.

A 'fast track reviewable decision' is a 'fast track decision' (other than one in respect of which the Minister has issued a conclusive certificate) made in relation to a 'fast track review applicant' or determined by the Minister to be reviewable.[73] A 'fast track review applicant' is a 'fast track applicant who is not an excluded fast track applicant'.[74] Every recipient of a fast track decision is individually assessed against the 'excluded fast track applicant' criteria even if the application for a protection visa was made as part of a family group.[75] A person is an 'excluded fast track applicant', if, 'in the opinion of the Minister', they have access to protection elsewhere, or they have previously been refused protection by a state authority or the Office of the United Nations High Commissioner for Refugees (UNHCR) anywhere. Further, a person is an 'excluded fast track applicant' if they have presented 'without reasonable explanation' a 'bogus document' to DIBP or to the Minister in support of their application; or if they have made a 'manifestly unfounded claim' for protection.[76]

Assuming that the IAA is able to review a decision, in the usual case it is required to do so on the basis of material provided to it by DIBP without accepting or requesting new information and without interviewing the applicant.[77] The IAA can consider new information if it is satisfied that there are 'exceptional circumstances' to justify this. In the case of information provided by the applicant, the applicant must show that the information either could not have been provided prior to the making of the primary decision, or is 'credible personal information which was not previously known and, had it been known, may have affected' consideration of the applicant's claims.[78] The IAA may interview an applicant to obtain new information from them or to obtain their comment on new information that it intends to consider and which 'would be a reason for an adverse

---

[72] *Ibid.* s. 473CC.

[73] *Ibid.* s. 473BB.

[74] *Ibid.* s. 5(1). The Minister may by legislative instrument give an excluded fast track applicant, or class to which they belong, access to the IAA (*ibid.* s. 473BC), but to date has not done so.

[75] DIBP, *PAM3 – Refugee and Humanitarian – Protection Visas – The Temporary Protection and Fast Track Assessment Process*, stack date 19 May 2016, available at https://legend.online.immi.gov.au/Pages/Welcome.aspx.

[76] Migration Act, s. 5(1). The definition of 'excluded fast track applicant' can be, but has not yet been, extended by legislative instrument.

[77] *Ibid.* ss. 473CB and 473DB(1).

[78] *Ibid.* s. 473DD.

decision'.[79] The IAA has indicated that such interviews will generally be conducted by phone.[80] At the time of writing, the IAA had not released any guidelines for dealing with minors or other vulnerable people.

Access to independent merits review is a minimum procedural safeguard against incorrect decisions. Therefore, the denial of such review to excluded fast track applicants is arguably incompatible with Australia's non-refoulement obligations.[81] While merits review by the IAA is better than no merits review at all, it is clearly inferior to merits review by the AAT MRD. It is to be doubted whether IAA review is robust enough to safeguard against the refoulement of applicants incorrectly rejected at primary stage. While all protection visa applicants do have access to judicial review, such review concerns itself only with errors of law and cannot therefore be relied upon as a safeguard in cases where a decision is incorrect on the facts but not the law.

5. INTEGRITY MEASURES

The POM Act made other amendments to the Migration Act directed at improving 'integrity within the protection status determination process'.[82] Section 5AAA of the Migration Act now provides that it is the responsibility of 'a non-citizen who claims to be a person in respect of whom Australia has protection obligations' to specify 'all particulars' of their claim and to provide 'sufficient evidence to establish the claim' and emphasizes that the Minister 'does not have any responsibility or obligation' to assist in specifying the particulars of the claim or establishing the claim. Coming close to imposing a positive onus on asylum-seekers to prove their claims, the system is particularly harsh, if not potentially unreasonable, in its application to children. The legislation, however, seems to be consistent with the general interpretative trend adopted by the courts.

---

[79] *Ibid.* ss. 473DC and 473DE.

[80] IAA, *Practice Direction for Applicants, Representatives and Authorised Recipients* (21 April 2016), available at www.iaa.gov.au/IAA/media/IAA/Files/Practice%20Directions/Practice-Direction-1-Applicants-Representatives-and-Authorised-Recipients.pdf.

[81] PJCHR, *Fourteenth Report of the 44th Parliament* (28 October 2014), para. [1.412]. See also M.Crock and H. Martin, 'Refugee Rights and the Merits of Appeals' (2013) 32 *University of Queensland Law Journal* 137.

[82] Explanatory Memorandum, Migration Amendment (Protection and Other Measures) Bill 2014.

In *MZAHU,* the child appellant had not made separate protection claims but had relied on her status as a member of the first appellant's family. Similarly, in *WZARN*,[83] a case involving protection visa applications by an Iranian man, his wife and their children, there were possible claims on behalf of the children that were vaguely discernible from the evidence but not squarely made. Even though both cases were decided on the basis of the law as it stood prior to the passage of section 5AAA, it was held in both that the decision-maker was not obliged to consider protection claims which had neither been articulated by or on behalf of the child applicant nor could be said to arise clearly from the material before them.[84] It may be the case, therefore, that section 5AAA simply reinforces the stance already taken by the courts even in cases involving child applicants.

Section 91WA of the Migration Act, inserted by the POM Act, provides that the Minister must refuse to grant a protection visa to an applicant, if they have provided a 'bogus document' as evidence of their identity, nationality or citizenship or have destroyed or disposed of documentary evidence of the same. Section 91W gives the Minister power to request an applicant to produce documentary evidence of identity, nationality or citizenship. The section was amended by the POM Act to prevent a protection visa being granted to an applicant who fails to comply with such a request or produces a bogus document in response. In both cases, the visa grant prohibition does not apply where the Minister is satisfied that the applicant has a 'reasonable explanation' for their previous action and either provides the requisite documentary evidence or has taken 'reasonable steps' to provide it.[85]

In the Explanatory Memorandum to the POM Bill, the Australian government acknowledged that some vulnerable individuals, such as unaccompanied minors, might find it difficult to discharge the responsibilities imposed by its integrity measures. It noted that applicants are able to seek assistance from an independent migration agent, with government funding under IAAAS or PAIS where warranted (see further below), and stated that decision-makers would take applicant vulnerabilities into account. The government also expressed confidence that the prohibitions in sections 91W and 91WA would not result in refoulement because the Minister for Immigration is able to avert such an outcome through

---

83 *WZARN* v. *Minister for Immigration and Border Protection* [2013] FCA 1299.

84 Both judges relied on the Full Federal Court ruling in *NABE* v. *Minister for Immigration and Multicultural and Indigenous Affairs (No. 2)* (2004) 144 FCR 1.

85 Migration Act, ss. 91W(2)–(4) and 91WA(2), (3).

exercise of one of their personal, non-compellable powers to grant a visa.[86] Unsurprisingly, the PJCHR placed little faith in the efficacy of this supposed safeguard. It expressed the view that sections 91W and 91WA were likely to be incompatible with Australia's non-refoulement obligations.[87] In relation to section 5AAA, the committee noted that there were good reasons for UNHCR taking the position that decision-makers share responsibility with applicants for establishing protection claims. It did not accept that the safeguards identified by the government were adequate to prevent incorrect decisions leading to refoulement.[88]

6. REPEAT APPLICATION BAR

In 2014, the long-standing statutory bar on repeat applications for protection visas was reinforced by the addition of section 48A(1AA) to the Migration Act. This provision clarifies that the bar applies to individuals included as minor children in previous applications. This is so even where the applicant did not know about,[89] or did not understand the nature of, the earlier application. The Australian government claimed that the amendment was necessary to forestall a possible interpretation of the Act which would allow the parent of a minor to make repeated unmeritorious applications on the minor's behalf for the purpose of delaying removal from Australia; result in different immigration outcomes for different members of the same family unit; and impose upon DIBP the 'unreasonable administrative burden' of inquiring into a minor's state of knowledge and understanding in order to ascertain whether the statutory bar applied.[90] It argued that where a minor had protection claims of their own which were not raised in the previous application, breach of Australia's various non-refoulement obligations could be avoided through exercise of the Minister for Immigration's personal power to lift the statutory bar. Again, the PJCHR did not accept that the Minister's non-compellable section 48B power was an adequate safeguard against

---

86 Explanatory Memorandum, Migration Amendment (Protection and Other Measures) Bill 2014, Attachment A.

87 PJCHR, *Ninth Report*, above n. 54, paras [1.207]–[1.208].

88 *Ibid.* paras [1.173]–[1.178]; PJCHR, *Twelfth Report of the 44th Parliament* (24 September 2014), para. [1.93].

89 It is only if an applicant is aged 16 or above that their signature is required on a visa application submitted by a family group.

90 Explanatory Memorandum, Migration Legislation Amendment Bill (No. 1) 2014, Attachment A.

refoulement.[91] The amendment was nevertheless accepted by Parliament and passed into law.

7. ACCESS TO APPLICATION ADVICE AND ASSISTANCE

There is no prohibition on protection visa applicants receiving application advice and assistance from a suitably qualified person.[92] However, if they cannot afford to pay for such services, their options are limited. Those who entered Australia lawfully are eligible for independent advice and assistance from a registered migration agent under the government-funded Immigration Advice and Application Assistance Scheme (IAAAS), if they are in immigration detention or they have a reasonable prospect of being granted a visa and are suffering financial hardship, and are experiencing some additional disadvantage.[93] Unaccompanied minors for whom the Minister for Immigration is guardian under the IGOC Act (IGOC minors) generally qualify and are 'routinely referred for IAAAS services'.[94] IAAAS covers advice relating to the primary stage of the protection visa application process, assistance with completing and lodging the application, and attendance at the visa interview.[95] With effect from 31 March 2014, only IGOC minors are eligible to access IAAAS services for the merits review stage.[96] At the merits review stage, IAAAS covers assistance with completing and lodging the review application, representation at the AAT hearing, and related advice.[97]

Since 31 March 2014, persons who enter Australia unlawfully, whether by air or by sea, have not been eligible for IAAAS funded services.[98] A small proportion of these unlawful entrants, who are unaccompanied minors, or 'exceptionally vulnerable' adults to whom DIBP considers it to be in the best interests of government to provide assistance, are given access to the government-funded Primary Application Information

---

[91] PJCHR, *Seventh Report of the 44th Parliament* (18 June 2014).

[92] With limited exceptions (e.g. for close family members and for lawyers giving legal assistance), only registered migration agents are allowed to provide immigration assistance: Migration Act, s. 280.

[93] DIBP, *Fact Sheet: IAAAS*, available at www.border.gov.au/about/corporate/information/fact-sheets/63advice#.

[94] DIBP, *Operations Manual*, above n. 42, para. [4.2.4].

[95] *Ibid.* para. [10].

[96] DIBP, *Fact Sheet: IAAAS*, above n. 93.

[97] DIBP, *Operations Manual*, above n. 42, para. [12].

[98] DIBP, *Fact Sheet: IAAAS*, above n. 93.

Service (PAIS) scheme.[99] Assessment for PAIS eligibility is made on an individual basis, but where an eligible person is a member of a family group, the whole family is referred for assistance.[100] As the name suggests, PAIS is generally only available at primary stage where it covers assistance with preparation and lodgment of the application, attendance at the visa interview, and related advice.[101] Unaccompanied minors for whom the Minister for Immigration is guardian under the IGOC Act have access to PAIS at merits review stage also.[102]

Even lawyers find it challenging to navigate the protection visa application process. The challenges are multiplied for asylum-seekers, who may well be wholly unfamiliar with Australian law and institutions, less than fluent in English, suffering from trauma, or some combination of the foregoing. Where the asylum-seeker is a child, the challenges are exacerbated by their not-yet-adult level comprehension and communication capacities.[103] In order to overcome these challenges, all asylum-seeking children, not just unaccompanied children, need assistance from a lawyer or other suitably qualified person.

8. AUSTRALIA'S COMPLIANCE WITH OBLIGATIONS UNDER THE CRC

The analysis which follows focuses on Australia's obligations under the following CRC provisions: Article 2 (non-discrimination); Article 3 (best interests of the child); and Article 12 (participation), which encapsulate general principles underpinning the whole treaty;[104] and Article 22 (treatment of asylum-seeking and refugee children), which is important in the present context.

Article 12(2) requires a child, 'who is capable of forming [their] own views',[105] to be 'provided the opportunity to be heard in any judicial and administrative proceedings affecting the child, either directly, or through

---

[99] DIBP, *The Temporary Protection and Fast Track Assessment Process*, above n. 75.

[100] *Ibid.*

[101] *Ibid.*

[102] *Ibid.*

[103] Evenhuis, 'Child-Proofing Asylum', above n. 5, at 539.

[104] UN Committee on the Rights of the Child, *General Comment No. 5 on General Measures of Implementation of the Convention on the Rights of the Child*, UN Doc. CRC/GC/2003/5 (27 November 2003), para. [12].

[105] The UNCRC has noted that children are capable of forming their own views even before they are able to communicate verbally: UNCRC, *General*

a representative or an appropriate body, in a manner consistent with the procedural rules of national law'.[106] Although it is contemplated that a child may be heard through a representative, the UN Committee on the Rights of the Child (UNCRC) has recommended that a child be heard directly 'wherever possible'.[107] The onus is on states to ensure that the hearing is an effective one by creating a child-sensitive setting, using appropriately trained staff, providing appropriate support, and using appropriate methods of verbal and/or non-verbal communication.[108] The guidelines relating to the interviewing of minors by DIBP and the giving of a hearing to minors by the AAT indicate that Australia does make some effort at the level of policy setting to comply with the requirements of Article 12(2) in those contexts, though more could be done in practice. However, there is no evidence that any such effort is made as a matter of policy or practice in the context of the unauthorized arrival screening process or in the context of IAA review involving child UMA applicants. Where a child is being heard through a representative, that representative needs to have 'sufficient knowledge and understanding of the various aspects of the decision making process' and be exclusively acting in the interests of the child.[109] While a parent may be a child's 'most obvious representative', they may not be an appropriate representative when regard is had to these requirements.[110] There is no evidence that Australia gives careful consideration to the question of whether the parents are appropriate representatives in cases involving accompanied children. Finally, in order for it to be said that a child has been heard through a representative, the representative must actually have conveyed the child's views to the decision-maker.[111] Preventing a child from making a repeat protection visa application even in a situation where they did not know about, or did not understand the nature of, the previous application therefore amounts to a denial of the child's right to be heard in proceedings affecting them.[112]

Article 2(1) requires states parties to ensure CRC rights to all children

---

Comment No. 12 on The Right of the Child to be Heard, UN Doc. CRC/C/GC/12 (20 July 2009), para. [21].

[106] The UNCRC has emphasized that the clause at the end should not be interpreted as permitting national law to derogate from the fundamental right: *ibid.* para. [38].

[107] *Ibid.* para. [35].

[108] *Ibid.*paras [21] and [24].

[109] *Ibid.* paras [36]–[37].

[110] *Ibid.* para. [36].

[111] *Ibid.*

[112] See also PJCHR, *Tenth Report of 44th Parliament* (26 August 2014), para. [1.259].

without discrimination. Non-discrimination is a general principle which underpins not just the CRC but all human rights treaties. The principle does not require that everyone be treated identically. However, it does require that differential treatment have an objective and reasonable justification. Such a justification will not exist if the aim to be achieved by the difference in treatment is not legitimate, or if the effects of the difference in treatment are disproportionate to the aim. As explained above, asylum-seekers who arrive without authorization risk being screened out and repatriated and, if allowed to make protection visa applications, are generally denied much needed access to free application advice and assistance even at primary stage. Within this cohort, asylum-seekers who are classified as UMAs face the additional risk of being transferred to a regional processing country. While UMAs in the legacy caseload are being allowed to apply for protection visas, most of these individuals are subject to fast track processing which is procedurally inferior to the standard determination process. Clearly, unauthorized arrivals and, even more so UMAs, are treated differently from authorized arrivals in a manner which impacts very negatively on them. Some effort is made to mitigate the impact of some of these measures on unaccompanied children but no such effort is made in relation to accompanied children. The aim of the differential treatment of unauthorized arrivals vis-à-vis authorized arrivals is to reinforce border control by deterring others from arriving without authorization in the future. Where UMAs are treated even worse than other unauthorized arrivals, the aim usually specified is that of deterring sea journeys, supposedly with a view to saving the lives of those who might otherwise be tempted to make these dangerous journeys. In both cases, the aim of differential treatment is one which cannot be accepted as legitimate for international human rights law. It can never be legitimate to use one group of people (asylum-seekers arriving in Australia without authorization) as a vehicle for sending a message of deterrence, however altruistic, to another group of people (asylum-seekers who may come to Australia without authorization). The policy involves implicit repudiation of the fundamental premise of international human rights law which is respect for the inherent and equal worth of every human being. The one instance in which deterrence is not the aim of differential treatment of UMAs is the fast track processing of the legacy caseload. This is because the measure has no application to future UMAs. Its aim must therefore be the legitimate one of administrative efficiency. That being said, the cumulative negative impact on unauthorized arrivals and UMAs of their differential treatment is so great that it cannot be described as proportionate to the aims (even if one or both of the aims are conceded to be legitimate).

Article 22(1) requires states parties to take appropriate measures to ensure that asylum-seeking children, whether accompanied or not,[113] receive appropriate protection in the enjoyment of rights under the CRC and other treaties to which they are party. In Australia's case, this must include taking appropriate measures to ensure that asylum-seeking children are protected from refoulement as required by the Refugee Convention and the other human rights treaties to which it is a party. However, as explained above, Australia's procedural safeguards against refoulement are inadequate at every stage, particularly in relation to unauthorized arrivals, and even more so in relation to UMAs. While there are additional safeguards in place for children, many only apply to unaccompanied children and none, especially as implemented in practice, can be relied upon to ensure that children at least are protected where adults are not.

Article 3(1) requires the best interests of the child to be 'a primary consideration' in all actions concerning children undertaken by courts, administrative authorities and legislatures, among other institutions. Actions concerning children include actions which indirectly affect them, so compliance with Article 3 requires systematic consideration to be given to the impact on children's rights of all proposed actions.[114] What constitutes a child's best interests must be determined by reference to the other rights contained in the CRC.[115] The measures identified above as being incompatible with Articles 12(2), 2(1) and 22(1) are therefore also measures which bring into question Australia's compliance with Article 3(1). Australia acts in the best interests of unaccompanied minors by giving them processing priority. However, UNHCR guidelines state that *all* child applicants 'should normally be processed on a priority basis'.[116] There is no evidence that Australia even considers whether the best interests of an accompanied child in a particular case require that they be given processing priority.

There are several other examples of Australia giving consideration to the best interests of unaccompanied children, but not those of accom-

---

113 The UNCRC defines an 'unaccompanied minor' as a person under the age of 18 years who has been separated from both parents and other relatives and is not in the care of an adult guardian: UNCRC, *General Comment No. 6*, above n. 4, para. [7].

114 UNCRC, *General Comment No. 5*, above n. 104, para. [12].

115 A. Lundberg, 'The Best Interests of the Child Principle in Swedish Asylum Cases: The Marginalization of Children's Rights' (2011) 3(1) *Journal of Human Rights Practice* 49, at 54.

116 UNHCR, *Guidelines on International Protection: Child Asylum Claims under Articles 1(A)2 and I(F) of the 1951 Convention and/or 1967 Protocol relating to the Status of Refugees* (2009), para. [66].

panied children. When making 'excluded fast track applicant' determinations, DIBP accepts that being an unaccompanied minor may be a reasonable explanation for experiencing difficulties in providing genuine documents.[117] Likewise, for the purposes of sections 91W and 91WA, DIBP accepts that being provided with bogus documents by family may be reasonable explanation for an unaccompanied minor presenting such documents.[118] By implication, DIBP makes no such allowances for accompanied children. Given that the independent capacity of an accompanied child to comply with documentation requirements is no greater than that of an unaccompanied child with the same characteristics, accompanied children are effectively being penalized for the actions or omissions of adult family members over which they have no control. The provisions which place sole responsibility on applicants to articulate their claims and provide evidence thereof, require the AAT to draw an adverse inference as to the credibility of new claims or evidence presented at merits review stage, and prevent the IAA considering new claims or evidence at all, have a particularly adverse impact on children because they are less likely than adults to understand what claims and evidence are important and may have less capacity than adults to put such claims and evidence forward.[119] In the case of unaccompanied children, these vulnerabilities are arguably offset by giving them access to free application advice and assistance at both primary and merits review stage. However, no such access is provided to accompanied children as a matter of course. Nor does Australia consider whether the best interests of an accompanied child in a particular case may require it. There is definitely no systematic consideration given to whether the best interests of an accompanied child in a particular case may require that they have separate representation from their family members.

While the Australian government acknowledges the best interests of the child principle, it is quick to point out that it is only *a* primary consideration. Moreover, it takes the position that the consideration would usually be outweighed by the need to maintain border control and the integrity of Australia's visa system. It is true that Article 3 CRC does not mandate that the best interests of the child trump all other considerations. However, the UNCRC takes the view that the best interests of the child can only be balanced against other rights-based considerations. Of particular relevance in the present context, it has emphasized that '[n]on-rights-based arguments

---

117 DIBP, *The Temporary Protection and Fast Track Assessment Process*, above n. 75.

118 DIBP, *Common Processing Guidelines*, above n. 10.

119 PJCHR, *Twelfth Report*, above n. 88, paras [1.123]–[1.127]; UNHCR, *Guidelines on International Protection*, above n. 116, paras [73]–[74].

such as those relating to general migration control, cannot override best interests considerations'.[120] Even if migration control considerations can legitimately be balanced against the best interests of the child, no systematic provision is made for case-by-case balancing. In fact, the Australian government has even gone to the extreme of deciding that, as a matter of policy, no consideration will be given to the best interests of the child when transferring UMAs who arrived on or after 19 July 2013 to regional processing countries. To the extent that the Australian government purports to have struck a balance upfront between migration control considerations and best interests of the child considerations in its protection visa application procedures, that balance is unacceptable from a human rights perspective because the likely negative impact on children, especially accompanied children, of the measures adopted seem to be disproportionate to the migration control gains. It follows that the Australian government is in breach of its Article 3(1) CRC obligation in its procedural treatment of asylum-seeking children.[121]

9. CONCLUSION

In its concluding observations on Australia's most recent CRC report,[122] the UNCRC urged Australia 'to bring its immigration and asylum laws into full conformity with the [CRC] and other international standards' having formed the view that such conformity was lacking at the time of the report.[123] Unfortunately, what this chapter has demonstrated is that in its procedural treatment of asylum-seeking children, Australia has moved further from, rather than closer to, conformity with the CRC since that time.

---

120 UNCRC, *General Comment No. 6*, above n. 4, para. [86].

121 See also PJCHR, *Ninth Report*, above n. 54, paras [1.214]–[1.217] and [1.225]–[1.227]; PJCHR, *Twelfth Report*, above n. 88, paras [1.118]–[1.121] and [1.129]–[1.1.31]; PJCHR, *Tenth Report*, above n. 112, para. [1.251].

122 CRC, Art. 44 requires state parties to make five-yearly reports to the Committee on the Rights of the Child on progress made in giving effect to CRC obligations.

123 UNCRC, *Concluding Observations on Australia*, UN Doc. CRC/C/AUS/CO/4 (28 August 2012), para. [81].

PART V

Children and immigration detention

19. Detention as a last resort: the implications of the Human Rights Committee's General Comment No. 35

Gerald L. Neuman*

1. INTRODUCTION

Improper confinement of children in migration contexts – unnecessary, prolonged or in harmful conditions – constitutes a severe and highly troubling phenomenon in the world today, and has reached crisis proportions in the United States. One of the tools that the international human rights system offers for combating this phenomenon is the prohibition of arbitrary detention. The Human Rights Committee's General Comment No. 35 on the right to liberty and security of person elaborates standards for characterizing detention as arbitrary, in this field as well as others.[1] It provides guidance to states, and support to advocates seeking to limit the use of detention against children who cross borders.

The standards do not, however, define every instance of detention of a person under 18 years of age in the course of migration enforcement as inherently arbitrary. The term 'detention' covers a range of forms and durations of control, applied in a variety of situations. The General Comment's treatment of the issue is consonant with Article 37(b) of the Convention on the Rights of the Child (CRC), which requires that '[t]he arrest, detention or imprisonment of a child shall be used only as a measure of last resort and for the shortest appropriate period of time'.[2]

* Although the author was a member of the Human Rights Committee from 2011 to 2014, this chapter does not speak on behalf of the Committee.

1 Human Rights Committee, General Comment No. 35, *Article 9 (Liberty and Security of Person)*, UN Doc. CCPR/C/GC/35 (16 December 2014).

2 Convention on the Rights of the Child, opened for signature 20 November 1989, 1577 UNTS 3 (entered into force 2 September 1990) (CRC) Art. 37(b). Every UN member state other than the United States has ratified this Convention.

This chapter will first introduce the Human Rights Committee and its case law restricting detention of children in the migration context. Then it will turn to the General Comment adopted in 2014, and reasons that favor the Committee's nuanced approach to the factors that make detention of a minor arbitrary.

2. HUMAN RIGHTS COMMITTEE AND ITS JURISPRUDENCE

The International Covenant on Civil and Political Rights (ICCPR) is one of the two principal human rights treaties at the global level.[3] It guarantees a range of rights, including life, fair trial, freedom of expression and equality. For the present chapter, the two most relevant provisions are Article 9, which protects liberty of person against arbitrary detention, and Article 24, which recognizes the right of children to special measures of protection. The ICCPR created the Human Rights Committee (HRC, or just 'the Committee') as an independent expert body empowered to monitor compliance by states parties with their obligations under the treaty. The HRC carries out this responsibility in three main ways: by engaging in dialogue with states over their periodic reports to the Committee on their implementation of the treaty; by deciding individual cases based on communications submitted by individuals claiming to be victims of a violation of the treaty;[4] and by issuing 'general comments' that summarize the Committee's interpretation of the treaty in light of its experience in evaluating reports and deciding communications. Although the HRC's decisions on communications are not legally binding in the strict sense, the HRC considers them 'authoritative', and the International Court of Justice has recognized the great weight owed to the interpretations adopted by the HRC in its individual decisions and General Comments.[5]

Article 9 asserts in its first paragraph the general rights of everyone to

---

[3] Opened for signature 19 December 1966, 999 UNTS 171 (entered into force 23 March 1976) (ICCPR). The other principal treaty is the International Covenant on Economic, Social and Cultural Rights, opened for signature 16 December 1966, 993 UNTS 3 (entered into force 3 January 1976) (ICESCR).

[4] This procedure is available only with regard to states that have also ratified the (First) Optional Protocol to the ICCPR, 999 UNTS 302, as roughly two-thirds of the 168 states parties to the ICCPR have done so far.

[5] HRC, General Comment No. 33, UN Doc. CCPR/C/GC/33 (25 June 2009), para. [13]; *Ahmadou Sadio Diallo (Republic of Guinea* v. *Democratic Republic of the Congo)*, Judgment [2010] ICJ Rep. 636, 664.

liberty and security of person, and prohibits arbitrary arrest and detention. Individuals can be deprived of liberty only on grounds established by law and through procedures established by law. Then four more paragraphs set forth specific safeguards against arbitrary or unlawful detention, and remedies in case of arbitrary or unlawful detention.

Article 24 guarantees to every child without discrimination 'the right to such measures of protection as are required by his status as a minor, on the part of his family, society and the State'.[6] This provision is generally worded, but it has acquired meaning over time through interpretation.[7] In that connection, the HRC has characterized the Convention on the Rights of the Child as 'a valuable source informing the Committee's interpretation of the Covenant'.[8]

Over the years, the HRC has decided a number of individual communications brought on behalf of children detained for purposes of migration control. One decision addressed an unaccompanied minor, and the others concerned children detained with one or more parents. The HRC's analysis of these cases was framed within its general approach to identifying arbitrary detention.[9] The fact that detention is lawful under domestic law does not necessarily mean that it is not arbitrary; the notion of arbitrariness includes elements relating to reasonableness, necessity and proportionality, as well as predictability and due process of law. Outside the criminal sentencing context, detention that extends in time must always be subject to periodic re-evaluation of whether it continues to be justified. Under the concept of proportionality, the longer the detention continues, and the greater its impact on the person detained, the greater the justification required.[10]

The HRC found no violation of the ICCPR in the first decision, *Jalloh* v. *The Netherlands* (2002).[11] Jalloh was an unaccompanied minor who sought asylum in the Netherlands. He described himself as 15 years old

---

[6] ICCPR, Art. 24, para. [1]. The following two paragraphs address every child's right to birth registration and a name, and the right 'to acquire a nationality'. ICCPR, Art. 24, paras [2], [3].

[7] See, e.g., HRC, General Comment No 17, *Article 24 (Rights of the Child) (1989)*, UN Doc. HRI/GEN/Rev.9 (2008), vol. I, p. 193.

[8] HRC, *Blessington and Elliot* v. *Australia*, UN Doc. CCPR/C/112/D/1968/2010 (22 October 2014), para. [7.11]. The HRC does not, however, simply treat the substantive provisions of the Convention on the Rights of the Child as incorporated into ICCPR, Art. 24.

[9] General Comment No. 35, above n. 1, paras [11]–[12].

[10] *Ibid.* See also HRC, *Baban* v. *Australia*, Communication No. 1014/2001 (6 August 2003), para. [7.2].

[11] Communication No. 794/1998 (23 March 2002).

and from the Ivory Coast, but he had no identification documents and the authorities were unable to confirm his nationality. He was put under guardianship and placed in an open reception facility while his application was being processed. After about a year he absconded from the facility and went into hiding to avoid deportation. His lawyer then persuaded him to submit to the authorities and reapply for asylum. This time he was ordered detained, for reasons including suspicion that he would not cooperate with his removal, and a court upheld the detention as lawful. Efforts to find a state that recognized him as its national failed, and after about four months the authorities ceased detaining him because there was no realistic prospect that he could be expelled. A court ordered medical and psychological examinations, which disclosed that he was not merely poorly educated but suffered from 'mental underdevelopment'. On that basis, he was granted a residence permit. The communication to the HRC amounted to a retrospective challenge to the few months of detention. The HRC concluded that, considering his flight from the open facility, it was not unreasonable to detain him for a limited time until the administrative procedure was completed; given that he was released once expulsion was not in prospect, the detention was not arbitrary within the meaning of Article 9 ICCPR. The HRC also found no violation of the duty to provide special measures of protection to a minor under Article 24. Details regarding the conditions of detention and possible efforts to raise the issue of 'mental underdevelopment' were lacking. The HRC noted that 'detention of a minor is not per se a violation of Article 24'. Given the doubts about his identity and his attempt to evade expulsion, the three and a half months of detention while investigation was ongoing did not entail a failure of protection.

The decisions about accompanied minors all arose within a long series of communications regarding detention of asylum-seekers in Australia. These cases deserve a fuller description of their origins in Australian asylum policy,[12] but the discussion here aims primarily at explaining the legal principles used by the HRC in deciding the communications. The HRC had earlier laid the foundations in *A* v. *Australia* (1997),[13] which concerned an adult from Cambodia who had been subjected to mandatory detention for more than four years because of his unauthorized arrival. Australia defended the detention primarily as preventing asylum-seekers

---

[12] On Australian asylum and detention policies, see, e.g., M. Crock, B. Saul and A. Dastyari, *Future Seekers II: Refugees and Irregular Migration in Australia* (Federation Press, 2006); J. McAdam and F. Chong, *Refugees: Why Seeking Asylum is Legal and Australia's Policies are Not* (UNSW Press, 2014).

[13] Communication No. 560/1993 (3 April 1997).

from absconding and disappearing into the community, while A's counsel argued that the real purpose was to deter other asylum-seekers from arriving and to induce detained asylum-seekers to abandon their claims. The HRC observed that it was not per se arbitrary to detain an individual who requested asylum, but that the concept of arbitrariness included an element of proportionality. Detention should not continue beyond the period for which the state can provide appropriate justification, and the state had not advanced any grounds particular to the individual that would justify his extended detention. Australia had therefore violated Article 9(1).[14]

The HRC applied these principles to the detention of a child in *Baban* v. *Australia* (2003).[15] An Iraqi Kurdish father and son were detained upon arrival in Australia in 1999, when the son was not yet two years old. They remained in mandatory detention for nearly two years while the father appealed the denial of refugee status, and then they escaped. The HRC found the detentions of both the father and the son to be arbitrary, because Australia had not shown an individualized justification for continuing the detention, particularly in light of the hardship of prolonged detention for the child. Australia had not shown (indeed had not explored) whether less invasive measures, such as reporting obligations or sureties, could have achieved its interests in migration control for these individuals.[16] The HRC accepted Australia's argument that its efforts to provide appropriate educational, recreational and other programs, within and outside the facility, satisfied some of its obligations of protection toward the child under Article 24, but dealt with the question of detention as such under the rubric of Article 9 rather than Article 24.

The next decision arose from a *cause célèbre* in Australia.[17] To summarize briefly a complex set of facts, the Bakhtiyaris were a Hazara family

---

[14] The decision is also noteworthy for its holding that the requirement of judicial review of the lawfulness of detention under Art. 9(4) includes the obligation for the courts to be able to order release from detention that is permitted under domestic law but that is arbitrary under the ICCPR.

[15] Communication No. 1014/2001 (6 August 2003).

[16] HRC member Ruth Wedgwood dissented from the conclusion that the mandatory detention regime was arbitrary. The HRC also found a violation of the right to judicial review of the lawfulness of detention, which should have included the power to remedy the violation of the ICCPR, but it dismissed claims alleging inhumane conditions of detention as unproven.

[17] See, e.g., D. Corlett, *Following Them Home: The Fate of the Returned Asylum Seekers* (Black Inc., 2005), pp. 13–47; M. Crock, 'Roqia's Story: Refugees and Natural Justice in the Court of Public Opinion' in H. Douglas et al. (eds), *Australian Feminist Judgments: Righting and Rewriting Law* (Hart Publishing, 2014), p. 101.

whose nationalities, Afghan or Pakistani, became a subject of dispute. The father reached Australia in 1999, and was granted a protection visa as Afghan and released. The mother arrived at the beginning of 2001 with her five children, aged from two to 11, not knowing the whereabouts of the father. The new arrivals were mandatorily detained, and they were kept in detention pending appeals because the government decided that the mother was from Pakistan and so not in need of protection. The government then proceeded to withdraw the father's visa, and eventually re-arrested him as well. The mother and the two eldest sons engaged in self-harm, but Australia rejected the HRC's request that they be taken outside the detention facility for assessment. The two elder sons escaped from the notorious Woomera detention facility and then were returned after the UK consulate refused to receive them. In the summer of 2003, the Family Court decided that it had jurisdiction to order the release of the Bakhtiyari children from migration detention if that order was in their best interests, despite statutory restrictions on judicial review, and they were placed in the custody of carers in Adelaide while their parents remained in detention. The Family Court's ruling was subsequently reversed as beyond its authority after the HRC had issued its Views.[18]

In *Bakhtiyari* v. *Australia* (2003),[19] the HRC decided several claims of the various family members. It found that the first period of detention of the father had been adequately justified under the circumstances, given that he was released two months after filing an application for protection.[20] The much longer detention of the mother and children, however, was arbitrary: after an initial period of detention for purposes of ascertaining identity and other issues, Australia had not shown the need for extended detention rather than less intrusive measures that would take into account the family's circumstances.[21]

The HRC also found that Australia had not provided the children with

---

[18] *Minister for Immigration and Multicultural and Indigenous Affairs* v. *B* (2004) 219 CLR 365.

[19] Communication No. 1069/2002 (29 October 2003).

[20] The father had not challenged the detention that followed the cancellation of his protection visa. The HRC did not rule on its propriety, and was in no position to resolve the dispute about his nationality.

[21] The HRC further held that the unavailability of judicial review for the mother, and for the children until the Family Court's novel assertion of jurisdiction, violated Art. 9(4), and that Australia's apparent intention to remove the mother and children to Pakistan before completing the proceedings with regard to the father violated family rights under ICCPR, Arts 17 and 23(1). According to later accounts Australia deported both parents and children, including a sixth child born in Australia, to Pakistan and they proceeded to Afghanistan.

the measures of protection required by Article 24. The principle that the best interests of the child must be a primary consideration in all decisions affecting the child formed an integral part of the state's obligations under Article 24. The demonstrable, documented and ongoing adverse effects suffered in particular by the two eldest sons prior to the Family Court's assertion of jurisdiction showed that the state's earlier actions had not been guided by the children's best interests.

The decision *D and E* v. *Australia* (2006)[22] adds little. An Iranian couple with children aged one and seven were mandatorily detained upon arrival in 2000, and unsuccessfully sought asylum. The detention of the entire family continued for over three years, and they ultimately received humanitarian visas in 2006. They challenged their detention as arbitrary, and the HRC agreed succinctly that it had violated Article 9.[23] Australia had not shown that extended detention beyond an initial period was justified, or demonstrated that less intrusive measures that would take into account the family's particular circumstances could not have achieved its purposes.

Finally, the 2013 cases *FKAG* v. *Australia*[24] and *MMM* v. *Australia*[25] combined claims on behalf of over 40 refugees, including two families with children. Australia recognized them as entitled to protection from return to their home countries but denied entry to the adults because of adverse security assessments. More than two years later, Australia had neither given them a fair opportunity to challenge the security assessments nor found another country willing to take them, and they remained in detention. Australia granted one of the children a protection visa almost three years after arrival, when he was roughly six years old, but his mother chose to keep him with her in detention; they were released a few months later after she received a more favorable security assessment. The other family included a mother and two children who were rescued at sea and brought to Australia, and a father who arrived separately. The parents were denied entry and chose to keep the children (a two-year-old, a five-year-old, and later a baby born in detention) with them. Both families were eventually

22 Communication No. 1050/2002 (11 July 2006).

23 The family also claimed that the prolonged detention of the children violated ICCPR, Art. 24, but the HRC found this claim unsubstantiated given Australia's efforts to provide appropriate educational, recreational and other programs, as in *Baban*. The HRC appears to have considered the question of detention as such in light of Art. 9 rather than Art. 24.

24 Communication No. 2094/2011 (26 July 2013). These cases were decided during the period when the HRC was deliberating on General Comment No. 35.

25 Communication No. 2136/2012 (25 July 2013).

placed in residential housing units within a detention facility, with opportunities for the children to go on escorted outings, and the second family remained in detention at the time of decision.

The HRC held in both decisions that the prolonged detention of the adults was arbitrary. Australia had not shown the need to keep the adults totally in the dark about the security risks attributed to them and to deprive them of opportunities for legal challenge, nor had it demonstrated that measures less intrusive than detention would not suffice to protect against the alleged risks. The arbitrariness of the detention extended to the consequences for the children, which also amounted to violations of Article 9(1) during the relevant periods. The HRC went further, noting the negative impact that prolonged indefinite detention, on grounds that the person is not even apprised of, can have on the mental health of detainees, as confirmed by medical reports concerning several of the refugees. Those reports included findings in relation to the mother and the middle child in the second family. The Committee concluded that the combination of the arbitrary detention, its protracted and/or indefinite character, the withholding of information, and the difficult conditions of detention, cumulatively inflicted serious psychological harm in violation of Article 7 ICCPR (which prohibits cruel, inhuman or degrading treatment as well as torture).

Together, this set of decisions on the detention of children spans a range of ages and situations and suggests a number of conclusions. The HRC does not regard detention as an improper instrument of migration control per se, even when the migrant is a child, but the detention must be reasonable, necessary and proportionate in the particular circumstances. A brief deprivation of liberty upon encountering an admittedly unauthorized migrant in order to begin the inquiry is normally justifiable. More extended detention requires individualized reasons, such as an actual risk of absconding or a threat of specific harm to others. Australia did not defend its detention policies before the HRC as contributing to the deterrence of other asylum-seekers, and the HRC would not have considered such a blanket justification for detention acceptable. When a child is being detained, the best interests of the child must be taken into account as a primary consideration. The demonstrated risk of the particular child's absconding may justify placement in closed accommodations, but less intrusive measures must be explored, and the conditions prevailing in the proposed placement matter greatly. The serious psychological harm to children from protracted confinement forms an important factor in the assessment of proportionality. When migrant parents pose a risk that motivates their own detention, the state may face a choice of temporarily separating parent and child or exposing the child to the effects of confinement; this dilemma does not automatically require release of the parent, but if the detention of the parent is not sufficiently justified the child may be a secondary victim of arbitrary detention. I should add that in light of subsequent Australian cases and deeper development of the rights of persons with disabilities, the *Jalloh* case might be decided differently on its particular facts today, placing greater emphasis on the state's duty to explore alternatives to detention and to evaluate more quickly the disability of an unaccompanied minor.

The HRC has also issued numerous Concluding Observations on state reports specifically addressing detention of migrants, and sometimes specifically focusing on detention of migrant children. For example, in its July 2013 evaluation of the periodic report of the Czech Republic, the Committee expressed concern that minors awaiting deportation could be held for up to 90 days in detention centers, and recommended that the state '[r]educe the maximum legal period of detention for foreign minors awaiting deportation and, in any event, ensure that the detention of children is permitted only as a last resort and for the shortest appropriate period'.[26] These Concluding Observations, however, are normally formulated as recommendations to the reporting state, and provide less legal guidance than the holdings in Views on communications and the HRC's General Comments.

3. GENERAL COMMENT NO. 35

Building on its experience in deciding communications and evaluating state reports, and after public input and two years of deliberations in open session, the HRC adopted a General Comment on Article 9 in 2014.[27] I will quote two key paragraphs of the General Comment here, before providing my own description of their implications regarding the detention of children.[28] The major passage on questions concerning detention in the migration context, paragraph 18, reads as follows:

> Detention in the course of proceedings for the control of immigration is not per se arbitrary, but the detention must be justified as reasonable, necessary

[26] *Concluding Observations on the Third Periodic Report of the Czech Republic*, UN Doc. CCPR/C/CZE/CO/3 (2013), para. [17].

[27] The 2014 General Comment replaced a much briefer General Comment from 1982. See General Comment No. 35, above n. 1, para. [1].

[28] The present author was the rapporteur on the General Comment, but the HRC as a whole debated and adopted the propositions it sets forth. My description of the General Comment's implications amounts to my own interpretation; it is not intended to speak on behalf of the HRC.

> and proportionate in the light of the circumstances and reassessed as it extends in time. Asylum seekers who unlawfully enter a State party's territory may be detained for a brief initial period in order to document their entry, record their claims and determine their identity if it is in doubt. To detain them further while their claims are being resolved would be arbitrary in the absence of particular reasons specific to the individual, such as an individualized likelihood of absconding, a danger of crimes against others or a risk of acts against national security. The decision must consider relevant factors case by case and not be based on a mandatory rule for a broad category; must take into account less invasive means of achieving the same ends, such as reporting obligations, sureties or other conditions to prevent absconding; and must be subject to periodic re-evaluation and judicial review. Decisions regarding the detention of migrants must also take into account the effect of the detention on their physical or mental health. Any necessary detention should take place in appropriate, sanitary, non-punitive facilities and should not take place in prisons. The inability of a State party to carry out the expulsion of an individual because of statelessness or other obstacles does not justify indefinite detention. Children should not be deprived of liberty, except as a measure of last resort and for the shortest appropriate period of time, taking into account their best interests as a primary consideration with regard to the duration and conditions of detention, and also taking into account the extreme vulnerability and need for care of unaccompanied minors.[29]

The discussion of the detention of children in paragraph 18 echoes the fuller observations on the rights of children in paragraph 62:

> Article 24, paragraph 1, of the Covenant entitles every child 'to such measures of protection as are required by his status as a minor, on the part of his family, society and the State'. That Article entails the adoption of special measures to protect the personal liberty and security of every child, in addition to the measures generally required by Article 9 for everyone. A child may be deprived of liberty only as a last resort and for the shortest appropriate period of time. In addition to the other requirements applicable to each category of deprivation of liberty, the best interests of the child must be a primary consideration in every decision to initiate or continue the deprivation. The Committee acknowledges that sometimes a particular deprivation of liberty would itself be in the best interests of the child. Placement of a child in institutional care amounts to a deprivation of liberty within the meaning of Article 9. A decision to deprive a child of liberty must be subject to periodic review of its continuing necessity and appropriateness. The child has a right to be heard, directly or through legal or other appropriate assistance, in relation to any decision regarding a deprivation of liberty, and the procedures employed should be child-appropriate. The right to release from unlawful detention may result in return to the child's family or placement in an alternative form of care that accords with the child's best interests, rather than simple release into the child's own custody.[30]

---

[29] General Comment No. 35, above n. 1, para. [18] (footnotes omitted).

[30] *Ibid.* para. [62] (footnotes omitted). One footnote includes an additional

These paragraphs of the General Comment should be understood against the background of the way that it defines detention. Article 9 ICCPR guarantees the right to liberty and security of person, and forbids arbitrary arrest or detention. Detention includes *any* form of deprivation of liberty of person,[31] and these terms are broadly defined in order to ensure that the prohibitions and safeguards that Article 9 provides for detained persons will be applicable. The General Comment explains 'liberty of person' as addressing freedom from confinement of the body, and deprivations of liberty of person are distinguished from mere limitations on liberty of movement by the fact that deprivations of liberty involve more severe restriction of motion within a narrower space.[32] An 'arrest' is any apprehension of a person that commences a deprivation of liberty.[33] The protections triggered by these broad definitions include the prohibition of arbitrary arrest or detention, notice of reasons for any arrest (Article 9(2)), the right to take proceedings before a court to determine the lawfulness of detention (Article 9(4)), and the right to compensation for unlawful or arbitrary detention (Article 9(5)).[34]

Paragraph 62 of the General Comment expands on this definition in relation to children. It was written with close attention to the Convention on the Rights of the Child and the General Comments of the Committee on the Rights of the Child. Unlike the normal restrictions that a child may face in family life, placement in institutional care can amount to deprivation of liberty. In other words, the definition of 'detention' includes some forms of deprivation of liberty that may actually serve as protection for the child in the particular situation. Even those forms of detention that serve the child's best interests should still be recognized as detention, and must be subject to the protective rules of Article 9 (among others). The HRC's interpretation of the requirements of some of those safeguards is stricter in the case of children than in the case of adults.

For children, as for some categories of adults, a broad definition of detention is important because it counteracts the tendency to apply

textual sentence: 'In contrast, normal supervision of children by parents or family may involve a degree of control over movement, especially of younger children, that would be inappropriate for adults, but that does not constitute a deprivation of liberty; neither do the ordinary requirements of daily school attendance constitute a deprivation of liberty.'

31 General Comment No. 35, above n. 1, para. [13].

32 *Ibid.* paras [3], [5]. Liberty of movement is protected by ICCPR, Art. 12.

33 General Comment No. 35, above n. 1, para. [13].

34 However, the right to notice of 'charges' under Art. 9(2), and the rights under Art. 9(3), apply only in the context of criminal proceedings.

euphemistic labels to restrictions of liberty in order to remove them from legal control. The broad definition also subjects the initial phase of detention to relevant safeguards, and helps limit abuse of any transition period between liberty and formalized custody.

The General Comment emphasizes that a child may be detained only as a last resort, and only for the shortest appropriate period of time.[35] The best interests of the child must be made a primary consideration in the decision whether and how to detain a child, and whether to continue, terminate or modify an ongoing detention.[36]

Sometimes, however, a deprivation of liberty – an appropriately limited form of detention – may itself be in the best interests of the child.[37] This proposition is not mere hypocrisy or a pretext for oppression; it is not an incitement to put children in prison to teach them a lesson. The proposition recognizes the vulnerability of children, particularly young children, and their need for the supervision and guidance of adults. It relies on the broad definition of detention employed in the General Comment, and the resulting attachment of safeguards to all forms of deprivations of liberty.

In addition, the HRC's understanding of the best interests standard is that the best interests of the child are not the sole consideration in all governmental decisions regarding children, or the single consideration that overrides all others. Particularly at the higher end of the age spectrum, the dangerous conduct of a person below the age of 18 may require a governmental response justified by the protection of the rights of others. A human rights approach must take into account the rights of other people, and not focus exclusively on the rights of the immediate claimant. A concrete threat to the rights of others may justify, as a last resort, some form of detention for the shortest appropriate period of time, with scrupulous attention to the vulnerability of juveniles in the procedure for making the determination and in the conditions of detention.[38] This reasoning is familiar in the field of juvenile justice for a state's own citizens, and it is sometimes also relevant in the migration context.

Paragraph 18 of the General Comment turns specifically to detention for purposes of migration control, with regard to adults as well as

---

[35] General Comment No. 35, above n. 1, para. [62].

[36] *Ibid.*

[37] *Ibid.*

[38] Several paragraphs of General Comment No. 35, and other General Comments such as the one on Art. 14, address safeguards for juveniles. See, e.g., General Comment No. 32, *Right to Equality Before Courts and Tribunals and to a Fair Trial*, UN Doc. CCPR/C/GC/32 (2007), paras [42]–[44] (on juvenile justice).

children.[39] It restates the rule applied in the HRC's decisions on communications involving migration, that detention by migration authorities is not per se arbitrary, but that any instance of such detention must be justified as reasonable, necessary and proportionate, and must be reassessed periodically.[40] It recognizes the legitimacy of a brief initial detention for such purposes as recording and identification, bearing in mind the broad definition of detention, and simultaneously making applicable the safeguards of Article 9, including notice of reasons for any 'arrest'. As the period of detention increases, greater individualized justification is required, and further safeguards such as the right to judicial review and limitations on the conditions of detention become more relevant than they would be in a short encounter. Both the notion of arbitrariness under Article 9 and the explicit guarantee of humane treatment in detention under Article 10 imply restrictions on conditions of detention, which must be appropriate in light of the purposes for which a person is detained.

The paragraph also summarizes the principles specific to the detention of migrant children:

> Children should not be deprived of liberty, except as a measure of last resort and for the shortest appropriate period of time, taking into account their best interests as a primary consideration with regard to the duration and conditions of detention, and also taking into account the extreme vulnerability and need for care of unaccompanied minors.

The General Comment seeks to regulate and restrict detention of children for migration control purposes, not to prohibit their detention absolutely. The 'last resort' and 'best interests' principles apply with sufficient flexibility to address different forms of detention and children of different ages and situations.

The brief initial detention that is justified for adult migrants may also be necessary for families and unaccompanied minors. Moreover, for some child migrants the initial deprivation of liberty may serve a protective function. Unaccompanied minors may need placement in a supervised residential setting, and restricting their movement during the short period required to make an initial assessment and find a placement may be necessary. Young children cannot simply be put on the street. When a

---

[39] The General Comment touches explicitly on migration matters in several other paragraphs (such as [3], [5], [14], [50], [58] and [60]), and many other paragraphs state general propositions that also apply to detention for migration control.

[40] General Comment No. 35, above n. 1, para. [18].

child is traveling with an adult who is not a parent, closer scrutiny may be required to determine whether the child needs protection against trafficking or other forms of abuse. The General Comment includes these protective interferences with liberty among the forms of detention, and subjects them to limitations and safeguards.

A longer detention may sometimes be justified to protect the rights of others. Older children may be involved in criminal activity or criminal gangs, and adults may use older children as agents of political violence. Concrete evidence that a particular minor poses danger may justify a form of detention, if it can be demonstrated that less restrictive measures would be insufficient. States should not exaggerate the threat posed by young migrants, but they should not be precluded from responding appropriately in exceptional individual cases. The conditions of any detention must be tailored to the needs and vulnerability of the minor, and a series of legal safeguards apply. Furthermore, children of any age may suffer from a highly contagious disease that requires isolation as a last resort, which is also a form of detention that Article 9 regulates.[41]

Finally, the needs of migration control may in certain instances justify detention for a limited time. The HRC does not deny the legitimacy of a state's interest in enforcing migration laws that are compatible with the ICCPR. As the *Jalloh* case indicates, when a particular minor resists the state's efforts to arrange less restrictive accommodation and supervision and succeeds for a time in evading enforcement, placement in a closed setting in order to allow proceedings to continue may become necessary, subject to appropriate conditions and safeguards. Moreover, once a decision to deport a child has become truly final, it may be necessary for the child to be physically returned to the child's home country in the custody of officials of the returning state. The General Comment recognizes and regulates such custody as a form of detention.[42]

In all these situations, if some form of detention is exceptionally appropriate as a last resort, the General Comment emphasizes that conditions in detention must take into account the best interests of the child and the extreme vulnerability of unaccompanied minors; duration must also be limited accordingly and reviewed for its necessity and proportionality on a continued basis. Procedural safeguards must be ensured and adapted to be child-appropriate. The General Comment did not have room to spell out in detail all the services and protections that must be provided – these may depend on a variety of factors such as the expected length of the detention,

---

41 *Ibid.* para. [5].

42 *Ibid.* paras [5], [30].

the age and health of the child, the presence and health of the parents, and the reasons why the child is being temporarily deprived of liberty.[43] The standards seek to reduce detention to the minimum duration necessary and to prevent avoidable harm.

To conclude, General Comment No. 35 explains the ICCPR as placing severe limits on detention of children in the migration context and requiring safeguards in the exceptional circumstances when children may permissibly be detained. It does not absolutely prohibit deprivation of the liberty of a minor altogether, but restricts and regulates detention as a last resort.

[43] General Comment No. 35 addresses ICCPR, Art. 9 as a whole, and its application across a wide range of contexts in which people of any age are deprived of liberty. Moreover, the General Comment was subject to a UN-imposed word limit of roughly 10,000 words on treaty body documents, imposed for budgetary reasons in light of translation costs. Cf. GA Res. 68/268 (9 April 2014), p. 5.

20. The impact of detention on the health, wellbeing and development of children: findings from the second National Inquiry into Children in Immigration Detention

Gillian Triggs*

1. INTRODUCTION

The Australian Human Rights Commission ('the Commission') has monitored and reported on conditions for people in immigration detention in Australia for almost 20 years, documenting numerous breaches of Australia's international human rights obligations. Some of the most serious breaches have related to the impacts of indefinite detention on the health, wellbeing and development of children.

Since 2004, the Commission has conducted two National Inquiries focusing specifically on the situation of children in immigration detention. This chapter examines the second of these inquiries, conducted between February and October 2014. It begins with an overview of international human rights obligations relevant to the detention of children, Australia's domestic legal framework for detention, and the outcomes of the first National Inquiry into Children in Immigration Detention. It then discusses the background to and key findings of the second National Inquiry. The chapter concludes with an overview of developments since the Second Inquiry and recommendations for further reform to prevent the detention of children into the future.

* Lucy Morgan, Specialist Adviser, Immigration at the Australian Human Rights Commission, assisted with the drafting of this chapter.

2. INTERNATIONAL LAW AND THE DETENTION OF CHILDREN

The right to freedom from arbitrary detention is enshrined in Article 9(1) of the International Covenant on Civil and Political Rights (ICCPR).[1] The United Nations Human Rights Committee (HRC) has repeatedly affirmed that this notion of arbitrariness is not to be simply equated with 'against the law' but should instead be interpreted more broadly to include elements of inappropriateness, injustice and lack of predictability. To avoid being arbitrary, detention must therefore not only be lawful but also necessary and reasonable in all the circumstances of the case, and a proportionate means of achieving a legitimate aim.[2]

Prevention of arbitrary detention thus requires an individual assessment of the necessity of detention for each person, taking into consideration their individual circumstances. While the use of immigration detention may be legitimate in some situations, such as to prevent flight or manage health and security risks, a person should only be detained if they are individually assessed as posing an unacceptable risk to the community which cannot be mitigated in a less restrictive way. If the person does not pose any identifiable risk, or the identified risk could be managed through less invasive means than detaining a person, then that person's detention will be arbitrary.

Article 37(b) of the Convention on the Rights of the Child (CRC) also prohibits arbitrary detention, and further requires that the detention of a child 'be used only as a measure of last resort and for the shortest appropriate period of time'.[3] In addition, the CRC mandates certain standards of treatment for children who are deprived of their liberty. Specifically, children should:

- be treated with humanity and respect for the inherent dignity of the human person, and in a manner which takes into account the needs of people their age;[4]

---

[1] International Covenant on Civil and Political Rights, opened for signature 16 December 1966, 999 UNTS 171 (entered into force 23 March 1976).

[2] *Van Alphen* v. *Netherlands*, Human Rights Committee, Communication No. 305/1988, UN Doc. CCPR/C/39/D/305/1988 (23 July 1990), para. [5.8]; *A* v. *Australia*, Human Rights Committee, Communication No. 560/1993, UN Doc. CCPR/C/59/D/560/1993 (3 April1997), para. [9.4].

[3] Convention on the Rights of the Child, opened for signature 20 November 1989, 1577 UNTS 3 (entered into force 2 September 1990), Art. 37(b) (CRC).

[4] *Ibid.* Art. 37(c).

- be separated from adults unless it is considered contrary to their best interests, and have the right to maintain contact with their family;[5]
- have the right to prompt access to legal and other appropriate assistance, as well as the right to challenge the legality of their detention.[6]

The abovementioned provisions apply generally to children deprived of liberty (including those held in corrective facilities) and do not specifically refer to immigration detention. In 2012, however, the Committee on the Rights of the Child provided specific guidance on the detention of children on the basis of their visa or migration status. The Committee affirmed that 'the detention of a child because of their or their parent's migration status constitutes a child rights violation and always contravenes the principle of the best interests of the child'. It called on states to 'expeditiously and completely cease the detention of children on the basis of their immigration status'.[7]

The CRC contains a range of additional obligations relevant to the detention of children. Article 3(1) requires states to ensure that in all actions concerning children, the best interests of the child shall be a primary consideration. States also have specific obligations to provide special protection and assistance to children who are in particularly vulnerable situations, including unaccompanied children (Article 20) and children who are seeking asylum or have been recognized as refugees (Article 22).

Broader obligations under the CRC related to ensuring that children can develop and thrive, and are protected from harm, are also highly relevant in a detention context. These include the right to freedom from discrimination (Article 2); the right to life, survival and development (Article 6); the right to privacy and family life (Article 16(1)); the right to protection from all forms of physical or mental violence, injury or abuse, neglect or negligent treatment, maltreatment or exploitation (Article 19(1)); the right to the highest attainable standard of health (Article 24(1)); the right to education (Article 28); the right to engage in play and recreational activities (Article 31); and the right to freedom from torture or cruel, inhuman or degrading treatment or punishment (Article 37(a)).

---

[5] *Ibid.* Art. 37(c).

[6] *Ibid.* Art. 37(d).

[7] Committee on the Rights of the Child, *Report of the 2012 Day of General Discussion: The Rights of All Children in the Context of International Migration* (28 September 2012), para. [78], available at www.ohchr.org/Documents/HRBodies/CRC/Discussions/2012/DGD2012ReportAndRecommendations.pdf.

3. IMMIGRATION DETENTION IN AUSTRALIA

The Migration Act 1958 (Cth) stipulates that all unlawful non-citizens must be detained until they are granted a visa or removed from Australia.[8] While section 4AA of the Act affirms that, as a general principle, children shall only be detained as a measure of last resort,[9] in practice detention of both adults and children occurs automatically before any individualized assessment of the need for detention is undertaken. The Act does not impose a time limit on detention or set out minimum standards for conditions of detention, nor does it provide for periodic judicial review of decisions to detain.

In addition, the breadth of the detention provisions in the Migration Act, which permit detention so long as a person is not a citizen and does not hold a valid visa, provide limited scope for challenging the lawfulness of detention. While the stated purpose of detention is 'to enable the identification and management of potential risks to the Australian community',[10] there is no legal requirement that a person must present some form of risk (health, security or flight) in order to be detained.

These aspects of Australia's detention policies on numerous occasions have led the UNHRC to conclude that Australia has breached its obligations under Article 9(1) of the ICCPR.[11] The Committee on the Rights of the Child has also expressed deep concern about Australia's maintenance of a policy of mandatory detention without time limits or judicial review.[12]

The High Court of Australia has suggested that immigration detention would become unlawful if its stated purpose, such as to consider a visa application or remove someone from Australia, was not being 'pursued and carried into effect as soon as reasonably practicable'.[13] The Court has

---

8 Migration Act 1958 (Cth), ss. 189, 196.

9 *Ibid.* s. 4AA.

10 DIAC, *Media, Fact Sheet 82: Immigration Detention* (May 2012), available atwww.border.gov.au/about/corporate/information/fact-sheets/82detention.

11 See *A v Australia*, above n. 2, para. [9.4]; *C* v. *Australia*, Communication No. 900/1999, UN Doc. CCPR/C/76/D/900/1999 (28 October 2002), para. [8.2]; *Shams and others* v. *Australia*, Communication Nos. 1255,1256,1259,1260,1266,1268,1270,1288 /2004, UN Doc. CCPR/C/90/D/1255,1256,1259,1260,1266,1268,1270 and1288/2004 (20 July 2007), para. [7.2]; *MMM and others* v. *Australia*, Communication No. 2136/2016, UN Doc. CCPR/C/108/D/2136/2012 (25 July 2013), paras [10.3]–[10.4]; *FKAG and others* v. *Australia*, Communication No. 2094/2011, UN Doc. CCPR/C/108/D/2094/2011 (26 July 2013), paras [9.3]–[9.4].

12 Committee on the Rights of the Child, *Concluding Observations: Australia*, 60th Sess., UN Doc. CRC/C/AUS/CO/4 (28 August 2012), para. [80(a)].

13 *Plaintiff S4-2014* v. *Minister for Immigration and Border Protection* (2014) 253 CLR 219, para. [28].

also indicated that the duration of detention 'must be fixed by reference to what is both necessary and incidental' to fulfil the purpose of detention.[14] However, these limitations have not yet been tested in court, and it remains to be seen whether they could trigger release in cases where a visa or removal outcome is not being actively pursued or is unlikely to be achieved.

In the interim, Australian law continues to permit the indefinite detention of all unlawful non-citizens, including children, for prolonged periods of time, regardless of whether they pose an identifiable risk to the Australian community.

4. FIRST NATIONAL INQUIRY INTO CHILDREN IN DETENTION

Under section 11(1) of the Australian Human Rights Commission Act 1986 (Cth), the Commission has a range of functions and responsibilities relating to the protection and promotion of human rights in Australia. These include powers to:

- examine enactments to determine whether they are inconsistent with or contrary with human rights;
- inquire into any act or practice that may be inconsistent with or contrary to any human right;
- promote an understanding and acceptance, and the public discussion, of human rights in Australia;
- report on laws which should be made by or actions which should be taken on matters relating to human rights; and
- report on action which needs to be taken by Australia to comply with relevant international instruments.[15]

In 2003, on the basis of these provisions, the Commission commenced the first National Inquiry into Children in Immigration Detention. The Inquiry was launched in response to increasing concern within the community about the impacts of detention on the health and wellbeing of children. This was the first time that any institution examining Australia's mandatory detention regime focused purely on the impact of detention on

---

14 *Ibid.* para. [29].

15 Australian Human Rights Commission Act 1986 (Cth), ss. 11(1)(e), 11(1)(f), 11(1)(g), 11(1)(j) and 11(1)(k).

children, and assessed the experience of children in immigration detention against all of the relevant provisions of the CRC.[16]

The Inquiry's report, entitled *A Last Resort?*, was published in 2004. The Inquiry made three major findings. First, Australia's immigration detention laws, as applied to children arriving in Australia without authorization, created a detention system that is fundamentally inconsistent with the CRC.[17] Second, children who are held in immigration detention for long periods of time are at high risk of serious mental harm, and the failure to remove certain children in accordance with recommendations from mental health professionals amounted to cruel, inhuman and degrading treatment.[18] Finally, the Inquiry found that at various times between 1999 and 2002, children in immigration detention were not in a position to fully enjoy a range of rights enshrined in the CRC.[19]

The Inquiry recommended the removal of all children from immigration detention facilities and urgent amendments to the Migration Act to ensure compliance with the CRC, including the introduction of a presumption against the detention of children for immigration purposes, a process of prompt and periodic judicial review of the detention of children and minimum standards of treatment for children in detention.[20]

Following the release of *A Last Resort?*, the Australian government gradually moved children and families out of high-security immigration detention facilities and placed significant numbers of children and families in community detention arrangements. Since that time, as a matter of policy, children have not been held in high-security Immigration Detention Centres[21] (although they continued to be held in lower-security closed facilities). The Federal Parliament also passed the Migration Amendment (Detention Arrangements) Act 2005 (Cth), which introduced the in-principle affirmation in section 4AA that children should only be detained as a last resort.[22]

While these were all welcome developments, they clearly fell far short of the Commission's recommendations. In particular, no substantive

---

[16] Human Rights and Equal Opportunity Commission, *A Last Resort? National Inquiry into Children in Immigration Detention* (2004), pp. 26–7, available at www.humanrights.gov.au/last-resort-report-national-inquiry-children-immigra tion-detention-2004.

[17] *Ibid.* 849–50.

[18] *Ibid.* 850.

[19] *Ibid.* 850.

[20] *Ibid.* 856–7.

[21] Department of Immigration and Border Protection, *Fact Sheet*, above n. 10.

[22] Migration Amendment (Detention Arrangements) Act 2005 (Cth), s. 1.

changes were made to the detention-related provisions of the Migration Act, with the result that the legal framework which had permitted harm documented in *A Last Resort?* remained in place – and with it, the risk that children would again be detained in large numbers for prolonged periods at some point in the future.

5. SECOND NATIONAL INQUIRY INTO CHILDREN IN DETENTION

5.1 Background to the Inquiry

Up until 2009, the number of children in detention remained relatively small. Following an increase in boat arrivals to Australia, the number of children in detention began to climb once more. At the end of 2009, there were around 100 children in closed detention facilities; by the end of 2010, the number was approaching 1,000.[23]

In October of that year, then Prime Minister Julia Gillard and Minister for Immigration and Citizenship Chris Bowen announced that significant numbers of children and vulnerable family groups would be moved out of closed immigration detention facilities into alternative community-based arrangements.[24] From that time, the number of children being held in community detention arrangements steadily increased.

As the number of people arriving by boat continued to rise, however, so too did the number of children in detention. At the end of July 2013, a record 1,992 children were being held in closed detention facilities across Australia. Notably, in the same month, the average length of detention in closed facilities dropped to 72 days, the lowest level since October 2010 (see Figure 20.1).[25]

---

[23] Department of Immigration and Citizenship, Answers to Questions on Notice (Q1–Q3) to Joint Select Committee on Australia's Immigration Detention Network, *Inquiry into Australia's Immigration Detention Network* (May 2011), pp. 379, 495.

[24] Chris Bowen, MP, Minister for Immigration and Citizenship and Julia Gillard, Prime Minister of Australia, *Government to Move Children and Vulnerable Families into Community-based Accommodation* (Media Release, 18 October 2010), available at http://parlinfo.aph.gov.au/parlInfo/search/display/display.w3p;query=Id%3A%22media%2Fpressrel%2F1927276%22.

[25] Department of Immigration and Citizenship, *Immigration Detention Statistics Summary* (31 July 2013), pp. 3, 7, 9, available at www.border.gov.au/ReportsandPublications/Documents/statistics/immigration-detention-statistics-july2013.pdf.

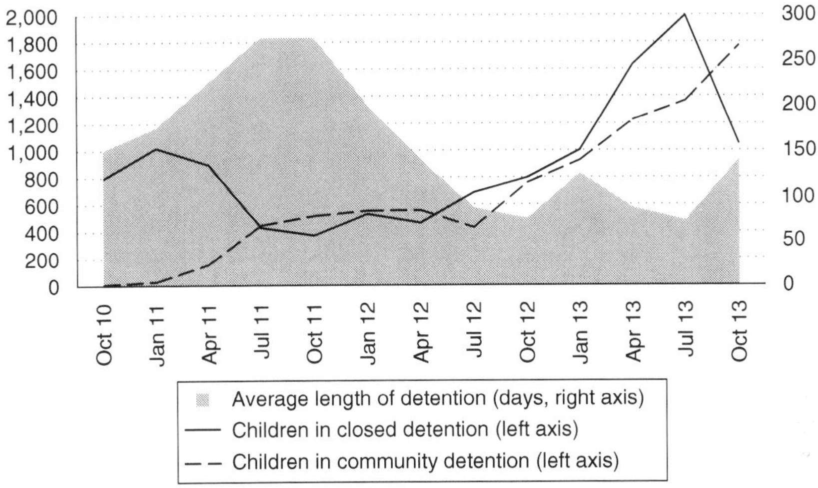

Note: * Figures compiled from Department of Immigration and Citizenship, 'Answers to Questions on Notice (Q1-Q3) to Joint Select Committee on Australia's Immigration Detention Network', *Inquiry into Australia's Immigration Detention Network* (May 2011), p. 379; and monthly immigration detention statistics summaries published by the Department of Immigration and Citizenship and the Department of Immigration and Border Protection, available at www.border.gov.au/about/reports-publications/research-statistics/statistics/live-in-australia/immigration-detention. Figures displayed for selected months due to inconsistencies in the publication of statistics. Figures on the average length of detention between October 2010 and January 2012 are estimates based on graphs in later summaries.

*Figure 20.1 Number of children in detention and average length of detention, October 2010 to October 2013**

As it had become increasingly clear that many of the issues raised in *A Last Resort?* remained unaddressed, the Commission had been planning to conduct a second National Inquiry into Children in Immigration Detention, marking the tenth anniversary of the first. With a Federal election imminent in the second half of 2013, it was decided that the launch of the Inquiry should be delayed until the outcome of the election had been determined and the incoming government had had sufficient time to implement any planned changes to detention policy.

In the six months following the Federal election in September 2013, it became clear that the new government's approach to detention policy had indeed changed. Boat arrivals began to slow, with the result that fewer children were entering closed detention facilities. However, releases of children already detained in these facilities also slowed. A significant number of the children in detention at that time were due to be transferred

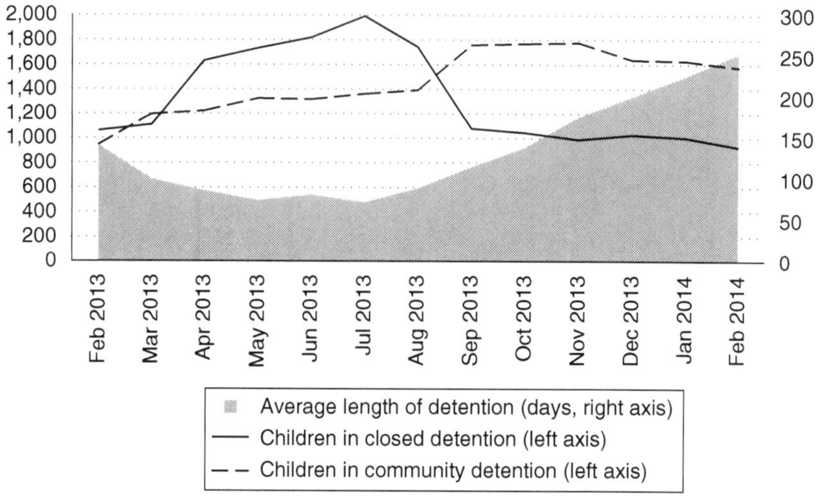

Note: * Figures compiled from monthly immigration detention statistics summaries published by the Department of Immigration and Citizenship and the Department of Immigration and Border Protection, available at www.border.gov.au/about/reports-publications/research-statistics/statistics/live-in-australia/immigration-detention.

*Figure 20.2 Number of children in detention and average length of detention, February 2013 to February 2014**

to Regional Processing Facilities, and therefore were not being considered for release. In addition, the average length of detention, which had previously been declining, began to increase dramatically, more than doubling between September 2013 and February 2014 (see Figure 20.2).[26]

In light of these circumstances, the Commission proceeded with launching the second National Inquiry on 3 February 2014.

5.2 Aims and Methodology

The second National Inquiry into Children in Immigration Detention had two key aims: to assess the impact of prolonged immigration detention on

[26] Department of Immigration and Border Protection, *Immigration Detention and Community Statistics Summary* (31 October 2013), p. 10, available at www.border.gov.au/ReportsandPublications/Documents/statistics/immigration-detention-statistics-oct2013.pdf; Department of Immigration and Border Protection, *Immigration Detention and Community Statistics Summary* (28 February 2014), p. 10, available at www.border.gov.au/ReportsandPublications/Documents/statistics/immigration-detention-statistics-feb2014.pdf.

children's health, wellbeing and development; and to promote compliance with Australia's international obligations to act in the best interests of children.

The Inquiry team was led by myself with assistance from Megan Mitchell, the National Children's Commissioner, and Tim Wilson, the Human Rights Commissioner, as well as independent paediatric and child mental health specialists. The team conducted 13 visits to detention facilities across the country. A total of 1,129 children and parents in detention were interviewed by the Inquiry team, along with 92 children and 12 parents who had previously been in detention and were living in the community.

The Commission issued a call for submissions, of which 239 were received, and held five public hearings to gather evidence from current and former Ministers for Immigration, representatives from the Department of Immigration and Border Protection, medical professionals, non-governmental organizations and former child detainees. A report detailing the Commission's findings and recommendations was provided to the Department of Immigration on 31 October 2014.[27]

5.3 Impacts of Detention on the Mental Health of Children

> I feel like I am in a prison. I am so bored and sometimes I think of killing myself. (12-year-old detained in Darwin)[28]

The Inquiry found that prolonged detention was having profoundly negative impacts on the mental and emotional health of children. Eighty-five per cent of children and parents interviewed by the Commission indicated that their emotional and mental health had been affected since being in detention.[29] Almost all children and their parents spoke about their worry, restlessness, anxiety and difficulties eating and sleeping in detention.[30]

Mental health screening of children conducted by detention staff

---

27 Australian Human Rights Commission, *The Forgotten Children: National Inquiry into Children in Immigration Detention* (2015), available at www.humanrights.gov.au/our-work/asylum-seekers-and-refugees/publications/forgotten-children-national-inquiry-children. Sections 5.3 to 5.6 of this chapter are based on the content of this report.

28 12-year-old child, Wickham Point Detention Centre, Darwin, 11 April 2014.

29 Australian Human Rights Commission, *The Forgotten Children*, above n. 27, at 58.

30 *Ibid.* 58.

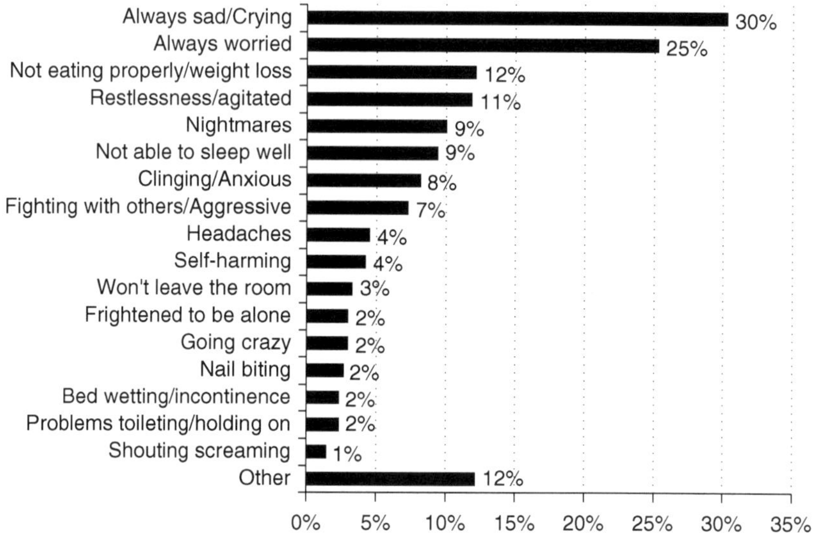

Note: * Australian Human Rights Commission, *Inquiry Questionnaire for Children and Parents in Detention, Australia 2014*, 327 respondents. (Note: respondents can provide multiple responses.)

*Figure 20.3 Responses by children and parents to the question: How has your emotional and mental health been impacted by detention?**

revealed alarming results both in the rates of mental disorder in these children and in the severity of their symptoms. Results from these assessments showed that 34 per cent of children had mental health disorders that would be comparable in seriousness to children referred to hospital-based child mental health out-patient services for psychiatric treatment.[31] Less than 2 per cent of children in the Australian population have mental health disorders at this level.[32]

Children had been exposed to danger through their close confinement with adults who suffer high levels of mental illness. From January 2013 to March 2014, there were numerous assaults and self-harm incidents in detention centres in Australia where children are held. They included 233 assaults involving children and 33 incidents of reported sexual assault, the majority involving children.[33]

---

[31] *Ibid.* 59.
[32] *Ibid.* 59.
[33] *Ibid.* 62.

The very high rates of self-harm amongst children in detention were of particular concern. Between January 2013 and March 2014, 128 children in detention engaged in actual self-harm and 171 children threatened self-harm.[34] The age of children involved in self-harm ranged from 12 to 17 years old.[35] 105 children in detention were assessed under the Department of Immigration and Border Protection's Psychological Support Program as being of 'high imminent risk' or 'moderate risk' of suicide or self-harm and required ongoing monitoring. Ten of these children were aged 10 years or younger.[36]

During interviews with the Inquiry team, children and their parents were asked to describe their experience of immigration detention in three words. Their responses revealed overwhelmingly negative sentiments. Many described the boredom and frustration of the detention environment with few opportunities for recreation or education.[37] Children spoke of the hopelessness which they felt about the future, the lack of certainty about a timeframe for the assessment of their refugee claims, and the fear of being sent to Nauru or Manus Island.[38]

The Commission considered that the mandatory and prolonged immigration detention of children is in clear violation of international human rights law. Australia's detention policies had not only breached its obligations to prevent arbitrary detention and ensure humane treatment in detention, but had also violated the right of children to the highest attainable standard of health as enshrined in Article 24(1) of the CRC.

5.4 Impacts of Detention on the Development of Children

> Our friends are going to school in Iran and we are not . . . [child crying]. This was a mistake to come to Australia. (Nine-year-old child detained on Christmas Island)[39]

The evidence gathered by the Inquiry clearly indicated that detention can impede the physical, social and emotional development of children. The inherently restrictive environment in detention facilities constrained opportunities for children to develop through play and exploration. There

---

34 *Ibid.* 62.
35 *Ibid.* 62.
36 *Ibid.* 62.
37 *Ibid.* 71.
38 *Ibid.* 71.
39 Nine-year-old girl, Construction Camp Detention Centre, Christmas Island, 2 March 2014.

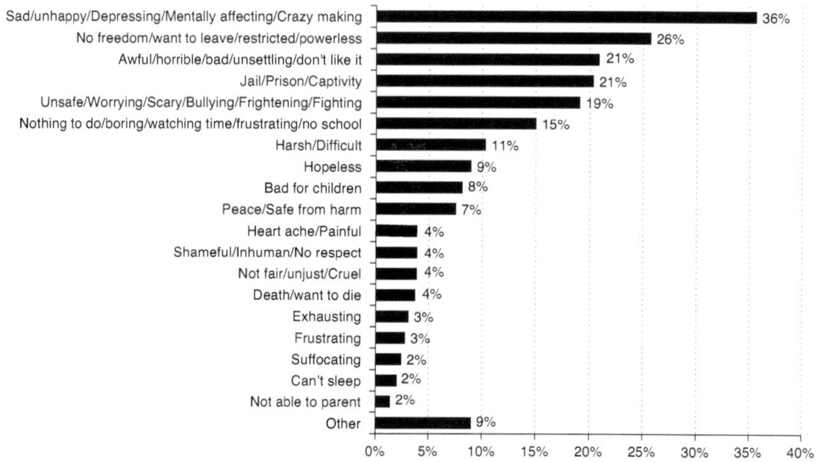

Note: * Australian Human Rights Commission, *Inquiry Questionnaire for Children and Parents in Detention*, Australia 2014, 723 respondents. (Note: respondents can provide multiple responses.)

*Figure 20.4 Responses by children and parents to the question: Use three words to describe the experience of detention**

was limited access to toys and recreation spaces such as playrooms, libraries and playground equipment, and children had limited opportunities to explore new places outside of the detention environment.[40]

In the detention facilities in Melbourne, Darwin and Christmas Island, families were being housed in converted shipping containers measuring between 2.5 x 3 metres and 3 x 3.5 metres.[41] These were extremely cramped spaces for energetic children but provided the only private spaces for families.[42] In Darwin and Christmas Island, the containers were the only private spaces that provided respite from the tropical heat.[43] At the Christmas Island detention facility, there was particular concern that the hard and stony terrain did not provide a safe environment in which babies could learn to crawl or walk.[44] At a time when children should have been

40 Australian Human Rights Commission, *The Forgotten Children*, above n. 27, at 134.
41 *Ibid.* 129.
42 *Ibid.* 107, 129.
43 *Ibid.* 107, 129.
44 *Ibid.* 95.

exploring their world and testing their abilities, many were being confined to cramped living quarters for many hours of the day.

At the detention facilities in Adelaide and Sydney, families and children were accommodated in houses which provided more space and a friendlier environment for children. Nevertheless, the physical environment in these facilities remained restrictive: children and families could not leave at will, remained subject to regular head counts, had limited opportunities to engage in activities outside the detention environment and had to be accompanied by a guard whenever they left the facility, including when travelling to and from school.[45]

One of the most concerning findings of the Inquiry was that children detained on Christmas Island had almost no access to school education between July 2013 and July 2014. During this period, two hours of schooling was provided on a rotational basis each day to all school-aged children. The Department of Immigration and Border Protection acknowledged this deficiency at the first public hearing held as part of the Inquiry, and the situation was rectified in July 2014.[46] Nonetheless, the lack of adequate education for a period of over a year had negative impacts on the learning of the children affected, and may have long-term impacts on their cognitive development and academic progress.

Prolonged detention was also found to have serious implications for the social and emotional development of children, particularly for those at critical life stages. For example, new mothers who are distressed or depressed in the detention environment can struggle to form healthy attachments with their babies, which can impede the social development of those babies.[47] For young children who are developing socialization skills, being deprived of a normal family environment and witnessing the distress of unwell adults in detention can have a significant impact on their ability to learn rules of behaviour and relate to others. Many parents of pre-schooler children, for instance, reported that their child was unable to get along with other children.[48]

The institutionalized structure and routine of detention also disrupts family functioning and relationships between parents and children. In the normal family environment, parents make most decisions about their child's care and development. In detention environments, by contrast, adults and children passively receive services rather than manage their

---

45 *Ibid.* 114, 130, 132–3, 138.
46 *Ibid.* 146–7.
47 *Ibid.* 87–8.
48 *Ibid.* 115.

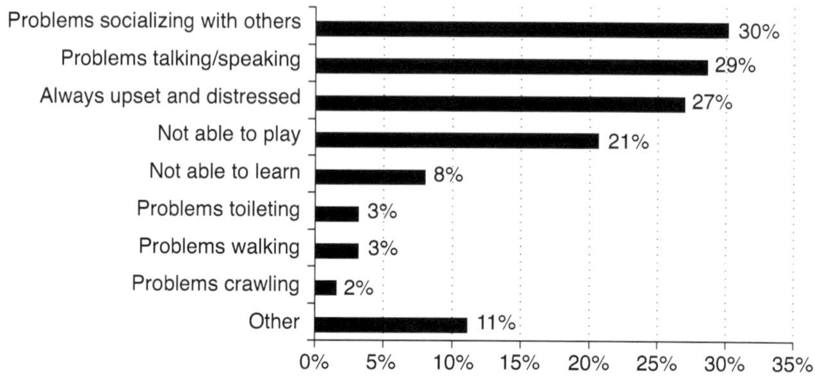

Note: * Australian Human Rights Commission, *Inquiry Questionnaire for Children and Parents in Detention*, Australia, 2014, 63 respondents. (Note: respondents can provide multiple responses.)

*Figure 20.5 Responses by parents of preschoolers to the question: What are your concerns about the development of your child?**

own environments. Adults are restricted in their ability to carry out routine parental functions and have limited decision-making authority. This distorts the relationship between parents and children, with a number of parents reporting that their children no longer respected their authority.[49]

The Commission considered that at various times, children in detention were not in a position to enjoy their right to development and their right to a standard of living adequate for their development. The failure to provide adequate education to school-aged children detained on Christmas Island also represented a violation of their right to education.

5.5 Unaccompanied Children in Detention

> I don't care about a visa any more. I want to finish everything. My life is very difficult. I don't understand why I am here. I am beginning to feel crazy; my situation is very bad and getting worse. I am alone, no family, nobody here. I've been here 15 months, I need to do something. (17-year-old unaccompanied child detained in Melbourne)[50]

In March 2014, shortly after the Commission commenced the National Inquiry, there were 56 children in Australian detention centres who had

---

[49] *Ibid.* 128, 144.

[50] 17-year-old unaccompanied child, Melbourne Detention Centre, 7 May 2014.

travelled to Australia without parents or a legal guardian. At that time, these children had been detained for an average of 217 days.[51]

Unaccompanied children require higher levels of emotional and social support because they do not have a parent in the detention environment. The evidence gathered by the Inquiry indicated that detention is not a place where these children can develop the resiliencies that they will need for adult life, nor can their particular vulnerabilities be addressed in an environment which exacerbates the effects of previous trauma.[52]

It was clear that being held in detention had placed an additional burden on these young people, who were already affected by their past experiences. When the Inquiry team asked unaccompanied children whether their emotional and mental health had been affected since being in detention, every one of the 42 respondents answered 'yes'.[53] When asked how they felt in detention, 48 per cent of the unaccompanied children said that they felt depressed all of the time and 45 per cent said that they felt hopeless all of the time.[54]

In July 2014, the Commission received case files from the Department of Immigration and Border Protection of 37 unaccompanied children who were either in detention or had been in detention. The case files revealed some alarming details about the nature of self-harm and suicide attempts amongst this group. Seven of the 37 children (19 per cent) had engaged in actual self-harm in detention and nine children (24 per cent) had threatened self-harm.[55]

The findings of the Inquiry also reinforced the Commission's long-standing concerns about the lack of effective guardianship for unaccompanied children who are seeking asylum. Under the Immigration (Guardianship of Children) Act 1946 (Cth) ('Guardianship of Children Act'), the Minister for Immigration and Border Protection is the legal guardian of certain 'non-citizen' unaccompanied children. In this role the Minister has the same 'rights, powers, duties, obligations and liabilities as a natural guardian of the child'.[56]

Under current arrangements, the Minister delegates their guardianship responsibilities to nominated Departmental officers, who are not required to have specific qualifications or experience relating to children.

---

51 Australian Human Rights Commission, *The Forgotten Children*, above. n. 27, at 151.
52 *Ibid.* 169–70.
53 *Ibid.* 153.
54 *Ibid.* 154.
55 *Ibid.* 156.
56 Immigration (Guardianship of Children) Act 1946 (Cth), s. 6(1).

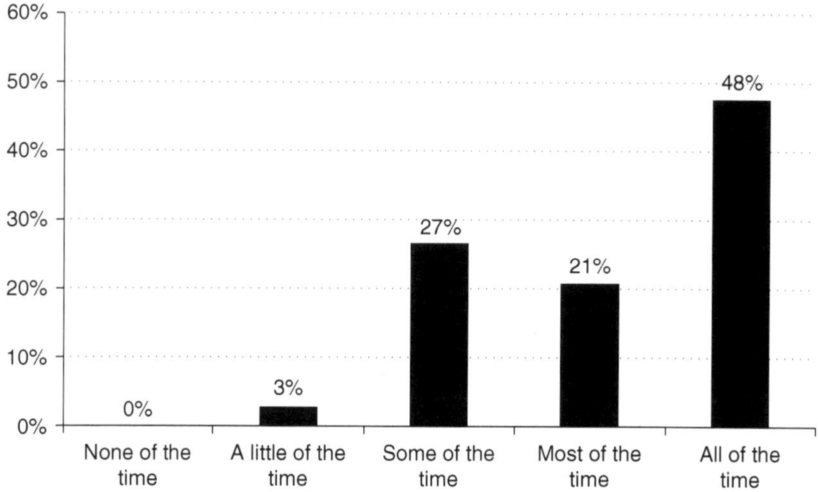

Note: * Australian Human Rights Commission, *Inquiry Questionnaire for Children and Parents in Detention*, Australia 2014, 33 respondents.

*Figure 20.6 Responses by unaccompanied children to the question: How often do you feel depressed?**

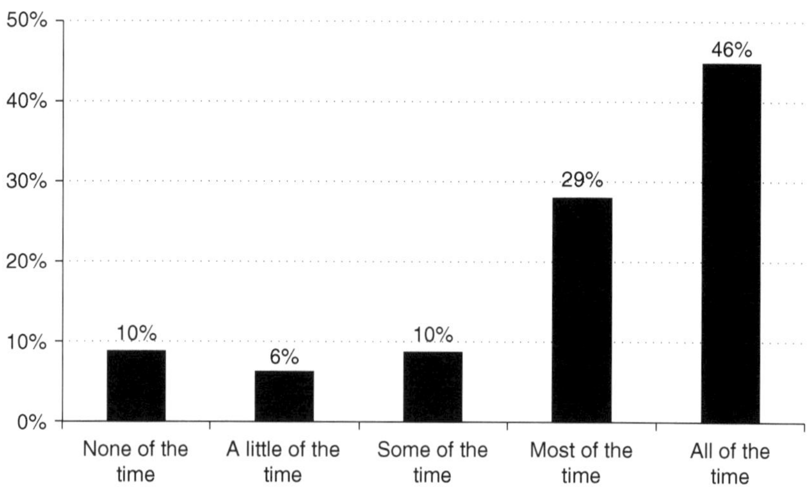

Note: * Australian Human Rights Commission, *Inquiry Questionnaire for Children and Parents in Detention*, Australia 2014, 31 respondents.

*Figure 20.7 Responses by unaccompanied children to the question: How often do you feel hopeless?**

The Commission remains concerned about the ability of the guardians to monitor properly and ensure the appropriate care and progress of an unaccompanied child without appropriate qualifications or specific child welfare experience.

The Commission has repeatedly stated that the effectiveness of the Minister's role as guardian of unaccompanied children conflicts with their additional responsibilities for administering the immigration detention regime under the Migration Act and for making decisions about granting visas, removals and transfers to Nauru and Manus Island. Given these multiple duties, it is difficult for the Minister, or their delegate, to make the best interests of the child the primary consideration in their decision-making about the child.

In the event of any conflict between guardianship obligations and migration policies, the Minister and their delegates must give priority to their roles under the Migration Act. The Guardianship of Children Act stipulates that the Minister or their delegates can only exercise their duties as guardians to the extent that those duties do not affect the performance or exercise of any function, duty or power under the migration law.[57]

There are clear shortcomings in Australia's framework for protecting unaccompanied children. These deficiencies have led to breaches of Australia's obligations to provide special protection and assistance to this particularly vulnerable group of children.

5.6 Children in Detention on Nauru

> Our marquees are very dirty. Because of the weather, after some time, there is mould in the marquees and because of the strong sun, the roof of the marquees has holes and when it rains, we get a lot of water inside the marquees. There is so much water that we have collected all our belongings and empty the water with buckets. (16-year-old detained in Nauru)[58]

In 2012, the Australian government reintroduced third country processing of asylum claims with the aim of deterring asylum-seekers from travelling to Australia by boat. Under this policy, asylum-seekers who arrive in Australia by boat are transferred to Australian funded Regional Processing Centres in Nauru and Papua New Guinea's Manus Island,

---

[57] *Ibid.* s. 8(2).

[58] Name withheld, 16-year-old detained in Nauru OPC, Submission No. 91 to the National Inquiry into Children in Immigration Detention 2014, p. 1, available at www.humanrights.gov.au/sites/default/files/Submission%20No%2091%20-%20Name%20withheld%20-%2016%20year%20old%20detained%20in%20Nauru%20OPC.pdf.

where their claims for refugee status are assessed. If they are found to be refugees, they will not be permitted to settle in Australia.

At the end of January 2014, just before the Inquiry commenced, there were 132 children detained in the Regional Processing Centre in Nauru.[59] While the Inquiry did not conduct a visit to this facility, it did receive substantial evidence about conditions of detention in Nauru and the impacts of prolonged indefinite detention on the children detained there.

Evidence provided to the Inquiry confirmed that conditions of detention in Nauru were harsh, characterized by cramped living quarters, overwhelming heat and limited privacy.[60] Children and families were being housed in tents situated on gravel terrain, with individual family areas within the tents separated only by vinyl partitions.[61] Numerous concerns were raised regarding the inadequacy of basic services, including hygiene facilities, provision of clothing and footwear, education and health services.[62]

The Inquiry also received significant evidence regarding the deteriorating physical and mental health of children in detention on Nauru. As on the mainland, prolonged and indefinite detention was seen to have a negative impact on the mental health of children, while crowded and unhygienic detention conditions and the limitations of healthcare on Nauru posed serious challenges to the physical health and development of children. Of perhaps greatest concern were reported incidents of harassment, bullying and abuse, including sexual abuse, involving children in detention on Nauru.[63]

There was no child protection framework in place in Nauru at the time of the Inquiry, and pre-transfer assessment processes in place for children sent to Nauru clearly lacked an adequate child protection focus. While a Best Interest Assessment was undertaken for children transferred to Nauru, this assessment had no bearing on whether that child was actually transferred. In all cases, the best interests of the child were determined to be outweighed by 'other primary considerations', such as the need to discourage dangerous boat journeys.[64]

---

[59] Department of Immigration and Border Protection, *Immigration Detention and Community Statistics Summary* (31 January 2014), p. 3, available at www.border.gov.au/ReportsandPublications/Documents/statistics/immigration-detention-statistics-jan2014.pdf.

[60] Australian Human Rights Commission, *The Forgotten Children*, above n. 27, at 181.

[61] *Ibid.* 181.

[62] *Ibid.* 182–5, 188–90.

[63] *Ibid.* 186–8.

[64] *Ibid.* 188, 190–93.

The evidence gathered by the Inquiry clearly indicated that children on Nauru were suffering from extreme levels of physical, emotional, psychological and developmental distress, resulting in multiple violations of Australia's international obligations.[65] So severe were the conditions under which children were detained in Nauru that the Commission determined Australia to be in breach of its obligation not to subject children to cruel, inhuman and degrading treatment.[66]

6. DEVELOPMENTS SINCE THE INQUIRY

The report of the second National Inquiry, entitled *The Forgotten Children*, was published in February 2015, around a year after the Inquiry had commenced. Over the course of that year, the number of children in closed detention facilities had reduced significantly, from close to 1,000 at the time the Inquiry commenced to around 200 at the time that *The Forgotten Children* report was publicly released.[67]

Following a steep decline in early 2015, releases of the small cohort of children remaining in detention stalled. The majority of these children were in detention because they had a parent who had received an adverse security assessment, and therefore was not being considered for release from detention, or because they had been temporarily transferred from Nauru to Australia so that they or a member of their family could receive medical treatment.

As the months went by, the Commission became particularly concerned about the welfare of the children in detention who faced return to harsh conditions and an uncertain future on Nauru. In mid-October 2015, the Commission conducted a visit to the Wickham Point detention facility to meet with these children and their families, assess their wellbeing and

---

65 *Ibid.* 195.

66 *Ibid.* 195.

67 The Inquiry was launched on 3 February 2014 and the report tabled in Parliament on 11 February 2015. The monthly immigration detention statistics summaries published by the Department of Immigration and Border Protection show that there were 1,006 children in closed detention as at 31 January 2014, and 211 children in closed detention as at 31 January 2015. See Department of Immigration and Border Protection, *Immigration Detention and Community Statistics Summary* (31 January 2015), p. 3, available at http://www.border.gov.au/ReportsandPublications/Documents/statistics/immigration-detention-statistics-jan2015.pdf.

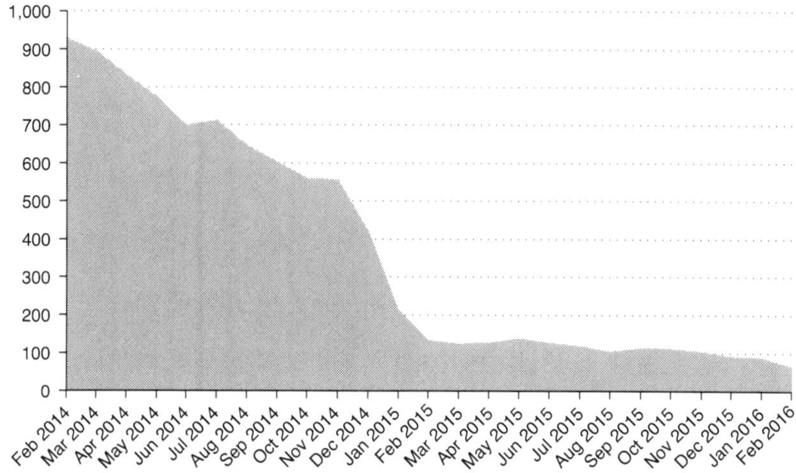

Note: * Figures compiled from monthly immigration detention statistics summaries published by the Department of Immigration and Citizenship and the Department of Immigration and Border Protection, available at www.border.gov.au/about/reports-publications/research-statistics/statistics/live-in-australia/immigration-detention.

*Figure 20.8 Number of children in closed detention facilities, February 2014 to February 2016**

monitor conditions of detention. At the time of the visit, there were 164 families with 76 children detained at Wickham Point.[68]

The Commission was accompanied by two consultant paediatricians, who reported that the children, most of whom had spent several months on Nauru, were amongst the most traumatized they had ever seen. Medical assessments revealed that many of these children were at risk of developmental delays and post-traumatic stress disorder, and were suffering from high levels of distress, hopelessness and despair. The paediatricians recommended that the children not be transferred to Nauru, and instead be released into alternative community arrangements.[69]

Earlier that month, the Government of Nauru had announced that the

[68] E. Elliott and H. Gunasekera, *The Health and Well-being of Children in Immigration Detention, Report to the Australian Human Rights Commission – Monitoring Visit to Wickham Point Detention Centre, Darwin, NT* (Australian Human Rights Commission, 2016), p. 7, available at www.humanrights.gov.au/our-work/asylum-seekers-and-refugees/publications/health-and-well-being-children-immigration.

[69] *Ibid.*

Regional Processing Centre had transitioned to an 'open' facility, from which people could come and go at any time.[70] However, the consultant paediatricians had determined that Nauru was an inappropriate place for asylum-seeking children to live, either in the detention centre or in the community.[71] Many of the people interviewed by the Commission team reported that they would not leave the Centre even though it is now 'open', due to concerns about their safety in the Nauruan community.[72]

In February 2016, the High Court of Australia delivered its judgment in this case of *Plaintiff M68/2015* v. *Minister for Immigration and Border Protection.*[73] The court ruled that Australian law provides the Australian government with the necessary legal authority to send asylum-seekers to Nauru for the purpose of processing their claims to asylum and to participate in a regime where they would be detained on Nauru while their claims were processed (albeit within limits).[74]

Following this decision, the Commission became concerned that the children at Wickham Point would be transferred to Nauru despite the risks this would present to their health and wellbeing. The Commission therefore decided to release the findings of its visit to Wickham Point in February 2016, urging the government not to return the children and families to Nauru.[75]

All of the children detained in the Wickham Point facility were subsequently released into alternative community arrangements. Although they remain at risk of being transferred to Nauru,[76] all remained in Australia at the time of writing. There was another welcome development in April 2016, when the Minister for Immigration and Border Protection

---

[70] Peter Dutton, MP, Minister for Immigration and Border Protection, *Australia Welcomes Nauru Open Centre* (Media Release, 5 October 2015), available at www.minister.border.gov.au/peterdutton/2015/Pages/australia-welcomes-nauru-open-centre.aspx.

[71] Elliott and Gunasekera, *The Health and Well-being of Children in Immigration Detention*, above n. 68, at 3.

[72] *Ibid.* 3, 12.

[73] *Plaintiff M68/2015* v. *Minister for Immigration and Border Protection* (2016) HCA 1.

[74] *Ibid.* para. [46].

[75] See Australian Human Rights Commission, *New Report: Experts Reveal Alarming Impact of Detention on Children* (Media Release, 4 February 2016), available at www.humanrights.gov.au/news/stories/new-report-experts-reveal-alarming-impact-detention-children.

[76] ABC Radio National, 'All children released from mainland detention: Peter Dutton', *RN Breakfast*, 4 April 2016 (Peter Dutton, MP, Minister for Immigration and Border Protection), available at www.minister.border.gov.au/peterdutton/2016/Pages/abc-rn-04042016.aspx.

announced that alternative community arrangements had been developed for all remaining children in detention who had arrived by boat to seek asylum.[77] At the time of writing, there were no children being held in closed detention facilities in Australia.[78]

Positive as these developments may be, the detention-related provisions of the Migration Act remain unchanged. Although releasing children from closed detention facilities may have resolved some of the immediate threats to their health and wellbeing, nothing has occurred to prevent other children from facing the same situation in the future. As with the response to *A Last Resort?*, the response to *The Forgotten Children* has again fallen well short of the Commission's recommendations.

7. WHERE TO FROM HERE?

It is clear that legislative amendments are critical to prevent the prolonged indefinite detention of children now and into the future. There does not appear to be any will for legislative reform amongst either of Australia's major political parties.

In late 2015, the Senate proposed several amendments to the Migration and Maritime Powers Amendment Bill (No. 1) 2015 (Cth). One of these amendments would require the Minister to release children from detention into community detention within 30 days.[79] This provision was not accepted by the majority of Senators without further amendments providing for broad exceptions.[80] The amended Bill was returned to the House of Representatives and has lapsed at the prorogation of Parliament.[81]

Two national inquiries, ten years apart, have unequivocally established that prolonged indefinite detention poses unacceptable risks to the health,

---

77 Peter Dutton, MP, Minister for Immigration and Border Protection, 'Doorstop Interview', Press Conference delivered in Brisbane, 3 April 2016, available at www.minister.border.gov.au/peterdutton/2016/Pages/doorstop-interview-03042016.aspx.

78 Department of Immigration and Border Protection, *Immigration Detention and Community Statistics Summary* (30 June 2016), p. 4, available at www.border.gov.au/ReportsandPublications/Documents/statistics/immigration-detention-statistics-30-june-2016.pdf.

79 Migration and Maritime Powers Amendment Bill (No. 1) 2015 (Cth), s. 197AAA.

80 *Ibid.* s. 197AAA(3A), (4).

81 Parliament of Australia, Migration and Maritime Powers Amendment Bill (No. 1) 2015 (15 April 2016), available at http://parlinfo.aph.gov.au/parlInfo/search/display/display.w3p;query=Id%3A%22legislation%2Fbillhome%2Fr5532%22.

wellbeing and development of children and violates Australia's international human rights obligations. Only legislative reform can ensure that there will be no need for a third inquiry. It is incumbent upon both major parties to show the political leadership necessary to definitively end the indefinite detention of children in Australia and bring our detention policies in line with international law.

21. The rise and rise of mandatory immigration detention

Daniel Ghezelbash

1. INTRODUCTION

Law-makers are increasingly drawing on the practice of other jurisdictions when developing immigration law and policy. This is due in part to the fact that the objectives of governments are converging. On the one hand, they seek to attract what they perceive as 'good' migrants, such as skilled workers and investors. At same time, they want to deter 'bad' migrants, such as asylum-seekers and irregular arrivals. The propensity to look abroad is made greater by the fact that migration policy decisions are *interdependent*.[1] Changes in the immigration policy settings in one jurisdiction can have ramifications for migratory flows in other jurisdictions. For example, deterrent measures introduced in one jurisdiction, can redirect irregular migratory flows to an alternate destination. In this context of 'competitive interdependence',[2] it makes sense to keep a close eye on what other jurisdictions are doing, and where appropriate, copy policies which are perceived as being successful. This tendency explains the rise of the policy of long-term mandatory detention of asylum-seekers. This has been facilitated by legal and policy transfer, which is the processes by which knowledge of laws, policies, administrative arrangements, institutions and ideas in one political system is used in another political system to develop its laws, policies, administrative arrangements, institutions and ideas.[3]

---

[1] See, generally, D. Ghezelbash, *Refuge Lost: Asylum Law in an Interdependent World* (Cambridge University Press, 2018).

[2] D. Ghezelbash, 'Forces of Diffusion: What Drives the Transfer of Immigration Policy and Law Across Jurisdictions?' (2014) 1(2) *International Journal of Migration and Border Studies* 139.

[3] D. Dolowitz and D. Marsh, 'Who Learns What from Whom: A Review of the Policy Transfer Literature' (1996) 44 *Political Studies* 343, at 334 (the definition of policy transfer put forward by Dolowitz and Marsh has been expanded to explicitly include the transfer of law, as well as policy).

I adopt Michael Flynn's definition of immigration detention as 'the deprivation of liberty of non-citizens for reasons related to their [immigration] status'.[4] This detention is generally of an administrative nature, rather than criminal incarceration which is carried out pursuant to a judicial order.[5] The detention of asylum-seekers who enter without authorization is a common policy response to irregular migration, practiced in numerous jurisdictions throughout the world.[6] In most countries where asylum-seekers are detained, the period of detention is restricted to the 'pre-admission' phase. This is where an asylum-seeker's identity is established and security checks are carried out. My focus in this chapter is on the more punitive policy of longer-term mandatory detention of asylum-seekers beyond the 'pre-admission' stage, with a particular focus on the detention of children. The concerns that such a policy raises under international human rights law are thoroughly examined in other chapters in this volume.[7] My focus here is on comparing the domestic legal frameworks governing the detention of children in the United States and Australia. Elsewhere, I have documented the process of legal and policy transfer which led to the spread of mandatory detention policies across these jurisdictions.[8] My objective here is to examine the impact of these transfers on child migrants.

---

[4] For a detailed discussion of this definition see M. Flynn, 'Who Must be Detained? Proportionality as a Tool for Critiquing Immigration Detention Policy' (2012) 31 *Refugee Survey Quarterly* 40, at 42–7.

[5] Note that in some jurisdictions, irregular migration is a criminal offence and thus detention in such a context can be criminal in nature.

[6] G.S. Goodwin-Gill, 'Article 31 of the 1951 Convention relating to the Status of Refugees: Non-Penalisation, Detention, and Protection' in E. Feller, V. Türk and F. Nicholson (eds), *Refugee Protection in International Law: UNHCR's Global Consultations on International Protection* (Cambridge University Press, 2003), pp. 185, 187. D. Ghezelbash and M. Crock, 'Out of Sight, Out of Mind? The Myths and Realities of Mandatory Immigration Detention' in D. Acosta and A. Wiesbrock (eds), *Global Migration Issues: Myths and Realities* (Praeger International, 2015), p. 23.

[7] See the contributions by Gerald Neuman, Chapter 19, and Gillian Triggs, Chapter 20.

[8] Ghezelbash, *Refuge Lost*, above n. 1; M Crock and D. Ghezelbash, 'Secret Immigration Business: Policy Transfers and the Tyranny of Deterrence Theory' in S.S. Juss (ed.), *The Ashgate Research Companion to Migration Theory and Policy* (Ashgate, 2013).

2. UNITED STATES

Provisions authorizing the detention of aliens seeking entry were first introduced in the United States in 1891.[9] However, the genesis of the current mandatory detention regime for unauthorized arrivals can be traced to the arrival of boats carrying Haitian asylum-seekers in the early 1980s. President Reagan implemented an informal rule in May 1981 that provided for the mandatory detention of all Haitians arriving by boat without documentation. After it was struck down by the courts on a technical point,[10] a fresh regulation was introduced that expanded mandatory detention to apply to *all* aliens arriving without proper documentation.[11] The regulations provided that:

> [a]ny alien who appears to the inspecting officer to be inadmissible, and who arrives without documents or who arrives with documentation which appears to be false, altered, or otherwise invalid . . . shall be detained.[12]

The regulations made it clear that, while parole was still available for 'emergent reasons' or on 'public interest' grounds, such conditional release was restricted to limited circumstance.[13]

The Illegal Immigration Reform and Immigrant Responsibility Act of 1996 (IIRIRA) broadened the classes of arriving aliens subject to mandatory detention and reduced access to parole.[14] It introduced new expedited removal procedures which remain in force today.[15] These allow aliens who arrive in the United States without valid documentation or with false documentation to be ordered removed without further hearings, reviews or appeals.[16] Judicial review of expedited removal decisions

---

9 Immigration Act of 1891, s. 8, ch. 551, 26 Stat. 1084, 1085–6.

10 *Louis* v. *Nelson*, 544 F. Supp. 973, 1003 (SD Fla, 1982) holding that the Immigration and Naturalization Service (INS) had violated the Administrative Procedure Act, 5 USC s. 553 (1982) by instituting a new rule without first publishing notice of the proposed change in the Federal Registrar and giving opportunity for interested parties to comment.

11 47 Fed. Reg. 30044-46 (9 July 1982) (codified at 8 CFR s. 212.5 (1982), additional regulations codified at s. 235.3 (1997)).

12 8 CFR s. 235.3(b) (1982).

13 8 CFR s. 212.5(a)(1), (2) (1982).

14 Pub. L No. 104-208, 110 Stat. 3009.

15 INA, s. 235(b)(1)(A)(i).

16 When introduced, expedited removal only applied to arriving aliens at ports of entry. In 2002, it was expanded to apply to aliens who arrive by sea who are not admitted or paroled. It was again expanded in 2005 to apply to certain unadmitted aliens intercepted within 100 miles of the US southern border.

is expressly barred. Aliens who indicate an intention to apply for asylum are referred to an asylum officer for a 'credible fear' interview. Only if the asylum officer agrees the claim is credible, can the person pursue their application for asylum through regular removal procedures. All persons subject to expedited removal procedures are to be mandatorily detained. Those awaiting their 'credible fear' determination and those found not to hold such a fear have no access to parole. Asylum-seekers who establish a 'credible fear' of persecution are no longer subject to expedited removal proceedings, but rather regular removal proceedings. As such, they may be eligible for parole under the normal parole criteria. However, recent practice indicates that even asylum-seekers in this category are routinely detained.[17]

Over the years, a number of special provisions have been made for children subject to detention. The original 1982 mandatory detention regulations authorized the release of juveniles on parole under the 'public interest' category.[18] The 1997 *Flores* settlement agreement arising out of a class action challenge to the detention of minors stipulated that children in immigration proceedings be placed in the 'least restrictive setting'.[19] This was initially applied to both accompanied and unaccompanied minors, who were generally released from detention. The application of this principle was formalized with respect to unaccompanied minors with the passage of the Trafficking Victims Protection Reauthorization Act 2008 (TVPRA). The law exempts unaccompanied children from expedited removal proceedings, providing them with the right to appear before an immigration judge to petition for humanitarian relief from removal.[20] Rather than being detained by the Department of Homeland Security like other undocumented migrants, unaccompanied minors are entrusted into

---

President Donald Trump announced plans in 2017 to expand expedited removal to apply to aliens intercepted anywhere in the United States who cannot show they have been present continuously in the United States for two years: DHS Secretary J. Kelly, *Memorandum Implementing the President's Border Security and Immigration Enforcement Policies* (17 February 2017), section G ('Kelly Memorandum').

[17] See notes 32–7 and accompanying discussion below.

[18] 8 CFR s. 212.5(a)(2) (1982).

[19] *Flores* v. *Reno* (CD Cal., Civ. No. 85-4544-RJK, Stipulated Settlement Agreement, 17 January 1997) ('*Flores* Settlement').

[20] See s. 235(c)(2), codified at 8 USC s. 1232(c)(2). Certain unaccompanied asylum-seeker children from Mexico and Canada can still be subject to expedited removal in certain circumstances: see M. Rosenblum, *Unaccompanied Child Migration to the United States: The Tension Between Protection and Prevention* (Transatlantic Council on Migration, April 2015), n. 19.

the care of the Office of Refugee Resettlement (ORR), which is required to 'promptly place' the children in 'the least restrictive setting that is in the best interest of the child'.[21] In practice, this has resulted in most unaccompanied minors being placed with a family member in the United States.[22] However, some unaccompanied minors are subject to long-term detention. The *Flores* settlement provides for an exception to the requirement of release where the Department for Homeland Security (DHS) determines that detention is necessary to ensure the child's safety or the safety of others, or is required to secure the juvenile's presence at immigration removal proceedings.[23] Detention takes place in ORR-contracted care facilities. Depending on the age, flight risk and whether the child poses a danger to themselves or others, the types of facilities include secure care, shelter care or foster care.[24] Secure care often means detention in juvenile criminal detention centres. Children could potentially be detained in these circumstances until the removal proceedings against them are concluded.[25] The government had argued that the placement decision and continued detention are completely at the discretion of the ORR. This position was upheld in a number of US District Court decisions.[26] However, in July 2017, the Ninth Circuit Court of Appeals affirmed the right of unaccompanied minors to have parole hearings to determine whether they can be released.[27] New rules announced by the Trump administration in February 2017 allow for the government to reassess children initially determined to be unaccompanied minors throughout the removal proceedings.[28] This means that children can lose the protections reserved for unaccompanied minors if they are placed with a parent or appropriate guardian in the United States, making them more likely to be detained.

In 2005, the George W. Bush Administration decided that the 1997 *Flores* settlement only applied to unaccompanied minors and began

---

21 Section 235(c)(2), codified at 8 USC s. 1232(c)(2).

22 Rosenblum, *Unaccompanied Child Migration to the United States*, above n. 20, at 9.

23 *Flores* Settlement, above n. 19, para. [11]. This is also reflected in DHS regulations: 8 CFR s. 236.3(b).

24 K. Manuel and M. Garcia, *Unaccompanied Alien Children – Legal Issues: Answers to Frequently Asked Questions* (Congressional Research Service, 27 January 2016), pp. 5–6.

25 *Ibid.* 14.

26 *DB* v. *Poston,* 119 F. Supp. 3d 472 (ED Va. 2015); *Re Rodriguez-Lopez* (BIA, WL 1398660, 29 March 2004); cf. *In Matter of A*, 2005 Immigration Reporter LEXIS 54924 (BIA, 23 September 2005).

27 *Flores* v. *Sessions*, 862 F.3d 863 (9th Cir. 2017).

28 See Kelly Memorandum, above n. 16, section L.

detaining children and their mothers for the entire duration of their status determination procedures. Most were held at the purpose-built T. Don Hutto Family Detention Center in Texas. It was not long before reports of serious mistreatment emerged in relation to this facility. These included claims that described 'young children forced to wear prison jumpsuits, to live in dormitory housing, to use toilets exposed to public view and to sleep with the lights on . . . while being denied access to appropriate schooling'.[29] These concerns were symptomatic of wider systemic problems resulting from the excesses of the mandatory detention regime. Reports of repeated incidents of human rights violations and denial of basic medical care prompted the administration of President Obama to embark on a program of detention reform,[30] with a series of changes announced in 2009.[31] The policy of detaining women and children was scaled-back and the controversial T. Don Hutto Family Detention Center was closed down. But the liberalization of the detention policies was short-lived. Detention of accompanied minors and their families was resumed in 2014 in response to an increase in the number of Central American asylum-seekers travelling irregularly to the United States. A reported 61,000 family units, as well as 51,000 unaccompanied minors crossed into the United States in 2014.[32] In June 2014, the DHS abandoned the policy of generally releasing asylum-seekers who have established a 'credible fear'. Instead, access to parole was restricted for accompanied children and their carers with the aim of deterring potential future migrants. In February 2015, the US District Court for the District of Columbia ordered a preliminary injunction to halt the continued application of the no parole policy, on the grounds that it

---

29 W.S. Hylton, 'The shame of America's family detention camps', *New York Times Magazine* (Online, 4 February 2015), available at www.nytimes.com/2015/02/08/magazine/the-shame-of-americas-family-detention-camps.html?_r=0.

30 For analysis of these reforms see A. Kalhan, 'Rethinking Immigration Detention' (2010) 110 *Columbia Law Review* 42; G. Heeren, 'Pulling Teeth: The State of Mandatory Immigration Detention' (2010) 45 *Harvard Civil Rights—Civil Liberties Law Review* 601, at 626–9; S. Gryll, 'Immigration Detention Reform: No Band-Aid Desired' (2011) 60 *Emory Law Journal* 1211.

31 See US Immigration and Customs Enforcement, *Fact Sheet: 2009 Immigration Detention Reforms* (6 August 2009), available at www.ice.gov/news/library/factsheets/reform-2009reform.htm; US Department of Homeland Security, *ICE Detention Reform: Principles and Next Steps* (6 October 2009), available at www.dhs.gov/xlibrary/assets/press_ice_detention_reform_fact_sheet.pdf. See also, D. Schriro, *Immigration Detention Overview and Recommendations* (US Department of Homeland Security, Immigration and Customs Enforcement, October 2009).

32 Hylton, 'The shame of America's family detention camps', above n. 29.

raised serious constitutional due process issues.[33] In response, the government announced that it would discontinue invoking general deterrence as a factor in custody determinations.[34] A subsequent ruling of the US District Court for the Central District of California held that the *Flores* settlement applied to both unaccompanied and accompanied children, and ordered DHS to begin releasing children and their families from detention.[35] This position was later affirmed by the Court of Appeals for the Ninth Circuit.[36] However, for now, detention of children and their families appears to be continuing.[37]

3. AUSTRALIA

Australian law has provided for the administrative detention of certain immigrants since 1925,[38] but these provisions were used sparingly until relatively recently. Just as in the United States, the policy change was triggered by the arrival of a particular cohort of asylum-seekers. In 1989, boats carrying Cambodian and Sino-Vietnamese began arriving in Australia. The Hawke Labor government responded by detaining all asylum-seekers, including children, who arrived by boat without authorization. Existing 'turn-around' laws were invoked under which persons arriving by boat who were suspected of not holding an entry permit could be detained until returned to their point of departure.[39] However, these provisions were not intended to authorize long-term detention. A legal challenge brought on behalf of 15 of the detained Cambodians who had been held for more than two years prompted amendments to the legislation in 1992.[40] These

---

[33] *RIL-R* v. *Jeh Charles Johnson* (DC, Civ. No. 15-11-JEB, 20 February 2015).

[34] ICE, *ICE Announces Enhanced Oversight for Family Residential Centers* (News Release, 13 May 2015), available at www.ice.gov/news/releases/ice-announces-enhanced-oversight-family-residential-centers.

[35] *Flores* v. *Lynch*, 212 F. Supp. 3d 907 (CD Cal. 2015).

[36] *Flores* v. *Lynch*, 828 F.3d 898 (9th Cir. 2016). Note, however, that the Ninth Circuit found that the District Court had erred in finding that the agreement provided an affirmative right to release for accompanying parents.

[37] *Flores* v. *Sessions* (CD Cal., Civ. No. 85-4544 DMG-AGR, 27 June 2017) (finding that children continue to be routinely detained in secure, unlicensed and inadequate facilities in violation of the *Flores* Settlement).

[38] See Immigration Restriction Act 1901 (Cth), s. 8C, inserted by Immigration Act 1925 (Cth), s. 8.

[39] See Migration Act, s. 88, inserted by Migration Legislation Amendment Act 1989 (Cth).

[40] *Chu Kheng Lim* v. *Minister for Immigration, Local Government and Ethnic Affairs* (1992) 176 CLR 1.

reinforced and formalized the policy of mandatory detention, with a nominal time limit of 273 days.[41]

The Migration Reform Act 1992 (Cth), which came into force on 1 September 1994, replaced these provisions with a scheme that provided simply that all 'unlawful non-citizens' must be detained until either granted a visa or removed from Australia.[42] This change broadened mandatory detention provisions, initially introduced as a temporary and 'exceptional' measure to deal with a particular cohort of boat arrivals, to apply to all persons who either arrived without a visa or who were in Australia on expired or cancelled visa. Significantly, the 273-day time limit which had applied under the earlier law was omitted. Unlike the US system, no provisions were made in the Australian laws for release on parole. Instead, a system of bridging visas was introduced which would allow the release of certain 'unlawful non-citizens' pending the determination of their claim for a substantive visa. Bridging visas were generally only made available to people who had entered the country lawfully.[43] Unauthorized arrivals, including children, were detained for the entire duration of their status determination procedures. Judicial challenges to the policy of mandatorily detaining children proved unsuccessful. An attempt to use the power of the Australian Family Court to make orders for the welfare of children as a means for releasing children from detention was struck down by the High Court in the 2004 decision of *Minister for Immigration and Multicultural and Indigenous Affairs* v. *B*.[44] Later the same year, the High Court upheld the constitutionality of mandatorily detaining children in *Re* v. *Woolley; Ex parte Applicants 276/2003*.[45] The Court rejected the argument that detaining children without consideration of anything other than their immigration status was punitive and therefore an action that could only be carried out by the judicial arm of government.[46]

Under pressure of mounting criticism surrounding the wrongful detention of lawful residents and Australian citizens,[47] and concerns about the

---

41 Migration Amendment Act 1992 (Cth), inserting the new Part 2 Div. 4B into the Migration Act. The time limit appeared in s. 54Q.

42 Migration Act, ss. 54W, 54ZD, inserted by the Migration Reform Act 1992 (Cth).

43 Migration Act, s. 54HS, inserted by the Migration Reform Act 1992 (Cth). Renumbered to s. 172 by the Migration Amendment Act 1994 (Cth).

44 (2004) 219 CLR 365.

45 (2004) 225 CLR 664.

46 *Ibid.* 32 (McHugh J).

47 See M. Grewcock, 'Slipping Through the Net? Some Thoughts on the Cornelia Rau and Vivian Alvarez Inquiry' (2005) 17 *Current Issues in Criminal Justice* 284.

cost of detention on the mental health of children and other detainees, the Liberal/National Coalition government announced a series of immigration detention reforms in June 2005.[48] These included a new community detention program for women and children;[49] the introduction of visas that provided an alternative to indefinite detention for persons who could not be removed from the country;[50] and giving the Commonwealth Ombudsman oversight of persons held in long-term immigration detention.[51] These reforms were extended by the Labor government when it took office in 2007. The new Immigration Minister, Chris Evans, announced a commitment to using detention as a last resort and for the shortest period of time, and avoiding indefinite detention and the detention of children.[52] The community detention program was further expanded,[53] as were the criteria for bridging visas. Asylum-seekers entering Australia irregularly became eligible for release, provided they had undergone health, security and identity checks.[54] Reflecting the practice of parole in the United States, reporting conditions could be imposed on those released. In February 2016, Immigration Minister Peter Dutton claimed that there were no more children in immigration detention in Australia.[55] It took 11 years to achieve this goal, which was first set by Prime Minister John Howard, and reiterated by every government since. While this is welcome news, there are concerns about the accuracy of this claim, as it ignores the significant number of children held in detention-like environments under community detention arrangements.[56] It also disregards the plight of children subject

---

48 For a detailed examination of these reforms, see S. Taylor, 'Immigration Detention Reforms: A Small Gain in Human Rights' (2006) 13 *Agenda* 49.

49 See Migration Act, Part 2 Div. 7 subdiv. B – Residence Determinations, inserted by Migration Amendment (Detention Arrangements) Act 2005 (Cth).

50 See Migration Regulations 1994 (Cth), Sch. 2, subclass 070 – Bridging (Removal Pending).

51 See Migration Act, Part 8C, ss. 486L–486Q, inserted by the Migration Amendment (Detention Arrangements) Act 2005 (Cth).

52 See C. Evans, Minister for Immigration, 'New Directions in Detention: Restoring Integrity to Australia's Immigration System', Speech delivered at Parliament House, 29 July 2008.

53 See notes 61–3 and accompanying text below.

54 See C. Bowen, Minister for Immigration, *Bridging Visas to be Issued for Boat Arrivals* (Media Release, 25 November 2011), available at www.chrisbowen.net/media-centre/media-releases.do?newsId=5240.

55 P. Dutton, *Doorstop Interview – Brisbane* (Media Release, 3 April 2016), available at www.peterdutton.com.au/Home/LatestNews/tabid/94/articleType/ArticleView/articleId/596/categoryId/5/Doorstop-interview--Brisbane.aspx.

56 See n. 79 and accompanying discussion below.

to Australia's offshore processing policies. As of August 2017, there were 43 children held on the tiny Pacific Island of Nauru.[57]

4. COMMON TRENDS

The United States and Australia have developed similar immigration detention policies. Both have a system of mandatory detention for persons that arrive without authorization, pending determination of their claims to a substantive visa. Both have provided grounds of release pending determination for certain classes of persons. In the United States, this is achieved primarily through parole or release on bond, although recent years have also seen the implementation of community-based models of detention.[58] In Australia, release is achieved through temporary bridging visas and community detention arrangements. The excesses of the mandatory detention policy gave rise to a similar backlash. Reforms were introduced in both countries in the mid-to-late 2000s, which provided more independent oversight over detention operations, broadened the categories of asylum-seekers who could be released pending a determination of their claims, and expanded community-based alternatives to detention (ATD). This liberalization was short-lived, with both countries reverting to more stringent detention provisions. In the United States, this has taken the form of a policy restricting access to parole for asylum-seeker women and children from Central American countries. In Australia, onshore detention has continued to be scaled back, but with the reintroduction of extra-territorial processing, asylum-seekers who attempt to travel to Australia by boat are transferred to facilities in Nauru or Manus Island in Papua New Guinea. While the Australian government has worked with the host governments to implement 'open centre' arrangements, asylum-seekers continue to be held in detention-like settings.[59]

These parallels are not a coincidence. Immigration law-makers in Australia and the United States regularly meet to discuss policy developments. Relevant forums include the United Nations High Commissioner for Refugees (UNHCR) Executive Committee meetings, the International Organisation for Migration (IOM) Dialogue on Migration and the informal bilateral talks that occur alongside these meetings; Regional

---

57 Australian Department of Immigration and Border Protection, *Immigration Detention and Community Statistics Summary* (31 August 2017).

58 See notes 63–9 and accompanying discussion below.

59 See Ghezelbash, *Refuge Lost*, above n. 1.

Consultative Processes such as the Five Country Conference and the Intergovernmental Consultations on Migration, Asylum and Refugees (IGC); and ad hoc bilateral meetings that occur as part of fact-finding missions and study tours. Another prominent channel for communication are the immigration representatives (or Immigration Consuls) based at the Australian Embassy in Washington and the US Embassy in Canberra. These officials provide a permanent means through which policy-makers from each country can request information regarding the operation or implementation of migration control policies.

These channels facilitated the recent spread of community-based ATD models for women and children. Community-based ATD programs were first trialed in the United States in the late 1990s. A number of studies demonstrated that these programs delivered high rates of compliance and significantly lower costs when compared to conventional detention.[60] Nevertheless, ATD programs were not rolled out on a large scale in the United States. The model did, however, gain traction in Australia. A community-based ATD program for women and children was introduced in 2005.[61] Persons held in community detention are not under guard and are free to move around the community, provided they spend their nights at the designated address. A crucial element of the Australian ATD program has been the provision of case management and support services provided by NGOs. The key elements of this model are the following:

First, there is an initial assessment phase were the client's needs are determined in conjunction with those of the case manager and a detailed plan is developed. The second stage centres on the establishment of a plan to meet those needs, and ensuring communication, education, advocacy and facilitation of appropriate service involvement. Finally, the case manager will continuously monitor the situation so any change in need can be identified and responded to accordingly.[62]

The use of community-based ATD has been progressively expanded over the years. The policy was instrumental in achieving the dramatic

---

60 See, e.g., Lutheran Immigration and Refugee Service, *Unlocking Liberty: A Way Forward for US Immigration Detention Policy* (2011); S. Weishar, 'A More Human System: Community-Based Alternatives to Immigration Detention (Part 2)' (2011) *Just South Quarterly* (Spring) 4; M. Golden, O. Root and D. Mizner, *The Appearance Assistance Program: Attaining Compliance with Immigration Laws Through Community Supervision* (Vera Institute of Justice, 1998).

61 See Migration Act, Part 2 Div. 7, subdiv. B.

62 International Detention Coalition, *Detention Reform and Alternatives to Detention in Australia: Case Management in the Community as an Innovative and Effective Alternative to Detention* (February 2010), p. 5.

reduction in the number of children held in onshore immigration detention facilities. It has now been expanded and is used for not only women and children, but also categories of detainees.

Australia's case management model of ATD appears to have in turn been influential in shaping recent ATD programs in the United States. The first large-scale ATD program was implemented in the United States in 2004. Known as the Intensive Supervision Appearance Program (ISAP), the focus was on ensuring compliance through intrusive reporting and electronic tagging.[63] It did not use individual case management services like in Australia.[64] This changed in 2009 with the introduction of the ISAP II, which included a 'needs-based case management component'.[65] These services were criticized as being rudimentary, and the over-arching enforcement focus appears to have impeded the ability of the program to foster trust with participants.[66] A more robust case management model of ATD was announced in September 2015, specifically targeting accompanied children and their families. Known as the Family Case Management program, it drew heavily on the Australian model, providing individualized needs assessments and service plans, information sessions on legal rights and immigration procedures, assistance in accessing legal assistance, housing, education and health services.[67] However, the Obama Administration was criticized for awarding the contract for the program to the GEO Group, which runs a for-profit network of private prisons, rather than NGO groups working in the sector.[68] The program was short-lived, with the Trump Administration abolishing it June 2017.[69]

There is ample evidence of the exchange of ideas between Australian

---

[63] Lutheran Immigration and Refugee Service, *Unlocking Liberty: A Way Forward for US Immigration Detention Policy* (2011), p. 30.

[64] *Ibid.*

[65] *Ibid.* 31.

[66] *Ibid.*

[67] M. Loiselle, 'GEO Care's Family Case Management Program' (2016) *GEO World* 2.

[68] See, e.g., American Immigration Council, *Obama Administration Again Hands Families Over to Private Prison Company* (Press Release, 18 September 2015); Grassroots Leadership, *Obama Administration Should Rescind Award for Family Case Management from Private Prisons* (Press Release, 18 September 2015); K. Obser, 'Missing the Point: Alternatives to Detention to be Run by Private Prison Contractors', *New America Media* (Online, 25 September 2015), available at http://newamericamedia.org/2015/09/missing-the-point-alternatives-to-detention-to-be-run-by-private-prison-contractors.php.

[69] A. Bendix, 'ICE Shuts Down Program for Asylum-Seekers', *The Atlantic* (Online, 9 June 2017), available at www.theatlantic.com/news/archive/2017/06/ice-shuts-down-program-for-asylum-seekers/529887/.

and US officials with regard to community-based ATD. The NGO working group set up by President Obama in 2008 to facilitate detention reform included an Australian representative: the Director of the International Detention Coalition, Grant Mitchell.[70] Mr Mitchell provided information to the Obama Administration about Australian detention reform measures.[71] The Obama Administration was purportedly very interested in Australia's use of alternatives to detention and Mr Mitchell has confirmed that he furnished detailed policy advice in relation to the operation of these policies in Australia.[72] Additionally, a number of NGOs directly lobbied the US government to follow the 'Australian model' of case managed community detention.[73]

There are also some interesting parallels in the public discourse on the detention of children and families. In Australia, NGOs like ChilOut and GetUp! have run long-standing campaigns to have all children released from immigration detention facilities. These campaigns played a significant role in pressuring successive governments to introduce reforms in this area. Efforts in this regard were assisted by a 2014 Australian Human Rights Commission report critical of continued detention of children.[74] The campaign to release children and families from detention has been largely successful.[75] In the United States, NGO lobbying played a crucial role in scaling back the detention of families in the late 2000s, which culminated with the closure of the T. Don Hutto Family Detention Facility in 2009. With the introduction of the no parole policy for asylum-seeker families from Central America in 2014, the NGO community again mobilized. Their efforts resulted in some important victories, including the closure of the controversial family detention centre in Artesia.

---

[70] Interview with Grant Mitchell, Director of the International Detention Coalition (telephone interview, 7 August 2012). See also, Ghezelbash, *Refuge Lost*, above n. 1, which provides further description and analysis of this interview.

[71] *Ibid.*

[72] *Ibid.*

[73] See, e.g., National Immigrant Justice Center, *Creating 'Truly Civil' Immigration Detention in the United States: Lessons from Australia* (May 2010); National Immigrant Justice Center et al., *Year One Report Card: Human Rights & the Obama Administration's Immigration Detention Reforms* (October 2010), pp. 9, 18; Detention Watch Network, *Community-based Alternatives to Immigration Detention* (August 2010).

[74] Australian Human Rights Commission, *The Forgotten Children: National Inquiry into Children in Immigration Detention* (2014); see also the contribution by Gillian Triggs, Chapter 20.

[75] See above n. 55 and accompanying discussion.

There are also some worrying similarities in government discourse. This is apparent in recent attempts in both countries to redefine detention spaces. In early 2016, in an apparent attempt to circumvent the court-ordered restriction of the detention of children,[76] the US federal government successfully lobbied Texas officials to licence the Karnes County Residential Centre as a 'child welfare' institution.[77] The process to issue a licence to a second family detention centre, the South Texas Residential Center in Dilley, was halted following a successful legal challenge.[78] In Australia, the announcement in April 2016 by Immigration Minister Peter Dutton that there were no longer any children left in immigration detention, was predicated on the reclassification of sections of detention centres where children were held as places of 'community detention'.[79]

Both countries are investing in offshore detention infrastructure. The United States has used offshore detention facilities in Guantanamo Bay, Cuba since the early 1990s. Asylum-seekers interdicted at sea on route to the United States, who voice a credible fear of persecution, continue to be transferred to the Guantanamo facility to have their claims processed.[80] In recent years, the US government has also provided hundreds of millions of dollars in financial aid to assist immigration enforcement and detention activities in Mexico.[81] There have even been reports of

---

[76] See above n. 35 and accompanying discussion.

[77] 'Health agency to press forward with licensing child detention centers', *Texas Observer* (Online, 12 February 2016), available at www.texasobserver.org/detention-center-child-care-to-hhsc.

[78] *Grassroots Leadership and others* v. *Texas Department of Family and Protective Services* (TX, Civ. No. D-1-GN-15-004336, 4 May 2016) (issuing a temporary restraining order); *Grassroots Leadership and others v. Texas Department of Family and Protective Services* (TX, Civ. No. D-1-GN-15-004336, 2 December 2016) (final judgement).

[79] B. Doherty, 'Asylum seeker children still in detention despite claims all have been released', *Guardian* (Online, 3 April 2016), available at www.theguardian.com/australia-news/2016/apr/03/asylum-seeker-children-still-in-detention-despite-claims-all-have-been-released.

[80] For a detailed analysis of the US government's use of Guantanamo Bay as a location for processing asylum claims, see A. Dastyari, *United States Migrant Interdiction and the Detention of Refugees in Guantanamo Bay* (Cambridge University Press, 2015).

[81] Petition for Interim and Permanent Measures regarding Systematic Violations of the American Convention on Human Rights and Other International Covenants against Central American Migrants in Mexico, Before the Inter-American Commission on Human Rights of the Organisation of American States (2016, Case No. P-652-16), pp. 26–7.

US immigration officers working inside Mexican detention facilities.[82] While Mexican law does not authorize the immigration detention of minors, in practice, children are routinely detained.[83] The US migrant processing facility in Guantanamo Bay was the model for Australia's offshore processing policy introduced as part of the Pacific Solution in 2001.[84] The policy of offshore processing was abandoned in 2007, only to be reintroduced in 2012. Current policy stipulates that all asylum-seekers who arrive without authorization by boat are liable to transfer to the offshore processing centres on Manus Island in Papua New Guinea, or the tiny Pacific island nation of Nauru. The Manus Island detention centre, an adult male only facility, was decommissioned in October 2017 as the result of a PNG Supreme Court decision finding the continued detention of asylum-seekers held there to be unlawful.[85] There are no plans to shut down the facility on Nauru, which caters for men, women and children (both accompanied and unaccompanied).[86] Australia has also directed tens of millions of dollars to fund immigration detention in Indonesia.[87]

Another common trend in the United States and Australia relates to the privatization of detention facilities. In December 2014, the company Serco was awarded a further five-year contract to run Australia's onshore detention facilities. The contract is estimated to be worth AUS$950 million to AUS$1.4 billion.[88] The Australian government paid Broadspectrum

---

[82] Centro de Derechos Humanos Fray Matias, *Privacion indefinida de libertad y violaciones de derechos, persisten en el centro de detencion para migrantes de Tapachula, ante la mirada y colaboracion de funcionarios Estadounidenses* (20 January 2016), available at http://cdhfraymatias.org/sitio/wp-content/uploads/2016/01/COMUNICADO_0116.pdf, cited in *United States Immigration Detention Profile* (Global Detention Project, May 2016), available at www.globaldetentionproject.org/countries/americas/united-states.

[83] V. Fernández, 'On the Way to the US, Children Seeking Asylum are Often Put in Mexico's Detention Centres', *PRI* (Online, 3 January 2017), available at www.pri.org/stories/2017-01-03/children-fleeing-violence-central-america-who-don-t-make-it-us-often-end-mexican.

[84] Ghezelbash, *Refuge Lost*, above n. 1; D. Ghezelbash, 'Lessons in Exclusion: Interdiction and Extraterritorial Processing of Asylum Seekers in the United States and Australia' in M. Guiffre, L. Tsourdi and J.P. Gauci (eds), *Exploring the Boundaries of Refugee Law: Current Protection Challenges* (Brill, 2015), p. 89.

[85] *Namah* v. *Pato* [2016] PJSC 13.

[86] See Gillian Triggs, Chapter 20 for further analysis of the detention of children in Nauru.

[87] A. Nethery, B. Rafferty-Brown and S. Taylor, 'Exporting Detention: Australia-Funded Immigration Detention in Indonesia' (2013) 26(1) *Journal of Refugee Studies* 88.

[88] J. Kollewe, 'Serco to continue running Australian immigration detention centres', *Guardian* (Online, 10 December 2014), available at www.theguardian.

(formerly Transfield) and G4S AUS$2.155 billion for services relating to its offshore processing facilities on Nauru and PNG between September 2012 and October 2016.[89] In the United States, the majority of the US$2 billion a year spent on the immigration detention network goes to private contractors.[90] It may even be that the private detention companies are acting as agents of legal and policy transfer. In June 2015, a leaked document revealed that Serco (which runs the onshore detention network in Australia) was lobbying to secure the contracts to run the family detention centres in the United States.[91] In the document, the company proposed that the United States adopt Serco's Family Residential Framework, which they claim has been 'proven for nearly a decade in the UK and Australia'.[92]

5. CONCLUSION

Long-term mandatory detention laws spread from the United States to Australia through a process of legal and policy transfer. More recently, the United States and Australia have learnt from each other's experiences with regards to ATD models for women and children. These types of transfers are not restricted to the United States and Australia. In recent years, mandatory detention provisions have spread to Canada and New Zealand.[93] At the same time, ATD models have been implemented in numerous countries, including the United Kingdom, Belgium, New Zealand, the Netherlands, Sweden, Poland, Croatia, Hong Kong, Indonesia, Thailand and Israel.[94] This demonstrates that transfers can be used to propagate

---

com/business/2014/dec/10/serco-australian-immigration-detention-centres-contract-christmas-island.

89 Australian National Audit Office, *Offshore Processing in Nauru and Papua New Guinea: Contract Management of Garrison Support and Welfare Services* (January 2017).

90 D. Cohen, 'Why the Immigration Debate is Also a Debate About Privatization', *Huffington Post* (Online, 4 February 2016), available at www.huffingtonpost.com/donald-cohen/why-the-immigration-debat_b_9161442.html.

91 O. Laughland, 'Controversial security firm Serco lobbies for US migrant detention contracts', *Guardian* (Online, 20 June 2015), available at www.theguardian.com/us-news/2015/jun/19/serco-immigration-detention-centers-united-states.

92 *Ibid.*

93 Protecting Canada's Immigration Act, SC 2012; Immigration Amendment Act 2013 (NZ). For analysis of these transfers see Crock and Ghezelbash, 'Secret Immigration Business', above n. 8.

94 R. Sampson and G. Mitchell, 'Global Trends in Immigration Detention and Alternatives to Detention: Practical, Political and Symbolic Rationales'

both regressive and progressive policies. In this context it is imperative that civil society actors, academics and immigration lawyers engage with the transfer process. These non-government actors need to share their experience about the practical implications and impacts of policy developments with their overseas counterparts. By engaging with developments abroad, these actors will not only be able to react appropriately to poor transfer proposals, but they can also play an active role in lobbying for and facilitating transfers of rights-sensitive policies based on substantiated evidence.

(2013) 1(3) *Journal on Migration and Human Security* 97; International Detention Coalition, *These Are the Alternatives* (2015).

PART VI

Challenges and solutions

22. Nowhere to turn: the protection needs of children defecting from criminal gangs

Farrin R. Anello*

Roberto was born in a gang-controlled neighborhood in Honduras.[1] His father subjected him to extreme physical abuse, and at the age of eight, he left home to escape the abuse and began living on the streets, feeding himself by working odd jobs or collecting discarded items to sell. The local gang leaders noticed that he was living without any family, and when he was 12, they began ordering him to serve as a lookout for drug transactions.[2] When gang members gave him an order, he understood that refusing would be suicidal. Gang members had killed one of Roberto's former classmates, a 13-year-old who had refused to join the gang. Going to the police was also out of the question, since corrupt local officers might inform gang leaders of his disloyalty.

The gang leaders next ordered Roberto to start selling drugs for them. At an initiation, adult gang leaders ordered other children to beat Roberto and forced him to stand silently and take the blows. Gang leaders later forced the children to watch the gang leaders beat a young man, telling

---

* Senior Staff Attorney, American Civil Liberties Union of New Jersey. This chapter was drafted in large part while I was a Visiting Assistant Clinical Professor at Seton Hall University School of Law. It does not necessarily reflect the views of the American Civil Liberties Union of New Jersey. I am grateful to Lenni Benson, Stacy Caplow, Jenny-Brooke Condon, Mary Crock, Dan Kesselbrenner, Robert E. Kopp, Maureen Sweeney, David Thronson, and the participants in the Clinical Law Review Writers' Workshop at New York University School of Law for their helpful advice and comments.

1 This story is fictional but is modeled on accounts of real children.

2 See, e.g., A. Hylton and S. Salvadore, 'They Said We Would Pay with Our Lives', *Slate*, 31 August 2016, available at www.slate.com/articles/news_and_politics/gender_and_migration/2016/08/as_central_american_gangs_target_younger_kids_more_minors_are_fleeing_to.html (explaining that the *maras* use boys to 'sell and run drugs' and extort people, and order girls to 'run drugs' and engage in sexual acts with gang members).

them that if they ever crossed the gang, worse would happen to them. One day, when Roberto was 14, a local gang leader ordered him to kill a man he knew from his neighborhood. Roberto panicked and fled, traveling to the United States by foot, by bus, and on the top of a train, working odd jobs along the way to survive.

Roberto was arrested after crossing the border and asked for protection. The asylum officer who interviewed him did not make a decision on his case and instead referred his asylum case to immigration court for a proceeding to determine if he should be sent back to Honduras. Several years later, a judge denied his claim for asylum and also found Roberto not eligible for any other protection. Roberto was deported. Three months later, he was killed by a member of the gang that had once conscripted him.[3]

The rise of transnational gangs in the Northern Triangle countries of Guatemala, El Salvador and Honduras has greatly increased the flow of child refugees seeking protection in neighboring countries and the United States. A 2016 UNHCR study showed that nearly 60 percent of children who had made the dangerous journey from the Northern Triangle or Mexico to the United States (US) on their own had been 'forcibly displaced because they suffered or faced harms that indicated a potential or actual need for international protection'.[4] It also reported that 72 percent of the children from El Salvador, which has seen particularly extreme gang violence, faced similar harms.[5] The children with claims for protection were most often fleeing violence by transnational gangs and/or extreme domestic violence.[6]

---

[3] Cf. S. De Leon, 'Guatemalan Youth Slain 17 Days After Being Deported From U.S.,' *L.A. Times*, 9 May 2004, available at http://articles.latimes.com/2004/may/09/news/adfg-deport9 (describing deportation and subsequent murder of Edgar Chocoy, a teenager who defected from a gang in Guatemala).

[4] UNHCR, *Children on the Run II* (2016), p. 6, available at www.unhcr.org/en-us/about-us/background/56fc266f4/children-on-the-run-full-report.html.

[5] *Ibid.* 6.

[6] *Ibid.* See also Center for Gender and Refugee Studies and Universidad Nacional de Lanus, *Childhood and Migration in Central and North America: Causes, Policies, Practices and Challenges* (2015), Executive Summary, i and iii, available at https://cgrs.uchastings.edu//Childhood-Migration-HumanRights. The report finds that in Honduras, '[c]hildren and adolescents primarily flee two types of violence: violence perpetrated by organized criminal syndicates and violence experienced in the home'. See also UNHCR, 'Children on the Run' in Center for Gender and Refugee Studies and Universidad Nacional de Lanus (eds), *Childhood and Migration in Central and North America: Causes, Policies, Practices and Challenges* (2015), p. 84, available at https://cgrs.uchastings.edu//Childhood-Migration-HumanRights.

These children frequently become the targets of gang violence if they attempt to refuse gang recruitment, witness a gang crime, or fail to meet gangs' extortion demands.[7] They may also be targeted because gangs are seeking to extort money from or retaliate against their family members, and girls are often targeted if they refuse gang members' sexual advances.[8]

US government officials and law-makers too frequently target immigrant children for deportation without addressing their unique vulnerabilities and protection needs. Children who flee Central America typically have no history of gang involvement and are fleeing gang violence or domestic abuse.[9]

This chapter focuses on a much rarer situation: that of a child who flees after having been conscripted or coerced into joining a gang. Such a child falls into what researcher Thomas Boerman calls the 'Trap of Gang Membership'. Gang leaders view renouncing gang membership as betrayal, and subject defectors from their ranks to torture and murder. Conversely, having been marked – and often tattooed – as a gang member, defectors cannot reintegrate into society in their countries of origin, and are often targeted for death by rival gangs and police.[10]

In 2004, 16-year-old Edgar Chocoy Gúzman, who had joined the Mara Savatrucha (MS-13) at the age of 12 and defected when he was only 14, was murdered 17 days after being deported from the United States to Guatemala.[11] Although broader data about violence against deportees is very limited, one study documents at least 83 deaths of deportees between 2014 and October 2015.[12]

---

[7] See S. Malik, *The Harrowing Lives and Traumas of Central American Refugees* (Center for American Progress, 2016), available at www.americanprogress.org/issues/immigration/news/2016/09/13/144027/the-harrowing-lives-and-traumas-of-central-american-refugees/. This publication contains a detailed list documenting numerous gang murders and attacks in the Northern Triangle.

[8] *Ibid.*

[9] *Children on the Run II*, above n. 4.

[10] T. Boerman, 'Central American Gangs: An Overview of the Phenomenon in Latin America and the US' (2007) 15(35) *Journal of Gang Research* 40.

[11] S. De Leon, above n. 3; and M. James, 'Fleeing the Maras: Child Gang Members Seeking Refugee Status in the United States' (2005) 25(1) *Child Legal Rights Journal* 1.

[12] See S. Brodzinsky and E. Pilkington, 'US government deporting Central American migrants to their deaths', *Guardian*, 12 October 2015; and Malik, *The Harrowing Lives and Traumas of Central American Refugees*, above n. 7; UNHCR, Roland/Marta, *Deported Children Face Deadly New Dangers on Return to Honduras* (29 January 2015), available at www.unhcr.org/en-au/news/latest/2015/1/54ca3289/deported-children-face-deadly-new-dangers-return-honduras.html (reporting on deaths of teenagers deported to Honduras, including an execution-style murder

Like former child soldiers in more traditional armed conflicts, formerly gang-involved children are frequently survivors of extreme violence and trauma. Adolescents, moreover, share a particular susceptibility to coercion and risk-taking – making them prime recruitment targets for both gang leaders and military leaders. On the other hand, young people also show a particular capacity for change and rehabilitation. In light of these factors, receiving governments can both protect children and provide them with the support structures needed to become contributing members of their communities.

1. FORMER CHILD SOLDIERS AND CHILDREN WHO DEFECTED FROM THE *MARAS*: PARALLEL EXPERIENCES

In recent years, scholars and some US courts have found that former child soldiers can qualify as refugees and that status determinations in such cases require individualized consideration of factors such as trauma, duress and coercion, and capacity.[13] Popular memoirs by child soldiers have also illustrated both the extreme cruelty and violence experienced by former child soldiers and their capacity for resilience and rehabilitation.[14]

Gang-involved children have often been excluded from both scholarly definitions and popular conceptions of child soldiers, since gangs are traditionally viewed as criminal rather than political entities.[15] Social scientists have only begun to explore the early and repeated victimization of child gang members.[16] The trauma, coercion and violence that children regularly face at the hands of the *maras* echo experiences of child soldiers in wartime, and emphasize the importance of seriously assessing claims for international protection.

The UNICEF Cape Town Principles define a 'child soldier' as anyone

---

of eight people, 'some of them aged 16 or 17', that was likely gang-related, and explaining that gang-related murders 'are usually linked to recruitment, unpaid debt . . . extortion, or turf wars').

[13] B. Lonegan, 'Sinners or Saints: Child Soldiers and the Persecutor Bar to Asylum After *Negusie v. Holder*' (2011) 31 *BC Third World Law Journal* 71, at 95–6; M.S. Gallagher, 'Soldier Boy Bad: Child Soldiers, Culture and Bars to Asylum' (2001) 13 *International Journal of Refugee Law* 310.

[14] See, e.g., I. Beah, *A Long Way Gone: Memoirs of a Boy Soldier* (Farrar, Strauss & Giroux, 2007).

[15] M. Wessells, *Child Soldiers: From Violence to Protection* (6th edn, Harvard University Press, 2006), p. 6.

[16] See D. Levenson, *Adios, Nino* (Duke University Press, 2013).

under 18 'who is part of any kind of regular or irregular armed force in any capacity', whether or not they carry arms.[17] The widespread use of child soldiers by Charles Taylor in Liberia and other forces in Africa came to worldwide attention in the 1990s, but this horrific practice has proliferated in other regions as well: in 2015, armed forces increasingly recruited children as soldiers in conflicts in the Middle East, with the United Nations reporting a two-fold increase in the number of children recruited to serve as soldiers in Afghanistan, a five-fold increase in Yemen, and 'massive recruitment and use' of children, including very young children, in the Syrian conflict.[18] In 2016, the US Department of State named 10 countries located in Africa, the Middle East and Asia using child soldiers in their armed forces.[19]

I use the term 'gang' here in a specific sense, to refer to the *maras* of Central America. Distinct from the smaller, more local *pandillas*, the *maras* are brutally violent transnational criminal organizations.[20] The *maras* originated as street gangs in Los Angeles in the 1980s.[21] Following the 1996 Immigration Reform Bills, the United States deported huge numbers of people to the 'Northern Triangle' countries of El Salvador, Guatemala and Honduras. Many of those removed had been members of gangs in the United States and were disconnected young people at risk of gang recruitment. The United States removed them to societies in post-conflict chaos, [22] with extreme poverty and violence and 'weak and

---

17 UNICEF, *Cape Town Principles and Best Practices* (1997), p. 12, available at www.unicef.org/emerg/files/Cape_Town_Principles(1).pdf; Wessells, *Child Soldiers*, above n. 15.

18 UNGA, *Children and Armed Conflict, Report of the Secretary General*, UN Doc. A/70/836–S/2016/360 (20 April 2016), paras 6, 21 and 149; see also P.R. Keefe, 'The Teen Killers of the Drug War', *The New Yorker*, 12 September 2016 (noting UN report that 'recruitment of child soldiers in Afghanistan doubled last year' and describing ISIS's 'cadre of juvenile conscripts, some as young as ten years old').

19 US Department of State, *Child Soldiers Prevention Act List* (2016), available at www.state.gov/j/tip/rls/tiprpt/2016/258691.htm. Listed countries include Burma, Democratic Republic of the Congo, Iraq, Nigeria, Rwanda, Somalia, South Sudan, Sudan, Syria and Yemen. Troublingly, as Wessells notes in his excellent book, the United States itself recruits 17-year-olds to its armed forces. Wessells, *Child Soldiers*, above n. 15, at 6.

20 See Boerman, 'Central American Gangs', above n. 10, at 37; C. Ribando Seelke, *Gangs in Central America* (Congressional Research Service, 2014), p. 2. *Pandillas* sometimes affiliate themselves with the *maras*.

21 Boerman, 'Central American Gangs', above n. 10, at 35.

22 Guatemala and El Salvador had particularly violent civil conflicts persisting through the 1980s, fueling migration to the United States, and into the 1990s.

corrupt justice systems'.[23] Moreover, the receiving countries had many ex-combatants who had been trained to use weapons and desensitized to violence.[24] In this environment, the *maras* grew from 'loosely structured street gangs' into exceedingly violent and wealthy transnational criminal organizations.[25] Elected officials in the region at first ignored the problem, allowing these gangs to amass power.[26] El Salvador and Honduras subsequently adopted *mano dura*, or 'firm hand', laws, which involve a militaristic approach to policing.[27] Scholars studying these laws have found that they not only fail to address root drivers of violent crime such as extreme poverty, domestic violence and corruption, but have encouraged police brutality and 'social cleansing' campaigns targeting anyone affiliated with gangs, have provoked retaliatory brutality by the *maras*, and have discouraged members from defecting.[28]

Today, the *maras* control significant territory in Northern Triangle countries, particularly Honduras and El Salvador, and trade drugs and arms. They exert near-complete control over the population within their territories, murdering and torturing rival gang members and civilians who refuse extortion demands or otherwise appear to question their authority.[29]

The experiences of children involved with gangs and children involved

---

See S.B. Coutin, 'Falling Outside: Excavating the History of Central American Asylum Seekers' (2011) 36 *Law and Social Inquiry* 575 (noting that by 1984, four years into the Salvadoran civil war, more than one-quarter of the population of El Salvador was displaced).

23 Boerman, 'Central American Gangs', above n. 10, at 36–7 (cataloguing scholarly explanations for the rise of the *maras*).

24 *Ibid.* 35–6.

25 See Seelke, *Gangs in Central America*, above n. 20, at 2–4 (explaining that the expansion of MS-13 and M-18 from Los Angeles to Central America 'accelerated' following increased removals from the United States following the enactment of the Illegal Immigrant Reform and Immigrant Responsibility Act of 1996, and that the low number of US removals to Nicaragua may explain why the *maras* lack significant presence in Nicargua); Boerman, 'Central American Gangs', above n. 9; L.E. Nagle, 'Criminal Gangs in Latin America: The Next Great Threat to Regional Security and Stability?' (2008) 14(7) *Texas Hispanic Journal of Law and Policy* 11 ('The spread of *mareros* into Central America is due in large measure to a US immigration and criminal justice policy that deports foreign-born criminal convicts back to their countries of origin following incarceration . . . for several years the US has been pouring tens of thousands of criminals, including extremely violent offenders, into Central America's weakest and most failing states').

26 Boerman, 'Central American Gangs', above n. 10, at 37.

27 *Ibid.* 37, 41–2.

28 *Ibid.* 37, 44–6.

29 See International Crisis Group, *Easy Prey: Criminal Violence and Central*

in more traditional armed conflict resemble each other in respects that help to explain why defectors from both types of groups face substantial danger. These commonalities illustrate the particular vulnerabilities of children to recruitment and manipulation, the trauma many children who commit bad acts in the name of a gang or militant group have suffered, and the potential for deadly retaliation following defection.[30]

The *maras* are criminal organizations,[31] but their activities and structure share many similarities with forces engaged in more overt political violence.[32] The *maras* arose in response to the military conflicts in Guatemala and El Salvador, and they have adopted terminology and structures that evoke military action. As a psychiatrist working with prisoners in Guatemala explained:

> The mareros' thinking is military thinking that is always reproducing war, they live in war with the logic of war, thinking of the enemy's attack. [They live within] a militarized culture of obedience, discipline, and the fulfillment of orders and missions.[33]

Both militant forces in armed conflicts and the *maras* often intentionally target children using violent and forcible recruitment practices. As Graça Machel documented in a ground-breaking 1996 UN report, child soldiers

---

American Migration (2016), available at www.crisisgroup.org/latin-america-caribbean/central-america/easy-prey-criminal-violence-and-central-american-migration.

30 'Where children are alleged to have committed crimes while their own rights were being violated (for instance while being associated with armed forces or armed groups), it is important to bear in mind that they may be victims of offences against international law and not just perpetrators.' UNHCR, *Guidelines on International Protection No. 8: Child Asylum Claims under Articles 1(A)2 and 1(F) of the 1951 Convention and/or 1967 Protocol relating to the Status of Refugees* (UNHCR, 22 December 2009), para. [59], available at www.refworld.org/docid/4b2f4f6d2.html.

31 See Wessells, *Child Soldiers*, above n. 15, at 6 (discussing commonalities between gang members and 'those viewed as more typical child soldiers' but advocating for a definition of 'child soldier' that focuses on 'mistreatment of children stemming from association with armed forces in the context of political violence').

32 Boerman, 'Central American Gangs', above n. 10.

33 Levenson, *Adios, Nino*, above n. 15, at 77 (quoting Rodolfo Kepfer). See also Center for Legal Research, Bristol Law School, *Youth and Violence: Drawing Parallels Between Child Soldiers and Youth in Gangs*, Working Paper (June 2013), p. 15 (reporting on discussion among legal scholars and other experts, who concluded that while urban and armed conflict generally had significant differences, the 'lines between' the two concepts 'have blurred' in the case of the 'drug wars in Latin America', where people often view themselves as being at 'war').

often enter armed forces by being kidnapped, conscripted or rounded up in groups ('press ganged').[34] In other cases, children turn themselves in to become soldiers, but they typically make this decision in response to extremely chaotic and life-threatening circumstances. They may join a militant force in order to address immediate survival needs, for example, to avoid starvation, to protect themselves and their families against war-time violence, or to escape extreme domestic abuse.[35] Others may seek to avenge atrocities against their families, respond to religious or ideological propaganda, or gain a sense of power and stability within a highly chaotic environment.[36]

Gangs in the Northern Triangle also recruit children, often targeting those who are particularly vulnerable due to a lack of family protection or extreme poverty.[37] Of a group of Central American children whom Human Rights Watch (HRW) interviewed in Mexico and Honduras, one-in-five reported that 'pressures to join gangs were the primary motive for them to migrate'.[38] In some areas, nearly all children were pressured

---

[34] Lonegan, 'Sinners or Saints', above n. 13, at 95–6 (proposing reforms to the interpretation of the persecutor bar in connection with child soldiers' cases) (citing G. Machel, *Impact of Armed Conflict on Children*, UN Doc. A/51/306 (20 August 1996)); see also Wessells, *Child Soldiers*, above n. 15, at 37–42 (collecting accounts by children who were abducted or press ganged by armed groups, which sometimes murdered and tortured their parents or siblings).

[35] Lonegan, 'Sinners or Saints', above n. 13, at 94–5; Wessells, *Child Soldiers*, above n. 15, at 3–4, 46–9, 54–5; and Machel, *Impact of Armed Conflict on Children*, above n. 34, paras [38]–[41].

[36] Lonegan, 'Sinners or Saints', above n. 12, at 94–5; Wessells, *Child Soldiers*, above n. 15, at 49–51, 53–4; and Machel, *Impact of Armed Conflict on Children*, above n. 34, paras [41]–[42]. See, e.g, Beah, *A Long Way Gone*, above n. 14, at 112 (describing training sessions for juvenile army recruits in Sierra Leone in which the adult commander trained orphaned children to imagine they were killing those rebels who had murdered their parents); and E. Braunstein, 'Are Gang Members, Like Other Child Soldiers, Entitled to Protection from Prosecution Under International Law?' (1999) 3(75) *UC Davis Journal of Juvenile Law and Policy* 89 (regarding US gangs).

[37] V. Rossi, 'Honduran Maras Recruit Children in Kindergarten', *InSight Crime*, (Online, 10 September 2002), available at www.insightcrime.org/news-briefs/honduran-maras-recruit-children-in-kindergarten-report (reporting that gangs in San Pedro Sula, Honduras were recruiting six-year-olds); UNHCR, *Guidance Note on Refugee Claims Relating to Victims of Organized Gangs* (31 March 2010), p. 10, para. [30], available at www.unhcr.org/refworld/docid/4bb21fa02.html; Declaration of Dr Ubaldo Herrera Coello, Expert on Children's Rights in Honduras, paras 32–33 (on file with the author and Center for Gender and Refugee Studies) ('Coella Declaration'), available upon request at https://cgrs.uchastings.edu/search-materials/cgrs-litigation-support-materials.

[38] Human Rights Watch, *Closed Doors: Mexico's Failure to Protect Central*

to join.[39] Gangs, like military and militant groups, routinely use force and coercion to recruit children.[40] Numerous children in the HRW study reported that they had fled after gangs threatened to kill them if they did not join; at least one reported a threat to kill family members; and two had been shot in the abdomen after they refused orders to join gangs.[41] In another example, a gang member stabbed a 15-year-old boy in the stomach and broke his nose when he declined to join them.[42] Two brothers, aged 13 and 15, fled from San Pedro Sula, Honduras, to the United States after gang members tortured or killed seven or eight children, all 15 years or younger, and then threatened to kill the brothers if they did not join the gang.[43] Another 13-year-old fled Honduras after a gang threatened to murder him and his six-year-old brother if he did not join and after two 14-year-old classmates were murdered and mutilated for refusing to join the MS-13.[44]

In light of the significant brain differences between children and adults, as discussed below, even a 'voluntary' decision by a child to join a gang is influenced by impulsive decision-making and coercion. The *maras*, moreover, like other armed forces, may offer struggling children financial security and protection from crime. They often target children without family protection. Such children desperately need a support network and are vulnerable to exploitation since they are willing to work for very little pay.[45] Moreover, the children recruited by the *maras*, like those targeted

---

American Refugee and Migrant Children (2016), available at www.hrw.org/report/2016/03/31/closed-doors/mexicos-failure-protect-central-american-refugee-and-migrant-children.

39 *Ibid.*

40 *Ibid.*; Inter-American Commission on Human Rights, *Violence, Children, and Organized Crime* para. 173 (2015), OEA/Ser.L/V/II. Doc.40/15, available at https://www.oas.org/en/iachr/reports/pdfs/ViolenceChildren2016.pdf ('There are often situations in which children and adolescents are pressured, threatened or beaten to force them to collaborate with the *mara* controlling the district where they live.').

41 *Ibid.*

42 N. Kristof, 'We're helping deport kids to die,' *New York Times*, 16 July 2016, available at www.nytimes.com/2016/07/17/opinion/sunday/were-helping-deport-kids-to-die.html.

43 J. Leland, 'Fleeing violence in Honduras, a teenage boy seeks asylum in Brooklyn', *New York Times*, 4 December 2014, available at https://nyti.ms/2lDqmZi.

44 N. Kristof, 'Obama's death sentence for young refugees', *New York Times*, 25 June 2016, available at https://nyti.ms/2tOBXaw>; see also Malik, *The Harrowing Lives and Traumas of Central American Refugees*, above n. 7 (documenting additional cases).

45 *Ibid.*

for recruitment or conscription by militant groups, are often uniquely vulnerable to coercion and pressure due to their own past trauma – often arising from child abuse, homelessness and extreme poverty.[46] One study identified 'affection, safety, survival and identity' as the primary reasons for Honduran children to join gangs.[47]

Next, militant leaders and gang leaders both use abusive tactics to ensure children's loyalty and desensitize them to extreme violence, so that they will not question their commanders' authority or balk at orders to execute violent acts on behalf of the group. Child soldiers are often 'subjected to brutal induction ceremonies in which attempts are made to harden children emotionally by punishing those who offer help or display feelings for others subjected to abuse'.[48] Militant groups beat new child soldiers and expose them to extreme violence 'so that they do not question the authority of the adults in the group'.[49]

Military commanders may make children kill others, including friends or members of their own families.[50] Such forced killings are intended to 'breed . . . complete obedience', inducing child soldiers, as a temporary survival mechanism, 'to devalue human life and to dehumanize themselves, relinquishing their independence and accepting their violations of previously embraced moral sanctions against killing a friend'.[51] In other words, such practices 'condition the children to violence', so that they experience 'as normal what most people would regard as abnormal'.[52] Such brutal practices quickly implicate children in the groups' violence, and cut them off from any possibility of alternate support from family or friends.[53]

The *maras* have similarly adopted initiation rituals 'characterized by violent and abhorrent acts', including sexual and physical violence against recruits.[54] The forced killings and violence that Wessells and

---

46 See James, 'Fleeing the Maras', above n. 11, at 4.

47 Interpeace et al., *De la prevención local a la nacional: propuestas para prevenir la violencia que afecta a la juventud en Honduras* (2011), p. 40 (quote translated).

48 Lonegan, 'Sinners or Saints', above n. 13.

49 *Ibid.*

50 *Ibid.*; Wessells, *Child Soldiers*, above n. 15, at 64–6 (teenage girl in a FARC militant group ordered to murder her close female friend after friend accused of unauthorized sexual activity).

51 Wessells, *Child Soldiers*, above n. 15, at 64–5.

52 Lonegan, 'Sinners or Saints', above n. 13, at 95.

53 *Ibid.* 95.

54 UNHCR Guidance Note, above n. 39 (gang membership viewed as a 'lifelong commitment' and former gang members who flee 'could fear retaliation and violence from their own and/or rival gangs').

others have described in the context of child soldiers mirror the types of psychological manipulation that gang leaders may use against children.

Forced drug use is a commonly reported experience for child soldiers,[55] and drug use among children involved in gangs is also common.[56] Although the nature of the drugs may differ, in both contexts the drugs may serve to overcome children's resistance to engage in violence and increase their sense of 'reward' for such engagement.[57]

Accounts from both contexts reveal that more established members of the gang or militant group often use sexual violence against girls as a way to incite fear and obedience. The use of rape as a weapon of war is well documented in many conflicts.[58] The *maras* have similarly used rape and sexual assault of girls to punish families that refused extortion or recruitment demands, or girls who have refused sexual demands.[59] Such tactics include forcing girls to enter ongoing relationships with gang members. The *maras* may treat sexual activity with older male gang members as a duty of female gang members. In one case reported in the *New York Times*, an 11-year-old girl became a gang member's 'girlfriend' after her friend was raped and shot in the stomach for refusing such an order.[60]

Although the level of psychological harm to former child soldiers and child gang defectors may vary from one circumstance to another, it is severe and widespread. Psychological studies have shown that child soldiers have rates of post-traumatic stress disorder much higher than civilian children living in war zones.[61] Like many children who become soldiers in armed conflicts, children recruited or conscripted by gangs suffer great trauma caused by repeatedly witnessing extreme violence. They live with

---

55 UNHCR, *Guidance Note*, above n. 37; Machel, *Impact of Armed Conflict on Children*, above n. 34.

56 Lonegan, 'Sinners or Saints', above n. 13, at 95–6.

57 *Ibid.* 95–6.

58 See, e.g., Amnesty International, *Sudan, Darfur: Rape as a Weapon of War: Sexual Violence and its Consequences* (2004), available at www.amnesty.org/en/documents/AFR54/076/2004/en/.

59 See, e.g., Hylton and Salvadore, 'They Said We Would Pay with Our Lives', above n. 2 ('Young women [recruited by gangs] understand their role would be to have forced sex with the gangs', Amoachi said. 'Girls become a vehicle for gang members to take revenge' against families who refuse recruitment or cannot pay extortion fees); Inter-American Commission, above n. 40 at para. [173].

60 *Ibid.*; N. Kristof, 'We're helping deport kids to die', above n. 42.

61 Wessells, *Child Soldiers*, above n. 15, at 131–3.

a constant expectation of imminent death.[62] On average, *mareros* (gang members) are dead by the age of 22.[63]

Just as a militant commander may use lethal violence against a child who defects from an armed force, gang leaders consider children who defect from gangs to be betraying a lifelong commitment to the gang.[64] Such children therefore face an extremely high likelihood of being tortured and killed if located by the gang.[65]

The United Nations High Commissioner on Refugees (UNHCR) has observed that former gang members who were forcibly recruited and later escape often 'fear retaliation and violence from their own and/or rival gangs and (will) not always benefit from the protection of law enforcement agencies'.[66] As local police carry out arbitrary killings, torture and other atrocities against people believed to be gang members, children previously associated with the *maras* are also at serious risk of government violence.[67]

For these reasons, children who escape after being recruited or conscripted by the *maras*, like former child soldiers who defect, are frequently themselves survivors of violence by the brutal organizations from which they have fled. The UNHCR has recognized that in 'certain circumstances, former and current gang members may be considered as victims of gang-related violence, in particular, as a result of forced recruitment, violent gang rituals and the enforcement of a gang's membership code'.[68]

While there is of course great variation among individual armed conflicts and gangs,[69] both groups have often experienced some form of trauma, violence and coercion.

---

[62] *Ibid.* 128–34 (describing effects of trauma in children of different ages and discussing extremely high prevalence of trauma and PTSD among former child soldiers); see also Braunstein, 'Are Gang Members, Like Other Child Soldiers', above n. 36, at 89.

[63] Levenson, *Adios, Nino*, above n. 16, at 6.

[64] UNHCR, *Guidance Note*, above n. 376.

[65] See Levenson, *Adios, Nino*, above n. 16; Coello Declaration, above n. 37, para. [34].

[66] UNHCR, *Guidance Note*, above n. 37, at 5, para. [13].

[67] Police or rival gangs may recognize former gang members by their tattoos, which are often on very visible areas such as their faces. See *ibid.*

[68] UNHCR, *Guidance Note*, above n. 37, at 5, para. [13].

[69] A UK working paper comparing the experiences of children in gangs across the world with those of children in armed conflict emphasized both similarities and differences between the two groups, Center for Legal Research, *Youth and Violence*, above n. 33, but because of their extreme levels of brutality against both recruits and the general population and military features, as discussed above, the *maras* present more similiarities to armed groups than smaller or less violent gangs.

2. REFUGEE CLAIMS BY CHILD GANG DEFECTORS

Even a very grave risk of death does not automatically lead to refugee protection. The basic asylum standard and the broader universe of children's asylum claims, the vast majority of which involve children who are fleeing from gangs or domestic violence, never having been affiliated with a gang, are addressed in another chapter of this book.[70] Here, I focus on two sets of evolving legal questions that demand attention in the small subset of cases involving children who defected from gangs.[71] First, I consider two ways in which such threats can meet the nexus requirement of the refugee definition, as incorporated in US asylum law: the analysis of 'membership in a particular social group' in the wake of restrictive administrative decisions, and the emerging theory of political opinion related to the *maras*. Second, I examine the criminal bars to asylum, which reflect the criminal exclusionary clauses of the Refugee Convention, and the concerns raised by applying a bar designed for adults to children.

2.1 Nexus to Protected Grounds

The question of whether children who have taken the dangerous step of deserting the *maras* have a refugee claim requires a careful analysis of the reasons their lives are at risk. First, deserting a gang can be an expression of political opinion.[72] The *maras* have evolved into complex transnational organizations that amass political power and perform quasi-governmental functions in areas that lack strong state control. For example, Honduras's 'political instability, deep poverty and a history of willfully weak judicial and security forces' have allowed the *maras* to 'explode ... in power

---

[70] See Timnah Baker and Kate Bones, Chapter 14.

[71] For an application of international refugee law principles to this type of claim, along with a discussion of bars to asylum and certain criminal law provisions that recognize the limited culpability of children, see James, 'Fleeing the Maras', above n. 11.

[72] See A. Goncalves-Peña, 'Challenging the "Political": U.S. Asylum Law and Central American Gang Warfare' (2008) 65 *Guild Practice* 242; and D. Uchimiya, 'Falling Through the Cracks: Gang Victims as Casualties in Current Asylum Jurisprudence' (2013) 23 (109) *Berkeley La Raza Law Journal* 145; L. Frydman and N. Desai, 'Beacon of Hope or Failure of Protection? U.S. Treatment of Asylum Claims Based on Persecution by Organized Gangs' (2012) 10 *Immigration Briefings* 1 (arguing that those fleeing gang recruitment may have political opinion claims); *Fuentes-Colocho* v. *US Attorney General*, No. 13-70470, Brief of *Amici Curiae* Harvard Immigration and Refugee Clinical Program et al. (2013).

and readily acquire military-grade weaponry'.[73] The Barrio 18 gang (also known as the Mara 18 or the 18th Street Gang) and MS-13 control extensive geographic territories. In those areas, they perform functions that mimic a governmental role, extorting residents for 'tax' or 'rent', and maintaining some measure of security in the absence of significant governmental law enforcement.[74] The *maras* have even funded political candidates and perpetrated violence in ways intended to influence political decisions. For example, in Honduras a *mara* carried out a massacre in which '28 people on a bus passing through the neighborhood were killed by gang members upset at plans to restore the death penalty'.[75] The gangs have also staged riots with specific political demands in Central American prisons.[76] The *maras* perpetuate political instability because it allows them to operate with impunity. They also engage in other activities designed to cement their far-reaching social control, including curfews, regulation of dress or personal grooming,[77] press intimidation,[78] and forced recruitment.[79] Thus, when a child or youth defects from a gang, this action may sometimes be an expression of anti-gang political opinion or opposition to the gang's political views.

Second, young people who have defected from gangs may qualify as refugees in the United States because they would face persecution on account of their membership of a 'particular social group', a protected ground that has been defined by many court and agency decisions over the years. Board of Immigration Appeals (BIA) decisions in *MEVG*

---

[73] R. Archibold, 'Hope dwindles for Hondurans living in peril', *New York Times*, 2 August 2014.

[74] *Ibid.*; A Goncalves-Peña, 'Challenging the "Political"', above n. 72, at 243–4.

[75] Archibold, 'Hope dwindles for Hondurans living in peril', above n. 73; see also Goncalves-Peña, 'Challenging the "Political"', above n. 72, at 244.

[76] *Ibid.* 244.

[77] M. Lohmuller, 'Honduras: Panic Ensues After MS13 Allegedly Prohibits Blonde Hair in Honduras Markets', *InSightcrime* (Online, 27 May 2015), available at www.insightcrime.org/news-analysis/ms13-allegedly-prohibits-blonde-hair-in-honduras-markets (gang 'is attempting to instate far-reaching social control'); M. Cawley, 'Gangs "Impose Curfew" in Honduran Capital', *InSightcrime* (Online, 6 February 2013), available at www.insightcrime.org/news-briefs/honduran-gang-curfew-security-barrio-18.

[78] See US Department of State, *Report on Human Rights Practices 2013* (2014), p. 11 (reporting that the Honduran press '"self-censored" due to fear of reprisal from organized crime or corrupt government officials').

[79] See Immigration and Refugee Board of Canada, *Honduras: The Recruitment of Mara Salvatrucha (MS) and 18th Street (Calle 18 or Mara 18) Gang Members* (2012) ('forced recruitment has been increasing over the last years because gangs want to maintain their influence and control over the neighborhoods they operate').

and *WGR* illustrate the Board's deep resistance to gang-related claims, including claims by former gang members.[80] In *WGR*, the BIA held that 'former members of the Mara 18 gang in El Salvador who have renounced their gang membership' did not qualify as a 'particular social group'.[81] In *MEVG*, the BIA rejected a proposed social group described as 'Honduran youth who have been actively recruited by gangs but who have refused to join because they oppose the gangs'.[82] But these decisions, read alongside Circuit Court precedents, in fact suggest that children who have defected from the *maras* can have strong asylum claims based upon their membership in a particular social group.

Several US Courts of Appeals have already recognized particular social groups for adults based upon former gang membership. As of this writing, the Fourth and Seventh Circuit have the clearest precedents, holding that former gang members can constitute a social group.[83] The Ninth Circuit rejected such a claim based upon the reasoning that bad acts should not be rewarded, but it emphasized in so doing that the respondent before the court had not renounced his gang membership, and in fact had testified that he remained an 'inactive' member.[84]

The federal Circuit Courts, the BIA, and many other courts have also recognized that being a former member of a group is an immutable characteristic, a core requirement for a social group claim, because membership occurred in the past and cannot be undone.[85] The *WGR* decision

---

80 *Matter of MEVG*, 26 I & N Dec. 227, 228 (BIA 2014); *Matter of WGR*, 26 I & N Dec. 208, 221–2 (BIA 2014).

81 *Ibid.* 221.

82 *Matter of MEVG*, above n. 80.

83 See *Martinez* v. *Holder*, 740 F.3d 902, 911 (4th Cir. 2014), as revised (27 January 2014); *Ramos* v. *Holder*, 589 F.3d 426, 430 (7th Cir. 2009); but see *Gonzalez v. US Atty. Gen.*, 820 F.3d 399, 406 (11th Cir. 2016); see also *Urbina-Mejia* v. *Holder*, 597 F.3d 360, 366 (6th Cir. 2010) (holding that former gang membership is an immutable characteristic).

84 *Arteaga* v. *Mukasey*, 511 F.3d 940 (9th Cir. 2007) (reasoning that '[t]he outlaw group to which the petitioner belongs is best described as an "antisocial group"', and that asylum law should not reward members of such groups); see also *Martinez* v. *Holder*, 740 F.3d 902, 912 (4th Cir. 2014).

85 See *Urbina-Mejia*, 597 F.3d 360, 366 (6th Cir. 2010) (citing *Gatimi* v. *Holder*, 578 F.3d 611, 614 (7th Cir. 2009) (former members of Mungiki, a criminal organization in Kenya); *Sepulveda* v. *Gonzales*, 464 F.3d 770, 771–2 (7th Cir. 2006) (former subordinates of the Attorney General of Colombia); *Koudriachova* v. *Gonzales*, 490 F.3d 255, 262–3 (2d Cir. 2007) (former KGB agents); *Cruz–Navarro* v. *INS*, 232 F.3d 1024, 1028–9 (9th Cir. 2000) (former members of the police or military); *Velarde* v. *INS*, 140 F.3d 1305, 1311–13 (9th Cir. 1998) (former bodyguards of the daughters of the president); *Chanco* v. *INS*, 82 F.3d 298, 302–3 (9th

rejected the UNHCR's social group definition in favor of one that requires both that a particular social group be defined with 'particularity' (that is, with specificity) and with 'social distinction' (that is, by showing that society would view the specified group as a discrete group). Yet in rejecting a proposed social group of 'former members of the Mara 18 gang in El Salvador who have renounced their gang membership', this decision also emphasized that the group in question was overbroad because it included 'persons of any age, sex, or background'.[86] Thus, a group defined with reference to age or other limiting factors could satisfy the particularity requirement.[87] The BIA noted, moreover, that social groups involving former membership could be 'defined with respect to the duration or strength of the members' active participation in the activity and the time frames relating to their active participation'.[88]

With respect to 'social distinction', the concerns the BIA raised in *WGR* and *MEVG* appear to rest largely on a lack of sufficient documentation in the record. In *WGR*, for example, 'the record contain[ed] scant evidence that Salvadoran society considers former gang members who have renounced their gang membership as a distinct social group'. But experts have observed that youth who leave the *maras* are in fact perceived as a group by their societies – and targeted as a group by the local police, their former gangs, and rival gangs alike.[89] Thus, the strength of the record in the individual case will prove a critical question in future cases. Finally, and critically for an asylum claim, these defections trigger retaliatory violence, as discussed in greater detail above.

Alternatively, courts and asylum officers may recognize other types of social groups that encompass children who have deserted gangs. In

---

Cir. 1996) (former military officers); *In re Fuentes*, 19 I & N Dec. 658, 662 (BIA 1988) (former members of the national police)); *Sepulveda* v. *Gonzales*, 464 F.3d 770, 771–2 (7th Cir. 2006) (collecting cases); *Lukwago* v. *Ashcroft*, 329 F.3d 157, 171–2 (3d Cir. 2003) (former child soldiers who have escaped); *Matter of CA*, 24 I & N Dec. 951 (BIA 2006); see W-G-R-, 26 I & N Dec, 221-22.

86 *WGR*, above n. 80, at 221–2.

87 In *MEVG*, above n. 80, the BIA held that asylum law did not recognize a 'particular social group' comprising 'Honduran *youth* who have been actively recruited by gangs but who have refused to join because they oppose the gangs', but the BIA omitted any express discussion of whether the age of the group members might make them sufficiently particular, as *WGR*, above n. 80, appears to suggest, so it is not clear that it considered this specific question. *MEVG*, above n. 80, at 228.

88 *Ibid.*

89 See Boerman, 'Central American Gangs', above n. 10; Coello Declaration, above n. 37, para. [34].

Lukwago, a case involving a former child soldier, the Third Circuit Court of Appeals held that 'the shared experience of abduction, persecution and escape' can serve as the basis for a social group.[90] In the context of juvenile gang defectors, UNHCR has recognized that a young person who resists gang orders often becomes a target 'because s/he lives in a poor neighborhood, and/or is without family or other social support networks'.[91] Likewise, the experience of surviving child abuse is an immutable characteristic that may also be used to define a social group.[92] Some adjudicators have recognized social groups involving former street children, a clearly identifiable group in Central American society that is often targeted for gang recruitment.[93]

In short, many children who have defected from gangs have viable social group claims, but these claims require thorough factual records.[94]

2.2 Criminal Bars to Asylum

US immigration law renders many people ineligible for asylum on the basis of two categories of past criminal activity, both derived from the Convention on the Status of Refugees. The first bar applies to an individual who, 'having been convicted by a final judgment of a particularly serious crime, constitutes a danger to the community of the United States'.[95] For purposes of asylum, particularly serious crimes are typically defined to include any 'aggravated felony', a term that includes a wide range of violent and non-violent offenses.[96] The second criminal bar applies when 'there are serious reasons for believing that the alien has committed a serious nonpolitical crime outside the United States prior to the arrival of the alien in the United States'.[97] A 'serious non-political crime' is defined

---

90 329 F.3d 157, 178 (3d Cir. 2003).

91 UNHCR, *Guidance Note*, above n. 37.

92 Coello Declaration, above n. 37.

93 See *Matter of Josue AG*, Center for Gender and Refugee Studies (CGRS) Database No. 3997 (EOIR); Matter of RD-, D, CGRS Database No. 3996 (Los Angeles EOIR). In addition, the BIA has recognized social groups based on family relationships, *Matter of LEA*, 27 I & N Dec. 40 (BIA 2017), so people who are targeted by the *maras* because they are relatives of individuals who have defected from gangs may also satisfy the refugee definition.

94 Additionally, children who desert based upon strongly-held religious beliefs or conversions may face persecution based upon religion.

95 INA, s. 208(b)(2)(A)(ii), 8 USC s. 1158(b)(2)(A)(ii) (emphasis added); INA, s. 241(b)(3)(B)(i), 8 USC s. 1231(b)(3)(B)(ii).

96 INA, s. 208(b)(2)(B)(i); 8 USC s. 1158(b)(2)(B)(i).

97 INA, s. 208(b)(2)(A)(iii); 8 USC s. 1158(b)(2)(A)(iii).

as one that is not committed out of genuine political motives, not seeking to modify the political organization or government structure, and having no direct, causal link between the crime and any political goals.[98] Whereas the 'particularly serious crime' bar statutorily requires a 'conviction', the 'serious non-political crime' bar does not.

US federal statutes, which govern the immigration consequences of state or federal criminal prosecutions, provide very limited guidance as to how the bars to asylum should apply to children who have convictions. In the seminal case on foreign convictions of children, the BIA held that a young man whom Cuba had prosecuted as an adult for theft at the age of 13 did not have a 'conviction' for purposes of US immigration law because his conviction would have been treated as a civil delinquency under the Federal Juvenile Delinquency Act (FJDA).[99] This statute governed the small proportion of juvenile or criminal proceedings charged in federal courts (as opposed to state courts, which handle most criminal prosecutions in the United States). Currently, federal law provides for the transfer of a child aged between 15 and 18 to adult criminal court where the child waives his or her right to be treated as a juvenile upon advice of counsel *and* where he or she is charged with specified offenses (primarily involving felony 'crimes of violence', controlled substances or firearm possession). Children between 13 and 15 may also be transferred to adult court, but only when charged with a small subset of violent offenses.[100] In either case, the court must find, after a hearing, that transfer to an adult court is in the 'interests of justice'.[101]

Each US State has its own laws governing when and if a child may be charged as an adult for purposes of criminal prosecution, and these laws vary widely. For example, Florida law gives prosecutors discretion to try children of *any* age as an adult,[102] whereas New York recently raised the age of criminal liability for misdemeanors to 18.[103] Some States have intermediate categories of adjudications that fall somewhere between criminal

---

[98] *McMullen* v. *INS*, 788 F.2d 591, 595 (9th Cir. 1986).

[99] *Ramirez-Rivero*, 18 I & N Dec. 135 (1981).

[100] 18 USC s. 5032.

[101] *Ibid.*

[102] See *Graham* v. *Florida*, 560 US 48, 67 (2010), as modified (6 July 2010) ('For example, under Florida law a child of any age can be prosecuted as an adult for certain crimes and can be sentenced to life without parole. The State acknowledged at oral argument that even a 5-year-old, theoretically, could receive such a sentence under the letter of the law.').

[103] E. Hager, 'The Fine Print in New York's Raise the Age Law', *The Marshall Project*, 14 April 2017, available at www.themarshallproject.org/2017/04/14/the-fine-print-in-new-york-s-raise-the-age-law.

and civil adjudications. In short, under current US law, determining whether a domestic action against a child should be treated as a 'conviction' for purposes of the bars to asylum has become nearly as complex as interpreting foreign adjudications of juvenile misconduct.

Next, while a full investigation of the question of whether adolescents can have the requisite mental state to have committed a disqualifying 'crime' exceeds the scope of this chapter, any such inquiry should address research showing that adolescent behavior differs significantly from that of adults, and that the adolescent brain differs in correspondingly significant ways from the adult brain. As a result of uneven development of different brain systems, adolescents often struggle with future goal-oriented planning and emotional self-regulation, and are more susceptible to peer pressure.[104] These characteristics make adolescents more likely to engage in risk-taking behaviors, especially in pressured situations.[105] However, as they mature, adolescents have the capacity to develop more mature impulse control and to decrease risk-taking behaviors, particularly when support networks are provided.[106] Because juveniles have a categorically different capacity from adults, adjudicators should and sometimes do recognize that they may lack the requisite mental state to have committed a crime. [107]

Moreover, adolescent susceptibility to peer pressure means adjudicators should give particular consideration to whether a child may have committed offenses under duress or coercion. Duress is a traditional exception to criminal liability and to the serious non-political crime bar,[108] and duress and coercion also are relevant to the question of whether a particular criminal offense is 'particularly serious'.

With reference to the criminal exclusionary clauses of the Convention

---

104 This conclusion finds support in a large body of research in neuroscience, developmental psychology, and other fields. See, e.g., National Research Council, *Reforming Juvenile Justice: A Developmental Approach* (2013), p. 2.

105 *Ibid.*

106 See, e.g., K. Monahan, L. Steinberg and A. Piquero, 'Juvenile Justice Policy and Practice: A Developmental Perspective' (2015) 44 *Crime and Justice* 577, at 585; S.J. Ordaz et al., 'Longitudinal Growth Curves of Brain Function Underlying Inhibitory Control through Adolescence' (2013) 33 *Journal of Neuroscience* 18109; see National Research Council, *Reforming Juvenile Justice*, above n. 104, at 90 ('[I]t is not possible to predict enduring antisocial traits on the basis of risky behavior during adolescence.').

107 See, e.g., *In Re E-O-* (BIA July 12, 2006) (unpublished) (holding that Ugandan child soldier was not subject to criminal bars to asylum because his juvenile status reflected diminished culpability) (on file with Center for Gender and Refugee Studies).

108 See *Urbina-Mejia* v. *Holder*, 597 F.3d 360, 369 (6th Cir. 2010).

on the Status of Refugees, which form the basis for the criminal bars in the US asylum statute, the UNHCR has recognized the need to consider 'the mental capacity of children and their ability to understand and consent to acts that they are requested or ordered to undertake'. The UNHCR does not apply the criminal exclusionary clauses to younger children, and, for children who have reached the age of criminal responsibility in receiving countries, it advises adjudicators to consider mental capacity as well as duress, coercion, defense of self or others, and proportionality.[109]

In short, adjudicators should approach children's cases with an understanding that adolescents' brains work differently from those of mature adults, and in light of children's particular vulnerability to future persecution. Categorical asylum bars designed for adults should not preclude protection for children who face persecution.

2.3 Discretion

In the United States, asylum is a discretionary form of relief. Whereas 'withholding of removal' implements the United States' non-refoulement obligation pursuant to Article 33(1) of the Convention on the Status of Refugees, our courts consider asylum to implement Article 34, which affords more benefits at the government's discretion.[110] Thus, even when someone meets the statutory eligibility requirements, an adjudicator may deny asylum in an exercise of discretion.

In making a discretionary asylum decision, adjudicators should look not only at past affiliations or past offenses, but also to questions such as the age and capacity of the child or young person at the time of any past bad acts and at factors such as child abuse, coercion and trauma that may have contributed to past offenses. They should also consider the young

---

[109] UNHCR, Guidelines on International Protection No. 8: Child Asylum Claims under Articles 1(A)2 and 1(F) of the 1951 Convention and/or 1967 Protocol relating to the Status of Refugees para. [62], available at http://www.refworld.org/docid/4b2f4f6d2.html. Although not the focus of this discussion, similar considerations would affect application of other bars to asylum. See Lonegan, 'Sinners or Saints', above n. 13, at 99. The BIA has held that a non-citizen who assisted in persecution solely for financial gain was subject to a 'persecutor bar' similar to that found in the asylum statute because the primary persecutors in that case were motivated by the victim's political opinion. *Matter of JM Alvarado*, 27 I & N Dec. 27 (BIA 2017). This decision, however, did not address any questions of duress or coercion, nor any allegations of limited capacity or understanding by the non-citizen who assisted in the persecution.

[110] *INS* v. *Cardoza-Fonseca*, 480 US 421 (1997).

person's more recent history, including evidence of rehabilitation and mental health treatment.

3. CONCLUSION

Because children who have defected from the *maras* are extremely likely to be killed if returned to their countries of origin, and because this persecution generally has a nexus to both anti-gang political opinions and to a 'particular social group' defined based on a defector's past membership, child defectors often have legitimate refugee protection needs. Their cases, like those of former child soldiers, should receive individualized adjudications, informed by an understanding of child psychology and brain development, and should not be subject to categorical bars to asylum designed to apply to adults. Law-makers and administrative officials should consider the evidence in each case to determine whether that child needs protection.

The argument set forth here comports with the need to protect public safety. As noted above, adolescents' still-developing brains make it possible for them to overcome traumatic and violent childhood experiences, as their capacities for long-term planning, risk avoidance and emotional self-regulation continue to mature. Although examination of strategies for supporting children who receive protection is beyond the scope of this chapter, receiving governments should learn from programs to reintegrate former child soldiers, and should support rehabilitation of children defecting from gangs by placing children in safe and secure living situations with supportive adult connections, and providing basic financial support, mental health and substance abuse programs, education and vocational assistance: opportunities to develop a sense of identity, belonging and purpose.[111]

[111] See, e.g., Center for Legal Research, *Youth and Violence*, above n. 33, at 40.

23. Don't look behind you: unaccompanied and separated children who have participated in armed conflict in South Sudan

Kasey Tyler and Shelly Whitman

1. INTRODUCTION

Children associated with armed forces and groups in various capacities are a unique group of migrant child. Where a child is affiliated with an armed force or group, there is an inherent risk that they will be subject to constant and extensive movement either within or over borders at the behest of their superiors. Unfortunately, despite a global yearning for straightforward and actionable data, obtaining authoritative figures for the number of children in this situation is near impossible due to the clandestine nature of many of the organizations that these children become associated with.[1] The best indicator of the prevalence of the use of recruitment of children in conflict situations comes from the UN Secretary-General's Annual Report on children and armed conflict which uses data from the UN-led Monitoring and Reporting Mechanism (MRM), a methodology detailed in section 4 of this chapter. As of August 2017, the United Nations is monitoring seven state forces and 54 non-state armed groups that currently recruit and use children.[2]

This chapter examines the challenges that exist in effectively protecting children who are members of an armed force or armed group under

[1] G. Kessler, 'The Zombie claim that 300,000 children are used as child soldiers', *Washington Post* (Online), 22 January 2016, available at www.washingtonpost.com/news/fact-checker/wp/2016/01/22/the-zombie-claim-that-300000-children-are-used-as-child-soldiers/; S. Whitman, 'How We Should Measure the Impact of War on Children', Huffington Post (Online), 6 July 2016, available at www.huffingtonpost.ca/shelly-whitman/impact-of-war-on-children_b_10336696.html.

[2] *Children and Armed Conflict: Report of the Secretary General*, GA 71st session, Security Council 72nd year, UN Doc. A/72/361-S/2017/821 (24 August 2017).

international law. The case study of South Sudan will be explored from the perspective of the authors' experience in that context. South Sudan, established as an independent nation in 2011, is estimated to have approximately 15,000 child soldiers within its borders and is one of the countries of concern highlighted in the UN Secretary-General's *Report on Children and Armed Conflict*. Kasey Tyler worked in South Sudan in the context of child protection for an international organization, while Dr Shelly Whitman is the Executive Director of the Romeo Dallaire Child Soldiers Initiative ('Dallaire Initiative'). The Dallaire Initiative is a global partnership that aims to progressively end the use of child soldiers globally through a unique security sector approach.[3]

This chapter will first examine the way in which the international community has struggled to define, and hence action, matters relating to children and armed conflict. The international protections in place for children affected by armed conflict will be detailed as will the related monitoring and reporting mechanism created by the United Nations. A short case study on the impact of conflict on children in South Sudan will conclude this chapter.

2. DEFINING THE PROBLEM

A child soldier is defined by the Additional Protocols to the Geneva Conventions[4] as someone who is recruited into or used by a military group whilst under the age of 15, though there is a push to increase the age under this definition to under 18 years.[5] The term 'child soldier' is often used interchangeably with 'child associated with armed force or armed group' (CAAFAG). The latter is a more contemporary term that seeks to emphasize the importance of including children who may be involved

---

[3] Security Sector refers to armed groups, armed forces, peace-keeping forces, police, military and prison personnel. For more information on this approach, see www.childsoldiers.org.

[4] Protocol Additional to the Geneva Conventions of 12 August 1949, and relating to the Protection of Victims of International Armed Conflicts (Protocol I), opened for signature 8 June 1977, 1125 UNTS 3 (entered into force 7 December 1978), Art. 77(2); Protocol Additional to the Geneva Conventions of 12 August 1949, and relating to the Protection of Victims of Non-International Armed Conflicts (Protocol II), opened for signature 8 June 1977, 1125 UNTS 609 (entered into force 7 December 1978), Art. 4(3)(c).

[5] Optional Protocol to the Convention on the Rights of the Child on the Involvement of Children in Armed Conflict, opened for signature 25 May 2000, A/RES/54/263 (entered into force 12 February 2002) (CRC-OPAC).

with an armed group in a role other than combat, such as a porter, a cook or a person in sexual servitude.[6] The use of young people in or for the interests of armed forces is not a recent phenomenon and there is undeniable evidence that a variety of cultures throughout history utilized the services of children during conflict.[7] The reasons for this are varied. First, the concepts of childhood as a distinctive period of one's life, and the child as an individual rights bearer, are relatively new achievements.[8] Secondly, in the context of culturally specific socialization, persons under 18 may be regarded as being of an appropriate age for combat or support roles.[9] The type of conflict may also affect the domestic and social roles of children: where a protracted conflict, for example, has seen the death or displacement of the adults and children are forced to adopt responsibilities that would usually be fulfilled by their elders.

The appropriate age for combat continues to be a matter for debate. Both the Additional Protocols to the Geneva Conventions and the UN Convention on the Rights of the Child (CRC) prohibit the military recruitment and use of children under the age of 15 rather than 18, the age to which most of the protections inherent in the CRC extend. In response, the Optional Protocol to the Convention on the Rights of the Child on the Involvement of Children in Armed Conflict (CRC-OPAC) was introduced in 2000. This required member states to ensure those below 18 years are not subject to conscription and do not take direct part in hostilities. Notably, only states are eligible to become a party to this CRC-OPAC, which has required alternative methods of advocacy to be used for non-state actors. No matter what culture or circumstances a child may reside within, recent science confirms that the brain continues to develop into early adulthood, thereby impacting one's ability to regulate moods, impulses and behaviours.[10] This makes children and teenagers more prone to faulty decision-making processes and taking unexamined

6 The Office of the Special Representative of the Secretary General for Children and Armed Conflict launched a 'Children, not Soldiers' campaign that opposes all forms of recruitment and use of children by national security forces in armed conflict; for more information, see https://childrenandarmedconflict.un.org/children-not-soldiers/.

7 M. Drumbl, *Reimagining Child Soldiers in International Law and Policy* (Oxford University Press, 2012), pp. 27–9.

8 S. Hart, 'From Property to Persons Status: Historical Perspective on Children's Rights' (1991) 46 *American Psychologist* 5.

9 Drumbl, *Reimagining Child Soldiers*, above n. 7, at 27–9.

10 I. Lambie and I. Randell, 'The Impact of Incarceration on Juvenile Offenders' (2013) 33(3) *Clinical Psychology Review* 448.

risks.[11] Further, recent research into underage recruits in the UK armed forces also shows that child recruits are more vulnerable to suicide, self-harm, post-traumatic stress disorders and alcohol abuse than adult recruits. They are also more likely to be injured or die in combat.[12] In addition, research demonstrates that military training is associated with a marked increase in stress-related mental health problems and that, relative to adults, children are more reactive to stressors.[13] As a result, this can impact the operational effectiveness of a military force.

The way in which children can become associated with armed forces and groups is varied. Children may be abducted, conscripted, tricked or otherwise coerced into joining an armed group or force. There is a perception that children have become increasingly vulnerable to such forced recruitment because of the growth of internal armed conflicts fought by state and non-state actors,[14] as well as the increased availability of lightweight weapons.[15] These weapons can be easily carried and discharged and therefore have increased the appeal of young people to armed forces and groups. There are also very clear strategic and tactical reasons as to why such groups are using and recruiting children. Children are attractive recruitment targets for armed forces and groups as they tend to obey orders without question, can be easily intimidated and are less costly than adult soldiers – eating less and sometimes serving without expectation of payment.[16] Children are also vulnerable to tactics that are designed to produce unquestioning obedience, such as coercion to harm or kill that both indoctrinates children into a culture of violence and discourages escape attempts due to the child's fear of social punishment or rejection.[17]

Alternatively, children may seek out membership of armed groups.

---

11 J. Giedd, 'The Amazing Teen Brain' (2015) 312(6) *Scientific American* 32.

12 R. Louise et al., *The Recruitment of Children by the UK Armed Forces: A Critique from Health Professionals* (Medact, 2016), available at www.medact.org/wp-content/uploads/2016/10/medact_childrecruitment_17-oct_WEB.pdf.

13 J.N. Gied, M. Keshavan and T. Paus, 'Why Do Many Psychiatric Disorders Emerge During Adolescence?' (2008) 9(12) *Nature Reviews Neuroscience* 947.

14 I. Cohn and G.S. Goodwin-Gill, *Child Soldiers: The Role of Children in Armed Conflict* (Clarendon Press, 1994), p. 63.

15 C. Nyamutata, 'Engaging or Shaming? An Analysis of UN's Naming and Shaming of Child Abusers in Armed Conflict' (2013) *Journal of International Humanitarian Legal Studies* 154; Drumbl, *Reimagining Child Soldiers*, above n. 7, at 27–9; M. Wessells, *Child Soldiers: From Violence to Protection* (Harvard University Press, 2006), pp. 18–19.

16 Drumbl, *Reimagining Child Soldiers*, above n. 7, 27–9; Wessells, *Child Soldiers*, above n. 15, at 18–19.

17 M. Steel, *Child Soldiers* (Vision, 2008), available at www.vision.org/visionmedia/social-issues/child-soldiers/6684.aspx.

Children in conflict zones may suffer from poverty, starvation, separation from their families, general displacement, sexual violence and insecurity.[18] Armed groups can present a sense of security for children who do not have family, food or accommodation.[19] Further, a child may be motivated to protect their community, earn a wage to support their family or to seek revenge for the harm caused to their community by the opposition.[20] One of the authors was challenged by a classroom of adolescent boys in a conflict zone to give them a viable alternative to joining an armed group that would address their hunger. In situations where there is no viable alternative, one learns to better understand the circumstances in which some children have to make very difficult decisions.

In addition to the Geneva Convention's Additional Protocols, the CRC-OPAC, the Cape Town Principles of 1997 and the Paris Commitments and Principles of 2007 all seek to address child recruitment, as well as the subsequent release and reintegration of the child soldier from armed groups and forces.[21] Specifically, they seek to guarantee that all signatories adhere to procedural safeguards that ensure enlistment procedures preclude the inclusion of persons under 18 and that, where children are identified in the ranks of armed groups and forces, they are reintegrated into the community in a way that reduces stigma and inspires rehabilitation and restoration. Sections 1 and 2 of this chapter will identify and examine the effectiveness of the international protections afforded to children associated with armed forces and groups.

3. INTERNATIONAL PROTECTIONS

The first international document addressing the rights of children, and the protections that should be afforded to them, was inspired by the suffering of young people during World War I. The Geneva Declaration of the Rights of the Child was adopted by the League of Nations in September

---

18 Wessels, *Child Soldiers*, above n. 15, at 23–30.

19 D.M. Rosen, 'Child Soldiers, International Humanitarian Law, and the Globalisation of Childhood' (2007) 109(2) *American Anthropologist* 298.

20 S. Hodgson, 'Whose Action Plan? An Analysis of the UN Security Council Resolution 1612 Action Plan and Monitoring and Reporting Mechanism in Nepal' (2012) 4(2) *Journal of Human Rights Practice* 174.

21 UNICEF, *Cape Town Principles and Best Practices* (April, 1997); UNICEF, *Paris Commitments to Protect Children from Unlawful Recruitment or Use by Armed Forces or Armed Groups* (February 2007); UNICEF, *The Paris Principles and Guidelines on Children Associated with Armed Forces or Armed Groups* (February 2007).

1924.[22] Powerful in its simplicity, the Geneva Declaration featured only five points that compelled signatories to recognize a duty to meet the basic needs of all children. Though the document does not mention conflict specifically, it seeks to ensure that children's needs are put first 'in times of distress'.[23]

The protection needs of children are also addressed in the four Geneva Conventions and the two Additional Protocols that guide modern international humanitarian law. The Fourth Geneva Convention specifically details special protections for children, and Protocols I and II (AP I and AP II) reinforce these requirements.[24] The potential for active participation by children in hostilities was first addressed by Article 51 of the fourth Geneva Convention, by which persons under 18 were exempt from compulsory labour, including forcible enlistment.[25] The Conventions remain silent, however, on voluntary recruitment and other types of participation. It was left up to Additional Protocols (AP) I and II, relevant to international armed conflicts and non-international armed conflicts, respectively, to specifically prohibit the participation of persons who had not reached 15 years and limit the involvement of young people between 15 and 18 years of age.

Article 77(2) of AP I requires parties to a conflict to take all feasible measures to ensure those below 15 years do not take direct part in hostilities and are not recruited into armed forces. Where persons are between 15 and 18 and recruitment is ongoing, the oldest of this group is to be given priority for active service positions. The restriction of the participation of children who have not attained 15 years is reiterated with reference to non-international conflicts in AP II, Article 4(3)(c) and is applicable to both armed forces and armed groups.[26] Cohn and Goodwin-Gill, one of the first authorities to examine the protection of children involved in armed conflict under international law, argue that while there are theoretical protections, the language of these protections is insubstantial, requiring

---

22 Available at www.un-documents.net/gdrc1924.htm.

23 *Ibid.*

24 For a brief overview, see R.K. Dixit, 'Special Protection of Children During Armed Conflicts under the Geneva Conventions Regime' (2001) 2 *Isil Yearbook of International Human and Refugee Law* 12.

25 International Committee of the Red Cross, *Commentary on Convention (IV) relative to the Protection of Civilian Persons in Time of War* (1958), available at https://tinyurl.com/y97bno5g.

26 'Whereas *armed forces* refer to official state militaries, *armed groups* refer to non-state entities distinct from those forces (notably, rebel or protest movements, dissident factions, and insurgents)', Drumbl, *Reimagining Child Soldiers*, above n. 7, at 4.

states to 'endeavour' or 'take all feasible measures' to protect and 'refrain' from endangering children.[27] It is also notable that these instruments do not seek to prevent an individual from seeking membership of an armed group, but instead impose a duty on those in charge of recruitment to decline a child's 'application for membership' of their organization. However, in the throes of conflict, it is difficult to believe that adhering to such an obligation would be at the forefront of the mind of local recruiters whose priorities may be far removed from those of command headquarters and implementation of international commitments. A further element of weakness inherent in the Geneva Conventions and Additional Protocols is that the parties to a conflict may not be signatories to these instruments, either because they are not a state party or because they are a non-state actor. Accordingly, unless Articles 77(2) and 4(3)(c) could also be classified as customary international law, the prohibition of children under 15 taking part in hostilities is unlikely to be legally enforceable.[28]

International humanitarian law (IHL) recognizes that a child's active involvement in a conflict, and the parameters of such involvement, should be restricted. International human rights law, too, largely reflects the protections set out in the above instruments. The CRC, which defines a child as every person under 18 years, echoes the IHL protections afforded to children in matters related to armed conflict in Article 38. The CRC is arguably the most compelling instrument of international law, receiving all but universal acceptance.[29] However, its protections also have limitations as they cannot be imposed upon non-state actors and the age of protection from participation is 15 years, not 18 years as is the preference of more recent and dedicated instruments. It also maintains the suggestive, rather than compelling, tone featured in the IHL instruments above:

Article 38
1. States Parties undertake to respect and to ensure respect for rules of international humanitarian law applicable to them in armed conflicts which are relevant to the child.
2. States Parties shall take all *feasible measures* to ensure that persons who have not attained the age of *fifteen years* do not take a direct part in hostilities.
3. States Parties shall *refrain* from recruiting any person who has not attained

27 Cohn and Goodwin-Gill, *Child Soldiers*, above n. 14, at 63.
28 *Ibid.* 65.
29 The Convention on the Rights of the Child has been ratified more quickly and by more governments than any other instrument. As of 25 October 2016, the United States is the only recognized UN state not to have signed the CRC. See www.unicef.org/crc/index_73549.html.

the age of *fifteen years* into their armed forces. In recruiting among those persons who have attained the age of fifteen years but who have not attained the age of eighteen years, States Parties shall *endeavour* to give priority to those who are oldest.

4. In accordance with their obligations under international humanitarian law to protect the civilian population in armed conflicts, States Parties shall take all *feasible measures* to ensure protection and care of children who are affected by an armed conflict. (Emphasis added)

It is important to note that one of the reasons Article 38 of the CRC defines the age for minimum recruitment at 15 years, rather than 18, was as a result of pressure from the United States and the United Kingdom,[30] both of whom used under 18s in their military. This was not the perspective of all the states involved in the drafting of the convention language. The CRC-OPAC (2000) was subsequently created to address this lacuna and ensure that every person categorized as a child by the CRC should be restricted from direct involvement in conflict.

Additional international principles applicable to children affected by and involved in conflict were created by the Cape Town Principles of 1997 and the Paris Principles of 2007. These sought to create specific guidelines for any state, group or organization that came into contact with recruited or demobilized children. Both sets of guidelines support increasing the age for participation in hostilities from 15 years to 18 years and seek to guide interventions in matters relating to recognition, release and reintegration of children associated with armed forces and armed groups. This push has subsequently been reinforced by the UN Secretary-General's 'Global Campaign for the universal ratification and implementation of the Optional Protocols to the CRC' in 2010 and the Office of the Special Representative of the Secretary-General for Children and Armed Conflict's campaigns 'Zero under 18' and 'Children not Soldiers'.

However, authors such as Julie McBride argue that these campaigns may also be hindering the progression of the law on children recruited and used as soldiers. McBride argues that children who are forcibly recruited by armed groups at 11 or 12 years of age are not in the same position as 17-year-olds who voluntarily enlist with parental consent.[31] The Dallaire Initiative also argues that while it is important to advocate for a cut-off age of 18 years, the progressive elimination of the use of children as

---

[30] J. McBride, *The War Crime of Child Soldier Recruitment* (Springer, 2014), p. 26.

[31] *Ibid*. 32.

soldiers should be grounded in the reality that children as young as five are being recruited, abducted and indoctrinated into the operations of war. As a result, the ultimate goal of ending the use of children as soldiers can only be realized via concrete and incremental action. This means that the very youngest children may need to be given priority attention in terms of protection from recruitment and use by armed groups and forces, as academic studies have shown that the younger a child is when recruited, the more difficult to successfully demobilize and reintegrate. When working within a delicate peace process in a fragile state it may be realistic that those using and recruiting children will agree only to make incremental steps towards an under 18 target. Due to challenging cultural and socio-economic situations on the ground it may take time to fully realise the under 18 target. Accordingly, it would be optimal if the international community could unite behind agreed incremental goals adapted to the circumstances of each nation-state and that ultimately culminate in a 'Zero under 18' target.

Despite the ongoing discussion as to the varying levels of protection for children between the ages of 15 and 18, on the whole there is a thorough package of international humanitarian law, international human rights law and international principles that seek to prevent and interrupt the participation of children in conflict. Section 4 will therefore go on to examine what has been done to actualize the protections afforded to children under these commitments.

4. INTERNATIONAL MONITORING AND ANALYSIS OF CHILDREN ASSOCIATED WITH ARMED FORCES AND GROUPS

In 1992, the Committee on the Rights of the Child initiated a dialogue about the impact of armed conflict on children. As a consequence, a report authored by Graca Machel on the Impact of Armed Conflict on Children was submitted to the United Nations General Assembly in 1996.[32] The report, known widely as the Machel report, detailed the way in which children were being directly targeted in major armed conflicts around the world. Machel determined that without wide dissemination, implementation and monitoring, no humanitarian or human rights law was going to

---

[32] United Nations General Assembly (UNGA), *Promotion and Protection of the Rights of the Child: Impact of Armed Conflict on Children*, 51st session, Agenda item 107, UN Doc. A/51/306 (26 August 1996).

be effective in actualizing the desired standards committed to by most of the international community. The report concluded by accusing governments, international organizations and civil society of failing to defend children against repeated violations of their human rights, labelling it as 'a fundamental crisis of our civilisation'.[33]

Machel's report was termed a 'comprehensive assessment of the multiple ways children were abused and brutalized during armed conflicts'.[34] In direct response to this report, the General Assembly was compelled to recommend the appointment of a Special Representative on the impact of armed conflict on children.[35] Initially established for a period of three years in 1997, the Office of the Special Representative of the Secretary-General for Children and Armed Conflict (SRSG-CAAC) remains the leading advocate for children in situations of armed conflict.[36] In 1999, the Security Council published its first resolution on the topic, noting that the impact of armed conflict on children had 'long-term consequences (for) durable peace, security and development'.[37]

The creation of a dedicated office for matters affecting children in armed conflict by the General Assembly was the beginning of a transformation for the monitoring and reporting of matters affecting children in armed conflict. The SRSG-CAAC coordinates the Security Council's response to violations against children in armed conflict, coordinating and verifying data from the field, creating annual reports on the status of children and armed conflict across the world, naming parties and triggering listings, and engaging in dialogue with listed armed groups to create Action Plans that set out time-bound measures for ending violations against children.[38] The SRSG-CAAC regularly reports to the General Assembly, the Human Rights Council and the Security Council and is tasked by the General Assembly with diplomatic and political engagements at the highest levels.[39]

---

33 *Ibid.* para. [317].

34 Office of the Special Representative of the Secretary General for Children and Armed Conflict, *The Six Grave Violations Against Children During Armed Conflict: The Legal Foundation*, Working Paper No. 1 (October 2009, updated November 2013), p. 4.

35 United Nations General Assembly, *Rights of the Child*, GA Res. 51/77, 51st Sess., Agenda item 106, UN Doc. A/Res/51/77 (20 February 1997).

36 See https://childrenandarmedconflict.un.org/.

37 United Nations Security Council, Resolution 1261, 4037th meeting, UN Doc. S/RES/1261 (30 August 1999).

38 For more information on Action Plans, see the website of the Office of the Special Representative of the Secretary General for Children and Armed Conflict, https://childrenandarmedconflict.un.org/our-work/action-plans/.

39 UNICEF, *Machel Study 10-year Strategic Review: Children and Conflict in*

In 2001, the Security Council asked the SRSG-CAAC to provide it with 'a list of parties to armed conflicts that recruit or use children in violation of the international obligations applicable to them'.[40] Recognizing that more needed to be done, in 2004 the Security Council compelled the SRSG-CAAC to devise an urgent and systematic:

> monitoring and reporting mechanism . . . in order to provide timely, objective, accurate and reliable information of the recruitment and use of child soldiers in violation of applicable international law and on other violations and abuses committed against children affected by armed conflict, for consideration in taking appropriate action.[41]

A year later, the Security Council ordered the formal instigation of a Monitoring and Reporting Mechanism on matters relating to children in armed conflict (MRM).[42] Created within an international legal framework that in and of itself supports the protection of children affected by armed conflict,[43] the MRM seeks to initiate both standardized data collection and constructive dialogue between the United Nations and offending armed groups. SRSG-CAAC promotes the MRM as a tool that can contribute towards the harmonization of interventions, strengthen systematic monitoring and reporting, assist in promoting accountability, and ensure coordinated responses by relevant stakeholders.[44]

The MRM is the mechanism with which specially trained child protection advocates document instances of specific types of offences against children in situations of armed conflict. Commonly referred to as 'the six grave violations', the offences are singled out both for their suitability for monitoring and reporting and their egregious nature and consequences on the lives of children.[45] The six grave violations consist of the following:

---

a Changing World (April 2009), p. 44, available at https://childrenandarmedconflict.un.org/publications/MachelStudy-10YearStrategicReview_en.pdf ('Machel Study').

[40] United Nations Security Council, Resolution 1379, 4423rd meeting, UN Doc. S/Res/1379 (20 November 2001).

[41] United Nations Security Council, Resolution 1539, 4948th meeting, UN Doc. S/RES/1539 (22 April 2004).

[42] United Nations Security Council, Resolution 1612, 5225th meeting, UN Doc. S/RES/1612 (26 July 2005).

[43] A. Nilsson, *Children and Youth in Armed Conflict* (Martinus Nijhoff Publishers, 2013), vol. 1, pp. 893–5.

[44] UNICEF, *Field Manual, Monitoring and Reporting Mechanisms (MRM) on Grave Violation Against Children in Situations of Armed Conflict* (June 2014), p. vi.

[45] Office of the Special Representative of the Secretary General for Children and Armed Conflict, Working Paper No. 1, above n. 34, at 9.

(i) *Recruitment and use of children*: recruitment or use of children by armed forces in any capacity, including as cooks, bodyguards, porters or 'wives', is a war crime.
(ii) *Killing or maiming of children*: the death or serious injury of a child incurred as a result of actions of an armed group; inherent in the prohibition of violence against civilians in international humanitarian law.
(iii) *Sexual violence against children*: rape or sexual violence incurred during or in the context of an armed conflict and constituted by a member of an armed group.
(iv) *Abduction of children*: an armed group or representative taking a child against their will, and/or the will of their guardian, either temporarily or permanently and without due cause – this often precedes recruitment into armed groups or trafficking.
(v) *Attacks against schools or hospitals*: reinforcement of international humanitarian and customary norms that hold that civilian institutions, particularly those that provide shelter and protection, are to be distinguished from military targets in all but extraordinary circumstances.
(vi) *Denial of humanitarian access*: parties to a conflict must not deny humanitarian assistance seeking to access children with aid, such as food and non-food items.

The Security Council Working Group on Children and Armed Conflict (SCWG-CAAC), also established by Resolution 1612, oversees the global development and implementation of the MRM and monitors the response of in-country taskforce to local trends.[46] As of June 2016, the SCWG-CAAC, via in-country taskforces, monitor 60 armed groups in 14 countries.[47] Armed forces and groups will be monitored if they are part of a conflict in which at least one party to the conflict is a listed group or force. To be listed, which is a reference to a party's name appearing in the appendix to the Annual Report of the SRSG-CAAC, there must be evidence of a party breaching one of the six types of grave violations as set out above.[48]

Part of the role of the in-country taskforce is to engage in dialogue with

46 Resolution 1612, above n. 42.

47 UN Secretary General, *Children and Armed Conflict, Report of the Secretary General*, GA 70th Sess., Security Council 71st Sess., UN Doc. A/70/836-S/2016/360 (20 April 2016).

48 Subsequent to the addition of abduction of children as a listing offence in 2015 (Security Council Resolution S/R/2225) the only grave violation that does not lead to listing is denial of humanitarian access.

listed parties (both state and non-state actors) with the aim to create a joint Action Plan that details the way in which that group can be delisted. One of the most common purposes of an Action Plan is the demobilization of children associated with armed forces or groups. This requires engaging with the armed force or group to form a joint agreement that the group or force will cooperate with UN representatives to design concrete and time-bound steps that will lead to compliance with international law and delisting.[49] The effectiveness and practical impact of Action Plans will be examined in the context of South Sudan in section 5.

In addition to practical tools for monitoring and reporting of children affected by conflict, increasing awareness of topics such as CAFAAG has advanced critical examination advocacy and policy development in the field. In 2009, a 10-year Strategic Review of the Machel Report was published by UNICEF. It positively reviewed the global action the Machel Report has inspired yet admitted that large gaps remain in the implementation and effectiveness of these initiatives, and that the associated data collection regarding CAAFAG remains 'still in its infancy'.[50]

An additional threat to the effectiveness and credibility of the MRM is the recent decision of the UN Secretary General Ban-Ki-Moon to remove a Saudi-led military coalition from the original June 2016 listing, following the threat of a loss of humanitarian funding for the Middle East and South Sudan.[51] This decision sent shock-waves through the international humanitarian community and suggests political and economic pressure can be imposed upon the United Nations to avoid the political embarrassment of being included on the list of state forces and armed groups that violate children's rights in conflict. As a result of the debates and pressure exerted in 2016, the new UN Secretary General, Antonio Guterres, and the newly appointed SRSG CAAC, Virginia Gamba, took their time to assess the 2017 report, which reports are typically released and presented to the UN Security Council in June of each year. In 2017, the report release was delayed until October and changes had been implemented in the listing format. As an example, the Annex of listed state and non-state violators of the six grave violations has now been broken into two parts, A and B, with the B list representing those countries which have put in place measures aimed at improving the protection of children. The Saudi-led coalition

---

[49] Office of the Special Representative of the Secretary General for Children and Armed Conflict, *Action Plans with Armed Forces and Armed Groups* (2016), available at https://childrenandarmedconflict.un.org/our-work/action-plans/.

[50] Machel Study, above n. 39, at 18.

[51] S. Sengupta, 'United Nations chief exposes limits to his authority by citing Saudi threat', *New York Times*, 9 June 2016.

was listed within the B list, to try to assuage concerns that the UN was not taking their violations against children in Yemen seriously, but also to temper the reaction of particular countries such as Saudi Arabia. Despite the value of the MRM, the vulnerabilities of the system (beyond those that exist in gathering information about incidents involving often invisible victims in conflict zones) have become even more obvious.

5. CASE STUDY ON THE CREDIBILITY AND IMPACT OF INTERNATIONAL PROTECTIONS ASSOCIATED WITH CAAFAG: SOUTH SUDAN

In the culmination of decades of tribal, religious, economic and political tensions, South Sudan was established and separated from Sudan by referendum in 2011.[52] Despite this apparent victory for the people of the South, in December 2013, a civil war broke out in the capital Juba and spread throughout the world's newest country.[53] Notwithstanding a Peace Agreement in 2015 and the recent reintegration of government and opposition leadership teams, fighting continues in numerous areas and state military spending has increased.[54] As a result, South Sudan's economy sits on a precipice, with all government efforts directed toward exchange rate and cost of living stabilization.[55] Displacement, malnutrition, food insecurity and disease are acute, as is the incidence of killing and gender-based violence imposed upon children.[56] These threats have led UNICEF to warn that South Sudan is at risk of 'losing a generation of children'.[57]

The established role of young people, particularly boys, in South Sudan

---

[52] For an efficient overview of a complex conflict see African Union Commission of Inquiry on South Sudan, *Final Report* (27 October 2015), paras [33]–[43], available at http://reliefweb.int/sites/reliefweb.int/files/resources/auciss.final_.report.pdf.

[53] Human Rights Watch, *We Can Die Too: Recruitment and Use of Child Soldiers in South Sudan* (December 2015), p. 15, available at www.hrw.org/report/2015/12/14/we-can-die-too/recruitment-and-use-child-soldiers-south-sudan.

[54] World Bank, *South Sudan: Overview* (20 October 2016), available at www.worldbank.org/en/country/southsudan/overview.

[55] O. Francis, *Hyperinflation Stalks War-Torn South Sudan as Prices Spike* (Bloomberg, 15 January 2016), available at www.bloomberg.com/news/articles/2016-01-14/war-ravaged-south-sudan-faces-new-crisis-of-hyperinflation.

[56] UNICEF, *Humanitarian Action for Children, Eastern and Southern Africa, South Sudan* (17 January 2017), available at www.unicef.org/appeals/south_sudan.

[57] UNICEF, *Humanitarian Action for Children, South Sudan* (2016), available at www.unicef.org/appeals/files/HAC_2016_South_Sudan.pdf.

also impacts the actualization of international standards for recruitment and reintegration at a national level. South Sudan is a signatory to the CRC and the national Constitution, as well as national legislation, reflects the international definition of a child as anyone under the age of 18. However, the actual role of a child, or childhood, in South Sudan is not as definitive. In fact, when training officials who are responsible for administering this legislation, it is unusual to get more than one or two correct answers in a full room to the question 'how old is a child under South Sudanese law'?[58] This is because childhood in South Sudan, as in many other countries, is traditionally defined not by age, but by the 'historical experiences of each society and culture'.[59] For males in some communities in South Sudan, tribal markings or the removal of teeth indicate a graduation from childhood and the capacity to take on new responsibilities.[60] Anthropologically, it is recognized that male socialization has often, throughout time and a variety of societies, been shaped through engagement in warrior groups or militias.[61] In South Sudan, these responsibilities have traditionally included defending their communities and cattle from attack, as well as participating in cattle raiding and revenge attacks.[62]

Both the government forces and opposition groups in South Sudan were listed by the United Nations as of October 2016. Accordingly, all groups involved in the conflict are monitored by the UN and its partners for grave violations against children in armed conflict. Additionally, both the government Sudan Peoples' Liberation Army (SPLA) and the main opposition group Sudan Peoples' Liberation Army in Opposition (SPLA-iO) have entered into Action Plans with the United Nations committing to the active release of child soldiers from their ranks.[63] Despite these agreements, there is little to show for the declarations. The Action

---

[58] T. Smith and L. Brownlees, *Age Assessment Practices: A Literature Review and Annotated Bibliography* (April 2011), p. 5, available at www.unicef.org/protection/Age_Assessment_Practices_2010.pdf: 'law enforcement has struggled to come to terms with the new definition of childhood and with it the new minimum age of criminal responsibility'.

[59] D.M. Rosen, 'Child Soldiers, International Humanitarian Law, and the Globalisation of Childhood' (2007) 109(2) *American Anthropologist* 296, at 297.

[60] African Union Commission of Inquiry on South Sudan, *Final Report*, above n. 52, para. [698].

[61] See Smith and Brownlees, *Age Assessment Practices*, above n. 58.

[62] Human Rights Watch, *We Can Die Too*, above n. 53, at 16 and 21.

[63] Both the SPLA (March 2012, recommitment July 2014) and SPLA-iO (December 2015) have signed Action Plans with the United Nations agreeing to halt the recruitment and use of children.

Plans keep being extended without their conditions changing or consequences for the offending parties. Listing continues and groups are listed for increasing violations, seemingly without consequence. Impeccably drafted laws reflect the greater expectations of international standards regarding recruitment age.[64] But they have failed to prevent over 15,000 children being associated with both government and opposition armed groups/forces.[65] Despite national legislation and dedicated Actions Plans agreeing to do so, neither side has ended the widespread recruitment and use of children in the armed forces or groups or started systematic demobilization.[66] This was illustrated by a publication from Human Rights Watch in which former child soldiers told of their recruitment at gun point and their arrest and detention until they agreed to fight for their captors.[67] Some were abducted, immediately armed and forced into battle. Still others joined willingly, though under duress, as they calculated that this was the best way to defend their community, participate in revenge or survive the conflict.[68]

The Dallaire Initiative responds to this challenge by researching practical solutions, advocating for policy change, and conducting comprehensive prevention-oriented training for security sector actors (this includes military, police, militia and peace-keepers) around the globe. The Dallaire Initiative has pioneered a unique approach to working with the security sector by framing the issues of vulnerable children in armed conflict as a specific priority that demands a unique security sector response. This approach requires the security sector to be effectively trained and prepared to interact with children as a key focus for effective peace-keeping and sustainable security sector reform at the national level. A key element to this training approach has been developed through research and collaboration with the military, former child soldiers and child protection advisors, and focuses on how to take away the perceived strategic and tactical advantages for those who recruit and use children. To be able to achieve this aim, the Dallaire Initiative not only educates the security sector on

---

64 See Child Act 2008, s. 31; Transitional Constitution of South Sudan 2012, art. 17; Sudan People's Liberation Army Act 2009, s. 22. Whilst the Convention on the Rights of the Child sets a minimum age for recruitment of 15, the Optional Protocol increases this expectation to 18 and reflects best practice as demonstrated by international principles such as the Cape Town Principles (www.unicef.org/emerg/files/Cape_Town_Principles(1).pdf) and the Paris Principles (www.unicef.org/emerg/files/ParisPrinciples310107English.pdf).

65 UNICEF, *Humanitarian Action for Children, South Sudan*, above n. 57.

66 Human Rights Watch, *We Can Die Too*, above n. 53, at 15.

67 *Ibid.*

68 *Ibid.*

the disadvantages of using children from a purely strategic and tactical perspective, but it aims to change the way the security sector perceives children used as soldiers through monitoring of attitude and behaviour change over time.

In November 2015, the Dallaire Initiative went to South Sudan, at the invitation of UNICEF, to identify areas where engagement with armed forces and groups could take place in relation to their accountability to their current peace agreement and more especially as it relates to the recruitment and use of child soldiers. A series of high-level meetings with various government and opposition force representatives, key civil society organizations and UN members took place in the capital, Juba. The Dallaire Initiative's engagement with the security sector and acceptance of their very real challenges, whilst maintaining a clear focus on prioritizing children's wellbeing, created potential for entry points for discussion and possible action.

The Dallaire Initiative met with the leadership groups of both the SPLA and the Cobra Faction in Pibor District to discuss their commitment to release the children that were associated with the armed groups. The fact that the Dallaire Initiative is led by a former military General, Roméo Dallaire, who has extensive experience in Africa, provided a unique opportunity, allowing discussions General to General. Frank discussions could take place about why using children is neither professional nor expedient from a tactical or strategic perspective. In cooperation with the United Nations, the Cobra Faction and SPLA released 145 children, the largest release since 2015 when 1,755 were disarmed and reintegrated into their community.[69]

The Dallaire Initiative specifically addressed the SPLA about the need for them to deposit a binding agreement on the minimum age of recruitment in line with the CRC-OPAC. Dr Whitman used this opportunity to talk about the challenges, in line with the realities of how children are often viewed as adults at a much younger age than 18 years in South Sudan. The Dallaire Initiative promotes a progressive elimination approach, which aims to incrementally realize the ultimate goal of ending the use of child soldiers through concrete and tangible actions. As an example, within a context such as South Sudan, the Dallaire Initiative puts forth potential incremental steps, such as protecting the youngest children from recruitment and use, and then using this benchmark to promote progress.[70]

---

[69] UNICEF, *145 Children Released Armed Groups in South Sudan* (Press Release, 26 October 2016), available at www.unicef.org/media/media_92960.html.

[70] Romeo Dallaire Child Soldiers Initiative, *Child Soldiers: A Handbook for Security Sector Actors* (2nd edn, 2014), pp. 4, 5.

Despite ongoing efforts, South Sudan continues to struggle with political and economic instability and widespread insecurity.[71] Unfortunately, this environment breeds further conflict, and within the first eight months of 2016, UNICEF reported the recruitment of an additional 650 children throughout the country.[72] Between the period of January to August 2017, UNICEF reported that boys released by the Cobra Faction in 2015 and 2016 were being mobilized to defend their communities against Dinka Bor armed elements. Some boys released from the Cobra Faction have also been recruited into the SPLA-iO (aligned with Taban Deng Gai).[73] South Sudan is a contemporary example of the urgent nature of the work to discourage the use of children in situations of conflict and the need to look at alternative approaches that may require new tools or innovative thinking.

6. CONCLUSION

This chapter has aimed to shed light on the challenges of protecting children associated with armed forces and groups through an examination of the law and practice that exists. The case of South Sudan highlights the urgency of these challenges and how it relates to a larger problem of achieving overall peace and security for the nation-state. International law relating to the treatment of children involved in conflict continues to develop, but so too must the practices to ensure adherence to these laws.

In November 2016, the Office of the Prosecutor of the International Criminal Court released their Policy on Children[74] created to improve the practice of the court applying a child-sensitive approach to all aspects of its work. It recognizes that in a given context, a child may be vulnerable and capable at the same time. The Court will aim to take into account the best interests of the child in an effort to close the impunity gap for the serious crimes against humanity, genocide and war crimes that highlight the plight of the children who are affected. In this way, it is hoped that the Court will assist in altering the perceptions that currently exist with respect to the use of children as soldiers and instead recognize their value to a

---

[71] F. Oloch, 'Is a UN Trusteeship the Solution?' (2017) 569 *The New African* 37.

[72] S. Kimbali, *South Sudan: A Generation Made to Fight: Saving South Sudan's Child Soldiers* (UNICEF, 28 October 2016), available at www.unicefusa.org/stories/generation-made-fight-south-sudans-child-soldiers/30738.

[73] Interview with Dr Whitman, UNICEF South Sudan, 20 September 2017.

[74] International Criminal Court, *ICC Prosecutor, Fatou Bensouda, Launches Policy on Children* (Press Release, 18 November 2016), available at www.icc-cpi.int/Pages/item.aspx?name=pr1257.

world that desperately needs to break cycles of violence if we are to seek a measure of peace for the future.

As Nelson Mandela stated, 'There can be no keener revelation of a society's soul than the way in which it treats its children'.[75] Globally we need to recognize that our failure to adequately address the needs of children has created conditions that push children towards roles and responsibilities that should be left to the realm of adults. Understanding how we address these violations of children's basic rights and put the resources towards their prioritization is critical to the future of humanity.

[75] N. Mandela, 'Launch of the Nelson Mandela Children's Protection Fund', Speech delivered at the launch, Pretoria, 8 May 1995, available at www.sahistory.org.za/archive/speech-president-nelson-mandela-launch-nelson-mandela-childrens-fund-mahlambandlopfu-pretori.

24. In search of solutions for unaccompanied children fleeing Central America

pamela goldberg

> I'm terrified because [the gangs] have taken girls from my school and raped them. (Cecilia N, aged 17, Honduras)[1]
>
> We couldn't go to school. There were too many risks. We couldn't stay in Guatemala anymore. (Johanna H, aged 17, Guatemala)[2]
>
> Life is ugly where I live. (Omar C, aged 11, Honduras)[3]

1. INTRODUCTION

Children living in the Northern Triangle of Central America (NTCA), comprising El Salvador, Guatemala and Honduras, are leaving their countries in alarmingly high record numbers, many of them unaccompanied by or separated from an adult parent or guardian. Large numbers of these children are fleeing harrowing, sometimes life-threatening harm and virtually all of them face grave danger throughout the treacherous journey north in their efforts to seek safety and security. Immediate action is essential to ensure the safety and well-being of these children. The urgent responses must also be linked to longer-term solutions or risk the continued spiraling of the dangers for these children and others in the NTCA.

This chapter discusses efforts to address the crisis of unaccompanied children fleeing from the NTCA by two key actors: the United Nations High Commissioner for Refugees (UNHCR), the UN agency

---

1 Human Rights Watch, *Closed Doors: Mexico's Failure to Protect Central American Refugee and Migrant Children* (2016), p. 24.

2 *Ibid.* 25.

3 *Ibid.* 28. See the full report for more detailed accounting of the stories of these and other children from the NTCA.

charged with the responsibility of overseeing the protection of refugees worldwide,[4] and the United States (US). The United States, where the large majority of these children attempt to migrate in the belief that it offers the greatest possibility for protection, has focused on short-term, small impact responses. UNHCR, true to its mandate and commitment, is undertaking a multilayered, multilateral, comprehensive approach that includes short-term programs to address the most immediate needs of the children and longer-term efforts that support addressing root causes of the crisis.

The background section of this chapter provides a snapshot of the often life-threatening reasons children are fleeing the region in such soaring numbers. The most compelling need for these children is to ensure they receive protection from harm. The meaning and sources of international and regional protection are presented next. UNHCR's efforts to address the crisis of children from the region, followed by US programs, are discussed in sections 4 and 5. The chapter concludes with a discussion of the effectiveness of this work to meet the short-term and longer-term protection needs of unaccompanied children fleeing the NTCA.

2. BACKGROUND

Tremendous violence and instability permeate the NTCA and have escalated dramatically in recent years. Armed criminal factions, many of which control territory throughout the states, are the perpetrators of this extreme, rampant brutality. These lawless groups often act with impunity due to lack of government accountability and effective systems of justice, corruption within the governments and brutal law enforcement practices. UNHCR has noted that the extraordinary epidemic of violence is compelling a diverse range of people to flee their homes and to seek international protection, particularly in bordering and nearby countries.[5]

---

[4] See, e.g., UN General Assembly, *Note on International Protection,* UN Doc. A/AC.96/830 (7 September 1994), paras 8, 10,11, 31,32. UNHCR's mandate also includes protection of returnees, internally displaced persons (IDPs) and stateless individuals. See, e.g., UNHCR, *Note on the Mandate of the High Commissioner for Refugees and his Office* (October 2013), available at www.refworld.org/docid/5268c9 474.html.

[5] UNHCR, *Regional Response to the Northern Triangle of Central America Situation, Supplementary Appeal* (June 2016), p. 6 ('*Regional Response*'). The *Regional Response* amplified the earlier UNHCR document, *Protection and Solutions*

The prevalence and dominance of these criminal factions have led to a blisteringly high homicide rate.[6] Women and girls are targeted for sexual violence and exploitation, often at risk of their lives, with the overwhelming majority of them between the ages of 10 and 19 years. Boys are also vulnerable, in particular to forced recruitment into violent gangs, frequently with life-threatening consequences for refusing.

Given these conditions, it is not difficult to realize that many of the children fleeing the region are in need of international protection and should not be returned to their home countries. In fact, a recent report by UNHCR found that at least 58 per cent of the children from the NTCA and Mexico arriving to the United States are potentially in need of international protection.[7] In further recognition of the dire situation in the region and the tremendous number of individuals seeking protection, UNHCR has issued guidelines for assessing eligibility for international protection for people from El Salvador, and from Honduras, with plans to issue them for Guatemala.[8]

Strategy for the Northern Triangle of Central America 2016–2018 (24 December 2015) ('*Solutions Strategy*').

6 *Regional Response*, above n. 5, at 6. The overall murder rate in the three countries in 2015 was 17,500, higher than in the armed conflict zones of Afghanistan, Iraq and Syria; in 2014 Honduras alone had more homicides than all the European Union states combined. See Letter to President Obama (25 January 2016) (signed by 275 organizations) ('NGO Letter'), available at www.refugeesinternational.org/advocacy-letters-1/2016/2/1/northern-triangle-temporary-protected-status-national-letter. For years Honduras had the highest murder rate in the world only to be surpassed by El Salvador in 2015, and Guatemala was ranked seventh highest. See, e.g., A. Gomez, 'El Salvador: World's New Murder Capital', *USA Today*, 8 January 2016, available at www.usatoday.com/story/news/world/2016/01/07/el-salvador-homicide-rate-honduras-guatemala-illegal- immigration-to-united-states/78358042/; J. Partlow, 'Why El Salvador became the hemisphere's murder capital', *Washington Post*, 5 January 2016, available at www.washingtonpost.com/news/worldviews/wp/2016/01/05/why-el-salvador-became-the-hemispheres- murder-capital/.

7 UNHCR, *Children on the Run: Unaccompanied Children Leaving Central America and Mexico and the Need for International Protection* (13 March 2014), available at www.refworld.org/docid/532180c24.html. Children are also leaving these countries due to violence in the home, deep poverty, lack of education and job opportunities, and inadequate healthcare. In most cases, the reasons children are fleeing to the United States are mixed. A discussion of the Mexican children fleeing the violence in Mexico is beyond the scope of this chapter.

8 UNHCR, *Eligibility Guidelines for Assessing the International Protection Needs of Asylum-Seekers from El Salvador*, UN Doc. HCR/EG/SLV/16/01 (15 March 2016), available at www.refworld.org/docid/56e706e94.html; UNHCR, *Eligibility Guidelines for Assessing the International Protection Needs of Asylum-Seekers from Honduras*, UN Doc. HCR/EG/HND/16/03 (27 July 2016), available

Long-term solutions for the crisis in these countries require addressing the fundamental root causes. This can be done by reinforcing the rule of law, strengthening the justice system and other democratic governance institutions, addressing corruption within the government, bringing to justice perpetrators of crime-related violence and corruption, and addressing the deep poverty and inequality.[9] Such efforts are essential to meaningfully change the dynamics in the NTCA. But these root causes are complex and deeply entrenched. Durable solutions demand an immense investment of resources, time and political will.[10] In the face of the current crisis, immediate actions must be taken to ensure the children fleeing El Salvador, Guatemala and Honduras receive protection, safety and security throughout their journeys, in countries of transit, and in final destination countries.[11]

---

at www.refworld.org/docid/579767434.html. Guidelines for Guatemala were issued in 2018. UNHCR, *Eligibility Guidelines for Assessing the International Protection Needs of Asylum-seekers from Guatemala*, January 2018, HCR/EG/GTM/18/01, available at http://www.refworld.org/docid/5a5e03e96.html. UNHCR has also issued guidelines for assessing a child's eligibility for asylum. See *Guidelines on International Protection No. 8: Child Asylum Claims under Articles 1(A)2 and 1(F) of the 1951 Convention and/or 1967 Protocol relating to the Status of Refugees* ('*Child Asylum Guidelines*'), UN Doc. HCR/GIP/09/08 (22 December 2009), available at www.refworld.org/docid/4b2f4f6d2.html.

[9] For a full discussion of the root causes in the NTCA countries, see, e.g. D. Restrepo and S. Mathema, *A Medium- and Long-Term Plan to Address the Central American Refugee Situation* (Center for American Progress, May 2016) ('CAP Report'). For a compelling and succinct description, see NGO Letter, above n. 6.

[10] A crucial issue is the need for the developed, wealthier countries to share the burden and responsibility for the protection of refugees. As set out in a recent report by Amnesty International: 'There are 193 countries in the world. And 21 million refugees. More than half of these refugees – nearly 12 million people – are living in just 10 of these 193 countries. This is inherently unsustainable. Countries hosting such high numbers of refugees cannot provide for them.' Amnesty International, *Tackling the Global Refugee Crisis: From Shirking to Sharing Responsibility* (October 2016) ('*Responsibility Sharing*'), pp. 4, 6, 7.

[11] In addition to the tens of thousands who have fled the region and crossed an international border there is an alarmingly high number of individuals in the NTCA who have had to flee their homes and communities but are still in their countries of origin. For example, it is estimated that in 2016 there were upwards of 174,000 IDPs in Honduras. See, e.g., UN General Assembly, *Report of the Special Rapporteur on the Human Rights of Internally Displaced Persons on His Mission to Honduras*, UN HR Council, 32nd Sess., UN Doc. A/HRC/32/35/Add.4 (5 April 2016) ('*Internally Displaced in Honduras*'), p. 7.

3. INTERNATIONAL AND REGIONAL PROTECTION FROM HARM

The principal form of international protection, and the one that offers the most security, is recognition of an individual as a refugee.[12] The 1951 Convention relating to the Status of Refugees and its 1967 Protocol ('Refugee Convention') recognize as refugees individuals who have fled their countries of origin because of a fear of persecution based on their race, religion, nationality, social group or political opinion, and are unable to return because their country is either unwilling or unable to provide them protection.[13] A fundamental tenet of the Refugee Convention is the prohibition of returning refugees to a country where their lives or freedom would be threatened.[14]

To ensure children – especially unaccompanied children – are identified and accorded international protection requires not only sensitivity to their particular needs but also to the ways in which violence, trauma and fear affect them and their ability to recall and recount these kinds of experiences.[15]

The 1984 Cartagena Declaration on Refugees ('Cartagena') is a non-binding statement of principles which, among its many important provisions, recognizes as refugees persons who have fled their country because their lives, safety or freedom have been threatened by generalized violence, foreign aggression, internal conflicts, massive violation of human rights or other circumstances which have seriously disturbed public order.[16] Cartagena came into being in response to the need for more effective measures to address the Central American refugee crisis in the 1980s, a result of civil strife, rampant human rights violations and armed conflict

---

12 A grant of asylum is the same as recognition of an individual as a refugee. For purposes of this chapter asylum and refugee status are used interchangeably.

13 Convention Relating to the Status of Refugees, adopted 28 July 1951, 189 UNTS 137 (entered into force 22 April 1954) and the attendant Protocol relating to the Status of Refugees, adopted 31 January 1967, 606 UNTS 267 (entered into force 4 October 1967). The Protocol universalizes the refugee definition by removing the date restrictions and otherwise incorporates by reference all the substantive provisions of the Convention. Refugee Convention, Art. 1.A(2); Protocol, Art. I(2) and (1), respectively.

14 Refugee Convention, Art. 33(1).

15 For a discussion of procedural and substantive child-sensitive approaches in refugee status determinations see *Child Asylum Guidelines*, above n. 8.

16 Cartagena Declaration on Refugees, Colloquium on the International Protection of Refugees in Central America, Mexico and Panama, 22 November 1984, available at www.refworld.org/docid/3ae6b36ec.html.

in the NTCA. It grew 'out of the ongoing need to establish and consolidate the "humanitarian practices and principles" to provide protection to a growing number of Central Americans compelled to leave their home countries'.[17] Cartagena linked humanitarian law, human rights and refugee rights into a framework for regional cooperation.[18] In the words of UNHCR:

> The Cartagena Declaration is the landmark regional refugee instrument, which broadened the refugee definition for Latin America and proposed new approaches to the humanitarian needs of refugees and displaced with a spirit of solidarity and cooperation.[19]

Although Cartagena does not contain any provisions specific to children, it endorses the principle that 'adequate provisions should be made for the protection of minors and unaccompanied children'.[20] The continued significance of Cartagena was recently consecrated at the Commemoration of its 30th Anniversary in the Brazil Declaration and Plan of Action.[21]

The United States, El Salvador, Guatemala, Honduras and Mexico are all bound by the Refugee Convention and Protocol, obliging them to ensure refugees are conferred international protection according to these instruments. The NTCA and Mexico have also adopted the Cartagena Agreement, manifesting a commitment to also apply the expanded refugee definition.[22]

UNHCR has determined that 'a significant percentage of those fleeing from the NTCA countries may be in need of international protection,

---

17 UNHCR, *The Cartagena Declaration on Refugees and the Protection of People Fleeing Armed Conflict and Other Situations of Violence in Latin America*, UN Doc. PPLA/2013/03 (June 2013), p. 9, available at www.refworld.org/docid/51c801934.html ('Cartagena Paper').

18 M. Esthimer, *Protecting the Forcibly Displaced: Latin America's Evolving Refugee and Asylum Framework* (Migration Policy Institute, 14 January 2016), available at www.migrationpolicy.org/article/protecting-forcibly-displaced-latin-americas-evolving-refugee-and-asylum-framework.

19 UNHCR, *+30 Cartagena: Latin America and the Caribbean Adopt a Common Roadmap to Address New Displacement Trends and End Statelessness Within the Next Decade*, available at www.acnur.org/cartagena30/en/background-and-challenges/.

20 Cartagena Paper, above n. 17, III, para. [8].

21 Brazil Declaration: A Framework for Cooperation and Regional Solidarity to Strengthen the International Protection of Refugees, Displaced and Stateless Persons in Latin America and the Caribbean (3 December 2014), available at www.refworld.org/docid/5487065b4.html.

22 Cartagena Paper, above n. 17, at 10.

in line with the 1951 Convention relating to the Status of Refugees as well as the 1984 Cartagena Declaration'.[23] Yet none of these countries is sufficiently fulfilling its obligations and commitments and instead are detaining unaccompanied children. They are also highly inconsistent in according them the opportunity to seek asylum, and in many instances, are returning them to their countries of origin where they may face grave harm without a review of their protection claims.

A broad array of UN agencies, international, regional, national and local non-governmental organizations and other stakeholders are working with governments to ensure these children receive protection. UNHCR is a fundamental and essential actor in these endeavours. The United States, situated at the heart of the region and the major receiving country of individuals fleeing the crisis in the NTCA, bears a particular responsibility to develop and implement programs that will meaningfully address the immediate needs, as well as build towards longer-term solutions. Several of each of their key programs are discussed below.

4. UNHCR

> The widespread risks for asylum-seekers, refugees, and returnees and IDPs [internally displaced persons] [from the NTCA] require an urgent, strategic and regional response in close coordination with all relevant stakeholders.[24]

With these words, UNHCR compellingly sums up the impetus underlying its overall strategy and approach for addressing the humanitarian crisis in the region.

UNHCR's strategy is framed in the context of the Brazil Declaration. Its purpose is:

> to enable UNHCR to support authorities in countries of origin, transit and asylum to create robust protection systems, preserve asylum space, and strengthen frameworks and policies on asylum, internal displacement and solutions.[25]

---

23 *Solutions Strategy*, above n. 5, at 6. This is consistent with findings in other recent UNHCR documents. See, e.g., *Children on the Run*, above n. 7; UNHCR, *Women on the Run: First-hand Accounts of Refugees Fleeing El Salvador, Guatemala, Honduras, and Mexico* (26 October 2015), available at www.refworld.org/docid/56307e2a4.html.

24 *Regional Response*, above n. 5, at 7.

25 *Solutions Strategy*, above n. 5, at 6.

It seeks to:

> ensure . . . that prevention, protection and solutions are embedded within comprehensive efforts to address root causes of displacement taking into account the magnitude and patterns of displacement and profiles of displaced people, *with a particular focus on the specific needs of children*, women, and LGBTI [individuals] including among them asylum-seekers and refugees in countries of asylum and in transit.[26]

'Children's rights are . . . at the heart of UNHCR's protection mandate' and the agency views its commitment to children as a 'moral imperative'.[27] UNHCR recognizes that forcibly displaced children are 'at greater risk than adults of abuse, neglect, violence, exploitation, trafficking or forced recruitment into armed groups'[28] and that events similar to those faced by adults often have greater impact on children.[29]

In 2007, the UNHCR Executive Committee issued its Conclusion on Children at Risk[30] The Child Conclusion affirms that forcibly displaced children are often more vulnerable than adults because of their age, social status and physical and mental development and acknowledges that similar factors to those faced by adults 'can put children in situations of heightened risk'. It identifies core principles that should underpin strategies and actions addressing forcibly displaced children. Among these are:

- Children should be among the first to receive protection and assistance.
- The best interests of the child must be the primary consideration in all actions concerning children.

---

[26] *Regional Response*, above n. 5, at 8 (emphasis added). A key objective of its strategy is to 'facilitate durable solutions for refugees . . . in the region'. *Solutions Strategy*, above n. 5, at 7.

[27] UNHCR, *A Framework for the Protection of Children* (2012) ('*Child Protection Framework*'), p. 7, available at www.unhcr.org/protection/children/50f6cf0b9/framework-protection-children.html.

[28] *Ibid.*

[29] See, e.g., *Child Asylum Guidelines*, above n. 8, para. 15.

[30] UNHCR, Conclusion on Children at Risk No. 107 (LVIII) (5 October 2007) ('Child Conclusion'), p. 1, available at www.unhcr.org/refworld/docid/471897232.html. The ExCom is UNHCR's governing body that, among its duties, advises on international protection matters; it comprises representatives from states parties to the Convention with 98 members for 2016–17, and includes among them the United States, which has been a member since the inception of the ExCom in 1959, and Mexico. See www.unhcr.org/en-us/executive-committee.html.

- Recognition of children's capacity and agency, and their participation in all actions concerning them, is integral to their protection.
- Children have the right to freely express their own views in all matters affecting them and these should be given due weight in accordance with their age and maturity.
- Gender equality is essential to the protection of children.[31]

In recognition of the growing plight of children around the world fleeing violence and war and their need for safety and protection, the High Commissioner for Refugees selected 'Children on the Move' for the theme of the 2016 annual UNHCR Dialogue on Protection Challenges.[32]

Although at present UNHCR has initiated relatively few programs designed for children alone, the Regional Strategy, as part of its overall commitment, identifies '[strengthening] the protection of unaccompanied children in line with best interest principles and practices' as a central priority,[33] and the needs of children are incorporated into many of UNHCR's efforts.[34] What follows is a snapshot of UNHCR's work in El Salvador, Guatemala, Honduras and Mexico, with a focus on programs addressing the protection needs of children.

---

[31] For the complete list of identified priorities, see *ibid.* para. (b).

[32] See UNHCR, *High Commissioner's Dialogue on Protection Challenges* (2016), available at www.unhcr.org/en-us/high-commissioners-dialogue-on-protection-challenges-2016.html. In addition, in July 2016, UNHCR co-convened the High Level Roundtable 'Call to Action: Protection Needs in the Northern Triangle of Central America'. Among the participants were representatives from the governments of El Salvador, Guatemala, Honduras, Mexico and the United States. The roundtable concluded with the issuance of the San Jose Statement, signed by all the government participants, which includes commitments made by most of the countries in attendance, some of which specifically address the needs of children. See www.refworld.org/docid/57a8a4854.html.

[33] UNHCR, *Operational Update for Central American and Mexico* (31 August 2016), p. 1, available at http://reporting.unhcr.org/sites/default/files/Operational%20 Update%20for%20Central%20America%20final%2011NOV16.pdf.

[34] The strategy also includes activities in Belize, Costa Rica, Nicaragua, Panama and the United States 'to ensure a comprehensive and harmonized regional approach'. See *Solutions Strategy*, above n. 5, at 6. For information and updates on UNHCR's work in the region, see UNHCR Global Focus, *Northern Triangle of Central America*, available at http://reporting.unhcr.org/node/14843.

4.1 El Salvador

El Salvador is situated on the west coast along the Pacific Ocean bordered by Guatemala to its north and Honduras to its south, with these two countries sharing a long border. As such, the number of children in transit on their way northward is very small. The primary issues are the safety and security of the children who are fleeing from there and those who have been returned after having fled. UNHCR has worked with state authorities to develop guidelines for determining the best interests of children to facilitate identifying their protection needs. In this context, it has worked with a variety of community-based organizations to help strengthen programs providing protection for children who have been returned to El Salvador. Similarly, it has supported reintegration efforts of returned individuals, including work with organizations that provide legal and psycho-social support. UNHCR has also provided general trainings on child protection and children's rights to 172 Government and organization staff members.[35]

4.2 Guatemala

Situated directly south of Mexico with a long border between the two countries and bordering El Salvador and Honduras to the south, Guatemala is both a refugee-producing country and a transit country for fleeing Salvadorans and Hondurans. Much of UNHCR's work in Guatemala has focused on children. Since June 2014, it has co-led the UN Task Force on Migration Issues with a focus on unaccompanied and separated children. It has also collaborated with UN agencies and other organizations in Guatemala to establish a broad-based child protection group. In addition, UNHCR has been working with government child welfare agencies on developing protection responses for returned children, as well as children passing through Guatemala on their northward journeys. UNHCR is also working with a variety of partners in Guatemala to build their capacity to provide protection, particularly to survivors of sexual and gender-based violence and to children more generally.[36]

---

[35] For more information on UNHCR's work in El Salvador, see *ibid.* and related links.

[36] For more information on UNHCR's work in Guatemala, see above n. 34 and related links.

4.3 Honduras

Along with the refugees fleeing Honduras, given its border with Guatemala to the north and El Salvador to the west, most of the children in transit there are Salvadoran. UNHCR's projects in Honduras include children, but as of this writing, there is no program devoted solely to them. It has provided technical assistance to government agencies in designing protocols for reception and responses for adults and children returned from Mexico. Another component of its work has been monitoring border areas and strengthening protection mechanisms in transit zones within Honduras. Due to the tremendous number of internally displaced persons in Honduras,[37] UNHCR has focused much of its efforts on this population.[38]

4.4 Mexico

Mexico is the primary transit country for many of the children fleeing the NTCA who seek to reach the United States, where they believe they will receive the greatest protection and best opportunity to live safe and productive lives. It is also, for many of them, the most accessible destination country.[39] Because of its pivotal role in the region, a brief background of the situation of refugee children from the NTCA in Mexico is presented to provide some context for UNHCR's efforts there.[40]

Over the past few years, Mexico has seen a staggering rise in the number of asylum-seekers, among them both accompanied and unaccompanied children. According to the Mexican Commission for Assisting Refugees (COMAR), the agency responsible for asylum screening and adjudication,[41] in 2016 Mexico received 'the highest number of individual claims registered [there] since the adoption of

---

[37] For information on the internally displaced in Honduras, as well as in El Salvador and Guatemala, see, e.g., above n. 10.

[38] For more information on UNHCR's work in Honduras, see above n. 34 and related links.

[39] Due to the dangerous conditions in Mexico, Mexican children are also fleeing the extreme violence in Mexico in search of protection. As noted above, discussion of these children is beyond the scope of this chapter. For information on these children, see, e.g., *Children on the Run*, above n. 7.

[40] For examples of Mexico's stringent deterrent efforts, in particular to block children arriving at its southern border with Guatemala from entering its interior, and US support of these measures, see above n. 1.

[41] For information about COMAR, see www.gob.mx/comar (available in Spanish).

its refugee protection law in 2011'.[42] About 94 per cent of the asylum-seekers are from the NTCA.[43]

Strikingly, less than 1 per cent of the estimated number of people from the NTCA who entered Mexico in 2015 applied for asylum.[44] COMAR has reported that 'although the number of unaccompanied children applying for asylum almost doubled in 2015 and again in 2016, the number of applications remains minimal'.[45] COMAR reported receiving 58 asylum applications from unaccompanied children, 55 from the NTCA, from 1 January to 30 April 2016. Forty-nine claims were adjudicated, 47 of these from the NTCA and of those 37 were recognized as refugees.[46] In stark contrast, 35,704 children were detained in Mexico in 2015, 52 per cent of them unaccompanied, and most of them children from the NTCA.[47]

The Law on the Rights of Girls, Boys and Adolescents ('Child Law'), which came into effect on 3 December 2015, guarantees the rights of all children in Mexico.[48] Among its many provisions, it established a comprehensive protection system as a means to implement the law. This includes special measures for addressing cases where a child's rights have been violated or threatened.[49] The law confers responsibility to identify children in need of protection to the family welfare agency.[50] In accordance with this law, Mexico established a Child Protection Authority (CPA)

---

42 UNHCR Mexico, *People of Concern: Population Trends* (2016) ('*Mexico 2016 Trends*'), available at http://reporting.unhcr.org/node/2536. This is also the highest recorded number of asylum applications since the 1980s when war and civil strife plagued the region.

43 *Ibid.*

44 Mexico, *Needs and Response: Protection and Operation Strategy* (2016) ('*Protection Strategy*'), available at http://reporting.unhcr.org/sites/default/files/Operational%20Update%20for%20Central%20America%20final%2011NOV16.pdf.

45 *Ibid.* Similarly, in 2015 asylum applications lodged from January to April rose by 259%, yet the total number of claims filed was only 2,100.

46 COMAR Statistics 2016 (data is preliminary and provided for information purposes only), available at www.comar.gob.mx/work/models/COMAR/Resource/267/6/images/ESTADISTICAS_2013_A_04-2016_act.pdf. Seven of the children from the NTCA were granted other forms of protection and three of the five claims denied were from the NTCA. Neither of the two claims brought by children from Nicaragua was granted. Cuba was the fourth country of origin and the claim remains pending at the time of writing.

47 Mexico, *Problem Assessment and Comprehensive Response* (2016).

48 General Law of the Rights of Girls, Boys, and Adolescents, Title 2, art. 13, para. XIX (English translation), Title 1, art. 1, para. II and Title 2, art. 13, para. [XIX].

49 *Ibid.* Title 1, arts 10 and 12.

50 *Ibid.* Title 2, art. 26, para. [IV].

tasked, among other things, with conducting Best Interests of the Child Determinations (BIDs). UNHCR's work has focused on strengthening the capacity of authorities to fulfil the obligations to refugee children under the Child Law. For example, UNHCR has been enhancing its support to the Mexican government for more effective implementation of child-sensitive protection screening mechanisms and BIDs and has provided technical guidance as part of this effort.[51]

UNHCR's child protection strategy for 2017 places even greater emphasis on implementation of the Child Law in collaboration with government agencies. One component of this strategy is to continue its support of the implementation of child-sensitive protection mechanisms with a particular focus on Mexico's border with Guatemala to enhance these efforts, and to work at both federal and local levels.

UNHCR also took part in webinars organized by COMAR that reached 398 immigration and family protection officials across the country. These individuals are implementing a protocol for identifying unaccompanied and separated children seeking asylum that was jointly developed by COMAR, UNHCR and UNICEF.[52] UNHCR has also worked with government entities to strengthen Mexico's capacity to monitor and certify shelters to accommodate unaccompanied children.[53]

5. UNITED STATES

In recent years, the United States has seen an unprecedented rise in the number of unaccompanied children from the NTCA, many of them 12 years and younger. The peak year was fiscal year (FY) 2014, when the number of these children apprehended at the US southern border was 51,705, close to a 1,300 per cent increase from 2011.[54] Following a drop to 28,387 in FY 2015, FY 2016 saw the second highest number ever

---

[51] UNHCR, *Mexico Progress Under the Global Strategy: Beyond Detention 2014–2019* (2016), p. 3, available at www.unhcr.org/57b583c57.pdf. UNHCR also continued the development and dissemination of child-sensitive materials on the asylum procedure in partnership with COMAR and the International Detention Coalition. See *ibid.* 3.

[52] *Ibid.* 5.

[53] *Protection Strategy*, above n. 44, at 7.

[54] US Citizenship and Immigration Services, *Ombudsman, Recommendation on the Central American Minors (CAM) Refugee/Parole Program* (21 December 2016) ('*Ombudsman Recommendation*'), available at www.dhs.gov/publication/cis-ombudsman-recommendation-central-american-minors-cam-refugeeparole-program.

recorded of apprehended unaccompanied children from the NTCA, at 46,893.[55] Although the United States has recognized the dire situation in the NTCA,[56] rather than focusing on protection and safety of the children fleeing these countries, it has instead taken an aggressive prevention and deterrence approach. In furtherance of this end, the US launched public information campaigns in the NTCA designed to discourage children from taking the journey to the US; augmented its assistance to Mexico in securing its southern border with Guatemala and its overall border enforcement; is using detention and expedited deportation procedures inside the country to decrease the ability of individuals to receive asylum; and has been conducting raids and arrests, targeting women and children in particular.[57] In addition, although the US does not provide a breakdown of asylum claim determinations by age or sex, it has been estimated that, as of January 2016, 63 per cent of claims brought by children from the NTCA countries had been denied.[58] It has also been reported that '85% of Central American families in detention have established threshold eligibility for refugee protection'.[59] Yet the flow of unaccompanied children to the US border with Mexico continued to rise in 2016, with 56,692 apprehended by US Customs and Border Protection in FY 2016.[60]

---

[55] *Ibid.*

[56] See, e.g., The White House, *Statement by Vice President Biden on the Budget Deal*, 18 December 2015, Office of the Vice President, available at www.whitehouse.gov/the-press-office/2015/12/18/statement-vice-president-biden-budget-deal.

[57] See, e.g., CAP Report, above n. 9. C.R. Seelke, *Mexico: Background and US Relations* (Congressional Research Service, 30 March 2016), available at www.fas.org/sgp/crs/row/R42917.pdf.

[58] A. Taxin, 'AP Exclusive: Children's asylum approvals vary by US region', Associate Press, 1 June 2016, available at http://bigstory.ap.org/article/b140ad95d4a646e9aff67b8c80708e57/ap-exclusive-childrens-asylum-approvals-vary-us-region. This figure only covers claims brought at the interview level, not the subsequent immigration court level.

[59] United States Congress Letter to President Obama (21 January 2016) (signed by 146 Members of the House of Representatives) ('Congress Letter'), p. 1, available at https://lofgren.house.gov/uploadedfiles/1.12.2016_ltr_to_president_on_family_enforcement.pdf.

[60] United States Border Patrol Southwest Family Unit, *Subject and Unaccompanied Alien Children Apprehensions Fiscal Year 2016*, available at www.cbp.gov/newsroom/stats/southwest-border-unaccompanied-children/fy-2016 (children aged 0–17 years). While this number is lower than the 'surge' of 68,541 unaccompanied children apprehended in 2014, it is substantially higher than the 39,970 apprehended in 2015. Family units, comprising largely women and children, also rose in 2016 to 77,674, surpassing the number in 2014 of 68,445 as well as the considerably lower 39,838 family units apprehended in 2015. These

The culmination of these prohibitive measures and denial of protection claims is to return these children to their countries of origin,[61] where they may continue to face danger and harm, including death.[62]

Many have criticized the US government's response to the crisis,[63] most notably members of the US Senate and the House of Representatives in letters to then US President Obama:

> We are deeply concerned that in its eagerness to deter additional arrivals from [the NTCA], the Department [of Homeland Security] is returning vulnerable individuals with valid protection claims to life-threatening violence. This is not hyperbole. There have been multiple reports of individuals, including children, being killed within days or weeks of their deportation. Moreover, we do not accept the argument that removing these individuals will deter additional children and families from fleeing the region.[64]
>
> [F]undamental American values have not been applied in your Administration's policies towards Central American refugee mothers and children. The brutality of violence in Central America is undeniable, and yet this Administration has failed to provide a comprehensive refugee solution for those seeking international refugee protection ... Thus far, your Administration

---

numbers include individuals from the NTCA and Mexico. *Ibid.* For the statistics on the NTCA alone without including Mexico, see above n. 54.

61 For example, in 2015 the United States and Mexico returned 75,875 Hondurans. More than 10% were children and adolescents. UNHCR, *Factsheet: Honduras* (July 2016), p. 1.

62 One recent study found that at least 83 individuals deported to an NTCA country were reported to have been subsequently murdered, the overwhelming majority within a year of deportation. J. Magana-Salgado, *Relief Not Raids: Temporary Protected Status for El Salvador, Guatemala, and Honduras* (Immigrant Legal Resource Center, 2016) (citing a forthcoming study by Elizabeth Kennedy), available at www.ilrc.org/sites/default/files/resources/01-13-2016_relief_not_raids_-_immigrant_legal_resource_center.pdf; S. Brodzinsky and E. Pilkington, 'US government deporting Central American migrants to their deaths', *Guardian*, 12 October 2015 (reporting that several murders occurred 'just days or months after their return'), available at www.theguardian.com/us-news/2015/oct/12/obama-immigration-deportations-central-america. Reported murder victims are principally but not exclusively adults.

63 See, e.g., Washington Office on Latin America, *Five Facts about Migration from Central America's Northern Triangle* (2016), p. 1 ('The administration's apparent belief that deporting families and children will send a message deterring other would-be migrants is short-sighted and inhumane'), available at www.wola.org/analysis/five-facts-about-migration-from-central-americas-northern-triangle/.

64 United States Senate Letter to President Obama (21 January 2016), p. 1 (signed by 22 Senators), available at www.durbin.senate.gov/newsroom/press-releases/durbin-leahy-senators-call-on-administration-to-halt-deportation-raids-and-consider-temporary-protected-status-for-vulnerable-families.

> has responded to the Central American refugee crisis with an emphasis on deterrence rather than the need for a regional refugee solution.[65]

These sharp criticisms reflect the inadequacy of the US protection-related response to the crisis in the region.

Recently, there have been several developments that, at least on their face, seem positive. On 19 September 2016, the United Nations convened the Summit for Refugees and Migrants (Refugee Summit).[66] At the conclusion of the Summit, the UN General Assembly (193 member states) signed the New York Declaration for Refugees and Migrants, expressing their commitment to strengthen the protections established under the Refugee Convention and Protocol.[67] The Declaration acknowledges that developing nations are hosting the vast majority of refugees and migrants and that greater sharing of the burdens and responsibilities to ensure the protection of refugees is essential.

According to some, these are promising indicators for the future, while others have been highly critical, in particular of the Refugees and Migrants Summit.[68] A principal concern expressed by critics is that, with no agreement for specific actions, the commitments made in the New York Declaration have no meaningful force behind them and are highly unlikely to result in coordinated improvements in policies and practices towards refugees on a global scale.[69] In particular, 'countries hosting large numbers of refugees are frustrated that the declaration has achieved no concrete measures, and concrete proposals will not be approved until 2018'.[70] The former Foreign Secretary of the United Kingdom, now presi-

---

[65] Congress Letter, above n. 59, at 1.

[66] For information on the Summit, see http://refugeesmigrants.un.org/summit. US President Barack Obama did not address the Summit; instead the United States was represented by then Secretary of State, John Kerry and Assistant Secretary of State, Anne Richard.

[67] Adopted by the General Assembly on 19 September 2016, UN Doc. A/RES/71/1 (3 October 2016), 71/1 ('New York Declaration for Refugees and Migrants'), available at www.un.org/en/ga/search/view_doc.asp?symbol=A/RES/71/1%20.

[68] See, e.g., J. Borger and P. Kingsley, 'Swift response to refugee crisis rests on Obama summit after UN talks fail: Leaders will have to make fresh pledges to take in more refugees or give more to countries in the developing world', *Guardian*, 19 September 2016, available at www.theguardian.com/world/2016/sep/18/refugee-crisis-rests-on-obama-summit-un-talks-fail. Very little information is publicly available concerning President Obama's Leaders' Summit or the meeting between the former US Vice President with the Presidents of El Salvador, Guatemala and Honduras.

[69] See, e.g., *Responsibility Sharing*, above n. 10, at 5, and n. 8.

[70] Above n. 68.

dent of the International Rescue Committee, one of the largest refugee aid organizations in the world, is quoted as having said:

> Any refugee reading the conclusions of the [Refugee Summit] is bound to say 'what is going to change?' and the answer they would have to be given is very little.[71]

Immediately following the UN Summit, then US President Obama convened the Leaders' Summit on Refugees ('Leaders' Summit').[72] Although the focus of the session was on Syrian refugees, President Obama mentioned in his remarks the violence in the NTCA, the many fleeing from the region, and the impact on Mexico, 'which is absorbing a great number of refugees from [there]'.[73] The Leaders' Summit was intended to strengthen plans among nations for sharing responsibilities and resources for refugees. In addition, the Presidents of El Salvador, Guatemala and Honduras, and then US Vice President Biden, met to discuss increasing collaboration and responsibility-sharing in the region.[74] Very little information has been made publicly available about these two sessions, including any outcomes or results they may have achieved.

A central factor in future US responses to the refugee crisis in the NTCA, as well as elsewhere in the world, is recently installed President Donald Trump, who has already made changes in US policy towards refugees that have taken a dramatic turn for the worse.[75] One such change,

---

[71] *Ibid.*

[72] US State Department, *Fact Sheet: Fiscal Year 2016 Refugee Admissions* (Bureau of Population, Refugees, and Migration, 20 January 2017), available at www.state.gov/j/prm/releases/factsheets/2017/266365.htm. The purpose of the Leaders' Summit was 'to galvanize additional humanitarian support, improve education and access to lawful work for refugees, and expand opportunities for refugee resettlement'. The Summit was intended to appeal to governments to pledge significant new commitments on refugees. It was co-hosted by UN Secretary General Ban Ki-moon, Canada, Ethiopia, Germany, Jordan, Mexico and Sweden. *Ibid.*

[73] Remarks by President Obama at Leaders' Summit on Refugees (20 September 2016), available at https://obamawhitehouse.archives.gov/the-press-office/2016/09/20/remarks-president-obama-leaders-summit-refugees.

[74] See Inter-American Development Bank, *The Presidents of El Salvador, Guatemala, and Honduras and the Vice President of the US to meet at the Inter-American Development Bank on Friday* (Press Release, 23 September 2016), available at www.iadb.org/en/news/news-releases/2016-09-22/northern-triangle-meeting-sept-23-media-update,11569.html.

[75] See, e.g., US President, 'Protecting the Nation from Foreign Terrorist

perhaps most relevant to the unaccompanied children coming to the United States from the NTCA, is a provision that targets undocumented immigrants in the US who assist or facilitate in unlawfully bringing their children to the US, which is sometimes the case with unaccompanied children from the NTCA. Under the policy changes, such parents could face deportation or prosecution for smuggling or human trafficking. Many have expressed deep concern about these changes in policy and practice. The *New York Times* has called them 'an assault on American values'.[76]

The previous Administration put into place two very limited protection-oriented programs for children in the NTCA. Assuming these programs continue under the present Administration, and if effectively implemented,[77] they will make a vital contribution to the safety, security and wellbeing of those few who are able to benefit from them.

Entry into the US' (Executive Order 13769, 27 January 2017), s. 5(a), (b) (among other provisions, suspending for 120 days the admission of all refugees recognized outside the United States and prioritizing international protection claims made by those fleeing harm based on being in a minority religion above all other grounds for seeking protection); and US President, 'Border Security and Immigration Improvements' (Executive Order 13676, 25 January 2017), ss. 4(d), 6, respectively (among other provisions, ordering designated agencies to take action to immediately increase immigration detention facilities to detain individuals at or near the border with Mexico and to 'ensure detention of aliens apprehended for violations of immigration law pending the outcome of their removal proceedings or their removal from the country'). In addition, the Department of Homeland Security (DHS) has issued a Memorandum, *Implementing the President's Border Security and Immigration Enforcement Improvements Policies* (20 February 2017). Among many other unduly restrictive and often punitive measures, the Memo instructs heads of agencies and departments responsible for immigration law enforcement to focus on stiffening the apprehension, detention and removal of non-US citizens, seriously impeding the ability of individuals to seek eligibility for release from detention, including asylum-seekers; returning to Mexico individuals who seek to enter or have unlawfully entered the United States from Mexico while their claim for admission, including asylum or other protection-oriented bases is pending, irrespective of the individual's country of origin. While none of these provisions is directed to children specifically, children accompanied by a parent or lawful guardian will be subject to the treatment of that adult. Other changes in policy and practice may develop that will have further negative impact on the immigrant population in the US, some of which may also affect children.

[76] 'Mr. Trump's "Deportation Force" prepares an assault on American values', *New York Times,* 21 February 2017, available at www.nytimes.com/2017/02/21/opinion/mr-trumps-deportation-force-prepares-an-assault-on-american-values.html.

[77] Many critics have included in their concerns the long delays in implementing the programs, limiting their reach even further.

5.1 Central American Minors Program

The Central American Minors Refugee/Parole Program (CAM)[78] was established in 2014.[79] CAM allows children under the age of 21 who are still living in their country of origin (El Salvador, Guatemala and Honduras) to enter the United States if they can meet the demanding criteria.[80]

While CAM has been touted by some as an important measure to provide protection to at least some small number of children and allows them to leave their countries safely, others have criticized it as inadequate and serving largely as yet another deterrence mechanism.[81]

The requirements under CAM are stringent.[82] The child must have a parent living in the United States with lawful immigration status.[83]

---

78 For a comprehensive discussion of the CAM Program, see *Ombudsman Recommendation*, above n. 54.

79 *Presidential Determination on Refugee Admissions for Fiscal Year 2015* (20 September 2014), available at www.whitehouse.gov/the-press-office/2014/09/30/presidential-memorandum-fy-2015-refugee-admissions. See also, Bureau of Population, Refugees, and Migration, *In-Country Refugee/Parole Program for Minors in El Salvador, Guatemala, and Honduras with Parents Lawfully Present in the United States* (US Department of State, 2014) ('DOS Fact Sheet'), available at www.state.gov/j/prm/releases/factsheets/2014/234067.htm.

80 The Obama Administration announced that the program would be expanded to allow other family members to apply. US Department of State, *US Expands Initiatives to Address Migration Challenges* (26 July 2016), available at www.state.gov/r/pa/prs/ps/2016/07/260507.htm.

81 See, e.g., National Public Radio, 'US Refugee Program ignores dangers children face, critics say' (Interview with Bill Frelick, 27 March 2015), available at www.npr.org/2015/03/27/395698425/u-s-refugee-program-ignores-dangers-waiting-children-face-critics-say; M.D. Shear, 'Red tape slows US help for children fleeing Central America', *New York Times*, 5 November 2015, available at www.nytimes.com/2015/11/06/us/politics/red-tape-slows-us-help-for-children-fleeing-central-america.html: '[A]t the time that it was proposed a year ago, a White House spokesman called it an "orderly alternative to the dangerous journey that children are currently undertaking to join relatives in the US"'. Still others, including some members of the US Congress, have charged that CAM is nothing more than an open admissions program for children not qualified to enter the United States. Perhaps among the most telling expression of this view is that in 2016 members of the US House of Representatives introduced a Bill calling for repeal of CAM. See also *Ombudsman Recommendation*, above n. 54, at 8.

82 For a full description of CAM eligibility requirements, see US Customs and Immigration Service, *In-Country Refugee/Parole Processing for Minors in Honduras, El Salvador and Guatemala (Central American Minors – CAM)* (16 June 2016) ('USCIS CAM'), available at www.uscis.gov/CAM.

83 Lack of lawful immigration status in the United States may seem a sound

Although there are several categories of immigration status that qualify, the large majority of individuals from the NTCA in the US are without lawful status. One recent study estimated the number and status of individuals in the US from the NTCA as of June 2015 as follows: 1.3 million Salvadorans of whom 436,000 are without qualifying status; of 902,000 Guatemalans, 704,000 are ineligible; and of 534,000 Hondurans, 317,000 are ineligible.[84]

The child must satisfy the definition of a refugee under US law. Since CAM provides for in-country processing, the child will not be outside the country of origin but will need to satisfy the rest of the criteria, including showing a reason for not being able to stay because of actual or fear of harm based on race, religion, nationality, social group or political opinion.[85] US law imposes a high burden on the individual to show she or he is a refugee.[86]

Those found ineligible for refugee status may qualify to be 'paroled' into the United States for 'urgent humanitarian reasons or significant public benefit' based on showing a 'risk of harm', which also imposes a high burden.[87] Unlike refugee status, parole is temporary and does not provide or lead to lawful residence in the US. If the child is allowed to enter under this program, the parent must pay travel and medical clearance costs, and someone must demonstrate the ability to financially support the child while in the US.[88]

---

basis to make a person ineligible to lawfully bring one's child to the US; however, there are two critical factors that outweigh this concern. First, these are children who are in fear for their lives, security and wellbeing; second, they are children who might otherwise undertake the treacherous journey to the US alone in search of protection and to be reunited with family. The tremendous need for safe haven and secure status belongs not to the parent but to the child.

[84] F. Hipsman and D. Meissner, *In-Country Refugee Processing in Central America: A Piece of the Puzzle* (Migration Policy Institute, 2015), pp. 6–8, available at www.migrationpolicy.org/research/country-processing-central-ame 00rica-piece-puzzle.

[85] US law allows the President to designate persons within their country of origin eligible to seek asylum under special circumstances. Immigration and Nationality Act (INA), s. 101(a)(42)(B), 8 USCA s. 1101(a)(42)(B).

[86] INA, s. 101(a)(42)(A), 8 USCA s. 1101(a)(42)(A). Although US law reflects the Refugee Convention's refugee definition, its terms are frequently interpreted strictly and narrowly, often in contradiction to international law standards. For some recent numbers on asylum claims brought by individuals from the NTCA, see above n. 54 and accompanying text.

[87] The basis for 'humanitarian parole' is found at INA, s. 212(d)(5)(A), 8 USCA s. 1182(d)(5)(A).

[88] These children are not eligible for medical and other benefits, but may

For either form of protection, the parent and child must undergo DNA testing to confirm the biological relationship, at their own expense,[89] and the child must pass a number of rigorous background and security clearances, including biometric and other investigatory checks, by multiple federal law enforcement and intelligence agencies.[90]

CAM also raises a concern about the degree of safety for the children who present themselves for an eligibility determination. Interviews are only conducted in the capital city of each country, requiring many children to undertake long and potentially dangerous journeys to have access to the process. The children must remain in the country of origin throughout the entire process, which may take many months if not longer. For many of them it would be unsafe to remain in the country during this extended period and leaves them vulnerable to further harm.[91] For those who are found ineligible, the mere fact that they sought protection under CAM may put them in jeopardy.

Disturbingly few children have been brought to the United States under CAM. According to the Deputy Secretary of the Department of Homeland Security, as of 26 July 2016, approximately 9,500 applications were filed,[92] 2,884 approved and a mere 'few hundred' had entered the US.[93]

CAM may provide protection for a limited number of children seeking safety outside their countries of origin, and the value to those few and their family members in the United States is undeniable. Overall, however, the disadvantages and limitations of CAM make it 'not likely to constitute

---

attend school and apply for employment authorization. Humanitarian parole under CAM will generally be for two years and renewal may be requested. DOS Fact Sheet, above n. 80.

[89] If DNA results confirm biological relationships the parent will be reimbursed. USCIS CAM, above n. 82.

[90] These same background and security clearances are mandatory for all individuals seeking asylum status in the United States.

[91] See Hipsman and Meissner, *In-Country Refugee Processing in Central America*, above n. 84. for a discussion of US in-country refugee processing.

[92] This is the same figure provided by DOS.

[93] See, e.g., T. Wilkinson and B. Bennett, 'US expands Refugee Program', *Los Angeles Times*, 26 July 2016, available at www.latimes.com/nation/la-na-refugees-20160726-snap-story.html. The *Washington Post* reported that 'US officials said that . . . 267 of them have entered the US . . . That number is minuscule compared with the thousands of children and families from those nations who are apprehended by US Border Patrol each month while trying to enter the country'. D. Nakamura, 'US to expand Refugee Program for Central American minors', *Washington Post*, 26 July 2016, available at www.washingtonpost.com/politics/us-to-expand-refugee-program-for-central-american-minors/2016/07/26.

a realistic alternative at a scale that can significantly reduce these flows to the US'[94] and does not provide a meaningful avenue to ensure the overwhelming number of unaccompanied children fleeing from the NTCA will receive safe passage to the US and the international protection many of them so desperately need.

5.2 Humanitarian Evacuation

In July 2016, the Obama Administration announced its participation in the Humanitarian Evacuation Program (HEV).[95] HEV is based on a Protection Transit Arrangement (PTA) between UNHCR, the International Organization for Migration and Costa Rica. HEV is an in-country program that provides individuals an opportunity to demonstrate an immediate protection need based on 'specific vulnerability'. Those found to have such need are to be brought to an Emergency Transit Center in Costa Rica temporarily until they can be resettled in the United States or elsewhere. Costa Rica has committed to host up to 200 individuals at any given time. The US government likewise committed to admitting up to 200 refugees at a time but did not indicate the maximum number of refugees it will accept under HEV.

UNHCR has been working in the NTCA countries with non-governmental organizations to identify particularly vulnerable individuals and refer them to US embassies in their countries of origin. The US staff would then conduct a 'pre-screening' to determine if these individuals are among those 'most in need of immediate protection'.[96] Those found to meet this criterion would be transferred to Costa Rica, where they would undergo a full refugee determination process by US officials. Those found to meet the refugee definition would then be resettled to the United States after they have cleared the same stringent security checks.

Individuals found not to require immediate evacuation but to be 'vulnerable residents' will be eligible for an in-country referral program to be considered for refugee protection. Those found eligible for resettlement under this provision are required to remain in the country of origin until

---

[94] Hipsman and Meisner, *In-Country Refugee Processing in Central America*, above n. 84.

[95] Department of Homeland Security (DHS), *US Expands Initiatives to Address Central American Migration Challenges* (Press Release, 26 July 2016) ('DHS HEV'), available at www.dhs.gov/news/2016/07/26/us-expands-initiatives-address-central-american-migration-challenges.

[96] *Ibid.* The United States has not articulated the standard for determining who is 'most in need of immediate protection'.

they have cleared the security checks and the United States is ready for them to enter the country.[97] As refugees identified as vulnerable, it seems evident that these individuals will be at a heightened risk of harm during what will likely be a protracted waiting period.

As with CAM, HEV and in-country processing for vulnerable refugees will be invaluable for those few who receive protection under it. As is also true of CAM, these measures come with risks and great limitations, and only a very tiny fraction of the thousands of children in immediate danger will receive protection under it.

6. CONCLUSION

The pervasive violence in Central America, and the unprecedented numbers of children fleeing their homes in search of protection, will only be resolved by addressing the complex and deeply embedded root causes, an endeavour that will take tremendous time, resources and political will. The difficulties inherent in a long-term approach underscore the need for immediate responses to ensure these children are protected in a child-sensitive, secure and just manner, with links or pathways to more lasting solutions. First and foremost, these children should not be deported unless their requests for protection have been fully and fairly considered, and safe passage and reintegration in their home countries is assured.

The programs implemented by the United States are important and valuable but pose potential risks, are extremely limited in their scope and will affect a mere fraction of the children in need of international protection. They are also vastly inadequate to surmount the deep repercussions of the US focus on prevention, deterrence, detention and deportation. The combination of meagre protection programs and punitive approach conveys a grievous disregard of the dire circumstances of so many of these children.

The United States must fulfil its international obligations to ensure these children receive protection within the US and from return to the violence and danger in their home countries, and it has the resources and capacity to do so. Under the new Administration, progress towards this end seems daunting and calls for pressure to be brought to bear by concerned individuals and organizations in the US and in the international realm.

UNHCR's strategy for the NTCA is comprehensive, with a multi-tiered

---

97 Individuals who flee to Costa Rica on their own are ineligible for HEV.

approach. Its approach has included working directly with the displaced children, governments, UN agencies, and international, regional, national and local organizations, consistent with its long history of working collaboratively with a wide range of stakeholders. Working across the region with a broad array of actors and menu of programs and activities means that the short- and long-term solutions will have broader consensus, greater acceptance and, as such, greater potential to achieve the desired results. Essential to the success of UNHCR's work is the cooperation and responsiveness of the governments in the region, including the United States.

Meaningful approaches to the crisis in the NTCA require a clear commitment to humanitarian and human rights principles and must focus on both the urgent needs and durable solutions. Concerted efforts by international, regional, national and local actors are vital to these efforts. The United States has the means and capacity to lead in these endeavours if it so chooses. UNHCR must continue to lead, influence and contribute to the safety, protection and wellbeing of these children.

Postscript

As this book was in the final stages of production, major changes were occurring in both the procedural and substantive legal protections for children seeking to migrate to the United States. First, the number of unaccompanied children and children traveling with at least one parent rose. Between October 2017 and May 2018 37,450 unaccompanied children were apprehended, along with 68,560 adults traveling with children.[1] Almost all came from three source nations: Guatemala, El Salvador, and Honduras.

In an unprecedented step, the US government began to separate children from their parents and to place the children in federal detention. The government then prosecuted many of these parents for entry without documents. The claim was made that the government had to take custody of the children while the parents served criminal sentences for illegal entry. Even where the parents were not prosecuted, the government began to detain parents and children in separate facilities. In March 2018, a national class action was filed challenging the separation practices. In *Ms. L. v. DHS*,[2] a federal district court judge ordered that the children be reunited with their parents. The US government failed to meet the judicially-imposed deadlines. It argued initially that separation of children was required because the courts had restricted the government's practice of detaining children in adult facilities not licensed to house children.[3] The policy was then justified as a measure necessary to deter people from seeking asylum in the United States or from trying to enter the United States

---

1 See https://www.cbp.gov/newsroom/stats/usbp-sw-border-apprehensions.

2 *Ms. L* v. *U.S. Immigration & Customs Enforcement*, No. CV 18-0428 DMS (MDD), 2018 WL 3129486 (S.D. Cal. June 26, 2018).

3 In 2016, the federal court had ruled that children could not be held in an adult detention facility that lacked certification as a juvenile facility. *Flores* v. *Lynch*, 828 F.3d 898 (9th Cir. 2016). After the order to reunited parents, the federal government sought a modification of the *Flores* order so that it could detain children and adults together. The federal court rejected this modification on July 9, 2018. See *Flores* v. *Sessions*, 2018 U.S. Dist. LEXIS 115488 (C.D. Cal. July 9, 2018). The District Court called the government request to modify the 20-year-old Flores settlement a "cynical" attempt to shift responsibility to the judiciary to resolve a problem created by the government's change in policy and Congressional inaction.

without visas. Following extensive public criticism, President Trump issued an Executive Order in June 2018 to officially halt the separation policy.[4]

Several lawsuits remained pending in summer 2018. In some, the parent has been deported without the children and the US government has refused to assist the parent in locating and securing return of the child.[5] As noted in earlier chapters, children are not appointed counsel. However, volunteer attorneys reported that the government would not facilitate reunification by providing children's attorneys with information about the location of the parent or the status of the adult's case. Conversely, the federal government reclassified the separated children as "unaccompanied minor children" which should trigger greater procedural protections.[6] A separate suit concerned forced medication and maltreatment of children in custody.[7] Another alleged that new procedures were delaying release of children to sponsors and unlawfully prolonging detention of children.[8] In July 2018 an estimated 11,800 children were being held by the US government.[9] Sadly, there is every indication that detention of families will become a US norm. As the Australian case demonstrates, once the carceral machine is built and practices become normalized they will be very hard to stop.

In response to the perceived crisis, the Attorney General vacated the

---

4 Executive Order 13841 dated June 20, 2018, available at www.gpo.gov/fdsys/pkg/FR-2018-06-25/pdf/2018-13696.pdf. The order did not address the estimated 2,700 children who had already been separated.

5 Caitlin Dickerson, Miriam Jordan and Don Nixon, '"I Want Her Back": Some Migrant Families Reunite, but Other Parents Grow Desperate', July 12, 2018, available at www.nytimes.com/2018/07/12/us/trump-migrants-children-border.html

6 See David Thronson, Chapter 13, discussing the US jurisprudence and Lenni B. Benson and Claire Thomas, Chapter 17, on the right to counsel and the treatment of children within the court procedures.

7 See *Lucas R.* v. *Azar*, 2:18-CV-05741 (filed June 29, 2018). The complaint is available at https://youthlaw.org/wp-content/uploads/1997/05/Flores-Supplemental-Complaint-June-2018.pdf.

8 See *L.M.V.* v. *Scott Lloyd, Director of the Office of Refugee Resettlement*, filed 16 Feb. 2018 and available at www.nyclu.org/sites/default/files/field_documents/ecf_1_class_action_complaint_and_petition_for_a_writ_of_habeas_corpus_2018-02-16_00062143xb2d9a.pdf. Previously, children were usually released to a relative within 30 to 40 days. The revised policy is to investigate the immigration status of the sponsors and to report those who are undocumented to DHS for possible arrest. See Mark Joseph Stern, "Trump's Office of Refugee Resettlement is Budgeting for a Surge in Child Separations," *Slate*, July 10, 2018 (discussing documents proposing detention bends for over 25,000 children), available at https://slate.com/news-and-politics/2018/07/trumps-office-of-refugee-resettlement-is-budgeting-for-a-surge-in-child-separations.html.

9 *Ibid.*

Board of Immigration Appeals rulings in several cases, substituting his own final decisions. This was a very unusual gesture, but is authorized by US statutes as the Attorney General is the head of the Department of Justice that contains the administrative immigration tribunals. In these cases, the Attorney General removed the power of the immigration judge to suspend or administratively close a removal case.[10] He vacated case law that precluded summary dismissal of asylum claims, and vacated an important case that found that women who were victims of pervasive domestic violence and unable to secure protection from their government could qualify for asylum protection.[11] This last case will make it much more difficult for children to apply for asylum where they have suffered violence from a family member or from a failure of their home country to provide adequate child protection.

In Chapter 24, pamela goldberg describes the Central American Minor Program (CAM). CAM presented a novel approach that offered legal resettlement to children who had at least one parent residing in a temporary or permanent lawful status within the United States. Sadly, it too has become a thing of the past. The program was eliminated by Executive Order in the first Travel Ban that suspended all refugee admissions. In June 2018, the US Supreme Court upheld the Presidential power to temporarily suspend refugee admissions.[12]

Lenni B. Benson and Mary Crock

---

[10] *Matter of Castro Tum*, 27 I&N Dec 271 (AG 2018). This case involved an unrepresented teenager who failed to appear at his immigration hearing. The immigration judge was not satisfied the youth had received notice and administratively closed the case. The Attorney General selected this case and ruled that immigration judges have no regulatory nor statutory authority to close cases without the consent of the DHS.

[11] See *Matter of –A-B, 27* I&N Dec. 316 (AG 2018) vacating *Matter of –A-R-C-G*, 26 I & N Dec. 388 (BIA 2014). The Attorney General's decision also suggests that people seeking protection due to private actor violence, such as threats from organized gangs, may also be in jeopardy. At least one federal court has approved of the Attorney General's interpretation in *Matter of –A-B*. See *S.E.R.L.* v. *AG United States*, No. 17-2031, 2018 U.S. App. LEXIS 18133 (3d Cir. 2018) (rejecting domestic violence based asylum claim and discussing Matter of –A-B positively).

[12] *Trump* v. *Hawaii*, 138 Sup. Ct. 2392 (2018) (rejecting challenges based on statements of religious bias and procedural challenges).

Index